THE NATURE OF UNDERDEVELOPMENT AND REGIONAL STRUCTURE OF NEPAL

The Nature of Underdevelopment and Regional Structure of Nepal

A MARXIST ANALYSIS

Baburam Bhattarai

ADROIT PUBLISHERS
Delhi-110 053

Published by
ADROIT PUBLISHERS
4675/21, Ganpati Bhawan, Ansari Road,
Daryaganj, New Delhi-110 002
Phones : 011-23266030, 23263506

Distributors
AKHIL BOOK DISTRIBUTORS
e-mail: akhilbooks@yahoo.com
akhilbooks@hotmail.com

Reprint 2011

ISBN : 81-87392-39-8

Printed in India on behalf of M/s Adroit Publishers by
Arpit Printographers E-mail : arpitprinto@yahoo.com

Foreword

Not only because he was a contemporary brilliant student of my formal education days but due to our common aim in life of 'understanding and changing the world', I had a special interest to read Com. Baburam Bhattarai's research work on "The Nature of Underdevelopment and Regional Structure of Nepal" prepared for the degree of Doctor of Philosophy. When we became co-travellers and co-fighters of a distinct political current after the historic people's movement of 1990 through completion of an important phase of ideological and practical struggle in the process of understanding and changing the Nepalese Society, I got the opportunity to read this research work about a decade ago. As the General Secretary of the Party making final preparations for revolutionary transformation of the Nepalese society with intense and decisive ideological struggle against rightist revisionism and with an attack on feudalism and imperialism through the medium of People's War (PW) I had read this research work with keen interest.

That perusal of this research work instantly had two deep impressions on me. Firstly, I felt that my perceptual impression of the intellectual brilliance of Com. Baburam Bhattarai had been transformed into a conceptual impression, and secondly, I realised that it had further strengthened my confidence in the politico-economic rationale of the PW we had been preparing for. We also discussed about the importance of publication of this research work, perhaps the first of its kind in Nepal carried out from a Marxist theoretical perspective. For this Com. Baburam Bhattarai had asked for about six month's time to update some of the old data. Though we realised its importance, as the Party was passing through a very sensitive phase of initiation of the PW and because he himself had to constantly discharge important roles and needs as a co-fighter, it was not possible to grant him the required time. Subsequently, with the initiation of the PW and its very fast pace of development we reached such a stage where we could not afford even six days, not to speak of six months.

Now, with the decision to publish the research work in its original form as per the demand and pressure of the time, Com. Baburam Bhattarai suddenly asked me to write a small foreword for this. I express heartfelt thanks to

Com. Bhattarai for this opportunity to give a perceptive opinion on the research work. I believe that even if the data may be somewhat old it won't have any adverse impact on the thought, significance and spirit of the research work. I believe that the publication of this research work that starts with the famous quotation of Karl Marx for 'changing the world' and concludes with the exhortation that development of Nepal is not possible without the structural transformation of society, will provide an important objective material to the serious and inquisitive readers, both inside and outside the country, desirous of understanding Nepal and the PW in its essential and scientific sense.

March 6, 2003.

Prachanda
Chairman,
Communist Party of Nepal (Maoist)

Preface

The Nepalese society at the beginning of the 21st century is passing through the greatest upheavals in its entire history in the form of the revolutionary People's War (PW) of the oppressed classes, regions, nationalities, gender and communities against the outmoded semi-feudal and semi-colonial social order. This has naturally raised the curiosity of many both inside and outside the country to understand the material basis or the politico-economic rationale of this epochal volcanic eruption. As a humble participant in this mass rebellion under the leadership of the CPN (Maoist), this author had long felt duty bound to attempt a sufficiently lucid exposition of the politico-economic foundation of the revolutionary movement for the convenience of the general public. However, both physical and mental constraints of an underground revolutionary life for the past seven years would not permit any such venture with ease. Hence, as the time was running out very fast, my close comrades and friends have suggested instead to publish this work which was completed as part of my doctoral thesis at Jawaharlal Nehru University (JNU), New Delhi, exactly ten years prior to the initiation of the historic PW in 1996. With usual trepidation and full knowledge that it may be a very poor substitute for the aspired project I have consented to place it before the discerning public for their critical dissection.

As the very first quotation of Karl Marx in the beginning of the book would suggest, the author has attempted an historico-materialist *interpretation* of the Nepalese society so that it may help to *change* it for the better. I have no claim and illusion that my interpretation is the most objective and scientific, but would humbly submit that I have tried to use the most scientific tool of Marxism-Leninism-Maoism for the said purpose without any apology and to the best of my ability; of course, within the limitations of an academic discourse in a mainstream university. In that sense I am extremely grateful to the liberal environment of JNU for providing me that liberty. I am aware that the text may appear too academic for the revolutionary political activists and a bit doctrinaire to the academicians and politically uninitiated. Also, I would have loved to unburden the readers with some very detailed portions and clumsy tables, but for the time to edit it thoroughly. Somewhat lengthy theoretical underpinnings and historical antecedents in each chapter, however, are kept in tact as they constitute the very essence of the historico-materialist method of the entire project.

Questions may be raised whether the research work done almost two decades earlier would stand the scrutiny of time in its theoretical approach, hypothetical propositions and basic conclusions and would bear relevance to the current global and national reality. It is the author's strong conviction that, though he would have preferred to update both the literature survey and statistical data, the basic propositions and conclusions would not only remain the same but they have been entirely validated by the subsequent course of events in the nineties of the last century and beginning of this century. Also, it may be relevant to note that the study is not confined to a particular time period but traces the history of development of Nepal from the beginning upto the nineteen-eighties and projects the trends to the future.

At the international plane, the subsequent events have only reinforced the validity of the Marxist concept of development of underdevelopment in the third world countries as a concomitant phenomenon resulting from imperialism as outlined in this work. Though after the nineteen-eighties the Bretton Woods system (i.e. the World Bank, IMF and later the WTO, etc.) parroted the worn out concept of imperialist 'globalization' and neo-Smithian 'liberalization' with increased vigour, and Huntingtons's ''clash of civilization" and Fukiyama's "end of history" trash was traded with impunity for some time among the intelligentsia in the immediate aftermath of the inevitable collapse of the revisionist Soviet system and its East European satellites, the burst of East Asian bubbles and implosion of Mexican and Argentinean debt-ridden economies in the nineties soon exposed the basically untenable imperialist system. Meanwhile, brutal aggression of imperialist 'globalization' in much of the third world countries further aggravated the process of underdevelopment and the gap between the rich and poor countries widened menacingly. According to the United Nation's *Human Development Report,* in 1970 the richest 20 percent of world's population had an average income 32 times that of the poorest 20 percent ; by 1991 that ratio had almost doubled to 61 times; and by the end of the nineties the ratio had reached to 74 times. Consequently Marxian concept of imperialism and underdevelopment was once again 'rediscovered' and popularised by different authors like Patnaik 1995, Singh, Randhir (2001), Magdoff 2002, Foster 2002, Amin 2003 and others, and it is reasonable to expect that the radical theories of development of underdevelopment would soon gain old currency in the underdeveloped world and elsewhere. The recent spate of massive anti –'globalisation' and anti-imperialist war movements throughout the world are significant pointers towards that.

In Nepal, a number of development studies have surfaced since the author's research work in the eighties. Among these may be cited Bista 1990, Bhattchan and Mishra 1997, Shrestha 1997, Dahal 1998, Pandey 1999, Bhattarai 1999 and Bhusal 2002. Despite valuable insights into particular aspects of development problematics, most of these studies continue to lack an objective and holistic approach and fail to locate the basic malaise in the internal and external social relations of production. Bhusal, following Mishra, attempts at a neo-Marxist analysis based on the 'dependency school', whose inadequacy has already been dealt with in the present work. Bhattarai's collection of politico-economic articles is generally based on the theoretical premise and conclusions of the earlier research work. Hence, the basic historico-materialist approach of this book which views 'underdevelopment' as "opposite condition of non-realisation of full potential of development and/or blockage to transformation to higher formation under the cumulative impacts of prevailing endogenous and exogenous conditions" remains as valid as ever.

The 1990 political change did not bring about any structural transformation of basic semi-feudal and semi-colonial structure of society. As Gurung rightly says: "Looking back after nine years of multiparty governance, it is apparent that the year of MRD(1990) was not a political watershed but a transition only in form while the socio-economic power structure remained in tact." (1999:iv). As a result the fundamental politico-economic characteristics of society or basic class relations cannot be assumed to have undergone any qualitative change, though some quantitative change could not have been arrested. Very low level of development of productive forces marked by low sectoral differentiation of the economy with the continued predominance of the primary production sector is there for all to see (Table 0.1). However, a discernible shift of both labour force and GDP away from the primary production sector to the economic integration sector in subsequent decades is a sign of growing comprador and bureaucratic capital and increasing integration with the metropolitan economy as envisaged earlier in this work. The spurious nature of the growth of secondary production

Table 0.1 Sectoral Distribution of Economically Active Population and GDP (at current prices) (1991 & 2001)

(%)

Sectors	*Economically Active Population*		*GDP*	
	1991	*2001*	*1990/91*	*2000/2001*
I. Production Sector	–	–	–	–
1. Primary Production	81.03	65.86	48.17	38.38
2. Secondary Production	2.67	13.20	17.04	20.87
	(2.52)	(8.81)	(6.80)	(9.04)
II. Economic Integration (circulation) Sector	18.25	20.71	34.78	40.75
1. Trade and Commerce	14.49	9.99	14.25	18.58
2. Services	3.76	10.72	20.53	22.17
III. Unknown/Others.	1.33	0.23	–	–
TOTAL	100.00	100.00	100.00	100.00

Note: Figures in parenthesis represent the share of 'Manufacturing'.

Source: Central Bureau of Statistic, *Population Census of Nepal* 1991&2001, and *Statistical Pocket Book, Nepal* (various issues), Kathmandu.

sector is quite apparent as the share of both labour force and GDP in the all important 'manufacturing' component is well below ten percent even now. The glaring disparity in the share of labour force and GDP in the primary production sector, i.e. agriculture sector, throughout is a sure sign of the pathetic and deteriorating condition of the rural economy. This has resulted in the increasing poverty unemployment and inequality in society in general. According to the *Nepal Human Development Report 1998* poverty has increased at an annual rate of 3% and the number of absolute poor has nearly doubled in the last two decades. Similarly, while the share of the bottom 40% of population in total income was 23% in 1985, it declined to 11% in 1996, and the share of top 10% has increased from 23% to 52%. This should adequately explain the material basis for raging rebellion of the poor peasant masses over the years.

As is well known, no substantial agrarian reform measure has been undertaken after the restoration of the parliamentary system in 1990. Rather the minimal state subsidies to the agricultural sector have been gradually withdrawn as per the dictation of the imperialist 'globalization' and 'liberalization' regime. It is therefore, axiomatic that the already backward and stagnant agriculture sector would further stagnate and retard in the subsequent decade. According to the annual *Economic Survey* reports, during the first half of the nineties when the GDP grew on an average rate of 5% or so, the agriculture sector grew only at 1.6%, and in the latter half of the decade the growth rate was negative for most of the years. In the current year, i.e. 2002/2003 too, the growth rate is reported to be negative. And Nepal, which had the highest yield rates of major crops in South Asia in 1960s, has now the lowest yield rates and has suffered decline in productivity in the 1990s (APROSC 1995). This all-round stagnation and decline would obviously be more pronounced in the Mountain and Hill regions than in the Terai. Also the backward and retrograde relation of production in agriculture as reflected in the pre-ponderence of 'owner-cultivated' subsistence peasantry amidst considerable disparity in the social distribution of the vital means of production, land, is continuously reproduced over the decade in the absence of any progressive land reform measure by the 'democratic' and 'left' governments. For example, even in the nineties per capita land holding was only 0.14 ha; 69.4 percent of landholdings were less than 1 ha. in size; 82.56 percent of households with 81.22 percent of cultivated land were registered as 'owner-cultivators', the ratio being expectedly higher in the Mountain and Hill regions than in the Terai and Kathmandu Valley (CBS 1993). The continued inequality in the distribution of land is expressed by the fact that the bottom 40 percent of the agricultural households operate only 9 percent of the total cultivated land, while the top 6 percent occupy more than 33 percent, and the concentration index for cultivated land is 0.54. (CBS 1997). Pre-capitalist ground-rent realised primarily through the system of share-cropping, continues to be the principal form of appropriation of social surplus thereby indicating a persistence of semi-feudal relations of production. For instance, in the nineties, of the 17.11 percent of tenant households that rented-in 9.04 percent of cultivated land, 56.57 percent practiced 'share-cropping' and only 5.60 percent paid fixed money rent (CBS 1993), which is only marginally different from the tenancy scenario in the seventies. In sum, the aggregate agrarian process is still found characterised by low technical level of production, pre-capitalist or semi-feudal relations of production and a general state of stagnation and retardation, which is the general finding of the research work done in the previous decade. As long as there is no revolutionary change in the agriculture sector that absorbs more than two-third of the total labour force, the country is not likely to break out of the vicious chain of underdevelopment, retardation and dependency. The rationale of the revolutionary PW raging since 1966 basically lies in this.

The process and nature of industrial retardation analysed in the nineteen-eighties also remains largely valid to this day with minor variations. The historically evolved endogenous and exogenous factors, i.e. retrograde semi-feudal production relations internally and a semi-colonial relations particularly with India externally, have continued to block and distort the industrial process. As a result the minimal industrial sector is further marked by a generalised pattern of chronically anemic and inverted structure reflected in excessively higher share of elementary processing consisting of agro-based and forest-based industries and a negligible share of production goods industries. There is yet no trace of 'capital' and 'basic' goods industries and the few 'intermediate' goods industries have decelerated growth rates. (CBS1998). The only notable difference in the industrial composition compared to the earlier decades is the sudden rise of woolen carpet manufacturing and garments industries essentially generated by exogenous factors. This pseudo-industrial process triggered and patronised through the so-called 'generalised system of preference' (GSP) by the metropolitan capital to exploit cheap labour of underdeveloped countries has already experienced worst scenario of 'dependency syndrome' in the form of erratic fluctuation of its fate over the years. Also most of the earnings from these industries are known to flow out for importation of raw materials, and Indian monopoly capital is said to be conveniently enjoying the real 'GSP' through the open border between the two countries. Hence the apparently bloated industrial growth without any sound internal foundation is likely to burst asunder as a bubble any time and the inverted and hollow industrial structure exposed thoroughly. Another significant negative development in the industrial sphere over the years has been the virtual dismantling of the small industrial base constructed under the state aegis in the past in the name of the so-called 'privatization' drive dictated by world imperialism. 17 out of the 45 public sector enterprises have been 'privatized' in one form or the other by the year 2002 at throwaway prices and most of them have virtually ceased to operate in the professed form (Ministry of Finance 2002). Thus without a basic restructuration of both endogenous and exogenous relations the aspired industrial revolution is not likely to materialise in the country.

The increasing tendency of proliferation of circulation capital (both in mercantile and financial forms) and its regressive role when dissociated with the internal production process, as forecasted in this research work, has been largely vindicated by the experiences of the subsequent years. With the introduction of the so-called Structural Adjustment Programme (SAP) and the neo-classical 'liberalization' regime under the world imperialist agenda since the nineteen-eighties, the past trend of proliferation of circulation capital in various forms was further intensified in the country. Whereas the articulation of merchant capital within was rather guarded due to the sluggish growth of the agriculture and industrial sector, the articulation with the metropolitan economy was more pronounced and with far greater vigour. However, the pattern of export-import trade with the major partner India and other countries followed the prevalent mode of dominance-dependence and 'unequal exchange' as adaquately stressed in the study. (See Table 0.2). While the dominance-dependance relations with India seemed to have slackened a bit by the end of eighties, it has progressively risen since then. It is well-known that the economic embargo imposed by India in 1989 had played a major role in precipitating the internal political crisis, which ultimately led to the political change of 1990. The 'unequal exchange' mechanism effectuated through the export of primary products or elementary processed products and import of finished products and capital and basic goods has continued to mark the underdevelopment process over the decade. Over dependence on export of elementary processed jute products in the earlier decades has now been replaced by that of all the more spurious carpets and garments exports. For example, carpets and garments combined constituted a hopping 83.91 percent and 83.43 percent of total exports to overseas countries (i.e. other than India) in the end-eighties and end-nineties respectively (Nepal Rastra Bank). The apparently favourable export scenario vis-a-vis India in the later years is just a manifestation of spurious growth of processing industries like vegetable ghee, which have no real roots in the indigenous economy of the country, but was the single largest export to India in 2002 (Nepal Chamber of Commerce).

Table 0.2 Pattern of Export-Import Trade (1977/78–2000/01)

(Rs. billion at current prices)

	*1977/78–1979/80**			*1988/89–190/91**			*1998/99–2000/01**		
	Export	*Import*	*Export/ Import Ratio %*	*Export*	*Import*	*Export/ Import Ratio %*	*Export*	*Import*	*Export/ Import Ratio %*
I. India	0.56 (47.78)	1.63 (55.49)	34.0	1.07 (23.80)	4.50 (27.88)	23.73	14.18 (37.65)	33.04 (34.77)	42.93
II. Other Countries	0.61 (52.22)	1.31 (44.51)	46.4	3.42 (76.20)	11.65 (72.12)	29.36	23.49 (62.35)	61.97 (65.23)	37.90
Total	1.17 (100.00)	2.94 (100.00)	39.5	4.45 (100.00)	16.15 (100.00)	27.79	37.67 (100.00)	95.01 (100.00)	39.65

Note: * Triennium averages
• Figures in parenthesis are percentages.

Source: Nepal Rastra Bank, *Quarterly Economic Bulletins* (various issues) Kathmandu.

The basic trends of articulation of financial capital within and without, too, has maintained the same pattern as predicted in the study, but with increased vigour. With the wind of financial 'liberalization' in full swing after the mid-eighties, the penetration of foreign financial capital was facilitated further and there mushroomed a number of 'joint-venture' commercial banks and financial companies in the country. By the end of nineties 13 new joint-venture commercial banks and 52 different financial companies had started operations mostly in large cities. (*Economic Survey*, 2002/2003). The deposit of commercial banks had risen from Rs. 4.28 billion in 1982 to Rs. 21.89 billion in 1990/1991 to further Rs 154.53 billion in 2000/01; i.e. 36 times in 18 years. (Nepal Rastra Bank). However, a glance at the sectoral distribution pattern of credits by commercial banks would confirm that they continued to strengthen the basically unequal integration of the country's economy with the metropolitan capital though in later years they seemed to finance the spurious 'industries' more. Meanwhile, aggravation of dependency and underdevelopment mechanism of the country through foreign 'aid' as analyzed in the study, took a graver turn in the subsequent decades. By the end of the century net foreign debt (both bilateral and multilateral, but increasingly latter) had crossed Rs 200 billion, which is more than 50 percent of the GDP. And the debt/export earning ratio was more than 600 percent, which according to IMF's own stipulated standard of not to exceed 200-250 percent, is quite critical. It is also quite noteworthy that whereas foreign 'aid' (i.e. both grant and loan) constituted 63.16 percent of the 'development' expenditure in 1965/66 and 57.20 percent in 1980/81, it was 55.19 percent in 2000/01 and further 64.43 percent in 2001/02. (*Annual Budget Speech*).

And finally, the configuration of the spatial structure of an underdeveloped semi-feudal and semi-colonial social formation, as picturised and analyzed in the research work, has completely stood the test of the time. Whereas overwhelming rurality has remained the hallmark of organisation of space in the country with only about ten percent of population in urban areas, horizontal migration from Mountain and Hill regions to the Terai has continued unabated, as nearly 50 percent of population is now living in the Terai. Also, an apparently contradictory, but typical of the physico-historical specificity of the country, scenario of spatial organisation marked by excessive polarisation around the capital city of Kathmandu, on the one hand, and outward-orientation towards India along a north-south dendrite stretching from Mountain to Terai, on the other, has been further accentuated over the years. The expanded transportation and communication networks in the nineties have conformed to the same mono-centred and extraverted spatial pattern. And most importantly, the spatial structure of development/ underdevelopment generalized from the spatial differentiation of composite levels of development of individual districts in the present study, have not only been confirmed by later academic studies (See, for example, ICIMOD 1997 and NESAC 1998), but also by the spatial pattern of eruption and spread of the revolutionary PW. The material basis for the development of the western Hills and Mountains into storm centres of revolution, followed by the eastern

Hills and Mountains and then other areas, have been amply highlighted in the study. Of course, subjective factors and the consciousness of the revolutionary vanguard have their distinct leading role in revolution, but a correct analysis of the objective basis has to accompany any effective subjective intervention. In that sense the author is extremely pleased with the subsequent revolutionary development in the country based on the correct fusion of objective and subjective factors. I wish the ongoing revolutionary PW would materialise the final conclusion of the thesis: "Hence without the basic restructuration of the society which would check the above tendencies as well as the forces abetting them, the social and spatial problems of development/ underdevelopment are not likely to be solved."

Baburam Bhattarai

Acknowledgements

I owe a lot of intellectual and otherwise debt to many individuals and institutions, both in Nepal and India, for the production of this book, which I hesitate to mention for obvious reasons, at least for the time being. However, since the basic content was produced in JNU, New Delhi, during 1980-85 I cannot do without publicly acknowledging the huge debt I owe to Dr. (Mrs.) Atiya Habeeb Kidwai, late Prof. Moonis Raza and other faculty members of the Centre for Study of Regional Development, JNU. Similarly, my active association with All India Nepalese Unity Society and thousands of emigrant Nepalese workers in India like Raju Nepali, Padam Rana, Bam Dev and others sharpened my perspective and resolve to step out of the narrow confines of the academics pre-occupied with mere 'interpretation' of the world and get involved in 'changing' it as well. I have also gained immensely from interactions with a host of luminaries and academics of Nepal including M.C.Regmi, Govind P. Lohani, Harka Gurung, Pitamber Sharma, V.B.S. Kansakar, Devendra R. Pandey, Sriram Poudyal, Deependra B. Chhetri and Bharat Devkota, though they may not entirely agree with my ideological-political persuasion. Important inputs from my friends Yogeshwar, Manu, Golak, Bishnu Pant, Madhav Devkota, K.K.Maharjan, Purusottam and others were instrumental during the original production work.

However, without the inspiration and encouragement of my Party comrades and gallant people's fighters in the later years, the study would not have seen the light of the day in this form after years of hibernation. I am extremely grateful to Com. Prachanda, Chairman of the Party, for writing a short but insightful 'foreword' for this book. Particularly I owe immense gratitude to Jagat, Sangeeta, Ramesh, Anju and Manushi for excellent logistical and other background work during the final publication stage. Of course, the management of Adroit Publishers, New Delhi, get full credit for daring to publish this work in these uncertain times.

And one name, which is usually recorded with 'the last but not the least' prefix but in my case has contributed the most intellectually, emotionally and physically from the beginning to the end of this work for the past more than two decades, I am hesitating to acknowledge publicly lest it be cliched and trivialised. Even if it may sound too personalised and emotional I should now let the public know that without Hisila Yami's selfless, constant and multi-faceted contribution this book would have never been completed and published, at least not in this form.

I humbly dedicate this book to thousands of great immortal martyrs of the historic PW, including Com. Suresh Wagle, Com. Rit Bahadur Khadka, Com. Rambrikshya Yadav and others, who have blazed the path of not only 'interpreting' but 'changing' the world.

March, 2003 **Baburam Bhattarai**

Contents

1 Introduction

"The Philosophers have only interpreted the world, in various ways; the point, however, is to change it."

—Karl Marx

- ***Rationale of the Study***
- ***Analytical Frame***
  - — Concept of development and underdevelopment
  - — Concept of space and spatial structure of under development
- ***Physical Setting and Definition of Spatial Units***
- ***Historical Setting***
- ***General Differentiation of the Economy***
- ***Hypothetical Propositions***
- ***Methods Used***
- ***Organisation of the Study***

1.1 RATIONALE OF THE STUDY

The issue of 'underdevelopment' has been rightly acknowledged as "the most important single issue of our time"[1]. The importance has not been attributed without reason. The waves of national liberation struggles and decolonisation in the post—World War II period, the rise of neo-colonialism to engulf the oppressed part of the world in a new guise, the unprecedented pace of polarisation between the haves and have-nots, both in inter- and intra-national plane, etc., have brought the issues of wide-spread deprivation, backwardness and lop-sided socio-economic structuration in Third World countries into sharp focus and the nomenclature 'underdevelopment' has been the epitomization of the consciousness of this reality. Similarly, colonialism's and subsequently imperialism's division of the world in physical terms into 'civilized' and 'uncivilized', or 'developed' and 'underdeveloped' parts, has imbued 'space consciousness' amongst people. It is also being increasingly realised that social and spatial attributes constitute inseparable elements of the composite development process both at macro and micro levels. However, the general intellectual hegemonisation by the possessing classes, on the one hand, and the tendency of the conventional 'philosophers' to merely 'interpret' the emperically observable world without attempting its 'change' on the other, have been reflected in the nature and quality of the current academic dialogue on the issue of underdevelopment. This is evident from the popularity of theoretical formulations which interpret 'underdevelopment' as the inevitable leaving behind of somebody in the great rat race or which introduce dualism in the social and spatial components of the process. Or others, who see 'underdevelopment' as an avoidable enigma of human creation where a 'country exploits country' or 'place exploits place'. Against these, the more objective and historically sustainable formulation that development/underdevelopment is a composite 'socio-spatial process' and the manifestation of contradictions in the mode of reproduction of life through a particular form of society under the cumulative impacts of 'endogenous' and 'exogenous' forces, is found still in a subdued and formative stage. Even in the professedly radical studies on underdevelopment, particularly those in the sphere of 'regional development', the primary role of prevalent social organisation of production or class relations in articulating the given social or spatial structure of underdevelopment is inappropriately and inadequately treated. Hence it was found imperative to make a case study of an underdeveloped formation with this latter perspective.

Selection of Nepal as the case study is more than a mere coincidence. For besides being a distinguished member of the 'poorest of the poor' club[2] and displaying attendant features of 'underdevelopment', it possesses several such specific attributes which should make its 'underdevelopment' simultaneously a typical and a rare case. Absence of direct colonial experience though a semi-colonial form of integration to British India and then to 'independent' India; unique physiographic diversity ranging from tropical plains of less than 100m. altitude to alpine Himalayan mountains of more than 8800m altitude within a horizontal expanse of less than 200km.; land-locked positioning between two hostile giant-size states of India and China; continuation of a medieval socio-political formation under the hegemony of a centralised despotic state since mid-18th century; are some of the specificities that would leave a definite stamp on the process of 'development of underdevelopment'. Consequently, whereas the core issues of 'underdevelopment' elsewhere have been non-realisation of productive potentials of society commensurate with the given historical stage of development, or distortions in the mode of development as compared to an ideal projection, the problematic of 'underdevelopment' in Nepal seem to be more of non-development of productive forces[3] and less of 'distorted' or 'dependent' development.

Non-development of productive forces is, however, just a manifestation and one facet of the problem. The other facet, and more important to unravel the causal mechanism of the underdevelopment process, is the retrograde form of organisation of society as manifested in extreme economic inequality within[4] and subjugated relations vis-a-vis the metropolitan economy. Concomitantly low absolute level of development of productive forces and high economic inequality are characteristic features of pre-capitalist, feudal society. On the other hand, deteriorating balance and terms of trade, unequal exchange relations in the export of primary products and import of manufactures, domination of foreign financial capital, etc., that are all to be found here are common characteristics of 'classically' underdeveloped economies. Thus the 'social' aspect of underdevelopment of Nepal seem to provide a fertile ground for scientific enquiry.

For the backward economy as is evident, spatial diversity and inequality, particularly in terms of dominant physico-ecological zones of Terai and hills, on the one hand, and capital centre of Kathmandu and rest of the country on the other, are truly remarkable and not inappropriately linked to the "gulf between the developed countries and the underdeveloped 'third' world".[5] The original spatial inequality as resulting from the use-value differentials of the soils would seem to have been systematically aggravated by subsequent socio-political factors and this provides enough scope for probing into the relative roles of natural and social factors in bringing about spatial inequality in development. Also, the spatial organisation of a backward, semi-colonial pre-capitalist economy interposed by the extremities of nature, should be a fresh domain to enquiry into.

As against these, the existing studies on the social and spatial aspects of underdevelopment process in Nepal have not only been remarkably sterile and devoid of a clear theoretical and analytical perspective, but have also been crude adaptations of schemas prescribed by the guardians of metropolitan capital, particularly the World Bank. Hence an attempt to go beyond these studies with a clear theoretical and analytical perspective becomes all the more imperative.

The objective of the present study, thus, may be defined as under:

- To bring into focus different factors which are responsible for, and accompany the processes of underdevelopment in a transitional, pre-capitalist society;
- To attempt towards a better understanding of the roles and interrelations of spatial and social factors in the development/underdevelopment process by integrating spatial analysis with politico-economic analysis;
- To contribute to the correction of short-comings in the developmental studies, particularly in Nepal, by adopting a clear theoretical and analytical approach and by highlighting the role of social relations of production in the articulation of the development/underdevelopment process.

The study is based on the premise that 'underdevelopment' is the distortion introduced in the sectoral and spatial dimensions of the social economy, and hence an attempt has been made to identify the characteristics and processes of these distortions through the concomitant sectoral (vertical) and spatial (horizontal) differentiation of the economy. Agriculture, industry and trade and finance are taken as the three principal sectors of the economy which would be subjected

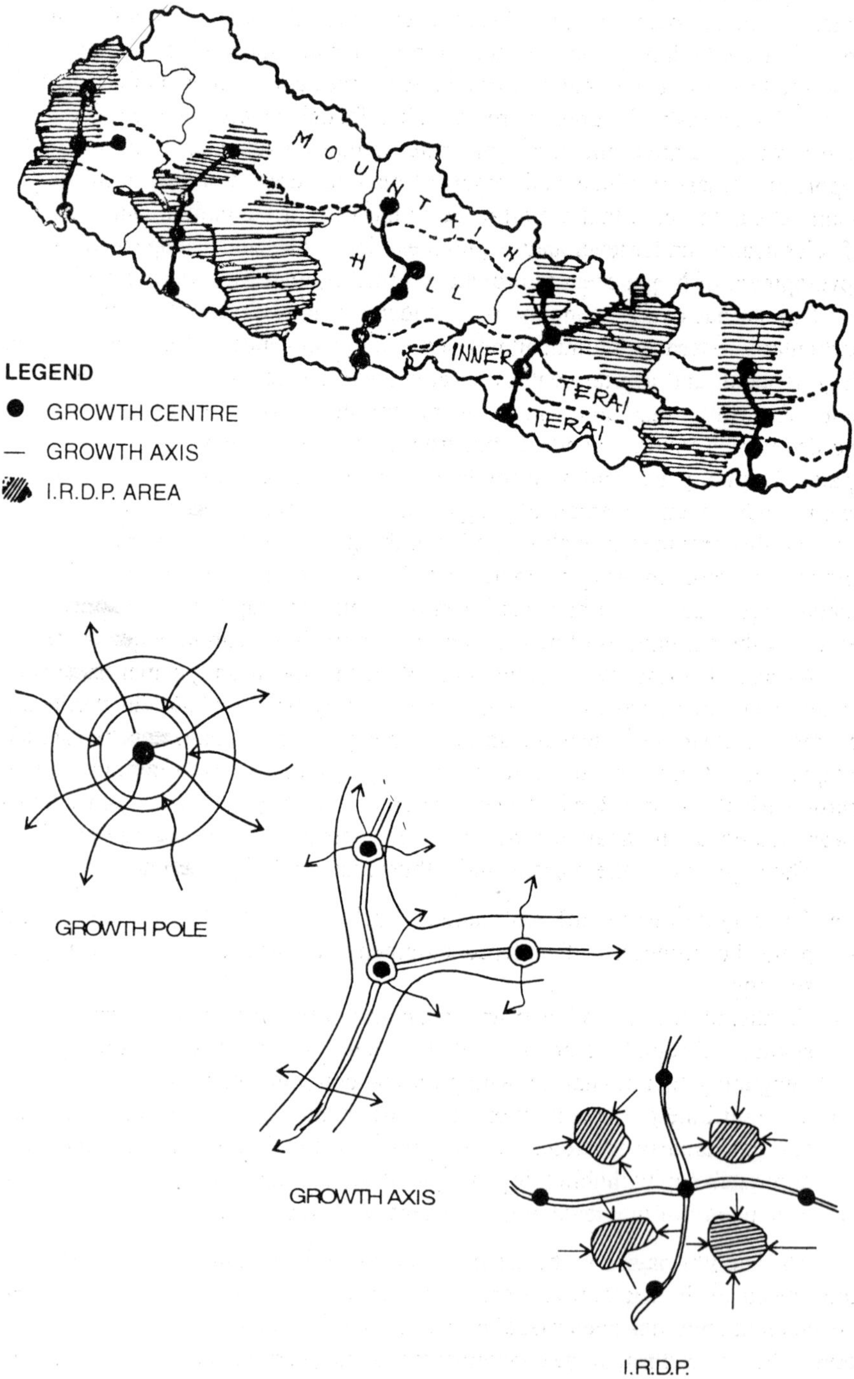

Fig. 1.1 Official 'Regional Development' Strategy.

to detailed analysis in their 'social' and 'spatial' dimensions. Finally an analysis will be made of the organisation of space which is considered here as the cumulative territorial manifestation of the social economy.

The study would encompass the whole territorial expanse of Nepal. Since the objective here is to understand the social and spatial structure of underdevelopment of a semi-colonial pre-capitalist economy a fragmentary approach would not be able to capture the totality of the political economy of Nepal, given its unitary structure and physio-economic diversity. Similarly, in view of the broad theoretical approach of the study and lack of sharp 'breaks' in the history of society for at least last two centuries, the study would attempt to trace the past historical legacy but would be practically confined to recent times for reasons of data constraints.

In order to proceed systematically with the analysis, we would first make a brief survey of the received theories on social and spatial dimensions of underdevelopment, with particular emphasis on the divergent approaches within the historico-materialist or Marxist framework, with a view to deriving an appropriate theoretical and analytical approach for the present study. This would be followed by a brief appraisal of the physical and historical specificities and economic structure of the country.

1.2 ANALYTICAL FRAME

"Concrete conditions do not validate concepts, it is the concept which makes possible and validates analyses of the concrete"[6].

1.2.0 It should be all the more true in the case of a social phenomenon like 'development' and 'underdevelopment' which is seen to have a myriad of connotations both in time and space frame. For a social phenomenon as this constitutes of so many variables interrelated in such a complex manner that in the absence of prior theorisation through distillation of facts from diverse historical and regional experiences to act as a frame of reference, not only is the objective analysis of the concrete phenomenon practically impossible but the consequent empiricist attempts would merely serve social opportunism. Hence prior defining of conceptual framework assumes paramount significance before venturing into empirical investigation of a concrete phenomenon in a concrete situation. For convenience we would take up the social and spatial aspects of the phenomenon separately.

1.2.1 Concept of Development and Underdevelopment

The history of the theory of development and under-development, particularly after World War II, has been the history of unceasing struggle between the two epistemological camps of Anglo-Saxon scholarship dominated by neo-classicism, on the one hand, and Marxist scholarship based on historical materialism, on the other, with a number of hybrids of the two lined on both sides. Though it would appear naive to attempt to pigeon-hole such wide array of literature in to two exclusive groupings the development and underdevelopment as understood by the two epistemological camps may be differentiated thus: The neo-classicists tend to define 'development' more in terms of economic 'growth' or as amorphous 'modernisation', and view 'underdevelopment' as its opposite, i.e. in terms of lack of economic growth or as an original state of 'backwardness'. This 'modern'-'traditional' dualism in sectoral, regional and inter-national terms is just seen as the result of natural historical and geographical differentials, or like 'original sin' which professedly can be overcome through more intimate integration of the backward and advanced sectors/areas. The radical view, on the other hand, regards 'development' as a cumulative *process* of progressive transformation of society to higher formations and sees 'underdevelopment' as the *concomitant process* of blockage to such transformation or distorted structuration primarily articulated through retrograde internal and external class configurations. As it would be virtually impossible, and also unwarranted, to encompass the whole gamut of definitions of the phenomenon from different ideological persuasions[7] in this limited space and context we would confine to the latter approach for the search of our model.

Of late there has been a virtual stampede of both theoretical and empirical works on the question of development and underdevelopment from scholars working within the Marxist tradition. Any serious observer pursuing the trails of the current debate[8] could single out the most relevent, and contentious issues thus: What is the 'prime mover' in social development? What are the mechanism and the nature of interrelations, if any, in getting some sectors/areas/nations retarded or underdeveloped while others get developed? What is the appropriate scale for the analysis of this phenomenon, i.e. a sub-nation, or a nation, or world? What is the role of endogenous and exogenous factors in the development of society in a particular manner? Can the process be explained only in terms of economic factors? etc. To get correct answer to these it may be necessary to recapitulate the basic methodological premises of Marxism and put the questions in historical perspective.

Materialist dialectics is the foundation of Marxist method of analysis of a social phenomenon. Calling it as the "doctrine of development", Lenin lists the basic features of dialectics as 'a development that proceeds in spirals, not in a straight line', 'a development by leaps, catastrophes and revolutions', 'the transformation of quantity into quality', 'inner impulses towards development, imparted by contradiction and conflicts within a given society', 'interdependence between *all* aspects of any phenomenon', etc.[9] The need to look 'inside' the thing to understand the development process has been hammered at more forcefully by Mao Tse-tung who categorically states the "fundamental cause of the development of a thing is not external but internal, it lies in the contradictoriness within the thing"...[10] The relative roles of 'internal' and 'external' causes in articulating development may be best summed up in the exposition, "external causes are the condition of change internal causes are the basis of change."[11]

Keeping within this broad philosophical base and following from Marx's well-known pronouncement on the mechanism of propelling or 'fettering' of forward march of society[12] it can be deduced that contradictions between 'material forces of production' and 'relations of production'[13] forming a determinate social mode of production constitute the 'prime mover' in the transition of societies to higher forms. This can be logically equated with the condition of 'development'. Similarly, the situation of 'fettering' or blockage of transition to higher forms of society could be seen as the condition of 'underdevelopment'. Even if there is no systematic exposition of the latter eventuality from careful observations of Marx and Engels' works on the then pre-capitalist non-European societies like India, China, Persia,[14] it can be amply seen that they attributed the backwardness or relative unchangingness of these societies to their retaining of archaic social structures marked by unshattered primitive communalism, extremely resilient symbiosis between craft industry and peasant agriculture, strong centralized and extractive state power, etc.[15] and to the extent colonialism destroyed these conditions of 'passiveness' they attributed to it a progressive role.

Important contributions to the theory of development, particularly with reference to the question of viability of capitalist development in backward societies with strong entrenchments of 'Asiatic' features and whether capitalist development by its inherent nature of lopsidedness and unevenness could be considered 'development' at all, were made in the course of vicious polemics between the Marxist Bolsheviks and populist Narodniks in Russia at the close of 19th century. Lenin not only asserted from a historico-materialist position the need to smash the retrograde pre-capitalist relations for progressive transformation of the society,[16] but did present a fully materialistic explanation of the essential nature of capitalist development thus:

> "This process of transformation must, by the very nature of capitalism, take place in the midst of much that is uneven and disproportionate: periods of prosperity alternate with periods of crisis, the development of one industry leads to the decline of another, there is progress in one aspect of agriculture in one area and in another aspect in another area, the growth of trade and industry outstrips the growth of agriculture, etc. A large number of errors made by Narodnik writers spring from their efforts to prove that this disproportionate, spasmodic development is not development."[17]

The significance and relevance of these observations for our current debate, when neo-populism occupies a formidable position, are obvious.

A new vista of enquiry in the development literature in general and the course of development to be followed by the dependent, pre-capitalist societies, in particular, was added with the advent of imperialism. The issue was particularly significant because henceforth the question of integration of pre-capitalist societies with metropolitan economy acquired a new meaning, in that the metropolitan economy realised surplus value from the colonies/dependencies not only by way of revenue and commercial profit as before but also by way of industrial profit through productive capital investment in colonies/dependencies. This was bound to have different impact on the course of development of dependent, pre-capitalist societies, and hence ensued different perceptions of the phenomenon.[18] Lenin the foremost exponent of the theory of imperialism maintained that despite the inherent 'parasitism and decay' of monopoly capitalism which would gain upper hand "in some branches of industry, in some countries, for certain periods of time"[19] the "export of of capital influences and greatly accelerates the development of capitalism in those countries to which it is exported".[20] Thus a dichotomous moribund-dynamic character of imperialism was envisaged by the most influential Marxist of the 20th century, which should prove of immense help to make a position on the current controversy on the role of imperialism in the dynamics of development/underdevelopment in the Third World countries.

The real issues of 'underdevelopment 'as viewed from the side of the dependent/pre-capitalist societies was brought into focus in the heydays of national liberation movements and the collapse of former colonial empires in the aftermath of World War II. Though a number of variations in the characterisation and explanation of the phenomenon have appeared since then, they can be broadly categorised into two streams, namely (i) neo-Marxist approach and (ii) mainstream Marxist approach, on the basis of the degree of affinity of their methodology to the original formulations and basic methodological premises of Marxism.

1.2.11 Neo-Marxist Approach

The neo-Marxist approach, or the 'dependency theory' has been the most influential theory of underdevelopment in recent times. It was Baran[21] who in a direct response to the neo-classicist apologetics of colonialism in the field of the theory of economic development during the tumultuous years of 'cold war' laid the foundation of a radical theory of underdevelopment which was brought to its 'pristine glory' as 'dependency theory' by Frank.[22] Though the theory has many off-shoots and has undergone many changes and adaptations to different situations[23] all-pervasive common feature can be summerised thus: 'Underdevelopment 'as distinct from 'undevelopment' is not an original state but the result of integration of the economy to the world capitalist system. Hence one can more appropriately talk of 'development of underdevelopment' rather than just 'underdevelopment'; the simultaneous underdevelopment of 'periphery' or 'satellites' and development of 'centre' or 'metropolis' is operationalised through systematic drain of economic surplus from the former to the latter aided by various mechanisms of 'dominance-dependence' including colonial, financial-industrial and technological-industrial; an unbroken hierarchical chain of metropolis-satellite or centre-periphery relations both at the social and spatial levels may be visualised to stretch from the direct producers in the remote areas of the periphery to the monopoly capitalists in the metropolis so that one can speak of only a global capitalist system but no separate national formations except that they may be distinguished as different forms of capitalist formations like 'peripheral capitalism', 'dependent capitalism' etc; the satellites experience their greatest economic development when their ties to their metropolis are weakest and hence as implied from this, what is desired for development is not the strengthening of integration with the metropolis as advocated by the neo-classicist 'dualists' but overhauling of the dominance-dependence relations.

Wallersteins' 'world systems' analysis,[24] though differing in its emphasis on structure and growth of a world economy, has similar causal explanations of underdevelopment and thus may be grouped with the general 'dependency theory'. Similarly, Emmanuel[25] and Amin[26] have advanced a more complex and sophisticated model of surplus extraction and transfer from the periphery to the centre, i.e. through 'unequal exchange' and 'unequal specialisation' respectively,[27] but their essential implications on the occurrence of underdevelopment in dependent/pre-capitalist societies remains the same and may be included in the 'dependency' camp.

Despite its historical contribution to shift the focus of development economics to dominated societies[28] and to establish the importance of taking international economy as the unit of analysis in the era of imperialism and seeing the phenomenon of development/underdevelopment "through a politico-historical lense"[29] the 'dependency theory' essentially represents a deviant 'neo-populist' current within the radical academics and has been appropriately taken to task by the better exponents of historico-materialist method.[30] As has been pointed out by earlier critics, the root of the problem with this theory lies in its eclectic perception of the world and its simplistic, deterministic model of society moving in a straight line as a result of mechanical pressure from exogenous forces, quite contrary to the scientific formulations of materialist dialectics on the law of motion of society as outlined earlier. In the realm of economics this fallacy is reflected in their seeing exploitation to take place not in the *essential* relations of production and between social classes but in the *apparent* relation of exchange and between countries or regions. As a result the theory is not only unable to explain the 'cause' of development/underdevelopment except for describing a 'zero-sum' process of development of one sector/ region/country at the cost of underdevelopment of the another thus presenting a static view of the world, but also advances a dangerous 'conspiracy theory' where there is no scope of 'reproduction' of the system[31] but only endless catastrophes. The anti-historic postures and fatalistic political implications of such a formulation are obvious. The basic historico-materialist position on the other hand is that the 'cause' of development/under-development should be sought within the reproduction logic of the particular mode of production and economic development is not just a quantitative amassing of surplus value but a qualitative leap made by the production system where capital, or accumulated surplus labour, is just one of the ensembles. The more important ensemble in this process of change is the class structure which "once established, will in fact determine the course of economic development or underdevelopment over an entire epoch" and the change in class structure is "incomprehensible in terms merely of market forces"[32]. Therefore, the "involvement of underdeveloped countries in the world economy was not significant in itself but only for the impact it had on the internal class structure of these countries, locking into position certain classes which stood in the way of a capitalist transformation"[33].

However, this should not be construed as total negation or minimisation of the significance of integration with metropolitan economy for the structuration of the dynamics of development of backward societies. For:

> "How a society moves from one stage to another will depend not only on the internal dynamics of the transition but also on how that society is inserted into the world system at a particular point in the development of that system"[34].

The 'external' nexus would be particularly significant when this 'particular point' happens to be the stage of 'primitive accumulation' in the case of 'peripheral' society and the mode of surplus appropriation by the metropolis be mercantilist.[35] Our only objections are with assigning a deterministic role to the 'external' factor, universalising a phenomenon largely true only in the case of particular stage of societies and in the mercantilist epoch and above all, the method of basing the reasoning on the relations of exchange rather than on the relations of production.

However, leaving aside the faulty analytical framework adopted and general characterisation of the peripheral economy as 'capitalist', many of the empirical observations of the social and spatial characteristics of underdeveloped economy, like retarded and distorted industrialisation, hypertrophy of tertiary sector, dominance of comprador capital, 'disarticulated' and 'extraverted' structure,[36] etc. as provided by them can be useful and may be judiciously adopted for empirical verification. Beside, without necessarily subscribing to the original connotations, some of the terminologies like 'dominance-dependence', 'centre-periphery; etc., coined or popularised by this sub-school can be selectively made use of.

1.2.12 Mainstream Marxist Approach

Parallel with the development of the neo-Marxist theories grew another body of literature on development/underdevelopment, which owed a closer allegiance to the classical Marxist method of analysis of the world. Since they avoided many of the pitfalls of 'dependency theory' and laid more emphasis on the structure of production and social classes to explain the dynamics of the structure of production and social classes to explain the dynamics of social development, they have come into increasing prominence over the debris of 'dependency theory' after the second half of the seventies. However, they are seen to be too abstract and general in approach to be of not much use for empirical application.

The most dominant and identifiable current within this stream of analytical approaches is perhaps what is commonly known as 'articulation of modes of production' approach.[37] This approach attempts to explain development/underdevelopment in terms of the nature of articulation of dominant mode of production with the dominated mode of production[38] and the resultant degree of 'conservation' and 'dissolution' of dominated mode of production and its restructuration with the implicit assumption that history should be essentially constituted as 'a science of discontinuous modes of production'. Though a number of varied interpretations of mechanism of articulation and their implications of or the nature of underdevelopment of pre-capitalist societies have been offered, the basic premises may be generalised thus: the underdeveloped society integrated to the world capitalist system can be visualised as a 'social formation'[39] constituting of more than one mode of production which are constantly interacting with each other and attempting to gain dominance over the other; during the period of transition of the modes the nature and speed of dissolution or conservation of the subordinate mode would vary depending upon the stage of development of the dominant mode, for example, if within the social formation capitalist mode of production is dominant there would be accelerated dissolution of other modes of production and if capitalist mode of production is not directly predominant the main tendency would be a guarded 'conservation-dissolution' of non-capitalist modes of production[40] or, in the case of capitalist penetration from outside the impact would vary according to the periodisation like, in period of merchant capital the tendency would be to strengthen pre-capitalist mode, in the period of industrial capital the disruption of pre-capitalist mode would be accelerated and in the period of finance capital (i.e. industrial plus banking capital) capitalist relations would be created but a pattern of uneven development would set in because of selective interests of imperialism.[41] The nature of articulation of capitalism with pre-capitalist modes of production would also vary by the forms of penetration of capitalism and the degree of resistance offered by pre-capitalist modes depending on the latter's internal structure.[42] A similar model of articulation between and transformation of sectoral structure of the economy can also be envisaged, in which "a dominant yet externally dependent sector restricts the development of other sectors..."[43]

Though the idea of explaining backwardness/underdevelopment in terms of uneven development of mode of production, both sectorally and spatially, appears logical and useful the model retains some of the fallacious premises of 'dependency theory' like assigning a deterministic role to the exogenous impulses and assuming transfer of value as 'cause' of underdevelopment, etc., and a number of other methodological discrepancies. Also, whereas the flavor of economic determinism in it is explicit, it also smacks of a form of 'dualism' in assuming non-capitalist modes as not having their own laws of motion. Concomitant with its excessive economism, the model also fails to tackle the role of class formation in development/underdevelopment in a satisfactory manner.

Of late some significant attempts have been made to reinterpret and adopt some of the newly arisen developmental issues within the Marxist frame, and there is seen an increasing trend to 'return to classical Marxism' or employ Marxist method to understand the phenomenon of development/underdevelopment.[44]

Despite some inconsistencies, not only do these works reassert the correct historico-materialist position of seeing underdevelopment as a manifestation of contradiction between the productive forces and production relations in a given formation[45] but also assign 'primacy' to production relations in articulating the process. Also discarding all forms of determinism and nihilism a correct assessment of the relative roles of 'endogenous' 'exogenous' variables in the development process is sought to be made. Among others, this is evident in Bagchi's apt characterisation of underdeveloped societies as "societies which have been hybridized under the dual stress of the logic of evolution of its pre-existing social structure and of the buffetings of an evolving world capitalist system".[46]

A parallel development in the contemporary Marxist academic world which has made a tremendous contribution to the understanding of the phenomenon of development/underdevelopment is the vigorous polemics and extensive empirical research on the interrelated questions of 'mode of production' (or popularly known as 'transition debate')[47] and imperialism.[48] Particularly the debate on 'transition from feudalism to capitalism' or characterisation of agrarian capitalism have thrown fresh light on the basic historico-materialist method of looking into the 'contradictoriness within the thing' and considering the phenomenon in totality to discern its laws of motion, which is synonymous with the laws of societal development/underdevelopment. Similarly, the debate on imperialism, particularly on the new developments since World War II seem to be increasingly taking the academics away from the 'stagnationist' viewpoint that ruled the roost earlier to the Leninist position of a dichotomous 'moribund-dynamic' character of imperialism which exercises a 'conservation-dissolution' role vis-a-vis pre-capitalist societies but the resultant growth is, sectorally and spatially, extremely uneven and distorted.

However, most of the existing literature on 'underdevelopment' has been based on the experience of societies that were under direct colonial domination or were subsequently integrated to world capitalist system for direct economic imperatives of imperialism. This has created a big hiatus and an analytical frame has not emerged through which we may analyse the dynamics of underdevelopment in societies which are only 'semi-colonies' (i.e which preserved juridicial independence, but were dependent economically upon imperialist powers) and have more of 'politico-strategic' than of economic utility to imperialism. On the basis of fragmentary literature on the subject[49] it can be surmised that such societies which are "at the bottom of the imperialist calculus", i.e. economic calculus, would be more "fossilized" than transformed to higher forms because of their own inherent passivity of archaic formations bolstered by the 'conservation' tendency of imperialism.

Moreover, in geographically marginal lands such as alpine areas or high mountains, the productive forces would be muffled/fettered more by nature than by social relations of production. Thus it would be appropriate to distinguish a situation marked more by low *absolute* level of productive forces as just 'retarded' and another with only *relative* low level or structurally deformed condition of productive forces as 'underdeveloped', after Bagchi, though he has used the connotations in slightly different context.[50]

All in all, there is a glaring need to charter a new course to apply the basic historico-materialist method of scientific enquiry for empirical investigation of the phenomenon of development/underdevelopment, in general and that in semi-colonial/dependent societies, in particular.

1.2.13 The Proposed Approach

On the basis of the foregoing survey the analytical approach for the proposed study can be summed up thus:

- The *method* of historical materialism should form the core of a scientific enquiry into a social phenomenon, for it goads one to see a phenomenon in its totality and in relation with all its surroundings, a phenomenon in constant motion and transformation of quantity into quality.
- Social development should be seen as a constant process triggered by the contradictions between forces and relations of production in the given mode of production. Development and underdevelopment may be seen as antithetical to each other in that, whereas, 'development' within a given social formation would be full realisation of productive potentials of the society or transition to higher social formation, 'underdevelopment' would be the opposite condition of non-realisation of full potential of development and/or blockage to transition to higher formations.
- A mode of production should be seen as the articulated combination of all or major ensembles of relations and forces of production and the temptation of generalisation through a single or few ensembles should be carefully checked to avoid wrong characterisation of stage or nature of development. Transition from one mode of production to another should not be taken as a linear and once-for-all event but a lengthy and discontinuous process, so that at a time there may be more than one mode of production but under the hegemony of one mode and in a dichotomous relation of unity-struggle-transformation.
- Development in one sector/area does not necessarily depend on or cause underdevelopment elsewhere. But at a particular stage of development of society, specially the stage of 'primitive accumulation' of capital, the transfer of absolute surplus value from one to another can prove important *but not the only* condition for the transformation of one into capitalism and relapse of another into pre-capitalist stage. Also, once capitalism is developed somewhere, by its nature of incessant drive towards expanded reproduction it tends to draw the whole world under its wings and thus intervenes in the development process elsewhere. But the impact on the pre-capitalist economy would vary according to the historical stage of development of capital and the mode of articulation with the pre-capitalist economy, i.e. whether

mercantile, industrial or financial, and also the internal structure of the pre-capitalist economy.

- No form of determinism or nihilism should be entertained as regards the relative roles of 'endogenous' and 'exogenous' factors in the process of development/underdevelopment, because in the era of imperialism no society can remain in a water-tight compartment unaffected by 'exogenous' factors, but in general conditions 'external causes become operative through internal causes'. Exploitation always takes place at the level of relations of production, though it may appear at the level of exchange. Therefore while talking of value transfer from one sector/region/country to another, the process should be located at the respective relations of production. Also no form of 'conspiracy theory' should be invented to explain exploitation of one by the other, but instead it should be sought within the reproduction logic of each. All sorts of determinism and reductionism, particularly economic, should be ruled out and the scope and role of subjective interventions through the superstructural level should be acknowledged, so that non-economic variables as like 'politico-strategic' considerations, can also be accounted for in the development/underdevelopment process and the theory can be realised in practice.
- Characteristics of underdevelopment would be different for different social formations. Therefore for empirical verification of the level and nature of development/underdevelopment characteristics of the different ensembles of forces and relations of production should be judiciously defined for each mode of production. Degree of differentiation of social division of labour and the extent of economic articulation can be taken as general indicators of higher mode of production, but the degree of unevenness, extravertedness, dysfunctionality, etc. should be qualified by their nature to identify with the particular mode of production/level of development.
- To differentiate the condition of backwardness in the *absolute* and *relative* sense or in pre-capitalist and capitalist social-formations respectively separate terminologies of 'retardation' and 'underdevelopment' may be used. In other words, the conventional usage of 'underdevelopment' (as made by the neo-Marxists) is particular to the capitalist social formations only; hence the term 'underdevelopment' here would have two connotations–one general and the other particular.
- Not necessarily complying with the technical connotations associated with them, it may be helpful to make selective and judicious use of terminologies thrown up by different branches of theories like: 'dominance-dependence' or 'core-periphery', to denote notional hierarchies of economies/areas and the unequal relations between them; 'unequal exchange' in the case of mechanism of value transfer between two economies of different labour productivity; or 'Asiatic' to denote remnants of pre-feudal structures particularly characterised by a strong centralised state.

1.2.2 Concept of Space and Spatial Structure of Underdevelopment

Not only because the phenomenon of development/underdevelopment takes place in terms of concrete physical space but also because there is an increasing realisation of an intricate interrelationship between social and spatial processes in the development process, that it is imperative to make a brief review of the relevant literature and lay the foundation for a theoretical framework for the study of Nepal. As in the case of every other social issue there is a deep ontological chasm on the spatial question as well. It may, therefore, be appropriate to survey the theories as developed by the two principal contending schools, namely the Anglo-Saxon school and the Marxist school.

1.2.21 The Anglo-Saxon School

Though we have not accepted the methodology of the Anglo-Saxon approach for the present enquiry, we deem it necessary to provide a brief critique of its position on the spatial issue, because, not only has it been the largest contributor on the subject but also because it exercises a monopoly hold on the academics in Nepal. The sway of neo-classical economics over the theories of 'regional development', however, is not surprising. The conventional 'regional development' theories mostly concern with the problem of regional unevenness in development and the locational aspect of economic activities of particular significance under capitalism. The neo-classical economics as the foundation of bourgeois-imperialist ideology should naturally come forward to prepare a theoretical recipe on 'regional question' for the consumption of the ruling classes. True to its a historical, segmented and linear view of the world, it sees only 'natural space' as space and regards it as 'external' but of deterministic significance, to the articulation of the social process. It identifies the question with the locational and mobility problem of different factors of production to be organised invariably on the capitalist basis. The main-stay of this group of theories on 'regional question' have, therefore, been the various streams of 'industrial location theories', dominantly of the Weberian tradition,[51] which provide a spatial configuration of economic activities determined by the mobility and transportation costs of different factors of production and by the distance to product market with a view to maximise profit for the capitalist. Spatial inequality in development are seen to result from the malfunctioning of equilibrium mechanism due to market imperfections and institutional bottlenecks that impede smooth factor and resource movements for bringing about an efficient spatial allocation of resources. This 'transitory aberration' is assumed to disappear in course of economic growth process when there would be greater unification of factor markets and economic integration among disparate spatial units.

The neo-classical general equilibrium theory in its spatial dimension reached its zenith in the works of 'regional science' group headed by Walter Isard.[52] The concept, however, stands largely rejected by academics of radical persuasions[53] on the grounds of not only its avowed ahistoricity and fallacious economic presumptions of equilibriating role of market mechanism in the current era of monopoly capitalism, but also for its incapacity to comprehend, the dynamics of space economy where the additional operation of 'monopoly of nature' would make the equilibrium doctrine of neo-classicism further redundant.

With the indefensible position of equilibrium doctrine thoroughly exposed by the realities of Third World countries in the post-World War II period, there arose from within the same epistemological camp a populist-reformist current to be commonly known as 'institutionalist' sub-school headed by Myrdal and ably supported and expanded upon by Hirschman, Friedman and others.[54] Based on principles like 'circular and cumulative causations', it recognises the tendency towards spatial inequality in the operation of capitalist market but falters at discerning the causal mechanism of the process. Its attempts to locate the formation of spatial inequality in the dichotomous 'spread' and 'backwash' effects, or, in 'trickling down' and 'polarisation' effects, in the flow of labour and capital between the advanced and depressed regions, makes a good description of the empirically observable phenomenon, but at close scrutiny turns out to be mere eclecticism as it tends to explain "effects in terms of effects."[55] In the absence of a correct historical and materialistic interpretation of why at different stages of social development and at different socio-physical conditions either of 'spread' or 'backwash' effects, mostly the latter, become predominant, the mere advocacy of a vague, classless 'state intervention' to balance the contradiction process is not going to make the populist pronouncements any better for concrete applications. A brief recapitulation of the constantly changing regional development planning strategies sold to the gullible Third World countries by the guardians of world monopoly capital should underscore this point; though the contextual circumstances permit us only the review of methodological approaches in dealing with the spatial question vis-a-vis the development process rather than vivisection of different models in the realm of policy making.

The single most influential model of 'regional development' during the 1960s and 1970s was 'growth pole' or 'growth centre'[56] approach. Primarily upholding the 'regional imbalance' thesis it sought to generalise the spasmodic growth dynamics of capitalism for all societies and places and put excessive faith on the ultimate positive effect to result from the 'natural' uneven growth. Consequently it advocated deliberate creation of growth enclaves or poles in selected localities from where in an umbrella like fashion growth impulses both in economic and spatial terms would spread to surrounding localities/areas. The marriage of convenience of 'general equilibrium' model of neo-classicists and 'circular and cumulative causation' of 'institutionalists' is amply apparent in the eclectic-romantic formulation. However, this spatial counterpart of 'green revolution 'model in fashion in neo-classical economics in the 1960s was to face the same fate of its economic counterpart by the 1970s. In the initial phases, to make it more palliative to the Third World countries with little internal articulation, entire areas along the principal transportation axes were envisaged as 'growth axes', or, the growth poles were divided into a series of smaller points and arranged into selective regional closures of 'growth foci' or 'decentralised concentration' of economic activities in a hierarchical spatial order.[57] The basic assumption throughout being that mechanical spread of economic activities along the geographical space within the same socio-political dispensation would produce 'growth with equity'. When these dreams were further belied and realisation dawned that further aggravated under the capitalistic economic logic there ensued a debate on 'development from above or below' and a large number of 'area' or 'target group' development and 'basic needs' approaches were flaunted to bring about 'development from below.[58] Not only was this an acknowledgement, though belated, of spatial inequality as a *fait accompli* under the capitalist system, but behind the apparent realisation there was no altruistic concern for the world's new found 'poor' but with the profit realisation crisis of capitalism.[59]

Pervading through all the works on 'regional question' of this branch of scholarship is their fallacious perception of space as 'external' to society and the failure to see spatial organisation in terms of historical forms of organisation of society. For this very reason we are compelled to turn to the alternative provided by Marxist scholarship.

1.2.22 The Marxist Approach

In view of the discernible divergence in the application of the basic tenets of Marxism in the recent times, as observed earlier, and in the absence of a coherent and comprehensive exposition of the 'regional question' in the traditional Marxist scholarship, it is necessary to have a cursory survey of the scanty and disparate literature on the subject and attempt to derive a methodology for the analysis of the 'regional question' based on the basic tenets of the scientific doctrine. The primary issues of our immediate concern are: notion of physical space/nature in social science, relation between space and society and identification of the spatial organisation of underdevelopment.

By the very nature of its being a 'materialist' philosophy and its method of seeing things in 'dialectical' relations the concept of physical space is immanent and any form of 'determinism' whether of natural or economic, is ruled out in the scheme of social development as perceived in the Marxist framework. This is amply reflected in one of the earliest works of Marx and Engels:

"We know only a single science, the science of history. One can look at history from two sides and divide it into the history of nature and the history of men. The two sides are, however, inseparable; the history of nature and the history of men are dependent on each other so long as men exist".[60]

Also Marx's well known definition of all production as 'appropriation of nature by the individual within and through a certain form of society' lays the foundation for constructing a theory of relation between nature and society as that of increasing interaction with and modification of nature with the development of higher social formations. This neither implies total irrelevance of nature in higher forms of society nor the impregnability of spatial barrier for social interactions given a certain level of development of capital. However, true to the experience in pre-monopoly phase of capitalism general emphasis of Marxist works of the day is found to be on the 'universalising tendency of capital' though they were not unaware of geographical differentiation but only gave it secondary importance compared to the universalising tendency of capital and the consequent drive toward equalization.[61] The notion of 'territorial division of labour' as a prerequisite for the development of productive forces and the emergence of economic regions to exploit 'every special advantage' in the form of geographic location of historical accumulations, etc. run through the classic works of Marxism.[62]

The real beginning of the construction of a Marxist theory of 'economic region', as the term is understood to mean today, can be said to have been made with Lenin's monumental study *Development of Capitalism in Russia* at the fag end of the 19th century. The way towards such a theory was paid by the first geographical differentiation of social processes in pre-revolutionary Russia, i.e. not in the sense of simple spatial comparison of economies but differentiation of such spaces as the "expression of the economic process of the territorial social division of labour and specialisation of the economy".[63] A far more significant methodological contribution in explaining spatial uneven development in terms of differences in their social organisation of production and in understanding dialectical connection between spatial and social processes, was made by his differentiation of economic regions in terms of long-inhabited parts of the country with 'intensive development of capitalism' and 'new lands' of the periphery with 'extensive development of capitalism.[64] This should provide an important insight for an analysis of the spatial structure of under-development in the Third World countries today. Also, as already noted in the preceding section, Lenin recognised inherent unevenness in the development of capitalism and when this is transposed to the geographical space we could come to fairly well articulated theory of spatial inequality under capitalism. Similarly his conceptualisation of imperialism as a 'stage' of capitalism is impregnated with territorial uneven development[65] and bears strong relevance for the current situation.

The onus of building a coherent and comprehensive theory of 'economic regions' and dynamics of regional formations from a historico-materialist perspective was left to the Soviet economic geographers in the aftermath of the October Revolution. Commonly referred to as the Baransky-Kolosovsky school, they synthesized historico-materialist formulations on relations between nature and society as one of dialectical interactions. Regions were viewed as 'socio-economic territorial systems' articulated through territorial division of labour and to be constantly altered by the dynamics of social mode of production. Regional inequalities were seen as territorial manifestations of social contradictions. However, with the political degeneration of the Soviet system the revisionist ideology is seen reflected in the treatment of the 'regional question' as well in the form of over-fascination with territorial organisation of productive forces and total discarding of the aspect of relations of production.

In the post World War II period in the face of renewed challenges from Anglo-Saxon scholarship, the fragmented Marxist scholarship is seen to have developed in diverse directions with no mainstream in sight. Of these diverse currents, the most easily recognisable are those who straight away adapt the formulations of neo-Marxist 'dependency theory' to construct a model of regional uneven development or spatial structure of underdevelopment. Based on 'surplus drain' scheme of dependency theory, this model invokes 'places exploiting places' theme to explain spatial inequality and romantically construct a spatial scenario of chains of 'satellitic centres' extending from a remote hamlet in the periphery to the 'metroplolitan centre' to articulate this 'exploitative' relationship.[67] Amin[68] presenting a variant on the theme bases his theory on a slightly different premises of 'auto-centric' development in the 'centre' and 'dependent' development in the 'periphery' and suggests an internally fragmented, or 'disarticulated', and externally integrated, or 'extraverted', spatial structure in the underdeveloped settings.

As in the case of the 'institutionalists' these models present correct descriptions of the outwardly observable spatial phenomenon, particularly in the case of countries with a colonial past or those closedly intertwined with the world capitalist system. They, however, present an erroneous explanation of the causal mechanism. Apart from the already criticised faulty, notion of occurrence of 'underdevelopment' and exploitation having taken place at the level of exchange, which may be ratified by showing "how the exploitative relations of wage labour is reproduced in the regional structure of production and exchange"[69] another inadmissible proposition is the theme of 'places exploiting places'. It may be useful to cite Walker to clear this confusion:

> "... the idea that places exploit places is based on a fundamental confusion of use and (exchange) value, similar to the mistaken notion that "nature" is exploited in value terms. The concrete physical and social attributes of places operate like forces of nature and means of production to augment (or diminish) value production, not to create value. If value flows from one area to another, it is owing to the concretely different use-value circumstances of capital and labour-power operating in those places. Surplus value is still passing from workers to capitalists and from capitalists to capitalists."[70]

The statement is self-explanatory. Of course, it does not deny that value flows from one area to another and one place may *appear* to 'exploit' another, but the disagreement with the neo-Marxist model is on the question of *essence* of value transfer and different forms it assumes under different historical circumstances. At a certain historical stage of society one place may appear to 'exploit' another place when the different places happen to be dominant locales of exploiting or exploited classes. For example, in a colonial set-up absolute surplus value may be transferred from the colony to the metropolis, or, in a semi-feudal society with a centralised state surplus value may be appropriated under direct or indirect coercion from the peasants in the countryside and transferred to the locales of state power or to 'feudal agglomerations'. But still the essence of value transfer lies in the class relations that fetish in space may result from the different use-valued circumstances of capital and labour power operating in those places, or from differences in the level of productivity of the factors of production in them. These differences may be a cumulative result of many instances including the geographical and historical advantages enjoyed by one place and not the other. Of course, once the differences are enshrined they would be cumulatively reproduced. Thus, while, agreeing with the description of the *appearance* of spatial inequality as provided by the neo-Marxists, the causal mechanism of the phenomenon would have to be replaced by the Marxist law of production, appropriation and circulation of surplus value under different historical stages of development of society.

In recent times, particularly after the mid-seventies, there has been a marked tendency, to attempt to return to the basic method of historical materialism to understand the relations between society and space in general and the phenomenon of spatial uneven development, in particular.[71] However, most of the works have been confined to the spatial problems of advanced capitalist countries and, there too, on the 'urban question'. Moreover, in the midst of various individualistic traits and obsession with excessive abstraction prevailing, there is no sight of emergence of a coherent Marxist approach to spatial analysis. Rather streaks of 'neo-Marxism' and populism run through many of the works.

Thus, without going into the methodological 'purity' of the individual authors, it would be relevant to summerise the dominant positions on the related issues, namely the concept of nature or space, relation between spatial and social problematics and spatial structure of underdevelopment.

As against the geographic fatalism or nihilism propagated by authors of other methodological persuasions, Marxists see an interactive and interdependent relation between nature and society. They recognise only a 'historical' or 'humanised' nature, but no unsullied 'external' nature as such. The concept of "production" or "production of space" and increasing domination in society by 'created space' in subsequent social modes of production[72] may be fully consistent with the historico-materialist theory. However, overzealous statements like "human societies create their own geography"[73] unless qualified by the 'stage' of "human societies", may smack of geographical nihilism. Hence not to err in scientific enquiry of 'regional question' the basic historical materialist formulations on the dialectical relations between nature and society need to be reasserted, as is explicit in the following observation by Baransky:

> "We must take into consideration the geographical factors not in isolation from everything else, not metaphysically, ... but dialetically, in relation to the current state of technology, to production relation and more generally to the overall socio-historical situation in which a country finds itself at a particular stage of its development"[74].

It is obvious that at lower stages of development geographical factors exercise considerable bearing on the social process, which get progressively diminished in higher formations.

Considerable divergence of opinion amongst Marxist scholarship is found on the second related issue of the nature of relationship between the spatial and social problematic in the development process. Soja[75] has attempted to differentiate three district approaches on this question namely:

1. those who attribute absolute primacy to class analysis, e.g. 'orthodox' Marxists;
2. those who present space as important but tend to defer the overriding significance of spatial social class, among whom he includes Castells, Harvey and Wallerstein, and
3. those who take the view of 'socio-spatial dialetic' or that "social and spatial relationship are dialetically interactive interdependent: that social relations of production are both space-forming and space-contingent", among whom are included Soja himself, Lefebvre and Mandel.

In the last category could also be included Santos and Mabgunje.[76]

However, we would contend that the classification is motivated and malafide, in that no 'orthodox' Marxist would ever totally negate the role of territorial space in the social development process.[77] Logically the classification can be only on the basis of relative weightages assigned to the social or spatial ensemble of the development process at the given stage of social formation and the specificities of the 'given' and 'created' spaces, without implying dualism in their relation. Though one should have no objection to the use of the term 'socio-spatial dialectic' in the sense that "social and spatial relationship are dialectically interactive and interdependent" and that " social relations of production are both space-forming and space-contingent", one cannot concur with the interpretation of 'dialectical relation' as implying that social and spatial problematic are "on the same level"[78] of significance in bringing about development/underdevelopment. To say that 'dialetical' interaction means statically 'equal' interaction and in mechanical order of succession, is not dialetics at all. Of course, spatial relations are immanent in the very concept of 'mode of production' or 'social formation'[79] and it is fully within the preview of 'dialetics' to envisage certain stages of social development or certain other exigencies when the spatial component would not only be 'on the same level' but of overriding importance in the development process. For example, in primitive societies or in cases of extreme localisation of potential natural resources, natural spatial conditions have been and will be the principal basis of territorial division of labour[80] and hence determinant of the development process. Therefore, any approach of treating social and spatial ensembles of the development process statically "on the same level" in the guise of "spatio-social dialectic' is bound to smack of 'spatial fetishism and determinism' and "unwittingly mimic the tendency within bourgeois social science to assign characteristics to places and things, rather than sticking to the dynamic of a process as the analytical focus."[81]

Another set of approaches of spatial analysis can be distinguished by their assigning of decisive importance to the social mode of production in defining the spatial structure or explaining "spatial organisation as a manifestation of the logic of the social system itself". The view is seen best articulated in the following observations by Peet:

> "A mode of production generates a typical set of relations with the physical environment, and a territorial structure which reflect the relations of production (especially the purposes of the owners of the means of production) and the level of development of the productive forces. Social formation structured by the same mode of production thus have generally similar geography. But given a mode of production express itself differently under varying physical conditions or in areas of varying cultural transmission from decayed modes of production, producing variations between and within the social formations it generates."[82]

Further he summerises:

> "Spatial relations are at base class relations; class relations contain the effects of space and environment."[83]

A greater emphasis on political economy for the articulation of particular nature of organisation of space is invoked by others, such as:

> "The regional political economist explains spatial organisation as a manifestation of the logic of the social system itself...
>
> To understand how those struggles to gain, maintain and increase control over surplus operate over space is to understand the logic behind the development of spatial organisation in a society. Spatial organization reflects those struggle and the underlying social relations of production".[84]

However, the views seeing spatial organisation as only the 'manifestation' of social formation, even though essentially based on a historico-materialist framework and providing scope for variations in different historical stages of development of society, tend to minimise the actively interacting role of space in the social process and give some currency to the charges of going to the other extreme of social determinism .[85] The more scientific and balanced approach, then, would be to view particular configuration of space both as the *manifestation* of and to a lesser degree a *causal factor* in the social process. But there should be no room for dualism or statism in the relation but should be in dialectical unison, ensuring constant dynamism and providing scope for accounting historical and other specificities. In this context, without being misunderstood of having tilted towards 'space determinism' or towards mechanistic "on the same level" thesis, it may be useful to envision the dynamics of space as a 'spatial process' and the combined dynamics of space and society as a 'socio-spatial process.'[86]

This brings us to the final task of synthesizing an analytical approach for defining and characterising spatial structure of underdevelopment. Prior to that we may have to sort out certain definitional problems, particularly that of 'spatial structure', 'spatial organisation' and 'spatial configuration'. Transposing the common definition of 'structure' i.e. an ordered relation between individual elements and the whole, to the realm of territorial space 'spatial structure' can be defined as the ordered relation, that exists between individual 'spatial forms' such as farmlands, settlements, factories, roads, etc. and the whole of which they form a part. By 'spatial organization' is meant spatial arrangement or distribution of activities or physical objects in sequences conforming with selected social ends. 'Spatial configuration' on the other hand means any distribution of activities or objects in the territorial space without consideration of goals or intervention of social processes. In other words, spatial organization refers to those spatial configurations that are mediated by social processes and that ultimately go to build spatial structure of particular social denomination.[87] Hence what we are interested at the moment is to unravel the logic of spatial organization of activities that constitute the spatial structure of underdevelopment.

Recent Marxist spatial analyses have been mostly confined to the advanced capitalist countries[88] and naturally their concerns have been confined to theories on the occurrence of spatial unevenness in development, which is but one, though major, aspect of distortions in spatial structure of underdeveloped countries. However, the general methods expounded therein could be of relevance for us. The dominant theme in these studies obviously has been to explain uneven development in terms of the immanent contradictory tendency of capital towards social and spatial 'differentiation' and 'equalisation'. As against the earlier experiences of more capital having moved to depressed areas to escape from falling rate of profit at the 'centre' and to take advantage of cheap labour, raw material, market etc. in the 'periphery', late experiences have shown the tendency of capital to 'concentrate and centralise', in order to be stronger. One also observes that "the accumulation of capital in one geographical area tends *ceteris paribus* to draw other capital to the same area".[89] Thus once capital is historically accumulated in one area the spatial inequality tends to be cumulatively reproduced as a result of increasing differentials in labour productivity, rates of profit, organic composition of capital etc. Further, exchanges between such unequal regions produce geographical transfer of value from backward to advanced and in that sense development of one region leads to further underdevelopment of another. This model of spatial inequality, though largely valid for capitalist countries, should have relevance in an underdeveloped country with a semi-feudal semi-capitalist economy.

Another approach to explain spatial uneven development has been in terms of uneven penetration of capitalism,[90] both at the sub-national scale and international scale. This analysis, which has its roots in the original works of Marx and Lenin, seeks to explain uneven penetration at different spatial points as due to a host of factors like nature of pre-existing modes of production and political formation differential features of nature, human resistence to incorporation as wage labour etc. Also, specially at the inter-national level the imperatives of creating a "geography of the industrial reverse army"[91] or to ensure a flow of cheap and/or docile workforce, tend to impede the process of capitalist penetration in labour reserve areas. Whatever may be the reason for non-penetration depending upon the endogenous and exogenous factors, the model offers varied possibilities for explaining spatial inequalities in transitional societies.

A spatial counterpart of the 'articulation of mode of production' model[92] has also been offered to explain spatial inequality, in a manner that 'a region is dominated when it is specialized in branches organized by dominated modes or by archaic stages of the dominant mode' etc. Though the model provides scope for explaining spatial inequalities in pre-capitalist societies integrated to the world capitalist system, the shortcomings of the economic modes of 'articulation of modes of production' as pointed out earlier, are seen further exacerbated by a mechanical transposition of social relations into spatial relations, making the model highly questionable.

The question of spatial inequality cannot be said to be insignificant in pre-capitalist societies,[93] though it is definitely aggravated under capitalism. However, the explanation of causative mechanism would have to be sought in the spatial logic of the particular social formation. On the other hand, by the very nature of domination of natural factors and historical exigencies in the formation of spatial structure of pre-capitalist societies, the apparent spatial differentials in them could be better accounted as 'diversity' than 'disparity'.[94]

Historico-materialist method of enquiry envisages different processes and characteristics of spatial structure of societies under different historical stages of development. Amidst the general paucity of literature on the subject based on the experiences of underdeveloped societies, the one by Salinas (1983) on Peru can provide significant insights for further enquiry. Though the focus appears to be tilted more towards the mechanism of surplus extraction and transfer across space than on organisation of production, it has been shown through a judicious combination of historical analysis of internal social mode of production and nature of integration with metropolitan economy that in different historical epochs like tribal communal formation (pre-Incan period), centralised state dominated early feudal formation (Incan period), colonial feudal-mercantile formation (Spanish colonial period), industrial capital and finance capital dominated neocolonial formations (British and U.S. capital dominated modern periods), different spatial logic of surplus production, appropriation and circulation do give rise to different spatial structures and areas dominant in one social formation do become peripheral in another. Basic inference to be derived is that the spatial structure of a society is to be analysed in terms of the production and reproduction logic of the prevailing politico-economic system.

A separate body of literature exists on the quantitative, methods of 'regionalisation' of the economy,[95] thanks to the 'empirico-positivist' wind fanned by the neo-classicists throughout the world. Since our present objective is to study the nature of social and spatial structure of underdevelopment from a politico-economic perspective rather than to 'regionalise' the economy suitable quantitative techniques will not be used *per se* but may be used to substantiate our arguments wherever necessary.

It may also be imperative to make a distinction of commonly used terminologies like 'region' which have quite different technical connotations. Even though in common parlance a 'region' has come to be used as any sub-national[96] spatial unit to be identified with a particular trait, a historico-materialist approach would define it as 'a spatial entity of sub-national scale, formed by an objective process of territorial division of labour, marked by internal heterogeneity but external homogeneity and linked to the system of national whole through the reciprocity of functions performed by each'. Hence it would be naive to speak of 'regions' where the system of 'national' whole, in the strict politico-economic sense, has not yet developed. The use of 'spatial structure' instead of 'regional structure' can save us from the embarrassment of technicality, but would be of peripheral significance to make a difference in the scientific enquiry. In the case of sub-national spatial differentiation of particular attributes like physiographic, administrative etc. the use of 'zone' instead of 'region' may be more appropriate. Similarly, establishment of differences from place to place and of spatial boundaries in the density of the distribution of a particular phenomenon over the surface of earth should not be considered 'regionalisation' but be called 'geographical differentiation'.

1.2.23 The Proposed Approach

On the basis of the foregoing discussion the proposed theoretical approach for spatial analysis in this study may be summed up thus:

- The historico-materialist theoretical framework should provide the most appropriate method for spatial analysis, for it envisions 'nature' and 'society' in constant interaction with each other and considers 'production' as 'appropriation of nature within and through a certain form of society' and views territorial 'space' as 'humanised' or 'historical' nature. Moreover, it rules out geographical determinism or nihilism in the social development process and visualises the dynamics of relation between nature and society as that of increasing interaction with and modification of nature with the development of higher social formations.
- Space should not be seen as 'external' to but as immanent in the development process such that one may define development as a combined 'socio-spatial process'. However, the implied dialectic of the relation between spatial and social processes should not be mechanistically interpreted as meaning equal roles of the two ensembles in articulating the development process. Barring

historical specifics, in general circumstances it may be more scientific to view spatial formation as the *manifestation* of and to a lesser degree a *causal factor* in the particular configuration of social formation, for it would be impossible to construct a logical historico-materialist theory in which spatial process as a rule is on equal footing with or has domination over the social process. The case of domination by 'natural space' in pre-capitalist formations, however, may not be confused with generalisations on organisation of 'created space' as the logic of the two are qualitatively different.

- Definition of spatial structure as a manifestation of prevailing social mode of production provides scope for searching the spatial logic of each mode in its production and reproduction logic. For example, in pre-capitalist societies and/or in those hegemonised by a centralised tribute-extracting state the spatial structure would be characterised by logic of *use-value* production and appropriation and circulation of *absolute* surplus value for consumption in 'feudal agglomerations' or parasitic urban places, and by the logic of policing needs of the extractive powers. With the increasing domination of circulation capital in the economy, there would be restructuration of space economy both in terms of change in pattern of territorial division of labour, i.e. increasing domination of sectors/areas producing exchange value, and in terms of spatial reorganisation largely geared to the swifter circulation of commodities; etc.
- Articulation of territorial division of labour is manifested in the emergence of 'economic regions' to exploit the special advantages accruing from geographic location and historical accumulation. The greater interaction among such 'regions' in terms of flow of goods and services, should constitute the essential criteria for characterisation of higher spatial formations. Any deviant development in spatial structure such as inequality, disarticulation or extrovertedness should be seen as territorial manifestations of social contradictions; and their causative explanation should be sought in conformation with the historical stage of social development. For example, inter-spatial disarticulation or non-development of territorial division of labour would be a general distinguishing feature of introverted pre-capitalist formation marked by low differentiation of social division of labour. Integration of pre-capitalist economy with the metropolitan economy, particularly in initial phases through mercantile relations, would result in the formation of 'disarticulated' and 'extraverted' spatial structure.

As regards spatial unevenness in development, the phenomenon would open through different social formations and its characteristics and causative mechanism would be different in different modes. For example, in capitalist formation the phonomenon of spatial inequality would be a logical extension of the very law of motion of capitalism, in as much that for its reproduction capitalism must proceed spasmodically and unevenly until it breeds its own negation. In pre-capitalist formations, spatial unevenness would result, on the one hand, from the differentiation of areas of 'production' and 'consumption', and on the other hand, quite significantly for that matter, from the geographical inequalities and historical exigencies favouring certain places so that it may be more relevant to talk in terms of spatial 'diversity'. The spatial disparateness in transitional societies, however, may be better explained in terms of uneven transition to higher modes at different spatial points due to a host of factors such as nature of pre-existing mode of production, natural barriers, or the logic of creation of 'geography of industrial reserve army' for the metropolitan capital. Moreover, once capitalist unevenness is introduced in the space economy, the inherent logic of capitalism tends to cumulatively reproduce spatial inequalities. But one should be cautious in explaining the causative mechanism of spatial inequality and not talk in terms of 'place exploiting place' even though value flow from one place to another. Rather the mechanism should be located in the social relations across space that fetishes in spatial relations.

Since the objective here is only to make spatial differentiation of underdevelopment rather than to 'regionalise' the economy, which is an altogether different proposition and demands a more rigorous enquiry into the inter-spatial economic relations, the study should proceed through a concomitant sectoral (vertical) and spatial (horizontal) differentiation, of the political economy and the points and nature of articulation identified to outline the nature of underdevelopment.

1.3 PHYSICAL SETTING AND DEFINITION OF SPATIAL UNITS

As this study covers the whole physical space of Nepal it may be relevant to make a brief appraisal of the physical specificities that have a direct bearing on the development/underdevelopment process. Accordingly we would here introduce the locational specificities, physiographic features and distribution of natural resources. Finally we would define the spatial units to be used for spatial differentiation of various attributes of development/underdevelopment.

1.3.1 Locational Specificities

Nepal covers 147181 Sq. Km. of area and is roughly rectangular in shape with an average width of 193 m. and an average length of 885Km. It has approximately north-west to south-east orientation between 80°15' and 88°15' east longitude and 26°20' and 30°10' north latitude. 22 times smaller than India and 75 times smaller than China, Nepal's sandwiched location between these two giant and mutually hostile neighbours has been metaphorically likened to 'a yam between two boulders' and often invoked as of decisive significance for guiding the path of social development. The more important aspect of the location perhaps is its spanning in a ladder-like manner the physical gap in between the Indo-Gangetic plain in the south and Tibetan plateau in the north, thus practically 'India-locked' from the three more accessible sides. No doubt the nearest access to sea is 1127 Km away beyond the Indian territory. Land-lockedness of Nepal in this sense is more acute in that the other similarly handicapped countries have alternate access to sea through more then one country. The physical extrovertedness of Nepal is also more pronounced in that whereas the other landlocked countries like Switzerland or Afghanistan have their most productive and strategic parts in the central heartland, that of Nepal lies along the border with India. (see Fig. 1.2).

Thus the political geography of location and politico-strategic considerations arising therefrom appear to be important variables in the development process of Nepal.

1.3.2 Physical Features

For its small size Nepal displays an incredible physical diversity as manifested in the altitudinal range spanning from about 100 m. in the southern most plains of Terai to more than 8800 m. in the Himalayan mountains of north within a horizontal distance of less than 200 Km, which has been very aptly and poetically described as "the stair steps to the sky". The transition to this amazing altitudinal distance is not, however, smooth and gradual, but interspersed with rugged and highly dissected terrains and criss-crossed by numerous river and tectonic valleys. As may also be evident from the contour map (Fig. 1.3) about 25% of the total area is above 3000 m, about 20% less than 300 m and the rest in between.[97] The 'ruggedness' is found increasing from south to north and from east to west.[98] In sum, about 79% of the territory is found to be occupied by hills and mountains and only 21% by the plains.

On the basis of topographical variations, four major physical zones from south to north can be differentiated; (i) Terai; (ii) Inner Terai; (iii) Hills; and (iv) Mountain. *Terai* is the southern most narrow strip of low-land of 15–40 Km. width stretching from east to west with two breaks at Chitwan and Dang-Deukhuri in between. Being Nepal's modest share of the Indo-Gangetic plain, this belt was previously thickly forested but is now turning into its most important habitation zone.

From the plains arise abruptly two parallel ranges of hills; the Churia range (1500 m) which is a continuation of Shivaliks in India and the Mahabharat range (1500–2700 m) with steep and jagged relief which form a natural barrier to interior parts of the country. At places these two parallel ranges diverge forming east west oriented Valleys or "Duns", which have a similar topography as that of Terai and hence are known as *Inner Terai.*

North of the Mahabharat range in a breadth of 50 to 100 Km. lies the *mid-hill* zone, which has been the backbone of the country, physically and historically. With elevations ranging from 600 m. to 3000 m, this zone is a complex of low-lying hills made up of ridges and ranges and river and tectonic valleys. Of the several tectonic valleys *Kathmandu Valley* is the biggest and has been the heart of the country since early times. The northern most physical unit is the great *Himalayan range*, which consists of the main, the inner and the Tibetan Himalayas.

LAND-LOCKEDNESS

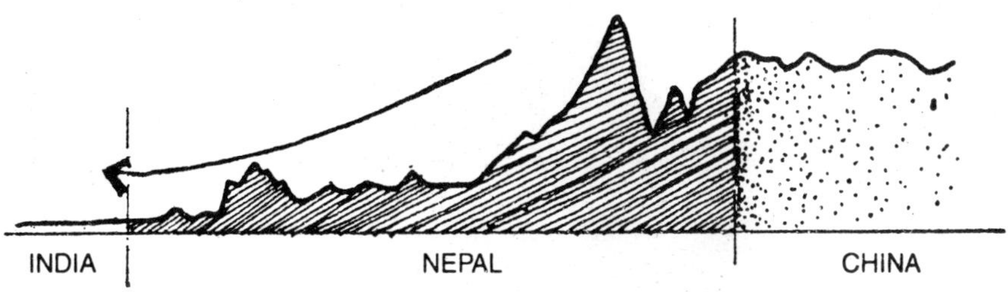

INDIA-LOCKED AND EXTRAVERTED STRUCTURE

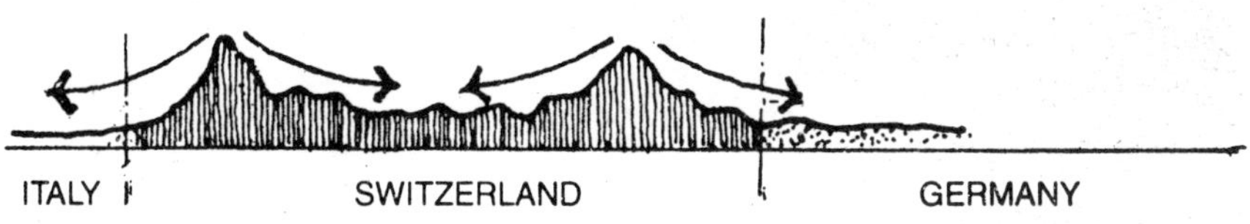

CONTRAST WITH LAND-LOCKED SWITZERLAND

Fig. 1.2 Locational Specification of Nepal.

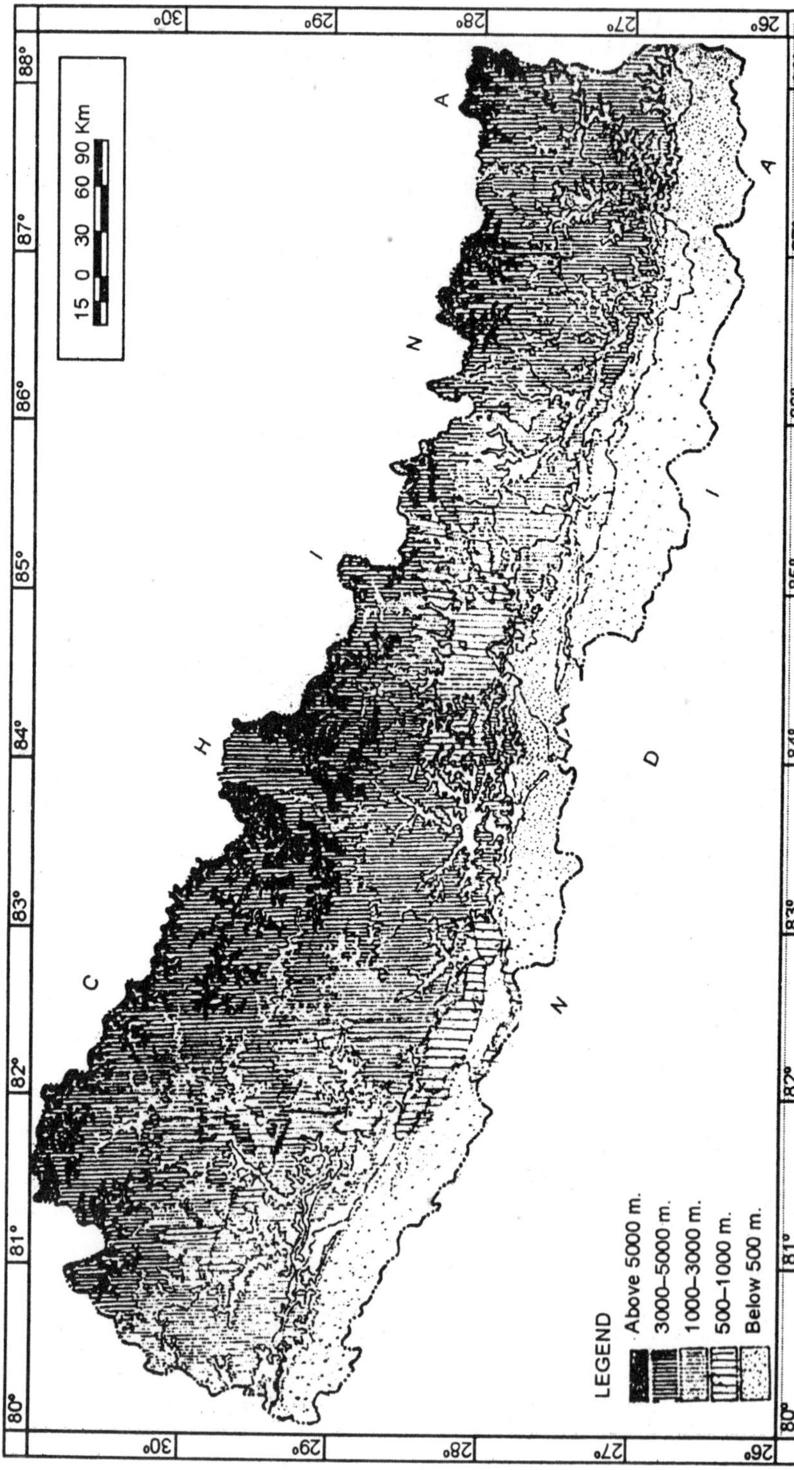

Fig. 1.3 Nepal: Altitudinal Zoning

These north-south physical zones and variations in their forms in the east-west direction may be better appreciated through Figs. 1.4 and 1.5. The geological zoning of the country also more or less tends to parallel with the above topographical zoning.

The drainage system of the country also would be largely governed by the physical features. Once the broad north-south orientation of rivers is determined by the topographical gradation in that direction, the geological history of later origin of southern hilly ranges, particularly the Mahabharat range, helps to understand the formation of dendritic pattern of major river systems. The three major drainage systems from east to west are the Kosi, the Gandaki and the Karnali, which have a single outlet each to the south through the Mahabharat range. These three river systems account for 80% of the drainage area in the country and divide the country into 3 more or less equal hydrographic zones that have been remarkably instrumental in guiding the course of history of the primitive society. Besides there are other minor drainage systems such as Mechi in the far-east, Kamala and Bagmati in centre-east, Rapti and Babai in the west and Mahakali in the far-west. (see Fig 1.6).

Thus on the basis of natural differentials 4 physical zones along north-south and 3 hydrographic zones along east-west can be clearly differentiated, thus giving a total of $3 \times 4 = 12$ physico-hydrographic zones.

1.3.3 Definition of Spatial Units

For the present study, the division of the country into appropriate spatial units is of significance. The various alternatives available are:

(i) Administrative Districts: 75 in number, these are unnecessarily clumsy for politico-economic analysis of development/underdevelopment for many of them have common physical and social attributes and are designed for mere administrative efficiency.

(ii) Development Regions: The official 'regional development planning' of the government envisages 5 (previously 4) 'development regions' arranged trom east to west and each constituting of three ecological belts of Terai, Hill and Mountain. Thus a total of 15 'sub-regions' can be assumed. But their division also, though sought to be based on physical and economic logic, does not exactly conform to the physico-historical logic of differentiation of spatial units for understanding the development/underdevelopment process.

A better differentiation of spatial units for the kind of empirical study we intend to make, i.e. following a historical-materialist method, would be the one which would take into account the physical and historical specificities of the units. On this count the differentiation into 12 physico-hydrographic zones as arrived earlier comes to the nearest proximation. On this could be added the Kathmandu Valley which possesses a distinct physical and historical identity.

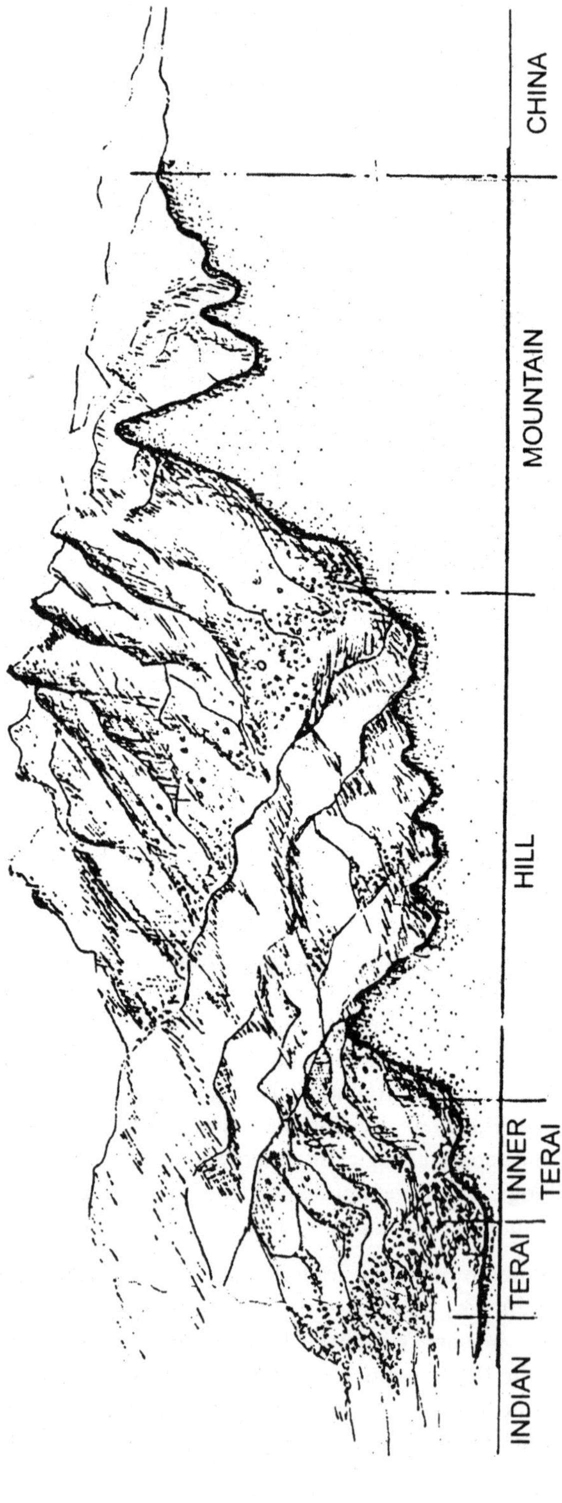

Fig. 1.4 Longitudinal Cross-Section Through Central Nepal.

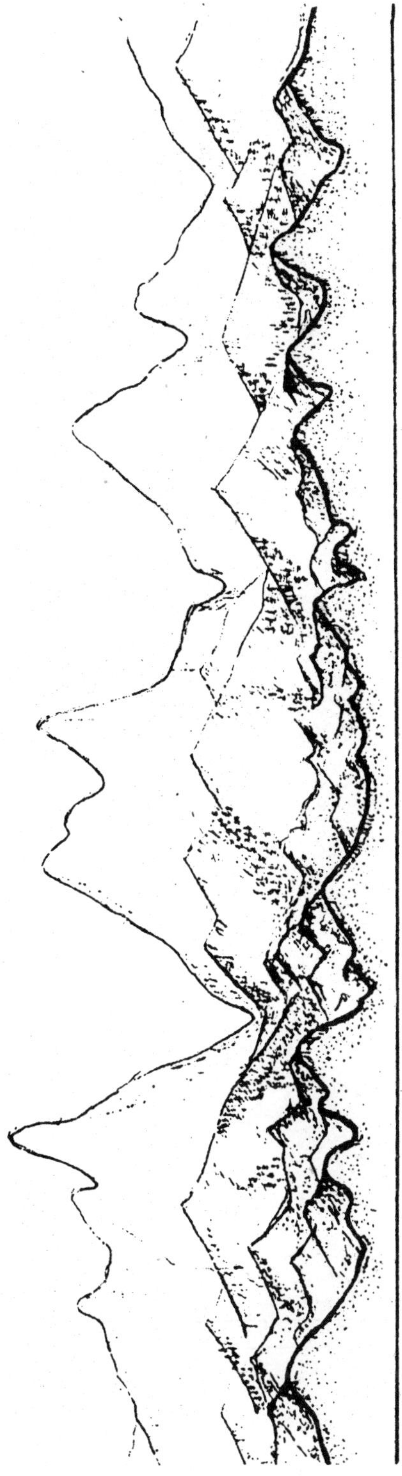

Fig. 1.5 Latitudinal Cross-Section Through Central Hill.

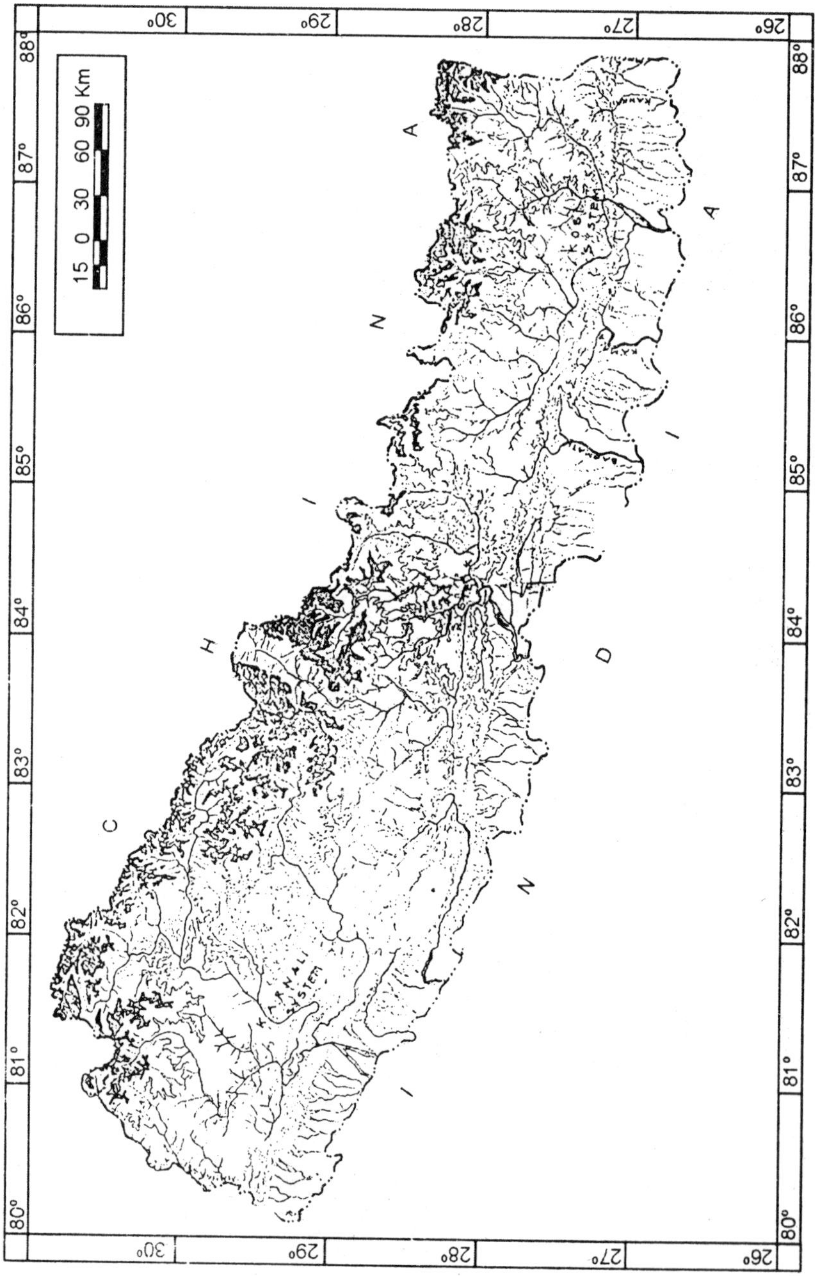

Fig. 1.6 Nepal: Drainage System.

Thus making 13 in all, these 'territorial zones' take into account the spatial diversities in physical features, distribution of natural resource endowments and for the primitive stage of society, different historical experiences. Also, on practical consideration, they could be constituted, with their areas and population, as given in Appendix-I.

But this spatial divisioning would also have certain deficiencies. The most glaring would be the non-conformation of district boundaries to the physical zoning in north-south direction which would be following definite contour lines. For example, many of the eastern Mountain districts intrude deep south beyond their assumed altitudinal barrier, and some Hill districts like Sindhupalchok and Gorkha possess areas almost equally divided into Hill and Mountain in terms of natural endowments. Similarly, Inner Terai districts intrude much deeper into Hill zone to encompass almost entire Mahabharat range. These limitations may distort some of the physico-historical determinants of the development process, but we have no means to redress them.

Also in view of the larger share of Terai area and total population and given the economic significance of it, the eastern Terai may be broken up into subzones i.e. Far-eastern, (Jhapa, Morang and Sunsari), Mid-Eastern (Saptari, Siraha, Dhanusha, Mahottari, Sarlahi) and Eastern (Rautahat, Bara and Parsa). Whenever a further micro-level analysis is required, the administrative districts can be taken as the basic spatial units.

1.4 HISTORICAL SETTING

Since this study intends to follow a historico-materialist method of analysis of social and spatial aspects of underdevelopment of Nepal, it would be pertinent to have a brief historical review of evolution of internal and external conditions that have a bearing on the current state of the space economy. The emphasis here, however, would be to trace only the general historical loci, that may provide an easy backdrop for a more detailed historical accounting by individual aspects of enquiry in each of the chapters that follow.

Though there is no authentic materialistic interpretation of Nepalese history available to date it may be reasonable to reconstruct the history from sundry findings and accounts and assume that the valleys of Nepal were the seats of very ancient people.[99] The real social history, however, can be traced only with the advent of 'hunting nomads' of Mongoloid stock (or the *Kirat*) from south-east and 'pastoral nomads' of Caucasoid stock (or the *Khas*) from north-west to meet at Nepal Valley (today's Kathmandu Valley) around first millenium B.C.[100] Whereas the evolutionary dynamics took its own slow course to varying forms of tribal communal formations in other parts of the territory, it was Kathmandu Valley with its excellent agro-climatic advantage for stabilized agriculture and primitive entrepot status for trade between Indian plains and Tibetan plateau that became the citadel of early civilization in line with the Greek city states. By the third century A.D. Kathmandu Valley under the Lichhavis had evolved a developed class society based on differentiation of social division of labour and diversified agricultural and craft production.[101] Except for the neighbouring hily areas in the vicinity of the Kathmandu Valley which must have been affected by the social processes of the Valley, other areas of the country seem to have followed their own dynamics of evolution to embroyonic proto-class formations out of the tribal communal society till the 10th–11th century.

A new social epoch was ushered in when after the 11th century there was a great influx of Hindu migrants from Indian plains in the wake of Moslem invasions there. Their introduction of superior production technology with the attendant social division of labour long stereotyped into hierarchical castes and the establishment of petty Hindu kingdoms through gradual assimilation of indigenous tribal communities in most of central and western hill regions by 14th, 15th century, marked a qualitative change into class society and emergence of state structure in the larger parts of the territory of Nepal. However, unlike in other instances of forcible conquest and imposition of alien social order, here the invaders themselves were 'refugees' and had to contend with entering into compromises with the existing social order dominated by tribal communalism. Moreover, the physical extremities of rugged terrains conducive for petty individuated property[102] had given rise to a peculiar form of tribal community from the beginning marked by common ownership of only a portion of the land such as meadows and woods and parcellized individual but nonalienable property on cultivated land like the *Kipat* system[103] existing till recently amongst certain communities. Hence even after the formation of petty states the process of 'detribalization' was not complete and the resulting social formation which was a hybrid 'state-communal'[104] type persisted with remarkable tenacity. In the eastern hill zones the tribal community lasted in more purer form because of its mere indirect and loose integration into the 'alien' states based in the southern Terai plains, e.g. Vijaynagar and Chaudandi. This physico-historic legacy of incomplete destruction of older formations may have significant relevance to the understanding of the later dynamics of the development process in Nepal.

By mid-18th century the present territorial expanse of Nepal was organised around sixty petty principalities, out of which the largest number 24 (hence '*Chaubisi*') were in the Gandaki region and 22 (hence '*Baisi*') in the Karnali region .Under the cumulative imperatives of the need to reorganise the society to meet the increased revenue demands of the state and proliferating non-labouring classes rallying around it and the threat of suction separately into the rising British empire in the south, led to the campaign for larger, unified state. The result was the establishment of the unified state of Nepal under the hegemony of the chieftain of a central Hill principality of Gorkha in thelater half of the 18th century. With its capital in Kathmandu the state extended all along the foot-hills of the Himalayas from the Teesta in east to the Sutlej in the west. The present state boundary consisting of hill tracts between the Mechi in east and the Mahakali in west with a narrow strip of plains in the south was defined when the expansionary drives of the Nepalese state and British colonialism had a head-long collision in 1814–16 resulting in the former's defeat and signing of a semi-colonial treaty formalising Nepali's semi-colonial integration into British India. Then ensued the concomitant dual– i.e. endogenous and exogenous imperatives on the development process of the Nepalese society.

To view the 'exogenous' dynamics first. The semi-coloinial mode of integration meant preservation of formal political independence but indirect political and economic subjugation to the dominant colonial power.[105] In the case of Nepal, as witnessed by the provision of unequal treaty of 1816 and subsequent developments since then, the relation of 'political dependency[106] to British India varied in degree according to the change in the international power balance of the colonialists and/or change in internal class structure of the society. Since Nepal's semi-colonial position in the early 19th century seems to have been governed by the colonialist calculus of maintaining it as a 'buffer zone' between the contending powers of British India and Imperial China, its political subservience to British India was aggravated after the 1850s.Still Nepal continued to remain a semi-colony rather than becoming a colony due to a number of factors. This was because the economic benefits of heavy colonial administration in the difficult terrains of mountains were not perhaps attractive enough to the Britishers and the Nepalese soldiers with their tribal 'non-feudalised' traits were better disposed to serve the 'non-Hindu' Britishers and hence the colonialists were more interested in procuring mercenary soldiers from a remote tribal land than in trading with the 'paupers' or antagonising the potential allies. Only after the extension of Indian railways to Nepal border by the end of 19th century possibilities of greater economic exploitation of Nepal were opened. The captive market potential of the country were further realised with the growth of industrial capital in India. This changing economic imperative over mere political one was symbolised with the signing of the treaty with British India in 1923 which recognised Nepal's political sovereignty but ushered in the concept of economic 'common market'. All through the economic exploitation from without took mercantile form, as there was nothing in Nepal which could offer higher profits to industrial capital than was provided in India. Only the global crisis in the capitalist economy brewed on the eve of World War II and its adverse effects on the British colonial economy, introduced foreign industrial capital in Nepal's Terai. Since it was a weak adjunct of metropolitan capital it could not flourish, the mercantile form of economic articulation continued to dominate, economic imperatives in the relations between Nepal and British India continued to be subdued and Nepal continued to remain a semi-colony when the Britishers left India in 1947.

Now coming to the 'endogenous' dynamics of development after state unification and semi-colonial integration to British India. The increase in the territorial size of the country and rise of the possibility of greater revenue extraction, should have naturally introduced fresher imperatives for reorganisation of the internal social structure. As the society was hegemonised by a centralised tributary state and the principal form of surplus extraction was direct 'tribute' or tax, the unmanageability of the territory led to vast expansion of the bureaucracy and policing machinery. Wide dispersal of these functionaries in remote areas practically cut-off from the central authority gradually led to their entrenchment into local 'autonomous' authorities and thus gradual 'feudalisation' of the tribal communal economy. On the other hand vast acquisition of fresher lands for cultivation also brought about spontaneous growth of 'feudalistic' structure of society. But the natural limitations of the rugged territory, strong, entrenchment of tribalism which was just 'adopted' but not 'shattered' by earlier conquests, and vast authority of the centralised state did check fuller growth of classical 'feudalism'. When vast territory of Terai was opened after the extension of Indian railways to the border, the mercantile interests had a heyday in both amassing direct commercial profits through timber exports and aligning with the feudals for a mercantile-feudal exploitation of the newly acquired land for 'commercial farming'. Thus a hodge-podge of class relations ranging from tribal communalism to 'commercial-feudalism' under the overall hegemony of a centralised state continued to be brewed. When the dominant merchant-feudal classes were directly aligned with the colonialists the growth of industrial capital was bound to be stunted. Moreover, after the 'de-industrialisation' of the countryside in the wake of unchecked inflow of factory-made goods from India and flight of pauperised craftsmen and peasants to work in Indian cities or British armies, the strength of mercantile-feudal interests was further enhanced and development of industrial capital was successfully checked.

After the departure of Britishers from India newer internal and external re-alignment of class relations was imperative, that brought about the political change of 1951 under direct Indian supervision without any substantial change in internal social structure. Then ensued a fresher era of semi-colonialism with increased economic imperatives, externally[107], and guarded 'conservation-dissolution' of hybrid pre-capitalist social structure, internally. Closer physical and economic integration with India since the 1950s is signified in the unequal political and economic treaty of 1950 with India,[108] construction of transportation and communication networks oriented towards India, increasing trade and financial interactions and exploitation of water resources through projects like Kosi and Gandak largely to the benefit of India, etc. On the other hand, revival of politico-strategic significance of the country in the aftermath of the Chinese revolution sought to perpetuate the semi-colonial status and brought in greater political and economic interventions of other imperialist powers.

Internally, the centralised despotic state structure continued unaltered and increased economic integration without resulted in strengthening the comprador mercantile and bureaucratic capitalist classes. Moreover, the gradual change in class configurations demanded concomitant restructuration of social relations of production and hence various "reforms" like land reform were brought in under the state aegis. Accumulating crises within the outmoded system were manifested in periodic revolts by the masses and heavy suppression of them by the state.

Meanwhile, Kathmandu remained the administrative, mercantile and financial capital of the country; vast countryside was articulated only under the political hegemony of the centre and continued to be physically cut-off from each other. Separate territorial units articulated independently with India.

Hence the current status of underdevelopment of Nepal would have to be seen in this historical setting to understand the essence of its dynamics.

1.5 GENERAL DIFFERENTIATION OF THE ECONOMY

As brought out in the discussion of the analytical frame earlier, higher stages of economic development of a society are marked by more pronounced economic and social differentiation, or a better articulation of social division of labour.[109] Hence to facilitate detailed probing into the characteristics and processes of different sectors of the economy in subsequent chapters it may be relevant here to make a general differentiation of the Nepalese economy.

The conventional typology of classifying economic activities into "primary", "secondary" and "tertiary" or "services" sectors and Colin Clark and Jean Fourastie's 'general theory of phases of evolution' based on them[110] is found inappropriate and inadequate to picturise the real state of the economy, particularly in the Third World Countries.[111] We have, therefore, sought to classify the available sectoral information according to the following typology derived from the Marxist methodology of viewing economic activities to consist of basically two components, i.e. 'production' and 'realisation' of value:[112]

A. Production Sector
   (i) Primary production (agriculture; forestry, fisheries; mining and quarrying);
   (ii) Non-primary (secondary) production (manufacturing; electricity, gas and water; construction);

B. Economic Integration (Circulation) Sector
   (i) Trade and Commerce (trade; finance and business services);
   (ii) Services and Administration (transport and communication; personal and community service).[113]

Within this framework we would briefly review the sectoral composition of 'economically active' population, gross social product (as measured in GDP) and state revenue (as a proxy for social surplus), to gauge the extent of differentiation of the Nepalese economy.

Sectoral distribution of total 'economically active' population (15 years and above) in a temporal frame is presented in Table 1.1 The abysmally low level of differentiation of the economy and overall backwardness of the society is amply reflected in the engagement of more than 93% of working population in primary production activities. The general primitiveness of the society is further compounded by the stagnant or deteriorating situation in the temporal frame.

Table 1.1 Sectoral Distribution of Economically Active Population (1952/54–1981).

(%)

Sectors	*1952/54*	*1961*	*1971*	*1981*
1. Production Sector				
(i) Primary Production	93.36	93.82	93.72	91.01
(ii) Secondary Production	2.19	2.04	1.32	0.54
2. Economic Integration Sector				
(i) Trade and Commerce	1.44	1.10	1.46	1.73
(ii) Service	2.87	2.28	3.51	4.67
(iii) Unknown	0.71	0.77	–	1.85
TOTAL	100.00	100.00	100.00	100.00

Source: Central Bureau of Statistics, *Population Census of Nepal*, 1952–54, 1961, 1971 and 1981, Kathmandu.

The most disturbing trend, however, is the consistent decline in the share of labour force in non-primary production activities, giving currency to the process of 'de-industrialisation' in the country. Nevertheless, unlike the general trend in most other 'underdeveloped' countries there is no marked shift of the labour force towards 'economic integration' activities. This should further indicate the specific nature of underdevelopment in Nepal.

Further quality of economic differentiation of a society ought to be measured by the productivity of labour-power engaged in and the extent of social surplus contributed by different branches of economic activities. Despite its inherent limitations of underestimating use-value production and relatively inflating exchange-value production, it is proposed here to make use of the Gross Domestic Product (GDP) as a proxy for the gross value of the social product.

From Table 1.2 it is evident that nearly two-third of the total GDP is contributed by the primary production sector and the remaining one-third more or less equally divided between non-primary production and 'economic integration' activities.[114] This lack of "hypertrophy of the tertiary sector" as observed in most of the other underdeveloped countries including the ones with lesser degree of integration with the world market,[115] seems to make the case of Nepal's 'underdevelopment' different from the usual.

However, the increasing share of the 'economic integration' activities in the total GDP (12.82% in 1964–65 to 26.31% in 1979–80) and their much higher growth ratio may be a sign of the country moving towards the same direction. Most disconcerting aspect of the phenomenon is again the decline of non-primary production sector both in terms of % share of GDP and the growth ratio. The apparent reduction in the share of primary production sector may be more due to its own absolute decline than the relative growth of other sectors.

Despite the not very significant proportion of social surplus directly appropriated by the state, its known absolutist-extractive nature makes the state the

Table 1.2 Distribution of GDP (at Current Prices)[1] by Sectors.

(amount in Rs. million)

	Production Sector						Economic Integration Sector									Total		
	Primary Production			Non-Primary[2] Production			Trade & Commerce			Services			Total					
	(i)	(ii)	(iii)	(i)	(ii)	(iii)	(i)	(ii)	(iii)	(i)	(ii)	(iii)	(i)	(ii)	(iii)	(i)	(ii)	(iii)
1964/65	3655	65.24		1229	21.94		306	5.46		412	7.35		718	12.82		5602	100.00	
			+10.15			7.03			3.48			12.82			9.22			9.37
1969/70	5926	67.59		1726	19.69		363	4.14		753	8.59		1116	12.73		8768	100.00	
			+14.29			8.85			15.18			16.86			16.32			13.58
1974/75	11557	69.74		2637	15.91		736	4.44		1641	9.90		2377	14.34		16571	100.00	
			3.25			–0.55			29.90			13.09			19.36			5.72
1979/80	13562	61.97		2566	11.72		2722	12.44		3036	13.87		5758	26.31		21886	100.00	

Note: (i) Amount, (ii) Percentage of the total; (iii) Annual compound growth rate (%).

1. B ecause of price inflation the actual figures of GDP and growth rates are misleading, and hence are meant for horizontal comparison only. The real growth rate of GDP for the period 1964/65–1979/80 comes to about 2.0% per annum. [Paudyal (1982), p. 16].
2. Non-primary production sector has been inflated with the inclusion of 'Ownership of dwellings', which contributes on the average 6.31% of the total GDP.

Source: HMG/N, Ministry of Food, Agriculture and Irrigation (1978). *Handbook of Agricultural Statistics of Nepal*, Kathmandu, and, Central Bureau of Statistics, *Statistical Pocket Book, Nepal, 1984, Kathmandu.*

typical representative of the parasitic surplus-appropriating class. Hence the structure of the appropriated social surplus should be by and large reflected in the structure of the state revenue (see Table 1.3 and Fig. 1.7). The increasing dependence of the state for revenue extraction on the "trade and commerce" sector, that too on custom duties on export-import trade (35–40% of total revenue), implies, on the one hand, the failure to keep pace with the required level of surplus generation or the absolute decline of the indigenous production sectors and, on the other, the increasing hegemony of merchant capital with exogenous base on the social process of Nepal. Figure 1.8 sums ups the increasing dichotomy in the interests of the producing class (labour) and the surplus-appropriating class and shows the differences in the level of sectoral productivity.

Spatial distribution of social product and 'social surplus' (state revenue here) have not been systematically studied as yet. According to the preliminary estimates of National Planning Commission for the year 1970–71, in the total GDP the share of Mountain-Hill, Terai and Inner Terai and Kathmandu Valley was 33.51%, 54.01% and 12.52% respectively, which shows a discernible ineqality in favour of the latter areas. As per the spatial distribution of state revenue, Gaige[116] had estimated for 1965–66 that 76% of the total domestically generated state revenue was provided by the Terai, including 75% of land revenue, 87% of timber revenue, 93% of excise revenue and 70% of customs revenue. In view of the progressive shift in the share of total revenue in favour of 'economic integration' activities since then and the known centralisation of these activities in Terai and Kathmandu Valley, the increased domination of these areas should be quite understandable.

This broad picture of the sectoral structure of the Nepalese economy in the spatio-temporal frame should provide adequate starting base to study the nature of underdevelopment in the socio-spatial dimensions.

1.6 HYPOTHETICAL PROPOSITION

When the natural and historical specificities of Nepal are refracted through the analytical lenses constructed above, a penumbric picture of the social and spatial structure of underdevelopment can be foreseen, which will have to be verified through detailed empirical investigation. To begin with it may be reasonable to assume the current Nepalese socio-spatial formation to be at a transitional pre-capitalist stage, whose motion is engineered by the interplay of a set of contradictory forces of both endogenous and exogenous kinds. Thus the problem of underdevelopment can be envisaged as the problem of articulation of forces and relations of production in a pre-capitalist mode and of smooth transition to higher mode, i.e. capitalism. This would be manifested in, sectorally and spatially, incoherent differentiation, unevenness in growth, general disarticulation within but excessive integration without, etc.

Table 1.3 Sectoral Origin of State Budget Revenue.

Fiscal year	Production Sector						Economic Integration Sector									Miscellaneous		Total		
	Primary Production			Non-Primary Production			Trade and Commerce			Services			Total							
	(i)	*(ii)*	*(iii)*	*(i)*	*(ii)*	*(iii)*	*(i)*	*(ii)*	*(iii)*	*(i)*	*(ii)*	*(iii)*	*(i)*	*(ii)*	*(iii)*	*(i)*	*(ii)*	*(i)*	*(ii)*	*(iii)*
1950/51 (actual)	15.95	56.83		5.30	18.83		4.07	14.48		0.85	3.04		4.92	17.52		1.90	6.76	28.07	100.00	
			2.32			1.26			8.87			8.24			8.76					3.47
1960/61 (revised estimate)	37.00	37.99	2.51	6.70	6.88	8.04	36.10	37.06	6.06	7.00	7.19	3.04	43.10	44.25	5.57	10.60	10.88	97.40	100.00	4.71
1970/71 (actual)	92.95	20.28	1.98	53.89	11.76	5.26	218.85	47.75	6.94	21.26	4.64	5.14	240.11	52.39	6.78	71.40	15.58	458.35	100.00	5.29
1980/81 (revised estimate)	184.00	7.58		283.5	11.69		1519.35	62.63		109.20	4.50		1628.55	67.13		330.05	13.60	2426.10	100.00	

Note: (i) Revenue in Rs. million: at current prices: (ii) % of total revenue; (iii) Decadal growth ratio.
Source: HMG/N, Ministry of Finance (1982), *Budget in Nepal (1951/52–1981/82)*, Kathmandu.

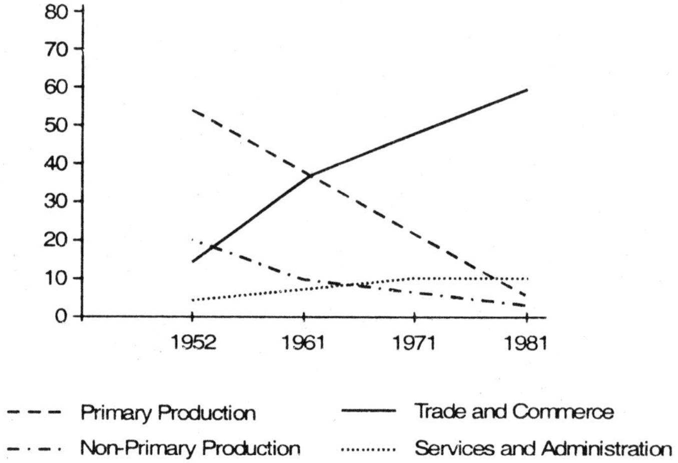

Fig. 1.7 Change in Structure of State Revenue.

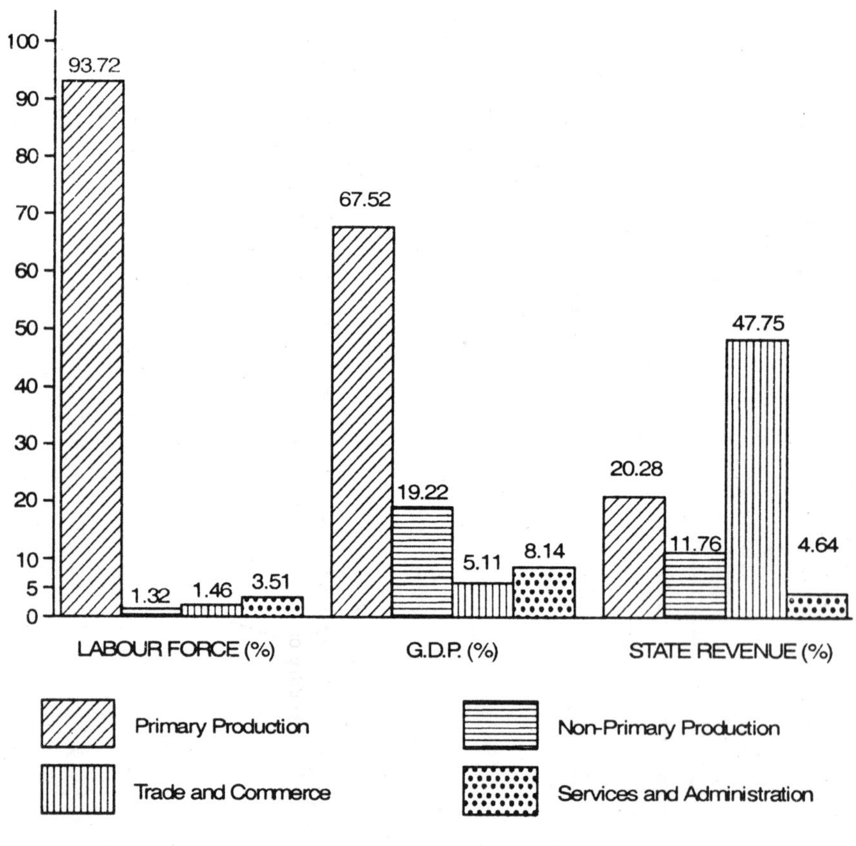

Fig. 1.8 Sectoral Composition of Labour Force, G.D.P. and State Revenue (1971/72).

Different interacting forces and their respective roles in the structuration of socio-spatial formation can be envisioned thus:

(i) Endogenous forces

- Extreme physical disparateness and natural fragmentation of productive space in rugged terrains tends to favour small-scale production that breeds conservative ideology and resistance to change; similarly physical inaccessibility/unconnectivity across rugged terrains would discourage spatial and social division of labour and impede development of productive forces.
- Historical absence of violent upheavals or sharp breaks in social continuity, e.g. through direct colonial annexation or through social revolutions, at least not since the formation of the unified state, has lead to the preservation of many outmoded social relations, including pre-feudal ones, which naturally impede the development of higher social formation.
- The existence of a powerful centralised state with a well-organised bureaucratic paraphernalia for extraction of absolute surplus value from the direct producers has, on the one hand, discouraged full-scale 'feudalisation' marked by parcellized sovereignty and spatial polarisation around the seat of state authority. This results is a dichotomous blockage of development of productive forces in large parts of the territory and aggravation of overall social and spatial inequality.
- Natural use-value differentials of different territorial units give rise to original spatial diversity and primitive inequality, but with the active interventions of subsequent social processes and unequal penetration of capitalism to different spatial points, these get aggravated and transformed into 'spatial disparity'.
- The form of spatial organisation is principally determined by the extractive and policing needs of the state and oriented towards the state capital, i.e. Kathmandu.

(ii) Exogenous forces

- The semi-colonial mode of integration with India since the British colonial period, has imposed on the space economy all the disadvantages of colonialism with none of the 'advantages', e.g. those deriving from productive investment of capital.
- The predominantly mercantile form of operation of metropolitan capital in the economy simultaneously gives rise to two dichotomous tendencies: one, the tendency of 'conservation' of pre-capitalist mode through 'de industrialisation' and hampering 'primitive accumulation of capital' by systematically draining away surplus value through 'unequal exchange'; and the other tendency of 'dissolution' of archaic mode by breaking its self-sufficiency and encouraging production of exchange value. The operation of this

dichotomous 'conservation-dissolution' mechanism leads to sectoral and spatial unevenness in development and general external orientation of the space economy.

- The politico-strategic motivation of rival imperialist powers to maintain 'stability' (or status quo) in a zone wedged between China and India have tended to work for general 'fossilization' of the space economy by not encouraging excessive economic depredation, by bribing the ruling classes through generous 'foreign aids' and by attempting to bring about controlled transformation of the economy to suit the imperialist calculus. Thus, again a dichotomous tendency of 'conservation-dissolution' of pre-capitalist mode is observed to be in operation.
- The cumulative effect of all these exogenous forces has been the acceleration of sectoral and spatial uneven development amongst general backwardness and increasingly outward orientation of the space economy.

Thus the social and spatial structure of underdevelopment in Nepal can be envisaged to have the following characterisatics:

(i) Socially: Low development of productive forces manifested in low articulation of social division of labour; uneven sectoral development reflected in general retardation of the 'productive' sectors and proliferation of 'circulation' activities; even within the same economic sector unequal development of activities catering to different social classes.

(ii) Spatially: Low social division of labour manifested in low territorial division of labour as seen in low territorial specialisation of economic activities and overwhelming rurality; in original geographical 'diversity' gradually developing into spatial 'disparity' as a corollary to the process of social uneven development; spatial organisation largely guided by the operation of merchant and bureaucratic capital in the economy as seen in general spatial disarticulation in the countryside but heavy orientation towards India and the metropolitan centre of Kathmandu.

Concomitant sectoral (vertical) and spatial (horizontal) differentiation of the economy by agriculture, industry and trade-finance sectors and evaluation of cumulative 'organisation of space' in the form of spatial distribution of population, settlement system and urbanisation and nature of social and spatial underdevelopment of the country.

1.7 METHODS USED

In view of the declared politico-economic approach of the present study the basic method throughout has been analytic and discursive. This is consciously resorted to out of compulsions of, firstly, the inadequacy of the most sophisticated quantitative techniques to measure many of the qualitative aspects in social science like the dialectics of relations between two phenomenon and, secondly, the unreliability of data in possession. However, extensive quantitative data has been used in simplest possible forms to support arguments flowing from a consistent analytical frame. Simple and common statistical techniques of frequency distribution, measures of inequality, dispersion, correlation, etc. in the temporal and spatial scale have been used whenever necessary. Simple matrices have been constructed to analyze inter-spatial relations.

Method of first principal component[117] has been used to construct composite indices of development at the district level for both sectoral development and overall socio-economic development. Of the different methods of synthesizing a number of development indicators into a composite index, this method has been preferred because the composite index obtained by this method is characterized as having the maximum sum of squares of correlation with the given variables. In other words, higher the correlations of a variable the greater would be its weight. This would be fully consistent with our definition of 'development', which is regarded as being characterised by greater articulation of social and spatial division of labour. The only precaution to be exercised in using this method is that the selected indicators should have high correlations with each other. In our context this was ensured by first constructing the correlation matrix and dropping the inappropriate variables.

In the case of sectoral indices of development, such as manufacturing industries, Kendall's method of additive ranking has been used for simplicity as here the idea of "maximization of the sum of the squares of correlation" was not very important.

Suitable cartographic methods and methods of visual presentation have been used to supplement the analysis, wherever necessary.

1.8 ORGANISATION OF THE STUDY

In the present chapter the rationale of the propose research work has been established and objectives of the study codified. Then an extensive survey of different theoretical and analytical approaches on the social and spatial aspects of development/ underdevelopment has been undertaken to ultimately define a scientific methodological approach for the proposed study. The physical, historical and general economic setting of the country has also been sketched.

In the subsequent chapters the process of development/underdevelopment in Nepal is first differentiated in the vertical (sectoral) dimension constituting of principal production and economic integration sectors, namely agriculture and industry/manufacturing, and trade and finance. Subsequently the country is differentiated in terms of horizontal (spatial) dimension. Before proceeding on to the analysis of the prevailing condition of each aspect, brief introduction of the conceptual issues and historical antecedents of the process are provided.

Chapter II is devoted to the analysis of the condition of the agriculture sector. According to the general methodological framework followed throughout 'production' and 'distribution' characteristics of the agrarian process are separately analysed in order to outline the nature of distortions in each. Their combined manifestations are ultimately summed up. In the 'production' aspect, first the condition of different factors of production including land, labour and other inputs by designated spatial units are examined. This is followed by assessment of level and growth of production and productivity (by land and labour) of major crops by spatial units. Agricultural zonings by 'production' characteristics is made by cross-classifying different attributes. Causal factors for the given state of development of productive forces in agriculture are sought to be indentified through a set of statistical measures. The 'distribution' aspect of the agrarian process is studied through the analysis of the ownership pattern of different means of production and of the tenurial condition of the operational land-holdings. Besides, other auxiliary modes of appropriation and utilisation of social surplus are examined. Finally, interdependencies between different aspect of the agrarian process are analysed in order to understand the nature of underdevelopment in the agriculture sector. Spatial differentiation of composite levels of development of agriculture is also made to bring out the nature of socio-spatial interdependence.

In Chapter III the condition of domestic proto-industry is first highlighted in its 'production' and 'distribution' characteristics, and then a detailed spatio-temporal observations is made of the manufacturing process. The 'production' characteristics are analysed with respect to firstly, the structural composition of industries based on standard industrial classifications by nature of inputs, use of end products, etc., secondly, the level and growth of production and productivity by different industrial classifications, and, thirdly, the level of technological development as manifested in level of capital intensity and nature of 'fixed capital assets', nature of power used, quality of labour employed, etc. The 'distribution' condition is observed in the same spatio-temporal frame in terms of scale of industrial production, ownership pattern of manufactories, condition of employment of labour, 'supply' and 'demand' market conditions, structure of industrial finance and the nature of state intervention in the industrial process. Finally, aggregate manifestations of industrial retardation is recorded, causal dependencies amongst different indicators of industrial process analysed, and spatial differentiation of composite level of industrial development/ underdevelopment made through the use of suitable statistical measures. Throughout, an effort is made to relate the industrial condition in Nepal with similar situations elsewhere and appropriate generalisation has also been attempted.

Chapter IV is devoted to the analysis of different ensembles of circulation capital, particularly merchant and financial capital, operating within and without the social economy, with the tacit assumption that in a transitional pre-capitalist economy integrated to the capitalist metropolitan economy various forms of circulation capital play an increasingly important role in the structuration of the indigenous economy. Accordingly, spatio-temporal articulation of merchant capital within is studied in terms of level of marketisation, structure of commerce and social and spatial relations of exchange. Articulation of merchant capital without is first analysed at the macro level with respect to the increasing hold of foreign trade in the economy, changing scale of trade with dominant partners commodity structure and terms of trade, and then the spatial implications of these social processes. Tourism is taken as a form of merchant capital and an adjunct of metropolitan capital and an attempt has been made to highlight its role in distorting the social and spatial structure of the indigenous economy. Subsequently the articulation of financial capital within and without in its social and spatial dimensions, is looked into. Internally, banking capital is taken as the key form of financial capital and its credit and deposit structure in the spatio-temporal frame analysed to find out the loci of emerging primitive capital in the economy. Externally, the so-called 'foreign aid' is considered as the main form of financial integration of the backward economy to the metropolitan economy and its various dimensions like sources of inflow, condition of disbursement, sectoral and spatial distribution,'class' bias, etc., analysed.

Chapter V is constructed to study exclusively the cumulative spatial manifestations of the sectoral processes analysed hitherto. First, the territorial spread and mobility of population is probed into as a general reflection of the emerging spatial organisation. Then the formation of settlement system and urbanisation is studied as a concrete manifestation of spatial redistribution of population as a response to the socio-economic processes. Characteristics of settlement system are viewed in terms of pattern of spatial distribution, population-size distribution and hierarchical arrangement of settlements. The urban processes are analysed with respect to the level and speed of the process and hierarchical structuring and economic basis of the designated urban places. The interdependence of 'spatial form' and 'social process' are sought to be discerned with the help of suitable statistical measures at the end of this sub-section. The next sub-section deals with the nature of spatial intergration in terms of evolutionary dynamics and current status of articulation of spatial linkages, particularly road and air ways, and generalisations are derived about the form of spatial organisation as a response to the socio-economic processes in keeping with the particular historical stage of development of Nepalese society. Finally, the nature of spatial unevenness is sought to be explained as a cumulative manifestation of socio-economic processes through spatial differentiation of composite levels of development/underdevelopment.

Summary and conclusions of the study are presented in Chapter VI.

REFERENCES

1. Brewer, A. (1980), *Marxist Theories of Imperialism*, Routledge and Kegan Paul, London, p. 21.
2. Of the 34 "Low (or Lowest !) income countries" classified by World Bank on the basis of their GNP per capita, Nepal ranked (13th from below), in 1976, slided to 7th

in 1981 and further slumped to 4th position by 1984. It was no surprise then, when one UN report in 1974 opened with the bleak statement: "Nepal is poor and is daily becoming poorer" (ARTEP 1974), *A Challenge to Nepal: Growth and Employment*, Bangkok, p.1). Another World Bank report in 1979 made further dour forecast for the whole remaining years of the century, saying: "Even by the year 2000, about one half of the population would be below or just at the minimum subsistence levels compared with a projected one-quarter for other low income countries" (The World Bank (1979), *Nepal Development Performance and Prospects*, South Asia Regional Office, Washington D.C., p. v).

3. This may be better understood in terms of some macro-economic indicators of development, such as: the per capita GNP in 1981 was more US$150; the average annual growth rate of GNP during 1960–81was 0.0%; 93% of economically active persons in 1980 were engaged in agriculture, which indicated the worst labour force composition in the world; the energy consumption per capita of 13 kg of coal equivalent in 1980 was the lowest in the world; etc. (The World Bank, *World Development Report 1983*, Oxford University Press, New Delhi).
4. This may be evident from the distribution of % share of house-hold income by percentile groups of house-holds for 1976/77 as under:

1st quartile	2nd quartile	3rd quartile	4th quartile	5th quartile	highest 10%
4.6	8.0	11.7	16.5	59.2	46.5

This was one of the most skewed distribution of income in the world. (The World Bank, *op. cit.*, Table 27. p. 200).

5. Malla, K.P. and Rana, P.S.J.B. " Introduction" in Rana P.S.J.B and Malla K.P. (1973), *Nepal in Perspective*, CEDA, Kathmandu, p. 20.
6. Hindess, B. and Hirst, P.Q. (1975), *Pre-Capitalist Modes of Production*, Routledge and Kegan Paul, London, p. 180.
7. For a review of definitions of 'development' and 'under-development' of different ideological persuasions, see Mabogunje A.L. (1980), *The Development Process: A Spatial Perspective*, Hutchinson, London, Chapter 2.
8. For summary of the debate raging within the 'Marxist' camp, see among others Brewer *op. cit.* and Forbes, D.K. (1984), *The Geography of Underdevelopment*, Croom Helm, London.
9. Lenin, V.I. (1914), "Karl Marx: A Brief Biographical. Sketch with an Exposition of Marxism", *Collected Works*, Vol. 21, Progress Publishers, Moscow, 1964, p. 54.
10. Mao Tse-tung (1937), *On Contradiction*, Foreign Language Press, Peking, 1967, p. 5.
11. *Ibid*, p. 7.
12. The celebrated passage from *Preface* to *Critique of Political Economy* reads:

    "At a certain stage of their development, the material productive forces of society come into conflict with the existing relations of production, or - what is but a legal expression for the same thing—with the property relations within which they had been at work hithereto. From forms which developed the forces of production, these relations now turn into their fetters. Then comes the period of social revolution" [Mc Lellan, D. (ed.) (1977), *Karl Marx: Selected Writings*, Oxford University Press, Oxford, p. 389].
13. The two ensembles 'forces of production' and 'relations of production' have been variously characterized by different authors. For example, Stalin regards forces of production to consist of 'instrument of production' 'people' and 'production

experience and labour skill' and relation of production as 'relation of men to each other in the process of production' [Stalin, J. (1938) *Dialectical and Historical Materialism*, New Book Center, Calcutta, 1976, p. 23]; Hindess and Hirst define forces of production as 'the mode of appropriation of nature' or 'the labour process in which a determinate raw material is transformed into a determinate product' and relations of production as 'mode of appropriation of surplus-labour and the specific form of social distribution of the means of production corresponding to that mode of appropriation of surplus labour'. (Hindess and Hirst, *op. cit.*, pp. 9–10).

14. See Marx, K and Engels, F. (1978), *On Colonialism*, Progress Publishers, Moscow.
15. These may be described as the characteristic features of 'Asiatic' society. Though Marx's concept of 'Asiatic Mode of Production' (AMP) was formally rejected by Comintern after 1931, the debate has been revived in recent times [see Bailey, A.M. and Llobera, J.R. (eds) (1981), *The Asiatic Mode of Production: Science and Politics*, Routledge and Kegan Paul, London] and without necessarily accepting it as a separate 'mode of production' it may be useful to distinguish between pre-capitalist societies with strong entrenchment of the 'Asiatic' attributes.
16. See particularly, Lenin, V.I. (1897a), "A Characterisation of Economic Romanticism (Sismondi and our Own Native Sismondis)", *Collected Works*, Vol. 2, Moscow, 1972.
17. Lenin, V.I. (1899), *Development of Capitalism in Russia*, Progress Publishers, Moscow, 1977, p. 597.
18. The main contributors to the development of the theory and participants in the debate were Hobson, Hilferding, Lenin, Luxemberg and Bukharin. Summary of their contribution and differing positions is available in Brewer *op. cit.*, and general survey of Marxist theory of capitalist development and crisis, in Sweezy, P.M. (1970), *The Theory of Capitalist Development*, Monthly Review Press, New York.
19. Lenin, V.I. (1916), "Imperialism, the Highest Stage of Capitalism" *Collected Works*, Vol. 22, Progress Publishers, Moscow, 1964. p. 276.
20. *Ibid*, p. 243.
21. Baran, P. (1957), *The Political Economy of Growth*, People's Publishing House, New Delhi (1962 edn).
22. The 'dependency theory' is best expounded in the classic work, Frank, A.G. (1967), *Capitalism and Underdevelopment in Latin America*, Monthly Review Press, New York. Frank's notable later works include Frank, A.G. (1969), *Latin America: Underdevelopment or Revolution*, Monthly Review Press, New York, and Frank, A.G. (1978), *Dependent Accumulation and Underdevelopment*, Macmillan, London.
23. It is virtually impossible to site all works expounding or based on the 'dependency theory'. Apart from the pioneering works of Frank, others who have sought to expand upon the theory or given their own interpretations like the 'structuralists' include Santos, T.D. (1970), " The Structure of Dependence" in Wilber, C.K. (ed)., *The Political Economy of Development/Underdevelopment*, Random House, New York; Santos, T.D. (1975), "The Crisis of Development Theory and the Problem of Dependence in Latin America" in Bernstein, H. (ed.). *Underdevelopment and Development: The Third World Today*, Penguin Books, Harmondsworth; Furtado, C. (1971), *Development and Underdevelopment*, University of California Press; and those who have applied the theory for a case study include Rodney, W. (1972), *How Europe Underdeveloped Africa*, Bogle-L'ouverture Publications, London; Keydar, C. (1981), *The Definition of a Peripheral Economy: Turkey 1923–1929*, Cambridge University Press, Cambridge; Ponnambalam, S. (1981), *Dependent Capitalism in Crisis: The Sri Lankan Economy, 1948–1980*, Zed Press, London; though the list could be

unending. Useful summaries and reviews of the theory are available in Palma, G. (1978), " Dependency: a formal theory of underdevelopment or a methodology for the analysis of concrete situations of underdevelopment?" *World Development*, No. 6; Scapini, J.C. (u.d), *Underdevelopment Theories in Latin America* (mimeo), Institute for Studies on Economic Development, Napoli (Italia); Roxborrow, I. (1979), *Theories of Underdevelopment*, Macmillan, London; Brewer, *op. cit.*; Bottomore, T. et al. (eds) (1983), *A Dictionary of Marxist Thought*, Basil Blackwell, Worcester.

24. See Wallerstein, I. (1974), *Modern World System*, Academic Press, New York.
25. Emmanuel, A. (1972), *Unequal Exchange: A Study in the Imperialism of Trade*, New Left Books, London.
26. Despite his progressively shifting positions with subsequent works, his most representative works remain, Amin, S. (1974), *Accumulation on a World Scale*, Harvester Press, Sussex, and Amin, A. (1979), *Unequal Development*, Oxford University Press.
27. See Chapter 4.1.1 below.
28. In fact, the theory of 'dependency' has been liened to 'the obverse side of the theory of imperialism' (Bodenheimer, 1970, cited in Roxborrow, *op. cit*., p. 43).
29. de Silva, S.B.D. (1982), *The Political Economy of Underdevelopment*, Routledge and Kegan Paul, London.
30. Good critiques of the method of 'dependency theory' are provided by Laclau, E. (1971), "Feudalism and Capitalism in Latin America," *New Left Review*, No. 67; Brenner, R. (1977), "The Origin of Capitalist Development: a Critique of Neo-Smithian Marxism", *New Left Review*, No. 104; Leys, C. (1977), "Underdevelopment and Dependency: Critical Notes", *Journal of Contemporary Asia*, Vol. 7, No. 1; Palma, *op. cit.* and General Critical reviews are also available in Roxborrow, *op. cit.*; Brewer, *op. cit.*; de Silva, *op. cit.* and Forbes, *op. cit.*
31. As Marx has observed, "...in order to be able to plunder there must be something to be plundered and this implies production" (quoted in de Silva, *op. cit*., p..11).
32. Brenner, *op. cit*., p. 27.
33. de Silva, *op. cit*., p. 11.
34. Roxborrow, *op. cit*., p. 25.
35. See Laclau, *op. cit*., p. 35.
36. See Amin (1979), *op. cit.* among others.
37. This body of literature which seeks to link its antecedents to the classical Marxist works of Marks, Engels, Lenin and Kautsky was initially associated with French economic anthropologists, such as Meillassoux, Terray and Rey. It made resurgence with Althusser, L.and Balibar, E. (eds.) (1970), *Reading Capital*, New Left Books, London (1979 edn.), and found full expression in Taylor, J. (1979), *From Modernization to Modes of Production*, Macmillan, London. Useful collection of representative works is available in Wolpe, H. (ed). (1980), *The Articulation of Modes of Production*, Routledge and Kegan Paul, London, and critical review of the literature in Foster-Carter A. (1978), "The Modes of Production Controversy," *New Left Review* No. 107; Brewer, *op. cit*, and Forbes, *op. cit.*
38. A 'mode of production' is commonly defined as: "integrated complex of social productive forces and relation linked to a determinate type of ownership of the means of production" (Laclau, *op. cit*., p. 33) or "an articulated combination of relations and forces of production structured by the dominance of the relations of production." (Hindess and Hirst, *op. cit*., p. 9), though there is wide variance in the usage of the term by different scholars. [See Wolpe, H. "Introduction", in Wolpe, H. (ed.) (1980), *op. cit.*].

39. 'Social formation' has been variously defined by different authors. The most common definition may be: "... a social formation–presents... a particular combination or a specific interlocking of several 'pure' Modes of Production" (Paulantza cited in Banaji, J. (1973), "Mode of Production in Indian Agriculture: A comment," *Economic and Political Weekly*, April 17, p. 679). Or in Amin's words: "Social formations are ... concrete, organized structures that are marked by a dominant mode of production and the articulation around this of a complex group of modes of production that are subordinate to it". [Amin (1979), *op. cit.*, p. 16].
40. See Bettelheim, C., "Theoretical Comments", in Emmanuel, A. (1972), *Unequal Exchange: A Study in the Imperialism of Trade*, New Left Books, London, Appendix I.
41. Taylor (1979) cited in Forbes, *op. cit.*, p. 95. Also see Bradby B. (1980), "The Destruction of Natural Economy", in Wolpe, H. (ed) (1980), *The Articulation of Modes of Production*, Routledge and Kegan Paul, London, p. 94–95, to understand the different needs of capitalism to articulate with pre-capitalist modes of production at different stages of capitalist development, e.g. for raw materials, land, labour power or market.
42. For example, Arrighi through his observations in Africa shows how normal articulation of externally implanted capitalism with backward primitive-communal formations is fully compatible in terms of supply of migrant labour from subsistence pre-capitalist sector without undermining its basic structure. [Arrighi, G., "International Corporations, Labour Aristocracies, and Economic Development in Tropical Africa", in Arrighi, G. and Saul, J.S. (eds) (1973), *Essays on Political Economy of Africa*, Monthly Review Press New York.] Similarly Bradby (*op. cit*, p. 118–126) illustrates the comparative nature of articulation of capitalist mode of Peru, and shows that Campa's 'tribal mode' is much more resistant to capitalist penetration than the 'peasant community' of Andean highlands.
43. Taylor, *op. cit*, p. 69.
44. Among these, though with their own different perceptions, can be cited as Bagchi, A.K. (1982), *The Political Economy of Underdevelopment*, Cambridge University Press, Cambridge; de Silva, *op. cit.*; Bardhan, P. (1984), *Political Economy of Development in India*, Oxford University Press, Delhi; Forbes, *op. cit.*
45. For example, de Silva acknowledges... "underdevelopment signifies a set of production relations which have become a barrier to the development of the productive forces" (*op. cit.*, p. 11).
46. Bagchi, *op. cit*, p. 19.
47. For the well-known Dobb-Sweezy 'transition debate', see Hilton, R., et. al. (ed) (1954), *The Transition from Feudalism to Capitalism*, People's Book House, Patna. For the on-going debate on development of capitalism in Indian agriculture, see Chapter 2.1.1 below.
48. See, among others, Owen, R. and Sutcliffe, R.B. (1972), *Studies in the Theory of Imperialism*, Longman, London; Brewer, *op. cit;* Warren, B. (1980), *Imperialism, Pioneer of Capitalism*, Verso, London; Lotta, R. and Shannon, F. (1984), *America in Decline*, Banner Press, Chicago.
49. For example, see, Halliday, F. (1979), *Arabia without Sultans*, Penguin Books, Harmondsworth; Blaikie, *op. cit*; Lotta, R. (1985), "On the Dynamism of Imperialism and Fettering of Social Development", *A World To Win*, No. 2, April, p. 71.
50. "We regard third world countries as *retarded*, because, in respect of the ability to transform their production capacities so as to meet the growing needs of the population they have fallen behind advanced capitalist countries...we call them

underdeveloped, because, not only does their actual development fall far short of their potential, but also because their capacity for exerting themselves to realize this potential is impaired by their internal social political structure, and by the dominating effect of the advanced capitalist countries which limit their choices all the time" (Bagchi, *op. cit.*, p. 20).

51. For a critical review of various streams of 'industrial location theory' from its founding father Weber, 1909 to Hotelling, 1929, and Losch, 1954, and its incorporation into the neo-classical regional development theory by Isard, 1956, and Moses, 1958, see Massey D. (1977), "Towards a Critique of Industrial Location Theory", in Peet, R. (ed.) *Radical Geography: Alternative Viewpoints on Contemporary Social Issues*, Maaroufa Press, Chicago.
52. Walter Isard has been the founding father and most prolific exponent of 'regional science' concept, dominant amongst the American geographers of Anglo-Saxon tradition. Of his many contributions to date the most representative remains, Isard, W. (1956) *Location and Space Economy*, MIT Press, Cambridge (1972 edn.).
53. For a critique of neo-classical spatial theory, see, among others, Chattopadhyay, B. and Raza, M. (1975), "Regional Development: Analytical Framework and Indicators", *Indian Journal of Regional Science*, Vol. II, No. 1; Holland, S. (1976) *Capital Versus the Regions*, Macmillan, London; Stilwell, F.J.B. (1978), "Competing Analyses of the Spatial Aspects of Capitalist Development", *Review of Radical Political Economy*, Vol. 10, No. 3 Fall; Saushkin, Yu. G. (1980), *Economic Geography: Theory and Methods*, Progress Publishers, Moscow.

    On its most glaring lacunae of a historicity and camouflaging of class relations in society, Saushkin writes: ".. what society's spatial organization do they have in mind? For there is no society in general but, concrete socio-economic formations, and the spatial organization within each is governed by the specific laws of these formations' development. With American geographers it is usually a matter of an abstract classless society in which the driving force is the behaviour of a man striving for the least expenditure of efforts and time in moving along the shortest route", (*op. cit.*, p. 91).
54. See, particularly, Myrdal, G. (1957), *Economic Theory and Under-Developed Regions*, Methuen, London (1969 Reprint); Friedman, J. (1966), *Regional Development Policy: A Case Study of Venezuela*, MIT Press, Massachusettes.
55. Chattopadhayay and Raza, *op. cit.*, p. 13.
56. It was Perroux, 1950, who first coined the term 'growth pole' while describing the uneven growth process under capitalism is in abstract economic space, with his by now well- known pronouncement; 'development does not appear everywhere and all at once: it appears in points or development poles with variable intensities; it spreads along diverse channels and has varying terminal effects for the whole of economy'. Boudeville, 1966, extened the concept to geographical space to define pole as 'geographical agglomeration of activities'. Since then many adaptation of and addition to the concept have been made. There is also considerable divergence in the use of words 'pole' and 'centre'. For example, whereas D.F. Darwent regards 'pole' as non-spatial or economic and 'centre' as 'spatial' or geographical concept, R.P. Misra and others differentiate them by their orders in the hierarchy of spatial points, i.e. 'pole' being higher than the 'centre'. (For a review of this literature see Bhattarai, B.R. (1979), *Development of Gandaki Growth Axis—A Planning Approach* (P.G. Dip. Dissertation), Department of Town and Country Planning, School of Planning and Architecture, New Delhi.

57. The 'growth foci' or hierarchy of growth poles approach can be seen as a hybrid of Perroux's growth pole, Christaller's hierarchy of central places and Friedman's 'stages theory' of spatial organization, which itself is an spatial adaptation of Rostow's 'stages of economic growth' theory. For further elaboration, see Patnaik, S.C. (1981), *Economics of Regional Development Planning in Third World Countries*, Associated Publishing House, New Delhi, pp. 55–68.
58. For a rather sterile polemics on 'development from above or below' but useful collection of information on different models of development 'from above' and 'from below' within the capitalistic socio-political dispensation see Stohr, W.B. and Taylor, D.R.F. (eds), (1981), *Development from Above or Below*, Wiley, Chichester.
59. This is well depicted in Carney's words thus:

    "The 'opening up' depressed rural areas through state intervention could be interpreted as a vital step in expanding the market for capitalist production and hence in laying the basis for rapid accumulation in the manufacturing sector. The destruction of the existing economy in such areas, assisted by state intervention, may well have been the only true purpose of such intervention in many cases".

    [Carney, J, "Regions in Crisis: Accumulation, Regional Problems, Crisis Formation" in Carney J. et al. (1981), *Regions in Crisis*, Croom Helm, London, p. 56, footnote 9]. There we may have to add only that in the case of Third World's dependent economies the 'market' thus created would be not for the indigenous industrial capital but for metropolitan capital.
60. Marx, K. and Engels, F., "The German Ideology", in Marx, K. and Engels, F. (1977), *Selected Works*, Vol. 1, Progress Publishers, Moscow, p. 21.
61. For further exposition on this theme, see Smith, N. (1984), *Uneven Development: Nature, Capital and Production of Space*, Basil Blackwell, Oxford.
62. See, for example, Marx, K. (1979), *Capital* Vol. 1, Penguin Books/New Left Review, Harmondsworth, p. 334.
63. Saushkin, *op. cit*, p. 31.
64. See Lenin (1899), *op. cit.*
65. See Lenin (1916), *op. cit.*
66. See for example, Saushkin, *op. cit.*, and Baransky, N. (1981), *Selected Works in Geography*, Progress Publishers, Moscow.
67. See, for example, Kundu, A. and Raza, M. (1982), *Indian Economy: The Regional Dimension*, Spektrum Publishers and Distributors, New Delhi, p. 2.
68. Amin (1979), *op. cit.*
69. Veltmeyer, H. (1978) "The Underdevelopment of Atlantic Canada" *Review of Radical Political Economy*, Vol. 10 No. 3 Fall, p. 96.
70. Walker, R.A. (1978), "Two Sources of Uneven Development Under Advanced Capitalism: Spatial Differentiation and Capital Mobility", *Review of Radical Political Economy*, Vol. 10 No. 3 Fall, p. 29.
71. See particularly the works of Peet, Slater, Soza, Walker, N. Smith, Massey, Harvey, Castells, Lefebvre and others. An annotated bibliography of the radical-Marxist 'geographical' literature is provided by King, R. "Marxist and Radical Geographical Literature in English: An Introduction" in Quaini, M. (1982), *Geography and Marxism*, Basil Blackwell, Oxford. Notable subsequent additions have been Moulaert and Salinas *op. cit.* and Smith *op. cit.* Concise review of relevant literature are available in Bottomore et. al. *op. cit.* and Forbes *op. cit.*

72. See Harvey, D. (1973), *Social Justice and the City*, Edward Arnold, London (1976 edn.), and Smith *op. cit.*
73. Smith, *op. cit.*, p. x.
74. Baransky, *op. cit.*, p. 24, footnote. See also Moonis Raza's model of 'triangle of forces' of Nature-Institution-Technology in the development process, as cited in Singh, H. (1978). *Ladhakh-Problem of Regional Development in the Context of Growth Point Strategy* (Unpublished Ph.D Dissertation), CSRD/SSS, J.N.U., New Delhi, p. 3.
75. Soja, E.W., (1980), "The Socio-Spatial Dialectic", *Annals of Association of American Geographers*, Vol. 70, No. 2, pp. 210–12.
76. For their respective positions, refer Mabogunje, *op. cit.*, pp. 52–54.
77. Since Soja and Co. have adopted and avowedly anti-Stalin posture and the charge of so-called 'orthodoxy' seems to have been directed towards him and the like, it may be relevant to quote from Stalin himself to disprove what Soja shoves down the throats of 'orthodox' Marxists a position no Marxist worth the name can hold. In his well known essay '*Dialectical and Historical Materialism*', Stalin writes:

    "Geographical environment is unquestionably one of the constant and indispensable condition of development of society and, of course, influences the development of society, accelerates or retards its development. But its influence is not *determining* influence, in as much as the changes and development of society proceeds at an incomparably faster rate than changes and development of geographical environment" (Stalin, *op. cit.*, p. 21).

    Though the reference here is on 'natural'/geographical space, it provides enough scope for evolving a stand on 'created' space as well.
78. This is implied by Soja's citing of Mandel immediately after making the above statement, which goes thus.

    "The unequal development between regions and nation is the very essence of capitalism, on the same level as the exploitation of labour by capital" [Mandel, E. (1976), "Capitalism and Regional Disparities" quoted in Soja, *op. cit.*, p. 211].
79. Perhaps the most forthright statement to the effect is from Walker (*op. cit.*, p. 29):

    "Human practice contains an indissoluble spatial element; it is not simply acted out with "all the world a stage". Of course, the social relations of a mode of production set limits and create pressures for a certain kind of appropriate spatial organization, but they do not determine spatial relations in a unique, uni-directional, non-contradictory—in short, non-dialectical-fashion. Indeed, space and spatial relations are part and parcel of the internally structured whole of a mode of production (or social formation)..."

    See also Harvey (1973), *op. cit.*, p. 11; Vieille quoted in Mabogunje, *op. cit.*, p. 59: Santos, M. (1977), "Society and Space: Social Formation as a Theory and Method", *Antipode*, Vol. 9, No. 1, 1 February, p. 5.
80. Saushkin, *op. cit.*, p. 225.
81. Ann Markusen, 1978, quoted in Soja, *op. cit.*, p. 219, f.n. 30.
82. Peet, R. (1979), "Societal Contradiction and Marxist Geography", *Annals of the Association of American Geographers*, Vol. 69, pp. 166–67.
83. *Ibid*, p. 167.
84. Salinas, P.W. and Moulaert, F., "Regional Political Economy: An Introduction and Overview" in Moulaert and Salinas, *op. cit.*, pp. 4–5. Similar views are also echoed in

Lipietz, A. "The Structuration of space, the Problem of Land and Spatial Policy" in Carney et. al., *op. cit.*, pp. 60–61.

85. For the critique of this approach, see Forbes, *op. cit.*
86. In fact Mabogunje (*op. cit.*, p. 50) defines 'development' as "essentially a socio-spatial process".
87. The definitions have been heavily drawn from Mabogunje (*op. cit.*, pp. 55–57) and Coraggio, J.L. "Social Spaceness and the Concept of Region" in Moulaert and Salinas (*op. cit.*, p. 25).
88. See particularly the Special Issue on 'Regional Uneven Development in Advanced Capitalism' of *Review of Radical Political Economy*, Vol . 10, No. 3, Fall 1978, and also Carney et. al., *op. cit.*, Smith, *op. cit.*, and O' Keefe, P. (ed.) (1984), *Regional Restructuring Under Advanced Capitalism*, Croom Helm, London.
89. Patnaik, P. (1973), "On the Political Economy of Underdevelopment" *Economic and Political Weekly*, Annual Number, February, p. 199.
90. See Stilwell, *op. cit*, and Markusen, A.R. (1978) "Class, Rent and Sectoral Conflict: Uneven Development in Western U.S. Boomtowns" in *Review of Radical Political Economy*, Vol. 10, No. 3.
91. Stilwell, *op. cit.*, p. 23.
92. See Lipietz, *op. cit.*
93. Rather, Mandel (*op. cit.*, p. 91) contends that the 'Law of uneven development' is "a universal law of human history". Althusser, drawing from Mao's *On Contradiction*, explains uneven development to encompass "everything in this world". (Althusser, 1977, cited in Smith, *op. cit.*, p. 172, f.n. 4).
94. Differentiating 'diversity' and 'disparity', Chattopadhyay and Raza (*op. cit*, p. 11) write:

    "Differences in initial resource endowments, largely of a *natural* or physiographic character, leading to territorial specialization and division of labour through exploitation of the resource advantage-comparative as well as absolute-constitute the basis and substance of inter-regional *diversity*, which is a concomitant of development. Inter-regional *disparity*, on the other hand, denote the failure of a region to exploit the development potential of its initial resource endowments, its latent comparative and absolute resource advantage, relative to another comparable region...."
95. See for example, Kundu, A. (1979) *Measurement of Urban Processes: A Study in Regionalisation*, Popular Prakashan, Mumbai.
96. Here 'nation' is used in the sense of 'state'.
97. Gurung, H. "The Land" in Rana P.S.J.B. and Malla, K.P. (1973), p. 25, *Nepal in Perspective*, CEDA, Kathmandu, p. 25.
98. For a statistical measurement of this, see Pant, B.D. (1982), *Statistical Analysis of Economic Activities for Regional Planning in Nepal* (Unpublished Ph.D Dissertation), Indian Statistical Institute, Calcutta.
99. Evidences of pre-historic man dating back to 200 thousand years have been unearthed in Nawalparasi area [Janchboojh Kendra (1974), *Mechi Dekhi Mahukali* (Nepali), Part-3 Kathmandu p. 14] and implements of neolithic age in Dang Valley (*op. cit.*, Part-4, p. 13). Very recently stone age relics haven been found in Kathmandu Valley (*The Times of India*, April 30, 1985, p. 18).
100. See Bista, D.B. (1982), "The Process of Nepalization", in *Anthropological and Linguistic Studies of the Gandaki Area in Nepal*, Monumentaserindica No. 10, Institute for the Study of Languages and Cultures of Asia and Africa, Tokyo.

101. See Bajracharya, D.B. (1974), *Lichchhabi Kalka Abhilekh* (Nepali), CNAS, Kathmandu.
102. See Engels, F. (1882), "The Mark", in Marx, K. and Angels, F. (1979), *Pre-Capitalist Socio-Economic Formations*, Progress Publishers, Moscow.
103. See Regmi (1976), *op. cit.*
104. Angels also talks of existence of different stages of communal property side by side and cites historical instances of "peoples' common land...claimed by the king as representative of the whole nation" (*op. cit.*, p. 275).
105. The term 'semi-colony' was originally coined by Lenin to describe those non-capitalist societies which managed to preserve a status of formal political independence, mainly as a result of international competition during the period of imperialist expansion during the 19th century, e.g. China, Japan, Turkey, Ethiopia, Thailand, Iran, Afghanistan. (See Seddon et. al. *op. cit*, p. 28).
106. Whereas 'political dependency' and 'semi-colony' seem to have been used interchangeably by Seddon et.al. (*-ibid-*), Sharma and Ojha have preferred to use 'political dependency' throughout while talking of Nepal's relations with British India (see Sharma and Ojha, *op. cit.*, pp . 24–25). We have, however, used the term in the sense of political manifestation of 'semi-colony'.
107. The political change of 1951, is seen as signifying the transition from semi-colony to 'periphery' by Seddon et al. (*op. cit.*) and transition from 'political dependency' to 'economic dependency' by Sharma and Ojha (*op. cit.*).
108. See Bhasin, A.S. (1970), *Documents on Nepal's Relations with India and China (1949–66)*, Academic Books Ltd..., Mumbai.
109. As Marx and Angels remark:
"How far the productive forces of a nation are developed is shown most manifestly by the degree to which the division of labour has been carried" [Marx and Engels (1979), *op. cit.*, p. 21].
110. This theory states that 'the larger the proportion of the active population engaged in the "tertiary" sector the higher is the national income'. See Mandel (1970), *op. cit.*, p. 204.
111. In the words of Baran: "...it is not the development of the services sector that is the *cause* of social development but social enrichment that is the cause of the development of services"; and "Just as obesity may be an indication of either affluence or squalor so large numbers of people engaged in the sphere of circulation (and services) may testify to both economic advancement and economic backwardness". (Baran *op. cit.*, p. 311, footnote-8).
112. See Marx, K. (1977a), *Grundrisse*, Penguin Books, Harmondsworth, pp. 88–89.
113. No separate break-up is available for useful services like health, education, etc. and activities of doubtful social utility like armed and police forces, etc. "Transport and communication" is include here because its development is said to be governed more by 'politico-strategic' and 'administrative' interest than by those of social production (See Blaiki et. al, *op. cit.*, p. 42).
114. According to the World Bank report the share in GDP of each sector is slightly different:

Year	*Agriculture*	*Industry*	*Service*
1976	65%	10%	25%

(The World Bank, *World Development Report 1983*, Oxford University Press, Delhi).

115. Amin (1979), *op. cit.*, p. 239.
The comparative sectoral distribution of GDP for other countries is as follows:

(%)

	Year	*Agriculture*	*Industry*	*Services*
1. 'Low Income Countries	1960	52	12	35
(34 in nos.)	1976	45	19	39
2. 'Industrialised Countries'				
(19 in nos.)	1960	9	41	47
	1976	6	41	52

(The World Bank, *op. cit.*).

116. Gaige, F.H. (1975), *Regionalism and National Unity in Nepal*, Vikas Publishing House Pvt. Ltd., New Delhi, p. 28.

117. See Dasgupta, B. (1971), "Socio-Economic Classification of Indian Districts—A Statistical Approach", *Economic and Political Weekly*, August 14, pp. 1763–74; Pal, M.N. (1975), "Regional Disparities in the Levels of Development in India", *Indian Journal of Regional Science*, Vol. II, No. 1, pp. 12–35; Kundu, *op. cit.*, among others.

2 Condition of the Agricultural Sector

2.1 INTRODUCTION

Before coming to the analysis of the present condition of the agriculture sector in Nepal, it may be necessary to clarify certain theoretical issues on the 'agrarian question' and make a brief historical review of the agrarian process in the country.

2.1.1 Theoretical Issues

In view of the well known theoretical and methodological disputes on the political economy of underdevelopment relevant to the agricultural sector[1] and the poor state of theory in the context of agricultural studies in Nepal, the theoretical premises to be dealt with here would be mainly related to the general law of motion in agriculture. Also, since our ultimate aim is to make a spatial differentiation of the agrarian process in Nepal, the basic postulates on the subject would be introduced.

2.2.11 Law of Motion in Agriculture

For our limited contextual purpose the discussion on the law of motion with particular reference to the transition from pre-capitalist to the capitalist stage of development in agriculture would be more important. Accordingly the issues can be broadly discussed under: (i) the question of 'prime mover' in agricultural development; (ii) operation of the laws of socialisation in agriculture; (iii) characterisation of 'peasant proprietorship'; and (iv) differentiation of the peasantry.

(i) The Question of 'Prime Mover' in Agriculture The transition from a lower to higher social formation is effectuated by the compulsions of restructuring the previously articulated combinations of the social forces and relations of production in keeping with the changed conditions in one or both the components of the production process, and to ensure the reproduction of the system in a more efficient form. The forces that play the primary role to bring about a rupture in the earlier system to the point of negating its very reproduction and lead towards the crystallisation of a superior formation may be termed as 'prime mover'.[2]

The decisive impact in the resolution of contradictions within the agricultural sector seems to have been mostly exercised by forces emanating from other sectors of the economy, specially industry. General backwardness of agriculture sector vis-à-vis other sectors is easily explicable in terms of the readiness with which various factors of production, e.g. labour, capital and instruments of production, can be combined and enlarged in the case of manufacturing and equal clumsiness in the combination and enlargement of the factors of production in the case of organisation of capitalist agriculture, principally due to the constraints posed by the pre-capitalist monopoly and market rigidity of the all important means of production, the land. Added to this general handicap of the agriculture sector is the symbiosis of peasant agriculture and handicraft production into a self-sufficient 'natural economy' that is impervious to capitalist penetration unless forcibly broken-up before hand. That is why Kautsky and Lenin seem to ascribe to "urban industry" the decisive role in the transformation of pre-capitalist agriculture to a higher mode.[3]

Kautsky-Lenin schema of agricultural development with urban industrial capital as the motor force has been inspired by the progressive nature of capitalism of the pre-monopoly, pre-imperialist era when it embodied a drive to 'create a world after its own image'. It was then quite logical for industrial capital to emit impulses of commodity production in the countryside in search of reciprocal markets for raw materials, capital and consumption goods and labour, and thereby accelerate the process of differentiation of peasantry. However, in the era of imperialism and neo-colonialism, the whole of the pre-capitalist economies of most of the Third World countries have come under the spell of metropolitan capital which has stood on the way of normal growth of indigenous industrial capital and thereby deprived agriculture its much-needed 'motor force'. In certain cases of natural advantage for agricultural production, extraverted agricultural enclaves with 'unequal specialization" in export crops or 'plantation economies' have mushroomed under the direct hegemony of metropolitan capital,[4] which constitute mere islands of growth in the vast ocean of all-round penury. In general, the entire pre-capitalist agricultural sector of the underdeveloped countries reel under the reactionary spell of metropolitan and local merchant and finance capital which have an inbuilt mechanism of perpetrating structural backwardness.[5] Hence, in view of the slackness of the internal drive of the agricultural sector for transition to higher modes of production and the continued stagnation of this vital economic sector threatening the very base of imperialist exploitation of the underdeveloped world, the guardians of metropolitan capital have of late devised ways of state interventions in the guise of 'land reforms', 'green revolutions', 'area or target group development programmes', etc., to ward off, 'revolution from below' by effectuating 'reform from the top'. Nevertheless, the agricultural sector without the support of an indigenous industrial base has not been able to extricate itself from the long spell of stagnation, and thus the theoretical formulations emphasizing the dialectical interlinkage of agriculture and industry remains as valid today as ever.

(ii) Operation of the Law of Socialisation in Agriculture The applicability to the agricultural sector of the law of increasing tendency of socialisation in production with higher levels of modes of production. has been questioned in recent times, as during the days of Kautsky and Lenin, on the basis of some empirical studies, which seem to confirm an inverse relation between productivity and *size* of a unit of production.[6] Since the current arguments are on similar lines, a return to Kautsky and Lenin[7] should suffice to refute them and put the original formulation in its proper perspective.

Certainly the law of increasing return to scale does not operate in the agricultural sector at a low level of technique of production due to some intrinsic limitations of agricultural production.[8] The problem arises when the observations with respect to the *size* of the units of production at a *determinate technical level* are misunderstood with those as applied to the *scale* of production on a *capitalist basis*.[9] Also, it is wrongly sought to extend the law of capitalist development to other modes of production, or compare the productivity of holdings cultivated at different technical basis.[10]

As per the tenacity of small farms by the side of large capitalist holdings, several explanations can be forwarded. Of these Marx's celebrated exposition in *Capital*, Vol III regarding the simultaneous playing of multiple roles of 'capitalist' 'landowner' and 'wage-worker' by the peasant,[11] remains a classic. From that Kautsky and Lenin synthesize the phenomenon of prevalence of "overwork" and "underconsumption" amongst small peasant households and attribute the so-called "superiority" of small-scale production to "the peasant art of starvation"[12] and to the "methods of sheer waste–waste of farmers' labour and vital energy, waste of strength and quality of the cattle, and waste of the productive capacities of land"[13]. In underdeveloped societies marked by rampant rural unemployment and underemployment and lesser opportunities of labour flight to urban industrial employment, this tendency of "overwork" and "underconsumption" amongst small peasants is more pronounced, and large landowners find it more rewarding to let out their land in small lots than to cultivate it as a large-scale capitalist enterprise.[14] This process is further accentuated through the practice of debt-bondage of semi-proletarianised peasants by the landlord-usurer to tie down the peasant-labourer to the land in semi-feudal relations.[15] Also merchant capital has a vested interest in perpetuating small peasant production, as "the grain prices are lower in countries with predominant small peasant land proprietorship than in countries with capitalist mode of production" because there "it is not necessary that the market price rise either up to the value or price of production."[16] When the ruination of peasantry goes too far and the emigration of rural population threatens labour scarcity, the big farmers tend to see or lease small lots of land remote from the centre of the estate in order to secure labour, and thus "rotation of concentration and parcellisation of the land" goes with capitalist development in agriculture.[17] The persistence of small peasant holdings by the side of large capitalist farms can also be explained in terms of not necessarily contradictory but complimentary nature of the two forms of production in that the peasants "are not competitors but customers" of commodities produced by larger farms and the "one commodity which they (i.e. small peasants) do possess in aboudance and which the bigger holdings need, is their labour power."[18] Thus, none of these factors contributing to the tenancity of small peasant holdings point towards the "superiority" or "viability" of small-scale production, but to their sheer condemnation into forced existence in the light of the weak, distorted and uneven development of capitalism, which is characteristic of the situation in the present-day underdeveloped countries.

However, there is some universal limitations of the development of capitalism in agriculture and the applicability of the attendant laws of development to this sector of the economy. The very essence of capitalist development, as already mentioned, is the 'free' mobility of the factors of production to unite at the highest level of productivity so that individual production units can reproduce themselves continuously at an expanded scale and compete successfully with other production units. This usually takes place under two broad movements-*accumulation* and *centralisation*, i.e. conversion of surplus value into capital and the amalgamation of several production units into a larger unit, respectively. Whereas in industrial production accumulation or concentration can proceed independent of centralisation, in agriculture the big landowner cannot generally increase his wealth except through centralisation and this presupposes a ready availability of surrounding small holdings for expropriation and their forming a *continuous* area,[19] which is less likely in reality specially in places of extreme physiographic diversity like Nepal. Thus, development of capitalism in agriculture is hampered by the two-fold monopoly on land at the beginning of the capitalist mode of production, a *natural monopoly* and a *property monopoly*.[20] Whereas the natural monopoly resulting from the *limitedness* of land creates obstacles on the way of centralisation and is inevitable in capitalist society, the property monopoly arising out of the seizure of ownership of land by a class of landowners claiming rent, i.e. absolute rent, prevents development of free market on land and has to be abolished for fuller development of capitalism.

(iii) Characterisation of 'Peasant Proprietorship' Characterisation of 'peasant proprietorship' as separate mode of production[21] has been another subject of controversy and needs to be discussed so that the real issues of underdevelopment in agriculture in a society marked by small-scale peasant production as in Nepal, may not be blurred.

A number of scholars[22] have already exposed the theoretical and methodological fallacy of the concept of 'peasant economy' mainly for its mere descriptive or ahistorical content as against the essentially analytical or historical content of the Marxist concept of mode or production. In the Marxist concept of mode of production,[23] the 'social relations of production' comprising a determinate type of ownership of means of production and determinate mode of appropriation of social surplus, is the crucial component. Contrary to this, the ahistorical notion of 'peasantry' as consisting of "small agricultural producers who, with the help of simple equipment and the labour of their families, produce mainly for their own consumption and for the fulfillment of obligations to the holders of political and economic power",[24] miserably fails to spell out a determinate social relations of production specific to a particular mode of production. What is important for the characterisation of the given mode of production is "*not* a theory of subsistence economy producing a little extra on the side but a theory of the mode of production organized around the production and appropriation of this surplus."[25]

'Peasants' possessing their means of production, exploiting their own family labour and producing primarily for their subsistence needs apart from parting away with a portion of their surplus labour by way of rent, tax and interest payment are known to have existed as important economic actors in diverse social formations from primitive societies of 'classical antiquity' to the advanced capitalist societies.[26] This makes the talk of 'peasantry' as a single homogenous whole identical in every society, totally farcical. Therefore, it is more logical to define peasants with respect to the dominant mode of production or 'agrarian system', they are subordinated to.[27] Characterisation of peasants would, thus, be a function of the determinate form of possession of the means of production (i.e. self-owned, vassalage or hired), a determinate form of appropriation of surplus labour above the subsistence needs of the direct producer (i.e. rent-money, kind, labour-tax or interest), etc. Consequently the historical 'peasant' could be variously termed as 'primitive agriculturist', 'serf peasant', 'tenant cultivator', 'peasant farmer' or 'disguised proletarian',[28] according to his subsumption under different historical epochs like 'classical antiquity', 'feudalism', 'semi-feudalism', or 'capitalism'.

(iv) The Differentiation of the Peasantry As evident from above, peasantry does not constitute a homogenous whole but summation of various class positions related with agricultural production under different historical epochs. The modality of measuring the process and identification of peasant classes has, therefore, generated intense debate amongst radical academics in recent years,[29] and hence demands familiarisation so that one does not go astray in the analysis of the situation in Nepal.

Despite the evolution of a set of satisfactory criterias for the identification of peasant classes at the *general* level, they are found to be of not much help at the particular level of the historically determined real world, where there exist "a variety of transitional forms, a complex interaction of developing capitalism with pre-capitalist organisations". For example, we find that "familly-labour-based holdings produce for the market, while wage-labour-based holdings do not necessarily invest in capital."[30] Similarly, labour services, the prinicpal form of appropriation of surplus labour under feudalism, can assume a capitalist relation of production if it is performed by a rural proletariat who has no implements.[31]

Thus peasants classes are usually sought to be characterised at the empirical level by the most significant attributes under the given circumstances. Whereas possession of the means of production and the mode of exploitation of labour are the most important criteria to distinguish class positions in general, the separation of labour from the means of production and subsistence,[32] or 'employment of wage-labour"[33] seems to be the single most important attribute distinguishing capitalist from non-capitalist relations. Of a number of attempts to evolve "the empirical approximation and methodological tool to pose and quantify class analysis of the peasantry" the ones by Patnaik (1976) based on 'labour exploitation ratio' or "the use of outside labour relative to the use of family labour", and by a Russian Statistician of the 1920s, Nemchinov, based on "the process of alienation of means of production from the direct producers and the expropriation of surplus value via control of means of production", appear to be more significant, despite their certain limitations.[34]

However, the poor and unreliable data base in most of the underdeveloped countries including Nepal would not permit the application of even these proximate tools and the peasant class structure there would have to be delineated through perceptive observations of a number of fragmentary aspects of class positions.

2.1.12 Spatial Differentiation of the Agrarian Process

By the very nature of direct appropriation of nature, which agricultural production is, agrarian process is more space contingent than any other economic process. Therefore, spatial differentiation should constitute an integral part of the study of underdevelopment of the agricultural sector.

The conventional spatial studies on agriculture have been mostly confined to territorial differentiation of crop structure, which have been erroneously called 'agricultural regionalisation' when in fact it is mere 'crop zoning'. Spatial studies on Nepalese agriculture[35] have displayed this error even more. Though the differentiation of crop zones, which are more the functions of natural factors than of the social ones, can be of some interest in a situation of extreme physiographic diversity like in Nepal, it is of little utility for a politico-economic study of the development/underdevelopment process as intended here. The more relevant study for our current purpose would then be the spatial differentiation of the total agrarian process manifested in the composite levels of development.

Measurement of the agrarian process, too, have often suffered from an ideological bias that puts excessive stress on the development of the productive forces and totally neglects the production relations aspect. Consequently, 'agricultural regionalistion' have often been attempted with respect to mere 'agricultural efficiency'[36] measured in terms of relative productivity of crops in particular area units. This has been justified on the ground that "agricultural efficiency is the interplay of a multitude of factors—environmental (climate and soils), socio-economic (size of holding, ownership and capital) and technological (irrigation facilities, cropping pattern, crop rotation, etc.)".[37] But the limitations of measuring the complex agrarian process by means of a single indicator of efficiency in production are too obvious to warrant explanations. Moreover, for a correct diagnosis of the process of underdevelopment in the agricultural sector the production relations aspect should be given adequate weightage. In this context, Sharma's[38] attempt at making spatial differentiation of 'distribution' aspects of agrarian process deserves particular attention.

The best way for discerning the underdevelopment process in the agricultural sector through a socio-spatial analysis would, however, be the spatial disaggregation of the composite levels of agricultural development constructed through a judicious combination of both the 'production' and 'distribution' components of the process.[39] But this may not be mistaken for 'agricultural regionalisation', which is a much more complicated process and is beyond the perview of our current exercise confined to the study of mere spatial distribution of sectoral underdevelopment. In a situation of lack of desirable data base like in Nepal, broad generalisations can be made from separate spatial differentiation of fragmentary aspects of the agrarian process.

As regards the spatial unevenness in agricultural development, there is discernible concurrence amongst different schools of thought on the fact of existence of wide unevenness, even when there is considerable divergence of opinion on the causative factors of the phenomenon. The unevenness in agricultural development, particularly at the capitalist stage of society, would be more pronounced because of the prevalence of two-fold pre-capitalist monopoly, i.e. natural monopoly and property monopoly (as explained earlier), on the all important factor of production, land. Whereas the neo-classicist location theorists[40] would extend the logic of 'industrial location theory' to the realm of agriculture and explain the uneven development of capitalism in agriculture in terms of rent differentials of different chunks of land, the Marxists[41] make a distinction between 'absolute rent' and 'differential rent' and concede the natural degree of unevenness only to the extent of the ability of certain land categories of particular fertility and favourable location to pay differential rent. The latter, in particular, ascribe the spatial unevenness in development of capitalism in agriculture more to the social factors like prevalence or not of labour service, burden of taxation, etc.[42] Nonetheless it is agreed that natural differentials do play a significant rôle in articulating spatial unevenness in agricultural development, more so at lower stages of organisation of society. However, from the point of view of political economy of underdevelopment the unevenness due to social differentials alone would demand our exclusive concern.

2.1.2 Historical Contours of Nepalese Agriculture

2.1.20 History of agriculture in pre-capitalist societies is in essence the history of the whole society, which is expressed in the evolution of the dominant mode of production. We will, therefore, attempt to decipher the complexities of this history in Nepal in keeping with the immediate objective of our study in terms of (i) the evolution of production relations in agriculture, practically summed up by the history of landownership, (ii) development of the productive forces, and (iii) the spatial configuration of their combined articulation.

2.1.21 Evolution of Social Relations of Production in Agriculture

As may be racollected from Chapter I, prior to the emergence of a centralised state of Nepal by the second half of 18th century various constituent spatial units disaggregated along the north-south ecological and east-west hydrographic zonings had traversed their own independent course from the primitive tribal-communal society into the proto-class, 'state-communal' formations. Hence, the effective history of agriculture on a countrywide canvass would be meaningful only since this period.

By the time of state unification the concept of state, or the king as its representative, as the sole repository of proprietorship of land within the domain is known to have been firmly established. Consequently except in a few areas of strong entrenchment of tribal communalism such as eastern hills and a few pockets of central hills, a system of state-landlordism, known as *Raiker* prevailed throughout the unified kingdom. In this system the actual cultivator enjoyed only occupancy and inheritable but inalienable right and made direct payment to the state.[43] The total appropriation by the state of the dominant means of production was, however, only the manifestation of final separation of tribal aristocracy and alien conquerors (the new 'ruling class') from the mass of the tribal peasantry and the culmination of collective exploitation of the primitive community.

A fresh restructuring of the relations of production based on parcellized sovereignty amongst members of the ruling classes and 'individual exploitation' of the peasantry was necessitated by the unmanageability of the newly acquired extensive territory and difficulty in maintaining harmony amongst the huge state bureaucracy and nobility at the prevailing level of development of productive forces confined to the production of use-values. Thus, with the gradual stabilization of its authority to be crowned by the establishment of Rana hereditary oligarchy in 1846, the state began alienating land in varying juridical independence to private individuals (*Birta*), religious and charitable institutions (*Guthi*), government employees (*Jagir*), royal vassals and former rulers (*Rajya*), local tax-collection functionaries (*Jirayat*, *Ukhada*, etc.) and others, giving rise to the rent-receiving landed intermediary interests in between the actual cultivator and the state; or the rise of incipient 'feudalism'.

A development of historical significance that brought about radical transformation of the economic life of the country by the late 19th century was the extension of Indian railway network to the border towns adjoining Nepal Terai, and the consequent massive clearance of forested Terai plains for 'commercial farming' through large-scale induced immigration of zamindars and peasants from neighbouring provinces of India.[44] This laid the material foundation for maturing of 'feudalism' during the Rana era,[45] which reached its peak by the beginning of the 20th century with the distribution in unprecedented scale of *Birta* lands in the newly opened-up Terai amongst the Rana family and the nobility[46] and the entrenchment of the oppressive *Jimidari* system.[47] However, because of the export-oriented and commoditised agricultural production the 'feudalism' that developed in Nepali Terai from the very beginning was not of the 'classic' type but a peculiar one that could be termed 'feudal-capitalist' similar to the mode of exploitation of forestry in Europe in the 15th century.[48]

Another line of development that introduced intermediary rent-receiving interests between the actual cultivator and the ultimate owner, the state, in the *Raiker* lands and encouraged social inequality by dispossessing the peasantry of their land and concentrating them into the hands of landlords, usures, mortgagers, etc. (who were mostly the village tax-collecting functionaries-*Chaudharies* and *Jimidars* in Terai; *mukhiyas and jimmawals* in the hills), was the gradual evolution of a set of factors including;

- Introduction of fixed-rent (*kut*) in place of previous crop-sharing (*Adhiya*) system;[49]
- Practice of realisation of rent in cash (confined to Terai and Western hills), with the result that moneyed interests could play into the financial difficulties of peasants;
- Abandonment of the practice of periodic redistribution and reallocation (*raibandi*) of rice-lands prevalent in the central hills by 1888;[50]
- Gradual evolution of property rights on *Raiker* lands from the early years of Rana period with the implicit provision of alienation by way of sale, mortgage or tenancy; to be explicitly recognised by law in 1927;[51]
- Full monetization of tax-assessment system on lands all over the country by the first decade of the 20th century and progressive decline in real value of taxes with the fixation of rates on a long-term basis in 1910 and only to be revised in 1934 and 1962,[52] thus introducing a layer of subinfeudation in land; etc.

Similarly, the *Kipat* system of communal ownership of land prevalent mostly in the eastern hill and juridically reaffirmed from time to time by the state for political expediency of keeping peace with the ethnic communities that were "voluntarily" integrated into the unified state rather than forcibly appropriated underwent gradual and fundamental changes under the impact of 'feudalisation' process going all around. "....(F) or all practical purposes, *Kipat* ownership ultimately developed into a system of freehold ownership like *Birta.* The communal character of the system was limited to non-alienability outside the community and the reversionary rights of the community in the event of the temporary absence or the extinction of the *Kipat* owner's family."[53] With the tacit design of the state, a large portion of the *Kipat* lands was temporarily alienated through possessory mortgages outside the community, to the extent of 70% of the cultivated area in one area of Ilam district in 1964–65[54] and only one-third of the total cultivated area in Pallokirat, or far-eastern hills, remained under *Kipat* tenure by 1951.[55]

The peak of 'feudalistic' development by the beginning of the 20th century was also marked by imposition on the peasantry of a number of extra-economic coercive measures and labour services such as *jhara* (i.e. casual unpaid labour for meeting occasional needs) and *rakam* (i.e. labour tax for the regular discharge of a specific function) by the state and other labour obligations by the *Birta* owners and tax-collection functionaries. However, there is no evidence of wide use of labour rent as in feudal Europe and to that extent 'feudalism' in Nepalese history can be taken only as a 'variant' of classical feudalism.[56]

The pattern of land tenure that crystallized by this period and continued till the 1950s can be schematically presented after Regmi (1963–68, 1976, 1978) as in Figure 2.1, and the distribution of land under different tenurial forms as in Table 2.0.

Table 2.0 Area Under Different Forms of Land Tenure Before 1950.

Form of Tenure	*Area (hectares)*	*% of Total Area*
Raikar	963,500	50.0
Birta	700,080	36.3
Guthi	40,000	2.0
Kipat	77,090	4.0
Rajya, Jagir, Rakam, etc.	146,330	7.7
TOTAL	1,927,000	100.0

Note: Since a part of land under *Birta* was used by individuals as *Guthi,* total area under *Guthi* tenure may have been much more.

Source: Zaman, M.A. (1973), *Evaluation of Land Reforms in Nepal,* HMG/N, Ministry of Land Reform, Kathmandu, p. 7.

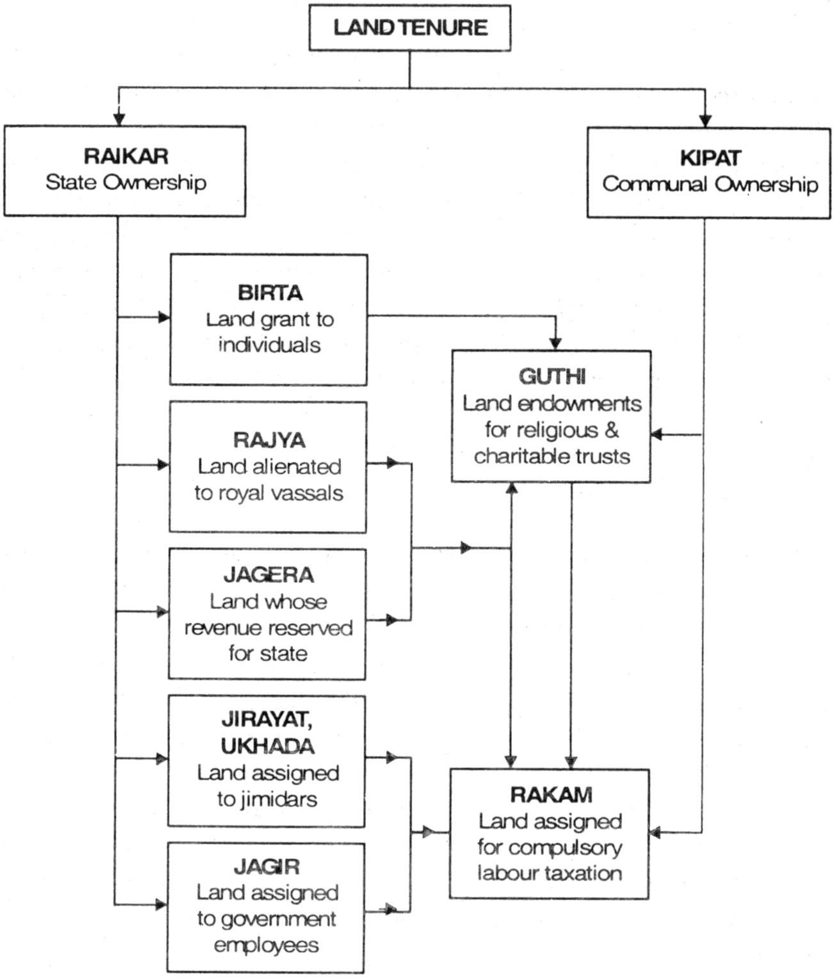

Fig. 2.1 Land Tenure System in Nepal.

As regards the actual cultivation of land before 1950, it has been estimated that 60% of the total cultivated land was tenanted by peasants paying rent to the various categories of intermediary owners on the basis of share-cropping (68% of tenanted land), fixed-rent (29%) and service rent (3%); the proportion of rent paid to the landowner under sharecropping tenancy not being less than half of the gross produce.[57]

With the downfall of the Rana regime, the biggest land-holding aristocracy in the country, in 1951 and with the ever increasing penetration of Indian merchant and industrial capital (the more of the former) after the Second World War, a remoulding of the land-tenure system amongst the various constituents of the possessing classes was imperative. Thus, the decade of 1950s and early 1960s saw the enactment of a number of legislative measures in the direction of 'land reforms' consisting of abolition of a number of tenure system such as *Jagir*, *Birta*, Crown lands, *Rajya* and *Rakam* in 1952, 1959, 1960, 1961, and 1963 respectively; improvement of the security of tenancy; rent control; and ceiling on land holdings.[58] The farcical nature of the cosmetic 'reforms' under the pressure of foreign 'aid' donors[59] is amply reflected in the mere "terminological reform"[60] of *Birta* tenure wherein 'A' class lands (mostly owned by dethroned Ranas) were nationalised *with compensation* and 'B' class ones just taxed. To crown it all, since the government did not possess any record of the size of such holdings, "the onus was left to the *Birta* holders to come forward with a declaration of their holdings."[61] However, even the partial implementation of the most comprehensive to date and much-publicised Land Act of 1964 is reported to have resulted in certain changes by way of diminution in the size of holdings and dispossession of tenancy rights of peasants[62] and facilitated penetration of exogenous foreign merchant and bureaucratic capital in the agriculture sector,[63] without bringing about any fundamental transformation in the agrarian relations.

With the enactment of legislations in 1968 abolishing all tenurial distinctions between *Kipat* and *Raiker* system, however, uniform tenurial conditions have been established all over the country. But religions prejudices have kept the *Guthi* system beyond the ambit of state 'control' (if the term can be used without misunderstanding:) on *Raiker* lines and made the Guthi corporation (the sole managing authority of all *Guthi* lands) the biggest landowner with about[66] thousand *bigha* of land[64] in the country and with all the worst features of absentee land-lordism.

2.1.22 Development of Productive Forces in Agriculture

The earliest available historical evidences of the Lichhavi period from around 3rd century A.D. onwards indicate a relatively high level of development of the forces of production in agriculture in the Kathmandu Valley, with a system of community (*gram-panchali*) operated irrigation channels, use of plough and cultivation of wheat and sugarcane.[65] Comparatively more handicapped both in natural attributes and social experiences, other parts of the present-day state can be safely assumed to have lagged behind Kathmandu Valley in the level of social development in general and that of agriculture in particular. In absolute terms, the tribal communities of the hills could not have progressed beyond the use of primitive tools and engaged in pastoralism and shifting cultivation.

Introduction of metal works, plough and technique of wet rice cultivation with the immigration of Hindus from the Indian plains to the central and western hills of Nepal from 11th century onwards gave tremendous boost to the development of productive forces in the region. With the establishment of petty principalities and increased social interactions across different zones for territorial expansion, the entire hills and the adjoining Terai plains gradually adopted the new production technologies. However, the single biggest boost to the hill economy since the great influx of immigrants from the plains, was provided by the introduction of American maize via India during the early 18th century. This enabled the unirrigated lands of the hills to yield at least two crops a year: maize during April-July and millet during August-December, and resulted in substantial growth of the population.[66]

A first-hand account of the economic situation in the unified state of Nepal from late 18th century onwards is provided by a number of Britishers visiting Nepal at different times since then, notably Kirkpatric (1811), Hamilton (1819),Wright (1877)and others. These accounts establish that during the 19th century the Nepali peasant produced not only such staple food crop as rice, wheat, maize and millet but also a number of commercial crops including cotton and cardamom in the hills, and indigo, opium, sugarcane and tobacco in the Terai. However, because of the scarcity of irrigation facilities and depredations by stray cattle and wild animals, multi-cropping appears to have been seldom practised. Rice was the main crop in both the Terai and central hills, where Hamilton estimated one-half of the total cultivation to consist in transplanted rice.[67] The production of crops in the Terai, particularly eastern Terai, exceeded the local needs and were exported in large quantities, specially rice and oilseeds, to Bihar, Bengal and elsewhere in India.[68] Jute production on a commercial scale was, however, to await the emergence of Indian jute industry and the extension of the railway system to the adjoining Indian towns accross the Nepal border towards the end of the 19th century.

As regards the all important factor for the advancement of productive forces in agriculture at a backward stage, i.e. the irrigation facilities, except for the long-standing provision of community-operated irrigation system in Kathmandu Valley and several districts of the central hills including Kaski, Nuwakot, Palpa and Syangja during the 19th century, there is little evidence to show that irrigation facilities were much developed in any party of the country.[69] The first modern irrigation project (Chatara Irrigation project) was initiated in eastern Terai only in the aftermath of increased demands of agricultural exports during and after the Second World War.

The absolute low level of development of productive forces in agriculture over the years can be summed up in the words of a highly-placed official scholar-functionary, that "the agricultural implements, which were found in use at least 150 years ago, are still being used virtually without any substantial improvement in respect of majority of farmers."[70]

2.1.23 The Process of Spatial Differentiation

As already mentioned, lower the level of development of the social productive forces stronger is the hold of nature over the social process. Hence the early spatial differentiation, howsoever marginal it was, of the social process in general and agrarian process, in particular, in Nepal was heavily governed by the natural attributes of the spatial entities. Also, particular historical experiences of each had important bearings in modifying the given spatial structure.

Kathmandu Valley, as already noted, was best favoured by both nature and history to take an early lead over the rest of the areas in the race for development, which it was able to maintain in the subsequent epochs till the recent times. Of the exceptionally highly developed state of agriculture for the given historical epoch in the Valley, then known as Nepal Valley, an European visitor had written in 1876:

> "The cultivation of the Nepal Valley is blessed with unequalled advantages and is carried on with utmost industry. In May we found a waving harvest of wheat awaiting the sickle and I was told that almost all these lands had already yielded an equally good rice harvest within the agricultural year, and that many of the fields would yet yield special crops, pepper, vegetables, and the like. In short, most of the lands yield two harvests in the year, and some yield even three.",[71]

However, Kathmandu Valley represented "an island of high agricultural productivity against a general background of inefficient and extensive farming practices",[72] and even there the pace of agricultural development seems to have bogged down for long primarily due to the retrograde production relations symbolized in *Guthi*, *Jagir* and *Birta* tenures on most of the lands and excessive rent and labour obligations on the peasantry till very recently.

The central east-west hilly spine of the country, the traditional habitation zone, can be said to have been differentiated into three distinct hydrographic sub-zones—the Koshi, the Gandaki and the Karnali basins-on the basis of both natural and social attributes since the dawn of civilization. Whereas the 'original' cultural differences of the *pastoral nomads* of the western hills and *hunting nomads* of the east, must have placed the west ahead of the east, with the centre acting as the bridge for quite some time, the superior natural attributes of the east must have ultimately compensated the original lag. The central zone endowed with best of the natural and social worlds did surge ahead of the rest in the long run. When the same central hills attracted the Hindu immigrants from the Indian plains with their better agricultural technology first, the ascendance of this territorial entity along with the Kathmandu Valley as the best agricultural region, was merely a matter of time. The subsequent crystallization of petty principalities, 24 in the central region (hence the name *Chaubisi*) and 22 in the western region (hence *Baisi*), further accentuated and articulated the internal spatial differences in the country. Whereas the broad, well-watered mountain valleys and moderately sloped, carefully-terraced hillsides of the *Chaubisi* region made it a predominantly rice-cultivating zone, the more rigorous terrain and poor agro-climatic attributes of the *Baisi* region permitted only marginally productive cultivation in maize, rice, millet and wheat, in that order.[73]

With the integration of the disjointed territorial entities into a loosely articulated centralised state and the subsequent intensification of surplus-appropriation drive by a number of landed interests from the state downwards to the village revenue-collection functionaries, the social factors took decisive precedence over the natural ones in the articulation of the agrarian spatial structure in the country. Discernible spatial variations in the land-tenure systems started surfacing and these tended to be a function of the distance from the central authority (quite a significant variable in the era of scanty transportation networks), tenacity of the tribal social structure and agronomic characteristics of the land. Consequently, the Karnali basin, lying farthest from the central authority at Kathmandu, enjoying the most extensive territories of relatively poor agronomic quality, possessing the feeblest remains of tribal-communal social structure (as it was mostly inhabited by the Indo-Aryan stock) and having the largest number of autonomous principalities (or, *rajyas*) till recently, was destined to develop the tracts of "feudalistic' agrarian structure to the highest degree amongst all the hill areas. This was marked by more widespread sub-infeudation and greater inequality of land-holdings because of early evolution of the right of alienation of *raiker* holdings by the peasants and the practice of extraction of rent/tax at a fixed rate (i.e. one-third of the total produce) and in cash.[74] At the other end, the eastern hills particularly its far-eastern section (i.e. pallokirat), experienced stiffest resistance from the tenacious relations based on private property on land, but was ultimately prevailed over by a number of subjective factors abetted by the hostile state to fall in line with the western parts of the country. The central hill region, which was the traditional home of the central ruling aristocracy, both military and civil, was to experience the heaviest direct interventions of the state in its agrarian development process. As this region mostly produced rice, the staple food of the nobility, almost the entire cultivated area there was controlled by *birta* owners and *jagirdars*[75] and the tenant-cultivators were required to pay half of the produce in kind as rent (*adhiya)* to their overlords against *chuni ryots* of *raiker* lands who paid 'taxes' to the state, thus virtually ruling out the emergence of intermediary landed interests or sub-infeudation of holdings. Even when the *adhiya* system was replaced by *kut* (i.e. fixed rent) system during the later period, the rate of rent to be paid reached as high as 75% of the rice crop,[76] sealing the fate of any prospective intermediary interests. Moreover, till the end of the 19th century a system of periodic redistribution and reallocation (*raibandi*) of rice-lands was practised in this region and the peasants held their land on short leases devoid of any right of alienation by way of sale, mortgage or allotment. Hence, the agrarian structure of the central hill region was marked by a prevalence of small cultivators against a greater degree of economic differentiation in other parts of the country.

As regards the presently all important Terai plains, larger parts of the area had remained thickly forested and economically not very significant till the mid-18th century, because of their hostile weather conditions for human habitation and their conscious preservation as barriers against foreign intrusion into the hills. But, with the establishment of the centralised state, its vast agricultural potentials were realised, and by the beginning of the 19th century parts of the eastern and central Terai, particularly the modern districts of Parsa, Bara, Rupendehi in centre-west, had become "outstanding agricultural regions" of Nepal. With the clearance of much of the Terai forest for cultivation after the extension of Indian railway networks to the Nepal border, the domination of Terai in the economic life of the country was fully established. The Terai, specially the eastern part, became not only the chief producer of staple food crop, rice but also of cash crops like tobacco, oilseeds, sugarcane and jute, out of which tobacco seemed to occupy a place of pride provoking Hamilton to describe it as "uncommonly good".[77] Of the different parts of Terai, the far-western section was to be the one last opened-up for cultivation when it was returned back to Nepal by the Britishers in 1858 since its seizure by them in the 1814–16 war. Its poorer agro-climatic attributes and remoteness from the central state authority in Kathmandu, made it economically less important till the recent decades.

The differentiation of the Terai from the rest of the country was also pronounced in the nature of production relations to be developed there. Till the last quarter of the 18th century the land tenure system of Terai seems to have paralleled with that prevailing in the adjoining regions of India. But with the "permanent settlement" in Bihar and Bengal in 1793 the *zamindari* system in the Nepal Terai started evolving on divergent lines. Whereas the *zamindars* in Bihar and Bengal acquired 'proprietory right' on their holdings, those in Nepal Terai remained only " a rural class other than, and standing above the peasantry".[78] Thus, by the 19th century the land in the Terai was normally in the possession of two categories of land-holders, *zamindars* and *chuni* ryots, who got their lands cultivated by share-croppers. As the state's share of the produce of the land appears to have been limited roughly to one-third of the gross produce assessed on the basis of crops and realised in cash as in Mughal India, there was widespread subinfeudation, and inequalities appear to be most pronounced in the Terai than in other parts of the country. After the intensification of large-scale *birta* grants during the Rana period and flourishing of the institution of *jimidars* as local tax-collection functionary, this inequality in land-holdings was further accentuated.

The valleys of inner Terai, due to their excessively humid and malarial climate remained marginal zones till the eradication of malaria in the 1950s and hence economically insignificant till then.

In the Himalayan mountain zone, the extreme physiographic conditions precluded stabilized agriculture there, and they remained marginal zones for human habitation throughout history. Barter trade across the Himalayas combined with animal husbandry and shifting cultivation, constituted the principal economic activities of this region and was prone to lesser degree of economic differentiation.

In the light of this historical contour of the agrarian process in the country, the current situation of the agriculture sector may be assessed in subsequent pages.

2.2 PRODUCTION CHARACTERISTICS OF AGRICULTURE

Without meaning to divorce the two components of a social phenomenon indissolubly bound together in a relation of dialectical interactions, for the sake of convenience and clarity of expression it would be worthwhile to depict first the 'production' and 'distribution' characteristics of the Nepali agriculture and subsequently articulate them. In the production characteristics it is sought to analyze the mode of appropriation of nature by the society, or the state of the forces of production, and in 'distribution' the mode of appropriation of the social product by the individual members of the society, or the nature of the relations of production.

Since appropriation of nature in primary production takes place through the interactions of the factors of production, namely land, labour, technique of production, etc., and our immediate aim is to delineate the spatial configuration of the development process in the agricultural sector, it would be befitting to start with the portrayal of major attributes of principal factors of production in the given spatial setting.

2.2.1 Conditions of Factors of Agricultural Production

2.2.11 Land

Land, the basic material element of production in agriculture, occupies a progressively more dominant place in the overall production process with the historically descending order of social mode of production. In the particular case of Nepal, marked by extreme natural differentiation of space and comparatively low social differentiation, the physical extent and agronomic qualities of distribution of cultivable land over the geographical space should exercise an even more important role in the articulation of the agrarian spatial structure.

As may be recapitulated from the earlier Chapter, there is extreme skewedness in the spatial distribution of cultivated land in the country. To have a better idea of the distribution pattern at the more disaggregated level, Table 2.1 has been constructed through the compilation of data from diverse sources.[79] The

Table 2.1 Distribution of Net Cultivated Area by Territorial Zones (1978/79).

Territorial Zones	*Net Area Under Cultivation*				
	Area[1] ('000 hect.)	*as % of total cultivated area*	*as % of geographical area*		*Per 1000 population[2] (hect.)*
			%	*L.Q.*	
MOUNTAIN	195.02	7.15	4.07	0.22	196
Eastern	78.17	2.87	6.52	0.35	170
Central	17.34	0.64	2.44	0.13	314
Western	99.51	3.65	3.46	0.18	207
HILL	965.35	35.40	17.44	0.93	171
Eastern	358.74	13.15	25.08	1.34	205
Central	399.36	14.64	17.52	0.94	163
Western	207.25	7.60	11.35	0.61	144

(Contd.)

(*Table 2.1 contd.*)

KATHMANDU VALLEY	47.04	1.72	42.88	2.29	68
INNER TERAI	239.36	8.78	15.52	0.83	239
Eastern	53.63	1.97	11.43	0.61	187
Central	82.47	3.02	17.37	0.93	208
Western	103.27	3.79	17.26	0.92	327
TERAI	1280.36	46.95	49.33	2.64	284
Eastern	842.00	30.87	59.02	3.15	253
Central	221.71	8.13	60.73	3.24	328
Western	216.64	7.94	26.96	1.44	429
NEPAL	2727.13	100.00	18.72	1.00	212

Note: 1. Net cultivated area for 1978/79 are calculated from data obtained from APROSC data bank and National Research Associates (1982), *Nepal District Profile*, Kathmandu, for different points of time, assuming a constant rate of growth.

2. Cultivated area for 1978/79 are weighted by 1976 mid-term census population; hence the absolute figures may be slightly on the higher side.

natural advantage enjoyed by the Terai over the rest of the country in the matter of agricultural production is once more confirmed. The high percentage of geographical area under cultivation in eastern (59.02%) and central (60.73%) Terai and Kathmandu Valley (42.88%) against a low (17.44%) in Hill and Inner Terai (15.52%) and exceedingly low (4.07%) in the northern-most Mountain, is easily explicable within the Ricardian frame of land-use pattern, and further helps to differentiate the zones of natural advantages in terms of distribution of vital means of agricultural production, the land. However, the comparatively low share of the geographical area in the centrall Hill (17.52%) should be accounted for by the non-precise delineation of zonal boundary with the inclusion of a large section of Mountain area in it (see Chapter I above); that in western Terai (26.96%) by the historical accident of late opening-up of the area for human habitation and that in Inner Terai (15.52%) by both the above factors (but inclusion of Hill areas in this case), and should not unduly underrate their potential for agricultural production.

Distribution of cultivated land relative to the population of the area expresses the population pressure on land, and this criteria too places the Terai (284 hectare per 1000 population) in a much better position than Kathmandu Valley (68 hectare/1000 population). And the Hill regions (171 hectare/1000 population). Though distribution of cultivated land relative to the *rural* population should have provided a better picture of the population pressure on land (Kathmandu Valley and Terai would have further improved their position with their higher share of urban population) in view of the high percentage of "urban" population in primary production activities (see Chapter V below) it was considered more judicious to view the pressure on land in terms of the total population. Distribution of cultivated land by quality is here analysed through its classification into conventional (i) irrigable lowland or *khet* or *dhanahar*, and (ii) non-irrigable upland or *pakho* or *bhit* and their further categorisation into *abal*, *doyam*, *sim* and *chahar*[80] in the decreasing order of agronomic capacity, as in Table 2.2 on next page 78.

Table 2.2 Distribution of Cultivated Land by Agronomic Classification and Territorial Zones (1978/79).

(%)

Territorial Zones	Total Cultivated Land			Irrigable Lowland/Khet Dhanhar					Non-Irrigable Upland/Pakho/Bhit				
	Total	Low-land	Upland	Total	Abal	Doyam	Sim	Chahar	Total	Abal	Doyam	Sim	Chahar
(1)	(2)	(3)	(4)	(5)	(6)	(7)	(8)	(9)	(10)	(11)	(12)	(13)	(14)
MOUNTAIN	100.00	7.90	92.10	100.00	1.93	52.70	43.24	2.12	100.00	8.51	38.84	46.26	6.39
Eastern	–	–	–	–	–	–	–	–	–	–	–	–	–
*Central	100.00	7.90	92.10	100.00	1.93	52.70	43.24	2.12	100.00	8.51	38.84	46.26	6.39
Western	–	–	–	–	–	–	–	–	–	–	–	–	–
HILL	100.00	23.04	76.96	100.00	6.68	25.90	52.90	14.52	100.00	6.18	21.35	51.16	21.31
Eastern	100.00	19.34	80.66	100.00	4.27	24.93	59.54	11.26	100.00	2.74	19.76	52.32	25.19
Central	100.00	27.99	72.01	100.00	8.79	26.88	46.93	17.41	100.00	11.08	23.82	48.41	16.69
**Western	100.00	13.66	86.34	100.00	2.49	19.36	70.34	7.82	100.00	2.02	16.32	70.24	11.41
KATH, VALLEY	100.00	50.15	49.85	100.00	24.65	30.26	37.19	7.89	100.00	37.36	62.64	–	–
INNER TERAI	100.00	40.63	59.37	100.00	21.69	46.62	30.24	1.44	100.00	48.73	30.94	19.22	1.11
Eastern	100.00	38.37	61.63	100.00	25.40	44.48	29.03	1.09	100.00	29.92	32.96	34.25	2.87
Central	100.00	34.43	65.53	100.00	30.88	45.37	23.35	0.40	100.00	51.45	29.56	18.34	0.66
Western	100.00	48.28	51.72	100.00	13.27	48.47	35.90	2.36	100.00	57.07	31.49	10.85	0.59
TERAI	100.00	77.69	22.31	100.00	25.28	53.37	20.60	0.74	100.00	93.38	5.27	1.07	0.28
Eastern	100.00	78.95	21.05	100.00	24.48	54.55	20.02	0.96	100.00	92.74	6.95	0.31	–
Central	100.00	81.34	18.66	100.00	25.89	58.83	15.07	0.21	100.00	89.35	2.79	5.95	1.91
Western	100.00	67.41	32.59	100.00	28.79	39.00	31.84	0.37	100.00	98.06	1.94	–	–
NEPAL	100.00	58.00	42.00	100.00	22.98	49.42	25.16	2.44	100.00	40.92	18.97	29.14	10.98

Note: *Only Mustang district.
**Only Dandelahura district.
(+)Total is biased in favour of Terai as all the 18 Terai districts are included in the 41 surveyed districts till 1978/79.

Source: Ministry of Land Reform, Department of Survey (Cadastral), HMG/N, Kathmandu.

The decreasing order from Terai to Mountain in the distribution of cultivated land by agronomic quality both in terms of upland-lowland classification and subsequent sub-classification into four grades, is quite unmistakable. In the east-west territorial dimension, however, no distinct trend is observable except for the discernible low quality of land in the western parts of the country.

2.2.12 Labour

Labour, the principal source of value in all production, assumes a more direct form in primary production, and lower the stage of social mode of production higher is the share of direct labour in production. The non-comparable definitions of 'economically active' population in the subsequent censuses would not permit a temporal analysis of the general attributes of the agricultural labour-force in a territorial frame. Hence our attempt here would be confined to the analysis of the same with reference to a single point of time, i.e. 1971 [Table 2.3].

Although it is difficult to generalise an ideal land-labour ratio for a given level of development of the social productive forces, the density of agricultural labour per cultivated hectare in Nepal (2.42) can be safely regarded to be on the higher side. In the territorial frame, the density figures for Hill (5.66) and Mountain (5.47), specially central Hill (6.28) and eastern Mountain (6.93), may be viewed as alarming. It may be useful to recapitulate in this context that whereas an optimal labour force in any production is an essential prerequisite, an excess labour is a drain on the value created by necessary labour and is both a cause and effect of structural underdevelopment.

Economically active persons in the age group of 15–59 (or 15–64) years are conventionally regarded as the real productive labour in any branch of industry, and in societies marked by extra-economic compulsions against the employment of female labour for productive activities, or because of the faulty definitions of 'economically active' population, the said age-group of productive labour may be further qualified by the inclusion of only the male labour. Hence the zone-wise index of the nature of agricultural labour force is sought to be constructed by calculating the percentages of male labour 15–64 years of age to the total agricultural labour, and expectedly the quality of labour is seen progressively declining from the south to the north. At the risk of pre-empting the verifications through the subsequent pages, this phenomenon could be tentatively explained two ways. Firstly, the higher share of male labour in Terai (86.68%) and Inner Terai (71.55%) compared to that in Hill (61.47%) and Mountain (60.51%) may be attributed to the higher degree of 'feudalization' in the south, or conversely, to the lesser degree of 'detribalization' in the north, and thus increasingly displacing the females from productive activities as one moves from north to south. Secondly, the higher share of child and old-age labour, i.e. labour below 15 years and above 64 years of age , in Hill (17.39%) and Mountain (16.13%) compared to that in Terai (13.32%) could be partly a reflection of higher magnitude of out-migration of adult labour from the former areas.[81]

Table 2.3 Distribution of Agricultural Labour Force by Territorial Zones (1971).

Territorial Zones	Agricultural Labour per Cultivated hectare		Nature of Agricultural Labour		
	All labour 10 yrs. and above	Male labour 15–64 yrs.	% of labour below 15 yrs. and Above 64 yrs. of age to total labour	% of male labour to total labour	% of male labour 15–64 yrs. of age to total labour
MOUNTAIN	5.47	2.78	16.13	60.51	50.90
	(2.26)	(1.93)	(1.01)	(0.87)	(0.86)
Eastern	6.93	3.40	18.55	59.98	49.14
	(2.86)	(2.36)	(1.16)	(0.86)	(0.83)
Central	4.29	2.14	15.19	57.78	49.83
	(1.77)	(1.49)	(0.95)	(0.83)	(0.84)
Western	4.70	2.48	13.98	(61.33)	53.01
	(1.94)	(1.72)	(0.88)	(0.88)	(0.90)
HILL	5.66	2.91	17.39	61.47	51.42
	(2.34)	(2.02)	(1.09)	(0.88)	(0.87)
Eastern	5.11	2.71	18.22	64.31	52.99
	(2.11)	(1.88)	(1.14)	(0.92)	(0.89)
Central	6.28	2.96	17.69	56.46	47.19
	(2.60)	(2.06)	(1.11)	(0.81)	(0.80)
Western	5.36	3.09	15.74	67.58	57.67
	(2.21)	(2.15)	(0.99)	(0.97)	(0.97)
KATH. VALLEY	2.81	1.71	12.55	68.83	60.80
	(1.16)	(1.19)	(0.79)	(0.99)	(1.03)

(Contd.)

(*Table 2.3 contd.*)

INNER TERAI	1.84	1.11	16.71	71.55	60.46
	(0.76)	(0.77)	(1.05)	(1.03)	(1.02)
Eastern	2.63	1.49	17.48	68.00	56.49
	(1.09)	(1.03)	(1.10)	(0.98)	(0.95)
Central	1.83	1.11	16.33	71.28	60.55
	(0.76)	(0.77)	(1.03)	(1.02)	(1.02)
Western	1.37	0.89	15.63	76.10	65.01
	(0.57)	(0.62)	(0.98)	(1.09)	(1.10)
TERAI	1.13	0.85	13.32	86.68	75.58
	(0.47)	(0.59)	(0.84)	(1.25)	(1.28)
Eastern	1.13	0.87	13.30	88.74	77.16
	(0.47)	(0.60)	(0.83)	(1.28)	(1.30)
Central	1.12	0.78	13.46	79.61	69.46
	(0.46)	(0.54)	(0.84)	(1.14)	(1.17)
Western	1.15	1.86	13.23	85.99	74.76
	(0.48)	(0.60)	(0.83)	(1.24)	(1.26)
NEPAL	2.42	1.44	15.93	69.60	59.22
	(1.00)	(1.00)	(1.00)	(1.00)	(1.00)

Note: Figures in parenthesis are Location Quotients.

Source: 1. Central Bureau of Statistics, Population Census-Nepal 1971, Kathmandu.
2. APROSC data bank (for cultivated area).

2.2.13 Other Factors of Production

(i) Irrigation In the absence of any authentic enumeration of indigenous informal irrigation systems that feed the bulk of the irrigable lowland as indicated in Table 2.2, the organised and government-sponsored irrigation system seems to cover a mere 0.198 million hectare, or less than 10% of the total cultivated land, by 1980 against 0.103 million hectare in 1975 and 0.0015 million hectare in 1955. This is a pathetic low by any standard of comparison. In the spatial frame the meagre provision is heavily concentrated in Terai and Inner Terai (Table 2.4), thus indicating the state's territorial bias in channelising development.

Despite the frequently invoked physiographic constraints of extreme ruggedness of terrain in the ready extension of irrigation facilities in the country, expert opinions concede a further 0.3 million hectare in Hill/Mountain and 1.1 million hectare in Terai as potentially irrigable cultivable land.[82]

(ii) Modern Inputs The extent of use of modern inputs, namely fertilizers, improved (HYV) seeds, pesticides, farm machinery and implements, etc., have become almost a standard measure for the development of productive forces in agriculture. In the context of Nepal, however, till the crystallization of agrarian 'crisis' in many of the underdeveloped countries by the mid-sixties and the subsequent state intervention to 'solve' the crisis within the status quoist frameworks under the able patronisation of international finance capital, use of modern inputs had been virtually unheard of. In the short period thereafter any amount of rhetoric of 'planned development' under the same archaic social dispensation could not have extricated the Nepalese agriculture from its abysmal conditions of stagnation. In spite of the impressive but spurious statistical projection of growth rates of use of modern inputs with a rock bottom datum line the absolute position of the agriculture economy as exemplified by the measure of use of chemical fertilizer per cropped area (GCA) remains the lowest amongst the community of countries in the region.[83] The very fact that the share of chemical fertilizers in the total value of modern inputs used in the country in 1970/71 and 1978/79 respectively constituted 94.35% and 90.69%, followed by 3.02% and 6.17% of improved seeds, 2.18% and 1.38% of agricultural machinery and tools and 0.45% and 1.76% of pesticides, should leave no illusion about the real state of use of other inputs and hence foreclose the need to disseminate their spatio-temporal distribution pattern separately. Farm Management Study carried out in 1968–69[84] had estimated only 3% of the total cultivated land under improved seeds and only one tractor for about 4300 hectares of cultivated land, whereas the more recent estimates put tractor horse power per 1000 agricultural workers (i.e. 2.59) in Nepal among the lowest in Asia.

In the horizontal dimension [Table 2.4] the concentration of use of modern inputs is seen heavily biased in favour of the already well-endowed agricultural zones of Kathmandu Valley, central Inner Terai and eastern and central Terai. Kathmandu Valley alone with only about 3.0% of the total cropped area is known to have consumed 56.26% and 32.05% of the total value of modern inputs in

Table 2.4 Distribution of Irrigation Facilities and Modern Agricultural Inputs by Territorial Zones.

Territorial Zones	Area Under Public Irrigation*			Value of Modern Inputs**				
	% of total irrigated area		Annual Growth Rate	1978/79		1970/71		Annual Growth Rate (%)
	1974/75	1981/82		per hectare (Rs.)	% of Total Value	per hectare (Rs.)	% of Total Value	
MOUNTAIN	–	–	–	5.22	0.49	N.A.	N.A.	
Eastern	–	–	–	9.83	0.42			
Central	–	–	–	3.16	0.03			
Western	–	–	–	0.94	0.04			
HILL	1.59	1.52	+23.38	22.85	11.98	1.24	1.54	+249.1
Eastern	–	0.02		22.75	4.06			
Central	1.59	1.15	+14.12	31.0	7.10			
Western	–	0.35		6.99	0.82			
KATHMANDU VALLEY	5.85	2.39	+1.17	529.44	32.05	363.35	56.26	+4.98
INNER TERAI	8.62	18.32	+69.28	31.85	8.04			
Eastern	–	0.03		12.45	0.70			
Central	8.25	18.15	+72.31	61.81	6.13			
Western	0.37	0.14	± 0	12.46	1.21			
TERAI	83.93	77.77	+22.17	36.0	47.44	12.79	42.20	+27.34
Eastern	73.49	60.89	+18.31	38.51	33.44			
Central	1.02	12.06	+451.8	43.22	10.41			
Western	9.42	4.82	++5.83	17.21	3.59			
NEPAL	100.00	100.00	+25.06	44.48	100.00	21.29	100.00	+18.18

Note: For want of separate break-up of value of modern inputs for 1970/71, 'Hill' include easteren Inner Terai and "Terai" include Central and Western Inner Terai.

Source: *APROSC, Kathmandu.
**Agriculture Inputs Corporation, Kathmandu.

1970/71 and 1978/79 respectively. Statistically, the glaring disparity in the use of modern inputs by the conventional ecological-hydrographic zones for 1978/79 is manifested in a staggering 308.75% coefficient of variation for the same. The only redeeming feature is the observed higher rate of growth of use of modern inputs in the Hill, which, however, could be a mere statistical illusion in view of the still abysmally low absolute value and a very low reference base.

2.2.14 Share of Factors in Aggregate Production

Relative share of primary (land, human and animal labour) and modern (fertilizer, machines, agro-chemicals etc.) factors in production should provide a ready generalisation of the state of productive forces in agriculture. Hence, in the absence of more polished inventory a simple measure of factor share constructed by an earlier scholar by way of dividing the value of each input by the sum of values of all material in puts at constant prices is sought to be reproduced as in Table 2.5, with the logical reservation about the method of measuring value through imperfect market prices.

The fact that traditional factors of production, namely land and human and animal labour, constitute nearly 99% of cost of production and 'modern' inputs only about 1% in the whole of Nepal eloquently speaks of the pathetic state of agriculture in the country. Insignificant variation in the composition over the territorial dimension, except perhaps the central Hill, which includes Kathmandu Valley, and central Terai, also signifies a yet lower level of social differentiation in the vertical and horizontal dimension in the country.

2.2.2 Level and Growth of Production

The absolute measure of level and growth of agricultural production is of crucial significance for a society dominated by use-value production, for it embodies the very basis of social reproduction. Hence it would be pertinent to evaluate the situation first with respect to the principal crops by the conventional ecological-hydrographic zones, and summarise the total picture subsequently.

2.2.21 Cropping Pattern and Cropping Intensity

Extreme agro-climatic differentiation and historico-cultural diversities reflecting on the dietary habits of the people have marked wide crop-combination types over the geographical space of Nepal. However, the use-value based economy could not have but depended heavily on the production of different staple food crops, of which paddy, maize, wheat, millet and barley account, for 90% of the total cropped area and 80% of the country's agricultural GDP.[85] In the Mountains potatoes also constitute a staple food item of nearly 30% of the population.[86] Among the 'non-cereal' crops (as the conventional terms 'cash crop' would be misnomer in a predominantly non-monetised economy) oilseeds, sugarcane, jute and tobacco would virtually cover the whole of the minimal area under cropping. Hence the aggregate study of these major ten crops should practically sum up the production condition of agriculture in Nepal.

Table 2.5 Factor Shares in Agricultural Production.

	Land	*Human Labour*	*Animal Power*	*Fertilizer Chemicals*	*Improved Seeds*	*Tractors*	*Pump Sets*	*Agro-Chemicals*	*Total*
HILL:									
Eastern	43.93	38.68	17.36	0.02	0.02	–	–	–	100.00
Central	33.15	53.00	11.02	2.13	0.30	–	–	0.01	100.00
Western	32.42	55.79	11.50	0.10	0.13	–	–	–	100.00
Far Western	34.31	49.00	16.68	–	0.01	–	–	–	100.00
TERAI:									
Eastern	36.51	44.00	19.04	0.12	0.22	0.03	0.01	0.01	100.00
Central	40.82	39.38	17.40	0.67	0.71	1.00	0.01	0.01	100.00
Western	36.51	35.96	26.35	0.23	0.80	0.12	0.02	0.01	100.00
Far Western	37.19	33.44	28.99	0.07	0.30	0.01	–	–	100.00
NEPAL	38.51	42.89	17.49	0.49	0.38	0.22	0.01	0.01	100.00

Source: Chapagain, D.P. (1976), "Agricultural Productivity Pattern in Nepal and its Regional Variations" in Dhungana, B. (ed.) *Research, Productivity and Mechanisation in Nepalese Agriculture*, CEDA, Kathmandu, p. 151.

Cropping intensity, i.e. the ratio of gross cropped area (GCA) to net sown or cultivated area (NSA), is a generally accepted measure of combined advancement of productive forces in agriculture, as it also largely accounts for the cropping pattern and different factors of production like irrigation, modern inputs, etc. In the case of Nepal, however, the absence of reliable statistical information on net cultivated area in a spatio-temporal frame has hampered a correct picturisation of this measure. Generalisations based on adhoc official estimates or independent fragmentary studies have been so divergent that they have done more to blurr than illuminate the real piçture.[87]

Our own estimation based on compilation of net cultivated area from diverse sources and gross cropped area under ten major crops (Table 2.6) seems to give a fairly accurate picture, except for slight bias against Mountain and Hill due to a less reliable data base and also perhaps due to non-inclusion of some specialised crops of these areas like buck wheat, etc. Generally, low figures for Mountain and Hill, specially the western sectors, may be explicable in terms of the low irrigation facilities, lesser amount of rainfall and weaker agronomic capacity of soil and, most importantly, as a result of agricultural 'involution' or ecological decline hastened by the cultivation of otherwise unsuitable mountain slopes to eke out a meagre existence for the impoverished peasantry. Needless to mention that the overall low cropping intensity is a reflection of the low development of productive forces in agriculture, and would in turn account for the low level of aggregate agricultural output and output per worker or per cultivated hectare.

Table 2.6 Intensity of Cropping (Avg. of 1977/78–1979/80).

Territorial Zones	*Intensity of Cropping (%)*
MOUNTAIN	52.71 (0.58)
Eastern	60.18 (0.66)
Central	55.29 (0.61)
Western	46.29 (0.51)
HILL	59.87 (0.66)
Eastern	54.89 (0.60)
Central	63.25 (0.70)
Western	61.97 (0.68)
KATHMANDU VALLEY	141.92 (1.56)
INNER TERAI	116.31 (1.28)
Eastern	115.86 (1.27)
Central	132.66 (1.46)
Western	103.49 (1.14)
TERAI	113.51 (1.25)
Eastern	113.73 (1.25)
Central	119.78 (1.32)
Western	106.25 (1.17)
NEPAL	90.91 (1.00)

Note: Figures in parenthesis are Location Quotients.

Sources: 1. National Research Associates (1982) *Nepal Disrict Profile*, Kathmandu.

2. APROSC Data Bank, Kathmandu.

Given the low intensity of cropping in the country, the study of cropping pattern would largely become an exercise in differentiation of crop zones on natural lines, which is beyond our current objective. Nonetheless it would be interesting to observe spatio-temporal variations in cropping pattern from Tables 2.7 and 2.8 below. The continued predominance of cereals and substitute crops production in the country-wide plane (i.e. 92.07% and 91.84% of cropped area in 1967/68–1969/70 and 1977/78–1979/80 respectively) is quite apparent, and to that extent points towards the backward nature of the agriculture sector largely geared to use-value production. Domination of single crop paddy (67.04%)* in Terai, paddy (34.42%) and maize (31.38%) in Inner Terai, wheat (34.69%), paddy (34.20%) and maize (22.93%) in Kathmandu Valley, maize (39.64%) and paddy (25.06%) in Hill and maize (32.75% and paddy 22.30%) in Mountain, broadly delineate the crop zones in the country, which can be explained in terms of both natural and social differentials. Greater rise in the share of wheat in the more advanced Terai, Inner Terai and Kathmandu Valley and consistent, but not very pronounced, decline in the share of millet and barley mostly patronised by lower strata of the populace indicate on increasing intervention of social factors in the articulation of cropping pattern. Looking at the spatial distribution of cash crops, areas of greater 'commodification' in agricultural production can be differentiated along Inner Terai and Terai. Total concentration of the single most important export crop jute in eastern Terai, the most externally integrated zone, further highlights the nature of distortion in agrarian spatial structure under the given mode of development/underdevelopment.

2.2.22 Level and Growth of Production by Major Crops

Tables 2.7, 2.8, and 2.9 have been constructed to provide the level and growth trend of agricultural production cropwise and by relevant spatial units for the decade between late-1960s and late-1970s. Area and output figures of triennium averages for 1967/68–1969/70 and 1977/78–1979/80 were adopted to minimise the effect of yearly fluctuation of crop production in a society heavily dependent on the vagaries of nature. Moreover, to standardize the value of production of different crops the output figures were weighted by the mean of national retail price for 1967/68–1977/78.

To view the level of production first, concentration of nearly 60% of cropped area and value of production in Terai with less than 20% of geographical area amply brings out the prevalent spatial inequality. The inequality is further manifest when the distribution of cereal and non-cereal production are observed separately [Figs. 2.2 and 2.3]. A more disturbing picture is the aggravation of the phenomenon over time.

True health of the agrarian economy may be gauged from the rate of change in agricultural production over time and space [Table 2.9]. Starting with the aggregate scenario of all crops over the entire physical space of the country, the moderate annual output increase of 0.93% cannot be regarded satisfactory by

Table 2.7 Level of Production of Principal Crops by Territorial Zones (Avg. of 1967/68–1969/70).

Territorial Zones		Cereal and Substitute Crops													
		Paddy		Maize		Wheat		Millet		Barely		Potato		Total	
		A	P	A	P	A	P	A	P	A	P	A	P	A	P
MOUNTAIN		13778	49354	29191	68171	25116	69679	210337	19532	8617	14058	8452	700032	95441	310826
	(a)	(14.15)	(15.74)	(30.09)	(78.12)	(25.89)	(22.23)	(10.66)	(6.23)	(8.80)	(4.48)	(8.71)	(22.34)	(98.38)	(99.14)
	(b)	(1.16)	(1.49)	(6.92)	(7.17)	(12.05)	(14.08)	(9.66)	(10.37)	(33.63)	(38.12)	(19.26)	(17.52)	(4.84)	(5.40)
Eastern		3072	14441	17516	55532	2857	6971	4814	9137	1525	2401	4367	36414	34961	124896
	(a)	(10.87)	(11.40)	(49.20)	(44.16)	(8.05)	(6.54)	(13.52)	(7.27)	(4.28)	(1.91)	(12.27)	(28.96)	(98.19)	(99.32)
	(b)	(0.33)	(0.43)	(1.15)	(4.51)	(1.38)	(1.41)	(4.50)	(4.85)	(5.95)	(6.51)	(9.95)	(9.11)	(1.77)	(2.23)
Central		1099	3658	3167	9004	1774	4017	1159	2761	1392	2331	1342	11479	10133	33750
	(a)	(10.76)	(10.00)	(31.00)	(26.60)	(17.36)	(14.23)	(11.34)	(6.68)	(15.58)	(7.48)	(13.14)	(33.91)	(99.19)	(99.69)
	(b)	(0.09)	(0.11)	(0.75)	(0.73)	(0.85)	(0.97)	(1.08)	(1.70)	(6.21)	(6.86)	(3.06)	(2.87)	(0.51)	(0.60)
Western		8757	31255	8508	23635	20475	57891	2364	6134	5500	9126	2743	22139	50347	152180
	(a)	(17.11)	(20.31)	(16.62)	(15.36)	(40.00)	(37.51)	(6.53)	(3.29)	(10.74)	(5.93)	(5.36)	(14.38)	(98.36)	(98.28)
	(b)	(0.75)	(0.94)	(2.02)	(1.92)	(9.82)	(41.59)	(4.08)	(4.32)	(21.47)	(24.75)	(6.26)	(5.54)	(2.56)	(2.66)
HILL		118405	434203	207894	643393	52731	144743	68937	178470	9192	14172	20220	171782	477379	1536243
	(a)	(24.21)	(27.89)	(42.50)	(41.30)	(10.79)	(9.29)	(14.09)	(8.25)	(1.88)	(0.01)	(4.13)	(11.03)	(97.60)	(98.64)
	(b)	(10.10)	(13.07)	(49.25)	(52.31)	(25.30)	(29.24)	(64.43)	(63.18)	(35.88)	(38.43)	(46.00)	(42.97)	(24.23)	(27.10)
Eastern		34951	129544	76693	242598	10774	25422	19277	35920	1323	2041	13441	115541	156409	552066
	(a)	(21.80)	(23.20)	(47.85)	(43.45)	(6.69)	(4.73)	(12.03)	(6.43)	(0.83)	(0.37)	(8.39)	(20.70)	(97.58)	(98.09)
	(b)	(3.00)	(3.90)	(19.17)	(19.22)	(5.15)	(5.34)	(18.02)	(19.05)	(5.16)	(5.53)	(30.63)	(28.90)	(7.94)	(9.73)
Central		56404	209425	87234	296420	10564	28522	38859	72680	2461	3677	4313	34860	199935	635684
	(a)	(27.59)	(32.47)	(42.66)	(44.40)	(5.22)	(4.44)	(19.01)	(11.27)	(1.20)	(0.57)	(2.11)	(5.40)	(97.78)	(98.54)
	(b)	(4.85)	(6.31)	(20.67)	(23.28)	(5.12)	(5.78)	(36.32)	(38.57)	(9.61)	(9.97)	(9.83)	(8.72)	(5.07)	(11.21)
Western		27050	99314	43967	114325	31343	89699	10001	19870	5408	8454	2466	21381	121035	349093
	(a)	(21.75)	(25.88)	(35.35)	(32.25)	(25.20)	(25.29)	(8.68)	(5.60)	(4.35)	(2.38)	(1.98)	(6.03)	(97.31)	(98.44)
	(b)	(2.33)	(2.87)	(10.42)	(9.30)	(15.04)	(18.12)	(10.10)	(10.54)	(21.11)	(22.93)	(5.62)	(5.35)	(6.14)	(6.15)

(Contd.)

(*Table 2.7 contd.*)

KATHMANDU VALLEY		25517	125282	17667	51532	19466	55354	4100	6578	28	38	2270	32532	69048	271326
	(a)	(36.32)	(45.79)	(25.15)	(18.03)	(27.71)	(20.23)	(5.84)	(2.40)	(0.04)	(0.01)	(3.23)	(11.89)	(98.29)	(99.16)
	(b)	(2.19)	(3.77)	(4.19)	(4.19)	(9.34)	(11.10)	(3.83)	(3.49)	(0.11)	(0.10)	(5.17)	(8.14)	(3.50)	(4.78)
INNER TERAI		84700	270462	71051	220692	14599	33963	6709	10871	905	1162	3865	35303	181829	572453
	(a)	(37.80)	(41.07)	(31.71)	(33.51)	(6.52)	(3.16)	(2.99)	(1.65)	(0.40)	(0.18)	(1.72)	(5.36)	(81.15)	(86.92)
	(b)	(7.28)	(8.14)	(16.83)	(17.94)	(7.00)	(6.86)	(6.27)	(5.77)	(3.53)	(3.15)	(8.81)	(8.83)	(9.23)	(10.09)
Eastern		17000	58567	15317	45180	1683	3745	2823	4247	133	159	1009	9264	37967	121163
	(a)	(35.22)	(41.04)	(31.73)	(31.66)	(3.49)	(2.63)	(5.85)	(2.98)	(0.28)	(0.11)	(2.09)	(6.49)	(78.66)	(84.91)
	(b)	(1.46)	(1.76)	(3.63)	(3.67)	(0.81)	(0.76)	(2.64)	(2.25)	(0.52)	(0.43)	(2.30)	(2.32)	(1.93)	(2.14)
Central		32800	108339	38300	122926	6316	14592	3267	5666	114	152	2240	20575	83037	272349
	(a)	(31.76)	(34.93)	(37.09)	(39.63)	(6.12)	(4.74)	(3.16)	(1.63)	(0.11)	(0.05)	(2.17)	(6.63)	(80.42)	(87.80)
	(b)	(2.82)	(3.26)	(9.07)	(9.99)	(3.03)	(2.97)	(3.05)	(3.01)	(0.44)	(0.41)	(5.11)	(5.15)	(4.21)	(4.50)
Western		34900	103556	17434	52587	6600	15526	617	958	658	851	616	5454	60825	178941
	(a)	(48.11)	(50.34)	(24.03)	(26.65)	(9.10)	(7.55)	(0.85)	(0.47)	(0.91)	(0.41)	(0.85)	(2.66)	(83.94)	(86.99)
	(b)	(3.00)	(3.12)	(4.13)	(4.28)	(3.17)	(3.14)	(0.58)	(0.51)	(2.57)	(2.31)	(1.40)	(1.37)	(3.09)	(3.15)
TERAI		920803	2442149	96281	226285	96506	191305	16909	22988	6879	7445	9069	90112	1146447	2980284
	(a)	(73.12)	(74.01)	(7.65)	(8.85)	(7.66)	(5.80)	(1.34)	(0.70)	(0.55)	(0.23)	(0.72)	(2.73)	(91.04)	(90.32)
	(b)	(79.16)	(73.52)	(22.81)	(10.40)	(46.30)	(38.64)	(16.00)	(12.20)	(25.95)	(20.19)	(70.67)	(22.54)	(58.19)	(52.55)
Eastern		642969	1693352	39720	91983	50638	98725	10908	15012	5008	5382	5872	57017	755115	1951472
	(a)	(76.90)	(76.51)	(4.75)	(4.16)	(6.06)	(4.46)	(1.30)	(0.58)	(0.50)	(0.24)	(0.70)	(2.58)	(90.31)	(88.52)
	(b)	(55.28)	(50.98)	(9.41)	(7.48)	(24.30)	(19.94)	(10.20)	(7.97)	(19.55)	(14.60)	(13.38)	(14.25)	(30.33)	(34.58)
Central		137257	421752	10767	54641	34101	66774	2242	2803	1862	2055	1638	19499	216897	567604
	(a)	(60.53)	(70.53)	(8.61)	(9.15)	(14.85)	(11.18)	(0.98)	(0.48)	(0.91)	(0.34)	(0.72)	(3.25)	(94.51)	(95.06)
	(b)	(13.52)	(12.70)	(4.68)	(4.44)	(16.35)	(13.49)	(2.10)	(1.54)	(7.27)	(5.57)	(3.78)	(4.88)	(11.01)	(10.01)
Western		120567	327045	36794	79661	11767	25805	3759	5093	9	8	1539	13595	174435	451208
	(a)	(62.25)	(66.86)	(19.00)	(16.29)	(6.27)	(5.28)	(1.94)	(1.04)	(–)	(–)	(0.79)	(2.79)	(90.06)	(92.25)
	(b)	(10.37)	(9.95)	(8.72)	(6.48)	(6.55)	(5.21)	(3.51)	(2.70)	(0.04)	(0.22)	(3.51)	(3.40)	(8.85)	(7.96)

(*Contd.*)

(*Table 2.7 contd.*)

Territorial Zones		*Cereal & Substitute Crops*													
		Paddy		*Maize*		*Wheat*		*Millet*		*Barely*		*Potato*		*Total*	
		A	*P*	*A*	*P*	*A*	*P*	*A*	*P*	*A*	*P*	*A*	*P*	*A*	*P*
NEPAL		1163153	3321530	422084	1230073	208413	495854	106992	198439	25621	35875	43075	399751	1970144	5671732
	(a)	(54.36)	(54.42)	(19.73)	(20.13)	(9.74)	(8.11)	(5.00)	(3.09)	(1.20)	(0.50)	(2.05)	(6.55)	(92.07)	(92.93)
	(b)	(100.00)	(100.00)	(100.00)	(100.00)	(100.00)	(100.00)	(100.00)	(100.00)	(100.00)	(100.00)	(100.00)	(100.00)	(100.00)	(100.00)

(*Contd.*)

Territorial Zones		*Cash Crops*											
		Oilseeds		*Sugarcane*		*Jute*		*Tobacco*		*Total*		*All Crops*	
		A	*P*	*A*	*P*	*A*	*P*	*A*	*P*	*A*	*P*	*A*	*P*
MOUNTAIN		1435	1739	72	66	–	–	111	879	1560	2684	97009	313510
	(a)	(1.40)	(0.55)	(0.02)	(0.02)			(0.11)	(0.28)	(1.62)	(0.86)	(100.00)	(100.00)
	(b)	(1.43)	(1.01)	(0.18)	(0.14)			(1.28)	(0.82)	(0.92)	(0.52)	(4.53)	(5.14)
Eastern		633	782	5	15	–	–	5	57	644	854	35605	125750
	(a)	(1.79)	(0.62)	(0.01)	(0.01)			(0.02)	(0.05)	(1.81)	(0.68)	(100.00)	(100.00)
	(b)	(0.63)	(0.46)	(0.04)	(0.03)			(0.07)	(0.05)	(0.38)	(0.20)	(1.56)	(2.06)
Central		83	105	–	–	–	–	–	–	83	105	10216	33855
	(a)	(0.81)	(0.31)							(0.81)	(0.31)	(100.00)	(100.00)
	(b)	(0.00)	(0.06)							(0.05)	(0.02)	(0.48)	(0.55)
Western		719	852	17	51	–	–	105	822	841	1725	51188	153905
	(a)	(1.40)	(0.55)	(0.03)	(0.03)			(0.21)	(0.53)	(1.64)	(1.12)	(100.00)	(100.00)
	(b)	(0.72)	(0.50)	(0.14)	(0.11)			(1.21)	(0.76)	(0.50)	(0.40)	(2.39)	(2.52)
HILLS		9754	13239	1720	5746	44	67	238	2068	11756	21120	489135	1557963
	(a)	(1.99)	(0.85)	(0.35)	(0.37)	(0.01)	(–)	(0.05)	(0.13)	(2.40)	(1.36)	(100.00)	(100.00)
	(b)	(9.70)	(7.70)	(14.07)	(12.44)	(0.00)	(0.06)	(2.75)	(1.92)	(6.93)	(4.89)	(22.86)	(25.53)

(*Contd.*)

(*Table 2.7 contd.*)

Eastern		3393	4452	404	1202	27	37	61	510	3885	6211	160294	558277
	(a)	(2.12)	(0.80)	(0.25)	(0.72)	(0.02)	(0.01)	(0.04)	(0.09)	(2.42)	(1.11)	(100.00)	(100.00)
	(b)	(3.38)	(2.600)	(3.29)	(2.60)	(0.00)	(0.04)	(0.70)	(0.47)	(2.29)	(1.44)	(7.49)	(9.15)
Central		3269	4932	1202	3931	–	–	60	524	4531	9307	204466	645071
	(a)	(1.60)	(0.76)	(0.59)	(0.61)				(0.00)	(2.22)	(1.460)	(100.00)	(100.00)
	(b)	(3.25)	(2.87)	(9.80)	(8.51)				(0.49)	(2.67)	(2.18)	(9.56)	(10.57)
Western		3092	3845	114	– 613	17	30	117	1034	3340	5522	124375	354615
	(a)	(2.49)	(1.08)	(0.09)	(0.17)	(0.01)	(0.01)	(0.09)	(0.29)	(2.69)	(1.56)	(100.00)	(100.00)
	(b)	(3.08)	(2.24)	(0.93)	(1.33)	(0.04)	(0.03)	(1.35)	(0.96)	(1.97)	(1.28)	(5.81)	(5.81)
KATHMANU VALLEY		1176	2716	28	82	–	–	–	–	1204	2298	70252	273624
	(a)	(1.67)	(0.81)	(0.04)	(0.03)					(1.71)	(0.84)	(100.00)	(100.00)
	(b)	(1.17)	(1.29)	(0.23)	(0.18)					(0.71)	(0.53)	(3.28)	(4.48)
INNER TERAI		39133	75585	586	1833	2014	3697	517	5059	42250	86144	224079	658597
	(a)	(17.46)	(11.40)	(0.26)	(0.28)	(0.90)	(0.56)	(0.23)	(0.77)	(18.85)	(13.08)	(100.00)	(100.00)
	(b)	(38.93)	(43.98)	(4.78)	(3.97)	(4.18)	(3.46)	(5.97)	(4.09)	(24.90)	(15.96)	(10.47)	(10.79)
Eastern		8033	16008	128	411	1992	3625	150	1408	10303	21532	48270	142695
	(a)	(16.64)	(11.22)	(0.27)	(0.29)	(1.40)	(2.54)	(0.31)	(1.04)	(21.34)	(15.09)	(100.00)	(100.00)
	(b)	(7.99)	(9.31)	(1.04)	(0.89)	(4.13)	(3.43)	(1.73)	(1.38)	(6.07)	(4.99)	(2.26)	(2.34)
Central		19633	35002	408	1240	22	32	160	1573	20223	37847	103260	310196
	(a)	(19.01)	(11.28)	(0.40)	(0.40)	(0.02)	(0.01)	(0.15)	(0.51)	(19.58)	(12.200)	(100.00)	(100.00)
	(b)	(19.53)	(20.37)	(3.33)	(2.68)	(0.05)	(0.03)	(1.85)	(1.46)	(11.92)	(8.77)	(4.83)	(5.08)
Western		11467	24505	50	182	–	–	207	1598	11724	26765	72549	205706
	(a)	(15.81)	(11.95)	(0.07)	(0.09)			(0.29)	(0.97)	(16.16)	(13.010)	(100.00)	(100.00)
	(b)	(11.41)	(14.30)	(0.41)	(0.39)			(2.39)	(1.85)	(0.91)	(6.20)	(3.39)	(3.37)
TERAI		49031	79077	9908	38461	46153	101938	7791	99041	112883	319317	1259330	3299601
	(a)	(3.89)	(2.40)	(0.79)	(1.17)	(3.66)	(3.09)	(0.62)	(3.03)	(8.96)	(9.68)	(100.00)	(100.00)
	(b)	(40.77)	(46.01)	(80.79)	(83.27)	(95.73)	(96.48)	(90.00)	(92.58)	(66.53)	(73.99)	(58.85)	(54.06)

(*Contd.*)

(*Table 2.7 contd.*)

Territorial Zones		*Cash Crops*											
		Oilseeds		*Sugarcane*		*Jute*		*Tobacco*		*Total*		*All Crops*	
		A	*P*	*A*	*P*	*A*	*P*	*A*	*P*	*A*	*P*	*A*	*P*
Eastern		21853	31396	5970	24138	45935	101580	7270	94703	81028	251897	836143	2213369
	(a)	(2.61)	(1.42)	(0.71)	(1.09)	(6.49)	(4.59)	(0.87)	(4.28)	(9.69)	(11.30)	(100.00)	(100.00)
	(b)	(21.74)	(18.77)	(48.68)	(52.26)	(95.78)	(96.14)	(83.98)	(87.89)	(47.76)	(58.37)	(39.08)	(36.27)
Central		8433	13423	3850	14025	118	195	193	1870	12594	29513	229491	597117
	(a)	(3.67)	(2.25)	(1.68)	(2.35)	(0.03)	(0.03)	(0.08)	(0.31)	(5.49)	(4.94)	(100.00)	(100.00)
	(b)	(8.39)	(7.81)	(31.39)	(30.37)	(0.24)	(0.18)	(2.23)	(1.73)	(7.42)	(6.84)	(10.72)	(9.78)
Western		18745	34258	88	298	100	163	329	3188	19261	37907	193696	489115
	(a)	(9.60)	(7.00)	(0.05)	(0.05)	(0.06)	(0.03)	(0.17)	(0.65)	(9.94)	(7.75)	(100.00)	(100.00)
	(b)	(18.65)	(19.93)	(0.72)	(0.63)	(0.71)	(0.15)	(3.79)	(2.96)	(11.35)	(8.78)	(9.05)	(8.01)
NEPAL		100529	171856	12254	46198	40211	105652	8557	107847	169661	431563	2139805	6103295
	(a)	(4.70)	(2.82)	(0.57)	(0.76)	(7.26)	(1.73)	(0.40)	(1.77)	(7.93)	(7.07)	(100.00)	(100.00)
	(b)	(100.00)	(100.00)	(100.00)	(100.00)	(100.00)	(100.00)	(100.00)	(100.00)	(100.00)	(100.00)	(100.00)	(100.00)

Note: A = Cropped area in hectares: P = Value of production in Rs. '000 (weighted by mean of national average retail price for 1968/69–1977/78). Figures in parenthesis are percentages: (a) Row percentage (Local Share) (b) Column percentage (National Share).

Source: HMGIN, Ministry of Food and Agriculture (1972), *Agriculture Statistics of Nepal*, Economic Analysis and Planning Division, Kathmandu.

Table 2.8 Level of Production of Principle Crops by Territorial Zones (Average of 1977/78–1979/80).

Territorial Zones		*Cereals and Substitute Crops*													
		Paddy 1		*Maize* 2		*Wheat* 3		*Millet* 4		*Barley* 5		*Potato* 6		*Total* 7	
		A	*P*	*A*	*P*	*A*	*P*	*A*	*P*	*A*	*P*	*A*	*P*	*A*	*P*
MOUNTAIN		22920	75282	33661	79761	12040	23131	13659	24419	8797	12329	10161	87427	101197	297349
	(a)	(22.30)	(25.03)	(32.70)	(26.52)	(11.71)	(7.69)	(13.29)	(8.12)	(8.52)	(4.10)	(9.89)	(27.40)	(98.45)	(98.86)
	(b)	(1.82)	(2.17)	(7.26)	(7.16)	(3.82)	(2.59)	(11.20)	(12.30)	(34.43)	(34.43)	(19.93)	(18.91)	(4.44)	(4.84)
Eastern		13071	44503	19263	49151	1467	3220	5655	10454	1160	1534	5881	48076	45515	156970
	(a)	(27.79)	(28.18)	(40.95)	(31.13)	(3.16)	(2.04)	(12.02)	(6.64)	(2.46)	(0.97)	(12.5)	(30.44)	(98.88)	(99.40)
	(b)	(1.04)	(1.28)	(4.15)	(4.41)	(0.41)	(0.14)	(4.64)	(5.28)	(4.55)	(4.28)	(11.55)	(11.03)	(2.04)	(2.55)
Central		362	2479	3467	9081	1178	2502	1580	2689	1605	2375	1460	12591	9647	31617
	(a)	(3.74)	(7.70)	(35.74)	(75.24)	(12.16)	(8.10)	(10.31)	(8.44)	(16.57)	(7.45)	(15.05)	(39.82)	(99.39)	(99.84)
	(b)	(0.29)	(0.07)	(0.75)	(0.61)	(0.32)	(0.20)	(1.30)	(1.35)	(6.31)	(6.63)	(2.86)	(2.91)	(0.42)	(0.52)
Western		9487	28290	10936	21609	9375	17329	6424	11246	5994	8420	2820	21660	45035	108562
	(a)	(20.60)	(25.49)	(23.74)	(19.47)	(20.35)	(15.61)	(13.95)	(10.13)	(13.01)	(7.59)	(6.12)	(19.51)	(97.78)	(97.80)
	(b)	(0.75)	(0.82)	(2.36)	(1.94)	(2.58)	(1.94)	(5.27)	(5.67)	(23.56)	(23.51)	(5.53)	(4.97)	(1.98)	(1.77)
HILL		144839	467024	229113	543532	73709	173912	60194	101935	9303	13819	27396	233660	664758	1563872
	(a)	(25.06)	(29.38)	(39.64)	(34.19)	(12.75)	(10.94)	(13.88)	(8.30)	(1.64)	(0.87)	(4.74)	(14.70)	(97.72)	(98.38)
	(b)	(11.49)	(13.46)	(49.39)	(48.76)	(20.30)	(19.50)	(63.77)	(65.40)	(37.38)	(38.59)	(53.73)	(53.61)	(24.80)	(25.44)
Eastern		47250	156640	85597	205859	16797	41503	24372	37866	1174	1636	18021	159602	192211	602906
	(a)	(24.00)	(25.59)	(43.47)	(33.63)	(8.02)	(6.79)	(12.36)	(6.15)	(0.60)	(0.27)	(9.15)	(26.07)	(97.67)	(98.50)
	(b)	(3.75)	(4.51)	(18.45)	(10.47)	(4.35)	(4.65)	(19.99)	(18.97)	(4.62)	(4.57)	(35.34)	(36.62)	(8.44)	(9.81)
Central		70401	223414	99657	220911	26632	67711	41629	70972	2541	3798	6679	52399	247619	639205
	(a)	(27.90)	(34.39)	(19.45)	(34.00)	(10.54)	(10.42)	(16.48)	(10.92)	(1.01)	(0.58)	(2.64)	(8.07)	(98.03)	(98.39)
	(b)	(5.59)	(6.44)	(21.40)	(19.82)	(7.34)	(7.59)	(34.14)	(35.75)	(9.99)	(10.51)	(13.10)	(12.02)	(10.87)	(10.40)

(*Contd.*)

(*Table 2.8 contd.*)

Territorial Zones		*Cereals and Substitute Crops*													
		Paddy 1		*Maise* 2		*Wheat* 3		*Millet* 4		*Barley* 5		*Potato* 6		*Total* 7	
		A	*P*	*A*	*P*	*A*	*P*	*A*	*P*	*A*	*P*	*A*	*P*	*A*	*P*
Western		27108	86970	43863	116762	31280	64698	14193	23297	5780	8386	2696	21649	124928	321761
	(a)	(21.11)	(26.63)	(34.15)	(35.62)	(24.35)	(19.74)	(11.05)	(7.11)	(4.51)	(2.56)	(2.10)	(6.60)	(97.97)	(98.16)
	(b)	(2.16)	(2.51)	(9.45)	(10.48)	(8.62)	(7.25)	(11.64)	(11.74)	(22.77)	(23.42)	(5.29)	(4.97)	(6.49)	(5.23)
KATHMANDU VALLEY		22829	113109	15309	46762	23157	76373	7898	4159	89	129	174	9817	65256	247349
	(a)	(34.20)	(46.15)	(22.93)	(17.47)	(34.69)	(30.48)	(4.34)	(1.65)	(0.13)	(0.05)	(1.46)	(3.92)	(97.75)	(98.23)
	(b)	(1.91)	(3.26)	(3.30)	(3.93)	(6.39)	(8.56)	(2.38)	(2.10)	(0.35)	(8.36)	(1.91)	(2.25)	(2.87)	(4.02)
INNER TERAI		95836	279160	87365	235358	141809	107039	17986	14116	1526	2118	4694	43335	239208	641126
	(a)	(34.42)	(36.47)	(31.38)	(30.75)	(15.02)	(13.98)	(2.87)	(1.94)	(0.55)	(0.28)	(1.58)	(5.66)	(85.92)	(89.99)
	(b)	(7.60)	(8.04)	(18.83)	(21.12)	(11.52)	(12.00)	(6.85)	(7.11)	(6.00)	(5.92)	(9.20)	(9.94)	(10.51)	(11.08)
Eastern		22309	67004	19283	50507	5618	14730	3409	5796	339	545	1330	11629	52288	160120
	(a)	(35.90)	(39.22)	(31.03)	(29.56)	(9.04)	(8.63)	(5.49)	(3.39)	(0.66)	(0.27)	(2.14)	(6.81)	(84.15)	(87.87)
	(b)	(1.77)	(1.93)	(4.16)	(4.53)	(1.55)	(1.55)	(2.80)	(2.92)	(1.33)	(1.27)	(2.61)	(2.67)	(2.30)	(2.44)
Central		34801	107560	40091	108351	15627	42979	3637	6665	310	408	2610	24857	97075	291430
	(a)	(31.01)	(34.14)	(36.64)	(34.59)	(14.28)	(13.64)	(3.32)	(2.12)	(0.28)	(0.13)	(2.39)	(7.89)	(88.73)	(92.51)
	(b)	(2.05)	(3.10)	(8.64)	(9.78)	(4.30)	(4.82)	(2.98)	(3.36)	(1.22)	(1.14)	(6.12)	(5.70)	(4.26)	(4.74)
Western		36726	101696	27991	15890	20560	49330	940	1595	876	1256	751	6849	89644	239576
	(a)	(36.24)	(37.42)	(26.19)	(27.15)	(19.24)	(17.65)	(0.80)	(0.59)	(0.82)	(0.45)	(0.70)	(2.45)	(84.07)	(85.70)
	(b)	(3.07)	(3.01)	(6.03)	(5.91)	(5.66)	(5.33)	(0.97)	(0.83)	(3.45)	(3.91)	(15.47)	(1.57)	(3.95)	(3.90)
TERAI		974399	2536391	98425	212195	212313	511420	17283	23083	5548	7411	7770	65604	1306658	3357906
	(a)	(67.04)	(80.22)	(6.77)	(6.61)	(14.61)	(13.51)	(1.13)	(0.63)	(0.36)	(0.20)	(0.53)	(1.75)	(89.90)	(88.71)
	(b)	(77.23)	(73.04)	(21.22)	(19.04)	(58.48)	(57.64)	(14.11)	(12.03)	(21.82)	(20.70)	(15.24)	(15.28)	(57.38)	(54.62)
Eastern		672588	1825214	31681	64372	136809	324029	11629	15815	4432	5924	5675	47741	862808	2293095
	(a)	(70.23)	(70.20)	(3.31)	(2.48)	(14.29)	(12.85)	(1.21)	(0.61)	(0.46)	(0.23)	(0.59)	(1.84)	(90.15)	(88.20)
	(b)	(53.35)	(52.51)	(6.93)	(5.73)	(37.60)	(37.45)	(9.64)	(7.97)	(17.43)	(16.54)	(11.13)	(10.95)	(37.89)	(37.30)

(*Contd.*)

(*Table 2.8 contd.*)

Central		174147	481622	16302	45066	49516	117007	2593	3264	704	890	725	6293	244047	574142
	(a)	(65.58)	(64.33)	(6.17)	(7.22)	(13.65)	(18.74)	(0.70)	(0.62)	(0.27)	(0.14)	(0.27)	(1.01)	(91.90)	(91.97)
	(b)	(13.81)	(11.57)	(3.53)	(4.04)	(13.64)	(13.12)	(2.13)	(1.64)	(2.77)	(2.49)	(1.38)	(1.44)	(10.72)	(9.34)
Western		127664	309556	41362	102757	25994	60384	2981	4805	412	697	1390	12570	199803	490689
	(a)	(55.46)	(59.17)	(17.97)	(18.31)	(11.29)	(10.76)	(1.30)	(0.86)	(0.18)	(0.11)	(0.60)	(2.24)	(85.80)	(87.44)
	(b)	(10.13)	(8.92)	(8.92)	(9.77)	(7.16)	(6.77)	(2.44)	(2.42)	(1.62)	(1.67)	(2.73)	(2.98)	(8.77)	(7.90)
NEPAL		1760823	3470966	463873	1114598	363924	891876	121948	196314	25423	35006	50992	435833	2277077	6147602
	(a)	(50.85)	(51.87)	(18.71)	(16.56)	(14.54)	(13.33)	(4.92)	(2.97)	(1.03)	(0.54)	(2.06)	(6.51)	(91.84)	(92.44)
	(b)	(100.00)	100.00()	(100.00)	(100.00)	(100.00)	(100.00)	(100.00)	(100.00)	(100.00)	(100.00)	(100.00)	(100.00)	(100.00)	(100.00)

(*Table 2.8 contd.*)

Territorial Zones		*Cash Crops*										*All Crops*	
		Oilseeds 8		*Sugarcane 9*		*Jute 10*		*Tobacco 11*		*Total 12*			
		A	*P*	*A*	*P*	*A*	*P*	*A*	*P*	*A*	*P*	*A*	*P*
MOUNTAIN		1350	1997	94	263	–	–	146	1176	1590	3436	102787	300285
	(a)	(1.31)	(0.66)	(0.09)	(0.09)			(0.14)	(0.39)	(1.56)	(1.14)	(100.00)	(100.00)
	(b)	(1.03)	(0.82)	(0.44)	(0.30)			(1.60)	(1.32)	(0.79)	(0.63)	(4.15)	(4.49)
Eastern		474	738	46	133	–	–	8	71	528	942	47043	157912
	(a)	(1.01)	(0.47)	(0.10)	(0.58)			(0.02)	(0.04)	(1.12)	(0.60)	(100.00)	(100.00)
	(b)	(0.36)	(0.30)	(0.21)	(0.15)			(6.10)	(0.08)	(0.26)	(0.17)	(1.90)	(2.36)
Central		40	51	–	–	–	–	–	–	40	51	9687	31868
	(a)	(0.41)	(0.16)							(0.41)	(0.16)	(100.00)	(100.00)
	(b)	(0.03)	(0.02)							(0.02)	(0.01)	(0.39)	(0.48)
Western		836	1208	48	130	–	–	138	1105	1022	2443	46057	111005
	(a)	(1.82)	(1.09)	(0.10)	(0.12)			(0.30)	(1.20)	(2.22)	(2.20)	(100.00)	(100.00)
	(b)	(0.64)	(0.49)	(0.22)	(0.15)			(1.72)	(1.24)	(0.61)	(0.45)	(1.86)	(1.66)

(*Contd.*)

(*Table 2.8 contd.*)

Territorial Zones		*Cash Crops*											
		Oilseeds 8		*Sugarcane* 9		*Jute* 10		*Tobacco* 11		*Total* 12		*All Crops*	
		A	*P*	*A*	*P*	*A*	*P*	*A*	*P*	*A*	*P*	*A*	*P*
HILL		11419	17964	1401	4647	–	–	376	3174	13196	25785	577953	1589657
	(a)	(1.98)	(1.13)	(0.74)	(0.20)			(0.07)	(0.20)	(2.28)	(1.620)	(100.00)	(100.00)
	(b)	(9.69)	(7.34)	(6.51)	(5.32)			(4.63)	(5.57)	(6.53)	(4.74)	(23.31)	(23.76)
Eastern		4263	7155	329	1140	–	–	110	964	4782	9259	196913	612165
	(a)	(2.16)	(1.17)	(9.17)	(0.10)			(9.86)	(0.16)	(2.39)	(1.50)	(100.00)	(100.00)
	(b)	(3.24)	(2.92)	(1.53)	(1.61)			(1.35)	(1.09)	(2.33)	(1.70)	(7.94)	(9.15)
Central		3871	6122	966	3178	–	–	146	1190	4903	10490	252602	649695
	(a)	(1.53)	(0.94)	(0.39)	(0.49)			(0.286)	(1.10)	(1.97)	(1.61)	(100.00)	(100.00)
	(b)	(2.94)	(2.50)	(4.49)	(1.64)			(1.80)	(1.34)	(2.45)	(1.93)	(10.19)	(9.71)
Western		3285	4687	106	329	–	–	120	1020	3511	6036	128438	327797
	(a)	(2.56)	(1.45)	(0.08)	(0.10)			(0.29)	(0.31)	(2.73)	(1.83)	(100.00)	(100.00)
	(b)	(2.50)	(1.91)	(0.49)	(0.36)			(1.58)	(1.15)	(1.74)	(1.11)	(5.18)	(4.90)
KATHMANDU VALLEY		1494	3164	5	15	–	–	–	–	1499	3179	66755	260528
	(a)	(2.24)	(1.26)	(0.01)	(0.01)					(2.25)	(1.27)	(100.00)	(100.00)
	(b)	(1.14)	(1.29)	(0.02)	(0.02)					(0.74)	(0.58)	(2.69)	(5.74)
INNER TERAI		38061	77573	732	2448	–	–	408	4286	39201	84294	278409	765410
	(a)	(13.67)	(10.13)	(0.25)	(0.32)			(0.15)	(0.56)	(14.08)	(11.01)	(100.00)	(100.00)
	(b)	(28.93)	(31.60)	(3.40)	(2.80)			(6.02)	(4.80)	(19.30)	(15.49)	(11.23)	(11.44)
Eastern		9516	18314	160	526	–	–	172	1885	9848	20725	62136	170845
	(a)	(15.31)	(10.72)	(8.76)	(0.31)			(0.26)	(1.10)	(16.85)	(12.13)	(100.00)	(100.00)
	(b)	(7.24)	(7.40)	(0.74)	(0.60)			(2.13)	(2.15)	(4.87)	(3.01)	(2.51)	(2.35)

(*Contd.*)

(*Table 2.8 contd.*)

Region													
Central		11772	21331	493	1693	–	–	63	587	12328	23598	109404	315018
	(a)	(10.76)	(6.77)	(0.43)	(8.34)			(0.080)	(0.18)	(11.27)	(7.49)	(100.00)	(100.00)
	(b)	(8.95)	(8.71)	(2.79)	(1.24)			(0.78)	(0.64)	(6.10)	(4.34)	(4.41)	(4.71)
Western		16773	37928	79	229	–	–	173	1814	17025	39971	106869	279547
	(a)	(15.69)	(13.57)	(0.07)	(0.08)			(0.16)	(0.65)	(15.93)	(14.30)	(100.00)	(100.00)
	(b)	(12.76)	(15.49)	(0.07)	(0.250)			(2.13)	(7.04)	(8.42)	(7.35)	(4.31)	(4.16)
TERAI		79259	144133	19294	79931	41092	123085	7193	80282	146738	427351	1453396	3765257
	(a)	(5.45)	(3.81)	(1.33)	(2.11)	(2.83)	(3.25)	(8.49)	(2.12)	(10.10)	(11.29)	(100.00)	(100.00)
	(b)	(60.70)	(58.87)	(89.63)	(91.56)	(120.00)	(160.80)	(90.38)	(90.59)	(72.56)	(78.55)	(58.62)	(56.57)
Eastern		33710	52842	13354	55208	41092	123085	6577	75612	94833	306247	957641	2599842
	(a)	(3.52)	(7.030)	(1.39)	(2.13)	(4.99)	(4.73)	(8.70)	(2.10)	(0.90)	(11.80)	(100.00)	(100.00)
	(b)	(25.64)	(21.60)	(62.93)	(93.19)	(100.00)	(100.00)	(82.72)	(83.02)	(46.98)	(56.38)	(38.63)	(38.85)
Central		15614	24117	5765	23891	–	–	243	2026	21622	50134	263669	624276
	(a)	(5.84)	(3.86)	(2.17)	(3.94)			(0.09)	(0.62)	(8.10)	(8.03)	(100.00)	(100.00)
	(b)	(11.80)	(9.85)	(26.79)	(27.48)			(2.99)	(2.28)	(10.64)	(9.22)	(10.71)	(9.33)
Western		29935	67174	175	632	–	–	273	2064	30383	70479	230186	561139
	(a)	(13.00)	(11.07)	(0.88)	(0.11)			(0.12)	(0.47)	(13.20)	(17.66)	(100.00)	(100.00)
	(b)	(22.70)	(27.44)	(0.81)	(0.72)			(3.06)	(3.90)	(15.02)	(12.95)	(9.29)	(8.39)
NEPAL		131472	244831	21525	87297	41092	123085	8123	85613	202294	544031	2479300	6691533
	(a)	(5.30)	(3.66)	(0.87)	(1.00)	(1.56)	(1.56)	(0.11)	(1.33)	(0.16)	(7.50)	(100.00)	(100.00)
	(b)	(100.00)	(100.00)	(100.00)	(100.00)	(100.00)	(100.00)	(100.00)	(100.00)	(100.00)	(100.00)	(100.00)	(100.00)

Note: A = Cropped area in hectare;
B = Value of production in Rs. 1000 (weighted by mean of national everage retail price for 1968/60–1977/70).
Figures in parenthesis are percentages: (a) Row percentage (local share); (b) Column persentage (national share).

Source: National Research Associate (1982), *Nepal District Profile*, Kathmandu.

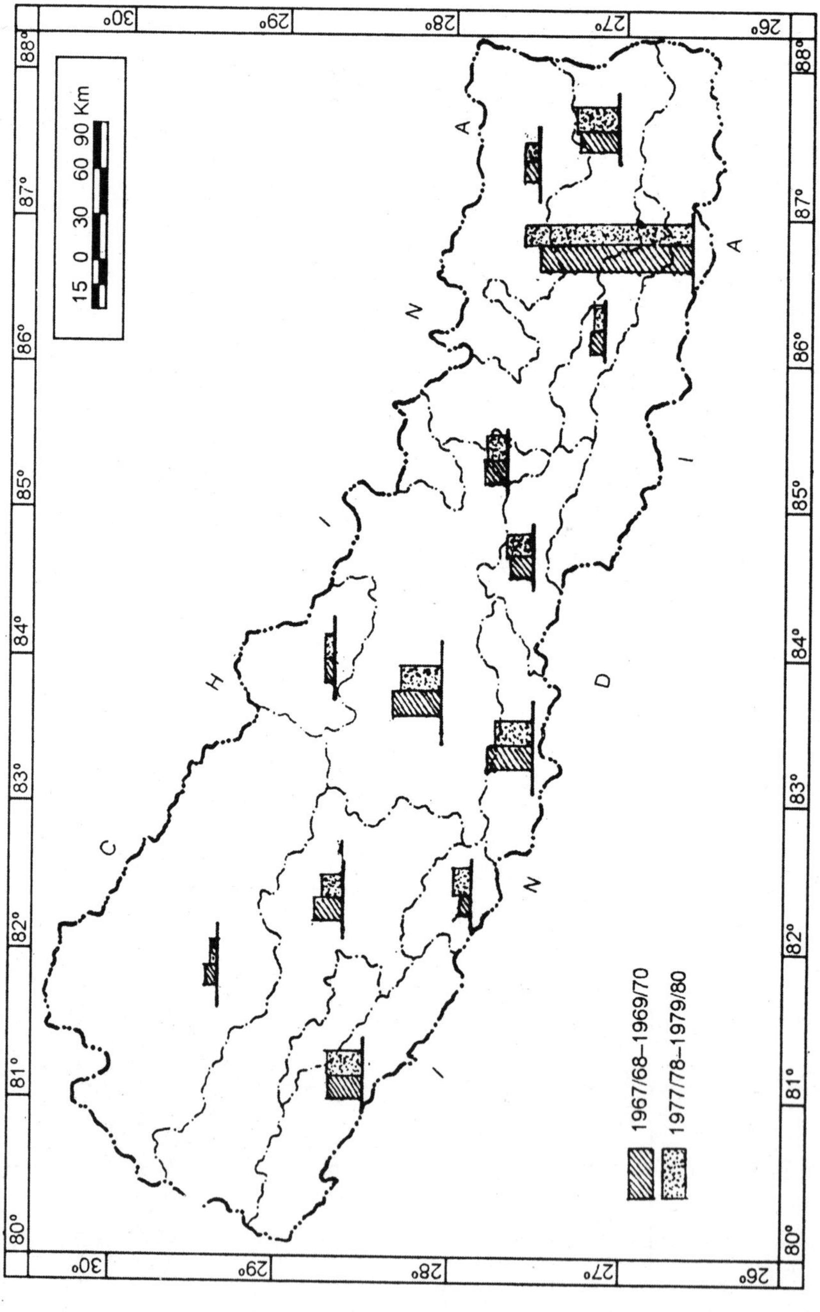

Fig. 2.2 Spatial Distribution of Cereal Crop Production (% Share).

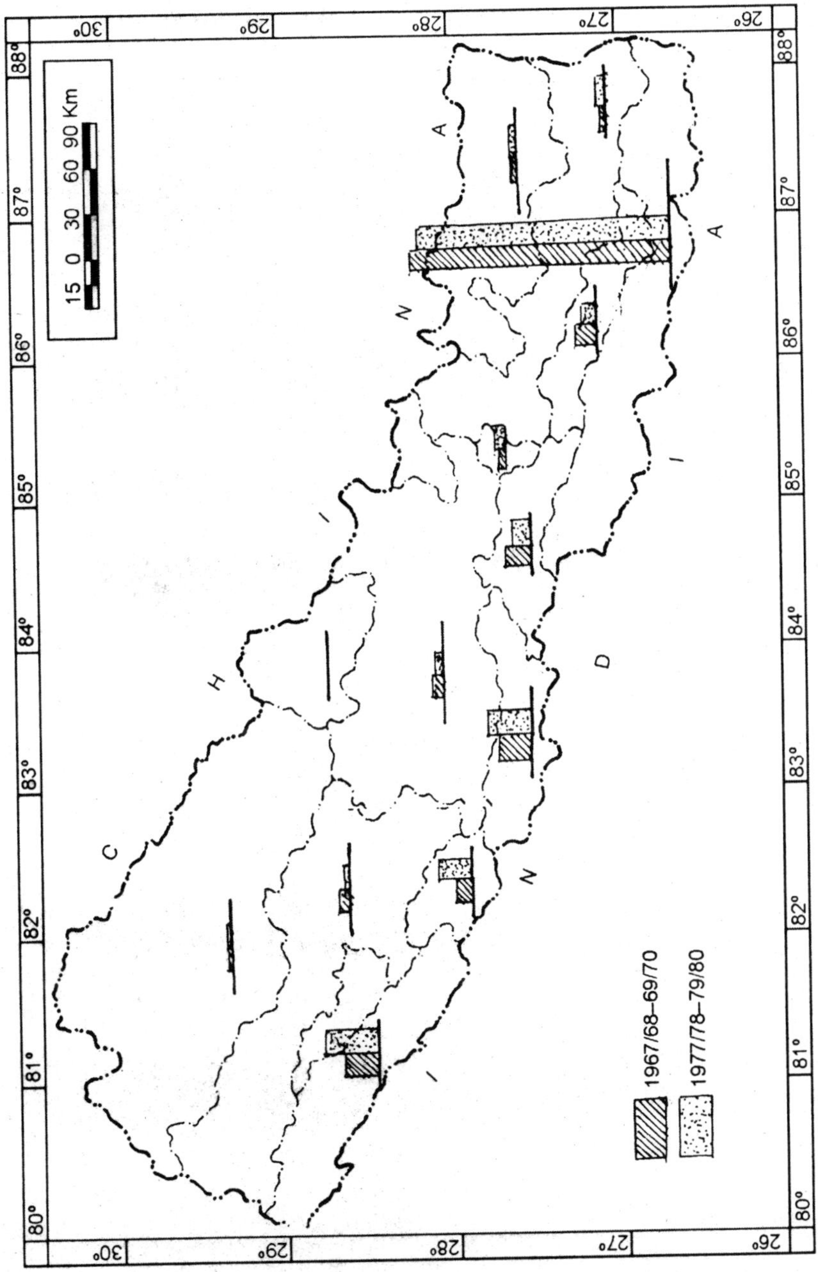

Fig. 2.3 Spatial Distribution of Cash Crop Production (% Share).

Table 2.9 Growth Rates* of Principal Crops by Territorial Zones.

Territorial Zones	Cereals and Substitute Crops													
	Paddy		Maize		Wheat		Millet		Barley		Potato		Sub-Total	
	A	P	A	P	A	P	A	P	A	P	A	P	A	P
(1)	(2)	(3)	(4)	(5)	(6)	(7)	(8)	(9)	(10)	(11)	(12)	(13)	(14)	(15)
MOUNTAIN	+5.26	+4.31	+1.45	−1.01	−7.63	−11.62	+2.83	+2.26	+0.16	−1.32	+1.86	+1.64	+0.60	−0.45
Eastern	+12.95	+11.91	+0.96	−1.23	−6.78	−8.03	+1.62	+1.38	−2.79	−4.58	+3.02	+2.82	+2.90	+2.32
Central	−11.75	−3.97	+0.90	−0.03	−4.18	−6.43	+3.15	+1.75	+0.08	−0.65	+0.87	+1.01	−0.50	−0.60
Western	+0.80	−1.00	+2.55	−0.90	−8.13	−12.82	+3.94	+3.30	+0.89	−0.81	+0.28	−0.22	−1.12	−3.43
HILL	+2.03	+0.73	+0.98	−1.70	+3.41	+1.96	+1.50	+0.27	+0.34	−0.25	+3.09	+3.09	+1.70	+0.18
Eastern	+3.07	+1.92	+1.10	−1.66	+3.95	+4.61	+2.37	+0.48	−1.20	−2.13	+2.98	+3.28	+2.08	+0.92
Central	+2.25	+0.65	+1.34	−2.64	+8.99	+9.00	+0.69	−0.24	+0.32	+0.32	+4.47	+4.16	+2.16	+0.06
Western	+0.02	−0.92	−0.02	+0.21	−0.02	−3.32	+2.77	+1.60	+0.70	−0.08	+0.93	+0.12	+0.32	−0.84
KATHMANDU VALLEY	−1.00	−1.03	−1.44	−1.65	+1.75	+3.27	−3.53	−4.71	+12.26	+13.00	−8.83	−12.73	−0.58	−0.96
INNER TERAI	+1.24	+0.32	+1.17	+0.64	+11.10	+12.17	+1.75	+2.66	+5.37	+6.19	+1.96	+2.06	+2.78	+1.75
Eastern	+2.75	+1.35	+2.34	+1.12	+12.80	+14.68	+1.90	+3.16	+4.47	+11.07	+2.80	+2.30	+3.26	+2.17
Central	+0.60	−0.07	+0.46	−1.21	+9.48	+11.33	+1.08	+1.64	+5.57	+10.38	+1.55	+1.91	+1.58	+0.70
Western	+1.05	+0.10	+4.85	+3.74	+12.03	+12.25	+4.30	+5.62	+2.90	+3.96	+2.00	+2.29	+3.98	+2.96
TERAI	+0.50	+0.38	+0.22	−0.65	+8.20	+10.33	+0.17	+0.39	−2.18	−0.04	−1.56	−3.07	+1.32	+1.20
Eastern	+0.44	+0.76	−2.29	−3.64	+10.45	+12.96	+0.66	+0.53	−1.23	+0.96	−0.34	−1.79	+1.34	+1.58
Central	+1.03	−0.50	−1.90	−1.95	+3.80	+5.77	+1.47	+1.25	−10.28	−8.72	−8.93	−11.97	+1.19	+0.12
Western	+0.58	−0.55	+1.18	+2.58	+8.25	+8.88	−2.35	−0.59	+19.14	+19.47	−1.02	−0.81	+1.36	+0.87
NEPAL	+0.78	+0.44	+0.95	−0.99	+5.70	+6.07	+1.35	+0.53	−0.07	−0.29	+1.50	+.90	+1.46	+0.84

Note: *Annual compound growth rates during 1967/68–1969/70 to 1977/78–1979/80.
A = Cropped Area J, P = Value of production.

Source: Derived from Tables 2.7 and 2.8.

any standard of comparison. It becomes fictitious when it is seen against the acreage increase of 1.48% for the same period. In the territorial dimension central and western Mountain, western Hill and Kathmandu Valley are seen to have registered actual decline in absolute crop production, central Hill and central Inner Terai are seen just in the margin; and only eastern and western Terai and Inner Terai appear to have registered any significant growth in absolute level of production. Whereas the decline in level of production accompanied by corresponding decline in acreage in Kathmandu Valley may be easily explained in terms of increasing use of cultivated land for non-agricultural purposes, mostly for construction, reasons for the same phenomenon (i.e absolute or near decline in aggregate output accompanied or unaccompanied by decline in acreage) in other areas will have to be sought in terms of the deeper structural crisis of the agrarian system.

Viewing the situation cropwise, the identical picture is instantly flashed in the case of aggregate cereals and substitute crops because of their overwhelming domination in total crop production. In the case of non-cereal crops, even a slightly better picture of 1.92% acreage growth and 2.61% output growth in the country-wide plane cannot be regarded as satisfactory or rosy by any international standard of comparison. In the territorial frame, the absolute decline both in acreage and output terms in Inner Terai may need deeper probe into its correlations, if any, with the export market trends. Only moderate growth (1.7% acreage growth and 2.18% output growth) in the supposedly most dynamic (in terms of manufacturing and export trade activities) eastern Terai would have to be seen in terms of broader inter-sectoral articulation of the economy.

To come to the analysis of production trends at the level of individual crops, discernible degree of slower growth or higher decline rates noticeable in the case of cereal crops like maize, millet and barley constituting the staple diet of mostly the lower classes and ethnic groups compared to that of paddy and wheat consumed mostly by the upper classes, immediately brings the issues of broader political economy of underdevelopment into the apparent technical process of agricultural production. Similarly the absolute decline in the acreage under jute, the single most important export item of Nepal, and decline in both acreage and output of tobacco another important industrial crop, point towards the lack of required impulses from other sectors of the economy for agricultural development as discussed earlier. Virtual elimination from the production scene of once the much widespread and celebrated cotton,[88] is another example of historical manifestations of exogenous underdevelopment process operating in the Nepalese society.

2.2.23 Net Food Balance

In a use-value based and subsistence-oriented agricultural economy net balance of food production per capita should practically sum up the condition of absolute level of social production and serve as a proxy measure of extent of social surplus available for appropriation. However, caution should be practised in

Table 2.10 Food Balance Condition by Territorial Zones (1970/71 and 1979/80).

Territorial Zones	*Net Food Balance ('000 m. ton)*		*Food Balance per 1000 population (m. ton)*			*No. of Food Deficit Districts*	
	1970/71	*1979/80*	*1970/71*	*1979/80*	*Annual Rate of Change (%)*	*1970/71*	*1979/80*
MOUNTAIN	–15.473	–30.959	–16.60	–29.25	–8.47	7	12
Eastern	–13.904	–9.762	–32.01	–20.17	+4.11	3	3
Central	+4.236	–2.086	+81.62	–43.12	–16.98	0	2
Western	–5.805	–19.111	–13.02	–36.36	–19.92	4	7
HILL	–127.753	–205.07	–24.90	–38.92	–6.26	25	29
Eastern	–29.216	–40.441	–18.24	–22.48	–2.58	9	9
Central	–66.101	–75.520	–29.70	–29.00	–0.26	9	10
Western	–32.436	–89.109	–24.91	–60.32	–15.79	7	10
KATH. VALLEY	+2.902	–80.763	+4.69	–105.32	–260.63	1	2
INNER TERAI	+72.872	+56.925	+82.79	+74.24	–1.15	2	1
Eastern	+3.291	+0.864	+12.66	+2.49	–8.93	1	1
Central	+58.200	+34.561	167.52	+69.22	–6.52	0	0
Western	+14.343	+21.500	+52.58	+49.78	–0.59	1	0
TERAI	+354.223	+379.084	+93.40	+62.80	–3.64	0	0
Eastern	+167.632	+270.604	+60.47	+63.72	+0.60	0	0
Central	+93.592	+52.248	+157.27	+54.47	–7.26	0	0
Western	+92.999	+56.232	+218.70	+67.72	–7.67	0	0
NEPAL	+294.051	+119.217	+25.90	+7.94	–7.70	35	44

Source: 1. HMG/N, Ministry of Food, *Agriculture and Irrigation, Agricultural Statistics of Nepal, 1972,* Kathmandu.
2. National Research Associates (1982), *Nepal District Profile*, Kathmandu.

Table 2.11 Net Food Balance per 1000 Population (1979/80) Cross-Classified by Annual Rate of Change (1970/71–1979/80).

	Annual Rate of Change (1970/71–1979/80)	*Net Food Balance (1979/80)*					
		Surplus (m. ton)			*Deficit (m. ton)*		
		High	*Medium*	*Low*	*Low*	*Medium*	*High*
		(> +60)	*(+25 to +60)*	*(< + 25)*	*(< –25)*	*(–25 to – 60)*	*(> –60)*
		(Abbreviations of Ecological Zones)					
+Ve Change	High (> +10%)				(5)		
	Medium (+2 to +10 %)		(1)		EM		
	Low (< +2%)	ET		(2)			(6)
–Ve Change	Low (< –2 %)	(3)	WIT			CH	
	Medium (–2 to –10 %)	WT CIT	CT	EIT	EH	(7)	(8)
	High (> –10%)			(4)		WM CM	WH KV

drawing serious conclusions from an empirical exercise based on arbitrary assumptions of ideal consumption standards and perfect equity in distribution.

Following the standards of per capita per annum requirement of edible food grains of 190 kg. in Terai, 160 kg. in Hill and 140 kg. in Mountain adopted by the Ministry of Food and Agriculture and allowing for standard deductions from gross value production due to various losses in storage, dehusking, milling, etc.[89] food balance estimates were drawn for 1970/71 and 1979/80 [Table 2.10]. It may be cautioned at the outset that despite our own intuitive judgement in cross-checking glaringly suspect results estimates on food balance cannot be relied upon and may be taken only as rough indication of the situation.

A quick glance at the Tables instantly brings to light the disturbing picture of declining food surplus or aggravating food deficit in absolute terms in almost all the territorial units of the country except the eastern Terai and western Inner Terai. Whereas central Mountain and Kathmandu Valley have changed from food surplus to food deficit zones, all the previously deficit areas, except eastern Mountain, have grown further deficit. When the change in absolute value of food balance is weighted by the corresponding change in population of the area, only eastern Terai is seen to have maintained a positive growth over the years. In terms of annual rate of change of food balance per 1000 population, the negative change in Kathmandu Valley (–260.63%), western Mountain (–19.92%) and Hill (–15.79%) and central Mountain (–16.98%) have been the most alarming.

Study of food balance situation at the district level reveals that the number of net deficit districts has increased from 35 to 44 out of a total of 75 districts during the 9-years period. From the ecological zone-wise breakup of the shift in the number of food deficit districts, the acute food situation of Mountain, Hill and Kathmandu Valley is confirmed at their micro-level as well.

To get a combined picture of food production (or by proxy total agricultural production) situation by spatial units in a dynamic frame, net food balance per 1000 population for 1979/80 was cross-classified with annual rate of change of the same for 1970/71–1979/80 to generate Table 2.11. The results of the bivariate analysis are interpreted as follows:

Category	*Definition*	*Spatial Units*
1. Surplus-Dynamic	With high or medium surplus and high or medium positive change	None
2. Surplus-Developing	With low surplus and all +ve change or, surplus and low +ve change	Eastern Terai
3. Surplus-Stagnant	With high or medium surplus and lower medium –ve change	Western Inner Terai, Western Terai, Central Inner Terai and Central Terai

(*Contd.*)

(Table contd.)

	Category	*Definition*	*Spatial Units*
4.	Surplus-Declining	With low surplus and –ve change, or surplus and less than medium –ve change	Eastern Inner Terai
5.	Deficit-Dynamic	With low or medium deficit but high or medium +ve change	Eastern Mountain
6.	Deficit-Developing	With high deficit and +ve change, or deficit and low +ve change	None
7.	Deficit-Stagnant	With low or medium deficit and low or medium –ve change	Eastern and Central Hill
8.	Deficit-Declining	With high deficit and –ve change, or deficit and high –ve change	Western and Central Mountain Western Hill, and Kathmandu Valley

The otherwise understandable results of the bivariate relationship (i.e. progressive decline in food balance from south to north and from east to west territorial dimensions) can be said to have been marred by the inclusion of traditionally 'rich' Kathmandu Valley at the bottom of the ladder as "deficit-declining". The apparent anomaly can be partly explained in terms of the faulty weighting of the gross value of food production by the total population of the area rather than only by the 'rural' or 'agricultural' population. Even then the implications of exclusion of "urban" population engaged in agricultural activities and the social obligation of the agricultural producers of feeding the entire population, would have remained open to question. Anyway the bitter truth of rapidly expanding urban agglomeration of the national capital eating into the agricultural land and lowering the level of gross output, on the one hand, and adding up the net consumers of foodgrains, on the other, cannot be lost sight of.

2.2.3 Level and Growth of Productivity

Measure of productivity by factor inputs should be the real test of development of productive forces in agriculture, or for that matter, any branch of production. In the absence of any significant use of other factors of production apart from land and labour in the case of Nepalese agriculture, we shall endeavour to analyse productivity with respect to these two factors only.

2.2.31 Level and Growth of Output per Hectare

To get a consolidated picture of land productivity, or output per hectare of gross cropped area,[90] average yield rates of ten major crops weighted by the mean of national average retail price for 1967/68–1977/78 were calculated separately and in relevant sub-groups for the 1960s and 1970s [Table 2.12] and their growth trends computed subsequently [Table 2.13]. Leaving aside the apparently low absolute value of yield rates, their spatio-temporal variations within the country would be of immediate interest for the present.

Table 2.12 Yield Rates of Principal Crops by Territories Zones.

Territorial Zones	Cereals and Substitute Crops													
	Paddy		Maize		Wheat		Millet		Barley		Potato		Sub-Total	
	Y1	Y2	Y1	Y2	Y1	Y2	Y1	Y2	Y1	Y2	Y1	Y2	Y1	Y2
(1)	(2)	(3)	(4)	(5)	(6)	(7)	(8)	(9)	(10)	(11)	(12)	(13)	(14)	(15)
MOUNTAIN	3595	3285	3020	2370	2774	1921	1890	1788	1631	1408	8286	8112	3257	2938
Eastern	3730	3405	3170	2552	2431	2165	1898	1854	1574	1325	8338	8175	3572	3375
Central	3328	6848	2843	2600	2715	2192	1951	1702	1590	1480	8554	8692	3331	3298
Western	3569	2983	2778	1976	2827	1848	1864	1751	1659	1405	8071	7681	3023	2411
HILL	3668	3224	3095	2372	2745	2359	1864	1645	1542	1454	8496	8529	3219	2769
Eastern	3706	3315	3163	2405	2464	2627	1863	1545	1543	1394	8596	8856	3530	3137
Central	3713	3170	3283	2217	2684	2542	1870	1705	1494	1495	8083	7845	3179	2581
Western	3524	3208	2601	2662	2862	2068	1840	1641	1563	1449	8670	8030	2884	2576
KATHMANDU VALLEY	4910	4955	2917	2859	2844	3298	1604	1435	1357	1449	14331	10079	3930	3790
INNER TERAI	3193	2913	3106	2694	2326	2560	1620	1768	1284	1388	9134	9238	3148	2847
Eastern	3445	3003	2950	2619	2226	2622	1503	1700	1195	1339	9181	8744	3191	2871
Central	3303	3091	3210	2718	2326	2750	1734	1833	1333	1316	9185	9524	3280	3002
Western	2967	2701	3016	2711	2352	2399	1553	1761	1293	1434	8870	9120	2942	2667
TERAI	2652	2603	2350	2156	1982	2409	1360	1388	1082	1336	9936	8572	2600	2570
Eastern	2634	2714	2316	2032	1950	2442	1376	1360	1075	1337	9710	8413	2598	2658
Central	2682	2306	2764	2751	1958	2363	1286	1259	1104	1264	11761	8926	2617	2353
Western	2713	2425	2165	2484	2193	2323	1355	1612	889	1449	8834	9043	2587	2456
NEPAL	2856	2753	2914	2403	2375	2457	1761	1628	1439	1408	9111	8547	2879	2700

(*Contd.*)

(*Table 2.12 contd.*) (*Rs./hect.*)

Territorial Zones	*Cash Crops*											
	Oil Seeds		*Sugarcane*		*Jute*		*Tobacco*		*Sub-Total*		*All Crops*	
	Y1	*Y2*	*Y1*	*Y2*	*Y1*	*Y2*	*Y1*	*Y2*	*Y1*	*Y2*	*Y1*	*Y2*
(1)	*(16)*	*(17)*	*(18)*	*(19)*	*(20)*	*(21)*	*(22)*	*(23)*	*(24)*	*(25)*	*(26)*	*(27)*
MOUNTAIN	1212	1479	3000	2798	–	–	7919	8055	1712	2161	3232	2926
Eastern	1235	1557	3000	2891	–	–	9500	8875	1326	1784	3532	3357
Central	1265	1275	–	–	–	–	–	–	1265	1275	3314	3290
Western	1185	1445	3000	2708	–	–	7829	8007	2051	2390	3007	2410
HILL	1357	1573	3341	3317	1523	–	8689	8441	1797	1954	3185	2750
Eastern	1315	1678	2975	3465	1370	–	8361	8764	1599	1969	3483	3109
Central	1509	1582	3270	3290	–	–	8733	8151	2072	2105	3155	2572
Western	1244	1427	5377	3104	1765	–	8838	8500	1653	1719	2851	2552
KATHMANDU VALLEY	1884	2118	2929	3000	–	–	–	–	1909	2121	3895	3753
INNER TERAI	1932	2038	3128	3340	1816	–	9785	10456	2039	2150	2939	2749
Eastern	1993	1925	3211	3288	1820	–	9920	10959	2090	2104	2956	2750
Central	1783	1812	3039	3428	1455	–	9831	9000	1871	1913	3004	2879
Western	2144	2261	3640	2899	–	–	9652	10486	2283	2348	2835	2616
TERAI	1613	1821	3882	4143	2209	2995	12815	11150	2829	2912	2620	2604
Eastern	1437	1568	4043	4142	2211	2995	13038	11309	3109	3235	2647	2715
Central	1592	1555	3643	4161	1653	–	9689	8337	2343	2329	2602	2351
Western	1828	2244	3386	3611	1630	–	9720	9758	1968	2319	2525	2438
NEPAL	1710	1862	3766	4055	2192	2995	12458	10934	2544	2690	2852	2699

Notes: Yield rates are with respect to gross cropped area (GCA).
Y = Average yield of 1967/68–1969/70.
Y2 = Average yield of 1977/78–1979/80.

Source: Derived from Tables 2.8 and 2.9.

Table 2.13 Change in Yield Rates* of Principal Crops by Territorial Zones.

Territorial Zones	Cereals and Substitute Crops							Cash Crops					
	Paddy	Maize	Wheat	Millet	Barley	Potato	Sub-total	Oil-seeds	Sugar-cane	Jute	Tobacco	Sub-total	All Crops
MOUNTAIN	–0.90	–2.45	–3.74	–0.56	–1.48	–0.21	–1.04	+2.01	–0.70	–	+0.17	+2.36	–1.00
Eastern	–0.92	–2.20	–1.16	–0.23	–1.75	–0.20	–0.57	+2.35	–0.37	–	–0.68	+3.01	–0.50
Central	+7.50	–0.90	–2.16	–1.37	–0.72	+0.16	–0.10	+0.08	–	–	–	+0.08	–0.07
Western	–1.80	–3.47	–4.34	–0.63	–1.68	–0.50	–2.29	+2.00	–1.03	–	+0.22	+1.55	–2.23
HILL	–1.30	–2.70	–1.53	–1.26	–0.59	+0.04	–1.52	+1.49	–0.07	–	–0.29	+0.84	–1.50
Eastern	–1.12	–2.78	+0.64	–1.89	–1.02	+0.30	–1.19	+2.47	+1.54	–	+0.48	+2.10	–1.15
Central	–1.60	–4.00	–0.55	–0.93	±0	–0.30	–2.10	+0.48	+0.01	–	–0.70	+0.16	–2.15
Western	–0.94	+0.23	–3.30	–1.15	–0.76	–0.77	–1.14	+1.38	N.A.	–	–0.39	+0.39	–1.10
KATHMANDU VALLEY	+0.10	–0.20	+1.50	–1.12	+0.66	–3.58	–0.36	+1.18	+0.24	–	–	+1.06	–0.36
INNER TERAI	–0.92	–1.43	+0.96	+0.88	+0.79	+0.11	–1.01	+0.54	+0.66	–	+0.67	+0.53	–0.68
Eastern	–1.38	–1.20	+1.66	+1.24	+1.15	–0.49	–1.16	–0.35	+0.24	–	+1.00	+0.07	–0.73
Central	–0.67	–1.68	+1.70	+0.56	–0.13	+0.36	–0.89	+0.16	+1.21	–	–0.89	+0.22	–0.43
Western	–0.94	–1.07	+0.20	+1.26	+1.04	+0.28	–0.99	+0.54	–2.30	–	+0.83	+0.28	–0.80
TERAI	–0.19	–0.87	+1.97	+0.20	+2.13	–1.49	–0.12	+1.22	+0.66	+3.09	–1.40	+0.29	–0.06
Eastern	+0.30	–1.32	+2.28	–0.11	+2.20	–1.44	+0.23	+0.88	+0.24	+3.08	–1.43	+0.40	+0.25
Central	–1.53	–0.05	+1.90	–0.21	+1.36	–2.80	–1.07	–0.24	+1.34	–	–1.52	–0.06	–1.03
Western	–1.13	+1.38	+0.58	+1.75	+5.00	+0.23	–0.52	+2.07	+0.65	–	+0.04	+1.66	–0.35
NEPAL	–0.37	–1.95	+0.34	–0.79	–0.22	–0.64	–0.65	+0.86	+0.74	+3.09	–1.31	+0.56	–0.65

Note: *Annual compound growth rates during 1967/68–1969/70 to 1977/78–1979/80.
Source: Derived from Table 2.13.

Contrary to the significant variation in gross value of production per capita in the horizontal dimension (coefficient of variation of net food balance per 1000 population for 1979/80 being a staggering 694.43%), the variation in gross output of total crops per hectare appears minimal and has remained virtually unchanged over the decade (C.V. 1960s=15.45%; C.V. 1970s=15.97%). This could be interpreted as the manifestation of low degree of social differentiation over the physical space in both static and dynamic frame. However, the marginal edge enjoyed by Mountain and Hill areas over Terai in land productivity (per GCA), though in a decreasing scale, needs deeper probe into other related aspects of scale of production, institutional structures, etc. before generalizing the distribution pattern of productivity in the horizontal dimension. This could also be explained in terms of underestimation of the "combined effect of all technological inputs on land" expressed through augmentation of cropping intensity, which would have been taken care of by using NSA in the denominator instead of GCA 91 as used by us for reasons already cited. A different trend visible in the distribution of land productivity with respect to NSA for the seventies and higher disparity in its distribution (C.V.=38.16%) gives a strong support to the above hypothesis.

The most distinct trend in the whole process is the declining yield rates of all crops combined in all the relevant spatial units except eastern Terai. The rates of decline per annum are seen progressively rising from Terai (–0.06%), Kathmandu Valley (–0.36%), Inner Terai (–0.68%) and Mountain (–1.00%) to Hill (–1.50%).

A cropwise study of level and growth of yield rates over the physical space would reveal an inverse distribution pattern of level of yield rates for cereal non-cereal crops. Whereas Mountain and Hill have higher yield rates for cereals than the Terai, the reverse is the case with yield rates for non-cereals. In absolute terms too, Mountain and Hill enjoy higher return per hectare in cereals over non-cereals, but its just the reverse with the Terai. Apart from indicating the natural and social importance of the particular crops in different territorial units, these observation also tend to confirm the Marxist explanation of the apparent higher land productivity in more backward and small-scale peasant production (here the reference is to Hill and Mountain areas) in terms of the higher 'exploitation' of themselves by the peasants to produce their subsistence needs. [See Section 2.1.11 above]. The growth pattern of yield rates, however, follow the identical trends for all areas, i.e. negative for cereals and positive for non-cereals, but in varying degrees of higher negative change in Hill and Mountain for cereals and higher positive change in Terai for non-cereals. By individual crops, only paddy and wheat among cereals and all but tobacco among non-cereals register a positive change of yield rates, which could be explained in technological terms by their better use of irrigation facilities and modern inputs and in political-economic terms by their patronisation by the upper classes and their subjection to growing market stimulations.

To assess the combined picture of levels and growth of agricultural productivity, output per hectare of GCA in the seventies was cross-classified by rate of change of the same during the preceding decade to generate the following table.

Table 2.14 Productivity Per Hectare (1970s) Cross-Classified by Change of Productivity per Hectare (1970s over 1960s).

Change in productivity per hectare (1970s over 1960s) (%)	*Productivity per Hectare (1970s)*		
	High (>Rs. 3500)	*Medium (Rs. 2700–3500)*	*Low (Below Rs. 2700)*
	(Ecological–Hydrographic Zones)		
+ ve		(1) Eastern Terai	
0 to –5	Kathmandu Valley	(2) Eastern Mountain Central Mountain Central Inner Terai	Western Terai
–5 to –15		Eastern Hill Eastern Inner Terai	(3) Western Hill Western Inner Terai Central Terai
Below – 15			(4) Western Mountain Central Hill

The above classification may be interpreted as follows:

Category	*Definition*	*Spatial Units*
1. Dynamic	With +ve growth rate and not less than medium productivity	Eastern Terai
2. Stagnant	0 to –5 growth rate and not less than medium productivity	Kathmandu Valley Eastern Mountain Central Mountain Central Inner Terai
3. Declining	0 to –15 growth rate and low productivity, other than stagnant	Western Terai, Eastern Hill, Eastern Inner Terai, Western Hill, Western Inner Terai, Central Terai
4. Collapsing	Below –15 growth rate and low productivity	Western Mountain, Central Hill

The spatial pattern obtained from the bivariate analysis has been plotted in Fig. 2.4. It may now be safely concluded after observing the spatio-temporal distribution pattern of agricultural productivity that not withstanding minor exceptions for certain spatial units the agricultural prospect of the country as a whole is extremely bleak. 'Stagnant' and 'declining' productivity pattern

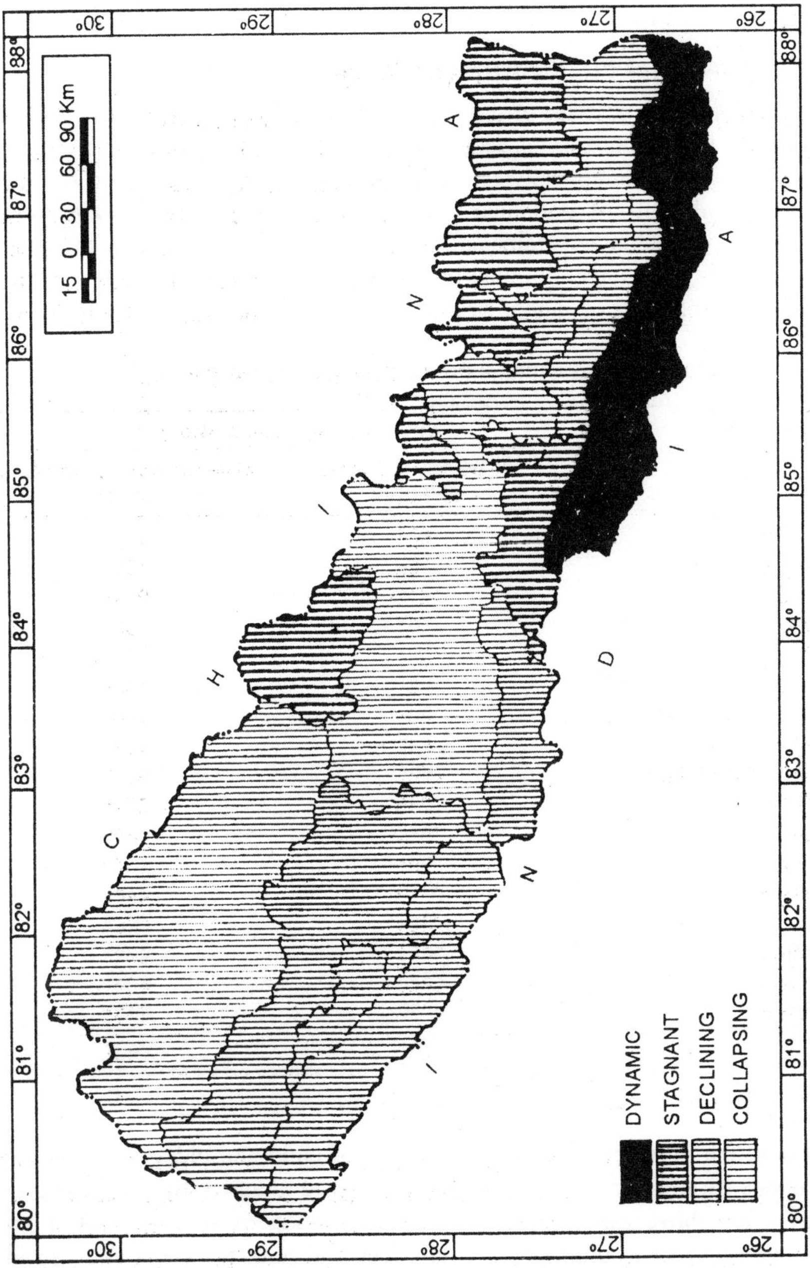

Fig. 2.4 Yield Rates of Crops Cross-Classified by Change in Yield Rates.

observable even in areas of highly favourable agronomic characteristics forces one to conclude that the economic ills of the country have to be diagnosed not in the hitherto fashionable 'natural' parameters but very much within the 'social' parameters.

2.2.32 Agricultural Productivity per Worker

A more enlightening account of the state of development of productive forces in agriculture in a labour surplus economy should be available from the measure of gross output per economically active person in the agricultural sector. But the usual non-availability of statistical information on agricultural workforce in the relevant spatio-temporal frame and non-comparability of available information due to changes in the definition of workforce, has forced us to study only the horizontal distribution of labour productivity in a static frame (Table 2.15).

Table 2.15 Agricultural Productivity per Worker (1970s).

Territorial Zones	*Output per Agricultural Workers (Rs.)*	
	All workers 10 years and over	*Male workers 15–64 years of age*
MOUNTAIN	651	1278
Eastern	752	1531
Central	1219	2445
Western	491	932
HILL	681	1324
Eastern	861	1625
Central	605	1282
Western	596	1034
KATHMANDU VALLEY	1867	3070
INNER TERAI	2246	3715
Eastern	1511	2676
Central	2391	3949
Western	2913	4481
TERAI	2894	3829
Eastern	2771	3591
Central	2825	4067
Western	3776	5051
NEPAL	1461	2467

Source: Tables 2.3 and 2.9.

Because of the presence of a large proportion of child and old-age labour and tremendous variation in sex ratio of labour engaged in agricultural activities as already noted above, separate indices of labour productivity were worked out firstly, with respect to total labour of all ages and both the sexes engaged in production and secondly with respect to the economically, more productive male labour of 15–64 years of age. Obviously greater variation in productivity was observed with respect to the total labour-force (C.V.=74.54%) than only with the male labour 15–64 years of age (C.V.=55.7%), both of which being substantially higher than the variations in land productivity (C.V.15.97%). This could be safely interpreted as the manifestations of greater social and spatial differentiation of agricultural productivity with respect to labour than with an immobile factor of production viz. land. The progressive decline in labour productivity from Terai to Hill and Mountain, on the other hand, displays the known pattern of high share of underemployed labour in Hill and Mountain agriculture marked by high man-land ratio, and exposes the falsity of observed higher land productivity (per GCA) in Hill and Mountain areas.

2.2.33 Combined Expression of Land and Labour Productivity

To have "a holistic view of the impact of environmental, technological, institutional and demographic factors on agricultural development"[92] productivity per hectare (1970s) has been cross-classified with productivity per worker (all workers, 1970s) to generate the following table.

Table 2.16 Productivity per Hectare (70s) Cross-Classified by Productivity per Worker (70s).

Productivity per Worker (70s)	*Productivity per Hectare (70s)*		
	High (> Rs. 3500)	*Medium (Rs. 3500–2700)* *(Ecological–Hydrographic Zones*	*Low (< Rs. 2700)*
High (> Rs. 2500)	(1)	Eastern Terai	Western Terai Central Terai Western Inner Terai
Medium (Rs. 1000–2500)	Kathmandu Valley	Central Inner Terai, Eastern Inner Terai, Central Mountain (2)	
Low (< Rs. 1000)		Eastern Mountain Eastern Hill (3)	Western Mountain Central Hill Western Hill

The above table may be interpreted as follows and depicted in Fig. 2.5.

Category	*Definition*	*Zones*
1. Healthy	With high value for one indicator and not less than medium in another	Eastern Terai Kathmandu Valley
2. Convalescent	With high value for one indicator and any value for another or not less than medium in both, other than the healthy zones	Western and Central Terai, all of Inner Terai, and Central Mountain
3. Chronic	Other than the healthy and chronic zones	All of Hill and Eastern and Western Mountain

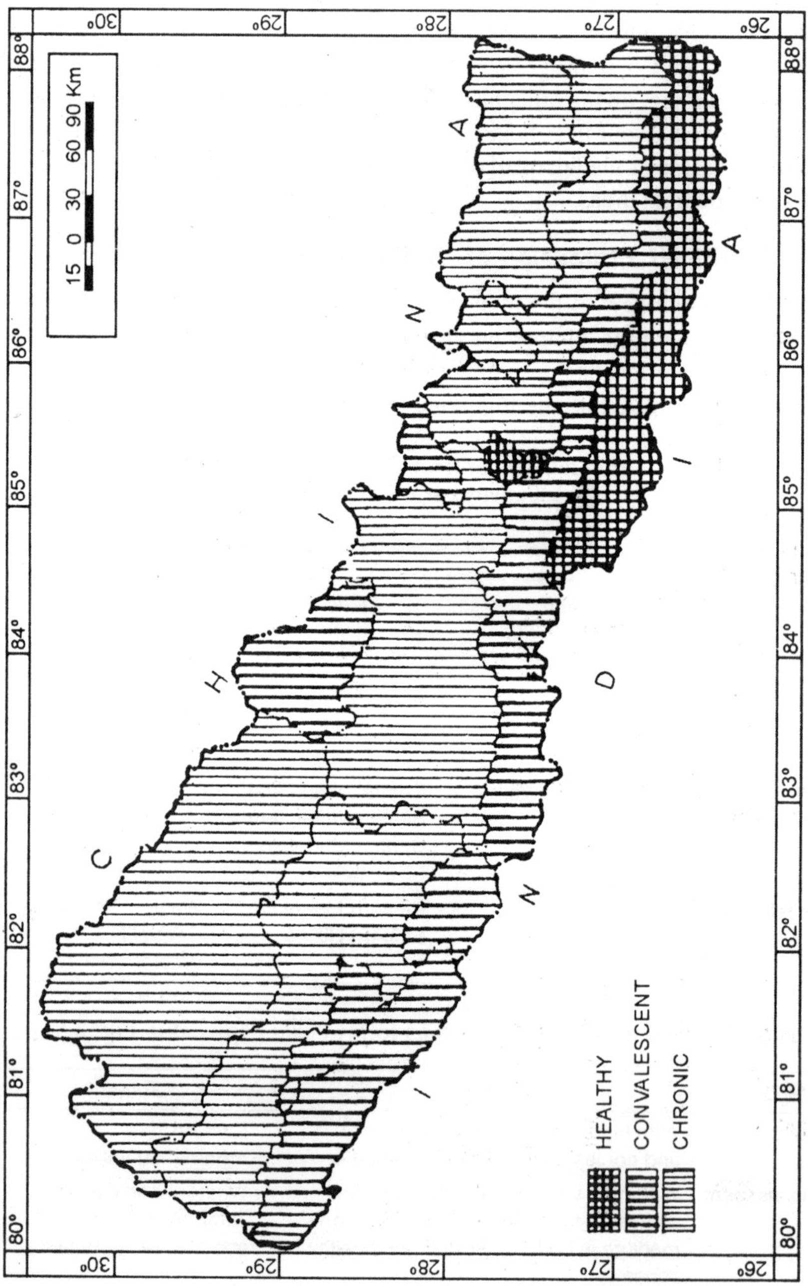

Fig. 2.5 Productivity per Hectare Cross-Classified by Productivity per Worker.

The agrarian spatial pattern obtained from the above analysis, more or less substantiates pending further probing into the interelated aspects, our initial assumption based on historical observation of the process of underdevelopment operating on the Nepalese space economy that except for spurts of spurious growth at points of superior natural attributes and integration with exogenous forces, i.e Terai, specially eastern part, and Kathmandu Valley, in the large territorial expansion of the country, specially Hill and Mountain, the predominant production sector, agriculture, is chronically morbid. The inclusion of central Mountain in the "convalescent" category should be taken as a special case of secluded marginal zones inhabited by scanty population and subjected to lesser stress and strain of underdevelopment process with its 'epi-centre' at points of greater socio-economic interactions.

2.2.4 Decomposition of Growth of Production and Productivity

While fully recognizing that "causal relationships should be rooted in logic, in the conceptual frame of the scholar which is evolved through the rigours of intellection and not through statistical exercises"[93] and realizing the havoc quantitative methods can play with simple logic when the data base is spurious, we ventured to probe statistical relationships in search of some pointers that would "*indicate* causal dependencies" between the different aspects of agricultural production process. Despite the not very encouraging, and at times spurious, results the empirical endeavour has yielded some important support to the basic theoretical frame to explain the growth process of Nepalese agriculture.

2.2.41 Analysis of Interdependencies

Of a series of correlations[94] worked out between different variables the following even when statistically not significant, may be useful in explaining the growth pattern of Nepalese agriculture:

- Apprehending a high influence of natural agro-climatic attributes on spatial variations in levels of agricultural development, a number of correlations were observed between land productivity and agronomic capacity of land (i.e.% of cultivated land of highest grade or '*abal*' category and % of irrigable lowland or *khet)* and between land productivity and distribution of rainfall. The positive but statistically not significant correlations between the said variables could be explained either in terms of greater role played by historico-cultural factors than the physiographic attributes in the selection of initial areas of habitation by the primitive cultivators, or, that the prevailing cropping pattern is more or less independent of availability of water or the agronomic quality of soil, or, that the data base may not be simply reliable.
- A negative but statistically not significant correlation between output per cultivated hectare and number of cattle units per hectare could indicate the traditional role of animal husbandry not complimentary to but as a substitute

of crop production in much of the remote Hill areas and Mountain highlands.

- A positive and highly significant (at 1% level) correlation of land productivity with intensity of cropping proves that spatial variations in gross output per cultivated hectare are more due to the differences in multiplication of cropping or expansion of gross cropped areas (GCA) than due to change in yield rate of crops in the relevant spatial units. This is also borne out by greater variation in land productivity with respect to NSA (C.V.=38.16%) than with respect to GCA (C.V.=15.97%). Differences in intensity of cropping, however, may arise as a result of differences in provision of irrigation facilities (eg. 96% of public irrigation systems in 1981/82 were located in Terai and Inner Terai with 59.5% of net cultivated area), natural advantage of agro-climatic conditions for multi-cropping (eg. in Kathmandu Valley), or, simple pattern.
- The correlation of output per hectare (GCA) with use of modern inputs per hectare was unexpectedly found to be positive and significant (at 5% level), despite the abysmally low absolute value of modern inputs per hectare (only N. Rs. 44.48 per hectare in 1978/79). On further checking it was detected that in the context of low spatial variation in land productivity with respect to GCA, the unproportionately high values of technological inputs per hectare and gross crop output per hectare in Kathmandu Valley had unduly exaggerated the correlation coefficient, and on its exclusion the correlation was found insignificant. This is a clear indication of negligible influence exercised by modern inputs in the overall agricultural development of the country, and of their catalytic role in aggravating disparity in spatial terms.
- Negative and highly significant (at 1% level) correlation between labour productivity and number of agricultural workers per hectare of NSA denotes high level of disguised unemployment prevalent in the agricultural sector.
- The positive and significant (at 5% level) correlation observed between land and labour productivity (male labour 15–64 years of age) implies that the development of productive forces in agriculture is not necessarily impeded by the corresponding increase in agricultural workers as feared by the "labour absorption" protagonists[95] but can be augmented by rise in labour efficiency. However, the implication may not be the same in the case of Nepal, as the areas of seemingly higher labour productivity (i.e. Terai and Inner Terai) have low man-land ratio due to historical accident of their opening-up late, for cultivation, and their so-called high 'labour productivity' is merely a measure of low man-land ratio in absolute terms than a relative measure of higher output per labour from a comparable piece of land.

2.2.42 Decomposition of Growth of Production and Productivity

The analysis of production characteristics of agriculture conducted so far and the preceding examination of interdependencies provide enough insights into the prevailing state of development of productive forces in Nepalese agriculture. However, lack of a detailed and systematic account of input-output relations have deprived us, within the obvious limitations of empirical verification of a social phenomenon, of clear quantitative disaggregation of related, causative factors of growth of production and productivity in the agriculture sector, when a number of quantitative tools to the effect have been quite successfully used in the context of other economies.[96] In the case of Nepal, too, a few preliminary attempts have been made to decompose growth components of agricultural production with limited success in view of the well-known data constraints.[97] Working within the same constraints of data and with our reservation for empirical methods that tend to exaggerate the role of natural or objective factors to the utter neglect of institutional or subjective factors in influencing a 'social' phenomenon like the change in agricultural production and productivity, we have not attempted a separate decomposition exercise but have only cited the relevant findings of previous scholars in support of our contention.

Pant and Sharma[98] basing themselves on the methodology of Bhalla and Alagh[99] have decomposed the growth of crop output for major ecological zones [Table 2.17]. Their findings tend to confirm our own intuition from results of the analysis so far. The excessive share (76.2%) of area increase in the moderate annual growth rate of 1.81% for the country as a whole corroborates our previous generalisation on the subject. The absolute decrease in the cropped area in the Kathmandu Valley with the rapidly expanding urban connurbation, reflecting on the overall decline in the agricultural growth rate in the Valley, however, is explicable in terms of the loss of best lands for non-agricultural use. Whereas, the high and moderate share of yield rate change in Kathmandu Valley and Terai in their growth rates speak of their relatively sounder health, the decline in yield rates and their consequent negative contribution in overall growth rates in the Mountain and Hill are of serious implications for the economy.

Table 2.17 Contributions of Different Components to the Growth of Crop Output in Nepal, 1970/71–1972/73 to 1980/81–1982/83.

Ecological Zones	*Exponential annual growth rate of crop output*	*Contribution to growth through*			
		Area	*Yield*	*Cropping pattern*	*Interaction between yield and cropping pattern*
Mountain	–0.38	0.26	–1.09	0.46	–0.01
Hill	1.29	2.02	–0.75	–0.03	0.06
Kathmandu Valley	–0.10	–1.49	1.65	–0.39	0.13
Terai	2.22	1.16	0.31	0.36	0.40
NEPAL	1.81 (100.00)	1.38 (76.2)	0.02 (1.1)	0.17 (9.4)	0.24 (13.3)

Note: Figures in parenthesis are row percentages.

Source: Adapted from Pant, B.D. and Sharma, P. (1984), "Growth of Agricultural Productivity in Nepal: A Regional Analysis", *Nepalese Economic Journal*, Nepal Rastra Bank. Kathmandu.

The share of cropping pattern (9.4%) and interactions between yield and cropping pattern (13.3%) in the agricultural growth rate of the country appear to be quite high and significant. Viewed in spatial terms, consistently high shares only in the Terai could be an indicator of positive adjustments of crop-combinations to maximise output as a result of the availability of better input supply, market stimulations and changing production relations in that particular territorial belt as against the rest of the country. However, a hasty generalisation would be unwarranted pending further probe into all the related aspects.

As regards the decomposition of component elements contributing towards the growth of productivity, which is variously picturised as 'sluggish' to outright declining,[100] no satisfactory results could be obtained from the production function model, and the insights gained from our earlier analysis of interdependencies had to be contented with.

However, it may be reaffirmed here that the study of the nature of growth of production and productivity, in essence the state of the productive forces, cannot be satisfactorily conducted except in league with the relations of productions to be unfolded subsequently.

2.3 DISTRIBUTION CHARACTERISTICS OF AGRICULTURE

As 'distribution' determines the conditions of appropriation of social surplus within the production system, its pivotal role in structuration of the underdevelopment process is self-evident. However, "before distribution can be the distribution of products, it is (1) the distribution of the instruments of production, and (2) which is a further specification of the same relation, the distribution of the members of the society among different kinds of production (subsumption of the individuals under specific relations of production)".[101] Hence, within the general limitations of an empirical exercise in correctly portraying a social process and specific limitations of data base in the context of Nepal, attempts would be made to delineate these concrete aspects of distribnution in the Nepalese agriculture.

2.3.1 Ownership of Means of Production

Determinate mode and extent of ownership of instruments of production may be regarded as the most important ensemble in articulating the relations of production. Due to lack of adequate information in the desired spatio-temporal frame, holding of assets per farm family provided by Agricultural Credit Review Survey is sought to be utilised to decipher broad trands in the distribution of means of production in agriculture. The most important factor, land, will subsequently be analysed. It may, however, be reminded at the outset that the conventional statistics giving merely the physical extent of distribution of material instruments of production in a static frame without simultaneously offering any clue to the determinate mode of organization of labour to complete the production process, should not be misunderstood as a convenient substitute for the measure of relations of production but accepted merely as fragmentary aspect of a broader phenomenon to be interwoven with prevailing labour relations to generalise the social process.

2.3.11 Holding of Assets per Farm Family

Material possessions of different size-group of farm families in the two broad territorial units, Hill (including Kathmandu Valley) and Terai (including Inner Terai), as obtained from the sample survey of 14 "accessible" districts conducted by Nepal Rastra Bank (1980) have been grouped under 'productive' and 'non-productive' (to be taken only in a relative sense) assets. Their horizontal (spatial) and vertical (size-group) distribution pattern [Table 2.18], proportion of individual assets to the total [Table 2.19] and their growth trend [Table 2.20] have also been analysed.

A glance at Table 2.18 would instantly eastablish a greater vertical disparity in the possession of total assets in Terai than in Hill, the ratios of values of total assets with the large and marginal farm households verying from 16.74 in Terai to 4.14 in Hill. The corresponding ratios are higher for 'productive' assets (17.35 in Terai and 8.45 in Hill) than for 'non-productive' ones (14.25 in Terai and 1.52 in Hill). The greatest relative disparity, though not quite significant in absolute terms, is, however, observed in the possession of machinery, tools and transport equipment in Terai (the relevant ratio being a staggering 73.55). All these could be safely interpreted as the manifestations of greater degree of social differentiation in Terai than in Hill.

In the distribution of assets by size-group in the horizontal (territorial) dimension, too, Terai scores over Hill in all the size-groups. The ratios of value of assets with Terai and Hill families, however, progressively decrease from 4.15:1 in large farm-size families 2.79:1, 2.67:1 and 1.98:1 in medium, small and marginal size families respectively. This is also an indicator of greater social differentiation together with the relatively higher level of development in Terai than in Hill.

Coming to the distribution of assets by quality (Table 2.19), despite the apparently encouraging scenario of nearly 75% of the total assets by value being categorised as 'productive', with slightly higher share for Terai (76.50%) and lower for Hill (69.94%), the glaring fact of 91.56% of total value of assets getting constituted by traditional possessions like land, livestock and building with negligible value of machinery, tools and transport equipments and financial assets speaks of the generally low level of social development in the absolute sense. Still disturbing trend of progressive decline in the proportion of 'productive' assets with farm size in case of small farm house-holds in Terai, which have lesser proportion of 'building' and correspondingly higher proportion of 'livestock', the trend being more marked in the case of Hill than in Terai, aggravates the already existing deprivation of the lower classes.

Table 2.18 Holding of Assets per Farm Family by Farm Size and Territorial Zones (1976–77).

(*Amount in Rs.*)

Assets		*Large*			*Medium*			*Small*		
Farm Size (1)	*Zones* (2)	*Overall* (3)	*Hill* (4)	*Terai* (5)	*Overall* (6)	*Hill* (7)	*Terai* (8)	*Overall* (9)	*Hill* (10)	*Terai* (11)
I. PRODUCTIVE ASSETS		73694	35408	146481	35617	16970	47776	21498	9062	24184
	(a)	(1.00)	(0.48)	(1.99)	(1.00)	(0.48)	(1.34)	(1.00)	(0.42)	(1.12)
	(b)	(2.53)	(1.69)	(4.51)	(1.22)	(0.81)	(1.47)	(0.74)	(0.43)	(0.74)
1. Land		62676	29849	125087	30525	14131	41212	17427	7404	19590
	(a)	(1.00)	(0.48)	(2.00)	(1.00)	(0.46)	(1.35)	(1.00)	(0.42)	(1.12)
	(b)	(2.56)	(1.71)	(4.58)	(1.25)	(0.81)	(1.51)	(0.71)	(0.42)	(0.72)
2. Live stock		7052	4938	11068	4078	2660	5003	3642	1507	4104
	(a)	(1.00)	(0.70)	(1.57)	(1.00)	(0.65)	(1.23)	(1.00)	(0.41)	(1.13)
	(b)	(1.96)	(1.60)	(2.92)	(1.14)	(0.86)	(1.32)	(1.01)	(0.49)	(1.08)
3. Machinery, Tools and Transport Equipment		3184	162	8931	622	110	957	329	119	375
	(a)	(1.00)	(0.05)	(2.80)	(1.00)	(0.18)	(1.54)	(1.00)	(0.36)	(1.14)
	(b)	(3.88)	(1.29)	(8.09)	(0.76)	(0.87)	(0.87)	(0.40)	(0.94)	(0.34)
4. Financial Assets and Cash in Hand		782	459	1395	392	69	604	100	32	115
	(a)	(1.00)	(0.59)	(1.78)	(1.00)	(0.18)	(1.54)	(1.00)	(0.32)	(1.15)
	(b)	(2.93)	(2.20)	(4.81)	(1.47)	(0.33)	(2.08)	(0.37)	(0.15)	(0.40)
II. NON-PRODUCTIVE ASSETS		22402	10225	45555	13893	9191	16957	6454	7943	6133
	(a)	(1.00)	(0.46)	(2.03)	(1.00)	(0.66)	(1.22)	(1.00)	(1.23)	(0.95)
	(b)	(2.29)	(1.14)	(4.56)	(1.42)	(1.02)	(1.70)	(0.66)	(0.88)	(0.61)
5. Building		17045	6492	37111	11317	6841	14234	4990	6544	4655
	(a)	(1.00)	(0.38)	(2.18)	(1.00)	(0.60)	(1.26)	(1.00)	(1.31)	(0.93)
	(b)	(2.25)	(1.00)	(4.63)	(1.49)	(1.06)	(1.77)	(0.66)	(1.01)	(0.58)
6. Other assets (gold, silver, utensils, etc.)		5357	3733	8444	2576	2350	2723	1464	1399	1478
	(a)	(1.00)	(0.70)	(1.58)	(1.00)	(0.91)	(1.06)	(1.00)	(0.96	(1.01)
	(b)	-(2.44)	(1.49)	(4.30)	(1.17)	(0.94)	(1.39)	(0.67)	(0.58)	(0.75)
III. TOTAL		96096	45633	192036	49510	26161	64733	27952	17005	30317
	(a)	(1.00)	(0.47)	(2.00)	(1.00)	(0.53)	(1.31)	(1.00)	(0.61)	(1.08)
	(b)	(2.47)	(1.53)	(4.52)	(1.27)	(0.87)	(1.52)	(0.72)	(0.57)	(0.71)

(*Contd.*)

(*Table 2.18 contd.*)

Assets		*Marginal*			*Average*		
Farm Size (1)	*Zones (2)*	*Overall (12)*	*Hill (13)*	*Terai (14)*	*Overall (15)*	*Hill (16)*	*Terai (17)*
I. PRODUCTIVE ASSETS		7908	4245	8482	29161	20921	32509
	(a)	(1.00)	(0.54)	(1.07)	(1.00)	(0.72)	(1.11)
	(b)	(0.27)	(0.20)	(0.26)	(1.00)	(1.00)	(1.00)
1. Land		6479	3239	6987	24481	17495	27319
	(a)	(1.00)	(0.50)	(1.08)	(1.00)	(1.71)	(1.16)
	(b)	(0.26)	(0.19)	(0.26)	(1.00)	(1.00)	(1.00)
2. Live stock		1242	936	1290	3592	3091	3796
	(a)	(1.00)	(0.75)	(1.04)	(1.00)	(0.86)	(1.06)
	(b)	(0.35)	(0.30)	(0.34)	(1.00)	(1.00)	(1.00)
3. Machinery,		111	63	118	821	126	1104
Tools and Transport	(a)	(1.00)	(0.57)	(1.06)	(1.00)	(0.15)	(1.34)
Equipment	(b)	(0.14)	(0.50)	(0.11)	(1.00)	(1.00)	(1.00)
4. Financial Assets		76	7	87	267	209	290
and Cash in Hand	(a)	(1.00)	(0.09)	(1.14)	(1.00)	(0.78)	(1.09)
	(b)	(0.28)	(0.03)	(0.30)	(1.00)	(1.00)	(1.00)
II. NON-PRODUCTIVE		3646	6705	3166	9774	8993	9986
ASSETS	(a)	(1.00)	(1.84)	(0.87)	(1.00)	(0.92)	(1.02)
	(b)	(0.37)	(0.75)	(0.32)	(1.00)	(1.00)	(1.00)
5. Building		2697	5747	2218	7577	6483	8022
	(a)	(1.00)	(2.13)	(0.82)	(1.00)	(0.86)	(1.06)
	(b)	(0.36)	(0.89)	(0.28)	(1.00)	(1.00)	(1.00)
6. Other assets		949	958	948	2197	2510	1964
(gold, silver,	(a)	(1.00)	(1.01)	(1.00)	(1.00)	(1.14)	(0.89)
utensils, etc.)	(b)	(0.43)	(0.38)	(0.48)	(1.00)	(1.00)	(1.00)
III. TOTAL		11566	10950	11648	38935	29914	42495
	(a)	(1.00)	(0.95)	(1.01)	(1.00)	(0.77)	(1.09)
	(b)	(0.30)	(0.37)	(0.27)	(1.00)	(1.00)	(1.00)

Note: (a) Ratio of zonal share to the overall.
(b) Ratio of size group to the average size within the same zone.

Source: Nepal Rastra Bank (1980), *Agricultural Credit Review Survey, Nepal*, Vol. I, Agricultural Credit Division, Kathmandu.

Table 2.19 Proportion of Holding of Assets by Farm Size and Territorial Zones (1976/77).

Assets / *Zones farm size*	*HILL*					*TERAI*									
	Average	*Large*	*Medium*	*Small*	*Margi-nal*	*Average*	*Large*	*Medium*	*Small*	*Margi-nal*	*Average*	*Large*	*Medium*	*Small*	*Margi-nal*
(1)	*(2)*	*(3)*	*(4)*	*(5)*	*(6)*	*(7)*	*(8)*	*(9)*	*(10)*	*(11)*	*(12)*	*(13)*	*(14)*	*(15)*	*(16)*
I. PRODUCTIVE ASSETS	69.94	77.59	64.87	53.29	38.77	76.50	75.88	73.81	79.77	67.53	74.9	76.68	71.94	76.91	68.44
1. Land	58.48	65.41	54.02	43.54	29.58	64.29	64.15	63.66	64.62	59.98	62.88	65.22	61.65	62.35	56.07
2. Livestock	10.34	10.81	10.17	8.85	8.55	8.93	5.76	7.73	13.52	5.82	9.22	7.34	8.24	13.02	10.75
3. Machinery, tools and transport equipments	0.42	0.36	0.42	0.69	0.58	2.60	4.65	1.48	1.24	1.01	2.11	3.31	1.26	1.18	0.96
4. Financial assets and Cash in hand	0.72	1.01	0.26	0.60	0.06	0.68	0.72	0.94	0.39	0.72	0.69	0.81	0.79	0.36	0.66
II. NON-PRODUCTIVE ASSETS	30.06	22.41	35.13	46.71	61.23	23.50	23.72	26.19	20.23	27.17	25.1	23.32	28.06	23.09	29.56
5. Building	21.67	14.23	26.15	38.48	52.48	18.88	19.32	21.99	15.35	19.04	19.46	17.74	22.86	17.85	23.34
6. Other assets (gold, silver, utensils, etc.)	8.39	8.18	8.98	8.23	8.75	4.62	4.40	4.20	4.88	8.13	5.64	5.58	5.20	5.24	6.22
III. TOTAL	100.00	100.00	100.00	100.00	100.00	100.00	100.00	100.00	100.00	100.00	100.00	100.00	100.00	100.00	100.00

Source: Nepal Rastra Bank (1980), *Agricultural Credit Review Survey Nepal*, Vol. I. Agricultural Credit Division, Kathmandu.

Table 2.20 Growth of Absolute Value of Assets (at Current Prices) Change in Proportion of Individual Asset to Total Assets (1976/77 Over 1969/70).

(%)

Zones	OVERALL								HILL		TERAI	
Assets Farm size	Large		Medium		Small		Average		Average		Average	
	(1)	(2)	(1)	(2)	(1)	(2)	(1)	(2)	(1)	(2)	(1)	(2)
(1)	(2)	(3)	(4)	(5)	(6)	(7)	(8)	(9)	(10)	(11)	(12)	(13)
I. PRODUCTIVE ASSETS	+56.83	–8.41	+81.76	–12.68	+121.20	–5.43	+108.96	–8.29	+74.02	–9.99	+118.27	–8.05
1. Land	+58.96	-6.18	+83.61	–10.08	+117.59	–5.49	+109.78	–6.69	+69.16	–10.28	+121.82	–5.62
2. Livestock	+95.18	-0.80	+117.38	+0.15	+186.56	+2.15	+153.98	+0.95	+194.38	+3.36	+144.90	+0.13
3. Machinery, tools and transport equipments.	+175.19	+1.22	+97.46	-0.10	+106.42	–0.16	+199.64	+0.48	+48.24	–0.14	+201.64	+0.52
4. Financial assets and Cash in hand	–72.00	–4.25	–50.88	–2.65	–55.72	–1.93	–57.21	–3.03	–61.65	–2.93	–50.19	–3.08
II. NON-PRODUCTIVE ASSETS	+172.10	+8.41	+287.96	+12.68	+202.01	+5.43	+246.72	+8.29	+197.88	+9.99	+266.73	+8.05
5. Building	+180.07	+6.72	+319.93	+11.23	+211.26	+4.59	+261.67	+6.97	+175.29	+6.01	+307.41	+7.71
6. Other assets (gold, silver, utensils, etc.)	+149.51	+1.69	190.74	+1.45	+175.68	+0.84	+203.45	+1.32	+278.01	+3.98	+160.48	+0.34
III. TOTAL	+74.01	±0.00	+113.62	±0.00	+137.30	±0.00	+132.12	±0.00	+98.88	±0.00	+141.22	±0.00

Note: 1. Growth of absolute value of assets (1976/77 over 1969/ 70).
2. Change in proportion of individual assets to total assets (difference in percentages for 1976/77 and 1969/70).

Source: Nepal Rastra Bank (1980), *Agricultural Credit Review Survey, Nepal,* Vol. I. Agricultural Credit Division, Kathmandu.

In the temporal frame, the observed growth trend for 1969/70–1976/77 [Table 2.20] is markedly higher for non-productive assets (+246.72%) than productive one (+108.96%); the identical pattern but with relatively slower rate for Hill (+197.88% for non-productive and +74.02% for productive assets) than for Terai (+266.73% for the former and +118.27% for the latter) being followed in the territorial dimension, and with respect to different farm-sizes. This differential growth rate has resulted in the decline in the share of productive components in the total assets (by –8.29 percentage points in average) and a corresponding rise in that of the non-productive ones over the seven years period. The most striking trend in the whole process is the decline in absolute value of financial assets and cash in hand, in all the area and for all the farm-sizes. The slower growth rate and decline in the proportion of productive assets compared to the unproductive one can be regarded as both the cause and effect of under development process operating in the Nepalese agricultural economy.

2.3.12 Distribution of Operational Land-Holding by Size-Class

The distribution pattern of operational land-holding by pre-determined size-classes is sought to be investigated here in a spatio-temporal frame to elicit information on trends of socio-economic differentiation taking place in the Nepalese society. It is also done in the belief that the physical extent of possession of this predominant material means of production in pre-capitalist societies can provide its possessor a decisive power to organise production in a determinate form.

It may be necessary to clarify at the outset that in view of the low reliability of absolute figures provided by the Sample Census of Agriculture undertaken in 1961 and 1971, the forthcoming analysis emanating from the same data base would be more useful for horizontal (spatial) comparison of the agricultural process than for the vertical (temporal) one. Hence, attempts would be made to cross-check the situation from other sources as well.

A glance at the distribution pattern of operational land-holding by relevant size-classes for 1961 and 1971 as presented in Tables 2.21 and 2.22 would suffice to bring out the low and declining level of possession of the vital means of production, land, by absolute value (the average size of holding per household was 1.09 hectare in 1961 and 0.96 hectare in 1971) and the considerable degree of vertical disparity within it (i.e. Gini Coefficient for 1971=0.624).

The decade of the 1960s having been marked by the introduction of the much-publicised government-sponsored 'land reform' programme of 1964, substantial changes would be expected in the distribution pattern of land holdings between 1961 and 1971. However, a comparative study of the relevant figures for the two points of time would establish that the marginal change in the overall distribution pattern of holdings (a slight decline in the Gini Coefficient from 0.644 in 1961 to 0.624 in 1971) and the discernible shift in the holding size towards the lower size (the share of farming population with less than 1 hectare of land increased from 73.89% to 76.77% of the total households and from 24.03% to 27.20% of total operated area during 1961 and 1971) may be more due to

Table 2.21 Distribution of Operational Land-Holdings by Size Classes and Territorial Zones (1961).

Territorial Zones		Size Classes of Land-holdings (hect.)								
		Landless	< 0.40	0.40–1.0	1–2	2–4	4–10	>10	>100	Total
1		2	3	4	5	6	7	8	9	10
MOUNTAIN	(i)	N.A.	N.A.	N.A.	N.A.	N.A.	N.A.	N.A.	N.A.	N.A.
	(ii)									
HILL	(i)	–	27.87	38.83	21.02	8.46	3.35	0.48	–	100.00
	(ii)	0.28	63.11	27.91	6.98	1.44	0.27	0.01	–	100.00
Eastern	(i)	–	23.34	37.00	24.41	10.63	4.12	0.50	–	100.00
	(ii)	0.15	58.57	29.71	9.11	2.06	0.38	0.02	–	100.00
Central	(i)	–	30.50	39.88	19.40	7.43	2.70	0.08	–	100.00
	(ii)	0.28	65.22	27.06	6.08	1.18	0.20	0.003	–	100.00
Western	(i)	–	31.36	40.26	17.88	6.45	3.02	1.03	–	100.00
	(ii)	0.46	66.00	26.78	5.50	1.02	0.23	0.02	–	100.00
KATHMANDU	(i)	–	25.24	48.78	19.99	5.10	0.90	–	–	100.00
VALLEY	(ii)	0.23	55.05	36.73	6.94	0.92	0.08	–	–	100.00
INNER TERAI	(i)	–	5.17	12.02	13.37	25.17	24.86	19.41	0.56	100.00
	(ii)	2.57	35.44	27.56	13.72	12.76	6.28	1.68	0.007	100.00
Eastern	(i)	–	10.86	16.82	14.27	25.72	20.56	11.77	–	100.00
	(ii)	0.34	51.39	25.54	9.63	9.00	3.40	0.71	–	100.00
Central	(i)	–	4.98	15.35	14.34	27.11	20.92	17.31	–	100.00
	(ii)	0.50	30.17	34.55	14.75	12.97	5.18	1.34	–	100.00
Western	(i)	–	0.80	3.61	11.33	22.11	33.66	28.46	1.77	100.00
	(ii)	13.09	10.52	14.17	20.60	21.00	15.80	4.79	0.04	100.00
TERAI	(i)	–	1.51	5.17	13.52	24.67	30.28	24.50	1.65	100.00
	(ii)	3.57	17.83	20.10	21.82	21.15	12.19	3.13	0.02	100.00
Eastern	(i)	–	1.98	6.14	13.87	27.29	31.46	19.37	0.81	100.00
	(ii)	3.59	20.39	19.94	20.69	21.26	11.75	2.39	0.01	100.00
Central	(i)	–	0.90	5.54	15.33	22.35	25.69	30.19	0.58	100.00
	(ii)	5.04	10.61	20.59	27.50	21.18	10.95	4.12	0.02	100.00
Western	(i)	–	0.28	3.52	7.41	13.15	30.03	45.61	7.931	100.00
	(ii)	2.62	6.08	20.87	21.49	19.91	19.97	9.05	0.14	100.00
NEPAL	(i)	–	8.81	15.22	15.37	20.31	22.62	17.67	1.13	100.00
	(ii)	1.43	47.97	25.92	11.72	7.84	4.10	1.02	0.007	100.00

Note: (I) Area; (II) Households.
Source: Central Bureau of Statistics, *Sample Census of Agriculture of Nepal*, 1961, Kathmandu.

Table 2.22 Distribution of Operational Land-Holdings by Size Classes and Territorial Zones (1971).

Territorial Zones		*Size Classes of Land-holdings (hect.)*								
		Landless	*< 0.4*	*0.4–1*	*1–2*	*2–4*	*4–10*	*>10*	*>100*	*Total*
(1)	*(2)*	*(3)*	*(4)*	*(5)*	*(6)*	*(7)*	*(8)*	*(9)*	*(10)*	*(11)*
MOUNTAIN	(i)	–	28.26	32.50	20.36	11.77	6.09	1.02	–	100.00
	(ii)	0.48	67.50	22.66	6.76	2.06	0.49	0.04	–	100.00
Eastern	(i)	–	24.63	36.67	21.24	9.80	5.82	1.79	–	100.00
	(ii)	0.32	59.80	29.13	8.17	1.95	0.55	0.07	–	100.00
Central	(i)	–	18.24	19.17	24.54	21.31	16.74	–	–	100.00
	(ii)	0.24	64.11	17.86	10.96	5.00	1.83	–	–	100.00
Western	(i)	–	35.97	28.66	18.11	12.91	4.35	–	–	100.00
	(ii)	0.68	76.16	16.29	4.76	1.84	0.27	–	–	100.00
HILL	(i)	–	43.05	34.87	13.93	4.52	1.91	1.72	–	100.00
	(ii)	0.20	76.10	19.34	3.60	0.60	0.12	0.03	–	100.00
Eastern	(i)	–	38.68	39.11	15.43	4.92	1.64	0.22	–	100.00
	(ii)	0.23	70.09	24.29	4.53	0.74	0.11	0.01	–	100.00
Central	(i)	–	44.84	32.90	12.83	4.13	1.77	3.53	–	100.00
	(ii)	0.20	78.58	17.42	3.11	0.53	0.11	0.05	–	100.00
Western	(i)	–	46.71	31.71	13.48	4.56	2.55	1.00	–	100.00
	(ii)	0.17	79.53	16.32	3.24	0.56	0.15	0.03	–	100.00
KATHMANDU	(i)	–	23.54	44.34	23.04	7.58	1.50	–	–	100.00
VALLEY	(ii)	1.24	53.75	35.10	8.36	1.42	0.13	–	–	100.00
INNER TERAI	(i)	–	6.89	14.46	21.54	23.62	21.63	11.87	–	100.00
	(ii)	1.36	37.82	26.23	18.53	10.53	4.58	0.93	–	100.00
Eastern	(i)	–	15.70	19.13	21.16	21.07	18.97	3.98	–	100.00
	(ii)	0.60	56.81	22.38	11.43	5.88	2.68	0.22	–	100.00

(*Contd.*)

(*Table 2.22 contd.*)

Central	(i)	–	7.70	21.02	30.07	24.50	12.15	4.56	–	100.00
	(ii)	0.39	33.44	31.97	22.12	9.51	2.25	0.29	–	100.00
Western	(i)	–	1.38	5.17	12.87	24.04	32.89	23.64	–	100.00
	(ii)	5.16	15.41	18.48	21.98	21.31	13.85	3.82	–	100.00
TERAI	(i)	–	2.44	7.75	17.43	27.75	28.03	16.60	0.35	100.00
	(ii)	1.72	21.57	21.65	23.40	20.00	9.52	2.09	0.003	100.00
Eastern	(i)	–	3.08	8.82	18.92	30.39	26.65	12.15	0.51	100.00
	(ii)	1.58	24.26	22.18	22.69	19.64	8.27	1.37	0.003	100.00
Central	(i)	–	1.77	8.12	18.84	27.02	25.79	18.46	–	100.00
	(ii)	1.62	16.53	23.36	26.71	20.47	8.92	2.39	–	100.00
Western	(i)	–	0.25	2.51	9.24	16.53	36.59	34.89	–	100.00
	(ii)	3.36	4.19	12.95	24.17	22.90	23.57	8.87	–	100.00
NEPAL	(i)	–	12.00	15.20	17.35	21.94	21.11	12.40	0.23	100.00
	(ii)	0.80	55.40	21.37	11.06	7.33	3.31	0.72	0.001	100.00

Note: (I) Area of Holdings.
(II) No. of Households.

Source: Central Bureau of Statistics, ***Sample Census of Agriculture of Nepal**, 1971*, Kathmandu.

absolute decline in the total availability of land per household than due to any structural change brought about by the cosmetic 'land reform'. Official circles themselves admit the nominal change in holding-size distribution due to "paper dispersal"[102] of ownership of excess land above ceiling[103] than as a result of genuine transfer. While others have cited the case of horizontal transfer of land amongst different factions of land-owning classes favoured and discriminated against by the political changes of 1951 and 1960,[104] without affecting the overall vertical composition of land-holding distribution. Apparently a more authentic report of the 'land reform evaluation advisor' deputed by the FAO[105] indicates a higher disparity in the ownership of land by size-classes (i.e. Gini Coefficient = 0.717); but the absolute value of average size of land-holdings provided [Table 2.23] may be grossly on the higher side because of the sampling bias in favour of the larger holdings.

In the territorial frame, the higher average size of holdings and greater disparity in their possession by size-classes (measured by Gini Coefficients, See Appendix 2) in Terai and Inner Terai than in Kathmandu Valley, Mountain and Hill can be expiained in terms of natural differences in land-man ratio and historical specificities of evolution of agrarian systems in different areas of the country as outlined previously. The least degree of social differentiation accompanied by the lowest average size of holdings found in the traditional habitation zones of central east-west territorial spine of the country i.e. the Hill, may be viewed as a typical manifestation of interactions between natural and social factors to operationalize underdevelopment through the perpetuation of a determinate backward social formation dominated by small peasant production. Almost uniform decline in the value of average size of holding and Gini coefficient of operational land holdings during 1961–1971, except in the Kathmandu Valley, may be taken as a reflection of negligible spatial veriation in the pace of economic differentiation taking place in the Nepalese society. On the contrary, this could be a mere statistical illusion precipitated by the faulty data base unable to capture the differential rate of change that should naturally go at least with the initial differences in the economic attributes of different spatial entities within the prevailing institutional frameworks that abet social and spatial inequality.

In sum, the low average size of holding, considerable vertical disparity in social distribution and negligible change over time provide a glimpse of the nature of stagnation of the backward agriculture sector under retrograde social dispensation.

2.3.2 Tenurial Conditions of Operational Land-Holding

Tenurial conditions of operational land-holdings and conjoint form of organisation of labour to effectuate production determine the principal mode of appropriation of social surplus in a predominantly agrarian economy, and hence the principal social relations of production. But in the absence of a systematic account of form of organization of labour in agricultural production, the prevailing social relations

Table 2.23 Territorial Distribution of Sample Household* and Area Owned After "Land Reform" by Size of Holding.

(%)

Size of Holding	*Kath. Valley*			*Eastern Terai*			*Western Terai*			*Eastern Hill*			*Western Hill*			*Overall*		
	H.H	*Area*	*Avg. size (hect.)*	*H.H.*	*Area*	*Avg. size (hect.)*	*H.H.*	*Area*	*Avg. size (hect.)*	*H.H.*	*Area*	*Avg. size (hect.)*	*H.H.*	*Area*	*Avg. size (hect.)*	*H.H.*	*Area*	*Avg. size (hect.)*
1 hect. (2.47 acre)	80.28	39.9	0.30	43.27	5.63	0.40	14.61	1.14	0.57	91.33	44.51	0.28	76.17	25.71	0.27	65.13	9.67	0.30
1–3 hectare (2.47–7.41 acre)	18.69	52.98	1.72	27.59	14.86	1.66	21.91	5.56	1.87	4.98	12.5	1.45	17.24	34.33	1.60	17.83	14.60	1.68
3–5 hectare (7.41–12.35 acre)	1.03	7.11	4.20	13.69	14.36	3.24	14.61	6.85	3.45	2.00	13.31	3.76	5.41	23.12	13.40	6.74	11.19	3.40
5–10 hectare (12.35–24.7 acre)	–	–	–	7.50	15.77	6.49	29.21	32.14	8.08	1.34	14.64	6.21	0.50	4.12	6.67	5.84	21.63	7.59
10–30 hectare (24.7–74.1 acre)	–	–	–	6.4	28.4	13.70	16.85	33.51	14.61	0.44	15.04	12.1	0.51	7.89	12.48	3.75	26.21	14.34
30 hectare and above (74.1 acre and above)	–	–	–	1.55	21.00	41.96	2.91	20.8	54.41	–	–	–	0.13	4.74	30.02	0.71	16.70	48.21
Total	100	100	0.61	100	100	3.09	100	100	N.A.	100	100	N.A.	100	100	0.80	100	100	2.05

Note: *The table excludes Tenant-Cultivator Households with no land ownership right and includes area belonging to Owner-cum Tenant households. But it also excludes area of land Rented in by this class.

Source: Zaman, M.A. (1973), *Evaluation of Land Reform in Nepal*, Ministry of Land Reforms, HMG/N, Kathmandu, pp. 93–94.

of production in the Nepalese space economy is sought to be broadly generalised with the help of an analysis of tenurial conditions of operational land-holdings and further disaggregation of the conditions of rented holdings.

2.3.21 Principal Forms of Land Tenure

Our earlier delineation of historical contours of evolution of agrarian structure in Nepal has clearly brought out the evolution of a countrywide uniform pattern of landownership as an alienable private property right under the overall de-jure sovereignty of the state (i.e. the *Raiker* system) by the decade of 1960s. Hence, except for *Guthi* land under institutional ownership of specified charitable trusts and religious bodies, which is invariably hired out to private cultivators but for which no authentic account is available for investigation, all the cultivable land in the country is either owner-cultivated for self-appropriation of the production or hired-out to tenant-cultivators to expropriate ground-rent, with the varying mixes of owner-cum-tenants in between. The conditions of rented tenure and actual form of organisation of production whether in self-owned or rented-in land, that constitute the real basis of appropriation of agricultural surplus shall be considered in the next sections after spatio-temporal variations in the principal forms of land tenure is analysed here.

The mysterious omission of the separate enumeration of non-cultivating land-owners, or landlords, in the Sample Census of Agriculture of both 1961 and 1971 has seriously hampered our study and limited it to the analysis of only owner-cultivators, owner-cum-tenants and tenant cultivators [Tables 2.24 and 2.25]. The glaring fact that 80.99% of total households with 73.65% of total area at an average rate of 0.88 hectare of land per household were enumerated as 'owner-cultivators' in 1971, speaks of the peculiar nature of general economy with a preponderance of subsistence peasantry. This poses serious dilemmas of characterisation of prevailing social formation to be woven around the determinate form of production, appropriation and utilization of social surplus, if one were to go only by the *quantitative* measures and outward *appearance* of the phenomenon without taking into consideration the non-quantifiable aspects and real *essence* of social relations as apprehended in Section 2.1.1. The sudden jump of this category of farming population from 59.64% in 1961 to 80.99% in 1971 with an addition of 21.35 percentage points in a decade marked by the official land reform programme of 1964 evokes serious doubts about the genuineness of the enumerated 'owner-cultivators'. Whereas certain degree of resumption of self-cultivation by the juridical owners in the aftermath of the much-publicised and populist 'land reforms' cannot be ruled out, much of the addition in the percentage of 'owner-cultivators' must be accounted to the forced or otherwise non-reporting or "voluntary surrender" of tenancy by the tenant-cultivators. This is further borne out by the more authentic land reform evaluation report, which cites a lower percentage of owner-cultivators (65.22%) and correspondingly higher ones for owner-cum-tenants (20.70%) and tenant-cultivators (10.77%) [Table 2.26]. Other estimates put 40% of the households and 30% of the area

Table 2.24 Distribution of Land-Holdings by Types of Tenure and Territorial Zones (1961).

(%)

Territorial Zones	Total		Types of Tenure: Owner-Cultivator		Tenant-Cultivator		Owner-cum-tenant Cultivator		
	HH	Area	HH	Area	HH	Area	HH	Area: Own	Area: Others
*MOUNTAIN	N.A.	N.A.	N.A.	NA	N.A.	N.A.	N.A.	N.A.	N.A.
HILL	100.00	100.00	65.62	56.56	2.95	2.19	31.43	27.56	13.68
Eastern	100.00	100.00	58.39	45.48	4.48	3.39	37.13	31.15	19.99
Central	100.00	100.00	74.41	67.04	1.28	0.97	24.30	23.75	8.24
Western	100.00	100.00	62.73	59.45	3.30	2.02	33.97	27.21	11.32
KATH. VALLEY	100.00	100.00	38.13	35.00	12.19	7.51	49.61	27.64	29.85
INNER TERAI	100.00	100.00	71.34	59.56	10.52	14.43	18.14	16.12	9.89
Eastern	100.00	100.00	74.79	50.89	3.97	3.91	21.24	27.39	17.81
Central	100.00	100.00	78.34	73.67	5.71	4.21	15.95	15.12	7.00
Western	100.00	100.00	41.49	47.64	42.21	36.77	16.30	8.27	7.32
TERAI	100.00	100.00	47.40	49.58	15.00	12.25	37.60	21.42	16.76
Eastern	100.00	100.00	51.04	48.24	9.93	10.06	39.03	23.38	18.32
Central	100.00	100.00	37.36	57.10	35.17	18.76	27.48	14.45	9.69
Western	100.00	100.00	30.00	46.66	25.59	15.56	44.40	20.10	17.68
NEPAL	100.00	100.00	59.64	51.84	7.17	9.79	33.19	22.64	15.72

Note: *Mountain is included in Hill.

Source: Central Bureau of Statistics, *Sample Census of Agriculture of Nepal, 1961*, Kathmandu.

Table 2.25 Distribution of Land-Holdings by Types of Tenure and Territorial Zones (1971).

(%)

Territorial Zones	Total		Types of Tenure						
			Owner-Cultivator		Tenant-Cultivator		Owner-cum-tenant Cultivator		
	HH	Area	HH	Area	HH	Area	HH	Area	
								Own	Others
MOUNTAIN	100.00	100.00	82.00	76.50	2.30	1.56	15.62	13.91	8.02
Eastern	100.00	100.00	77.50	72.10	3.39	2.28	19.11	14.87	10.75
Central	100.00	100.00	91.00	84.99	0.66	0.48	8.32	9.86	4.66
Western	100.00	100.00	85.76	81.69	1.33	0.65	12.75	13.23	4.40
HILL	100.00	100.00	89.32	84.26	1.03	0.67	9.63	9.74	5.68
Eastern	100.00	100.00	81.64	75.60	1.89	1.28	16.47	14.6	9.65
Central	100.00	100.00	93.78	89.50	0.45	0.20	5.71	7.20	3.10
Western	100.00	100.00	91.55	88.60	0.90	0.50	7.55	6.80	4.50
KATHMANDU VALLEY	100.00	100.00	54.27	58.19	19.96	12.89	25.77	15.84	13.09
INNER TERAI	100.00	100.00	88.88	81.22	5.35	8.66	5.95	5.27	4.96
Eastern	100.00	100.00	90.27	78.65	1.83	2.05	8.42	11.13	8.69
Central	100.00	100.00	96.61	96.56	1.04	0.84	2.35	1.50	1.10
Western	100.00	100.00	65.72	66.63	23.32	20.27	10.95	6.09	7.01
TERAI	100.00	100.00	68.59	69.96	8.46	7.99	22.95	11.18	10.87
Eastern	100.00	100.00	65.30	64.84	8.68	9.08	26.02	12.95	13.14
Central	100.00	100.00	84.72	88.00	5.31	3.00	9.97	5.11	3.88
Western	100.00	100.00	69.80	74.65	12.69	8.16	17.51	9.40	7.79
NEPAL	100.00	100.00	80.99	73.65	4.38	6.48	14.61	10.62	9.32

Source: Central Bureau of Statistics, *Sample Census of Agriculture of Nepal, 1971*, Kathmandu.

under tenant-cultivators and owner-cum-tenants after the 'land reform' against a staggering 60% each of households and area before it.[106] Another unpalatable reality is that 3.1% of the households reported as landlords corner 26.91% of the total cultivated area with an average holding size of 18.33 hectares per household against an average holding size per household of 1.67, 1.64 and 1.74 hectares respectively for owner-cultivator, owner-cum-tenant and tenant-cultivators [Table 2.26]. This provides a useful indication of the relative position of domination of different land tenure types in the economy of the country.

The unbelievably high percentage (66.17%) of holdings reported by landlords as personally cultivated[107] puts the actual position of landlords in some doubt. But the fact that this percentage is much higher for remoter areas like western Terai (84.14%), western Hill (81.53%) and eastern Hill (46.89%) where the hegemony of the landlords over the tenants would be expectedly more articulated, than in more integrated and 'open' Kathmandu Valley (14.32%) and eastern Terai (28.35%), where the tenants would enjoy a better bargaining position, amply demonstrates the doubtful nature of such reporting.

The scenario in 1971 in the horizontal dimension expectedly displays a distinct higher share of rented tenure (tenant-cultivators plus owner-cum-tenants) in Kathmandu Valley (25.98% of area and 45.73% of households), Terai (18.86% of area and 31.41% of houscholds) and Inner Terai (13.62% of area and 11.30% of households) compared to Mountain (9.58% of area and 17.93% of households) and Hill (6.34% of area and 10.66% households) and vice versa for owner-cultivators. An identical pattern prevailed in 1961 but with substantially higher share of rented tenure in all areas. In the east-west dimension of the same ecological zone, a discernably higher percentage of rented tenure prevailed in the eastern and western sections compared to the central one; thus giving the highest percentages of rented areas for 1971 in western Inner Terai (27.28%), eastern Terai (22.22%) and western Terai (15.95%), with an obvious exception of Kathmandu Valley (25.98%). If the extent of rented tenure is to be accepted as a proxy indicator for 'detribalisation' or development of 'feudalism'[108] then the prevailing spatial pattern of areas of better agro-climatic conditions (e.g. Terai, Kathmandu Valley and Inner Terai) and away from the central state authority (e.g. western and eastern sections) exhibiting higher degree of feudalisation fully conforms to the Marxist theoretical position on the question and the historical sequence of evolution of the agrarian process as outlined previously. As regards the expected inverse relations between land-man ratio and rentability of land,[109] the normal pattern seems to have been offset in Nepal because of the peculiar historical specificities of areas of lesser agronomic capacities and harsher physiographic conditions (i.e. Hill) having been subjected to earlier colonisation and constituted the principal zones of habitation till recent history.

2.3.22 Conditions of Rented Tenure

Even when the extent of renting of land by itself cannot be a criterion in characterising a social mode of production in agriculture, the conditions of

Table 2.26 Land Tenure Distribution After 'Land Reform'.

Land Tenure Group	*% of Households*		*% of Cultivated Area*	*Average Size of Holding (hect.)*
	Total Households	*Households with Land Holdings*		
I. With Land Holdings	92.2	100.00	100.00	–
1. Land lords	1.8	3.31	26.91	18.33
2. Owner-Cultivators	62.0	65.22	49.11	1.67
3. Owner-cum-Tenants	19.1	20.70	15.36	1.64
4. Tenant-Cultivators	2.3	10.77	8.62	1.74
II. Landless (including non-agricultural population)	7.8	–	–	–
TOTAL	100.00	100.00	100.00	100.00

Source: Compiled from Zaman, M.A. (1973), *Evaluation of Land Reform in Nepal*, HMG/N, Ministry of Land Reforms, Kathmandu.

renting or forms of realisation of ground-rent by the landowner, can provide valuable insight into it. However, as already cautioned, the possibility of existence of identical rental forms under different modes of production should not be ruled out, and the conditions of rented tenure ought to be viewed in the broader historical perspective and a logical conceptual frame.

Tables 2.27 and 2.28 provide the distribution pattern of various types of rented tenure of land in the space economy of Nepal for 1961 and 1971. In the countrywide plane a preponderance of share-cropping tenancy (i.e. 60.78% of total rented area in 1961 and 64.53% in 1971) is evident. In view of the raging debate[110] on the possibility of existence of share-cropping tenancy under different historical stages of organisation of production, on the one hand, and the lack of sharing adequate recorded information on the terms and conditions of crop-sharing and input-sharing arrangements by size of holdings, on the other, it may not be easy to socially characterise the existing tenancy form in the country. However, when the historical legacy of general backwardness in Nepalese agriculture is matched with the generally known pattern of excessive rent[111] to be paid to the landowner without his having made any contribution in production by way of input-sharing etc., and the no known evidence of 'reverse tenancy',[112] the retrograde pre-capitalist nature of share-cropping tenancy is not hard to generalise. On the other hand, the increase in the share of cultivated area under share-cropping during 1961–71 and the higher proportion of area under this tenancy in the generally more advanced Terai and Inner Terai than in the backward Hill and Mountain can tempt one to suspect whether the tenancy relation belongs to a higher historical organisation of production. This can be discounted at first hand when the general labour scarcity in the former areas due to historically-determined low man-land ratio there and higher labour demand for rice-cultivation (the predominant crop there), is realised. On further probing when the falsity of higher percentage of supposedly better form of fixed-rent tenancy (both in money and in-kind) in the more secluded and backward Hill and Mountain, specially the remotest western part, is traced to historical reasons [see Section 2.1.2 above] and the historical possibility of commutation of more retrograde form of labour services into money-rent to intensify exploitation of cultivators through additional debt-bondage under the same social form of production is recollected,[113] the grounds for doubting the precapitalist nature of share-cropping tenancy get considerably weakened.

The high proportions of tenancy under mortgage conditions in Mountain and Hill, specially the western and eastern sections, further confirm the apprehensions about the retrograde nature of money-rent prevailing in those areas. When this reactionary cash-nexus is linked with the high rate of labour out-migration from these areas for petty cash remittances,[114] the social implications usually associated with these various tenancy types get really blurred in the context of Nepal. Here 'forms' of different social relations tend to masquerade in a

Table 2.27 Distribution of Rented Holdings by Conditions of Tenure and Territorial Zones (1961).

(%)

Territorial Zones	Rented Holdings as % of total Holdings		Conditions of Tenure of Rented Holdings (% of area)				
	H.H.*	Area	Total	Fixed Rent	Mortgage	Crop-sharing	Exchange for Services
MOUNTAIN	N.A.	N.A.	N.A.	N.A.	N.A.	N.A.	N.A.
HILL	34.38	15.88	100.00	28.72	50.51	18.43	2.33
Eastern	41.61	23.38	100.00	48.65	35.57	14.95	0.83
Central	25.59	9.21	100.00	39.72	28.38	29.53	2.36
Western	37.27	13.34	100.00	9.97	66.20	17.37	6.46
KATHMANDU VALLEY	61.87	37.36	100.00	95.76	1.69	1.60	0.95
INNER TERAI	28.66	24.32	100.00	29.11	2.39	62.69	5.79
Eastern	25.21	21.72	100.00	22.57	4.20	72.34	0.89
Central	21.66	11.21	100.00	16.39	4.86	64.23	14.51
Western	58.51	43.05	100.00	36.96	0.84	59.72	4.89
TERAI	52.60	28.99	100.00	23.16	2.98	71.47	2.40
Eastern	48.96	28.38	100.00	13.96	3.03	81.86	1.16
Central	62.64	28.44	100.00	75.04	2.93	20.61	1.45
Western	70.00	33.34	100.00	5.77	2.82	81.92	9.49
NEPAL	40.36	25.51	100.00	26.11	10.37	60.72	2.59

Note: * Mountain is included in Hill.

** Renting households include both Tenant-cultivators and Owner-cum-Tenant cultivators.

Source: Central Bureau of Statistics, *Sample Census of Agriculture of Nepal, 1961*, Kathmandu.

Table 2.28 Distribution of Rented Holdings by Conditions of Tenure and Territorial Zones (1971).

(%)

Territorial Zones	Rented Holdings as % of total Holdings		Conditions of Tenure of Rented Holdings (% of area)							
				Fixed Rent						
	HH*	Area	Total	Money	Others	Total	Mortgage	Crop sharing	Exchange for Services	Others
MOUNTAIN	17.93	9.58	100.00	11.78	18.53	30.31	29.27	36.20	1.01	3.00
Eastern	22.5	13.03	100.00	12.62	19.12	31.74	18.98	45.97	0.76	2.55
Central	8.99	5.14	100.00	2.15	83.52	85.67	5.44	8.07	–	0.81
Western	14.08	5.05	100.00	10.35	2.65	13.00	76.99	2.58	2.24	5.28
HILL	10.66	6.34	100.00	12.51	18.59	31.10	26.31	35.15	2.38	5.13
Eastern	18.36	10.94	100.00	14.08	24.01	38.09	23.37	34.70	1.01	2.82
Central	6.18	3.30	100.00	10.79	13.52	24.31	21.23	47.18	2.21	5.07
Western	8.44	4.60	100.00	8.91	5.32	14.23	42.65	22.28	7.41	13.42
KATHMANDU VALLEY	45.72	25.98	100.00	18.94	77.60	96.54	0.19	2.10	0.16	1.00
INNER TERAI	11.30	13.62	100.00	10.15	2.74	12.89	0.39	84.55	0.31	1.72
Eastern	10.25	10.74	100.00	5.78	5.43	11.21	0.20	87.10	0.08	1.41
Central	3.38	1.94	100.00	17.22	11.80	29.02	3.69	57.38	0.67	9.24
Western	34.28	27.28	100.00	10.55	1.51	12.06	0.18	86.20	0.34	1.23
TERAI	31.14	18.86	100.00	10.29	11.81	22.10	0.58	70.24	0.99	6.22
Eastern	30.70	22.22	100.00	11.30	11.23	22.53	0.31	73.18	0.69	3.29
Central	15.28	6.89	100.00	10.78	6.32	17.10	4.02	30.62	3.30	44.95
Western	30.20	15.95	100.00	4.14	12.26	16.40	0.74	75.15	1.63	6.07
NEPAL	19.00	15.80	100.00	10.75	13.39	24.14	3.24	66.17	0.99	5.42

Note: *Households include both Tenant-cultivators and Owner-cum-Tenant cultivators.

Source: Central Bureau of Statistics, *Sample Census of Agriculture of Nepal, 1971*, Kathmandu.

misleading fashion without any concurrence with the 'essence' they are supposed to manifest. Only the negligible and declining extent of labour-service tenancy in all the territorial units of the country may imply non-existence or modification of 'classical' feudal relations in the Nepalese agriculture. Also consistently the high proportion of fixed-rent tenancy in Kathmandu Valley (95.76% and 96.54% in 1961 and 1971 respectively) can be matched with the prevailing favourable productivity conditions there to regard it as the manifestation of a higher relation of production.

Thus, in the absence of a more systematic analysis of rented tenure by farm sizes in a wider spatio-temporal frame, the general picture of social relations of production in the Nepalese agriculture to be surmised from this cursory study is the prevalence of backward pre-capitalist (i.e. presumably semi-feudal) relations with little spatio-temporal variations.

2.3.23 Labour Relations in Production

As noted earlier, the actual mode of organisation of labour in production or the determinate mode of appropriation of surplus labour from the direct producer constitutes the essence of social relations of production and hence the social mode of production; of course, setting aside the rare specificities like use of slave labour in essentially a capitalist mode of production, etc. But again, the virtual absence of any inventory on the form of labour use in agricultural production in Nepal has forced us to take recourse to drawing implied inferences from fragmentary information on the subject.

From the analysis, of distribution of size-classes and tenurial conditions of operational land-holdings, it has been established that the principal mode of organisation of labour in agricultural production in Nepal has been the petty 'peasant proprietorship', or a form of 'self-exploitation in a small family enterprise'. But as hammered upon during the theoretical discussions earlier, the core issue in the analysis of the dynamics of a social process in class society consists in understanding the mode of appropriation and utilisation of *surplus labour*, howsoever, marginal it may appear quantitatively. We would, therefore, be more interested in knowing the nature of labour relations in production involving 'outside' labour other than the family labour.

Starting with the total labour involved in 'outside' relation, the only information available on the form of labour use in agriculture is in terms of the 'non-cultivators' as against the actual cultivators. If this is to be taken as the measure of 'free' (in the real sense) labour, which should be a gross underestimate, its role in the social organisation of production is obviously insignificant. However, taking the entire landless households (Table 2.29) as sellers of labour power and another 76.77% of households with less than 1 hectare of land [Table 2.22] as partial sellers of labour power, the size of labour power available for sale gets quite inflated. But the real question is about the extent and mode of utilisation of this potential labour power in production.

The middle owner-or tenant-cultivators are generally known to consume their own labour power with occasional hiring of others on reciprocal basis or through outright purchase.[115] Only the big land-owners display in their mode of organisation of labour for production certain variations commensurate with the differing land-labour ratios and the level of development of the productive forces in agriculture. On the basis of a number of micro-level studies[116] and our own personal acquaintances of different areas, it can be safely deduced that a type of servile attached-labour system, whether on a legal contract for a stipulated time against a fixed wage in cash or kind (e.g. the *kamaiya* system[117] in large parts of Terai and Inner Terai) or through debt bondage or other extra-economic coercions, constitutes the predominant form of extraction of surplus labour from the direct producer other than the small tenant-cultivator. However, in areas of greater development of communications and availability of landless or migrant labour, from within or outside the country, an increasing practice of wage labour use is discernible over the years. This is specifically true for the Terai region, where migrant labour mostly from the neighbouring areas of India is hired during the peak seasons.

Looking at the available statistics in the territorial frame, the higher shares of both landless households [Table 2.29] and large land-owners [Tables 2.21 and 2.22] in Terai and Inner Terai, should provide a better objective basis for these areas to develop a higher (i.e. capitalistic) form of organisation of labour in agricultural production. Same should be the implication of the higher proportion, though negligible in absolute sense, of 'non-cultivators' [Table 2.29] in these areas, and also in the Kathmandu Valley. But this is significant only in the relative sense of inter-regional variation. In the absolute sense, the use of wage labour in agricultural production is negligible to make a difference in the mode of production.

The backward labour relations in agriculture is seen aided by non-release of surplus labour from the agriculture sector, which is manifested in significant degree of unemployment and extremely high degree of underemployment in rural areas.[118] Also, though no systematic statistical information is available to empirically verify the contention, it can be reasonably assumed that the significant scale of seasonal or otherwise outmigration[119] of semi-proletarianised peasants from hilly areas of Nepal mostly to Indian cities for supplanting meagre family income from non-economical peasant holdings, has retarded the process of differentiation of the peasantry and reproduced archaic relations of production in the Nepalese agriculture.[120]

2.3.24 Spatial Pattern of Social Differentiation in Agriculture

To get a combined picture of the extent of social differentiation at the level of social relations of production by spatial units, Gini coefficients of operational land-holding (1971) were cross-classified with the area under rented tenure (1971) [See Appendix-2] to generate the following table:

Table 2.29 Distribution of Landless Households and Non-cultivators* by Territorial Zones.

Territorial Zones	*Landless Households*						*No. of Non-cultivator per 100 thousand of Agricultural Labour force (1971)*
	1961			*1971*			
	No.	*%²*	*L.Q.*	*No.*	*%²*	*L.Q.*	
MOUNTAIN	N.A.	N.A.	N.A.	148	0.48	0.60	3
Eastern	N.A.	N.A.	N.A.	245	0.32	0.40	4
Central	N.A.	N.A.	N.A.	20	0.24	0.30	0
Western	N.A.	N.A.	N.A.	483	0.68	0.85	2
HILL	2657	0.28	0.20	1757	0.20	0.25	9
Eastern	491	0.15	0.10	637	0.23	0.29	13
Central	986	0.28	0.20	742	0.20	0.25	8
Western	1180	0.46	0.32	378	0.17	0.21	5
KATHMANDU VALLEY	129	0.23	0.16	812	1.24	1.55	142
INNER TERAI	2115	2.57	1.80	1428	1.36	1.70	31
Eastern	109	0.34	0.24	210	0.60	0.75	7
Central	179	0.50	0.35	196	0.39	0.49	43
Westran	1827	13.09	9.15	1022	5.16	6.45	42
TERAI	17051	3.75	2.62	9107	1.72	2.15	27
Eastern	12573	3.59	2.51	6468	1.58	1.98	30
Central	3651	5.04	3.52	1302	1.62	2.03	18
Westran	827	2.62	1.83	1337	3.36	4.20	21
NEPAL	21952	1.43	1.00	13852	0.80	1.00	19

Note: * Non-cultivators among agricultural labour force include: Professional/Technical workers, Administrative workers, Clerical workers, Sales workers, Service workers and Production/Labour workers, according to the census definition of 1971.

** % Refers to that of the total households in the respective zones. For 1961 Landless households in Mountain are included in the Hill.

Source: Central Bureau of Statistics, *Sample Census of Agriculture of Nepal*, 1961 and 1971 and *Population Census*, 1971, Kathmandu.

Table 2.30 Gini Coefficient of Operational Land-holdings (1971) Cross-classified with % of Area under Rented Tenure (1971).

% of Area under Rented Tenure (1971)	*Gini Coefficient of Land-holdings (1971)*		
	High (> 0.500)	*Medium (0.400–0.499) (Territorial Zones)*	*Low (< 0.399)*
High (> 20%)	Western Inner Terai, Eastern Terai (1)		Kathmandu Valley
Medium (10–20%)	Eastern Inner Terai Western Terai	Eastern Mountain (2)	Eastern Hill
Low (< 10%)	Central Mountain Central Terai	Western Mountain, Central Inner Terai	Central Hill Western Hill (3)

The above cross-classification may be interpreted as follows:

Category	*Definition*	*Spatial units*
1. High	With high value for one indicator and not less than medium in another	Western Inner Terai; Eastern Terai; Eastern Inner Terai; Western Terai
2. Medium	With not less than medium value for both, excluding High	Kathmandu Valley; Eastern Mountain; Central Mountain; Central Terai
3. Low	Other than High and Medium	Eastern Hill; Western Mountain; Central Inner Terai; Central Hill; Western Hill

The spatial pattern of the degree of social differentiation obtained from the above bivariate analysis is plotted in Fig. 2.6 from which the following observations can be made:

- Areas of abundance of agricultural land and away from the central state authority exhibit highest degree of social differentiation.
- All the Hill areas are marked by low social differentiation. This may be due to the prevalence of small parcellized landed property which does not favour consolidation of land and socialisation of production.
- Even if the nature of the level of differentiation cannot be ascertained whether progressive or retrograde without incorporating the conditions of rented tenure in the analysis, higher social differentiation should generally provide an objective basis for organisation of production on higher technical basis. Hence, Terai and Inner Terai logically appear to be more ripened for restructuring social organisation of production in agriculture.

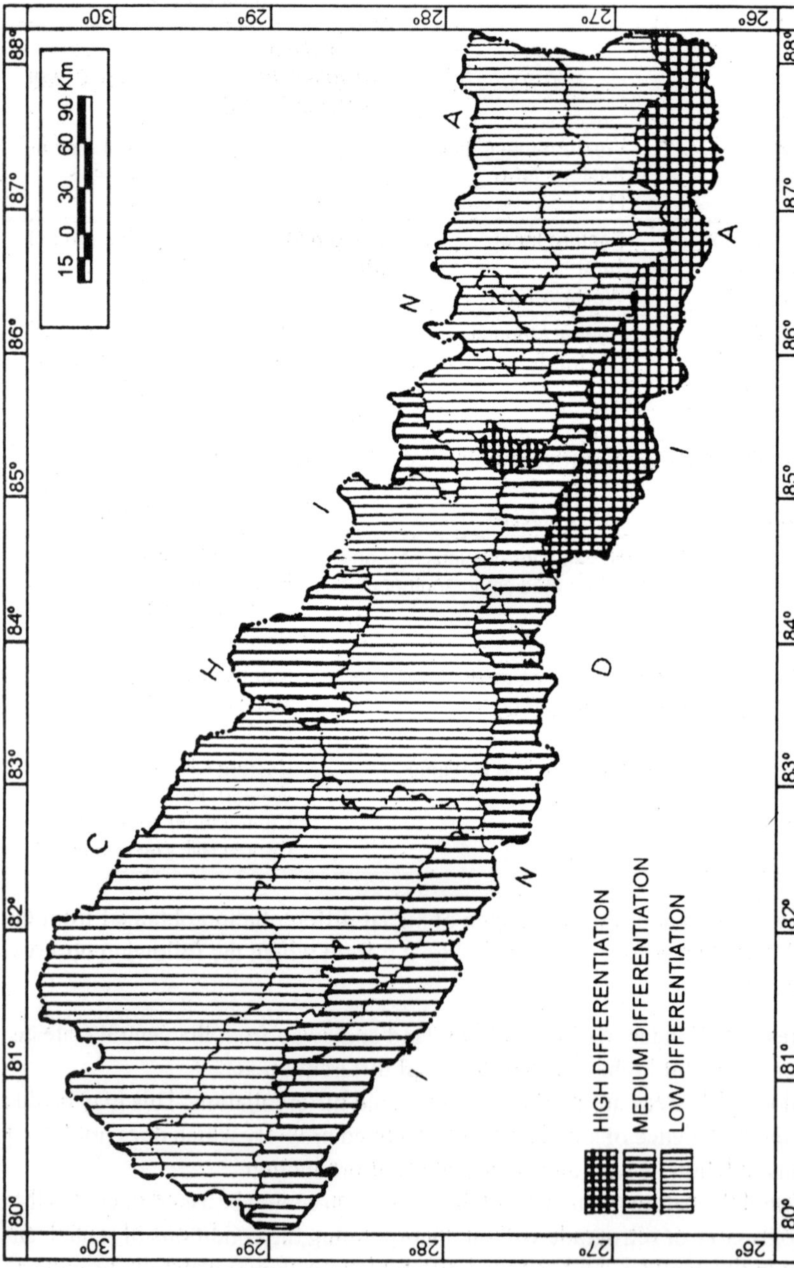

Fig. 2.6 Gini Coefficient of Operational Land-Holding Cross-Classified by Percentage of Area under Rented Tenure

2.3.3 Auxiliary Mechanisms of Appropriation of Social Surplus in Agriculture

Apart from the principal mechanism of surplus appropriation in agricultural production as pre-capitalist ground-rent, other auxiliary modes operating in Nepalese society include direct state taxation (direct extraction as land revenue and various 'development' taxes, and indirect extraction as 'deed registration fee', etc.), interest payment to various credit agencies and transfer of value through unequal terms of trade with other branches of production (both within and outside the national economy).

2.3.31 As already observed in Chapter I, in spite of land acquiring the juridical status of property of the state, the relative importance of social surplus appropriated from the primary production sector (mostly agriculture, and that too, cropping) has gradually declined in the total share of state revenue over the years. Also the fact that the proportion of agricultural surplus directly appropriated by the state constitutes a negligible share of total produce (i.e. less than 1% of gross value of produce as 'direct' extraction and less than 2% of it as 'indirect' extraction) makes the role of this aspect of social relation less significant in the structuration of overall process of under-development in Nepal. The discernible spatial variation in the ratio of percentage share of land revenue and gross value of agricultural production (i.e higher in Terai and Inner Terai than in Hill and Mountain) also appears not significantly inconsistent with the spatial differences in social productivity.

2.3.32 The transfer of value from agricultural production through market relations, within the agriculture sector (i.e. between different social classes and different spatial units) and outside the sector, should constitute an important dimension of social relations of production. But the generally known prevalence of use-value production, and absence of reliable quantitative inventory of marketed surplus and terms of trade has rendered our venture into the analysis of the phenomenon less meaningful and difficult. Hence, to avoid duplicity of efforts this aspect would be dealt within the relevant sections of trade relations in Chapter IV. However, it would be necessary to introduce at this stage the adverse market position of agricultural output vis-a-vis the inputs originating in the industrial sector, that too of the metropolitan economy; thereby illustrating the mechanism of surplus drain out of the primary production sector to an alien economy. Table 2.31 provides the fluctuations in the prices of chemical fertilizers (all of which are imported) and grains and their terms of trade over the years. It is abundantly clear that the terms of trade are turning against the agriculture sector, more markedly with respect to the predominant crop paddy.

2.3.33 Role of Credit Agencies

Whereas debt-bondage of peasantry through usurious money-lending has been one of the prominent universal practices of exploitation under pre-capitalist

Table 2.31 Terms of Trade Between Agricultural Inputs and Outputs.

Year	Output Price Index (O_i)		Inputs (Fertilizers) Price Index (I_i)			Terms of Trade ($O_i/I_i \times 100$)	
	Paddy	Wheat	A. Sulphare	Urea	Complex	Paddy vs Urea	Wheat vs Urea
1970/71	100.0	100.0	100.0	100.0	100.0	100.0	100.0
1971/72	111.9	115.3	117.6	114.4	147.3	97.8	100.8
1972/73	131.0	159.0	117.6	114.4	147.3	114.5	139.0
1973/74	139.7	171.5	195.1	163.4	209.5	85.4	105.0
1974/75	134.1	216.0	195.1	163.4	209.5	82.1	132.2
1975/76	138.1	174.3	220.0	181.8	214.8	76.0	95.9
1976/77	126.2	150.7	220.0	181.8	214.8	69.4	82.9
1977/78	152.4	170.8	220.0	181.8	214.8	83.8	93.9
1978/79	157.9	180.6	220.0	181.8	214.8	86.9	99.4
1979/80	153.2	189.6	231.8	181.8	214.8	84.3	104.4
1980/81	203.2	213.2	282.4	231.0	264.9	88.0	92.3

Source: Agriculture Inputs Corporation (1983), *Basic Statistics of Agriculture Inputs in Nepal*, Kathmandu.

relations, the arch-reactionary role of usury capital to perpetuate various retrograde production relations in the countryside, specially semi-feudalism, has been well documented by now.[121] To examine this important relation in the Nepalese agrarian economy, in the absence of a systematic micro-level account of the phenomenon the Agricultural Credit Survey and Review Survey conducted by Nepal Rastra Bank in 1969/70 and 1976/77 respectively have formed the data base of our study. It may again be reiterated at the outset that because the Survey were conducted in only the "accessible" and hence more well-off areas, the picture presented here would be brighter than the actually existing one in the country as a whole.

A cursory glance through Tables 2.32 to 2.34 and Agricultural Credit Review Survey reports should immediately bring out the enormous extent of indebtedness amongst the farming households (i.e. 62.29% of all families in 1976/77), high proportion of debt to the value of gross produce (i.e. 14.46% for all families in 1976/77) and greater grip of private agencies in extending credit (i.e. 75.98% of all borrowers borrowed from private agencies in 1976/77) and enforcing indebtedness (i.e. 58.94% of all debtors were indebted to private creditors in 1976/77). In the temporal frame, though the extent of indebtedness seems to have decreased by 2.9 percentage points over the seven years period the total amount of debt as proportion of the value of gross produce has correspondingly increased by 0.51 percentage points.

In terms of the farm-size class, of all the borrowing families the small, medium and large farm households constituted 64.45%, 16.67% and 18.88% respectively. The retrograde nature of credit, exercising the highest pressure on the small peasants becomes evident from the fact that the small and medium farm households were forced to borrow 42.57% and 56.43% respectively of the total

Table 2.32 Proportion of Indebted Farm Families by Size Group (1969/70 and 1976/77).

(%)

Zones	All Families		Large		Medium		Small	
	1969/70	*1976/77*	*1969/70*	*1976/77*	*1969/70*	*1976/77*	*1969/70*	*1976/77*
HILL	69.02	61.41	51.47	80.18	64.38	55.50	73.20	44.41
Terai	63.33	62.65	45.56	69.13	62.14	62.79	66.69	61.90
Overall	65.19	62.29	47.47	76.37	62.91	59.91	68.85	59.08

Source: Nepal Rastra Bank (1980), *Agricultural Credit Review Survey*, Vol. I, Agricultural Banking and Credit Division, Kathmandu.

Table 2.33 Proportion of Debt to the Value of Gross Produce by Size Group (1969/70 and 1976/77).

(%)

Zones Size Group	All Families		Large		Medium		Small	
	1969/70	*1976/77*	*1969/70*	*1976/77*	*1969/70*	*1976/77*	*1969/70*	*1976/77*
HILL	33.10	17.14	27.10	14.94	27.94	22.11	39.61	21.76
Terai	8.68	13.85	6.14	17.62	7.34	9.89	12.37	13.08
Overall	13.95	14.46	10.10	16.76	11.08	11.56	19.58	13.72

Source: Nepal Rastra Bank (1980), *Agricultural Credit Review Survey*, Vol. I, Agricultural Banking and Credit Division, Kathmandu.

Table 2.34 Proportion of Outstanding Debt of Farm Families to Different Credit Agencies–by Farm Size and Territorial Zones (1969/70 and 1976/77).

(%)

Zones	Overall								Hill		Terai	
Farm size	Large		Medium		Small		All Families		All Families		All Families	
Credit Agency	1969/70	1976/77	1969/70	1976/77	1969/70	1976/77	1969/70	1976/77	1969/70	1976/77	1969/70	1976/77
I. INSTITUTIONAL	33.65	66.40	15.63	27.20	10.74	17.79	16.99	41.06	3.51	26.07	44.70	45.28
1. Corperatives, Sajha institutions and local bodies	10.37	7.58	12.17	7.80	9.15	6.84	10.07	7.15	2.98	3.72	14.90	8.10
2. Agricultural Development Bank	19.00	50.52	0.24	12.10	0.20	8.33	4.50	27.95	–	16.81	28.65	31.11
3. Commercial Banks	4.28	8.80	3.22	7.30	1.39	2.62	2.42	5.96	0.53	5.54	1.15	6.07
II. PRIVATE	66.35	33.60	84.37	72.80	89.26	82.21	83.09	58.94	96.49	73.93	55.30	54.72
4. Village and Professional money lenders	30.13	20.48	34.13	41.16	50.69	30.50	42.56	29.34	49.79	46.31	29.81	24.53
5. Landlords	7.44	1.67	4.30	1.72	3.18	3.24	4.51	2.19	0.53	3.55	4.80	1.81
6. Agricultural Traders	2.29	2.89	2.98	4.80	1.79	7.71	2.11	4.97	0.85	5.19	6.95	4.90
7. Friends and relatives and others	26.49	8.56	42.96	25.12	33.60	40.75	33.83	22.44	45.32	18.88	13.74	23.48
TOTAL	100.00	100.00	100.00	100.00	100.00	100.00	100.00	100.00	100.00	100.00	100.00	100.00

Source: Nepal Rastra Bank (1980), *Agricultural Credit Review Survey, Nepal,* Vol. I, Agricultural Banking and Credit Division, Kathmandu.

amount for 'consumption expenditure' against 16.18% by the large ones. The higher and increasing proportion of large farm families indebted against the lower and decreasing proportion of medium and small ones, however, may be explained in terms of the more progressive role of credit to the larger farms, as indicated by the excessively high percentage of debt of large farms, having got settled with 'institutional' or public agencies (i.e. 66.40% of outstanding debt in 1976/77) compared to a similarly high proportion of indebtedness of medium and small peasants to private agencies (i.e. 72.80% and 82.2% respectively of outstanding debt in 1976/77). Moreover, the greater degree of indebtedness of small and medium farm households to different moneylenders, landlords and agricultural traders (i.e 41.45% and 47.68% respectively of outstanding debt in 1976/77), who charge enormously usurious interest rated ranging from 100% to 150% against the institutional rates of 8–18%,[122] further confirms the greater burden of usury capital borne out by small and medium peasants.

Spatially, we observe that in 1976/77 the degree of indebtedness is greater among large farm households and is less among medium and small ones in the Hill than in Terai against a uniform higher indebtedness for all size-classes in Hill in 1969/70. The observation is slightly intriguing. This may be explained to some extent by the higher rise in percentage points of institutional debt in Hill (i.e. + 22.56%) than in Terai (i.e. + 0.58%). However, the higher indebtedness in absolute percentage term to private agencies in Hill (i.e. 73.93%) than in Terai (i.e. 54.72%) fails to account for lesser indebtedness among small and medium peasants in Hill. High but declining indebtedness of both Hill and Terai peasants to village and professional moneylenders (i.e. 46.31% and 24.53% respectively of outstanding debt in 1976/77) and the rise in proportion of debt to landlords and agricultural traders amongst Hill peasants (but a decline amongst Terai peasants), should give some indication of rising entanglement of merchant and financial capital in the Hill economy.

2.3.4 Mode of Utilisation of Social Surplus

The mode of ultimate utilisation of social surplus appropriated from the direct producers through various means as outlined above, complete the circuit of the social process and helps to characterise the social formation. For this not only a detailed inventory of sectoral input-output figures but also a complete accounting of the extent and structure of expenditure pattern of society is needed. Setting aside such tall orders, as may be evident from the foregoing experiences, we lack even the preliminary accounting of the social surplus appropriated from the agricultural sector through various means. However, in view of the known, predominantly pre-capitalist methods of surplus extraction in the Nepalese agriculture sector we cannot faintly hope to encounter a more progressive method of its utilization and its retrograde nature is generally accepted.[123] Within this framework we have sough to infer some pattern of utilization of surplus *within* the agricultural sector from the fragmentary information provided by the Nepal Rastra

Bank (1980). Tables 2.35 and 2.36 provide glimpses of the extent of 'capital formation'[124] and structure of capital expenditure by different farm sizes and territorial zones for 1969/70 and 1976/77. Though the actual extent of 'capital formation' may not be very reliable in view of its liberal definition and sample bias of the survey in favour of more developed parts of the country, the pattern of expenditure of farm households on different items related with farming activities provides some pointers to the level of development of forces and relations of production in agriculture. The very fact that more than 75% of the expenditure in an average is still made for purchasing land, livestock and construction of farm houses and cattle sheds, which are not necessarily an "addition" to the "capital" assets, speaks of the backward nature of organization of production. Viewing across farm sizes and physical spaces, the relevant scenario for small and medium farm households and Hill areas, that constitute the bulk of the agricultural population and areas, are more bleak.

Table 2.35 Extent of Agricultural 'Capital Formation' by Territorial Zones (1969/70 and 1976/77).

Territorial Zones	*% of Families with 'Capital formation'*		*Average Gross 'Capital Formation' per Farm Family (Rs. at current prices)*	
	1969/70	*1976/77*	*1969/70*	*1976/77*
HILL	30.02	65.58	123	917
Terai	33.23	62.24	135	989
Overall	32.18	63.20	132	967

Source: Nepal Rastra Bank (1980), *Agricultural Credit Review Survey*, Vol. III, Agricultural Banking and Credit Division, Kathmandu.

Thus, from the foregoing analysis of different components of 'distribution' aspect of agriculture in the available spatio-temporal frame it can be generalised that Nepalese agriculture continues to stagnate under retrograde, pre-capitalist (presumably semi-feudal) social relations of production with little variations in the territorial dimensions.

2.4 ARTICULATION OF THE AGRARIAN PROCESS AND SPATIAL DIFFERENTIATION

Having separately dealt with the 'production' and 'distribution' aspects of the agrarian process in the relevant spatio-temporal frame, the logical follow-up would have been the documentation of the articulated combination of the two aspects to get the resultant social process in its totality. This could also provide the complete measure of the levels of agricultural development. However, as cautioned earlier, not only are there methodological reservations in mechanically attempting to separate and then combine the two already intertwined and inseparable

Table 2.36 Proportion of Average Gross Capital Expenditure by Farm Size and Territorial Zones (1969/70 and 1976/77).

(%)

Item	*Zones*	*Overall*								*Hill*		*Terai*	
	Farm Size	*Large*		*Medium*		*Small*		*All Families*		*All Families*		*All Families*	
		1969/70	*1976/77*	*1969/70*	*1976/77*	*1969/70*	*1976/77*	*1969/70*	*1976/77*	*1969/70*	*1976/77*	*1969/70*	*1976/77*
1.	Purchage of Land	44.54	9.17	52.36	8.65	31.92	20.69	41.38	13.24	29.25	6.10	45.99	15.71
2.	Purchase of Livestock and Poultry	22.35	34.84	33.49	34.58	51.06	48.86	35.63	39.93	50.34	47.44	29.94	37.31
3.	Purchase of Machinery tools and transport equipment	10.23	23.45	2.36	8.65	1.06	5.17	5.17	13.24	0.68	2.56	6.95	16.91
4.	Development of irrigation	1.04	2.65	0.47	1.91	–	1.15	1.16	1.87	–	1.34	1.08	2.11
5.	Land reclamation and improvement	5.2	5.84	3.30	6.81	2.13	5.74	3.44	6.13	2.04	1.95	4.27	7.46
6.	Construction of farm houses, cattle sheds	15.60	20.51	7.08	38.98	12.77	16.47	12.64	23.41	17.69	35.00	10.70	19.45
7.	Laying of orchards etc. other capital expenditure	1.04	3.54	0.94	0.42	1.06	1.92	0.58	2.18	–	5.61	1.07	0.95
	TOTAL	100.00	100.00	100.00	100.00	100.00	100.00	100.00	100.00	100.00	100.00	100.00	100.00

Source: Nepal Rastra Bank (1980), *Agricultural Credit Review Survey, Nepal*, Vol. I, Agricultural Credit Division, Kathmandu.

components of a social process, but we also lack empirical devices for such an exercise. Also in our specific case, as must have been clear by now, the temporal and spatial units of our analysis of the different aspects have not always been comparable and hence additive. Within these limitations, we have tried to amalgamate selected indicators of agricultural development belonging to both the 'production' and 'distribution' aspect into a composite index and delineate spatial configuration of the process in the smallest micro-spatial units, the districts.

2.4.1 Choice of Indicators

To get a complete picture of the multi-dimensional phenomenon like the nature and level of articulated combination of the agrarian process in a given spatial frame, a maximum possible number of related dimensions ought to be aggregated through suitable empirical means. However, in our case it has to be frankly admitted at the outset that besides sticking to the fair representation of both the 'production' and 'distribution' aspects, our choices of relevant indicators have been grossly limited by the availability of data, into the following:

- A-5 Output per hectare of net sown area (NSA);
- A-6 Percentage of area under cash crops to gross cropped area (GCA);
- A-7 Value of modern inputs per hectare of GCA;
- A-8 Percentage of households having more than 5 acres (2 hectares) of cultivated land to the total cultivating households.

As has already been highlighted in the previous section, the question of measuring the agricultural yield rate (as a development indicator) relative to either the NSA or GCA has been subjected to a vehement debate focussing in the differences of basic theoretical positions on upholding or denying the operation of the law of socialisation in agricultural production. We have, however, found it prudent to measure productivity with respect to the NSA, basing on the theoretical validity of the general operation of the law of socialisation in agriculture and also considering that it would take care of the effect of cropping intensity and irrigation, which we have not been able to incorporate separately. Land productivity would naturally be a good indicator of the development of productive forces in agriculture, but in the present case some allowance would have to be made for the less reliability of data particularly on the districtwise NSA.

Integration of the backward 'peripheral' economy with the advanced 'metropolitan' economy as a net supplier of primary products and importer of manufactured products is cited as one of the principal causes and effects of 'underdevelopment'. Also as a prelude to the generalised production of commodities under capitalism, the initial phases of transition from pre-capitalist to capitalist stages are marked by increased commodity production. To capture the extent of the articulation of both these processes, percentage of area under cash crops to GCA is included here as an indicator representing the 'distribution' component of the agrarian process. However, it may be cautioned that in a self-exploiting, subsistence peasant economy marked by domination of use-value production the cultivation of certain amount of 'non-cereal' crops for self-consumption is perfectly logical and should not be misunderstood as exchange-value production. Similarly arrangements of territorial or social division of labour does often compel areas or societies to produce more of cereals than the so-called cash crops as exchange value. But every empirical exercise has its own limitations and can cater to only the 'general' situation.

Increased use of modern technological inputs like chemical fertilizers, pesticides, improved seeds, machinery and implements etc. invariably go with higher development of productive forces in agriculture. Also, the commercial motives of international finance capital in sponsoring pockets of 'green revolution' dependent on imported agricultural inputs in the underdeveloped countries are by now well-known. To capture these aspects aggregate monetary value of modern inputs per hectare of GCA is sought to be incorporated as a development indicator. Since more than 90% of the gross value of these inputs was found to consist of chemical fertilizers that need to be replenished for every additional crop, the GCA and not the NSA was considered more relevant to be weighted against.

The distribution pattern of farm-sizes amongst the households constitutes an important element in the combined articulation of the agrarian process. Though contradictory interpretations have been made about the relative efficiency of the small or large farm-sizes and though there is the unsettled controversy regarding their usage as a positive or negative indicator of development,[125] consistent with the position held throughout about the validity of the law of socialisation in agricultural production we have included percentage of households owning more than 5 acres (2 hectares) of land to the total cultivating households as a positive contributor in the development process.

2.4.2 Analysis of Interdependencies

Before proceeding to the construction of the composite index out of the given indicators, it would be worthwhile to analyse the matrix of the correlations among different indicators of agricultural and other sectoral development [Appendix-9], for "an alalysis of correlations backed by an appropriate theoretical frame can indicate causal dependencies".[126]

Starting with correlations among different indicators of agricultural development, it is interesting to note that output per hectare of NSA (i.e. net land productivity) has positive and significant correlations with all the remaining variables, which is a healthy sign by any reckoning. However, delving into further details and recapitulation of earlier observations would substantially undermine our premature optimism.

- Particularly high and positive correlations of land productivity with value of modern inputs per hectare (A-7) would indicate a significant contribution of modern inputs in the overall land productivity. But in view of the overall low value of these inputs and extreme disparity in their spatial distribution (c.v.=2.275), the incongruity of such observations gets more apparent. Hence, the relevant explanation will have to be sought elsewhere specially in the greater contribution of cropping intensity in determining the net land productivity (see, Section 2.2.41), which in turn is a function of irrigation and other forms of water availability. When it is realised that more than 90% of the value of modern inputs is composed of chemical fertilizer which is highly multi-collinear with water availability, the said relation appears to be mostly coincidental.

- The positive significant, but not very high, correlation of land productivity with percentage of area under 'cash crops' (A-6) also appears a bit incongruous in view of the low overall percentage (8.16% in average) of area under such crops. Though a part of the explanation will have to be sought in the high multi-collinearity of this indicator with cropping intensity, its positive contribution to the net agricultural productivity will have to be acknowledged.
- Low but positive significant correlations of land productivity with percentage of households owning land more then 2 hectares (A-8) would tempt one to conclude that the law of socialisation operates in the Nepalese agriculture. But that would be presumptions, in view of the low absolute size of the holding (i.e. 0.96 hectare per household in average) and the methodological problems in equating 'size' of the holding with the 'scale' of production [see Section 2.1.11 above]. Though larger size of land-holdings would definitely facilitate the organization of production in a more efficient manner, the relation may have been exaggerated here by other factors such as historical concentration of larger size holdings in areas which are also more conducive for multiple cropping.
- The insignificant correlation between percentage of area under cash crops (A-6) and value of modern inputs per hectare (A-7) could be an indicator of not only the low volume of cash crop production or use of modern inputs, but also the low level of organization of production of cash crops.
- The correlation of percentage of area under cash crops (A-6) with percentage of households owing land more than 2 hectares (A-8) works out positive and significant. In view of the apparent low level of organization of production of cash crops, this relation may be interpreted to substantiate the fact that cash crops are produced only as subsidiary crops on 'extra' land that can be spared only by the larger size holdings.
- The percentage of households owning land more than 2 hectares (A-8) exhibits no significant correlation with value of modern inputs per hectare (A-7). This, apart from indicating the overall insignificant use of modern inputs in agricultural production, could imply a generally low level of organisation of production in larger size holdings.
- Coming to the correlations with indicators of industrial development, only the indicators of 'production' aspect of agricultural development (A-5 and A-7) are seen to have significant positive correlations with the 'size' of industrial development (I-9). On the other hand, there is no or marginal

interdependence between the quality or organisation of production aspects of the two processes. This could be a pointer towards the primitive nature of articulation of agricultural and industrial processes in the country. No significant correlation of cash crop production (A-6) with industrial production (A-6) further underscores this sectoral disarticulation.

- As per the association with indicators of general economic base and social infrastructure, again the 'production' aspect of the agrarian process is found better articulated with them than the 'distribution' aspect. Whereas a part of the explanation may lie with the faulty data base, this could well substantiate our apprehensions regarding the deep sectoral disarticulation in the economy.

On the basis of the above system of interdependencies certain generalisations can be made about the conditions of the Nepalese agricultural sector:

- The general technical level of production is low, largely unaffected by modern technology:
- The general level of social organisation of production is yet to attain a stage of generalised commodity production and be responsive to the law of socialisation of production;
- The forces and relations of production do not seem to be articulating in unison, thereby further aggravating structural underdevelopment.
- There is considerable sectoral disarticulation, such that other sectors of the economy particularly industry have little impact in changing the backward structure of agriculture.

2.4.3 Spatial Differentiation by Levels of Agricultural Development

2.4.31 Following from the theoretical frame of the study an articulated combination of the different aspects of production and distribution components of the agrarian process should constitute the levels of development in the abstract space. Therefore, to get the spatial configuration of the process its selected dimensions as embodied in the indicators of development already highlighted, have been composited through principal component analysis for each of the micro-spatial units, i.e. the districts.

In the absence of relevant data in the temporal frame only a static picture of the levels of development by districts has been obtained. This will obviously hamper a more meaningful picturisation of the agrarian process in a dynamic frame. This lag is, however, sought to be compensated by subsuming the static quantitative measures under a coherent theoretical frame and the historical canvass already drawn.

It must be clarified at the outset that our choice of relevant development indicators has been more influenced by the desire to evaluate the structural position or quality of the agrarian economy over the physical space than to gauge its absolute size. This was considered necessary in order to weigh down the natural advantages of certain areas over the others and to be in line with the basic theoretical position that the social factors should be placed over the natural ones in a study of the social process like agricultural underdevelopment. Also, the immediate concern of our study is merely to delineate the spatial configuration of the nature of underdevelopment operating in the agricultural sector, and not to delimit comprehensive agricultural 'regions' of the country which would have much wider ramifications and need much more rigour than the present exercise.

To view the composite index of development at the general level, it is interesting to note that, following from the basic postulates of principal component analysis as applied on the correlation matrix of the variables, which lays spacial emphasis on the interrelatedness of the variables, higher weights should be assigned to productivity indicator A-5 (0.60856) followed by cash crop, A-6 (0.50533) distribution of land-holding by size, A-8 (0.47820) and modern inputs, A-7 (0.38160). 127 This not only conforms with our earlier observations on the relative merits of the indicators but ensures equity between the 'production' and 'distribution' aspects of the agrarian process.

2.4.32 Factor scores of first principal components for each district are arranged in the descending order of their value, and ranks assigned to them to generate Table 2.37.

Table 2.37 Spatial Differentiation of Levels of Agricultural Production.

Class	*Rank*	*Factor Scores of First Principal Component*	*District (Territorial zone)*	
(1)	*(2)*	*(3)*	*(4)*	
	1.	4.05410	Bhaktapur	(KV)
	2.	3.13535	Chitwan	(CIT)
	3.	3.09837	Morang	(FET)
	4.	3.00721	Sunsari	(FET)
	5.	2.93009	Kathmandu	(KV)
I.	6.	2.67087	Jhapa	(FET)
	7.	2.60134	Kailali	(WT)
	8.	2.47717	Lalitpur	(KV)
	9.	2.43900	Bardiya	(WT)
	10.	2.13915	Dang	(WIT)
	11.	2.09854	Udaipur	(EIT)
	12.	1.67129	Sindhuli	(EIT)
	13.	1.59567	Persa	(ET)
	14.	1.51953	Bara	(ET)
II.	15.	1.47370	Makwanpur	(CIT)
	16.	1.27859	Nawal Parasi	(CT)
	17.	1.11932	Rupendehi	(CT)
	18.	1.08632	Banke	(WT)
	19.	1.08056	Saptari	(MET)
	20.	0.84817	Sarlahi	(MET)
	21.	0.73544	Siraha	(MET)
	22.	0.70769	Kanchanpur	(WT)

(Contd.)

(*Table 2.37 contd.*)

III.	23.	0.60014	Dhanusha	(MET)
	24.	0.59902	Mahottari	(MET)
	25.	0.59685	Kapilvastu	(CT)
	26.	0.58173	Rautahat	(MET)
	27.	–0.14049	Surkhet	(WIT)
	28.	–0.36324	Manang	(CM)
	29.	–0.36468	Sankhuwasabha	(EM)
	30.	–0.43790	Kaski	(CH)
	31.	–0.52777	Lamjung	(CH)
IV.	32.	–0.55805	Dhankuta	(EH)
	33.	–0.59957	Pyuthan	(WH)
	34.	–0.60597	Solukhumbu	(EM)
	35.	–0.62118	Ilam	(EH)
	36.	–0.70540	Rolpa	(WH)
	37.	–0.72230	Okhaldhunga	(EH)
	38.	–0.74582	Tanahu	(CH)
	39.	–0.76046	Kavre	(EH)
	40.	–0.79407	Dolakha	(EM)
	41.	–0.84439	Gulmi	(CH)
	42.	–0.86213	Sallyan	(WH)
	43.	–0.87814	Arghakhanchi	(CH)
	44.	–0.88293	Dolpa	(WM)
	45.	–0.90187	Myagdi	(CH)
	46.	–0.90276	Tehrathum	(EH)
V.	47.	–0.91988	Gorkha	(CH)
	48.	–0.92280	Rukum	(WH)
	49.	–0.92592	Dhading	(CH)
	50.	–0.95031	Sindhupalchok	(EH)
	51.	–0.97837	Doti	(WH)
	52.	–0.97925	Rasuwa	(CM)
	53.	–1.00895	Mustang	(CM)
	54.	–1.01068	Bhojpur	(EH)
	55.	–1.03254	Panchthar	(EH)
	56.	–1.06538	Nuwakot	(CH)
	57.	–1.06678	Jajarkot	(WH)
	58.	–1.06917	Humla	(WM)
	59.	–1.07549	Dandeldhura	(WH)
VI.	60.	–1.09906	Baglung	(CH)
	61.	–1.11366	Baitadi	(WH)
	62.	–1.11535	Palpa	(CH)
	63.	–1.12038	Darchula	(WM)
	64.	–1.12812	Taplejung	(EM)
	65.	–1.13720	Syangja	(CH)
	66.	–1.17260	Parbat	(CH)
	67.	–1.17593	Achham	(WH)
	68.	–1.20074	Bajura	(WM)
	69.	–1.24684	Khotang	(EH)
	70.	–1.26264	Dailekha	(WH)
VII.	71.	–1.31713	Ramechhap	(EH)
	72.	–1.32155	Jumla	(WM)
	73.	–1.44402	Bajhang	(WM)
	74.	–1.48892	Kalikot	(WM)
	75.	–1.58644	Mugu	(WM)

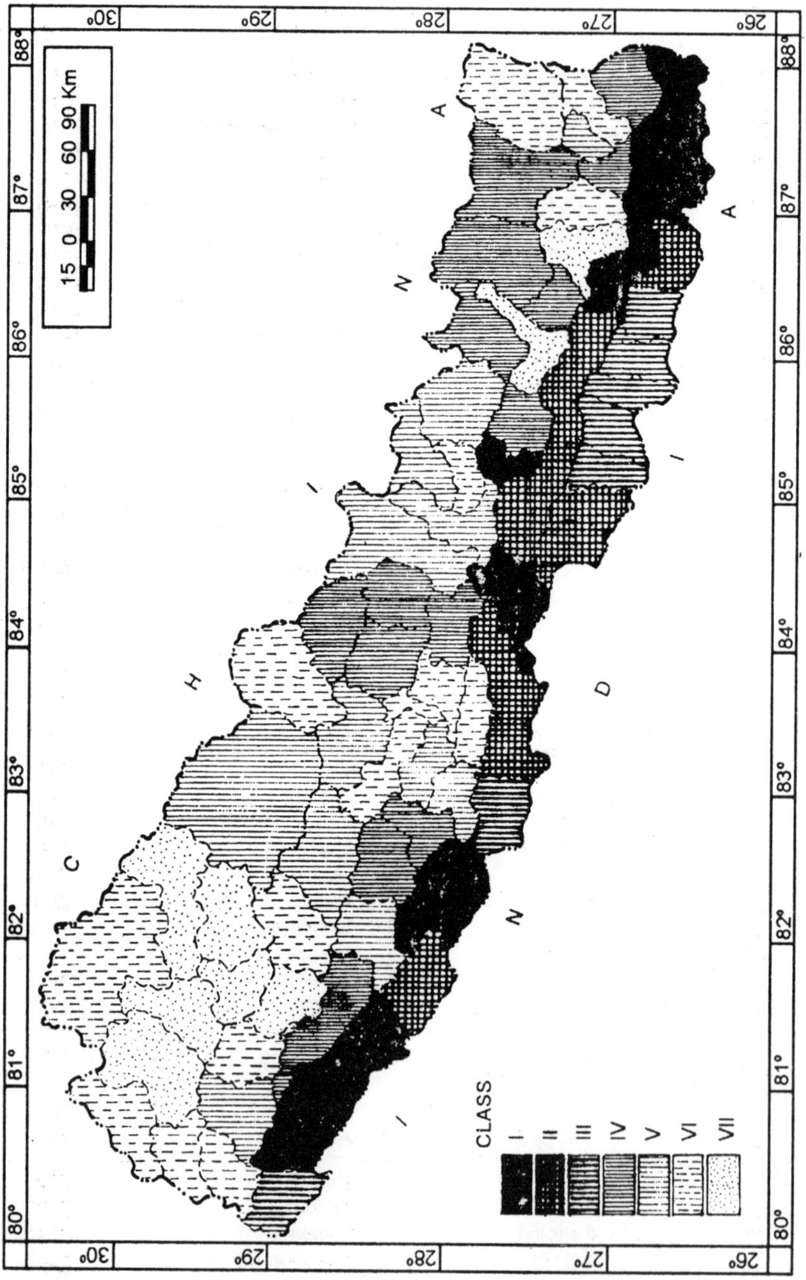

Fig. 2.7 Levels of Agricultural Development.

Exercising our own subjective judgements in determining suitable cut-off points, the districts have been sub-grouped into homogenous categories in the order of their levels of development and plotted in Fig. 2.8.

Standard Deviations (S.D.) and Coefficients of Variations (C.V.) of composite index values (Factor Scores) are calculated for each sub-group to ascertain absolute and relative dispersion of index values within the sub-groups. Greater dispersion at the higher levels than at the lower levels, howsoever marginal they may be in absolute terms, may be the manifestations of greater disparities with increasing levels of development and could be a correct reflection of the inherent logic of development process under the current socio-economic dispensation. However, the not so pronounced differences in the composite index values of each district may indicate the still low level of socio-economic differentiation viewed in a countrywide plane.

The rankings of the districts and their distribution by ecological zones display a distinct spatial pattern of agricultural development and by and large substantiate the earlier observations made in the course of analysis of the agrarian process. Also the spatial pattern obtained here is seen to conform to the historical contours of development sketched earlier and appear nearer to the objective reality than the ones obtained by earlier studies.[128] This may have been partly due to the considerations given to the 'distribution' aspect of the process in the selection of indicators which have been long neglected in Nepal, and partly due to the better aggregation technique adopted.

It is interesting to note that all the 26 districts in the first category with composite index values higher than the national average are from Kathmandu Valley, Terai and Inner Terai. Among the 27 districts in these zones only Surkhet, a late entrant to the race for development falls below the national average. Even within these zones distinct spatial pattern of areas of high and low development are discernible. Incorporation of all the three districts each of Kathmandu Valley and Eastern Terai in the first category of highly developed districts conform to the historical and natural pattern of economic development in the country. These are not only the areas of best agronomic qualities, but historically best placed to score over others in the race of economic development. Kathmandu Valley has been not only the home of centralised state power but also the mercantile and financial capital of the country for a long time, and hence a beneficiary of all the attendant stimulants for agriculture development. The Far-Eastern Terai, for its proximity to the Calcutta port has been historically groomed as an enclave of high economic prosperity to mediate in the 'metropolitan-periphery' chain of economic interactions. Apart from these enclaves of high prosperity, the inclusion of three Inner Terai and two Western Terai districts in this category, signifies the rapid rate of exploitation of their vast agricultural potentials untapped till recently for their hostile climatic conditions and due to their preservation in the natural state for strategic reasons of protecting the Hills from intrusions from the plains.

The second sub-group comprises mostly of districts of Central Terai and Inner Terai which have been historically most advantaged due to their strategic positioning along the trade routes joining India and Tibet via Kathmandu Valley, but have recently lost their position to the Eastern Terai with the change in the pattern of economic interaction with the outside world. It may be noted that these areas constitute the immediate hinterland of traditional trading outpost of Birgunj, Bhairahawa and Nepalgunj.

In the third sub-group are almost all the districts of Mid-Eastern Terai, which have been historically overshadowed by the Far-Eastern and Central Terai because of the latters' more advantageous location as explained earlier. The earlier advantage enjoyed by mid-Eastern Terai in the matter of production of export-oriented cash crops like tobacco etc. was lost when the pattern of external trade changed [Refer Chapter IV below].

In the sub-groups of Hill and Mountain districts, the formation of development hierarchy has been less articulated indicating low spatial differentiation. The marginal differentiation amongst individual districts appears to have been governed by a combination of factors including their agro-climatic attributes, external physical linkages and specific historical experiences. Eastern and central Zones are seen to be better of than the west as they enjoy a definite advantage in all these conditioning factors.

Because of greater emphasis placed on measuring the *quality* rather than *quantity* of the agricultural attributes consistent with our theoretical frame adopted throughout, many of the otherwise remote districts of eastern and central Mountains are seen to be placed favourably in the overall development matrix.

The most backward position of western Hill and Mountain is perhaps the most pronounced feature observable in the present analysis. This is quite understandable in view of their disadvantaged position with respect to both natural and social factors. However, a recapitulation of the historical contours of agricultural development in different physical units of the country will convincingly drive home the point that the western Hill and Mountain areas have been historically 'fossilized' at a low level of development because of their location far away from the centralized state authority at Kathmandu Valley and areas of centralisation of industrial and commercial activities.

Thus, the agrarian spatial structure to be generalised from the above distribution of levels of agricultural development is the differentiation of areas of 'extraverted development' along Terai, Inner Terai and Kathmandu Valley, and areas of absolute backwardness or retardation in the vast hinterland of Hill and Mountain. This spatial formation can be taken as a typical manifestation of the underdevelopment process operating in the Nepalese space economy.

2.5 CONCLUSIONS

- The current socio-spatial structure of the agriculture sector is largely conditioned by the peculiar specificities of the Nepalese history marked by late and induced 'feudalisation' and incomplete 'detribalisation' of society under a strong state power. Also, the historical role played by 'social' factors in articulating spatial differentiation, e.g. greater persistence of communal formation in the east, greater degree of feudalisation in the west and more direct state intervention in the central region, etc., would have its bearing on the present structure.

- Very low development of productive forces in the agriculture sector is reflected in overwhelming domination of traditional factors of production like land and human and animal labour in total factor inputs. Marked unevenness in the spatial distribution of natural factors of production is compounded by extreme spatial disparateness in the use of modern inputs.
- The backward and retarded state of agriculture is also manifest in low cropping intensity, predominance of subsistence (cereal) crops in total area and value of production, sluggish growth rate of crop output, declining food surplus (or aggravating food deficit), etc. The spurious nature of even this marginal growth is evident in higher rate of acreage increase than the output increase. The minimal 'cash crop' production is highly centralised in the more extravertedly integrated Terai; but not only is its growth rate extremely sluggish but some important export-oriented cash crops like jute is seen declining in the absolute sense. The decline of the few industrial crops like tobacco points towards the lack of required impulses from other sectors of the economy (i.e. industry) for agricultural development.
- The yield rates of crops, or land productivity, are found not only low but are seen consistently declining over time. Whereas gross land productivity declines from the more depressed Mountain-Hill to Terai, net land productivity and labour productivity vary the other way round; thus giving currency to the Marxist explanation of apparent 'superiority' of small-scale peasant agriculture as due to 'overwork' and 'under-consumption' by the hapless peasants. The spatial differentiation of the holistic picture of the 'health' of the agriculture sector as obtained by cross-classification of spatial distribution of land and labour productivities reveal that only the eastern Terai and Kathmandu Valley, the traditional area of centralisation of merchant-bureaucratic and industrial capital, are 'healthy' in the midst of chronic morbidity of the vast hinterland.
- Spatial variations in gross output per cultivated hectare are more due to the differences in the multiplication of cropping or horizontal expansion of gross cropped area than due to change in yield rates of crops. More than three-fourths of the marginal increase in gross agricultural output is found accounted for by area increase and an insignificant share of less than 2% by yield increase. Modern inputs are seen to have exercised negligible influence in the overall structuration of the agriculture sector, except for their catalytic role in aggravating spatial disparateness.

- The backward and retrograde relations of production in agriculture is found reflected in the extremely low and declining average size of land-holding per farm household and pre-ponderance of 'owner-cultivator' subsistence peasantry amidst considerable disparity in the social distribution of vital means of production-land. The stagnant structure is also manifest in the negligible change in the distribution pattern of land-holding even in a decade marked by the much-publicised official 'land reform programme' except for the rise in fragmentation of land-holdings. The low degrees of social differentiation accompanied by pre-ponderence of 'owner-cultivator' households as well as the lowest average size of holding to be found in the traditional habitation zone of central east-west hilly spine of the country, may be cited as the typical example of social retardation operationalized through the perpetuation of a marginalized peasantry.
- Pre-capitalist ground-rent realised primarily through the system of share-cropping constitutes the principal form of appropriation of social surplus in the agriculture sector. However, a number of historical and natural specificities of different parts of the country do make the characterisation of different rented tenure according to premedited concepts not as simple. In the territorial dimensions, areas of better agro-climatic conditions (i.e. Terai, Kathmandu Valley and Inner Terai) and those away from the central state authority (i.e. eastern and western sectors) exhibit higher degree of 'feudalisation' than the rest; thus complying with the Marxist theoretical position on the conditions of development of feudalism and with the historical sequence of evolution of agrarian process in Nepal.
- Of the auxiliary forms of appropriation of social surplus from the agriculture sector such as state taxation, mercantile exploitation and usury practices, the last form is found widespread in both space and time frame and quite retrograde in character.
- Various types of servile attached-labour system are known to prevail as the mode of extraction of surplus labour from the direct producer other than the small tenant-cultivator. Moreover, rampant under-employment and seasonal out-migration has slackened the process of peasant differentiation and perpetuated, the archaic social relations of production. In view of greater polarisation of classes and greater articulation of social contradictions, Terai and Inner Terai logically appear to be more ripened for restructuring of social organisation of production in agriculture.
- The aggregate agrarian process in Nepal is thus found characterised by low technical level of production, pre-capitalist (or semi-feudal) relations of production, disarticulation with other sectors of the economy, particularly industry, and a general state of stagnation and retardation. In the territorial dimension it is manifested in the marginally differentiated vast hinterland of Hill and Mountain surrounded by areas of 'extraverted development' along Terai, Inner Terai and Kathmandu Valley.

REFERENCES

1. Of the more notable debates on the 'agrarian question' are the ones amongst German and Russian Marxists at the end of the 19th and the beginning of the 20th century, amongst Bolsheviks in Russia in the 1920s and recently amongst Indian Marxists beginning with the late 1960s.
2. Lenin seems to use the term 'carrier of technical process' interchangeably for 'prime mover' (See Lenin V.I. (1900) "Capitalism in Agriculture", *Collected Works*, Vol. 4, Progress Publishers, Moscow, 1964.
3. This is explicitly expressed by Kautsky as follows:

   "*Industry* forms the motor force not only of its own development, but also of the development of agriculture. It was urban industry that smashed the unity of industry and agriculture in the countryside, that converted the peasant into a pure agriculturalist, a commodity producer tied to an unknown market, that established the possibility of his proletarianisation. The agriculture of the feudal epoch ended in an impasse, from which it could not escape through its own dynamism. It was urban industry that generated the revolutionary forces that were bound to, and could break down the feudal regime and open a new path of development for itself and agriculture. It was industry, moreover, that produced the scientific and technical condition of the new agriculture, that revolutionized it with machinery and chemical fertilizer and established the dominance of large capitalist holdings over the small peasant exploitation." [Banaji, J. (1980) "Summary of Selected Parts of Kautsky's *The Agrarian Question*" in Wolpe, W. (ed). *The Articulation of Modes of Production*, Routledge and Kegan Paul, London, p. *89*].
4. See Amin, S. (1979), *Unequal Development*, Oxford University Press, Delhi.
5. See Kay, G. (1975), *Development and Underdevelopment: A Marxist Analysis*, Macmillian, London, and Bhaduri, A. (1984), *Economic Structure of Backward Agriculture*, Macmillian, London, for the mechanism of operational of merchant and financial/usury capital to perpetuate underdevelopment. Bhaduri, in particular, provides an illuminating exposition of the operation of "forced commerce" in the structuration of backwardness in pre-capitalist agriculture.
6. Since the 1960s a number of studies by Indian scholars including Sen, A.K. (1962), "An Aspect of Indian Agriculture", *The Economic Weekly*, Annual Number, February; Rao, C.H.H. (1968), "Farm Size and Yield per Acre: A "Comment", *Economic and Political Weekly*, September 14; Bhattacharya, N. and Saini, G.R. (1972), "Farm Size and Productivity: A Fresh Look", *Economic and Political Weekly*, June 24; Bharadwaj, K. (1974), *Production Conditions in Indian Agriculture*, Cambridge University Press, London; and others, have confirmed an inverse relation between farm *size* and productivity.
7. See Banaji, *op. cit.*, Lenin (1900), *op. cit.*, and Lenin, V.I. (1901), "The Agrarian Question and the Critics of Marx", in *Collected Works*, Vol. 5, Progress Publishers, Moscow, 1973.
8. As Kautsky observes: "In agriculture... the expansion of a given enterprise on the *same technical basis* amount to a mere extension of the area under cultivation, and thus entails a greater loss of material, a greater deployment of effort resources, time, for the transport of material and men." (Banaji, *op. cit.*, p. 74; emphasis added.)
9. The distinction between *size and scale* may be clear from another of Kautsky's observations: "...with intensive farming, production can be carried on upon a larger

scale on a small estate than on a large estate extensively farmed." (Kautsky quoted in Lenin (1900) *op. cit.*, p. 132).

10. "Small-scale production becomes predominant only in those places where agriculture is in a state of decline, or where pre-capitalist large-scale production enters into competition with peasant production". (*Ibid.*)
11. The of-quoted passage reads:

    "For the peasant owning a parcel, the limit of exploitation is not set by the average profit of capital, in so far as he is a small capitalist; nor, on the other hand, by the necessity of rent, in so far as he is landowner. The absolute limit for him as a small capitalist is no more than the wages he pays to himself, after deducting his actual costs. So long as the price of the product covers these wages, he will cultivate his land, and often at wages down to a physical minimum." [Marx, K. and Engels, F. (1979), *Pre-Capitalist Socio-Economic Formations*, Progress Publishers, Moscow, p. 219].
12. Lenin (1900), *op. cit.*, p. 130.
13. Lenin (1901), *op. cit.*, p. 179.
14. Mandel, E. (1970), *Marxist Economic Theory*, Vol. I, Monthly Review Press, New York, p. 289.
15. See Bhaduri, A. (1973), "A Study in Agricultural Backwardness Under Semi-Feudalism", *The Economic Journal*, Vol. 83, No. 329, March.
16. Marx and Engels, *op. cit.*, p. 220.
17. Lenin (1900), *op. cit.*, p. 136.
18. Banaji, *op. cit.*, p. 77, and Davey, B. (1975), *The Economic Development of India: A Marxist Analysis*, Spokesman Books, Nottingham, p. 38.
19. Banaji, *op. cit.*, p. 73, and Lenin (1900), *op. cit.*, p. 134.
20. Lenin (1901), *op. cit.*, p. 125–26 and Mandel, *op. cit.*, p. 275.
21. For a brief review of the conceptual position on 'peasant mode of production' or 'peasant economy', see Kerblay, B. (1971), "Chayanov and the Theory of Peasantry as a Specific Type of Economy" in Shanin, T. (ed.) (1971), *Peasants and Peasant Societies*, Penguin Books, Harmondsworth and Thorner, D. (1971), "Peasant Economy as a Category in Economic History" in *Ibid.*
22. See, for example, Bernstein, H. (1979), "African Peasantries: A Theoretical Framework", *Journal of Peasant Studies*, Vol. 6, No. 4, July; Gordon, A. (1979), "Stages in the Development of Java's Socio-economic Formations 700–1979 A.D.", *Journal of Contemporary Asia*, Vol. 3, No. 2; Harris, J. (1982), *Capitalism and Peasant Farming*, Oxford University Press, Delhi. The most devastating critique, however, has been provided by Utsa Patnaik, which reads as: "the peasant economy" is not a set of production relations at all, it is simply an aggregation of individual, atomistic production units—the family farms–all identical with each other: the micro unit blown up *n* times. [which has] never existed... What has actually existed, is *petty production* as the basis of feudalism and *petty commodity production*—in transitional forms to capitalism as feudal economy disintegrates–both of which do constitutes social relations of productions". [Patnaik, U. (1979), "Neo-Populism and Marxism: The Chayanovian View of the Agrarian Question and its Fundamental Fallacy", *Journal of Peasant Studies*, Vol. 6, No. 4, *July*].
23. For the definition of 'mode of production', see Section 1.3 above.
24. Shanin, T. "Peasantry as a Political Factor" in Shanin, *op. cit.*, p. 240.
25. Gordon, *op. cit.*, p. 129.

26. According to Mandel's evidence [cited by Shanin, *op. cit.*, p. 248], even in the present day (i.e.1964), U.S.A. there are 1,250,000 small farms exhibiting the features of a mainly natural economy.
27. Roxborough, I. (1979), *Theories of Underdevelopment*, Macmillan, London, pp. 95–96.
28. See, Saul, J.S. and Woods, R. "African Peasantries" in Shanin (ed.), *op. cit.*, p. 103, and Harriss, *op. cit.*, p. 290.
29. The Indian debate on the mode of production in Indian agriculture and identification of peasant classes has been particularly noteworthy. Of the numerous participants in the continuing debate the more significant may be cited as: Rudra, A. et. al. (1969), "Big Farmers of Punjab", *EPW*, September 20 and December 27, Rudra, A. (1970), "In Search of the Capitalist Farmer", *EPW*, June 27; Chattopadhyay, P. (1972), "On the Question of Mode of Production in Indian Agriculture: A Preliminary Note", *EPW*, March 25; Banaji, J. (1973), "Mode of Production in Indian Agriculture: A Comment" *EPW*, April 27; Sau, R. (1973), "On the Essence and Manifestation of Capitalism in Indian Agriculture", *EPW*, March 31; Alavi, H. (1975), "Indian and the Colonial Mode of Production", *EPW*, special Number, August; Patnaik, U. (1971), "Capitalist Development in Agriculture: A Note", *EPW*, September 25; Patnaik, U. (1976), "Class Differentiation within the Peasantry: An Approach to Analysis of Indian Agriculture", *EPW*, September.

    A later contributor on measuring 'peasant capitalism' has been Shanin, T. (1980), "Measuring Peasant Capitalism" in Hobsbawn, E.J. *et. al.* (ed.) (1980), *Peasants in History*, Oxford University Press, Calcutta.
30. Patnaik, U. (1971), *op. cit.*, p. A–127.
31. Lenin (1899), *op. cit.*, pp. 205–6.
32. Brenner, R. (1977), "The Origins of Capitalist Development: A Critique of New-Smithian Marxism", *New Left Review*, No. 104, pp. 73–74.
33. Lenin (1901), *op. cit.*, p. 163.
34. For a comparative and critical evaluation of the two approaches, see Shanin (1980), *op. cit.*
35. See, for example, Amatya, S.L. (1973–74), "A Study of Agriculture Crop Combination in Nepal", *The Himalayan Review*, Vol. VI, No. 5–6, Nepal Geographical Society, Kathmandu, and Pant, B.D. (1982), *Statistical Analysis of Economic Activities for Regional Planning in Nepal* (Unpublished Ph.D. Dissertation), Indian Statistical Institute, Calcutta.
36. Agriculture effeciency was first measured by Kendal in terms of output per unit area. He used the ranking device all the areal units were ranked according to acre-yields of different crops and estimated average rank and termed it as the ranking coefficient for each unit. This was further refined by Sapre and Deshpande by a weighted average of the ranks of all crops in respect of their share to the total cropped area in each areal unit. Its further refinement was attempted by Bhatia through the weightage of acre-yield in respect of the proportionate share of each crop to the total cropped acreage of any areal unit, which was also used by Sengupta and Sdasyuk for 'agriculture regionalisation' of India. [See Sengupta, P. and Sdasyuk, G. (1968), "Economic Regionalisation of India: Problems and Approaches" in *Census* of India–1961, Vol. I, No. 8, New Delhi, p. 110].
37. *Iloc. Cit.*

38. Sharma, P.S. (1982), *Inequality in Land Holding and Agricultural Development in India–A regional Analysis* (Unpublished Ph.D. Dissertation), CSRD/SSS/JNU, New Delhi.
39. For an attempt on Indian agriculture on the same line, see Kundu A. and Raza, M. (1982), *Indian Economy: The Regional Dimension*, Spektrum Publishers and Distributors, New Delhi.
40. See, particularly, Isard, W. (1956), *Location and Space-Economy*, MIT Press, (1972 edn.), pp. 189–90.
41. See Marx, K. "Capital, Vol. III, Ch. XLVIII–Genesis of Capitalist Ground-Rent" in Marx and Engels (1979), *op. cit.*, pp. 213–14.
42. See Lenin, V.I. (1899), "Development of Capitalism in Russia", in *Collected Works*, Vol. III, Progress Publishers, Moscow, 1964, pp. 624–25.
43. Regmi, M.C. (1971), *A Study in Nepali Economic History 1968–1846*, Manjusri Publishing House, New Delhi, p. 28.
44. See Lohani, G.P. (1967), "Nepalma bhoomi–sambandhama sudhar tarfa bhaeko gatibidhi ra aja sammako upalabdhi" (Nepali), HMG/N, Ministry of Information and Broadcasting, Department of Information, Kathmandu; Lohani, G.P. (1977), "Nepalko arthik chintanma bhoomi ra janako sthitile prastut gareka kehi bisangatiharu" (Nepali), *Roop-Rekha*, Vol. XVIII, No. 8, Kathmandu; and Feldman, D. and Fournier, A. (1976), "Social relations and Agriculture Production in Nepal's Terai," *The Journal of Peasant Studies*, Vol. 3, No. 4, July; among others.
45. Anand Bahadur (1981), "Marxko 'ek bora alu' ko siddhanta ra kisan kranti ko samasya" (Nepali), *Jhilko*, Vol. I, No. 1, Kathmandu.
46. Regmi , M.C. (1963–68), *Land Tenure and Taxation in Nepal*, Ratna Pustak Bhandar, Kathmandu (1978 edn.), p. 274.
47. '*Jimidar*' may not be confused with '*Zamindar*', despite their phonetic similarities. *Jimidar* was a mere tax-collection functionary, whereas *Zamindar* also enjoyed different rights over land. [See Regmi (1971), *op. cit.*, p. 8, and Regmi, M.C. (1978), *Thatched Huts and Stucco Palaces: Peasants and Landlords in 19th Century Nepal*, Vikas Publishing House Pvt. Ltd., New Delhi, p. 87].
48. See Banaji (1980), *op. cit.*
49. Regmi, M.C. (1976), *Landownership in Nepal*, University of California, Berkley, p. 129.
50. *Ibid.*, p. 175.
51. *Ibid.*, pp. 176–77.
52. *Ibid.*, pp. 138 and 180.
53. *Ibid.*, p. 91.
54. Caplan, L. (1970), *Land and Social Change in East Nepal: A Study of Hindu–Tribal Relations*, Routledge and Kegan Paul, London, p. 111.
55. Regmi (1976), *op. cit.*, p. 95.
56. Dasgupta has proposed a similar distinction while characterising mode of production in pre-British Bengal. But the Nepalese case seems to be all the more 'variant' in that the centralized structure of state authority here was more pronounced than in Bengal, among other differences. [See Dasgupta, B. (1984), "Mode of Production and the Extent of Peasant Differentiation in Pre-British Bengal", *Social Scientist*, Vol. 12, No. 8, August.]
57. Zaman, M.A. (1973), *Evaluation of Land Reform In Nepal*, HMG/N, Ministry of Land Reforms, Kathmandu, p. 8.

58. For brief historical reviews of different 'land reform' measures and critical assessment of their impact, see Zaman *op. cit.*; Regmi (1963–68 and 1976), *op. cit.*; Scholz, J.T. (1977), *Policy Processes and Rural Development: A Study of Land Reform in Nepal* (Unpublished Ph.D. Dissertation), University of California, Barkley; among others.
59. Gaige, F. (1975), *Regionalism and National Unity in Nepal*, University of California Press, Berkley and Los Angeles, p. 172 and Scholz, *op. cit.*, pp. 44–47.
60. Regmi (1963–68), *op. cit.*, p. 374.
61. Zaman, *op. cit.*, p. 9.
62. *Ibid.*, pp. 31–36.
63. Anand Bahadur, *op. cit.*, p. 12.
64. Lohani (1977), *op. cit.*, p.141.
65. For a detailed account of the situation, see Bajracharya, D.B. (1974), *Lichchhavi Kalka Abhilekh* (Nepali), Centre for Nepal and Asian Studies, Tribhuvan University, Kathmandu.
66. Regmi (1978), *op. cit.*, p. 8, and Regmi, M.C. (1984), *The State and Economic Surplus: Production, Trade and Resource Mobilisation in Early 19th Century Nepal*, Kathmandu, p. 66.
67. Regmi (1978), *op. cit.*, p. 75.
68. Regmi (1971), *op. cit.*, p. 16.
69. Regmi (1978), *op. cit.*, p. 11.
70. Shrestha, B.P. (1962), *An Introduction to Nepalese Economy*, Ratna Pustak Bhandar, Kathmandu (1981 edn.) p. 62.
71. Richard Temple, "Remarks on a Tour Through Nepal in May 1876" in *Journals Kept in Hyedrabad, Kashmir, Sikkim and Nepal*, London, W. H. Allen, 1887, Vol. 2, p. 251, cited in Regmi (1978), *op. cit.*, p. 12.
72. Regmi (1978), *op. cit.*, p. 12.
73. *Ibid.*, p. 5.
74. Regmi (1971), *op. cit.*, p. 30.
75. Regmi (1984), *op. cit.*, p. 56.
76. Regmi (1976), *op. cit.*, p. 129.
77. Hamilton, F.B. (1819), *An Account of the Kingdom of Nepal*, Manjusri Publishing House, New Delhi, 1971, p. 64.
78. Habib, I. (1963), *The Agrarian System of Mugal India (1556–1707)*, Mumbai, p. 14.
79. In the absence of a comprehensive land-use survey of the country which only now seems to be under way, total area under cultivation compiled from various sources vary widely and may not be very reliable. For instance, Asian Development Bank cites it at 3.1 million hectares [Asian Development Bank, (1982), *Nepal: Agricultural Sector Strategy Study*, Vol. II, Bangkok, Kathmandu, p. 40]; Pant and Thapa give 2.3 million hectares of 'cropped area' [Pant, T.N. and Thapa, G.B. "Development Potentials of Nepal's Hill Agriculture", in HMG/N, Ministry of Food and Agriculture (1981), *Nepal's Experience in Hill Agriculture Development*, Kathmandu, pp. 19–20]; Shah gives 2.5 million hectares for 1978–79 [Shah, S. (1981), "Developing an Economy; Nepal's Experience", *Asian Survey*, Vol. XXI, No. 10, October, p. 1078]; whereas our own computation of data obtained from various sources gives 2.7 million hectares for 1978–79.
80. For the precise definition of the traditional grades of land by agronomic capacity, see Regmi (1976), *op. cit.*, pp. 148–49.

81. See, among others, Weiner, M. (1971), "The Political Demography of Nepal", in *Seminar on Population and Development* (July 28–30, 1971), CEDA, Kathmandu; Kansakar, V.B.S. (1974), *Population Change in Nepal: A Study of Mobility During 1911–1961* (Unpublished Ph.D. Dissertation), Patna University; Zevering, K.H. (1974), *Agricultural Development and Agrarian Structure in Nepal*, ARTEP, Bangkok.
82. Asian Development Bank, *op. cit.*, p. 117.
83. The position of various countries of Asia in the use of chemical fertilizers per hectare of arable land is as follows:

(In 100 grams)

Country	*1961–65*	*1967*	*1972*	*1977*
Bangladesh	44	106	200	371
India	37	71	167	253
Japan	3052	3874	3895	4281
Nepal	4	14	49	73
Pakistan	34	99	228	351
Sri Lanka	408	542	487	536
Asia	118	185	310	454

Source: FAO, *Fertilizer Year Book*, 1978.

84. HMG/N, Ministry of Food and Agriculture (1971), *Farm Management Study in the Selected Regions of Nepal, 1968–69*, Economic Analysis and Planning Division, Kathmandu.
85. Gurung, H. (1981), *Food Systems and Society in Nepal: An Overview*, New Era, Kathmandu, p. 31.
86. National Planning Commission (1980), *Draft Sixth Plan (1980–85)* (Nepali), HGM/N, Kathmandu, pp. 18–52.
87. HMG/N, Ministry of Food, Agriculture and Irrigation (1978) gives the cropping intensity figures for the whole country as 98.6% for 1961/62, 112.7% for 1970/71 and 106.6%. 1977/78 [*Handbook of Agricultural Statistics of Nepal*, Agricultural Statistics Division, Kathmandu, p. 8.] Nepal Rastra Bank, on the basis of a survey of different size farms in 14 "accessible" districts of Terai and Hill in 1976/77, provides cropping intensity figure as follows:

Zones	*All Size Farms*	
	Irrigated	*Unirrigated*
HILL (including Kathmandu Valley)	157.98	129.81
TERAI (including Inner Terai)	146.26	124.71
Overall	147.24	133.84

The sample being avowedly biased in favour of the "accessible", and thus more developed, parts of the country these figures would be highly exaggerated. [Nepal Rastra Bank (1980), *Agriculture Credit Review Survey Nepal*, Vol. IV, Agricultural Credit Division, Kathmandu, p. 8]. Banskota on the other hand claims the overall cropping intensity in the country to have declined from 95% in 1961 to 82% in 1974. [Banskota, M. (1979) *Basic Needs and Agriculture in Nepal: The Role of Agriculture Inputs*, CEDA, Kathmandu, p. 13].

*Cropped area in 1977/78–1979/80.

88. See Regmi (1984), *op. cit.*, p. 62.
89. Gurung, *op. cit.*, p. 33.
90. Whether to measure land productivity with respect to net sown area (NSA) or gross cropped area (GCA) has remained a controversy amongst the academics for quite some time. [For a brief review of arguments in favour of or against the two approaches, see Bharadwaj, *op. cit.*, and Kundu, *op. cit.*, among others]. Despite our individual preference for the first approach as rooted in the theoretical frames outlined earlier, the lack of reliable data on NSA in the desired spatio-temporal dimensions has compelled us to use the second approach for larger part of the present study. Nevertheless, whenever the study is to be carried out in a static frame and only for the aggregate products, land productivity with respect to NSA is considered.
91. See Kundu and Raza, *op. cit.*, p. 15.
92. *Ibid.*, p. 66.
93. Raza, M., "Introduction" in Mahmood, A. (1977), *Statistical Methods in Geographical Studies*, Rajesh Publications, New Delhi, p. XIV.
94. Unless otherwise mentioned the correlations are for the seventies and land productivity whenever encountered refers to that with respect of the NSA.
95. See Kundu and Raza, *op. cit.*, p. 75.
96. For example, Minhas and Vaidyanathan analysed growth of crop output in India through an additive decomposition of the growth of production into four components: changes in acreage, yield rate, cropping pattern and interactions due to yield and cropping pattern [Minhas, B.S. and Vaidyanathan, A. (1965), "Growth of Crop Output in India, 1951–4 to 1958–61: An Analysis by Component Elements", *The Journal of the Indian Society of Agricultural Statistics*, Vol. XVII, No. 2]. Bhalla and Alagh, on the other hand, studied a districtwise growth of agricultural production in India by decomposing production into its major components of area change, yield change, cropping pattern change, and cropping pattern and yield change interaction through a multiplicative scheme [Bhalla, G.S. and Alagh, Y.K. (1979), *Performance of Indian Agriculture: A Districtwise Study*, Sterling Publishers Pvt. Ltd., New Delhi].
97. See, Rana, R.S.J.B. (1971), "Regional Variations in the growth Structure of Crop Production in Nepal", *The Himalayan Review*, Vol. IV, Nepal Geographical Society, Kathmandu; Pant, B.D. and Sharma, P. (1984), "Growth of Agricultural Productivity in Nepal: A Regional Analysis" *Nepalese Economic Journal*, Nepal Rastra Bank, Kathmandu.
98. *Op. cit.*
99. *Op. cit.*, Appendix 6, p. 215.
100. Whereas Pant and Sharma [*op. cit.*] cite the 'sluggish' growth of average productivity from 2803.89 (Rs./ha.) in 1970/71–72/73 to 2997.08 (Rs./ha.) in 1980/81–82/83, our own figures show the absolute decline from 2852 (Rs./ha.) in 1967/68–69/70 to 2699 (Rs./ha.) in 1977/78–79/80 [refer Table 2.12 above].
101. Marx, K. (1977), *Grundrisse*, Penguin Books, Harmondsworth, p. 96.
102. Zaman, *op. cit.*, p. 31.
103. The land–ceiling limits per farm family fixed by the Land Act, 1964, vary according to the territorial zones within the country as follows:

	Agriculture Land	*Homestead*
(i) Terai and Inner Terai	16.4 hectares	2.0 hectares
(ii) Kathmandu Valley	2.7 hectares	0.4 hectares
(iii) Rest of the country	4.1 hectares	0.8 hectares

These ceiling limits are generally regarded to be grossly on the higher side, both with respect to similar comparisons elsewhere and the prevailing land-man ratio in the country.

104. See Rana, P.S.J.B. and Malla, K.P., "Nepal in Perspective: An Introduction", in Rana, P.S.J.B. and Malla, K.P. (ed.) (1973), *Nepal in Perspective*, CEDA, Kathmandu, pp. 21–22; and Scholz, *op. cit.*
105. Zaman, *op. cit.*
106. APROSC (1978), *Agrarian Reform and Rural Development in Nepal* (Country Review Paper), Kathmandu, p. 9.
107. Zaman, *op. cit.*, Table 9, p. 85.
108. Though it is methodologically wrong to generalize a mode of production through a single 'indicator', and we fully concur with the familiar Marxist position highlighted by Marx himself in the classic case of capitalist ground rent that rented tenure can assume a number of forms spanning into different social modes of production (see also Section 2.1.11 above), it is being tentatively hypothesised here in view of the historically late and incomplete transformation of the initial 'tribal-communal' formation in Nepal into a higher social formation presumably, but not necessarily, 'feudal'.
109. See Dobb, M. (1946), *Studies in the Development of Capitalism*, Routledge and Kegan Paul, London (1978 edn.) p. 88.
110. Share cropping tenancy, generally accepted as "a transitional form between pre-capitalist and capitalist rent [Mandel, *op. cit.*, p. 289], is known to have existed in substantial degree even in advanced capitalist societies. This has given rise to an interesting debate amongst radical academics on the question of characterization of this tenancy type. Whereas one line of argument would see it essentially as a 'semi-feudal' relation, the other would regard it fully compatible under capitalist relations in a labour-scarce situation. However, the general consensus appears to be that it is a vestige of pre-capitalist relation and would go on declining with the development of productive forces in agriculture. For different theoretical positions on the question and accounts of concrete situations, see, among others, Bhaduri (1973), *op. cit.*; Bagchi, A.K. (1982), *The Political Economy of Underdevelopment*, Cambridge University Press, Cambridge, pp. 167–172; Byres, T.J. (1983), "Historical Perspectives on Share Cropping", *Journal of Peasant Studies*, January–April, pp. 7–40; Pearce, R. (1983), "Sharecropping: Towards a Marxist View", *Journal of Peasant Studies*, January–April, pp. 42–70; Dasgupta, B. (1984–a), "Sharecropping in West Bengal during the Colonial Period", *Economic and Political Weekly*, Review of Agriculture, March 31, pp. A–2 to A–8; Dasgupta, B. (1984–b), "Sharecropping in West Bengal: From Independence to Operation Barga", *Economic and Political Weekly*, Review of Agriculture, June 30, pp. A–85 to A–96.
111. The official Land Act, 1964 itself provides for a maximum of 50% share in the gross produce to the landowner; which is excessive by all economic logic and prevailing standard elsewhere.
112. 'Reverse tenancy' denotes tenancy holdings of the larger farmers rented–in from the smaller farmers [See Dasgupta (1984 – b), *op. cit.*, p. A–91].
113. For the methodological expositions on this historical possibility, see Dobb, *op. cit.*, and Hindess, B. and Hirst, P.Q. (1979), *Pre-Capitalist Modes of Production*, Routledge and Kegan Paul, London.
114. See, among others, McDougal, *op. cit.*, and Caplan, *op. cit.*

115. For the rural areas of Nepal as a whole, during the peak agriculture season, 62 out of the required 174 family male labour days (i.e. 35.63%) and 49 out of 125 family female labour days (i.e. 39.20 %) are known to be hired. Similarly, an average of 29 labour days of male and 32 labour days of female per household per year are obtained under mutual exchange arrangements. [National Planning Commission Secretariat (1978), *A Survey of Employment, Income Distribution and Consumption Patterns in Nepal* (Summary Report, Vol. IV), HMG/N, Kathmandu].
116. Among others, see, McDougal, *op. cit.*, for Western Hill and Terai; Caplan, *op. cit.*, for eastern Hill; Feldman and Fournier, *op. cit.*, for central Terai; Bista, D.B. (1968), *Padipur: A Central Terai Village of Nepal* (mimeo.), USAID/N, Kathmandu, for mid-eastern Terai; and Ishi, H. (1982), "Agricultural Labour Recruitments in a Parbate Village in Nepal," in *Anthropological and Linguistic Studies of the Gandaki Area in Nepal*, Institute for the Study of Language and Culture of Asia and Africa, Tokyo, for central Hill.
117. This hybrid 'feudal-capitalist' relation is reminiscent of 'Munshi system' in Bengal [See Bhaduri (1973), *op. cit.*].
118. This may be evident from the following official figures of percentage of under-employed days in the rural households of Nepal by principal geographic regions:

Geographic Region	*% of Unemployed Days*		
	Male	*Female*	*Total*
Mountain	57.04	65.70	61.45
Hill	62.05	67.88	65.04
Terai	54.13	71.89	61.90
NEPAL	57.88	68.69	63.10

Source: National Planning Commission Secretariat (1978), *A Survey of Employment, Income Distribution and Consumption Pattern in Nepal* (Summary Report Vol. IV), HMG/N, Kathmandu.

119. A number of micro-level studies have established the significant scale of out-migration of labour and remittances of non-agricultural income into peasant households in Nepal hills. For example, see, McDougal, *op. cit.*; Caplan (1970), *op. cit.*, pp. 115–117; Caplan, A.P. (1972), *Priests and Cobblers: A Study of Social Change in a Hindu Village in Western Nepal*, Chandler Publishing Company, San Francisco, pp. 40–41; Khadka, R.B. (1979), *Emigration in Nepal (A Micro Level Study of Bayalpata Village Panchayat, Achham)*, Tribhuvan University, Kathmandu.
120. For theoretical expositions on the role of different types of labour migration in reproducing or changing retrograde production relations in the countryside, see, among others, Lenin (1900), *op. cit.*; Banaji (1980), *op. cit.*; Meillassoux, C. (1980), "Farm Reproduction to Production: A Marxist Approach to Economic Anthropology", in Wolpe, *op. cit.*; Standing, G. (1981), "Migration and Modes of Exploitation: Social Origins of Immobility and Mobility", *The Journal of Peasant Studies*, Vol. 8, No. 2, January; Bhattarai, B.R. (1985) "Prabasi mazdoorharuko dohoro bhoomika: kehi saiddhantic prasnaharu" (Nepali), *Nepali Ekta Sandesh* (Organ of All India Napalese Unity Society), Vol. 5, No. 1.
121. See, among others, Bhaduri, *op. cit.*
122. Nepal Rastra Bank (1980), *op. cit.*, Vol. I, p. 179.

123. As in all such transitional formations, the surplus from agricultural production is known to be squandered in conspicuous consumption of imported luxury goods or investment in real estate in urban areas and in export-import mercantile activities or in hoarding and usury practices, by the non-producing classes. Feldman and Fournier, *op. cit.*, provide glimpse of this in a case study of central Terai rural households.
124. 'Capital formation' is defined here as "... an additional to fixed capital assets such as plant and machineries, buildings, raw materials, etc., which means that the formation of physical capital or asset is capital formation". [Nepal Rastra Bank (1980), *op. cit.*, Vol. III, p. 74].
125. See Kundu, A. (1980), *Measurement of Urban Processes: A Study in Regionalisation*, Popular Prakashan, Mumbai, pp. 46–77.
126. Kundu and Raza, *op. cit.*, p. 70.
127. Figures in parenthesis are weights, which statistically are elements of the eignvector associated with the highest eignvalue.
128. Specially compare with Pant (1982), *op. cit.*, and National Council of Science and Technology (1980), *Nepal: Atlas of Economic Development*, HMG/N, Mapping Sub-Committee, Kathmandu, pp. 126–27.

3 The Nature of Industrial Retardation

3.1 INTRODUCTION

In this chapter we shall investigate the nature of underdevelopment in the industrial sector (in the strict sense) as manifested in the social and spatial dimensions. Following the general scheme, first a brief introduction of the theoretical underpinnings and a historical review of the industrial process in Nepal shall be made followed by a detailed investigation in spatio-temporal frame of the 'production' and 'distribution' conditions of the domestic proto-industry and manufacturing industry. Finally the aggregate condition of the industrial sector shall be summed up and its spatial differentiation made to generalise the nature of industrial underdevelopment.

3.1.1 Theoretical Underpinnings

To ensure that the sectoral analysis attempted in this chapter follows the broad analytical frame outlined earlier it may be necessary to introduce here certain theoretical issues related to the industrial process.

3.1.11 Though a qualitative process like industrialisation cannot be defined in strict quantitative terms, it would be safe to view it as the process of vertical transfer of labour from activities of 'direct appropriation of nature' (i.e. primary production) to 'indirect appropriation of nature' (i.e. secondary production) and the concomitant qualitative change in the social structure. The higher social formations, as explained earlier, are characterised by greater share of labour force engaged in and social product contributed by the non-primary production sector. But the common misconception of equating industrial activities *per se* with capitalist mode of production would have to be set at rest first to have proper understanding of the dynamic of development/underdevelopment in the industrial sector. Historical study of industrial activities would bring to light an array of different forms of activities ranging from 'domestic industry'–'artisan' and 'handicraft' production– to 'manufacture' and 'modern factory' industry[1], and each marking a progressive change to higher form of social organisation It is only with the advent of the stage of 'manufacture' that the material base is prepared to organise industrial production on a capitalist basis; i.e. it is only now that the concomitant process of "the transformation of labour-power into a commodity and the transformation of the means of production into capital"[2] takes place. Still in the earlier stages of manufacture capital just takes over a 'mode of labour developed before the emergence of capitalist relations' and there is only 'formal subsumption of labour under capital'; the 'real subsumption' takes place at the stage of factory production and only then true capitalist relations blossom.[3]

The possibility of easy enlargement of scale of production due to greater factor mobility and operation of law of increasing return to scale to a quite high levels of output[4] and absolute increase though relative decrease of variable capital (i.e. labour) with the increase in constant capital (i.e. machinery etc.) in industrial production as against the opposite tendency in agricultural production[5], does provide for a faster rate of expansion and development of higher relations of production in the industrial sector. The nature and speed of development, however, would vary with the internal structure of society and its articulation with outside economies, because the prerequisites of development of industrial capitalism, namely sufficient concentration of capital in the hands of a bourgeois class that would put it to productive use, dispossession of labour from the means of production so that he is 'free' to still his labour-power at will and formation of a commodity market which can absorb a continuously increasing volume of production, *concomitantly*[6], can be fulfilled only with the total restructuration of the old society.

3.1.12 The question of underdevelopment in the industrial sector in the present Third World countries, therefore, implies the problem of fulfillment of above preconditions for the development of industrial capitalism within the interventionist impact of imperialism from without and conservative social structure within. The issue has been fairly extensively discussed amongst radical academics [7], and despite discernible divergence in their analytical approaches some common generalisations can be made about the characteristics and causes of industrial underdevelopment in Third World countries.

The characterisation of industrial underdevelopment may vary from 'de-industrialisation' in the earlier colonial context to 'distorted' or 'dependent' industrialisation in later colonial and neo-colonial context. De-industrialisation is the absolute decline in the share of labour force engaged in and social product contributed by the industrial sector and the reversal of technological development in the social economy.[8] It is the direct consequence of the breaking up of the symbiotic links between agriculture and household industry in the wake of penetration of factory-made goods from the colonial country. Distorted or dependent industrialisation, on the other hand, is characterised by spurious 'growth' in industrial activities and production but no independent 'development' in the real sense. In other words, it is marked by predominance of export-oriented elementary processing activities or production of import-substitution consumer goods, inverted industrial structure (i.e. negligible proportion of production or capital goods industries), excessive dependence on technological or capital goods imports, disarticulation among different branches of industries, extreme unevenness in distribution of productivity, etc.[9] A general industrial scenario marked by low and disparate growth and with mixed characteristics of both de-industrialisation' and 'distorted'/'dependent' industrialisation may be tentatively referred to as 'industrial retardation'.

The causal mechanism of industrial underdevelopment have been quite disparately explained and may be better understood in terms of problems associated with the principal elements of the industrial process, namely accumulation of capital, availability of 'free' labour and formation of a home market.

The original or primitive accumulation of capital in the hands of a bourgeois class that would use it for productive purposes is known to be hampered in the Third World countries by: (i) draining away of social surplus by colonial plunder, or through profit repatriation by foreign investors, or through 'unequal exchange' in trade relations, or through debt-servicing in financial transactions;[10] (ii) squandering of accumulated surplus in conspicuous consumption or hoarding in foreign banks or investment in real estate and usurious practices, by landlord and mercantile-bureaucratic bourgeois classes;[11] (iii) conversion of indigenous merchant capital into comprador mercantile and bureaucratic capital;[12]

(iv) existence of pre-capitalist monopoly in trade which would lock-up the capital in the hands of monopoly trader and prevent from passing on to more enterprising industrial entrepreneur[13]; (v) entrenchment of capital under the arbitrary power of a despotic and all-powerful state that would thwart the rise of an independent capitalist class[14]; (vi) backwardness of agricultural sector and shortage of absolute surplus value; (vii) non-concentration of capital into fewer hands due to low class differentiation.[15]

Similarly, the formation of industrial proletariat is blocked by: (i) retention of labour in backward agriculture through servile ties and debt-bondage; (ii) reproduction of uneconomic peasant agriculture through augmentation of income from seasonal out-migration of labour;[16] (iii) slackening of dispossession of a small producer from the means of production due to ineffective process of capital concentration.[17]

The third necessary condition of development of industrial capitalism, i.e. the formation of an ever-expanding commodity market, may be thwarted by any or all of these factors;

(i) Both supply and demand market may be constricted due to prevalence of use value production or as yet unshattered symbiotic link between peasant agriculture and household industry;
(ii) The created 'home market' may be preempted by foreign capital either by force or by subtle economic manipulation as its higher labour productivity and cheap prices of products cannot be matched by indigenous capital in the absence of the protective umbrella of a state;
(iii) Backwardness of agricultural sector would deprive market for both articles of consumption for the workers and of means of production for the agricultural bourgeoisie;[18]
(iv) High inequality in income distribution would constrict the market for mass consumption goods, and the narrow consumer durable demands of the minority rich would not sustain desirable level of industrialisation;[19]
(v) The foreign market for industrial products is virtually closed due to low competitiveness vis-à-vis developed industrial economies, except in times of crisis for the latter, like war etc. The only advantage enjoyed by underdeveloped economies may be in elementary processing industries, which would trap them in a perpetual 'unequal exchange' relation.

In the light of these general experiences and the internal and external specificities of a particular social formation, the state of industrial process prevailing in it may be studied.

3.1.13 As regards the spatial aspects of industrial underdevelopment, the conventional 'industrial location theories'[20] provide very little light. Since the prime concern of much of these theories is the locational behaviour of individual firms in an ahistoric, or a static capitalist setting, their utility for a politico-economic appraisal of the industrial process, as the current study is, would be naturally peripheral. Nevertheless, keeping within our general analytical approach of seeing spatial organisation as both 'manifestation' and to a lesser extent 'causal factor' in the social process, the spatial dimensions of industrial underdevelopment in the present Third World context may be briefly introduced.

By the very nature of 'indirect' appropriation of nature, industrial activities would be less space-contingent and more space-forming. But the degree of space contingency and the nature of space formation would depend on the historical stage of development of industries. Thus emergent 'locational problem' of industries may be seen as "spatial manifestation of contradiction of capitalism."[21]

In the case of Third World countries the spatial organisation of industrial activities would depend on the nature of industrial underdevelopment. An industrial structure marked by predominance of simple raw materials processing would give rise to a disarticulated and dispersed spatial organisation, and the location of individual industry would be mainly 'rooted'[22] to the sources of raw materials. On the other hand, industrial growth under the overriding influence of external colonial/neo-colonial imperatives would give rise to a distorted spatial structure marked by growth of dysfunctional industrial enclaves along points of superior articulation with outside economies and stagnation of vast indigent hinterland.[23] In the general situation of underdeveloped countries, however, a complex pattern would prevail which can be discerned through a systematic analysis of both spatial and a-spatial factors concomitantly.

3.1.2 Historical Antecedents

The historical overview here consists of a brief sequential analysis of the process of industrial retardation followed by an assessment of the principal elements of the process, namely capital, labour and market, and the resultant spatial implications.

3.1.21 A Review of the Process of Industrial Retardation

The fragmentary historical accounts on the territorial entities constituting the present day Nepal are replete with positive references about the state of artisan and craft productions in the country. Laudatory remarks about the Nepalese woolen products by Kautilya, the renowned Indian economist, in 4th century B.C. is an oft-cited case in point.[24] Similarly, numerous inscriptions of the Lichchavi era (3rd to 7th century A.D.) and the travel accounts of the celebrated Chinese traveller of the 7th century, Yuan Chwang, confirm the flourishing of textile industries and circulation of locally minted copper and silver coins in Kathmandu Valley during the time.[25] Discernible 'urban' and mercantile culture of the Greek-like city states of the Valley also bear adequate testimony to the fairly high state of artisan and craft production then. Though no authentic accounts of the differentiation of the economy in those early years is available for the rest of the countryside, the invasion of the hill tracts by the fleeing Hindus from the Indian plains with their well defined occupational caste structure from 11th century onwards, must have bolstered and diversified the artisan production inherent in the prevailing natural economy.

A fairly reliable picture of the healthy state of secondary production activities in the country after its political unification in the second half of the 18th century, can be reconstructed from the reports and travelogues of a number of well-known Britishers associated with Nepal during the 19th century. These sources portray a very encouraging scenario, though varying with time and space, of artisan, handicraft and manufacturing production of different metal-works, munitions, cotton and other textiles, brown sugar, paper, etc. in different parts of the country.[26] Whereas there is adequate evidence of importation of factory-made luxury consumption goods primarily from British India, in increasing volume and diversity from late 18th century onwards, the disjointed economic subsystems during the period are known to have been self-sufficient in different non-primary goods and even exported some craft products to Tibet and India. Particularly high level of achievement in industrial production for the given era was recorded in the field of mineral (specially iron, copper, zinc and lead) processing and munition production, which is reported to have attained the stage of factory production of fire arms and ammunitions sufficient to equip an army of more than 100 thousand men.[27] However, the lopsided nature of the so-called industrial development guided by the impulses of the militarist ruling oligarchy is underscored by the "primitive technique" of artisan and handicraft production of mass consumption goods like cloth, boats and canoes, etc. and by the overwhelming dependence of the population on agriculture all through the 19th century.[18]

Extension of Indian railway networks to the Nepalese border by the end of the 19th century and greater economic integration of the country with the colonial British economy culminating in the formal signing of "Treaty of Friendship" between Nepal and Britain in 1923, facilitated the inundation of the Nepalese captive market with the British-Indian manufactured goods, which led to the gradual decline and near collapse of age-old artisan and handicraft production in the country. Serious students of economic history of Nepal are unanimous on the disastrous impact the unrestricted integration with the more advanced Indian economy had on the traditional industries of Nepal and in arresting and distorting the natural growth process of the country's economy. To cite Seddon et. al. on the situation in central Nepal in this context:

> "By the late 1930's the small-scale production of cloth by urban manufacturers in Nepal had almost entirely disappeared and the brass and copper workers of such centres as Tansen and Pokhara were beginning to suffer from rising prices of imported raw materials and competition from Indian and other foreign manufacturers. Around 1940 attempts were made to revive the once vigorous cotton weaving industry of Bandipur and skilled workers

were imported from the Kathmandu Valley to operate the looms, which at one time reputedly numbered over 200; but a combination of disputes among the shareholders of the company concerned and restrictions imposed by India on the export to Nepal of the cotton thread now used extensively brought about a rapid decline."[29]

However, the peculiar specificities of global capitalist crisis of the 1930's and the exigencies of pre-World War II situation paved the way for the rise of modern manufacturing activities in Nepal charged by the fabulous demands of the war, specially for jute and forest products, on the one hand, and compelled by the dislocation of the British imperial economy, on the other, a section of the Indian monopoly capital found it prudent to literally jump over the political border to the Nepalese side to join hands with the indigenous feudal-mercantalists. The result was the establishment of a series of manufacturing industries as "joint stock public limited companies' in the eastern Terai across the Indian border, starting with the largest manufacturing unit in the country, the Biratnagar Jute Mills, in 1936.[30]

Table 3.1 provides a glimpse of the growth pattern of "Joints Stock Public Limited Companies" in different phases of the war upto the political change of 1950–51 marked by the installation of a regime more amenable to the 'new' rulers in India in place of the old pro-British Rana regime. It is interesting to note that immediately after the war 4 out of 5 cotton mills were closed and further elementary-processing, export-oriented industries like rice and oil mills, jute mills, mining, etc. were incorporated. This provides an inkling of the ensuing nature of industrial retardation in the country under the shadow of more developed industrial capitalism in India. Also, the fact that most of these industries were located in the Terai adjoining the Indian rail-head and an overwhelming share of capital investment in them was made by the Indian monopolists,[31] further substantiates the real nature of the 'extra-verted' industrial growth.

The period immediately after the political change of 1950/51 was a period of intensification of economic integration of Nepal with India and a period of further industrial retardation in Nepal. By 1956 , when the first five-year 'plan' was launched, out of 68 public companies registered 24 had been dissolved "due to lack of equity capital", 19 were in liquidation, 15 reported operation at a loss and only a few apparently reasonably successful.[32]

Only the combined effect of a set of historical coincidences in the late 1950's and early 1960's marked by the sudden rise of imperialist interest to maintain 'stability' in the Himalayas in the wake of Tibetan revolution, temporary loosening of the hold of Indian monopoly capital in Nepal in the aftermath of India's military clash with China over the Himalayas and the generation of a populist, pseudo-nationalist wave[33] inside the country by the rivalry over exercising political supremacy of the two dominant factions of the ruling classes represented by the Nepali Congress Party and the absolute monarchy, brought about a relatively more congenial atmosphere for industrial growth in the country. These

Table 3.1 Growth of Joint Stock Public Limited Companies in Nepal (1936/37–1950/51).

	Industry	*Pre-war Period (1936/37–1938/39)*		*War Period (1939/40–1944/45)*		*Post-war Period (1945/46–1950/51)*		*Total (1936/37–1950/51)*	
		Incorporated	*Wound-up*	*Incorporated*	*Wound-up*	*Incorporated*	*Wound-up*	*Incorporated*	*Wound-up*
1.	Jute Mills	1	–	–	–	2	–	3	–
2.	Cotton Mills	–	–	2	–	3	4	5	4
3.	Sugar Mills	1	–	–	1	1	–	2	1
4.	Rice and Oil Mills	2	1	2	–	15	–	19	1
5.	Cigarette Factory	–	–	–	–	1	–	1	–
6.	Match Factory	1	–	–	–	2	–	3	–
7.	Mining	–	–	1	–	3	–	4	–
8.	Wood Work	–	–	3	–	1	–	4	–
9.	Power Supply	–	–	1	–	1	–	2	–
10.	Miscellaneous	1	–	5	1	6	2	12	3
	ALL INDUSTRIES	6	1	14	2	35	6	55	9

Source: Adapted from Shrestha, B.P. (1967), *The Economy of Nepal*, Vora and Co. Publishers, Mumbai, P. 164.

years, subsequently, saw increased industrial investment primarily through 'aid' from diverse external sources and backed by a half-hearted though attempt at agrarian reforms. However, the basically undisturbed retrograde social structure backed by external props could not have conceivably promoted genuine industrialisation in the country, and by the 1970s the industrial scenario was back to square one.

3.1.22 Condition of Principal Elements of the Industrial Process

The historical process of industrial retardation may be understood in greater depth if it is viewed in terms of deficiencies embedded in the principal component parts of the industrial process, namely primitive accumulation, availability of 'free' labour and formation of a perfect commodity market.

(i) Barriers to Primitive Accumulation In the true sense of the term 'primitive accumulation' refers to the polarisation of the social classes and the concentration of capital in the hands of the nascent bourgeoisie. But in the case of Nepal, the process seems to have been historically marred by the following specificities:

- Despite a fairly well-articulated class of merchant capitalists mostly confined to the Kathmandu Valley and engaging in entrepot trade, they had over the time developed into powerful monopolists and hence were not inclined to play a "revolutionary" role in seizing over the production process. Moreover, common to most of the non-European societies,[34] the 'Asiatic' state was heavily involved in economic activities, specially trade, and hence the growth of independent merchant class that could subsequently graduate into the industrial bourgeoisie was grossly inhibited.
- As it was more of an 'artisan' than 'handicraft' production (see Section 3.1.1 above) of domestic proto-industries that prevailed in most parts of Nepal, it was more difficult for the small artisans to graduate into the industrial bourgeoisie than had they been small handicraftsmen.
- Overdependence of the traditional merchant class on entrepot trade between Tibet and India rather than on the internal commodity trade, virtually sealed their economic fate after the opening up of the trade route to Tibet via Chumbi Valley in Sikkim in 1904 and the consequent decline in entrepot trade through Nepal.
- The new merchant class that had emerged in the Terai in the wake of extension of Indian rail-heads to the Nepalese border, was either alien or/and an appendage of imperialism; hence he could not play a progressive role of readily switching over to production capital.
- Due to the concentration of mercantile activities in the hands of the same group of powerful feudal lords, like the Ranas, the appropriated surplus continued to be squandered in conspicuous luxury consumption, construction of numerous palatial buildings, etc.[35]

- The unrestricted link-up of the Nepalese economy with the more advanced Indian economy through periodic unequal Treaties, control of fiscal policies by the Indian Reserve Bank till the late 1950s, compounded by the political uncertainties in the country, paved the way for the absolute drain of accumulated surplus to India in the form of investments and bank deposits.[36]

(ii) Lack of Industrial Proletariat In the Nepalese history, the growth of industrial proletariat appears to have been hampered by the twin, and apparently contradictory, processes of non-release of surplus labour from the backward agricultural sector, and the drain of released labour away from the indigenous economy as follows:

- Historical survey of the agricultural processes (see Section 2.1.2 above) has clearly brought into light the predominance of small-scale peasant production and the changing forms of chaining the survile peasantry to their meager holdings. Such institutionalised condemnation of the peasantry to 'self-exploitation' not only directly abated the perpetuation of the prevailing retrograde production relations but also contributed in arresting the development of the industrial sector by not releasing the required 'free' labour. Rather there are evidences of ruined artisans and craft producers from the beginning of 20th century onwards reverting back to agriculture and adding to further fragmentation of land-holdings in the hills.[37] Apart from the social factors, natural topographical barriers of the hills also came in the way of concentration of land-holdings and resultant class differentiations, thereby strengthening the retrograde forces and industrial retardation.
- On the contrary, beginning with the cessation of state expansion campaign in the first quarter of the 19th century and crowning with the ruination of artisan and craft production in the wake of fatal onslaughts by the British-Indian manufactured goods, there arose a sizeable body of unemployed or under-employed labour force in the economy. To this, preferential recruitments of Nepalese hill-dwellers in British-Indian army, unlimited mercenary service opportunity offered by the two World Wars and gradual development of industrial capitalism in India, etc., acted as strong 'pull' factors for the emigration of Nepalese semi-proletarialnised labour. Thus ensued a steady migratory flow of Nepalese labour to India,[38] and the growth of industrial proletariat within the country was stunted.

(iii) Preemption of the 'Home Market' 'Periods of rapidly expanding markets as well as of expanding labour supply are the periods *par excellence* of industrial expansion'.[39] The formation of markets for industries in Nepal, however, seem to have been historically impaired by the following factors:

- The historical backwardness of the agriculture sector and low differentiation of peasantry as delineated earlier, seem to have deprived the much-needed 'home market' for the rise of indigenous industries. Moreover the continued survival of 'natural economy' with a symbiotic link between the primitive agriculture and artisan production in large parts of the physically secluded areas, constricted the size of potential market for large-scale manufacturing.

- The only consumers of industrial products, the ruling feudal oligarchy, consumed luxury goods which could not be locally manufactured but had to be imported from outside.

  The most prominent indigenous production, was perhaps the munitions production, which lost its rationale after the cessation of state expansion drive after the 1st quarter of the 19th century.
- Whatever market for manufacturing products did develop in the country in the beginning of the 20th century, specially after World War I, did not become the 'internal market' for the Nepalese industries. After the Treaty of 1923 allowing for virtually unrestricted inflow of British-Indian manufactured goods, it became an appendage to the 'internal market' of Indian industries, as apprehended by Baran[40] for all the underdeveloped countries integrated to the metropolitan economy. With the subsequent unequal Treaties with 'independent' India in the same vein of the 1923 Treaty,[41] Nepal continued to remain a virtual captive market for Indian manufactured goods.
- The total absence of modern transportation and communication network prior to the 1950s and the negligible extent of the same since then, has provided a formidable physical barrier for commodity circulation in the country and hindered the formation of an integrated 'national' market for indigenous industries.
- Except for a brief interlude of World War II, Indian or overseas markets for Nepalese industries were practically ruled out because there was no commodity which was not manufactured in India at a higher level of social productivity that could be manufactured in Nepal. Furthermore, till the 1960s economic relations of Nepal with countries other than India were virtually non-existent. The traditional Tibetan market for the Nepalese industries declined after the opening up of direct India-Tibet trade route via Chumbi Valley in 1904, and finally closed after the consolidation of revolution there in the 1950s.

3.1.23 Locational Implications

The historical process of industrial underdevelopment in Nepal is seen to be characterised by corresponding locational shift and distortions inflicted in the earlier spatial distribution of industries. A general overview of the industrial process over the years would establish that a nominal vertical shift in the production pattern from the traditional artisan and handicraft types to the modern manufacturing type has been accompanied by a more than proportionate degree of locational shift from the mid-Hills to the Terai along the Indian border.

The traditional industries in Nepal dominated by mineral processing, munition production, cotton weaving and spinning, etc. are known to have had a dispersed locational pattern along important centres of mid-Hills; or mainly 'rooted' to their raw material base. Followed by Kathmandu Valley, central and eastern

Hills seem to have been the most significant zones of industrial activities during the 19th and the first quarter of the 20th century. The three major cities, Kathmandu, Lalitpur and Bhaktapur in Kathmandu Valley, Pokhara-Bandipur-Palpa-Baglung-Gorkha-Lamjung in central Hill, Banepa-Dhulikhel-Chautara-Bhojpur-Dhankuta in eastern Hill, were the principal craft-production centres specialising in cotton textiles and metal products, before their decline in the face of onslaughts from mill-made goods from British India after the first quarter of the 20th century[42]. Those in eastern Hill and Pyuthan in western Hill were the better known centres for mineral-processing and munition production.

With the advent of modern manufacturing in the 1930s and '40s, a decisive shift in the locational pattern of industries took place in favour of the Terai, particularly its eastern, rather far-eastern, sector. Out of the 56 joint-stock industrial enterprises incorporated as 'public limited companies' between 1936 and 1963 as many as 45 had selected their sites in the Terai and about 3/4th of private firms registered or licensed between 1944–45 and 1963 were concentrated in the Terai[43]. Some idea of literal physical proximity of Nepalese industries to India can be had from the fact that of the two most important jute mills of the country located in Biratnagar, the one is only a few yards and the other a few hundred yards away from the Indian border.

This pronounced historical shift in industrial location may be explained in terms of the following:

- The so-called modern, industrial development stirred by the temporary exigencies of World War II, as already noted, was heavily 'extra-verted', both for import of heavy machineries and export of finished products, and needed to be located nearest to the rail-heads across the Indian border to economise on transport cost.
- The far-eastern Terai, being the closest to the nearest Calcutta port and the most well integrated with the Indian railway system, provided the most suitable location for such 'extra-verted' industries.
- The emphasis of industrial production having been shifted to agro-processing activities, the Terai naturally scored over other areas in the matter of suply of raw materials, viz. jute in far-eastern Terai, sugar in central Terai, tobacco in mid-eastern Terai, grains and oil-seeds all over Terai, etc.
- As the Indian monopolists were the principal owners of the industrial enterprises, they quite understandably preferred physical proximity to India.
- Because of early growth of monopolies, or rather 'transferred' monopolisation from India, in the infantile industrial sector, the monopolist owners tended to centralise industrial activities at one place even when rationally not always warranted; e.g. location of sugar mill in Biratnagar.

The net result was a highly skewed and extra-verted location pattern of industries not commensurate with the early stage of their social development. This historically transmitted spatial distortion would naturally weigh quite significantly on the present or future industrial spatial structure in the country.

3.2 CONDITIONS OF DOMESTIC PROTO-INDUSTRY[44]

Notwithstanding the historical decline of artisan and handicraft production in the wake of fatal onslaughts of foreign factory-made goods, the general persistence of domestic proto-industry in Nepal on a significant scale, both in the social and spatial dimensions, demands a comprehensive understanding so that all the aspects of the underdevelopment process may be understood. The fact that 24% of all households in the country are still engaged in 'cottage type manufacturing'[45] and about 95% of the total industrial employment of slightly more than one million persons[46] is provided by 'cottage industry'[47], amply highlights the social and economic importance of this sub-sector.

In the absence of a comprehensive census or record of the domestic proto-industry in the desired spatial and temporal dimensions, the present study has been based on fragmentary information obtained from diverse sources and may exhibit the lack of desired level of rigour. Nonetheless we have attempted to stick to the general methodological framework adopted throughout and sought to analyse the 'production' and 'distribution' aspects of the phenomenon separately.

3.2.1 'Production' Characteristics

Basically an adjunct of peasant agriculture, the scope of domestic proto-industry encompasses the production of a wide range of goods and services varying with urban or rural areas or divergent ecological zones, but invariably complimenting and reproducing the respective 'natural economy'. Moreover, with the increasing integration of the economy with the outside world through merchandise trade and tourist flows, this sub-sector has been made to produce export-oriented crafts. Since it would be too unwieldy to analyse different attribute of individual items produced [48] it would be worthwhile to group them with respect to certain common attributes like input base, use of output, etc. In the absence of comparable data base in a temporal frame, we have adopted a 'mixed' classification made by Industrial Services Centre for 1977/78 (Table 3.2) and devised our own input- and use-based classification[49] for 1972/73 (Tables 3.3 and 3.4).

3.2.11 From Table 3.2 it is evident that 'agro-based' followed by 'cotton and woolen textiles', 'forest-based' and 'metallic' products in that order, constitute the most important domestic proto-industries in Nepal. In fact the three principal sub-groups, namely agro-based, forest-based and cotton and woolen textile industries, together account for 95.37% of registered units, 93.85% of total employment, 88.49% of fixed investment, 88.89% of gross value of production and 86.07% of value added. The negligible share of more advanced metallic, plastic and chemical products, amply speaks of the structural infirmities embedded in the domestic proto-industrial sector.

Though the absolute figures may not be comparable due to changed definition of industry classes, a cross-classification of 'input-based' and 'use-based'

Table 3.2 General Characteristics of Domestic Proto-Industry (1977–78).

Mixed Classification of Industries / *Attributes*	*No. of HH or Registered Unit Engaged*	*Employment*	*Fixed Investment (in Rs. '000)*	*Annual Production (Rs. '000)*	*Value Added (in Rs. '000)*
1. Agro-based	340527 (45.37)	432729 (41.86)	111666 (32.74)	316290 (44.36)	56450 (25.80)
2. Forest-based	193078 (25.72)	263316 (25.47)	66553 (19.51)	70018 (9.82)	31468 (14.33)
3. Non-Metallic Products	5665 (0.75)	13465 (1.30)	6299 (1.85)	17220 (2.42)	7820 (3.58)
4. Metallic Products	24751 (3.30)	43413 (4.20)	25936 (7.61)	50523 (7.09)	17843 (8.16)
5. Cotton and Woolen Textile	182217 (24.28)	274071 (26.52)	123602 (36.24)	24747 (34.71)	100500 (45.94)
6. Leather and Leather Products	3383 (0.45)	4750 (0.46)	3618 (1.06)	3865 (0.54)	1430 (0.65)
7. Plastic Products	102 (0.01)	382 (0.04)	861 (0.25)	2507 (0.35)	1108 (0.51)
8. Detergent and Chemicals	30 (0.004)	185 (0.02)	1083 (0.32)	1317 (0.18)	520 (0.24)
9. Drugs and Medicines	5 (–)	49 (0.005)	139 (0.04)	446 (0.06)	278 (0.13)
10. Miscellaneous N.E.S.	817 (0.11)	1275 (0.12)	1293 (0.38)	3290 (0.46)	1343 (0.61)
TOTAL	750575 (100.00)	1033636 (100.00)	341050 (100.00)	713001 (100.00)	218761 (100. 00)

Note: Figures in parenthesis are column percentages.
Source: Industrial Services Centre (1982), *Industrial Sectoral Plan Study (1980/81–1990/91)*, Vol. I, (Revised Edition), Kathmandu.

sub-groups (Tables 3.3 and 3.4) among themselves would enable one to discern a changing structural composition of domestic proto-industries in favour of agro-based units at the cost of other sub groups.

Spatial differentiation of gross value of production by input-based and use-based classifications should provide further insights into the nature of structural retrogression experienced by the domestic proto-industries. Looking at the input-based classification (Table 3.3) first: the higher share of agro-based, specially crop-based and correspondingly low share of mineral-based, and forest-based industries in the supposedly more 'developed' eastern and central zones could be a manifestation of greater differentiation of non-primary production activities in these areas both as a result of their greater articulation with outside economy and comparatively higher levels of agricultural development in them. In the absence of relevant data disaggregated along the more diverse north-south ecological zones it would be presumptuous to venture definite conclusions, but from the observed fact of the lowest share of metallic mineral based activities in the minerally better endowed central zone, which happens to be the earliest and best integrated with the superior Indian economy, it can be safely surmised that traditional domestic proto-industries have been worst affected in areas most inundated with Indian factory productions. The same conclusion can be drawn from the analysis of spatial distributional pattern of domestic proto-industries by use-based classifications (Table 3.4). The lower shares of 'agricultural tools and equipments' and 'household equipments and accessories', which are mostly mineral and forest-based, in the central and eastern zones are cases in point[50].

The rather intriguing spatial distribution pattern of 'textiles and allied' industries, i.e. higher share of value of production in both intra- and inter-zonal terms in the most and the least externally integrated central and far-western zones respectively (Table 3.4), perhaps permits us to draw another set of conclusions about the realignment of internal structure of industries in the light of external integration. The higher share of textiles in the central zone, which has traditionally excelled in this craft specially in cotton and woolen weaving, can be interpreted as the manifestations of greater resistance offered by it to the onslaughts of imported manufactured products, or alternatively, as the survival resulting from its capacity to adjust, though in a dominated form, to the new international division of labour. However, the explanation should be viewed only in relation with other zones, for, at the absolute level there are enough evidences of decline of traditional handloom textiles in their most celebrated 'home' of Kathmandu Valley in central zone[51]. On the contrary, the survival of more backward textile proto-industries in the far-western zone may be attributed to the insufficient penetration of imported factory made products, or to the greater stability of 'natural economy' which have been historically more pronounced than in other zones because of its greater natural and social seclusion.[52]

Table 3.3 Input-based Classification of Domestic Proto-Industry by Territorial Zones (1972–73).

Classification of Industries		*Value of total Production (Rs. '000)*								
Territorial Zones		*I Forest-based*	*II Agro-based*			*III Mineral-based*			*IV Miscella-neous*	*Total*
			Crop-based	*Animal based*	*Sub - Total*	*Metallic-mineral*	*Non-metallic mineral*	*Sub-Total*		
1. Eastern Zone		4203	56705	11079	67784	4914	122	5036	11069	88092
	(i)	(4.77)	(64.37)	(12.58)	(76.95)	(5.58)	(0.14)	(5.72)	(12.56)	(100.00)
	(ii)	(9.16)	(32.24)	(22.76)	(30.19)	(40.08)	(2.42)	(29.09)	(71.64)	(29.05)
2. Central Zone		6282	68561	4444	73005	417	314	731	13	80031
	(i)	(7.85)	(85.67)	(5.55)	(91.22)	(0.52)	(0.39)	(0.91)	(0.02)	(100.00)
	(ii)	(13.69)	(38.98)	(9.13)	(32.51)	(3.40)	(6.22)	(4.22)	(0.08)	(26.39)
3. Western Zone		17344	21583	4439	26022	2289	2315	4604	3575	51545
	(i)	(33.65)	(41.87)	(8.61)	(50.48)	(4.44)	(4.49)	(8.93)	(6.94)	(100.00)
	(ii)	(37.78)	(12.27)	(9.12)	(11.59)	(18.66)	(45.85)	(26.59)	(23.14)	(17.00)
4. Far-Western Zone		18073	29024	28705	57729	4644	2298	6942	794	83538
	(i)	(21.63)	(34.74)	(34.36)	(69.11)	(5.56)	(2.75)	(8.31)	(0.95)	(100.00)
	(ii)	(39.37)	(16.50)	(58.98)	(25.71)	(37.87)	(45.51)	(40.10)	(5.14)	(27.55)
NEPAL		45902	175873	48667	224540	12264	5049	17313	15451	303206
	(i)	(15.14)	(58.00)	(16.05)	(74.05)	(4.04)	(1.67)	(5.71)	(5.10)	(100.00)
	(ii)	(100.00)	(100.00)	(100.00)	(100.00)	(100.00)	(100.00)	(100.00)	(100.00)	(100.00)

Note: Figures in parenthesis are percentages; (i) Raw percentage (ii) Column percentage.

Source: Central Bureau of Statistics, *Sample Survey of the Cottage and Small Scale Industries 1972–73*, Kathmandu.

Table 3.4 Use-based Classification of Domestic Proto-Industry by Territorial Zones (1972–73).

Classification of Industries		*Value of Production (Rs. '000)*						
Territorial Zones		*Food and Allied*	*Textiles and Allied*	*Agricultural tools and equipments*	*Household equipments and accessories*	*Jewelleries and ornaments*	*Miscellaneous*	*Total*
1. Eastern Zone		46436	23186	2092	2980	2329	11069	88092
	(i)	(52.71)	(26.32)	(2.37)	(3.38)	(2.64)	(12.57)	(100.00)
	(ii)	(91.85)	(14.89)	(9.11)	(5.63)	(41.57)	(71.64)	(29.05)
2. Central Zone		3959	68837	379	6843	–	13	80031
	(i)	(4.95)	(86.01)	(0.47)	(8.55)		(0.02)	(100.00)
	(ii)	(7.83)	(44.21)	(1.65)	(12.93)		(0.08)	(26.39)
3. Western Zone		162	5255	11402	30900	251	3575	51545
	(i)	(0.31)	(10.19)	(22.12)	(59.95)	(0.49)	(6.94)	(100.00)
	(ii)	(0.32)	(3.37)	(49.65)	(58.39)	(4.48)	(23.14)	(17.00)
4. Far-Western Zone		–	58433	9092	12197	3022	794	83538
	(i)		(69.95)	(10.88)	(14.60)	(3.62)	(0.95)	(100.00)
	(ii)		(37.53)	(39.59)	(23.05)	(53.95)	(5.14)	(27.55)
NEPAL		50557	155711	22965	52920	5602	15451	303206
	(i)	(16.67)	(51.35)	(7.57)	(17.45)	(1.85)	(5.10)	(100.00)
	(ii)	(100.00)	(100.00)	(100.00)	(100.00)	(100.00)	(100.00)	(100.00)

Note: Figures in parenthesis are percentages; (I) Row percentage, (II) Column percentage.
Source: Central Bureau of Statistics, *Sample Survey of the Cottage and Small Scale Industries 1972–73*, Kathmandu.

The greater structural change of domestic proto-industries in the more externally integrated central and eastern zones compared to the remote far-western zone is also reflected in the greater specialisation of products in the former than in the latter, though the process cannot be discerned too emphatically in the absence of micro-level and time series data.

3.2.12 The very nature of "small scale" production and primary reliance of family labour devoid of automation, also the absence of competitive impulses of a 'free' market in the case "artisan" production, the domestic proto-industry in its generalised form is marked by a primitive technique of production and low production and low productivity of factors involved. The scenario in the case of Nepal as evident from Tables 3.5 and 3.6, is no exception. Rather, the very low average values of return to labour, capital and industrial unit and use of machinery and fuel per unit indicate a very rudimentary form of production.

A study of the structural positions of the domestic proto-industries by relevant groups (Table 3.5) would bring out significant inter-group variations despite their overall low absolute values. The more important (volume-wise) subgroups of agro-based and forest-based proto-industries are found to be structurally the most depressed, whereas the next important ones of woolen and cotton textiles and metallic products are seen to be in a comparatively better position. The apparently impressive productivity and structural base of the three sub-groups including drugs and medicines, detergent and chemicals and plastic products do not amount to much in view of their negligible share in the total volume of domestic proto-industries. Whereas much of these inter-group differences in productivity could be explained in terms of the differences in their "natural" attributes, the distortions inflicted by 'social' factors also seem to be no less important. Sounder structural base and higher productivity in the proto-industry sub-groups catering to the export market and consumption of the upper classes than in those producing mass consumption goods, should be a pointer towards that.

Spatial configuration of basic structural attributes of the domestic proto-industries (Table 3.6) provide further insights into the process of structural retrogression afflicting the sub-sectoral economy in question. Whereas the sounder position of central zone by any yardstick is unmistakable and is easily explicable in terms of the socio-historical advantage enjoyed by it over the rest of the territorial zones, the most depressed state of western zone even behind the generally most laggard far-western zone provides grounds for serious thought. Leaving aside the far-western zone as a chronic case of 'autarchic stagnation', the polarisation of central and western zones to extreme positions from a not so markedly different beginning deserves a probing in terms of the dynamics of endogenous and exogenous forces interacting on them. In the lack of time series data and pending the analysis of internal social relations of production, it can only be hypothesised on the basis of earlier observations that these may be ideal cases of 'absolute ruination' and 'dependent restructuration' of domestic proto-industrial production in territorial zones of differing social structures in the face of

Table 3.5 Structural Attributes of Domestic Proto-Industry by Types (1977–78).

Structural Attributes Types of Industries	*Labour/Unit (Persons)*	*Output/Unit (NRs.)*	*Output/Labour (NRs.)*	*Capital/Unit (NRs.)*	*Capital/Labour (NRs.)*	*Value added/unit (NRs.)*	*Value added/labour (NRs.)*
Agro-based industries	1.27 (0.92)	929 (0.98)	731 (1.06)	328 (0.72)	258 (0.78)	166 (0.57)	130 (0.61)
Forest-based industries	1.36 (0.99)	303 (0.32)	200 (0.29)	345 (0.76)	253 (0.77)	163 (0.56)	120 (0.57)
Non-metallic Products	2.38 (1.72)	3040 (3.20)	1279 (1.85)	1112 (2.45)	468 (1.42)	1380 (4.74)	581 (2.74)
Metallic Products	1.75 (1.27)	2041 (2.15)	1164 (1.69)	1048 (2.31)	597 (1.81)	721 (2.48)	411 (1.94)
Woolens Cotton Products	1.50 (1.09)	1358 (1.43)	903 (1.31)	678 (1.49)	451 (1.37)	552 (1.90)	367 (1.73)
Leather and Leather Products	1.40 (1.01)	1142 (1.20)	814 (1.18)	1069 (2.35)	762 (2.31)	423 (1.45)	301 (1.42)
Plastic Products	3.75 (2.72)	24578 (25.87)	6563 (9.51)	8441 (188.59)	2254 (6.83)	10862 (37.33)	2901 (13.68)
Detergents and Chemicals	6.17 (4.47)	45700 (48.11)	7411 (10.74)	36100 (79.52)	5854 (17.74)	17333 (59.56)	2811 (13.26)
Drugs and Medicines	9.8 (0.71)	89200 (93.89)	9102 (13.19)	27800 (61.23)	2837 (8.60)	55800 (191.75)	5694 (26.86)
Miscellaneous	1.56 (1.13)	4027 (4.24)	2580 (3.74)	1583 (3.49)	1014 (3.07)	1644 (5.65)	1053 (4.97)
Overall Average	1.38 (1.00)	950 (1.00)	690 (1.00)	454 (1.00)	330 (1.00)	291 (1.00)	212 (1.00)

Note: Figures in parenthesis are location factors.
Source: Derived from Table 3.2.

Table 3.6 Structural Attributes of Domestic Proto-Industry by Territorial Zones (1972–73).

Structural Attributes / *Territorial Zones*	*Labour/Unit*	*Capital/Labour (Rs.)*	*Output/Labour (Rs.)*	*Capital/Output (Rs.)*	*Machinery/Unit (Rs.)*	*Fuel/Unit (Rs.)*
1. Eastern Zone	2.09 (0.76)	478.50 (3.48)	754.93 (2.59)	0.63 (1.34)	42.18 (1.32)	33.24 (3.85)
2. Central Zone	1.76 (0.64)	636.16 (4.63)	3728.79 (12.77)	0.17 (0.36)	55.46 (1.74)	14.13 (1.64)
3. Western Zone	3.23 (1.17)	57.23 (0.42)	75.37 (0.26)	0.76 (1.62)	25.14 (0.79)	3.13 (0.36)
4. Far-Western Zone	2.26 (0.82)	156.30 (1.14)	383.40 (1.31)	0.41 (0.87)	38.01 (1.19)	5.70 (0.66)
TOTAL	2.76(1.00)	137.48(1.00)	291.96(1.00)	0.47(1.00)	31.95(1.00)	8.63(1.00)

Note: Figures in parenthesis indicate Location Factors.
Source: Central Bureau of Statistics, *Sample Survey of the Cottage and Small Scale Industries, 1972–73*, Kathmandu.

onslaughts of factory made goods from outside. Whereas the central zone with its more developed and diversified mercantile and industrial base marked by stronger social adaptability and resilience can be said to have 'restructured' its productive capacity to adjust to the new international division of labour, the western zone with its fragile social base dominated by petty peasant production may be said to have failed to readjust itself to the new situation and finally ruined or collapsed in the absolute sense.

3.2.2 'Distribution' Characteristics

Domestic proto-industries are known to exist in different historical forms characterised by different modes of ownership of means of production, realisation of value of labour, accumulation of surplus labour, etc. As different historical forms have different ramifications in the articulation of the underdevelopment process, it would be pertinent to attempt to generalize the existing forms through the analysis of important 'distribution' characteristics.

3.2.21 Since the size of production units have a great bearing on the overall organization of production, the sizes with respect to labour engaged and capital invested have been cross classified with the legal status of ownership in Table 3.7. The extremely small size of production units is evident from the fact that as many as 92.08% of all units employ five or less workers per unit and 95.28% of them have a capital investment of less than Rs. 1000 per unit. It is therefore quite understandable that 99.92% of all the units are under 'individual proprietorship', which would naturally reflect a low level of organization of production. Also since small-scale enterprises are more conducive for self-exploitation of owner-labourers, and contrary to the arguments of the votaries of "small is beautiful" it is often found that they tend to be more exploitative of labour in a labour-surplus economy[53], this phenomenon may partly explain the resilience of domestic proto-industry in the country.

3.2.22 The change from 'artisan' to 'handicraft' to capitalist commodity production, marks a great step in the break-up of 'natural economy' and development of industrial capitalism. For a correct diagnosis of this process a detailed information on whether the domestic industrial producers possess agricultural land or not and whether they produce for private customers or 'buyers-up' or the free market,[54] would be warranted. In the absence of the desired data base, we have constructed a table showing the share of home consumption to total production by 'use-based' classification of proto-industries and territorial zones (Table 3.8). It is seen that for the country as a whole and for all industry groups, only 17.07% of total value of production is for home-consumption, and an impressive 82.93% is for sale or exchange. Among the important industry groups, textiles and allied (91.89%) have the highest share of sale and food and allied (61.82%) the lowest. In the territorial dimension the highest share of sale or exchange is expectedly seen in central zone (98.83%), closely followed by

Table 3.7 Distribution of Domestic Proto-Industry by Legal Status and Size (1972–73).

Legal Status		*Number of Establishments*									
		Capital Size (in Rs.)					*Labour Size (No. of Persons engaged)*				
		Up to 100	*101–1000*	*1001–10000*	*10001–200000*	*Total*	*1*	*2*	*3–5*	*6–9*	*Total*
1. Individual Proprietorship		239396	119204	15994	1745	376339	94883	117706	133904	29846	376339
	(i)	(63.61)	(31.67)	(4.25)	(0.46)	(100.00)	(25.21)	(31.28)	(35.58)	(7.93)	(100.00)
	(ii)	(99.99)	(99.82)	(99.85)	(98.48)	(99.92)	(99.92)	(99.86)	(99.96)	(100.00)	(99.92)
2. Partnership		33	96	24	27	180	66	88	26	–	180
	(i)	(18.33)	(53.33)	(13.33)	(15.00)	(100.00)	(36.67)	(48.89)	(14.44)		(100.00)
	(ii)	(0.01)	(0.08)	(0.15)	(1.52)	(0.05)	(0.07)	(0.07)	(0.02)		(0.05)
3. Others		–	113	–	–	113	11	80	22	–	113
	(i)		(100.00)			(100.00)	(9.73)	(70.80)	(19.47)		(100.00)
	(ii)		(0.10)			(0.03)	(0.01)	(0.07)	(0.02)		(0.03)
TOTAL		239429	119413	16018	1772	376632	94960	117874	133952	29846	376632
	(i)	(63.57)	(31.71)	(4.25)	(0.47)	(100.00)	(25.21)	(31.30)	(35.57)	(7.92)	(100.00)
	(ii)	(100.00)	(100.00)	(100.00)	(100.00)	(100.00)	(100.00)	(100.00)	(100.00)	(100.00)	(100.00)

Note: Figures in parenthesis are percentages; (i) Row percentage, (ii) Column percentage.
Source: Central Bureau of Statistics, *Sample Survey of the Cottage and Small Scale Industries, 1972–73*, Kathmandu.

Table 3.8 Share of Home-Consumption to Total Production of Domestic Proto-Industry by Use-based Classification and Territorial Zones (1972–73).

Use-based Classification of Industries Territorial Zones	*Share of Home-consumption to Total Production (%)*						
	Food Allied	*Textiles and Allied*	*Agricultural Tools and Equipments*	*Household Equipments and Accessories*	*Jewelleries and Ornaments*	*Miscellaneous*	*Total*
1. Eastern Zone	41.52 (1.09)	23.85 (2.94)	11.23 (0.47)	12.58 (0.66)	0.69 (0.92)	30.36 (1.33)	32.39 (1.90)
2. Central Zone	0.10 (0.00)	0.90 (0.11)	24.80 (1.05)	3.19 (0.17)	– –	38.46 (1.69)	1.17 (0.07)
3. Western Zone	10.49 (0.27)	30.87 (3.81)	36.48 (1.54)	24.91 (1.31)	2.39 (3.19)	4.17 (0.18)	28.04 (1.64)
4. Far-Western Zone	–	8.32 (1.03)	10.53 (0.44)	14.82 (0.78)	0.66 (0.88)	0 (0.00)	9.28 (0.54)
NEPAL	38.18 (1.00)	8.11 (1.00)	23.71 (1.00)	19.08 (1.00)	0.75 (1.00)	22.75 (1.00)	17.07 (1.00)

Note: Figures in parenthesis indicate Location Factors.
Source: Central Bureau of Statistics, *Sample Survey of the Cottage and Small Scale Industries, 1972–73*, Kathmandu.

far-western (90.72%) and significantly trailed by western (71.96%) and eastern (67.61%) zones. In the absence of information on the precise modes and conditions of exchange and in view of the generally believed state of economic backwardness marked by predominance of use-value production, it is difficult to venture a satisfactory explanation to the seemingly high share of value of proto-industrial productions 'exchanged'. However, the persistence to a significant degree of traditional 'artisan', or a modified *Jajmani* relations operationalised through an ossified division of labour on caste lines in much of the countryside, the more so in the more remote areas of the hills[55] should explain much of the share of 'sale' or exchange noticed specially in the far-western zone as being spurious. Only the high share of products 'sold' or exchanged in the central zone could be to a large extent attributed to a genuine "commodification", because over the years the contribution of domestic proto-industrial products in the export trade has been quite significant[56] and most of the trade takes place in this zone (see, Section 4.2 below). Thus much of the larger share of the "marketed" proto-industrial products seems to be a mere illusion, and even where genuine "commodification" has taken place in the present era of neo-colonialism circulation of commodities alone cannot contribute much to transform the economic base of underdeveloped societies and herald industrial capitalism.

3.2.23 The real test of the social relations of production in the given sub-sector of the economy is, however, provided by the nature of labour relations in the actual production process. Even though by the very definition of "domestic" proto-industry exploitation of family labour should constitute the major component of labour in production, the degree of hiring of outside labour has come to be accepted as a measure of higher level of social mode of production. Besides, the divorcing of domestic industrial producers from agricultural production is regarded an important step towards the revolutionization of proto-industrial production. But, in the case of Nepal there are said to be "a negligible number of full-time craftmen"[57], a sure sign of social backwardness of industrial production. Also, as revealed in Table 3.9 there is a negligible share (i.e.1.62%) of wage-labour to total labour and a very low absolute value (i.e. NRs. 363.18) of annual wages per labour. In the territorial dimension the central zone expectedly shows the highest percentage (i.e.15.68%) of wage-labour to total labour. However, the lowest value of wage per labour (i.e. NRs. 48.72) in this zone does seem to confirm tentatively the contention that the capacity of the "informal sector" to draw upon the "ample reservoir of cheap, unorganised labour and money-lending debt linkages to generate significantly high profit margin" provides it "resilient competitiveness" to effectively subvert the consolidation of the modern mill industry.[58] Whether the phenomenon of persistence of proto-industry is more due to the 'subversion' of the proto-industry or due to the inherent weakness of factory industry to destroy and restructure the former, more research would be required.

Table 3.9 Nature of Production Relations in the Domestic Proto-Industry by Territorial Zones (1972–73).

Territorial Zones	*Number of Wage-labour*	*Wage-Labour to total Labour (%)*	*Wage per Labour (Rs.)*	*Home Consumption to total Production (%)*	*Individual Proprietorship to total Establishments (%)*
1. Eastern Zone	93.17 (0.55)	7.93 (4.90)	562.31 (1.55)	32.39 (1.90)	99.57 (0.996)
2. Central Zone	3366 (0.20)	15.68 (9.68)	48.72 (0.13)	1.17 (0.07)	99.79 (0.999)
3. Western Zone	162 (0.01)	0.02 (0.01)	2672.84* (7.36)	28.04 (1.64)	99.09 (1.001)
4. Far-Western Zone	4020 (0.24)	1.85 (1.14)	71.89 (0.20)	9.28 (0.54)	100.00 (1.001)
TOTAL	16865 (1.00)	1.62 (1.00)	363.18 (1.00)	17.07 (1.00)	99.92 (1.00)

Note: Figures in parenthesis indicate Location Factors.
* Appears too influted, hence not reliable.

Source: Central Bureau of Statistics, *Sample Survey of the Cottage and Smell Scale Industries, 1972–73*, Kathmandu.

3.2.24 On the basis of the foregoing analysis of the 'production' and 'distribution' conditions of the domestic proto-industry in Nepal certain generalisations can be made about the retardation of this sub-sector both in the social and spatial dimensions.

Despite the general historical decline of indigenous industrial production in the aftermath of unrestricted flooding of the economy by Indian factory made goods since the 1920s, the persistence of a significant degree of indigenous domestic proto-industry and considerable spatial variations in the destruction and restructuration of the 'natural economy' provide important insights into the process of industrial retardation in the country. It is seen that areas of greater economic and physical accessibility and integration to outside world have experienced greater destruction of the 'natural economy'. Secondly, amongst the areas of greater destruction the ones with greater inner social resilience, e.g. the central zone particularly Kathmandu Valley, have been able to restructure their proto-industrial production by entering into the new international division of labour albeit in a subjugated position. Against this background the domestic proto-industry can be seen to have simply collapsed in areas of more fragile social base. Thus, as elsewhere[59] in similar situations, areas of absolute backwardness but resistant to change and areas of extroverted development can be seen to be emerging, the process depending upon the nature of integration to outside economy and internal solidity.

3.3 'PRODUCTION' CHARACTERISTICS OF MANUFACTURING

In this section we shall discuss the state of productive forces in manufacturing[60] as reflected in the structural composition of industries, level and growth of production and productivity and the level of technology.

3.3.1 Structure of Manufacturing

Structural composition of industries based on standard industrial classifications by nature of inputs, use of end products, etc., provides a fairly accurate measure of level of development of productive forces in the industrial sector. In Nepal, however, neither the International Standard Industry Classification (ISIC) schedule has been strictly followed nor an indigenous classification has been evolved, thereby creating a virtual chaos of inconsistent and adhoc industrial groupings which render any classification into meaningful categories in a spatio-temporal frame extremely difficult. Nevertheless we have attempted to classify the disparate manufacturing activities by 'input-based' and 'use-based' typologies[61] as defined earlier in this chapter. We have also adopted other classifications wherever available, so as to study the structural characteristics of the Nepalese manufacturing industries in greater depth.

3.3.11 The extremely fragile and inverted structure of the manufacturing sector is evident from the study of composition of industries and their subsequent input-based (Tables 3.10) use-based (Tables 3.11 and 3.12) classifications.[62] The virtual absence of the basic goods and capital goods industries was reflected in their combined share which was as low as 6.81% of employment and 7.79% of 'financial investment' in the 'public' sector. This in turn accounted for a mere 19.25% of employment and 34.68% of 'financial investment' in the total manufacturing sector in 1976/77. The overwhelming dominance of non-durable consumer goods industries is a sure indicator of primitive stage of industrialisation[63]. Also, the steep fall in the already low shares of intermediate-goods industries since 1965 points towards a deeper structural malady and retrogression marked by intra-sectoral disarticulation[64].

Similarly, the structural inversion and chronic anaemia afflicting the manufacturing sector is amply reflected in the input-based classification. The predominant position of agro-based industries followed by the forest-based ones, which are invariably the elementary processing activities with a low share of value-added content, entails a recurrent industrial backwardness tied to the dynamics of agricultural underdevelopment. The declining share of mineral-based production, specially the metallic mineral-based one, and the stagnation of the infant chemical-based and service-based industries, further confirm the ill-health of the industrial sector.

Another classification by 'technique-based' typology into 'elementary' and 'secondary' processing activities[65] would have probably brought into focus the predominance of elementary processing activities in conformity with the general pattern of the primitive industrial structure as a veiled extension of the agricultural sector and an adjunct to the metropolitan semi-colonial/neo-colonial economy. But, the non-availability of data about the "level of skill", mechanised and non-mechanised methods of operation, etc., in individual industrial units, did not permit us to undertake the exercise.

Yet another typology of classification of industries based on the ISIC schema, which could be tentatively termed as 'use-cum-input-based', (Table 3.13) further highlights the inverted structure of the Nepalese manufacturing sector, wherein rice and oil milling alone are found to contribute more than two-third of the industrial gross output and nearly half the gross value-added.

Nepal's subjugated position vis-à-vis other 'developing' countries in terms of comparative industrial structures is quite apparent. The fact that the combined share of value-added in important industries like (i) chemicals plastic, rubber (ii) non-metallic mineral products and (iii) basic metals and engineering industries in Nepal in 1977/78 (i.e. 12.4% of the total) was less than one third of the share in total of the same industries in 'developing' countries in 1960 or 1970 (i.e. 39.2% of the total in 1960 and 46.1% in 1970) amply substantiates this.[66]

3.3.12 The spatial configuration of the structural characteristics of the manufacturing sector analysed in terms of the distribution of manufacturing establishments (in the absence of relevant information by other production attributes) by

Table 3.10 General Attributes of Manufacturing Industries by Input-based Classification.

	No. of establishments				No. of persons engaged				Gross fixed capital (Rs.'000)				Gross output (Rs. '000)				Value added (Rs. '000)			
	1965	1972/73	1976/77	Change*	1965	1972/73	1976–77	Change*	1965	1972/73	1976–77	Change*	1965	1972–73	1976–73	Change*	1965	1972–73	1976–77	Change*
Agro-based	979	2014	2898	+4.26	9603	34483	31958	−2.94	89037	112489	384154	+7.03	381516	988113	1609999	−1.79	46305	126249	170791	−6.39
	(77.88)	(82.74)	(82.14)		(66.70)	(72.39)	(63.7)		(81.48)	(65.62)	(88.51)		(91.57)	(84.39)	(89.78)		(76.86)	(60.80)	(70.47)	
I. (i) Crop based	979	1998	2860	+3.19	9603	33194	30323	−6.20	89037	107942	381949	+6.52	381536	982802	1602894	−2.19	46305	124691	168040	−7.52
	(77.88)	(82.09)	(81.07)		(66.70)	(69.68)	(60.50)		(81.48)	(62.97)	(88.00)		(91.57)	(83.94)	(89.38)		(76.86)	(60.05)	(69.34)	
(ii) Animal based	–	16	38	–	–	1289	1635	–	–	4547	2205	–	–	5311	7104	–	–	1558	2751	–
	–	0.66	(1.08)			(2.71)	(3.26)			(2.65)	(0.51)			(0.45)	(0.40)			(0.75)	(1.14)	
II. Forest based	63	112	213	+1.0	1231	3052	4072	−0.43	5269	13538	6792	−3.26	10639	31466	58170	+0.69	3673	14230	17939	+1.30
	(5.01)	(4.60)	(6.04)		(8.55)	(6.41)	(8.12)		(4.82)	(7.90)	(1.56)		(2.55)	(2.69)	(3.24)		(6.10)	(6.85)	(7.40)	
Mineral based	105	120	132	−4.61	2330	6357	7160	−1.90	2034	12604	11339	+0.75	12833	47512	30031	−1.41	5369	29215	10731	−4.48
	(8.15)	(4.93)	(3.74)		(16.18)	(13.34)	(14.28)		(1.86)	(7.35)	(2.61)		(3.08)	(4.06)	(1.67)		(8.91)	(14.07)	(4.43)	
(i) Metallic mineral	13	37	35	−0.04	218	1057	1141	+0.77	1212	5113	6868	+0.47	5117	16014	20491	−0.09	2020	5531	6497	−0.67
	(1.03)	(1.52)	(0.99)		(1.51)	(2.22)	(2.28)		(1.11)	(2.98)	(1.58)		(1.23)	(1.37)	(1.14)		(3.35)	(2.66)	(2.68)	
III. (ii) Non-metailic mineral	92	83	97	−4.57	2112	5300	6019	−2.66	822	7491	4471	+0.28	7716	31498	9340	−1.32	3349	23684	4234	−3.81
	(7.31)	(3.41)	(2.75)		(14.67)	(11.13)	(12.01)		(0.75)	(4.37)	(1.03)		(1.85)	(2.69)	(0.53)		(5.56)	(11.41)	(1.75)	
IV. Chemical based	11	11	22	−0.26	59	124	441	+0.47	89	262	1513	+0.27	1212	2093	5700	+0.03	140	164	2137	−0.65
	(0.82)	(0.45)	(0.62)		(0.41)	(0.26)	(0.88)		(0.08)	(0.15)	(0.35)		(0.29)	(0.18)	(0.32)		(0.23)	(0.08)	(0.88)	
V. Serviced based	70	103	151	−1.29	334	990	1969	+1.61	4859	3126	6784	−2.89	3760	19042	7010	−0.51	1371	7181	2186	−1.38
	(5.57)	(4.23)	(4.28)		(2.32)	(2.08)	(3.93)		(4.45)	(1.82)	(1.56)		(0.90)	(2.63)	(0.39)		(2.28)	(3.46)	(0.90)	
VI. Miscelleneous	29	74	112	+0.86	803	2632	4519	+1.44	7985	3420	23436	−1.97	6672	82597	82484	−3.00	3390	30619	38561	+10.28
	(2.31)	(3.04)	(3.17)		(5.58)	(5.53)	(9.02)		(7.31)	(2.00)	(5.34)		(1.60)	(7.05)	(4.60)		(5.63)	(14.74)	(15.91)	
TOTAL	1257	2434	3528	±	14397	47638	50120	±0	109273	171422	434017	±0	416652	1170822	1793334	±0	60248	207658	242345	±0
	(100.00)	(100.00)	(100.00)		(100.00)	(100.00)	(100.00)		(100.00)	(100.00)	(100.00)		(100.00)	(100.00)	(100.00)		(100.00)	(100.00)	(100.00)	

Note: Figures in Parenthesis are percentages, *Change in % share in 1976/77 over 1965.
Source: Central Bureau of Statistics, *Census of Manufacturing Establishments* 1965, 1972/73, 1976/77, Kathmandu.

Table 3.11 General Attributes of Manufacturing Industries by Use-based Classifications.

Industry Group	No. of Establishments			No. of Persons Engaged			Fixed Capital (Rs. '000)			Gross Output (Rs. '000)			Value Added (Rs. '000)		
	1965	1972/73	1976/77	1965	1972/73	1976/77	1965	1972/73	1976/77	1965	1972/73	1976/77	1965	1972/73	1976/77
Consumer Goods	1116 (88.78)	2237 (91.91)	3258 (92.35)	8541 (59.32)	33999 (71.37)	34904 (69.64)	82829 (75.80)	124983 (72.91)	387450 (89.27)	366429 (87.95)	1001110 (85.50)	1629033 (90.84)	46657 (77.44)	146379 (70.49)	184577 (76.16)
I. (i) Durable	53 (4.22)	97 (3.99)	164 (4.65)	572 (3.97)	1989 (4.18)	2405 (4.80)	1826 (1.67)	6174 (30.60)	7735 (1.78)	7181 (1.72)	22655 (1.93)	33763 (1.88)	2957 (4.91)	11532 (5.55)	12558 (5.18)
(ii) Non-durable	1063 (84.57)	2140 (87.92)	3094 (87.70)	7969 (55.35)	32010 (67.19)	32499 (64.84)	81003 (74.13)	118809 (69.31)	379715 (87.49)	359248 (86.22)	978455 (83.57)	1595270 (88.96)	43700 (72.53)	134847 (64.94)	172019 (70.98)
II. Intermediate Goods	112 (8.91)	133 (5.46)	186 (5.27)	5053 (35.10)	11503 (24.15)	10834 (21.62)	18449 (16.88)	27461 (16.02)	23668 (5.45)	43551 (10.45)	93604 (7.99)	82151 (4.56)	10201 (16.93)	33165 (15.97)	19231 (7.94)
III. Capital and Basic Goods*	–	–	–	–	–	–	–	–	–	–	–	–	–	–	–
IV. Miscellaneous	29 (2.31)	64 (2.63)	84 (2.38)	803 (5.58)	2136 (4.48)	4381 (8.74)	7985 (7.31)	18970 (11.07)	22922 (5.29)	6672 (1.60)	76116 (6.50)	82150 (4.58)	3390 (5.63)	42213 (20.33)	38537 (15.90)
TOTAL	1257 (100.00)	2434 (100.00)	3525 (100.00)	14397 (100.00)	47638 (100.00)	50120 (100.00)	109273 (100.00)	171422 (100.00)	434017 (100.00)	416652 (100.00)	1170822 (100.00)	1793334 (100.00)	60248 (100.00)	207655 (100.00)	242345 (100.00)

Note: Figures in parenthesis are percentages.
*Because of the units being 2 or less in number, no separate information available.

Source: Central Bureau of Statistics, *Census of Manufacturing Establishments*, 1965, 1972/73, 1976/77, Kathmandu.

Table 3.12 Use-based Classification of Manufacturing Industries in the 'Public' Sector (1977/78).

Use-based Classification	*No. of Units*	*No. of Employees*	*Financial Investment (Rs. '000)*
Basic Goods	3 (13.64)	386* (4.00)	12966** (3.92)
Capital Goods	2 (9.09)	271 (2.81)	12811 (3.87)
Intermediate Goods	4 (18.18)	3263 (33.82)	14428*** (4.36)
– Consumer Goods:	13 (59.09)	5727 (59.37)	290501 (87.84)
– Consumer Durables	–	–	–
– Consumer Non-durables	13 (59.09)	5727 (59.37)	290501 (87.84)
TOTAL	22 (100.00)	9647 (100.00)	330706 (100.00)

Note: * Figures not available for Hetauda Cement Factory, which is yet to start operating.
** Figures not available for Himal Cement Co. Ltd. Chovar.
*** Figures not available for the Timber Corporation of Nepal Ltd., Hetauda and Raghupati Jute Mills Ltd., Biratnagar.
– Figures in parenthesis are percentages.

Source: HMG, Ministry of Finance (1980), *Highlights of Public Enterprises in Nepal For the F.Y. 1977/78*, Corporation Coordination Division, Kathmandu.

Table 3.13 General Attributes of Manufacturing Industries by Use-cum-Input Based Classification.

(%)

	1965/66			1972/73			1977/78		
	Employment	*Gross output*	*Value added*	*Employ-ment*	*Gross output*	*Value added*	*Employ-ment*	*Gross output*	*Value added*
Food and allied	31.6	81.2	62.0	36.8	76.7	52.4	35.8	73.5	57.5
Rice, oil mills share	36.6	78.9	61.7	27.1	73.3	47.8	24.2	65.0	44.3
Drink and tobacco	4.2	3.8	4.9	14.2	4.86	5.7	14.9	5.1	5.6
Textiles and allied	25.2	7.2	7.8	17.4	4.36	2.9	16.7	8.3	12.3
Jute goods share	23.6	6.1	7.77	11.9	3.5	N.A.	8.6	3.9	8.3
Wood Paper, Printing and allied	9.5	3.3	5.1	9.3	4.16	9.8	13.5	6.6	12.1
Chemicals, Pharmaceuticals, Plastics and rubber	0.24	0.3	0	0.3	0.17	0.1	1.4	0.8	2.1
Non-metallic mineral products	8.1	1.5	3.4	12.8	2.63	11.1	14.3	3.6	7.0
Metals, fabrication	2.3	1.7	N.A.	2.0	1.25	2.3	3.0	2.0	3.4
Jewellery curios	1.1	0.1	0.4	0.5	0.15	0.5	0.3	0.0	0.0
Miscellaneous	17.8	0.8	16.4	6.2	6.86	14.2	0.1	0.1	0.1
TOTAL	100.00	100.00	100.00	100.00	100.00	100.00	100.00	100.00	100.00

Notes:

I. 1. Food and allied: Rice, oil; Bakery, Confectionary; Tea; Suger; Dairy products; Animal feed; Other food.
2. Drink and .tobacco: Bidi; Cigarettes; Beer, Soft-drink; Liquour.
3. Textiles and allied: Carpet, Rugs; Textiles, Yarn; Knitwear; Jute goods; Leather shoes; Other apparel and Textile goods.
4. Wood, paper, printing; Catuhu; Saw mills; Plywood board; Wood furniture and equipment; Printing; Other wood & paper products.
5. Chemicals and Pharmaceuticals: Soap; Drugs, Medicines; Other chemicals and Plastic products.
6. Non-metallic minerals: Brick, Tiles; Cement products; other non-metallic mineral products.
7. Metals, fabrication: Metal utensils; Fabrication repair; Metal furniture.
8. Jewellery curios
9. Miscellaneous: any other.

II. The estimates for 1977/78 are on the basis of1976/77 census, with revisions. 1972/73 is also revised upwards for cigarettes and jute (value added).

Source: Industrial Services Centre (1982), *Industrial Sectoral Plan Study (1980/81–1990/91)*, Vol. I (revised edition), Kathmandu.

input-based types, is depicted in Table 3.14. In keeping with its overall higher share (i.e. 63.75%) in the total manufacturing establishments, the Terai zone is seen to account for higher proportions of almost all sub-groups of industries except the forest-based and service-based ones. The higher share of agro-based (specially crop-based) establishments in the Terai may be easily explicable in terms of its corresponding domination in crop production but a disproportionately higher share of chemical-based (54.55%) and mineral-based (48.48%) establishments in a territorial zone with no distinct advantage in raw-material availability, points towards the systematic distortion of industrial spatial structure by some other extraneous factors. However, the generalised pattern of chronically anaemic and inverted industrial structure with a dangerously fragile base (reflected in excessively higher share of elementary processing agro-based and forest-based industries and a negligible share of higher quality metallic mineral, chemical and service based ones), is seen to be more or less uniformly spread over the physical space, with the slight exception of the Kathmandu Valley; thus confirming the more disturbing situation of 'absolute backwardness' rather than a sort of 'distorted development' of industries in the country.

The spatial concentration of the three 'basic' and two 'capital' goods industries in the 'public' sector along the Birgunj-Hetauda-Kathmandu Valley axis in the central zone[67] may give some inkling of an emerging 'inward-looking' industrial spatial structure with Kathmandu Valley, the centre of state authority, at the apex; but the conclusion would be too presumptuous given the very low absolute scale of industries in the 'public' sector.

3.3.2 Level and Growth of Production

From the abysmally low proportions of economically active persons engaged in and gross domestic product contributed by the non-primary production sector in the total economy of the country as cited in Chapter 1.5, the low absolute scale of industrial production at the macro level should never be in doubt. It would, therefore be relevant here to analyse spatio-temporal variations of the same to unfold the inner dynamics of the observed industrial retardation.

3.3.21 Level of Production

The embarrassingly low level of industrial production even by "major" industries is evident from their very low gross volume as recorded in Table 3.15. Viewed against the total population of the country at about 15 million in 1980/81, the per capita production of individual industrial goods would be insignificant ironically except perhaps for the production of cigarettes. Talking of the more important (by volume of production and economic significance) of the "major" industries, for example, the gross volume per capita in 1982/83 (weighted against 1981 population) comes to about 1.26 kg. of jute goods, 1.49 kg. of sugar, 2136 sticks of cigarettes, 0.53 metres of cotton textiles, 2.46 kg. of cement, 0.78. kg. of iron goods, 0.057 kg. of fertilizer and so on. Assuming the most equitable social

Table 3.14 Spatial Distribution of Manufacturing Establishments by Input-based Classifications (1976–77).

Territorial Zones	*No. of Establishments by Input-based Classifications*										
	Agro-based			*Forest based*	*Mineral based*			*Chemical based*	*Service based*	*Miscella-neous*	*Total*
	Crop based	*Animal based*	*Total*		*Metallic*	*Non-metallic*	*Total*				
(1)	(2)	(3)	(4)	(5)	(6)	(7)	(8)	(9)	(10)	(11)	(12)
I. MOUNTAIN	1	20	21	9	–	–	–	1	–	2	33
(i)	(3.03)	(60.61)	(63.64)	(27.27)				(3.03)		(6.06)	(100.00)
(ii)	(0.00)	(52.63)	(0.72)	(4.23)				(4.55)		(1.79)	(0.94)
Eastern	–	5	5	6	–	–	–	–	–	–	11
(i)		(45.45)	(45.45)	(54.55)							(100.00)
(ii)		(13.16)	(0.17)	(2.82)							(0.31)
Central	–	–	–	–	–	–	–	–	–	–	–
Western	1	15	16	3	–	–	–	1	–	2	22
(i)	(4.55)	(68.18)	(72.73)	(13.64)				(4.55)		(9.10)	(100.00)
(ii)	(0.00)	(39.47)	(0.55)	(1.41)				(4.55)		(1.79)	(0.62)
II. HILL	279	9	288	27	10	10	20	1	13	12	360
(i)	(77.50)	(2.50)	(80.00)	(7.50)	(2.78)	(2.78)	(5.56)	(0.28)	(3.61)	(3.33)	(100.00)
(ii)	(9.76)	(23.68)	(9.94)	(12.68)	(28.57)	(10.31)	(15.15)	(4.55)	(8.61)	(10.71)	(10.20)
Eastern	78	4	82	7	5	1	6	–	2	–	97
(i)	(80.41)	(4.12)	(84.53)	(7.22)	(5.15)	(1.03)	(6.19)		(2.06)		(100.00)
(ii)	(2.73)	(10.53)	(2.83)	(3.29)	(14.29)	(1.03)	(4.55)		(1.32)		(2.75)
Central	199	3	202	15	5	9	14	1	11	11	253
(i)	(78.66)	(8.19)	(79.84)	(5.93)	(1.98)	(3.56)	(5.53)	(0.40)	(4.35)	(4.35)	(100.00)
(ii)	(6.96)	(7.89)	(6.97)	(7.04)	(14.29)	(9.28)	(10.61)	(4.55)	(7.28)	(9.82)	(7.17)
Western	2	2	4	5	–	–	–	–	–	1	10
(i)	(20.00)	(20.00)	(40.00)	(50.00)						(10.00)	(100.00)
(ii)	(0.00)	(5.26)	(0.14)	(2.35)						(0.89)	(0.28)

(Contd.)

(*Table 3.14 contd.*)

Territorial Zones		No. of Establishments by Input-based Classifications										
		Agro-based			Forest based	Mineral based			Chemical based	Service based	Miscella-neous	Total
		Crop based	Animal based	Total		Metallic	Non-metallic	Total				
(1)		(2)	(3)	(4)	(5)	(6)	(7)	(8)	(9)	(10)	(11)	(12)
III. KATHMANDU		356	7	363	97	18	19	37	7	81	23	608
VALLEY	(i)	(58.55)	(1.15)	(59.70)	(15.95)	(2.96)	(3.13)	(6.09)	(1.15)	(13.32)	(3.78)	(100.00)
	(ii)	(12.45)	(18.42)	(12.53)	(45.54)	(51.43)	(19.59)	(28.03)	(31.82)	(53.64)	(20.54)	(17.23)
IV. INNER		234	–	234	10	1	10	11	1	7	15	2 7 8
TERAT	(i)	(84.17)		(84.17)	(3.60)	(0.36)	(3.60)	(3.96)	(0.36)	(2.52)	(5.40)	(100.00)
	(ii)	(8.18)		(8.07)	(4.69)	(2.86)	(10.31)	(8.33)	(4.55)	(4.64)	(13.39)	(7.88)
Eastern		18	–	18	–	–	1	1	–	–	–	19
	(i)	(94.74)		(94.74)			(5.26)	(5.26)				(100.00)
	(ii)	(0.63)		(0.62)			(1.03)	(0.76)				(0.54)
Central		152	–	152	10	1	6	7	1	6	12	188
	(i)	(80.85)		(80.85)	(5.32)	(0.53)	(3.19)	(3.72)	(0.85)	(3.19)	(6.38)	(100.00)
	(ii)	(5.31)		(5.24)	(4.69)	(2.86)	(6.19)	(5.30)	(4.55)	(3.97)	(10.71)	(5.33)
Western		64	–	64	–	–	3	3	–	1	3	71
	(i)	(90.14)		(90.14)			(4.23)	(4.23)		(1.40)	(4.23)	(100.00)
	(ii)	(2.24)		(2.21)			(3.09)	(2.27)		(0.66)	(2.68)	(2.01)
V. TERAI		1990	2	1992	70	6	58	64	12	50	60	2249
	(i)	(88.40)	(0.09)	(88.57)	(3.11)	(0.27)	(2.58)	(2.85)	(0.53)	(2.22)	(2.67)	(100.00)
	(ii)	(69.58)	(5.26)	(68.74)	(32.86)	(17.14)	(59.79)	(48.48)	(54.55)	(33.11)	(53.57)	(63.75)
Eastern		1410	2	1412	47	5	24	29	10	35	43	1577
	(i)	(89.41)	(0.13)	(89.54)	(2.98)	(0.32)	(1.52)	(1.84)	(0.63)	(2.22)	(2.73)	(100.00)
	(ii)	(49.30)	(5.26)	(48.72)	(22.07)	(14.29)	(24.74)	(21.97)	(45.45)	(23.18)	(38.39)	(44.70)
Far-Eastern		374	2	376	30	2	9	11	6	8	16	447
	(i)	(83.67)	(0.45)	(84.12)	(6.71)	(0.45)	(2.01)	(2.46)	(1.34)	(1.79)	(3.58)	(100.00)

(*Contd.*)

(*Table 3.14 contd.*)

	(ii)	(13.08)	(5.26)	(12.97)	(14.08)	(5.71)	(9.28)	(8.33)	(27.27)	(5.30)	(14.29)	(12.67)
Mid Eastern		678	–	678	10	–	7	7	1	4	15	715
	(i)	(94.83)		(94.83)	(1.40)		(0.98)	(0.98)	(0.14)	(0.56)	(2.10)	(100.00)
	(ii)	(23.71)		(23.40)	(4.69)		(7.22)	(5.30)	(4.55)	(2.65)	(13.39)	(20.27)
Eastern		358	–	358	7	3	8	11	3	23	12	415
	(i)	(86.27)		(86.27)	(1.69)	(0.72)	(1.93)	(2.65)	(0.72)	(5.54)	(2.89)	(100.00)
	(ii)	(12.52)		(12.35)	(3.29)	(8.57)	(8.25)	(8.33)	(13.64)	(15.23)	(10.71)	(11.76)
Central		375	–	375	10	1	29	30	2	12	15	444
	(i)	(84.46)		(84.46)	(2.25)	(0.23)	(6.53)	(6.76)	(0.45)	(2.70)	(3.38)	(100.00)
	(ii)	(13.11)		(12.94)	(4.69)	(2.36)	(29.90)	(22.73)	(9.09)	(7.95)	(13.39)	(12.59)
Western		205	–	205	13	–	5	5	–	3	2	228
	(i)	(89.91)		(89.91)	(5.70)		(2.19)	(2.19)		(1.32)	(0.88)	(100.00)
	(ii)	(7.17)		(7.07)	(6.10)		(5.15)	(3.79)		(1.99)	(1.79)	(6.46)
NEPAL		2860	38	2898	213	35	97	132	22	151	112	3528
	(i)	(81.07)	(1.08)	(82.14)	(6.04)	(0.99)	(2.75)	(3.74)	(0.62)	(4.28)	(3.17)	(100.00)
	(ii)	(100.00)	(100.00)	(100.00)	(100.00)	(100.00)	(100.00)	(100.00)	(100.00)	(100.00)	(100.00)	(100.00)

Note: Figures in parenthesis are percentages (i) Row percentage (ii) Column percentage.
Source: Central Bureau of Statistics, *Census of Manufacturing Establishments*, 1976/77, Kathmandu.

Table 3.15 Gross Volume and Growth of Production in Major Industries (The Growth Index has been Calculated with 1977–78 as Based Year)

Industry (Unit)		*1961–62*		*1964–65*		*1967–68*		*1971–72*		*1974–75*		*1977–78*		*1979–80*		*1982–83*	
		Vol.	*Index*	*Vol.*	*Index*	*Vol.*	*Index*	*Vol.*	*Index*	*Vol.*	*Index*	*Vol.*	*Index*	*Vol.*	*Index*	*Vol.*	*Index*
1. Jute Goods	('000 m.t.)	15.0	0.92	18.7	1.15	14.0	0.86	18.9	0.79	12.3	0.75	16.3	1.0	15.5	0.99	18.96	1.16
2. Sugar	('000 m.t.)	2.3	0.09	7.3	0.28	6.4	0.24	7.6	0.29	11.9	0.45	26.5	1.0	14.2	0.54	22.36	0.84
3. Cigarettes	('000 million)	0.25	0.02	0.41	0.06	1.17	0.07	28.4	1.37	30.00	1.84	16.3	1.0	16.11	1.11	32.09	1.97
4. Matches	('000 gross)	314	0.46	361	0.53	427	0.63	527	0.78	649	0.96	677	1.0	854	1.26	858	1.27
5. Liquor	('000 litre.)	N.A.	(0.16)	122	0.18	45.5	0.06	124.4	0.18	224	0.33	687	1.0	898	1.31	334	0.49
6. Seed	(m.t.)	N.A.	(0.50)	8.34	0.63	360	0.27	898	0.68	691	0.68	1317	1.0	1712	1.30	5100	3.87
7. Shoes	('000 pcs)	N.A.	N.A.	1.1	0.02	28.6	0.49	70.0	1.19	70.0	1.19	59.0	1.0	76.0	1.29	68.15	1.49
8. Leather	(m.t.)	N.A.	N.A.	3.0	–	64.0	0.05	171.0	0.14	54.9	0.04	(1256)	1.0	(1965)	1.49	2800	2.23
9. Agricultural Tools	(m.t.)	–	–	–	–	–	–	124	0.36	300	0.96	313	1.0	132	0.42	368	1.28
10. Tea	(m.t.)	N.A.	N.A.	N.A.	N.A.	13.6	0.03	34.4	0.08	46.7	0.11	413	1.0	387	0.94	714	1.73
11. Stainless steel and utensils	(m.t.)	–	–	–	–	738	4.27	133	0.77	13.6	0.9	173	1.0	613	3.54	374	2.16
12. Utensils	(m.t.)	–	–	–	–	–	–	775	1.03	1022	1.36	749	1.0	930	1.24	737	0.98
13. Bricks, tiles	(Million pcs)	N.A.	(1.0)	N.A.	(1.0)	N.A.	(8.0)	27.9	1.4.	25.6	1.26	20.0	1.0	36.7	1.76	30.69	1.53
14. Beer	('000 litre)	–	–	–	–	–	–	137.4	0.17	688.0	0.87	788	1.0	1311	1.65	1992	2.53
15. Cotton Textiles	(M. Million)	N.A.	(0.2)	N.A.	(0.3)	N.A.	0.4	N.A.	(0.5)	4.24	1.02	3.9	1.0	4.0	1.02	7.97	2.04
16. Synthetic Textiles	(")	–	–	1.0	0.5	2.69	1.54	0.48	–	–	–	2.7	1.0	2.7	1.41	3.02	1.78
17. Cement	('000 m.t.)	–	–	–	–	–	–	–	–	29.9+	(0.80)	37.6	1.0	30.6	0.81	36.96	0.98
18. Plastic Goods	(m.t.)	–	–	–	–	–	–	–	–	39+	(0.50)	44	1.0	139	3.16	130	2.95
19. PVC Pipes	('000 m.)	–	–	–	–	–	–	–	–	–	–	185	1.0	426	2.3	2772	14.98
20. Plywood	('000 sq.m.)	–	–	–	–	–	–	–	–	–	–	184	1.0	194	1.05	230.6	1.25
21. Biscuits/Bakery	('m.t..)	–	(0.5)	–	(0.5)	932	0.78	1095	0.91	NA	(0.92)	1197	1.0	2396	2.00	2279	1.90
22. Iron Goods	('000 m.t.)	–	–	–	–	1.3	0.36	N.A.	N.A.	4.9+	N.A.	3.6	1.0	6.3	1.75	11.69	3.25
23. Fertilizers/ Bone meal Tools	(m.t.)	–	–	–	–	–	–	N.A.	N.A.	5.76+	N.A.	423	1.0	268	0.63	863	2.04
Weighted total index			0.60		0.79		1.70		0.85		0.95		1.0		1.34		N.A.

Note: + For 1975–76.
* Figures in parenthesis are approximate estimates.

Sources: 1. Industrial Service Centre (1982), *Industrial Sectoral Plan, Study (1980–81, 1990–91)*, Vol .1 (Revised Edition) Kathmandu.
2. Central Bureau of *Statistical Pocket Book, Nepal, 1984*, Kathmandu.

distribution pattern, the per capita availability of the manufactured products speaks for itself the shameful state of material culture prevalent in the society.

In the temporal frame, the picture is more disturbing. The fact that the total index[68] of industrial production by "major" industries has actually declined compared to the late 1960s, is a case in point. The abrupt rise in the index value in 1967/68 may be attributed to the by now infamous stainless steel utensils and synthetic textiles boom triggered by a peculiar pseudo-industrialisation strategy based on simple processing of semi-finished imported goods for re-export to a third country. The change in total index value since then leaves much to be desired. Viewed items-wise, the country made a humble beginning with some elementary 'basic' and 'capital' goods industries like cement, agricultural tools, ets. in the late 1960s and early 1970s. However, their negligible size in both absolute and relative sense renders this growth ineffective. In fact the index of production of the single most important export-oriented industry, viz. the jute goods, is seen to have consistently declined from 1.15 in 1964/65 to 0.75 in 1974/75, to rise only marginally since then.

The spatio-temporal variations in levels of selected production attributes of all manufacturing activities including the predominant rice and oil mills are given in Table 3.16 and Figs. 3.1 and 3.2. The low absolute values of industrial productions at the aggregate level are seen to be further compounded by their extreme localisations in few areas like the Terai, bordering India, and the Kathmandu Valley, the seat of state capital. Though there are some indications of dispersion of industrial location over the years specially in favour of Inner Terai and Hill. However, the Terai and Kathmandu Valley together account for phenomenal 80.98% of establishments, 83.01% of labour employed, 86.58% of value-added, 88.58% of gross output and 98.33% of fixed capital. Within the Terai, the eastern section is still seen to occupy a predominant position in industrial production with its share of more than 60% of the fixed capital and gross output and over 50% of the industrial labour and value added in the country. However, a discernible shift in industrial location around the central part of the country, specially the Birganj-Hetauda-Kathamndu axis, may provide some pointers of changing socio-spatial dynamics of economic development in the country. Pending further probing into other aspects of the industrial process, specially the nature of social relations of production, it may be hypothesised at this stage that the changing locational pattern may be a horizontal response to the 'vertical' shift in the industrial structure. The hypothesis gets important support from the administrative zone-wise distribution pattern of types of industries with fixed capital above N Rs. 2 lakhs[69]. It is found that of a total of 1672 industrial units[70] registered till 1983 as many as 1011 (i.e. 60.47%) are located in Bagmati (which includes Kathmandu Valley) and Narayani (which includes Hetauda and Birgunj) zones, and they house both the cement factories, 28 out of 46 steel and iron mills, 21 out of 28 electric accessories, 28 out of 48 cotton and synthetic textile mills, 17 out of 24 hosiery and 11 out of 12 garment units, 22 out of 30 paper and paper board mills, 78 out of 107 construction and 400 out of 546 miscellaneous industries

Table 3.16 General Attributes of Manufacturing Activity by Territorial Zones (1965, 1972–73 and 1976–77).

Territorial Zones	No. of establishments			No. of Persons engaged			Gross Fixed Capital (Rs. '000)			Gross Output (Rs. '000)			Value Added (Rs. '000)		
	1965	1972–73	1976–77	1965	1972–73	1976–77	1965	1972–73	1976–77	1965	1972–73	1976–77	1965	1972–73	1976–77
MOUNTAIN	–	12 (0.49)	33 (–.94)	–	359 (0.75)	770 (1.54)	–	1335 (0.78)	245 (0.06)	–	725 (0.06)	2595 (0.14)	–	330 (0.16)	1398 (0.58)
– Eastern	–	12 (0.49)	11 (0.31)	–	359 (0.75)	357 (0.71)	–	1335 (0.78)	132 (0.03)	–	725 (0.06)	1026 (0.06)	–	330 (0.16)	459 (0.19)
– Central	–	–	–	–	–	–	–	–	–	–	–	–	–	–	–
– Western	–	–	22 (0.62)	–	–	413 (0.82)	–	–	223 (0.03)	–	–	15.69 (0.09)	–	–	339 (0.69)
HILL	–	167 (6.86)	360 (10.20)	–	1189 (2.50)	4261 (8.50)	–	3062 (1.79)	5749 (1.32)	–	57867 (4.92)	133363 (7.44)	–	9640 (4.64)	10594 (4.37)
– Eastern	–	56 (2.3)	97 (2.75)	–	203 (0.43)	1121 (2.24)	–	643 (0.49)	1387 (0.32)	–	30086 (2.57)	11598 (0.05)	–	5008 (8.41)	2762 (1.14)
– Central	–	111 (4.56)	253 (7.17)	–	986 (2.67)	3024 (6.63)	–	2019 (1.29)	4329 (1.00)	–	27481 (2.35)	120728 (6.73)	–	4653 (2.23)	7723 (3.29)
– Western	–	–	10 (3.28)	–	–	116 (0.23)	–	–	33 (0.01)	–	–	1028 (0.06)	–	–	110 (0.03)
KATHMANDU VALLEY	291 (23.13)	441 (18.12)	606 (27.23)	2361 (16.34)	6668 (14.00)	8078 (16.12)	17813 (16.50)	24285 (14.17)	84437 (19.45)	39681 (9.57)	138203 (11.80)	207729 (11.58)	9361 (15.49)	37933 (18.27)	34649 (24.30)
INNER TERAI	26 (2.07)	167 (7.68)	276 (7.68)	191 (2.33)	2796 (5.87)	3488 (6.96)	1557 (1.42)	26039 (10.52)	11687 (2.69)	9608 (2.31)	65420 (5.93)	68738 (3.83)	2031 (4.89)	7384 (3.56)	20540 (8.48)
– Eastern	–	8 (0.33)	19 (0.54)	–	32 (0.07)	70 (0.14)	–	042 (0.08)	389 (0.09)	–	1560 (0.13)	3901 (0.22)	–	223 (0.20)	1055 (0.44)
– Central	26 (2.07)	133 (6.46)	188 (5.33)	191 (1.33)	1353 (2.84)	1912 (3.82)	1557 (2.42)	16392 (9.56)	9898 (2.28)	9608 (2.31)	57419 (4.90)	53563 (2.99)	2931 (4.86)	6339 (3.05)	16839 (6.97)

(*Contd.*)

(*Table 3.16 contd.*)

	– Western	–	46 (1.89)	71 (2.01)	–	1411 (2.36)	1505 (3.00)	–	1505 (0.88)	1400 (0.32)	–	10442 (0.89)	00274 (0.63)	–	832 (0.40)	2586 (1.07)
TERAI		940 (74.76)	1627 (66.64)	2249 (83.75)	11625 (62.24)	36626 (78.88)	33523 (66.89)	63903 (82.27)	124794 (72.50)	342366 (78.88)	367163 (88.12)	904906 (77.29)	2360928 (77.00)	47966 (79.62)	152357 (73.37)	175183 (72.28)
	– Eastern	650 (51.71)	1173 (48.19)	1577 (44.70)	9952 (69.13)	31762 (60.72)	23947 (91.77)	79090 (72.39)	97381 (56.81)	261164 (60.17)	307523 (73.81)	733597 (62.66)	1149980 (64.13)	38126 (63.29)	109167 (52.67)	121197 (50.01)
	• Far-Eastern	178 (14.16)	323 (13.27)	447 (12.67)	6351 (44.11)	13474 (28.28)	21769 (23.46)	44315 (40.66)	46374 (27.03)	273723 (40.03)	180442 (43.31)	319788 (27.31)	417916 (23.30)	21060 (34.96)	31610 (15.24)	34868 (14.39)
	• Mid-Eastern	292 (23.23)	500 (20.54)	715 (20.27)	2303 (16.00)	12869 (27.01)	7853 (25.67)	27678 (25.33)	25273 (11.74)	46308 (11.13)	74549 (27.89)	274155 (23.42)	121836 (17.95)	8494 (14.90)	66748 (33.11)	56147 (23.17)
	• Eastern	180 (14.32)	350 (14.38)	415 (11.76)	2298 (9.02)	5439 (11.42)	6325 (12.62)	7106 (6.50)	25734 (15.01)	39131 (9.02)	52532 (12.61)	139648 (11.93)	410227 (22.88)	8574 (14.23)	8779 (4.23)	30182 (12.43)
	– Central	195 (15.51)	274 (11.26)	444 (12.59)	1045 (7.26)	3708 (7.78)	5050 (10.08)	4986 (4.56)	19349 (11.29)	698281 (16.09)	35464 (8.51)	87950 (7.48)	137116 (7.65)	5765 (9.57)	34021 (16.38)	30593 (12.62)
	– Western	95 (7.56)	180 (7.40)	228 (6.46)	828 (5.76)	1136 (2.38)	2526 (5.04)	5818 (5.32)	8065 (4.70)	11302 (2.62)	24176 (5.80)	83759 (7.15)	93832 (5.23)	4093 (6.79)	9169 (4.42)	23373 (9.64)
NEPAL		1257 (100.00)	2434 (100.00)	3528 (100.00)	14397 (100.00)	47638 (100.00)	50120 (100.00)	109273 (100.00)	171422 (100.00)	434017 (100.00)	416652 (100.00)	1170822 (100.00)	1793334 (100.00)	60248 (100.00)	207655 (100.00)	242345 (100.00)

Note: • Values are at constant prices.
• Figures in parenthesis are percentages.

Source: Central Bureau of Statistics, *Census of Manufacturing Establishments*, 1965, 1972–73 and 1976–77, Kathmandu.

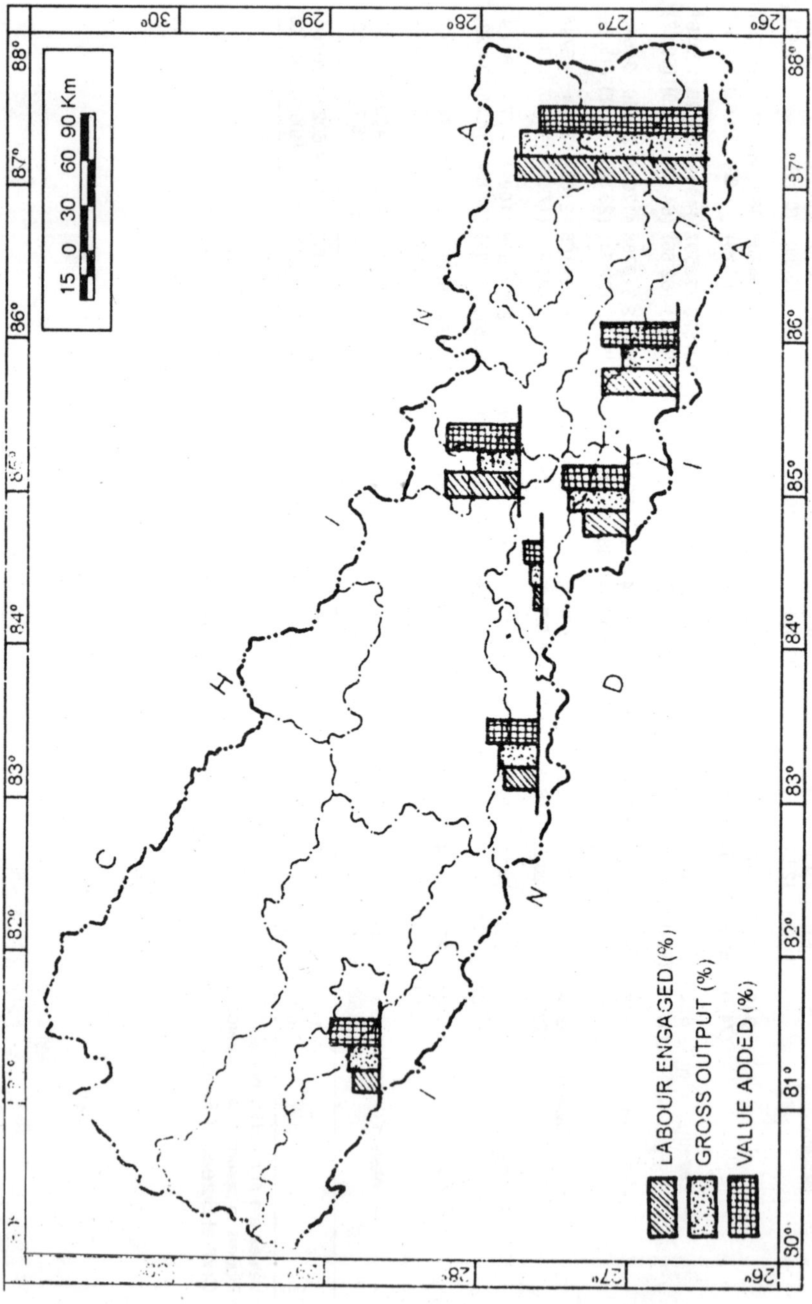

Fig. 3.1 Spatial Distribution of Manufacturing Industries (1965).

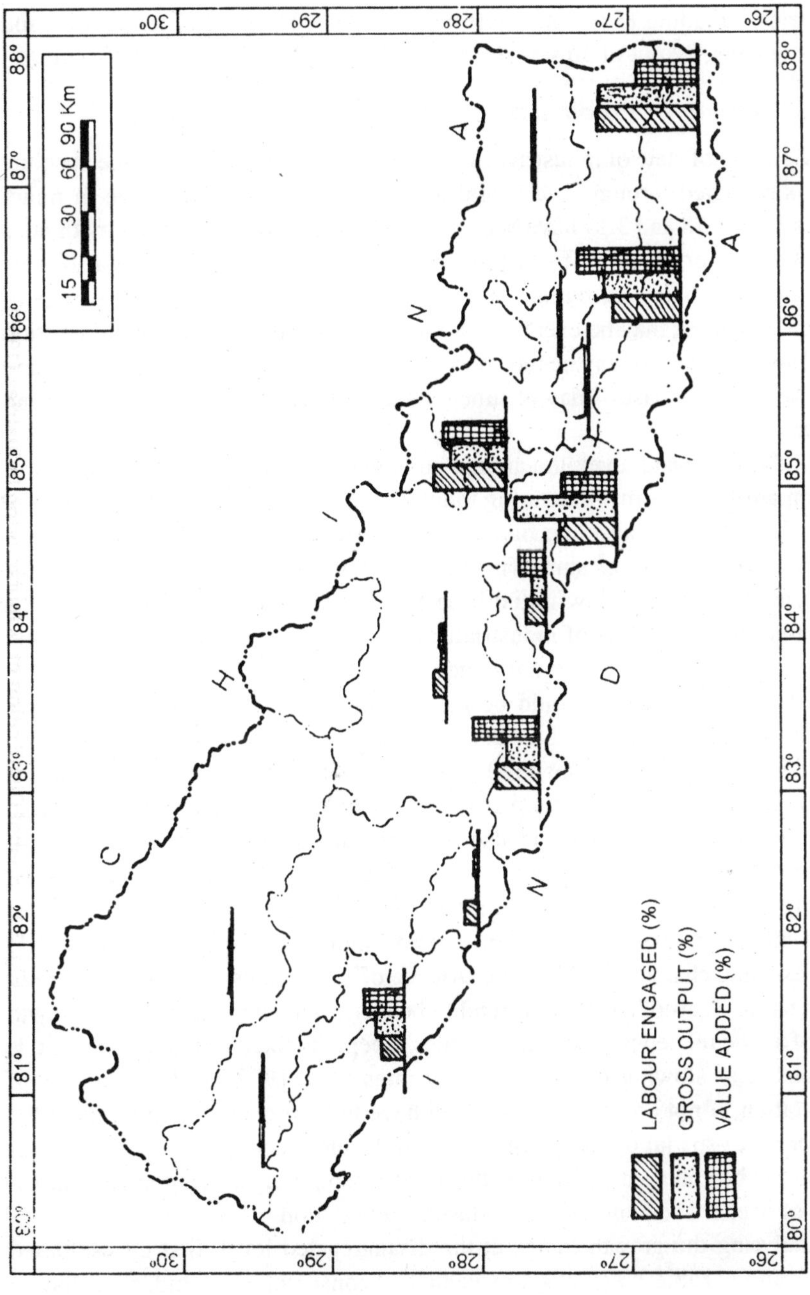

Fig. 3.2 Spatial Distribution of Manufacturing Industries (1976/77).

including workshops, cold storage, press, transport, engineering, etc. On the contrary, the traditional industrial homeland of far-eastern Terai (included in Mechi and Kosi zones here) are seen to house the largest number of export-oriented industries, including 15 out of 16 jute manufactures, 11 out of 17 tea packing and blending units, 22 out of 56 saw mills and 75 out of 203 rice, oil and flour mills.

3.3.22 Growth of Production

A real picture of state of industrialisation can be obtained only when the absolute level is refracted through a temporal lense. With the same objective in mind, Tables 3.17, 3.18 and 3.19 have been constructed to give compound growth rates of industrial production by input-based and use-based classifications of industries and their distributions over the identified territorial zones. A note of caution, however, may be exercised at the outset that the time frame in question (i. e. 1965 to1976/76) may be too short to discern a meaningful growth trend and the spurious data base[71] may at times impair a fair judgment on the observed growth trend.

At the aggregate level, the annual compound growth rates of different production attributes of manufacturing industries at constant prices are found quite high[72]. However, the absolute figures may be grossly misleading in view of the inclusion of a number of simple processing proto-industries a "manufacturing" industries[73] and a very low initial base to be weighted against. Moreover, the economies at a low level of industrialisation are known to exhibit a higher and erratic rate of growth at the initial stages than the highly industrialised and stable economies. Therefore, it would be more illuminating to analyse comparative growth rates of the same attribute at two points of time, or growth rates of different industrial attributes at one point of time. Comparatively speaking, the rate of growth of industrial employment is found not only to lag behind the growth in output and value-added but it is also observed that when and where the rate of growth of fixed capital investment is high that of industrial employment is invariably low. This tendency is entirely in keeping with the characteristic features of the industrial growth process in underdeveloped societies, which Sutcliffe terms as being characterised by "the absence of a bourgeoisie and the absence of a proletariat"[74]. Another distinct trend to be observed with respect to the growth rates of all the related production attributes except the fixed capital investment, is the consistent slowing down of growth rates after 1972/73. This process of deceleration, if not absolute decline, will have to be probed into in terms of the broader socio-spatial dynamics of industrial development before a definite conclusion can be ventured on whether this is mere temporary aberration or manifestation of deeper social process of industrial retardation.

Analysing the growth trends at the disaggregated level, first by use-based classification (Table 3.17), it is noticeable that consumer goods industries have a consistently higher rates than the intermediate goods industries[75]. Among the former, durable goods have higher rates than the non-durable goods. This is a

Table 3.17 Annual Growth Rates* of Manufacturing Industries by Use-based Classification.

(%)

Industry Group	*Labour Employed*			*Gross Output*			*Value Added*		
	1965/ to 1972/73	*1972/73 1976/77*	*1965 to 1976/77*	*1965 to 1972/73*	*1972/73 1976/77*	*1965 to 1976/77*	*1965 to 1972/73*	*1972/73 1976/77*	*1965 to 1976/77*
I. Consumer Goods	21.82	0.66	13.65	15.45	11.48	14.52	17.75	6.00	13.32
(i) Durables	19.49	4.86	13.95	17.85	10.50	15.12	21.46	2.15	14.05
(ii) Non-durables	21.97	0.38	13.63	15.40	11.50	14.62	17.47	6.28	13.27
II. Intermediate Goods	12.48	–1.49	7.18	7.20	–3.21	5.95	18.35	–12.74	5.93
III. Capital and Basic Goods**	–	–	–	–	–	–	–	–	–
IV. Miscellaneous	15.00	19.67	16.68	41.59	1.93	25.64	43.37	3.94	24.73
TOTAL	18.64	1.30	12.00	15.90	11.25	14.20	19.34	3.95	13.50

Note: * Compound growth rates at constant prices.

** Because of their small numbers, no separate information given in the census. They are included in the "Miscellaneous" category.

Source: Derived from Table 3.11.

Table 3.18 Annual Growth Rates* of Manufacturing Industries by Input-based Classification.

(%)

Input-based Classification of Industries	Labour Employed			Gross Output			Value Added		
	1965 to 1972/73	1972/73 to 1976/77	1965 to 1976/77	1965 to 1972/73	1972/73 to 1976/77	1965 to 1976/77	1965 to 1972/73	1972/73 to 1976/77	1965 to 1976/77
I. Agro-based	20.04	–1.88	11.55	14.57	13.00	14.00	15.40	7.85	12.60
(i) Crop-based	19.39	–2.23	11.02	14.47	13.00	13.95	15.20	7.75	12.43
(ii) Animal Husbandry-based	–	6.12	–	–	7.55	–	–	15.27	–
II. Forest-based	13.85	7.48	11.49	16.75	16.60	16.70	21.35	5.95	14.61
III. Mineral-based	15.42	3.01	10.75	20.56	–10.83	8.04	27.38	–22.15	6.50
(i) Metallic mineral	25.30	1.93	16.24	17.70	6.37	13.43	15.47	4.10	11.20
(ii) Non-metallic mineral	14.05	3.23	9.99	22.26	–25.81	1.95	32.24	–34.98	2.15
IV. Chemical-based	11.19	37.33	20.07	8.11	28.46	15.11	2.30	89.99	28.12
V. Service-based	16.79	18.76	17.50	26.08	–22.11	5.83	26.69	–25.72	4.33
VI. Miscellaneous	18.48	14.47	17.01	43.25	–0.05	25.68	36.94	5.93	24.74
TOTAL	18.64	1.30	12.00	15.90	11.25	14.20	19.34	3.85	13.50

Note: *Compound growth rates at constant prices.

Source: Derived from Table 3.10.

Table 3.19 Annual Growth Rates* of Manufacturing Industries by Territorial Zones.

(%)

Territorial Zones	Labour Employed			Gross Output			Value Added		
	1965 to 1972/73	1972/73 to 1976/77	1965 to 1976/77	1965 to 1972/73	1972/73 to 1976/77	1965 to 1976/77	1965 to 1972/73	1972/73 to 1976/77	1965 to 1976/77
MOUNTAIN	–	21.02	–	–	37.55	–	–	43.47	–
Eastern	–	–0.05	–	–	9.07	–	–	8.60	–
Central	–	–	–	–	–	–	–	–	–
Western	–	–	–	–	–	–	–	–	–
HILL	–	37.59	–	–	23.37	–	–	2.39	–
Eastern	–	53.29	–	–	–21.20	–	–	–13.82	–
Central	–	32.34	–	–	44.78	–	–	13.63	–
Western	–	–	–	–	–	–	–	–	–
KATHMANDU VALLEY	15.85	4.91	11.75	19.43	10.72	16.19	22.18	–2.24	12.67
INNER TERAI	46.69	5.68	30.22	32.65	–0.25	19.59	14.15	29.10	19.36
Eastern	–	21.61	–	–	25.75	–	–	47.48	–
Central	32.27	9.03	23.30	29.10	–1.72	16.90	11.65	27.78	17.28
Western	–	1.64	–	–	1.95	–	–	32.78	–
TERAI	17.53	–2.19	9.94	13.75	11.30	12.80	18.00	3.6	12.50
Eastern	18.04	–4.94	9.10	13.30	12.00	12.75	16.20	2.65	11.09
Far-Eastern	11.34	–3.33	5.77	8.50	7.00	7.97	5.99	2.46	4.69
Mid-Eastern	27.86	–11.62	11.80	20.45	4.00	14.35	34.81	–4.94	18.73
Eastern	22.71	3.84	15.49	15.00	30.92	20.54	0.34	36.17	12.12
Central	19.83	8.03	15.40	13.80	11.95	13.08	28.87	–2.62	16.38
Western	4.62	22.11	10.67	19.42	2.90	13.12	12.21	26.36	17.16
NEPAL	18.64	1.30	12.00	15.90	11.25	14.20	19.34	3.85	13.50

Note: *Compound growth rates at constant prices.
Source: Derived from Table 3.16.

very significant pointer to the nature of industrial development in the country, because, on the one hand, the lower growth rates of intermediate goods industries (not to speak of the basic and capital goods industries) reflect the continued disarticulated and inverted industrial structure and, on the other, higher growth rates of durable consumer goods industries means an industrial growth geared to the demands of a narrow upper echelon of the populace, which ultimately leads to a cul-de-sac of industrial stagnation for want of a sufficiently large market base for the industrial products. Another important observation to be made on the growth dynamics of industries is the deceleration, and in some cases absolute decline, in the growth rates of all the industry sub-groups and in all the production attributes except for the fixed capital investment, since 1972/73. That the observed pattern of deceleration or decline is not a mere historical accident but the manifestation of a deep seated structural malady embedded in the economy, is evident from the fact that the decline is most severe in the case of intermediate goods industries. Also, greater deceleration of the durable consumer goods industries[76] already indicates the limitations of the industrial growth tied to the conspicuous and constricted demands of the smaller upper classes of society.

The growth rates of manufacturing industries by input-based classification (Table 3.18) also provides useful pointers to the dynamics of industrial underdevelopment in the country . Whereas the higher growth rates of mineral-based and service-based industries (compared to the agro-based and forest-based ones) in the initial phases provide a hopeful sign, even if they could be highly exaggerated in view of their low starting base. Their greater deceleration, rather absolute decline, in the later phase reflects a disturbing structural retrogression afflicting the Nepalese industrial sector. Moreover, the wide and incoherent fluctuations in growth rates for almost all categories of industries in the short period in question (i.e. from 1965 to 1976/77), speak of the fragility of the industrial base and their over-dependence on the vagaries of exogenous factors.

The spatial variations in growth rates of different production attributes at the aggregate level of industries (Table 3.19) , also tend to confirm the nature of the malady afflicting the Nepalese industrial sector. However, extreme values of growth rates are more observable in the spatial dimensions because of non-existent or negligible initial base in all the Mountain and Hill and some Inner Terai areas. Hence too much should not be read into the seemingly high growth rates in such areas. Nevertheless, the definite decline or deceleration in growth rates since 1972/73 in all the spatial units except a few, are distinctly observable and to that extent confirm the aggravation of industrial stagnation since then. Leaving aside the extreme values of growth rates in the backward Hill and Mountain as simply spurious, the higher overall growth rates accompanied by greater fluctuations in the Inner Terai and central and western sections of Terai may be viewed as manifestations of general industrial instability goading capital to roam around in hitherto unchartered areas in search of higher profitability. Only the consistently higher growth rates in the axes, 'eastern' Terai-central Inner Terai-Kathmandu Valley, i.e. the Birgunj-Hetauda-Kathmandu axis, provides further confirmation of a gradual shift in the industrial location pattern to central Nepal near the seat of state authority.

Amidst the confusing scenario of incoherent and inflated growth rates abated by an extremely low initial base, a distinct trend in industrial growth rates is their deceleration or decline in the 1970s . Though it would be premature to venture hypothetical explanations of this trend pending the study of other aspects of the industrial process, valuable inferences may be drawn from the lively debate on the phenomenon of industrial stagnation in India since the mid-1960s.[77]. However, in view of the significantly different historical experience of the two countries and discernible variations in the current industrial structure, the explanations for industrial retardation in Nepal may have to be sought more in the overall socio-economic backwardness and structural deformations manifested in "the absence of a bourgeoisie and the absence of a proletariat", preemption of available home market by exogenous industries, technological dependence on foreign economies, etc., which we shall discuss in the subsequent sections.

3.3.3 Level and Growth of Productivity

The real measure of development of forces of production in any sub-sector of economy is provided by the measure of gross and net return to different factors of production and pattern of change over time. Since labour (i.e. 'live' labour) and capital (i.e. 'dead' labour) constitute the two most important factors of industrial production we propose in this section to study the level and growth of gross and net return per unit of labour and capital in the relevant social and spatial dimensions so as to contribute further in unraveling the nature of underdevelopment in the Nepalese industrial sector.

3.3.31 At the aggregate level (Tables 3.20 and 3.21) gross output per labour is found to be fairly high and increasing over time[78]. But a low value of net output, or value added, per labour[79] and low growth rate suggests the illusory nature of the observed high productivity as the result of a mere 'transfer' of value from the primary production sector and not due to genuine addition of value in the secondary sector itself. Very low capital/output ratio (i. e. 0.262 and 0.242 in 1965 and 1976/77 respectively), on the other hand, may be a manifestation of either high efficiency of capital use or low absolute value of capital in industrial production[80]. From the study of capital intensity in Table 3.22, it appears that the latter is the most likely case in the context of Nepal.

At the disaggregated level of use-based classification industries (Table 3.20), the incidence of higher rates of gross and net output per labour in consumer goods, specially non-durable consumer goods industries than in intermediate goods industries further qualifies the primitive nature of industrialisation in Nepal dominated by production of subsistence goods. The high intra-industry differentiation of gross output per labour is not, however, reflected in the moderate differentiation of net output (value added) per labour. This is a clear indication of prevalence of elementary processing activities with proportionately low value added

Table 3.20 Industrial Structure and Productivity by Use-based Classifications.

Industry Group	*Capital/Labour (Rs '000)*			*Capital/Output*			*Output/Labour (Rs '000)*			*Value Added/Labour (Rs '000)*		
	1965	*1972/73*	*1976/77*	*1965*	*1972/73*	*1976/77*	*1965*	*1972/73*	*1976/77*	*1965*	*1972/73*	*1976/77*
I. Consumer Goods	9.70	3.68	11.10	0.226	0.125	0.238	42.90	29.45	46.67	5.46	4.31	5.29
(i) Durables	3.19	3.10	3.22	0.254	0.273	0.229	12.55	11.39	14.04	5.17	5.80	5.22
(ii) Non-durables	10.16	3.71	11.68	0.225	0.121	0.238	45.08	30.57	49.09	5.48	4.21	5.29
II. Intermediate Goods	3.65	2.39	2.18	0.424	0.293	0.288	8.62	8.14	7.58	2.02	2.88	1.78
III. Capital and Basic Goods*	–	–	–	–	–	–	–	–	–	–	–	–
IV. Miscellaneous	9.94	8.88	5.23	1.197	0.249	0.279	8.31	35.63	18.75	4.22	19.76	8.80
TOTAL	7.59	3.42	8.66	0.262	0.146	0.242	28.25	24.58	35.78	4.18	4.36	4.84

Note: *No separate information available.
–Because of suspected overestimation of labour employed in 1972/73, the relevant figures for the year are not reliable.

Source: Central Bureau of Statistics, *Census of Manufacturing Establishments*, 1965, 1972/73,1976/77, Kathmandu.

Table 3.21 Industrial Productivity by Territorial Zones (1965, 1972/73 and 1976/77).

	Capital/Output			Output/Labour (Rs '000)			Value Added/Labour (Rs '000)		
	1965	*1972/73*	*1976/77*	*1965*	*1972/73*	*1976/77*	*1965*	*1972/73*	*1976/77*
I. MOUNTAIN	–	1.840	0.095	–	2.02	3.37	–	0.92	1.82
(1) Eastern	–	1.840	0.129	–	2.02	2.87	–	0.92	1.29
(2) Central	–	–	–	–	–	–	–	–	–
(3) Western	–	–	0.072	–	–	3.80	–	–	2.27
II. HILL	–	0.053	0.043	–	48.42	31.30	–	8.11	2.49
(1) Eastern	–	0.028	0.120	–	148.21	10.35	–	24.67	2.46
(2) Central	–	0.081	0.036	–	27.87	39.92	–	4.70	2.55
(3) Western	–	–	0.032	–	–	8.86	–	–	0.95
III. KATHMANDU VALLEY	0.447	0.176	0.406	16.75	20.73	25.72	3.92	5.69	4.29
IV. INNER TERAI	0.162	0.260	0.170	50.30	24.83	19.71	15.35	2.64	5.89
(1) Eastern	–	0.091	0.100	–	48.74	55.73	–	6.97	15.07
(2) Central	0.162	0.285	0.185	50.30	42.44	28.01	15.35	4.69	8.84
(3) Western	–	0.144	0.124	–	7.40	7.49	–	0.59	1.72
V. TERAI	0.245	0.138	0.248	31.05	24.71	41.19	4.06	4.16	5.23
(1) Eastern	0.257	0.133	0.227	30.90	23.08	44.32	3.83	3.43	4.67
(i) For-Eastern	0.246	0.145	0.416	28.41	23.73	35.51	3.32	2.35	2.96
(ii) Mid-Eastern	0.371	0.092	0.150	32.37	21.30	40.98	3.69	5.34	7.15
(iii) Eastern	0.135	0.184	0.095	40.47	25.68	64.86	6.61	1.61	4.77
(2) Central	0.141	0.221	0.509	33.94	23.61	27.15	5.52	9.18	6.06
(3) Western	0.241	0.096	0.121	29.20	73.73	35.73	4.94	8.07	9.25
NEPAL	0.262	0.146	0.242	28.25	24.58	35.78	4.18	4.36	4.83

Source: Central Bureau of Statistics, *Census of Manufacturing Establishments*, 1965, 1972/73 and 1976/77. Kathmandu.

content in non-durable consumer goods sector, which is also the dominant industry group in the country. However, a lower capital/output ratio accompanied by higher capital intensity in the non-durable consumer goods sector dominated by rice and oil milling activities, seems to merely emphasise the absolute backwardness of 'production' goods sector than the so-called advancement of the subsistence goods sector. This is also reflected in the declining output/labour ratio in the intermediate goods sector against a moderately rising ratio in the consumer goods sector. Except for the durable consumer goods, the value added/ labour ratio is seen declining for all other sub-groups; a further confirmation of the deteriorating health of the infantile industrial sector.

3.3.32 Level and growth of industrial productivity in the spatial dimension (Table 3.21) also tends to follow the general pattern of overall development marked by progressive decline from South to North and from East to West with some significant exceptions of pockets of higher productivity scattered at random. The said pattern is more pronounced in the case of gross output/labour than in other attributes. The spatial distribution pattern of gross and net output per labour do not tend to articulate well; thus suggesting either a gross deformation of the industrial structure of some serious flaws in the data base. Given the overwhelming domination of simple cereal-processing activities in all the territorial zones, the latter could be the more probable case. Also, some extreme values like high output/labour and value added/labour ratios in eastern Inner Terai may be a simple statistical illusion resulting from a spurious data base.

In the combined spatio-temporal frame, the distribution of industrial productivity seems to have grown more disparate over the years. For example, coefficient of variation of output/labour is seen to have changed from 29.28% in 1965 to 67.51% in 1976/77. The disparateness, however, may be explained more in terms of physical seclusion and disarticulation of different areas inhibiting the mobility of capital in its natural drive for equalisation of profit than as a result of the crystallisation of pre-capitalist territorial and social monopoly.

From the foregoing analysis it is evident that the industrial productivity in the country is not only low at the absolute aggregate level, but there are wide intra-sectoral and intra-territorial variations in them indicating high social and spatial disarticulation of the industrial economy.

3.3.4 Level of Technology

As highlighted previously, the higher stages of industrial production are marked by an increased division of labour '*within* each craft and each production process' and an increased replacement of living labour with 'dead labour', i.e. rising organic composition of capital. For, that is the only way open to individual capitalists to enable them to constantly reduce the costs of production and improve the productivity of labour and survive under the system of competitive capitalism. In the absence of the relevant data base such a comprehensive study in the case of Nepal is not possible hence we have sought to arrive at certain generalizations about the level of technological development with the help of the following set of measures:

(i) Capital intensity and nature of 'fixed capital assets';
(ii) Nature of power used; and
(iii) The quality of labour employed.

3.3.41 Capital Intensity and Nature of 'Fixed Capital Assets'

Capital, by definition, is "nothing but the crystallisation of unpaid labour"[81]. Also since expanded reproduction of capital is one of the basic characteristics of capitalist mode of production, the development of higher forms of industrial production should be accompanied by increasingly higher proportion of capital (i.e. constant capital) to labour (i.e. variable capital), though not necessarily the absolute decrease in the latter[82]. To examine the trends in capital/labour ratio in the combined spatio-temporal frame in the manufacturing industries of Nepal, Table 3.22 has been constructed. At the aggregate national level the ratio is found quite low as compared to other Third World economies at different level of development[83]. Leaving aside the 1972/73 ratio as grossly deflated due to over-estimation of labour employed, the marginal growth of the ratio from NRs. 7590: 1 to 8660: 1 during 1965 to 1976/77, i.e. a rise of 14.1% over 11 years, should amply reflect on the absolute backwardness and retrogression of the manufacturing sector[84].

In the horizontal territorial dimension, though there is no discernible pattern observable in the distribution of capital/labour ratios in 1965, there is observed a distinct pattern of progressive decline form South to North and from East to West in 1972/73 with visible enclaves of higher ratios in far-eastern and central Terai and Kathmandu Valley (the traditionally more industrialised pockets in the country). Viewed in the combined spatio-temporal frame, the declining capital intensity in the Mountain and Hill region and in some pockets of Inner Terai, and Terai, further underscores the primitive and retrograde nature of the so-called industrial development.

Decomposition of "fixed capital assets" into their different component elements (Table 3.23) also brings out the structural weaknesses of the Nepalese industrial sector. Not only is there a high proportion of 'unproductive' assets like land and buildings (combined share of 40.8% and 36.01% in 1965 and 1976/77 respectively), but there is observed an actual decline in the share of machinery and tools (from 49.89% in 1965 to 45.46% in 1976/77) in the total capital assets.

The low and stagnant capital intensity ratio accompanied by lower proportion of modern assets like machinery and tools, thus, is a very strong indicator of low state of forces of production in the manufacturing sector.

3.3.42 Nature of Power Used

The direct reflection of capital or labour-intensive techniques of production can be seen in the nature of power used in the manufacturing industries. Though a

Table 3.22 Spatio-temporal Variations in Capital Intensity in Manufacturing Industries.

	Capital/Labour Ratio (Rs. '000)			% Change in 1976/77 Over 1965
	1965	1972/73@	1976/77 1965	
MOUNTAIN	–	3.72	0.32	–91.4*
Eastern	–	3.72	0.37	–90.05*
Central	–	-	–	–
Western	–	–	0.27	–
HILL	–	2.58	1.35	–47.67*
Eastren	–	4.15	1.24	–70.1*
Central	–	2.25	1.43	–36.4*
Western	–	–	0.29	–
KATHMANDU VALLEY	7.48	3.64	10.45	39.7
INNER TERAI	8.15	6.45	3.35	–58.9
Eastern	–	4.43	5.56	25.5*
Central	8.15	12.12	5.18	–36.4
Western	–	1.07	2.04	90.7*
TERAI	7.60	3.41	10.21	34.3
Eastern:	7.95	3.06	10.07	26.7
– For-Eastren	6.98	3.44	14.76	111.5
– Mid-Eastren	12.02	1.96	6.15	–48.8
– Eastren	5.47	4.73	6.19	13.2
Central	4.77	5.22	13.83	189.9
Western	7.03	7.10	4.51	–35.8
NEPAL	7.59	3.60	8.66	14.1

Note: @ Capital/labour ratios for 1972/73 are not reliable because of suspected overestimation of labour employed.
* % change over 1972/73.

Source: Central Bureau of Statistics, *Census of Manufacturing Establishments*, 1965, 1972/73 and 1976/77, Kathmandu.

Table 3.23 Composition of Fixed Assets in the Manufacturing Establishments.

(%)

Fixed Assets	Value of Fixed Assets	
	1965	1976/77
1. Land	6.56	3.95
2. Building	34.24	32.06
3. Transport Equipment	2.29	2.06
4. Machinery	49.89	38.48
5. Furniture	0.84	7.45
6. Tools	N.A.	6.98
7. Others	6.18	8.99
TOTAL	100.00	100.00

Note: For 1965, 'machinery' and 'tools' are perhaps combined.

Source: Central Bureau of Statistics, *Census of Manufacturing Establishments*, Nepal, 1965 and 1976/77, Kathmandu.

substantially high percentage (i.e. 89% in 1976/77) of manufacturing establishments are reported to have had power equipments, their capacities do not appear to be very high (i.e. on an average of 13.37 H.P. of prime movers except generators, 10.67 H.P. of electric motors and 5.17 K.W. of generators per establishment 'with power equipment').

A study of type of fuels used also provides significant pointers towards the low technique of industrial production. For 1976/77, the share of different fuel types in the total value of fuels used was reported as follows: wood = 21.29%; coal/charcoal = 16.25%; diesel/patrol = 21.69%; fuel oil, lubricating and kerosene oil = 31.90%; other = 8.88%. The actual energy value share of traditional fuel items of wood and coal (charcoal would be much higher if the comparatively higher unit price value of different oils (which are all imported) are taken into account.

Use of electricity is perhaps the single most significant indicators of level of technology in industrial production. However in Nepal, one of the richest countries in hydro-electric power potential, the share of electricity in total value of industrial inputs was found to be as low as 0.56% and 0.45% in 1965 and 1976/77 respectively. In absolute terms the per capita use was equivalent of NRs. 306.40 in 1976/77.

Table 3.24 provides a spatial configuration of establishments which use power equipments and also the total and per capita use of electricity in industrial production. It is interesting to note that none of the scanty manufacturing establishments in Mountain and western Hills use power equipments and the ratios of establishments with power equipments tends to follow the by now familiar general pattern of progressive decline from South to North, the significant exception being the Kathmandu Valley. In the consumption of electricity both in aggregate and per capita terms a similar general pattern is discernible though the spatial differentiation in both intra- and inter-ecological zonal terms is more pronounced. Far-eastern Terai and Birgunj-Hetauda-Kathmandu Valley axis stands out as an enclave of technological superiority amidst general backwardness of technique of industrial production in the country.

Spatial distribution of generation and consumption of electricity (Table 3.25) exhibits further disparateness, though the figures include non-industrial consumption as well. Whereas central and eastern Hill are the principal locales of generation of electricity Kathmandu-Birgunj corridor and far-eastern Terai consume the larger share.

Table 3.24 Use of Power Equipment and Consumption of Electricity in Manufacturing Industries by Territorial Zones (1976/77).

Territorial Zones	% of Establishments with Power Equipments	Consumption of Electricity	
		Total Value (Rs. '000)	Per Person Engaged in Manufacturing (Rs.)
	(1)	(2)	(3)
MOUNTAIN	0	0	0
	(–)	(–)	(–)
Eastern	0	0	0
	(–)	(–)	(–)
Central	–	–	–
Western	0	0	0
	(–)	(–)	(–)
HILL	73.89	330	77.45
	(0.830)	(2.15)	(0.253)
Eastern	70.10	208	185.55
	(0.788)	(1.35)	(0.606)
Central	78.26	122	40.34
	(0.879)	(0.79)	(0.132)
Western	0	0	0
	(–)	(–)	(–)
KATHMANDU VALLEY	90.13	2309	285.84
	(1.013)	(15.04)	(0.933)
INNER TERAI	86.69	1152	330.28
	(0.974)	(7.50)	(1.078)
Eastern	94.74	0	0
	(1.064)	(–)	(–)
Central	86.17	1118	584.73
	(0.968)	(7.28)	(1.908)
Western	85.92	34	22.58
	(0.965)	(0.22)	(0.074)
TERAI	92.71	11566	345.02
	(1.043)	(75.31)	(1.126)
Eastern	93.15	9463	364.70
	(1.047)	(61.62)	(1.191)
– Far-Eastern	93.06	6457	548.64
	(1.046)	(42.05)	(1.791)
– Mid-Eastern	92.45	688	87.61
	(1.039)	(4.48)	(0.286)
– Eastern	94.46	2318	366.48
	(1.061)	(15.09)	(1.196)
Central	90.32	1810	358.42
	(1.015)	(11.79)	(1.170)
Western	94.30	293	115.99
	(1.060)	(1.91)	(0.379)
NEPAL	39.00	15357	306.40
	(1.00)	(100.00)	(1.00)

Note: Figures in parenthesis in columns 1 and 3 are location factors and those in column 2 are percentages.

Source: Central Bureau of Statistics, *Census of Manufacturing Establishments*, Nepal, 1976–77, Kathmandu.

Table 3.25 Generation and Consumption of Electricity by Territorial Zones (1976/77).

	Generation of Electricity Total (MWH)	*Consumption of Electricity* Total (MWH)	*Ratio of Consumption to Generation*
	(1)	(2)	(3)
MOUNTAIN	–	–	–
Eastern	–	–	–
Central	–	–	–
Western	–	–	–
HILL	133.694	6426	0.048
	(74.11)	(4.88)	(0.066)
Eastern	36737	1928	0.052
	(20.36)	(1.46)	(0.071)
Central	96957	4498	0.046
	(53.75)	(3.42)	(0.063)
Western	–	–	–
KATHMANDU VALLEY	4781	71117	14.875
	(2.65)	(54.00)	(20.377)
INNER TERAI	1744	5145	2.950
	(0.97)	(3.91)	(4.041)
Eastern	–	–	–
Central	1601	5009	3.129
	(0.89)	(3.80)	(4.286)
Western	143	136	0.951
	(0.08)	(0.10)	(1.303)
TERAI	40179	49006	1.220
	(22.27)	(37.21)	(1.671)
Eastern	29100	41047	1.411
	(16.13)	(31.17)	(1.933)
– Far-Eastern	22090	20578	0.932
	(12.25)	(15.63)	(1.277)
– Mid-Eastern	4019	2872	0.715
	(2.23)	(2.18)	(0.979)
– Eastern	2991	17597	5883
	(1.66)	(13.36)	(8.059)
Central	7120	4623	0.649
	(3.95)	(3.51)	(0.889)
Western	3959	3336	0.843
	(2.19)	(2.53)	(1.155)
NEPAL	180398	131694	0.730
	(100.00)	(100.00)	(100.00)

Note: Figures in parenthesis in columns 1 and 2 are percentages and those in column 3 are location factors.

Source: Nepal Electricity Corporation, Kathmandu.

3.3.43 Quality of Labour Employed

Higher levels of techniques of industrial production should be marked by greater division of labour within the production units and higher proportion of skilled to unskilled labour. In the absence of systematic data, proportions of 'technical administrative' labour to total labour (both 'paid' & 'unpaid') by territorial zones are presented in Table 3.26.

Table 3.26 Percentage of 'Technical-Administrative' Labour to total Labour by Territorial Zones (1965 and 1976/77).

	% of Technical-administrative Labour to Total Labour				
	1965			1976/77	
	Technical	Adminis-trative	Technical + Adminis-trative	Technical + Adminis-trative	
	1	2	3	4*	5
MOUNTAIN	–	–	–	10.38	12.86
Eastern	–	–	–	4.79	8.96
Central	–	–	–	–	–
Western	–	–	–	13.96	16.22
HILL	–	–	–	13.85	33.80
Eastern	–	–	–	27.09	28.54
Central	–	–	–	6.98	36.18
Western	–	–	–	20.00	22.41
KATHMANDU VALLEY	5.88	19.19	25.07	22.57	23.83
INNER TERAI	24.08	29.84	53.92	12.09	18.20
Eastern	–	–	–	15.69	24.29
Central	24.08	29.84	53.92	18.81	26.30
Western	–	–	–	4.07	7.63
TERAI	8.61	21.83	30.44	18.64	18.30
Eastern:	7.64	21.40	29.04	19.20	24.99
– For-Eastern	5.16	19.78	24.94	22.56	25.19
– Mid-Eastern	11.51	23.97	35.48	14.06	27.24
– Eastern	12.87	24.81	37.68	18.46	21.82
Central	11.87	19.62	31.49	14.45	19.60
Western	10.63	29.71	40.34	20.93	26.92
NEPAL	8.04	21.50	29.54	18.36	24.45

Note: *Figures are only for "paid" technical-administrative labour to total 'paid labour'.
Source: Central Bureau of Statistics, *Census of Manufacturing Establishments*, 1965 and 1976/77, Kathmandu.

Even if no comparative data are available for 1976/77, from the composition of labour types for 1965 the low share of 'technical' labour in the industrial production is self-evident. The combined share of technical-administrative labour in *total* industrial labour i.e. both hired and a family labour is highly inflated and misleading because of the inclusion of less productive family labour engaged in 'administrative' activities. Thus a better idea of quality of industrial labour may be provided by the percentage share of only *hired* 'technical-administrative' labour (for want of a separate break-up for 'technical' labour 'alone') to total hired labour (see Column 4 in Table 3.26). Nevertheless, the fall in percentage share of technical-administrative labour over time is very visible and the increasing use of non-technical operative labour, signifies the deterioration in levels of technique of industrial production in the country.

In the spatial dimension, no definite trend in the distribution of quality of labour is discernible from the available data, because of the suspected higher proportions of unpaid 'administrative' labour in the more backward areas, specially the Hills. However, a pattern with higher proportions of higher quality labour in the industrially more advanced areas of Terai, specially the far-eastern section, and Kathmandu Valley can be distinguished when only the hired labour is taken into consideration.

A more reliable account of the quality of labour by principal industrial groups is available from the *Industrial Survey Report* of Nepal Rastra Bank[85]. At the aggregate level it is found that 21.01% of total labour is engaged in 'administrative and managerial activities' and of the remaining 'operative' labour as high as 68.49% is 'unskilled'. By principal industry groups, only the sugar refineries, milk products and machine and tools industries are seen to have high percentages of both administrative and managerial labour and skilled operative labour.

3.4 'DISTRIBUTION' CHARACTERISTICS OF MANUFACTURING

As already highlighted in the earlier chapter, the 'distribution' (or social relations of production) conditions constitute the most vital elements for articulating the process of underdevelopment in the industrial sector. In view of the paucity of relevant data in the desired frame and the obvious theoretical complexities of empirically measuring the social relations of production, we have sought in this sub-section to study fragmentary aspects of the 'distribution' conditions separately.

3.4.1 Scale of Industrial Production[86]

While acknowledging analytical reservations in equating 'size' of production unit with 'scale' of operation, the changing scales of production and the process of concentration and centralisation expected to be associated with higher stages of industrial production is sought to be examined here, for convenience, with respect to the spatio-temporal variations in the size of the manufacturing establishments. It may also be relevant to reassert at the outset that the process of socialisation of production in the industrial (in the strict sense!) sector should be more pronounced than in the other sectors of the economy and non-compliance to the general law should signal the disruptive interventions of extraneous factors, both exogenous and endogenous.

Table 3.27 Size of Manufacturing Establishments by Territorial Zones (1965, 1972/73 and 1976/77).

Territorial Zones	*Labour/Manufacturing Establishment*		
	1965	*1972/73*	*1976/77*
MOUNTAIN	–	29.92	23.33
Eastern	–	29.92	32.45
Central	–	–	–
Western	–	–	18.77
HILL	–	7.12	11.84
Eastern	–	3.63	11.56
Central	–	8.88	11.95
Western	–	–	11.60
KATHMANDU VALLEY	8.18	15.12	13.29
INNER TERAI	7.35	14.95	12.55
Eastern	--	4.00	3.68
Central	7.35	10.17	10.17
Western	–	30.67	21.21
TERAI	12.58	22.51	14.91
Eastern:	15.31	27.09	16.45
– Far-Eastern	35.68	41.72	26.33
– Mid-Eastern	7.89	25.74	10.98
– Eastern	7.21	15.24	15.24
Central	5.36	13.53	11.37
Western	8.72	6.31	11.08
NEPAL	11.45	19.57	14.21

Note: Ratios for 1972/73 are not reliable because of suspected over-estimation of labour engaged.

Source: Central Bureau of Statistics, *Census of Manufacturing Establishments*, 1965, 1972/73 and 1976/77, Kathmandu.

The spatio-temporal variations in average size of labour per establishment and distribution of establishments by size based on labour engaged have been presented in Tables 3.27 and 3.28. The fact that nearly 80% of the units employ less than 10 persons each and less than 3% of them engage 100 or more persons each with the average number of labour per establishment being as low as 11.45 in 1965 and 14.21 in 1976/77 , amply demonstrate the dominance of small-scale production and also the implied general backwardness of industrial economy[87] in Nepal. Viewed across time and space, an identical pattern is discernible, except in the Mountain zone where the recently established manufacturing units seem to go for larger sizes. In fact the larger number of labour per establishment in Mountain and some more developed enclaves of eastern Terai appear to be a function of better structural composition of industries comparatively less dominated by rice and oil milling units. The slight increase in the shares of small and large establishments at the cost of medium ones and in the average size of the establishments over the years may be interpreted as some signs of ongoing differentiation within the diminutive industrial sector. The former trend can be discerned more clearly for the period 1965–1972/73 than for 1972/73–1976/77. Though the rise in the share of smaller units in the latter period may tempt one to view it as the manifestation of the 'process of ancillarisation[88], the overwhelming domination of small agro-processing unit, since the beginning and a negligible share of 'intermediate goods' industries in the total manufacturing sector should preclude any conventional explanation used to explain the higher stages of development of industrial capitalism. The phenomenon of increase in the share of smaller units in the case of Nepal may be a simple manifestation of structural retrogression marked by proliferation of small agro-processing units[89] at the cost of bigger size 'production' goods industries. However, as agro-industries are also "subject to the laws of concentration and centralisation; scale economies and the law on increasing firm size... like other industries"[90] the contrary situation in Nepal may be the result of interventions of the "monopsonist power of the factory"[91] (located primarily in India in our case!), or a mark of the "initial process of capitalist development" in industry[92], or both.

A study of growth trend of manufacturing establishments by size based on labour engaged by the year of commencement of initial production as recorded in the census of 1972/73 and 1976/77 (Table 3.29), reveals an interesting pattern of higher share of larger size establishments in the preceding than the following years. Whereas a part of the phenomenon may be explained by the higher rate of liquidation of smaller size establishments initiated during the Fifties and Sixties which had ceased operation by the time of census enumeration in the Seventies, general validity of the pattern can be ascertained by the higher, or not significantly lower, absolute numbers of bigger size establishments in the preceding years, specially the Sixties, than in the Seventies. This gives further credence to the hypothesis of falling concentration of indigenous industries under the "monopsonist power of the (foreign) factory".

To gain more insight into the mechanism of falling, or not significantly rising, concentration of manufacturing industries in Nepal, some conventional 'structural ratios' of industries by size of labour employed have been calculated for a single point of time for want of relevant information in a time series (Table 3.30). Even if no distinct pattern of association of plant size with various structural ratios are observable, perhaps due to spurious data or as a reflection of intra-sectoral disarticulation typical of primitive industries, some negative correlations between plant size and technological structure (i.e. capital intensity and extent of fuel used) and labour productivity can be discerned[93]. The phenomenon may appear slightly intriguing as it tends to go against the basic tenets of the general law of socialisation of production (or, the law of increasing return to scale'). However, as already noted in the context of 'peasant production' in agriculture in the earlier chapter, the apparent higher 'efficiency' of small-scale production is a mere camouflage for greater and more direct exploitation of labour and a

Table 3.28 Labour-Sile Distribtion of Manufacturing Establishments by Territorial Zones.

Territorial Zones		Manufacturing Establishments by Number of Persons Engaged														
		Up to 9			10–99			100 and Over			1000 and Over			All		
		1965	1972-73	1976-77	1965	1972-73	1976-77	1965	1972-73	1976-77	1965	1972-73	1976-77	1965	1972-73	1976-77
MOUNTAIN			2	1		9	31		1	1					12	13
	(a)	–	(0.10)	(0.04	–	(2.09)	(4.91)	–	(1.54)	(1.12)	–	–	–	–	(0l.49)	(0.94)
	(b)		(16.67)	(3.03)		(75.00)	(93.94)		(8.33)	(3.03)					(100.00)	(100.00)
Eastern			2			9	10		1	1					12	11
	(a)	–	(0.10)	–	–	(2.09)	(1.55)	–	(1.54)	(1.12)	–	–	–	–	(0.49)	(0.31)
	(b)		(16.67)			(75.00)	(90.91)		(8.33)	(9.09)					(100.00)	(100.00)
Central	(a)	–	–	–	–	–	–	–	–	–	–	–	–	–	–	–
	(b)															
Western				1			21									22
	(a)	–	–	(0.04)	–	–	(3.26)	–	–	–	–	–	–	–	–	(0.62)
	(b)			(4.55)			(95.45)									(100.00)
HILL			148	260		16	95		3	5					167	360
	(a)	–	(7.63)	(9.30)	–	(3.72)	(14.75)	–	(4.62)	(5.62)	–	–	–	–	(60.86)	(10.20)
	(b)		(88.62)	(72.22)		(9.58)	(26.39)		(1.80)	(1.39)					(100.00)	(100.00)
Eastern			53	74		2	23		1						56	97
	(a)	–	(2.75)	(2.75)	–	(0.47)	(3.57)	–	(1.54)	–	–	–	–	–	(2.30)	(2.75)
	(b)		(94.64)	(76.29)		(3.57)	(23.71)		(1.79)						(100.00)	(100.00)
Central			95	185		14	63		2	5					111	253
	(a)	–	(4.90)	(6.62)	–	(3.26)	(9.78)	–	(3.68)	(9.62)	–	–	–	–	(4.56)	(7.17)
	(b)		(85,59)	(73.12)		(12.61)	(24.90)		(1.80)	(1.58)					(100.00)	(100.00)
Western				1			9									10
	(a)	–	–	(0.04)	–	–	(1.40)	–	–	–	–	–	–	–	–	(0.28)
	(b)			(10.00)			(90.00)									(100.00)
KATHMANDU		233	306	462	53	125	130	5	10	16				291	441	668
VALLEY	(a)	(23.53)	(15.78)	(16.52)	(21.03)	(29.07)	(20.19)	(33.33)	(15.38)	(17.95)	NA	–	–	(23.15)	(18.12)	(17.25)
	(b)	(80.07)	(69.39)	(75.99)	(18.21)	(28.9)	(21.38)	(1.72)	(2.27)	(2.63)				(100.00)	(100.00)	(100.00)
INNER		21	171	230	5	12	40		4	8				26	187	278
TERAI	(a)	(2.12)	(8.82)	(8.23)	(1.98)	(2.79)	(6.21)	–	(6.15)	(8.99)	–	–	–	(2.07)	(7.68)	(7.88)
	(b)	(80.77)	(91.44)	(82.73)	(19.23)	(6.42)	(14.39)		(2.14)	(2.88)				(100.00)	(100.00)	(100.00)

(Contd.)

(*Table 3.28 contd.*)

Easterm		–	7	18	–	1	1	–	–	–	–	–	–	–	8	19
	(a)		(0.36)	(0.64)		(0.23)	(0.16)								(0.33)	(0.54)
	(b)		(87.50)	(94.74)		(12.50)	(5.26)								(100.00)	(100.00)
Central		21	119	154	5	10	29	–	4	5	–	–	–	26	133	188
	(a)	(2.22)	(6.14)	(5.51)	(2.98)	(2.33)	(4.50)		(6.16)	(5.62)				(2.07)	(5.46)	(5.33)
	(b)		(87.50)	(94.74)		(12.50)	(5.26)							(100.00)	(100.00)	(100.00)
Western		–	45	58	–	1	10	–	–	3	–	–	–	–	46	71
	(a)		(2.32)	(2.08)		(0.23)	(2.55)			(3.37)					(1.89)	(2.01)
	(b)		(87.50)	(94.74)		(12.50)	(5.26)								(100.00)	(100.00)
TERAI		736	1312	1842	194	268	348	10	47	59	NA	7	4	940	1627	2249
	(a)	(74.34)	(67.66)	(65.90)	(76.98)	(62.33)	(54.04)	(66.67)	(72.31)	(66.29)		(100.00)	(100.00)	(74.78)	(6.68)	(63.75)
	(b)	(78.30)	(80.64)	(81.90)	(20.64)	(16.47)	(15.47)	(1.00)	(2.89)	(2.62)		(0.43)	(0.18)	(100.00)	(100.00)	(100.00)
Western		495	936	1293	146	200	237	9	37	47	NA	7	4	650	1173	1577
	(a)	(50.00)	(48.27)	(46.26)	(57.54)	(46.51)	(36.80	(60.00)	(56.92)	(52.81)		(100.00)	(100.00)	(51.71)	(48.19)	(44.70)
	(b)	(76.15)	(79.80)	(81.99)	(22.46)	(17.65)	(15.03)	(1.38)	(3.15)	(2.93)		(0.60)	(0.25)	(100.00)	(100.00)	(100.00)
–Far Eastern		105	208	321	65	94	101	5	21	25	NA	2	2	176	323	447
	(a)	(10.61)	(10.73)	(11.48)	(26.98)	(21.86)	(15.68)	(33.33)	(32.31)	(28.09)		(28.57)	(50.00)	(14.16)	(13.27)	(12.67)
	(b)	(58.99)	(64.40)	(72.79)	(38.20)	(29.10)	(22.60)	(2.31)	(6.50)	(5.59)		(0.62)	(0.45)	(100.00)	(100.00)	(100.00)
–Mid Eastern		249	430	627	39	62	74	4	8	14		3	1	292	823	715
	(a)	(25.15)	(22.18)	(22.43)	(15.48)	(14.42)	(11.49)	(26.67)	(12.31)	(15.73)		(42.86)	(25.00)	(23.23)	(33.81)	(20.27)
	(b)	(85.27)	(52.25)	(87.69)	(13.36)	(7.53)	(10.36)	(1.37)	(0.97)	(1.96)		(0.36)	(0.14)	(100.00)	(100.00)	(100.00)
–Eastern		141	298	345	39	44	62	–	8	8	–	2	1	180	350	425
	(a)	(14.24)	(15.37)	(12.34)	(15.48)	(10.23)	(9.63)		(12.31)	(8.99)		(28.57)	(25.00)	(14.32)	(14.38)	(11.76)
	(b)	(85.27)	(52.25)	(87.69)	(13.26)	(7.53)	(10.35)	(1.37)	(0.97)	(1.96)		(0.36)	(0.14)	(100.00)	(100.00)	(100.00)
Central		165	239	366	30	29	69	–	6	9	–	–	–	195	274	444
	(a)	(16.67)	(12.33)	(13.09)	(11.90)	(6.74)	(10.71)		(9.23)	(10.11)				(15.51)	(11.26)	(12.59)
	(b)	(84.62)	(87.23)	(82.43)	(15.38)	(10.58)	(15.54)		(2.19)	(2.03)				(100.00)	(100.00)	(100.00)
Western		76	137	283	18	39	42	1	4	3	–	–	–	95	180	228
	(a)	(7.68)	(7.07)	(6.55)	(7.14)	(9.07)	(6.52)	(6.67)	(6.15)	(3.37)				(7.56)	(7.40)	(6.46)
	(b)	(80.00)	(76.11)	(80.26)	(18.95)	(21.67)	(18.42)	(1.05)	(2.22)	(1.32)				(100.00)	(100.00)	(100.00)
NEPAL		990	1939	2795	252	430	644	15	65	89	NA	7	4	1257	2434	3528
	(a)	(100.00)	(100.00)	(100.00)	(100.00)	(100.00)	(100.00)	(100.00)	(100.00)	(100.00)		(100.00)	(100.00)	(100.00)	(100.00)	(100.00)
	(b)	(78.76)	(79.66)	(79.22)	(20.05)	(17.67)	(18.25)	(1.19)	(2.67)	(2.52)		(0.29)	(0.11)	(100.00)	(100.00)	(100.00)

Note: Figure in perenthesis are percentages: (a) Column percentage, (b) Row percentage.
Source: Central Bureau of Statistics, *Census of Manufacturing Establishments*, 1965, 1972–73 and 1976–77, Kathmandu.

Table 3.29 Growth of Manufacturing Establishments by Size Based on Number of Persons Engaged.

Size Based on Number of Persons Engaged		*No. of Establishments by Year of Commencement of Initial Production*											
		1973/74–1976/77		*1963/64–1972/73*		*1953/54–1962/63*		*Prior to 1953/54*		*Not Reported*		*Total*	
		(i)	*(ii)*	*(i)*	*(ii)*	*(i)**	*(ii)*	*(i)*	*(ii)*	*(i)*	*(ii)*	*(i)*	*(ii)*
1–9		1519	–	1077	1730	134	144		55	65	20	2795	1939
	(a)	(80.88)		(80.73)	(83.09)	(54.25)	(61.02)	N.A.	(63.95)	(94.20)	(66.67)	(79.22)	(79.66)
	(b)	(54.35)		(38.53)	(89.22)	(4.79)	(7.43)		(2.84)	(2.33)	(1.03)	(100.00)	(100.00)
10–99		324	–	222	321	94	76		23	4	10	644	430
	(a)	(17.25)		(16.64)	(15.42)	(38.06)	(32.20)	N.A.	(26.74)	(5.80)	(33.33.)	(18.25)	(17.67)
	(b)	(50.35)		(34.47)	(74.65)	(17.67)	(17.67)		(5.35)	(0.62)	(2.33)	(100.00)	(100.00)
100–999		35	–	35	37	15	15		6	–	–	85	58
	(a)	(1.87)		(2.62)	(1.78)	(6.07)	(6.36)		(6.98)			(2.41)	(2.38)
	(b)	(41.18)		(41.18)	(63.79)	(17.65)	(25.86)		(10.34)			(100.00)	(100.00)
1000 and over		–	–	–	4	4	1		2	–	–	4	7
	(a)				(0.19)	(1.62)	(0.42)		(2.33)			(0.11)	(0.29)
	(b)				(57.14)	(100.00)	(14.29)		(28.57)			(100.00)	(100.00)
TOTAL		1875	–	1334	2082	247	236	N.A.	86	69	30	3528	2434
		(100.00)		(100.00)	(100.00)	(100.00)	(100.00)		(100.00)	(100.00)	(100.00)	(100.00)	(100.00)
		(53.23)		(37.83)	(85.54)	(7.00)	(9.70)		(3.53)	(1.96)	(1.23)	(100.00)	(100.00)

Note:
- (I) Establishments in operation during 1976/77; (II) Establishments in operation during 1972/73.
- Figures in parenthesis are percentages; (a) Column percentage; (b) Row percentage.

* Established prior to 1962/63.

Source: Central Bureau of Statistics, *Census of Manufacturing Establishments*, 1972/73 and 1976/77, Kathmandu.

Table 3.30 Structural Ratios of Manufacturing Industries by Size (1976/77).

(Rs. '000)

	Total	Size based on Labour Engaged			
		0.9	10.99	100.999	1000 and over
1. Capital/Labour (Rs.)	19.03	25.85	23.68	11.53	27.22
	(1.00)	(1.358)	(1.244)	(0.606)	(1.430)
2. Fuel/Unit (Rs.)	0.748	1.188	0.928	0.389	1.00
	(1.00)	(1.588)	(1.241)	(0.520)	(1.337)
3. Capital/Output (Rs.)	0.242	0.128	0.331	0.354	0.444
	(1.00)	(0.529)	(1.368)	(1.463)	(1.835)
4. Output/Labour (Rs.)	78.61	201.27	71.63	32.54	61.35
	(1.00)	(2.560)	(0.911)	(0.414)	(0.780)
5. Value Added/ Labour (Rs.)	10.62	0.178	21.97	5.91	17.67
	(1.00)	(0.017)	(2.069)	(0.556)	(1.664)

Note: Figures in parenthesis are ratios to the total.
Source: Central Bureau of Statistics, *Census of Manufacturing Establishments*, 1976/77, Kathmandu.

reflection of the essential 'inefficiency' of the larger-scale production under the existing retrograde social relations of production which would thwart the operation of the general law of socialisation of production. Higher profit rate accompanied by lower wage rate to be observed in the smaller industries in Nepal provide instant empirical support to this analytical position. The illusory nature of higher capital intensity associated with smaller enterprises has been rightly exposed as due to over-valuation of non-productive assets like buildings[94] in then and should hold true in Nepal as well, as indicated by the structure of capital assets in the previous section. Only the better technological structure and higher labour productivity to be seen in the largest size (i.e. with more than 1000 labour/unit) establishments as compared to the middle sized ones, could be taken as manifestations of genuinely higher modes of industrial production since they all happen to be public limited companies under total or dominant state control.

The differentiation of industries by the size of fixed capital investment (Table 3.31) also reflects an identical pattern of overwhelming domination of small industries (77.09%) over medium (17.46%) and large (5.44%) ones[95]. Viewed in the territorial dimensions, whereas the general prevalence of 'small' industries is discernible in all the territorial zones, the central zone (including the Birgunj-Hetauda-Kathmandu axis) accounts for a higher share of large and medium industries while the far-eastern zone occupies the lowest rung of the plant-size ladder.

Thus, the important inference to be derived from the foregoing analysis of size-distribution of manufactories is the stagnant or falling rate of already very low concentration of industries primarily as a result of structural retrogression marked by over-dependence on elementary agro-processing activities and failure to transform the prevailing backward and distorted relations of production.

Table 3.31 Distribution of Manufacturing Industries by the Size of Fixed Capital Investment (1982/83).

Territorial Zones		*Number of Industries by Size of Capital*			
		Small	*Medium*	*Large*	*Total*
1. Eastern Zone		293	47	7	347
	(i)	(84.44)	(13.54)	(2.02)	(100.00)
	(ii)	(22.72)	(16.10)	(7.69)	(20.75)
2. Central Zone		764	205	77	1046
	(i)	(73.04)	(19.60)	(7.36)	(100.00)
	(ii)	(59.27)	(70.21)	(84.62)	(62.56)
3. Western Zone		135	24	5	164
	(i)	(82.32)	(14.63)	(3.05)	(100.00)
	(ii)	(10.47)	(8.22)	(5.49)	(9.81)
4. Far-Western Zone		97	16	2	115
	(i)	(84.35)	(13.91)	(1.74)	(100.00)
	(ii)	(7.53)	(5.48)	(2.20)	(6.88)
NEPAL		1289	292	91	1672
	(i)	(77.09)	(17.46)	(5.44)	(100.00)
	(ii)	(100.00)	(100.00)	(100.00)	(100.00)

Note: Figures in parenthesis are percentages:
(I) Row percentages.
(II) Column percentages.
Source: HMG, Ministry of Industry (1983), *Industrial Profile*, Kathmandu.

3.4.2 Ownership Pattern of Manufactories

3.4.21 A determinate mode of ownership of the industrial means of production, which is " the power to appropriate and dispose of the product obtained"[96], constitutes one of the basic ensembles of the relations of production in the industrial sector. However, the lack of a detailed and authentic information on the essential form of ownership of individual means of production in Nepal, has driven us here to attempt to generalise the same through the analysis of the 'juridical' (not necessarily the 'essential') forms of ownership of the registered manufactories by principal official catagories[97].

A glance at Table 3.32 instantly brings out the essential nature of organisation of industrial production in Nepal, namely the predominant bias in favour of private appropriation of the social surplus. Though all the given juridical forms of ownership of industrial establishments basically relate to the different forms of private ownership, a substantial number of 'public limited' enterprises are known to be controlled by the state through its total or majority shares in them[98]. Even when both the private and public limited forms of ownership of industries by the state are taken into account, the overall share of the state (in essence the coalition of dominant feudal, comprador and mercantile classes), as frequently talked about in the case of many Third World countries, does not amount to be very significant. However, the larger shares in the total labour and capital engaged and in the bigger size enterprises with more than 100 labour each (commanded by the

Table 3.32 Ownership Pattern of Manufacturing Establishments (1976/77).

Legal Status	No. of Establishments	No. of Persons Engaged	Gross Fixed Capital (Rs '000)	Gross Output (Rs '000)	Value Added (Rs '000)	No. of Establishments by Size based on No. of Persons Engaged			
						1–9	10–99	100–999	1000 and over
1. Individual proprietorship	3043 (86.25)	25960 (51.80)	401297 (42.09)	2822129 (71.62)	230161 (43.23)	2540 (90.88)	470 (72.98)	33 (38.82)	–
2. Partnership	327 (9.27)	5060 (10.10)	130117 (13.65)	386224 (9.80)	144761 (27.19)	233 (8.34)	86 (13.35)	8 (9.41)	–
3. Public Limited	20 (0.57)	5042 (10.06)	186566 (19.57)	276419 (7.02)	642338 (12.07)	2 (0.07)	6 (0.93)	12 (14.12)	–
4. Private Ltd.	127 (3.60)	12704 (25.35)	209838 (22.06)	415059 (10.53)	88255 (16.58)	17 (0.61)	79 (12.27)	27 (31.76)	–
(i) Govt. owned	115 (3.26)	11490 (22.92)	176747 (18.54)	363280 (9.22)	79336 (14.90)	15 (0.54)	72 (11.18)	24 (28.24)	4 (100.00)
(ii) Pvt.-owned	8 (0.23)	871 (1.74)	10963 (1.15)	20463 (0.52)	5082 (0.95)	1 (0.04)	5 (0.78)	2 (2.35)	–
(iii) Both Govt. and Pvt. owned	4 (0.11)	343 (0.68)	22128 (2.32)	31316 (0.79)	3837 (0.72)	1 (0.04)	2 (0.31)	1 (1.18)	–
5. Others	11 (0.31)	1354 (2.70)	25987 (2.73)	40124 (1.02)	5017 (0.94)	3 (0.11)	3 (0.47)	5 (5.88)	–
ALL	3528 (100.00)	50120 (100.00)	953535 (100.00)	3939955 (100.00)	532432 (100.00)	2795 (100.00)	644 (100.00)	85 (100.00)	4 (100.00)

Figures in parenthesis are percentages.
Source: Central Bureau of Statistics, *Census of Manufacturing Establishments*, 1976/77, Kathmandu.

public limited and government-owned private limited establishments) highlight the crucial role exercised by the state in the industrial destiny of the country.

A study of use-based classification of manufactories organised as public limited companies (Table 3.12 above), further underscores the structural dependence of the infantile industrial sector on the state. Not only are the negligible number of 'basic' and 'capital' goods industries organised under the state aegis, but also a substantial number of important 'intermediate' and 'consumer non-durable' goods industries[99] owe their existence in the 'public' sector.

Viewed in a temporal frame by cross-classifying legal status and the year of commencement of initial production of the manufacturing establishments (Table 3.33), the drastic decline in the share of state-collaborated units (both private and public limited companies) to total industrial units in the successive decades since the initiation of modern manufacturing in the 1930s upto 1970s[100] and gradual rise in those of the fully private and individually owned enterprises (both 'individual proprietorship' and 'partnership') during the same period amply illustrates the nature of the so-called industrialisation in the country. This manner of state initiating the 'industrialisation' process only to prepare ground for future individual private investment, is not perhaps surprising in view of the long entrenchment of the despotic state and the historical accumulation of primitive capital in the hands of the big land-lords and comprador mercantile bourgeoisie jointly exercising the state power.

The role of state in promoting the given nature and condition of the industrial process in Nepal can also be understood from the study of sectoral allocation of total outlay under different periodic 'plans' from 1956 to 1985[101]. The highest share of 32.17% and 27.9% of the total plan outlay have been allocated to the 'Industry, Power and Mining' sector in the Second Plan (1962–1965) and Third Plan (1965–1970) respectively, and the share of industrial outlay has been consistently declining since the early Sixties only to rise marginally in the Eighties.

3.4.22 Since no recorded information is available about the ownership pattern of industrial enterprises by dominant firms or individuals and their socio-political bases to delineate the flow of social surplus across dominant social classes and national boundaries, we have sought to draw a generalised picture through fragmentary data from diverse sources.

Table 3.34 provides the distribution of fixed capital by dominant social groups generally known to be exercising hegemony in the Nepalese economy. Allowing for slight discrepancies in deducing social groups from the caste surnames and allowing for a heavy underestimation of Indian nationals or people of Indian origin in the official records of the Department of Industries[102], it can be seen that Marwaris and people of Indian origin own as much as 40% of the total fixed capital investment in industries. The traditional indigenous mercantile community of Newars come next, followed by the two ruling dynasties of Ranas and Shahas.

Table 3.33 Ownership Pattern of Manufacturing Establishments by Year of Commencement of Initial Production (1972/73).

S. No.	*Legal Status*		*Year of Commencement of Initial Production*				*Total*
			0–9	*10–19*	*20 and Over*	*Not Reported*	
1.	Individual		1774	180	65	26	2045
	Proprietorship	(i)	(86.75)	(8.80)	(3.18)	(1.27)	(100.00)
		(ii)	(85.21)	(76.27)	(75.58)	(86.67)	(84.02)
2.	Partnership		221	34	9	4	268
		(i)	(82.46)	(12.69)	(3.36)	(1.49)	(100.00)
		(ii)	(10.61)	(14.41)	(10.47)	(13.33)	(11.01)
3.	Private Limited		73	16	2	–	91
		(i)	(80.22)	(17.58)	(2.20)		(100.00)
		(ii)	(3.51)	(6.78)	(2.33)		(3.74)
4.	Public Limited		8	–	9	–	17
		(i)	(47.06)		(52.94)		(100.00)
		(ii)	(0.38)		(10.47)		(0.70)
5.	Others		6	6	1	–	13
		(i)	(46.15)	(46.15)	(7.69)		(100.00)
		(ii)	(0.29)	(2.54)	(1.16)		(0.53)
	ALL		2082	236	86	30	2434
		(i)	(85.54)	(9.70)	(3.53)	(1.23)	(100.00)
		(ii)	(100.00)	(100.00)	(100.00)	(100.00)	(100.00)

Note: Figures in parenthesis are percentages;
(i) Row percentage (ii) Column percentage.

Source: Central Bureau of Statistics, *Census of Manufacturing Establishments*, 1972/73, Kathmandu.

Table 3.34 Fixed Capital Investment* by Dominant Social Groups.

Social Groups	*Total Capital Investment*		
	Amount (NRs. million)	*% of Total Investment*	*% of Private Investment*
1. Newars	492.844	13.09	20.77
2. Ranas and Shahs	388.977	9.01	14.28
3. Hill Brahmins and Chhetris	340.358	9.04	14.34
4. Terai Brahmins and Chhetris	105.666	2.81	4.45
5. Marwaris and Indian Origins	942.586	25.04	39.72
6. Others	152.845	4.06	6.44
Total Private Investment	2373.276	63.05	100.00
Public Investment	1390.723	36.95	–
TOTAL	3763.999	100.00	–

Note: * As registered with Department of Industries upto 1982, excluding hotels and other tourism-oriented activities.

Source: Department of Industries, Ministry of Industry and Commerce, HMG, Kathmandu.

A study of share-holding pattern of principal 'public limited companies' has also brought into focus the monopolistic hold of a small number of people in the shares of the companies. It has been found that a mere 3.19% of total number of share-holders owning more than 1% of shares in the company control nearly 60 to 80% of the shares in the respective companies[103]. This monopolistic hold of foreign capitalists and comprador-landlord classes in the infant industrial sector should give enough pointers to the rampant industrial retardation in the country[104].

3.4.23 Territorial distribution of juridical ownership pattern of manufactories reflects a higher concentration of public and private limited state-owned enterprise in Kathmandu Valley, followed by Terai specially its far-eastern section[105]. Also, the spatial bias in favour of the Central Zone, or Kathmandu-Hetauda-Birgunj axis, in the allocation of industrial plan outlay is evident from the fact of a share of 50.81% of total industrial outlay in the Sixth Plan (1980/85) going to this already favoured zone. Such abatement of the supposedly 'neutral' state to further aggravate the distortions in spatial distribution of the industrial process thoroughly exposes the superficiality of the 'regional development' strategies of judicious industrial dispersion advocated by the state.

Spatial distribution of share-holders of principal public limited manufacturing establishments also reflects a heavy concentration in Kathmandu Valley (i.e. 73.24% of total share-holders) followed by Biratnagar-Dharan (i.e. 13.83%) and Hetauda-Birgunj (i.e. 5.69%) corridors[106].

Though a pronounced spatial differentiation of the ownership pattern of manufactories would be too much to expect in view of the absolute backwardness of the industrial sector, the discernible concentration of public limited companies and other state sponsored industrial units in the traditional habitation zones of big land-lords and comprador mercantile bourgeoisie reflects the harmony of vertical (social) and horizontal (spatial) differentiation of the industrial process in the country.

3.4.3 Condition of Employment of Labour

The actual mode of extraction of surplus labour from the direct producer entails a key condition for defining social relations of production. Hence it would be worthwhile to analyse different aspects of the conditions of employment of labour in the manufacturing industries, viz. separation or otherwise of labour power from the means of production, form and extent of realisation of value to the owner of labour power, etc., so as to contribute towards generalizing the nature of underdevelopment in the industrial sector of Nepal.

The initial stages of industrialisation or development of capitalism are universally known to be characterised by the yet unbroken tie of industrial labour with agricultural production in a "half-peasant, half worker"[107] relation, in the countryside, and with the means of industrial production to consummate petty commodity production, in the urban areas. To ascertain the situations in Nepal, Table 3.35 have been constructed to provide percentage share of 'paid' labour and 'unpaid' family labour disaggregated into 'administrative-technical' and 'operative' labour by territorial zones. At the aggregate national level, the

Table 3.35 Nature of Labour Employed in Manufacturing Industries by Territorial Zones (1976/77).

	% of Labour Employed						
	Total	*Paid Labour*			*Unpaid Family Labour*		
		Admn. Technical	*Operative*	*Sub-Total*	*Admn. Technical*	*Operative*	*Sub-Total*
	1	*2*	*3*	*4*	*5*	*6*	*7*
MOUNTAIN	100.00	8.83	76.23	85.06	4.03	10.91	14.94
Eastern	100.00	7.00	90.20	97.2	1.96	0.84	2.80
Central	–	–	–	–	–	–	–
Western	100.00	10.41	64.16	74.57	5.81	19.61	25.42
HILL	100.00	9.13	56.77	65.90	24.67	9.43	34.10
Eastern	100.00	21.94	59.05	80.99	6.60	12.40	19.00
Central	100.00	4.20	55.99	60.19	31.98	7.84	39.82
Western	100.00	13.79	55.17	82.13	8.62	22.41	31.03
KATHMANDU VALLEY	100.00	19.37	66.46	85.83	4.46	9.71	14.17
INNER TERAI	100.00	10.92	79.44	90.36	7.28	2.35	9.63
Eastern	100.00	11.43	61.43	72.86	12.86	14.29	27.15
Central	100.00	16.47	71.13	87.60	9.83	2.56	12.39
Western	100.00	3.85	90.84	94.69	3.78	1.53	5.31
TERAI	100.00	16.93	73.90	90.83	7.39	1.78	9.17
Eastern	100.00	17.55	73.87	91.42	7.44	1.14	8.58
Far-Eastern	100.00	21.53	73.90	95.43	3.66	0.91	4.57
Mid-Eastern	100.00	11.64	71.12	82.76	15.60	1.64	17.24
Eastern	100.00	17.49	77.22	94.71	4.33	0.96	5.29
Central	100.00	12.63	74.81	87.44	6.97	5.58	12.55
Western	100.00	19.16	72.41	91.57	7.76	0.67	8.43
NEPAL	100.00	16.12	71.67	87.79	8.33	3.89	12.22

Source: Central Bureau of Statistics, *Census of Manufacturing Establishments, 1976/77*, Table No. 23, Kathmandu.

prevalence of a substantial share of unpaid family labour (i.e. 12.22%) even the so-called manufacturing industries amply high-lights the primitive nature of 'peasant' production in the overall industrial sector. Viewed in the spatial dimension, a higher share of unpaid family labour in the more backward Hill (34.10%) and Mountain (14.94%) than in more advanced Inner Terai (9.63%) and Terai (9.17%), with some exception of Kathmandu Valley (14.17%) (which has a different history of domination of petty commodity production since earlier times) provides enough credence to the tenet that "only where labour has been separated from possession of the means of production, and where labourers have been emancipated from any direct relation of domination... are both capital and labour power 'free' to make possible their combination at the highest possible level of technology".[108] This is further substantiated by the higher share in central (39.82%) and western (31.03%) Hill, western Mountain (25.42%), eastern Inner Terai (27.15%) and mid-eastern Terai (17.24%) , which are generally believed to be at lower stages of development or more underdeveloped within the respective ecological zones. In the absence of more detailed information on the socio-economic conditions of labour employed, particularly of 'paid' labour, it is not possible to conclusively establish causal relations between given degree of wage-labour and general levels of development in the manufacturing industries. But, from the observed high degree of seasonal labour employed (i.e. 19.89% of total labour)[109], it can be safely assumed that the undissolved tie with agriculture largely accounts for the preservation of backward relations of production in industries[110]. This is also supported by similar observations of earlier scholars[111] and our own previous generalisations on the non-agricultural earnings of the agricultural labour force.

A study of the industrial labour force by their 'nationality' further tends to confirm the adverse impact of the lower level of differentiation of the peasantry, or for that matter traditional domestic proto-industry, on the overall backwardness of the industrial sector. Whereas as much as 26.26% and 18.75% of the total labour force in the manufacturing sector in 1972/73 and 1976/77 respectively were 'non-Nepali', i.e. mostly Indians, their proportion was higher in the Terai and in some key industries like jute processing. In the most industrially advanced district of Morang in far-eastern Terai, the proportion of non-Nepali workers was a staggering 77.43% with some *biri*-factories employing 100% of non-Nepali workers[112]. It may be intriguing to note that whereas there is heavy out-migration of semi-pauperised peasants from Nepal hills to Indian cities for petty unskilled jobs, much of the industrial labour force in Nepal Terai consist of immigrant workers from India. On recapitulating the historical process of development of 'centre-periphery' relations between India and Nepal and on closer examination of the political economy of relations between the two social formations at different levels of development as at present, this phenomenon of cross-migration of unskilled labour from Nepal to India and more skilled ones from India to Nepal[112], could be seen as a corollary to the broader 'unequal exchange' relations existing between the two economies. Moreover, the addititional advantages accruing to capital from migratory labour[113], namely the possibility of "super-exploitation" offered by the lower reproduction cost of such labour because of its getting subsidized by peasant earnings back home, their reactionary role as "strike-breakers" and of impeding unionisation of indigenous workers, their contribution in constantly replenishing the reserve army of labour and thus depressing the wage rate, etc. could not have been lost on the bourgeoisie on the two sides of the political border to encourage and perpetuate such retrograde relations of industrial production.

An analysis of spatio-temporal variations in the share of wages in total manufacturing value-added (Table 3.36) and real wage rate of labour (Table 3.37) provides important insights into the degree of exploitation of labour as well as the nature of pseudo-industrialisation based on maximisation of 'absolute' as against 'relative' surplus value[114]. Looking at Table 3.36 first, despite the unreliability of some extreme values and incoherent trends reflecting on the spurious data base on value-added, a decrease in the share of wages from Terai to Hill, with the exception of Mountain, and over the years at both aggregate and disaggregate level, is quite unmistakable and demands careful interpretations based on a sound theoreticalframe. Since share of wage bill is both a reflection on the

Table 3.36 Wage* as Percentage of Value Added by Territorial Zones.

	Wage as % of Value added		
Territorial Zones	*1965*	*1972/73*	*1976/77*
MOUNTAIN	–	107.26	52.67
Eastern	–	107.26	96.53
Central	–	–	–
Western	–	–	31.22
HILL	–	8.20	20.56
Eastern	–	1.50	19.81
Central	–	15.44	20.08
Western	–	–	73.44
KATHMANDU VALLEY	40.30	18.86	30.64
INNER TERAI	14.77	29.82	13.15
Eastern	–	6.57	6.77
Central	14.77	32.19	10.43
Western	–	18.01	33.52
TERAI	5 6.21	23.30	25.25
Eastern	62.01	28.41	30.59
–Far-Eastern	79.91	56.16	71.87
–Mid-Eastern	42.97	7.50	10.30
–Eastern	36.90	92.16	20.65
Central	27.82	7.34	14.43
Westren	42.18	21.68	11.69
	51.73	22.16	24.95

Note: *'Wage' includes all emoluments paid to workers and management employees, and both cash and kind payments.

Source: Central Bureau of Statistics, *Census of Manufacturing Establishments*, 1965, 1972/73 and 1976/77, Kathmandu.

Table 3.37 Real Wage Rate of Labour by Territorial Zones (1965, 1972/73 and 1976/77).

Territorial Zones	*Annual Wage per Labour*			*Change in 1976/77 over 1965 (%)*
	1965	*1972/73*	*1976/77*	
MOUNTAIN	–	986 (1.02)	956 (0.79)	–3.04**
Eastern	–	986 (1.02)	1241 (1.03)	25.86**
Central	–	–	–	–
Western	–	–	709 (0.59)	–
HILL	–	665 (0.69)	511 (0.42)	–23.16**
Eastern	–	369 (0.38)	488 (0.40)	32.25**
Central	–	725 (0.75)	513 (0.43)	–29.24**
Western	–	–	698 (0.58)	–
KATHMANDU VALLEY	1579 (0.73)	1073 (1.11)	1314 (1.09)	–16.78
INNER TERAI	2267 (1.05)	789 (0.82)	774 (0.64)	–65.86
Eastern	–	469 (0.49)	1014 (0.84)	116.20**
Central	2267 (1.05)	1508 (1.56)	922 (0.76)	–59.33
Western	–	106 (0.11)	576 (0.48)	443.40**
TERAI	2281 (1.05)	969 (1.003)	1319 (1.09)	–42.17
Eastern:	2376 (1.10)	976 (1.01)	1420 (1.18)	–39.86
Far-Eastern	2650 (1.22)	1319 (1.37)	2129 (1.77)	–19.66
Mid-Eastern	1585 (0.73)	401 (0.41)	736 (0.61)	–53.56
Eastern	2438 (1.13)	1488 (1.54)	986 (0.82)	–59.56
Central	1535 (0.71)	674 (0.70)	874 (0.72)	–43.06
Western	2085 (0.96)	1749 (1.81)	1082 (0.90)	–48.11
NEPAL	2165 (1.00)	966 (1.00)	1206 (1.00)	–44.30

Note: * 'Labour' includes all employees in manufacturing industries.
** Change over 1972/73: Figures for 1972/73 may not be reliable because of suspected overestimation of labour employed.
Wages are at constant prices.
Figures in parenthesis are location factors.

Source: Central Bureau of Statistics, *Census of Manufacturing Establishments*, 1976/77, Kathmandu.

extent of expropriation of surplus labour and the rate of return to different factors of production[115], the declining share of wage bill in the horizontal dimension, i.e. from Terai to Hill, may be seen as a manifestation of increasing rate of extraction of 'absolute' surplus labour from Terai to Hill and the same trend in temporal dimension, i.e. decrease in share of wage bill in 1976/77 over 1965, may be viewed as the result of relatively lower rate of return to labour than other factors of production, specially capital, over the period. The relatively higher share of wage bill in Mountain may, however, be regarded as the mark of both lower level of extraction of surplus labour because of the known labour scarcity in this zone and lower return to other factors of production, which would be negligible.

The pattern of variation in the absolute value of real wage rate over time and space (Table 3.37) also enables us to draw the same set of inferences. Whereas a part of the state of lower wages in Hill and Mountain than in Terai and Kathmandu Valley may be explained in terms of differences in the productivity of labour, the situation is quite understandable in view of the higher degree of socialisation of production and correspondingly greater articulation of bargaining power of labour through unionisation in Terai and Kathmandu Valley than in rest of the country. The absolute decline in real wages of labour over the years, however conclusively establishes the increasing rate of expropriation of 'absolute' surplus value from the direct producer; and higher is the rate of exploitation the more backward is the area, except for the Mountain zone which is not effectively integrated with the rest of the country.

The differentiation of wage rate by size of establishments and forms of juridical ownership of manufactories (Table 3.38) also brings out that the wage declines in more or less direct proportion to the size and with the movement in juridical ownership pattern from 'public' and collective to private and individual. Thus the observed increase in the proportion of smaller enterprises and private-individual ownership over the years are seen to be guided by their capacity for more expropriation of 'absolute' surplus labour than for raising productivity.

Thus, the state of industrialisation in Nepal is still seen to be characterised by what Marx calls 'formal subsumption' rather than 'real subsumption of labour under capital'[116]

3.4.4 The Market Condition

By definition, industrial production, specially in its manufacturing and higher stages, entails the act of adding use value to the primary products and its realisation in the form of exchange value so as to reinvest in production at constantly higher scales. The act of exchange or circulation of commodities, or the market mechanism, there is endogenous to the "circuit of production'[117]. Also, since industrial capital has to go through the market process both in the beginning and end of the circuit of production to acquire means of production and dispose off finished products, both these spheres of market assume significance in articulating the industrial process.

In the context of Nepal this vital aspect of the industrial process is sought to be studied with respect to:

Table 3.38 Annual Wage Rate by Size and Form of Ownership of Manufacturing Establishments (1976/77).

(Rs.)

Size based on Labour Employed	*Annual Wage Rate/Form of Juridical Ownership of Establishments*							
	Individual Proprietorship	*Partnership*	*Public Limited*	*Private Limited*			*Others*	*Total*
				Govt. Owned	*Privately Owned*	*Both Govt. and Privately Owned*		
1–9	2121	1719	1182	4476	2375	1750	1733	2100
10–19	1393	2482	22813*	2931	3227	–	6500	1862
20–49	2686	2517	4311	3932	2821	–	1290	2890
50–99	2411	1728	2677	5310	1434	3006	–	2807
100–499	3112	5280	2394	348*	4470	2778	1844	1735*
500–999	456*	–	6925	57*	3704	–	–	2289*
1000 and over	–	–	–	6248	–	–	–	6248
TOTAL	2172	2913	5071	2572*	3493	2872	1872	2650

Note: Figures do not appear to be reliable.
Wages are at current prices.

Source: Central Bureau of Statistics, *Census of Manufacturing Establishments*, 1976/77, Kathmandu.

(i) the supply market for raw materials and instruments of production; and
(ii) demand market for finished products; though the two markets are not necessarily exclusive.

3.5.41 Supply of Raw Materials and Instruments of Production

Natural resource base specially mineral resources in Nepal is not very encouraging and whatever potential exists largely remains to be explored and economically exploited. Given such natural constraints abetted by a dominated and retarded social process, the structure of the primitive industries was earlier seen to be overwhelmingly agro-based. However, within the known structural limitations of the vital agricultural sector marked by domination of use-value production of subsistence crops, it may not be surprising to find the nascent industries chronically afflicted by a dearth of raw materials.

Table 3.39 Demand and Supply of Raw Materials by Type of Industries* (1977).

(%)

Sl. No.	Industry Groups	No. of Establishments	Raw Material demands	Supply of Raw Materials			Deficit
				Local	Foreign	Total	
		1.	2.	3.	4.	5=(3+4)	6=(2–5)
1.	Food (rice**, flour and oil)	38	100.00	52.93	–	52.93	47.07
2.	Bakeries, etc.	6	100.00	61.17	29.20	90.37	9.63
3.	Sugar Refineries	5	100.00	56.57	0.57	57.14	42.86
4.	Tea Packing	6	100.00	29.76	–	29.76	70.24
5.	Milk Products	2	100.00	60.07	11.00	71.07	28.93
6.	Distilleries	4	100.00	47.35	21.69	69.04	30.96
7.	Cigerette, Biri, etc.	6	100.00	64.02	35.98	100.00	–
8.	Animal Feeds	3	100.00	45.38	21.76	67.14	32.86
9.	Textiles and Allied	12	100.00	-	76.44	76.44	23.56
10.	Handicraft Products	8	100.00	62.22	20.37	82.59	17.41
11.	Saw Mills and Furnitures	14	100.00	33.08	4.18	37.26	62.74
12.	Leather and Leather Products	6	100.00	29.44	5.53	34.97	65.03
13.	Jute and Jute Products	2***	100.00	86.44	–	86.44	13.56
14.	Chemical Products	6	100.00	34.38	42.16	76.54	23.46
15.	Matches	4	100.00	28.45	68.91	97.36	2.64
16.	Plastic Products	3	100.00	–	45.63	45.63	54.37
17.	Metal Products (excluding construction materials)	6	100.00	0.15	5.41	5.56	94.44
18.	Machines and Tools	3	100.00	8.11	63.43	71.54	28.46
19.	Construction Materials and Allied (excl. contract Services)	15***	100.00	4.09	35.58	39.67	60.33
20.	Miscellaneous	9***	100.00	18.53	36.15	54.68	45.32
	TOTAL	**158**	**100.00**	**31.96**	**12.53**	**44.49**	**55.51**

Note: * All Industries with fixed capital above NRs. 2 lakhs.
** Only 25% of rice mills.
*** Information not available for rest of the establishments.

Source: Nepal Rastra Bank (1977), *Industrial Survey Report* (Nepali), Kathmandu.

Table 3.39 provides the demand and supply position of raw materials for principal industries surveyed by Nepal Rastra Bank in 1977. At the aggregate level, only 44.49% of total requirements of raw materials is founds to have been met, 31.96% from local and 12.53% from foreign sources. There is, however, wide fluctuation in the scenario by individual group of industries; thus providing significant clues to the nature of structural retrogression undergone over the years. It is interesting to note that only the important import-substituting and consumer-goods industries like cigarette and *biri*, matches, bakeries, etc. and export-oriented ones like jute and jute products, handicraft products, etc. have high proportion of their raw materials demands met from both internal and external sources. Viewed by principal sources of acquisition of raw materials, the traditionally more significant industries with strong local raw material base, such as textiles (mostly cotton) and metal products, are now seen to be totally dependent on the foreign sources. As observed earlier, this is a clear indication of the distortions inflicted on the indigenous production structure after the integration of the economy with the developed capitalist world. Also, the important import-substituting industries like machine and tools, plastic products, construction materials, matches, cigarettes, etc. have high proportions of imported raw material, which reveals the fallacious nature of such pseudo-industrialisation with continued but veiled external dependence. Only the export-oriented industries like jute and jute products, handicraft products, food processing, etc. seen to get total or pre-dominant share of raw material supply from local sources.

As regards the apparent causes for the import of raw materials, the *Census of Manufacturing Establishments, 1976–77*, cites "absence of production in the country and comparative cheapness of imports" as decisively scoring over "absence of required quality and standard in local market" (by 92.13% against 7.87% of total establishments using imported raw materials), thereby directly indicting the sluggishness of the agricultural sector as responsible for aggravating the external dependence of the industrial sector. However, the phenomenon has to be viewed not in a static but a dynamic historico-materialist frame, so that the so-called "absence of production in the country" can also be seen as historically conditioned by the articulation of endogenous and exogenous social processes, viz. the decline and final cessation of production of cotton in the country in the light of the annihilation of indigenous textiles industry at the hands of the imported factory-made textiles from India.

Analysis of the structure of imports by principal manufacturing industries (Table 3.40) provides further substance to the position that external dependence for both technological and raw material inputs has increased with the rise in so-called industrialisation. In the absence of a spatio-temporal disaggregation of the structure of total industrial imports, the apprehended trend cannot be empirically established, but from the fact of higher value of total imports in the industrially more advanced regions of far-eastern and eastern Terai, Kathamandu Valley and central Inner Terai till 1982/83, the trend appears quite unmistakable. Moreover, it is interesting to not that except for 'eastern' Terai, in all these enclaves of higher industrial development the share of raw material imports is higher than the understandable high technological (i.e. machinery and parts) imports. This could safely be interpreted as the manifestation of distorted industrial development geared to the conspicuous consumption demands of the minority upper classes at the cost of strengthening productive base through the promotion of capital and basic goods or providing mass consumption goods. The much-maligned stainless steel utensils and synthetic fibre industries of the late 1960s and the recent watch and transistor assembling units based on imported semi-finished products, can be cited as incontrovertible examples of pseudo-industrialisation as an adjunct of metropolitan capital.

Table 3.40 Structure of Imports of Principal Manufacturing Industries by Territorial Zones (1983).

(Rs. '000)

	Industrial Imports			
	Machinery and Parts	*Raw Materials*	*Others*	*Total*
MOUNTAIN	N.A.	N.A.	N.A.	N.A.
HILL	7040	968	–	8008
	(87.91)	(12.09)		(100.00)
Eastern	4620	–	–	4620
	(100.0)			(100.00)
Central	2420	968	–	3388
	(71.43)	(28.57)		(100.00)
Western	N.A.	N.A.	N.A.	N.A.
KATHMANDU VALLEY	14019	60115	4007	78141
	(17.94)	(76.93)	(5.13)	(100.00)
INNER TERAI	20249	28390	6600	55239
	(36.66)	(51.39)	(11.95)	(100.00)
Eastern	N.A.	N.A.	N.A.	N.A.
Central	20185	28390	6600	55175
	(36.58)	(51.45)	(11.96)	(100.00)
Western	64	–	–	64
	(100.00)			(100.00)
TERAI	111717	104236	9476	225429
	(49.56)	(46.24)	(4.20)	(100.00)
Eastern:	102035	95494	9476	207005
	(49.29)	(46.13)	(4.58)	(100.00)
Far-Eastern	43656	72248	9476	125380
	(34.82)	(57.62)	(7.56)	(100.00)
Mid-Eastern	530	35	–	565
	(93.81)	(6.19)		(100.00)
Eastern	57849	23211	–	81060
	(71.37)	(28.63)		(100.00)
Central	2833	3742	–	6575
	(43.09)	(56.91)		(100.00)
Western	6849	5000	–	11849
	(57.80)	(42.20)		(100.00)
NEPAL	153025	193709	20083	366817
	(41.72)	(52.81)	(5.47)	(100.00)

Note: Figures in parenthesis are percentages.
Source: HMG/N Ministry of Industry (1983) *Industrial Profile*, Kathmandu.

The increasing extent of imports of technological inputs specially machinery and transport equipments, over the years[118], however, illustrates the common case of technological dependence of all underdeveloped countries. The virtually non-existent and snail-paced growth of production goods industries in the country as highlighted earlier ensures the perpetuation of this condition of external dependence for quite some time.

Thus, contrary to the experience of most of the other underdeveloped countries Nepal is seen to have been reduced to a peculiar dilemma of having to import even the basic industrial raw materials along with the other common technological inputs.

3.4.42 Market for Finished Products

As highlighted in the historical review earlier, the initiation of modern industrial production in Nepal in the wake of disruption in the established imperialist world market during the 2nd World War, was stimulated both by the 'export-promotion' and 'import-substitution' possibilities. But when both the avenues got overruled with the restoration or restructuration of the global domination of the metropolitan capital and perpetuation of the retrograde internal social structure by the 1950s, the strategy of pseudo-industrialisation in Nepal has either tended to oscillate between the two poles or has been a contrived hybrid of the two, depending on the vagaries of the world capitalist crisis and internal socio-political upheavals.

The temporary spurt of import-substitution industrialisation in the early 1960s brought about by a combination of internal and external factors mentioned previously, could not have proceeded further because of the essentially constricted 'home market' comprised of the peculiar consumption demands of a narrow upper strata of the populace. Thus the later half of 1960s had seen a gradual shift towards the manufacture of luxury consumption goods of the nature of stainless steel utensils and synthetic textiles out of imported semi-processed raw materials from Japan and Hongkong and geared to the vast market of India opened by certain ambivalent provisions of the 1960 Indo-Nepal trade and transit treaty. However, with the vigilant sealing of Indian market for Nepalese manufactures based on third-country raw materials as per Trade Protocal of 1968, drastic industrial decline set in[119] and the market base got directed predominantly towards the inside and partly to third countries other than India.

For the essentially export-oriented industries like jute processing, the period after the mid-sixties saw a gradual diversification of markets away from India, thanks to the much abused EEE (Export Earner's Entitlement) scheme[120]. Apart from the incentive under the EEE scheme, the lower prices commanded by Nepalese jute and jute products in the traditional Calcutta market[121], must have compelled Nepalese manufacturers to seek third-country export market.

Table 3.41 Market Base of Manufactured Products (1976/77).

(Value in Rs. '000)

	Total	*Inland Sales*	*Export to India*	*Export to Third Countries*
I. FOOD AND ALLIED	641376	632682	6283	2411
	(100.00)		(0.98)	(0.38)
1. Oil and Grain Mill Prod.	510119	504007	5825	287
	(100.00)	(98.80)	(1.14)	(0.06)
2. Bakery Products	29962	29504	458	–
	(100.00)	(98.47)	(1.53)	
3. Sugar Refineries	93321	91784	–	1537
	(100.00)	(98.35)		(1.65)
4. Tea Packing	7360	6773	–	587
	(100.00)	(92.02)		(7.98)
5. Ice and Ice Cream	614	614	–	–
	(100.00)	(100.00)		
II. DRINK and TOBACCO	56640	56640	–	–
	(100.00)	(100.00)		
6. Distilleries	10290	10290	–	–
	(100.00)	(100.00)		
7. Biri Making	46350	46350	–	–
	(100.00)	(100.00)		
III. TEXTILES AND ALLIED	92219	77291	932	13996
	(100.00)	(83.81)	(1.01)	(15.18)
8. Yarn and Textiles	70098	61389	85	8624
	(100.00)	(87.58)	(0.12)	(12.30)
9. Knitting Mills	2043	2043	–	–
	(100.00)	(100.00)		
10. Carpets and Rugs	11046	7819	803	2424
	(100.00)	(70.79)	(7.27)	(21.94)
11. Caps	1252	1208	44	–
	(100.00)	(96.49)	(3.51)	
12. Footwear Shoes	7780	4832	–	2948
	(100.00)	(62.11)		(37.89)
IV. WOOD, PAPER, PRINTING AND ALLIED	90531	71985	18546	–
	(100.00)	(79.51)	(20.49)	
13. Saw Mills	53118	35825	17293	–
	(100.00)	(67.44)	(32.56)	
14. Furniture-Wooden	16143	14924	1219	–
	(100.00)	(92.45)	(7.55)	
15. Paper Manufacturing	809	792	17	–
	(100.00)	(97.90)	(2.10)	
16. Printing Press	9006	8989	17	–
	(100.00)	(99.81)	(0.19)	
17. Matches	11455	11455	–	–
	(100.00)	(100.00)		
V. CHEMICALS AND PHARMACEUTICALS	13014	13014	–	–
	(100.00)	(100.00)		
18. Drugs and Medicines	7082	7082	–	–
	(100.00)	(100.00)		
19. Soaps	5932	5932	–	–
	(100.00)	(100.00)		

(Contd.)

(*Table 3.41 contd.*)

VI. NON-METALLIC MINERAL PRODUCTS	25072 (100.00)	25056 (99.94)	16 (0.06)	–
20. Bricks and Tiles	25072 (100.00)	25056 (99.94)	16 (0.06)	–
VII. METALLIC PRODUCTS AND REPAIRS	40254 (100.00)	37846 (94.02)	2258 (5.61)	150 (0.37)
21. Furniture-Steel	21810 (100.00)	21810 (100.00)	–	–
22. Metallic Vessels	17466 (100.00)	15124 (86.59)	2249 (12.88)	93 (0.53)
23. Jewellery and Curios	871 (100.00)	805 (92.42)	9 (1.03)	57 (6.54)
24. Repairing Works	107 (100.00)	107 (100.00)	–	–
VIII. MISCELLANEOUS	873641 (100.00)	828574 (94.84)	8190 (0.94)	36877 (4.22)
TOTAL	1832747 (100.00)	1743088 (95.11)	36140 (1.97)	53434 (2.92)

Note: Figures in parenthesis are row percentages.
No particulars available for jute processing, Cigarette factory, animal feeds and fruit canning and bottling, to maintain 'secrecy' as their manufacturing units number only two each. They are included in 'Miscellaneous' category, hence the figures unduly inflated.

Source: Central Bureau of Statistics, *Census of Manufacturing Establishments, 1976/77*, Kathmandu.

Table 3.41 provides a commodity-wise market-base for the manufactured products in 1976/77. The fact that 95.11% of the total product is sold 'inland' should amply speak of the importance of the 'home market'. Of the meagre share of exported value of 4.89%, a larger proportion (i.e. 2.92%) is exported to countries other than India thereby confirming the earlier trends of diversification of markets away from India. Individual commodity-wise, 'miscellaneous' articles (which include jute products), forest-based and textiles and allied products have the highest share in the exports.

To get a better picture of the nature of constriction of foreign market for Nepalese manufactured products, the change in export/import ratio by major commodity groups as presented in Section 4.3 below may be read with the present study. Despite a gradual rise in the share of manufactured products in the total volume of export trade which reached a peak in the 1960s and progressively declined thereafter, the relevant export/import ratio is seen to be too meagre; i.e. less than 20%. This is quite understandable and is in keeping with the position of most of the underdeveloped countries which cannot compete with the products of metropolitan capitalist countries with their higher productivity of labour and better capital/output ratios.

Thus the principal market base of Nepalese industrial products is bound to be its own internal base. However, because of its retrograde social structure marked by a stunted agricultural sector and an extreme income inequality, the effective demand of the local populace is limited to a narrow stratum of upper classes, which is already a captive client of metropolitan capital. Moreover, because of physical and economic seclusion of a large proportion of territories and societies in fragmented sub-economies, the home market confined to the upper strata of the populace is further disarticulated and limited. Thus nowhere does the significance of widening home market through modernisation of agriculture and basic structural changes of society as hammered by a number of scholars[122] to stimulate industrial growth seem to assume more relevance than in the case of Nepal.

3.4.5 Structure of Industrial Finance

As noted earlier, the very logic of industrial development under the capitalist social dispensation is to constantly replace 'living labour' with 'dead labour' in the production process. The surplus labour that is crystallised and articulated in the form of instruments of production or money capital tends to get accumulated in diverse sectors and spaces of economic activities and needs to be channelised into the industrial production process through various mechanisms of financial transfer. Hence the realm of industrial financial flows could be one of the more significant arenas to discern the nature of underdevelopment process operating in the society, specially in the context of imperfect capital market situation dominated by international financial oligarchies working to the further detriment of underdeveloped societies.

3.4.51 In a predominantly agrarian economy such as in Nepal the major share of meagre surplus labour crystallised into capital is bound to originate in the agricultural sector, though a minor share may be contributed by craft production or trade with outside economies (the latter is likely only in circumstances of favourable entrepot trade position, otherwise generally acting as a net drainer of indigenous social surplus). Since it is impossible in the absence of relevant information on inter-sectoral flows to ascertain the source of primitive capital that has found its way into the fragile manufacturing sector, it can be safely assumed to have been largely originated in the agricultural sector even though there may have been different modes of its realisation. The fact that the beginning of modern manufacturing in the country was made by the collaboration of Indian capitalists with the ruling Rana landed oligarchy in the sphere of export-oriented agro- and forest-processing activities in the zones of abundance of those raw materials in eastern Terai than by the indigenous merchant capitalists or craftsmen independently in the traditional fields of secondary production based in the Kathmandu Valley, gives strong credence to this hypothesis. Continued overwhelming domination of elementary agro-processing activities in small manufacturing units scattered all over the agriculturally more prosperous zones confirms the same pattern of agricultural surplus getting transferred to the infantile industrial activities. However, within the prevalent structural maladies in the agricultural sector characterised by predominantly pre-capitalist relations of production and accompanying low social productivity of labour, the deficiency of disposable social surplus and the inherent tendency of the usurpers of this surplus to fritter it away in immediately more profitable speculative or trading activities, has created a "self-perpetuating"[123] dearth of industrial investment in the country. Consequently the state with the help of foreign 'aid' seems to have tried to play a mediatory role in redeeming the situation by establishing institutions of industrial finance like the NIDC to stimulate private sector investment and directly investing on certain key industries like agricultural tools, sugar, cigarette, tannery and shoes, bricks and tiles, etc. It would therefore, be interesting to study the trends and structure of industrial finance in the country with the help of some empirical support.

In the absence of information on detailed sources of finance for initial investment (i.e. whether 'private' or 'public', and whether indigenous or foreign), the term 'internal' and 'external' sources used here are only with respect to the particular production unit and not with the economy in general. Viewed in this broad catagorisation at the aggregate level of all manufacturing activities, the percentage share of 'internal' finance appear to be quite high and is found to have risen abruptly by 20 percentage points over the four-year period from 1972/73 to 1976/77[124]. While different theoretical explanations may be forwarded to correlate progressively or regressively the internal/external financial ratios with levels of industrial development[125], the high and rising share of internal sources in the context of Nepal will have to be accepted as a negative indicator of distress reversion to self-containment in the dearth of external sources of finance. Within the known low and anaemic state of industrialisation, weak condition of the industrial bourgeoisie overshadowed by the rising comprador mercantile bourgeoisie and deceleration of industrial growth rates after the beginning of the Seventies, no other explanation would enjoy reasonable degree of conviction. The assertion would be further substantiated if the absolute value and change of proportions of different sources of finance in individual manufacturing activities are analysed. The comparatively higher share of external sources in 1972/73 (when industrial production was in a relatively better state) at the aggregate level of industries is seen to be accompanied by higher contribution of foreign agencies and individual and private institutions (clubbed with 'others' in the census) at the cost of government and related agencies, whereas the sudden slump in the share of external sources in 1976/77 has been accompanied by a reverse trend in the component sources as well. In other words, the foreign agencies[126] and individual and private institutions which constituted a dominant external source had shied away in the aftermath of failure of export-oriented industrialisation strategy in the late 1960s and the relatively weak government and related agencies could not fill in the void. The scenario gets further clarified when the situation is observed with respect to the principal industry groups. Whereas cereal-processing is seen to continue to command a sizeable share from all sources, some significant shift particularly from individual and private agencies in favour of yarns and textiles and preference of foreign agencies for sugar refineries, distilleries, carpet and rugs, etc. (i.e for luxury consumption goods), are discernible. On closer observation it is found that the apparent change in the structure of industrial finance was mostly brought about by the increase in the share of internal finances in cereal-processing industries, which could be regarded as a favourable sign of growing capitalist class from amongst the agriculturists.

The external financing ratio in the selected 57 "companies" during 1972/75 by one study [127], were found much higher than in the present case, specially in 'fast-growing' industries like cement, dairy, tea, jute, electricity, etc. The apparent anomaly may be easily explained in terms of greater accessibility enjoyed by private and public limited companies to the external sources of finance. However, such exessively high dependency on external sources may be regarded as an indicator of the failure to attain a self-sustained growth and hence a net liability.

When the condition of industrial finance is seen in the territorial dimension[128], a wide variation in internal/external financing ratio is observed but with no definite trend discernible. Accepting the hypothesis that a high internal/external financing ratio in the initial stages of industrialisation would be a negative indicator of development and vice versa in the later stages, the lower values in Mountain and Hill and higher ones in Terai and Kathmandu Valley would both be manifestations of different processes of underdevelopment; viz. the former that of *lack of credibility* for external finance and the latter that of *over dependence* on the same. Whereas the higher share of external financing contributed by NIDC, commercial banks and individual and private institutions in Terai (particularly far-eastern Terai), Inner Terai and Kathmandu Valley indicate a comparatively better state of industrialisation in these zones, greater concentration of direct HMG and foreign agencies financing in the Birgunj-Hetauda-Kathmandu axis reflects the well-known spatial bias of the state in the matter of so-called industrialisation in the country.

The spatial and sectoral bias of the state is seen further articulated in the disbursement pattern of finance by the foremost state sponsored industrial financing body with active collaboration of Western metropolitan capital, i.e. the NIDC,[129]. The thin veil of pseudo-industrialisation strategy adopted in the country gets shattered when it is realised that since its inception this premier agency has invested as much as 34.62% of its finances in tourism-based 'industries' (or, traditing activities?), mostly in the construction of luxury hotels, 95% of which is concentrated in the central zone, i.e. in and around Kathmandu Valley.

3.4.52 To get a correct picture of the nature of industrial underdevelopment in the era of imperialism and neo-colonialism it would be important to analyse the structure of capital invested in the country by dominant nationalities. However, because of the continued semi-colonial position of Nepal vis-à-vis India the economic interest of metropolitan capital in the country has been peripheral to that of India. Also, with the declared or implied common market link existing between the two economies, it has not been possible to document with any degree of authenticity the extent and nature of economic interactions across the formal political border. Furthermore, in keeping with the highest profitability of capital in its circulatory from than in the productive form in the backward economies, the operation of foreign capital in Nepal has assumed more of mercantile than an industrial form. In such a situation any attempt at quantification of foreign capital investment in the country is not only bound to be an underestimation but would fail to capture real extent and nature of the foreign economic domination.

As sketched out in the section on historical antecedents, Indian capital has played a significant role in determining the course of industrialisation in Nepal. According to one study[130], private Indian investment in the joint stock companies in Nepal prior to 1951 had constituted nearly 50% of the total authorised capital and since then in 1969 alone, the peak year of bourgeoning of export-oriented stainless steel utensils and synthetic fibre industries, total Indian investment in Nepal was worth Rs. 8 million, or 26.2% of total Indian investment of Rs. 29.42 million in Colombo plan countries, which was only next to that in Malayasia in volume[131]. The slow but consistent rise in private Indian investment in Nepal was mainly characterised by its investment in export-oriented industries like jute, stainless steel utensils, synthetic textiles, etc., and a few import-substituting industries like the one collaborated upon by the Birlas in cotton textile manufacturing in the 1960s never saw the light of the day. Moreover, Indian industrial capital was more inclined to cross the political border to take advantage of custom and tax loopholes[132], thus never seeking to strike deep roots there. Also, because of no or negligible restrictions on profit repatriation the capital accumulated in the hands of the Indians found its way back to India for safer deposits or more varied investment opportunities.

As noted earlier, the early 1960s was a period of considerable inflow of foreign industrial capital other than the traditional private Indian investment in Nepal. Whereas USSR and China found it prudent to help establish a number of basic and import-substituting industries like agriculture and machine tools, cigarette, sugar, leather and shoe, brick and tile, and other industries in the 'public' sector, the rival Western block, mainly the USA, sought to strengthen the private sector by funneling funds through the NIDC. However, no significant private industrial investment from countries other than India is known to have taken place in Nepal to the present day. Sundry investments by the MNCs are known to have been made invariably through their subsidiaries in India[133]

After a momentary full of the early Seventies in the aftermath of the failure of export-oriented industrialisation, Indian capital seems to have made a fresh bid to enter the market in a big way in the form of 'joint ventures' in a number of mineral-extracting, tourism-oriented and consumer goods industries. The beginning of the Eighties have also been marked by concerted official attempts at welcoming the foreign private investors, but with little success.

Thus the position with regard to the vital industrial finance after more than three decades of 'industrialisation' is a continued fall back upon the meagre surpluses from a moribund agriculture sector and the unpredictable merciful deeds of the comprador mercantile bourgeoisie of both Indian and Nepalese origin.

3.5 ARTICULATION OF INDUSTRIAL RETARDATION AND SPATIAL DIFFERENTIATION OF LEVELS OF DEVELOPMENT

Since industrial retardation is the sum total of infirmities, limitations and distortions embedded in the 'production' and 'distribution' components of the industrial process, it would now be pertinent to sum up the aggregate process in its vertical (sectoral) and horizontal (spatial) dimensions. However, because of the methodological problems involved in empirically deriving a composite social process from its component elements as mentioned in the earlier chapter, we would refrain from any such attempts but try to generalise the composite picture through the analysis of interdependencies between different elements of the social process in question. We would, thus, first summerise the aggregate manifestations of industrial retardation and then would follow it up by an analysis of interdependencies and spatial differentiation based on the districtwise composite indices of industrial development.

3.5.1 Aggregate Manifestions of Industrial Retardation

Considering the inadequacies of available statistical techniques in general, and in the absence of relevant data base in the desired spatio-temporal frame in particular, we have sought to treat the level of 'capacity utilisation' and extent of 'temporary closure' of production units over time and space as proxy measures for summerising the net condition of industrial process in the country. This would give us an accurate quantitative measure of industrial retardation. Despite the obvious methodological objections to such over-simplifications of a complex social process and in view of the 'backward' rather than 'underdeveloped' structure of the industrial sector in Nepal we have considered any such transgressions to be less palpable.

Table 3.42 provides the percentage share of capacity utilisation of registered manufactories (with capital investment above NRs 2 lakhs) by use-based classification. When capacity utilisation is seen as an end result of the efficiency of different production variables rather than a mere measure of attainment of technically specified production level of a unit,[134] it may be possible to ascribe to it a definite meaning. The overall low level of capacity utilization is evident from the fact that only 14.81 percent of total industries utilise above 85% of their capacity and as many as 51.85% of industries below 55% of their capacity. Thus the average capacity utilisation in the country is about 52.0%, which is a pathetic low for the already low capacity of production units. By industry classes, deep structural malady is reflected in the lower capacity utilization in intermediate and non-durable consumption or mass consumption goods industries. This should bear adequate testimony to the prevailing intra-sectoral disarticulation and constricted 'home market' for the industries. Viewed by individual commodities[135],

Table 3.42 Percentage of Industries with Use-based Classification by Percentage of Capacity Utilisation (1978).

Industry Group	*% of Industries by Capacity Utilisation*					*Total*
	Upto 10%	*10–25%*	*25–55%*	*55–85%*	*85–100%*	
I. Consumer Goods	7.70	12.50	29.81	33.65	16.35	100.00
(i) Durables	21.43	21.43	14.28	21.43	21.43	100.00
(ii) Non-durables	5.56	11.11	32.22	35.56	15.56	100.00
II. Intermediate Goods	7.41	18.52	29.63	37.04	7.41	100.00
III. Capital Goods	15.79	15.79	15.79	31.57	21.05	100.00
IV. Miscellaneous	–	8.33	58.33	25.00	8.33	100.00
TOTAL	8.02	13.58	30.25	33.33	14.81	100.00

Source: Nepal Rastra Bank (1977), *Industrial Survey Report* (Nepali), Kathmandu, Table No. 13.

the once premier export-oriented industries like stainless steel utensils (3.61% of capacity), and synthetic textiles (7.95%) are seen to have had the lowest capacity utilisation and the conspicuous industries of the type of alcoholic drinks (66.67%) and *biri*-making (100%) have enjoyed the highest patronage. On the other hand, the more economically significant export-promoting and import substitution industries like rice-husking (53.68%), sugar (54.63%) and other had a low capacity utilization. As regards the declared impediments in full capacity utilization, 67.68% of the total units are reported to have cited dearth of raw materials as the prime cause and another 43.9% of them as the market problem[136]. This is a clear indictment of the lop-sided development taking place in an agrarian society engaged in massive imports of foreign manufactured goods.

Literal shutting down of industrial units may be regarded as a more serious manifestation of maladies afflicting the industrial process. It is disquieting to note that in Nepal the extent of temporary closure of the already small number of manufacturing units had increased from 35.95% of total units in 1972/73 to 52.49% in 1976/77. Viewed by industry groups (Table 3.43), the non-durable consumer goods or mass consumption goods industries, which are also overwhelmingly agro-based, are seen to fare the worst with as high as 53.49% of units in 1976/77 temporarily closed. The depressing scenario is not significantly better for other groups of industries either. When the recorded 'causes' of closure are analysed, the foremost cause is again found to be lack of raw materials (37.58% of units closed), followed by lack of market (6.97%). Among industries citing lack of market as the reason for temporary closure, the durable consumer goods industries, mostly patronised by the minority upper strata of the society, and intermediate-goods industries, which should stimulate further industrial production, are found to number the most. This once again fully substantiates our earlier observation that industrial retardation is primarily a function of the sluggishness of the agricultural sector and prevalent social inequality, which in turn are a function of the retrograde internal class structure that is directly abetted by the exploitative machinations of the metropolitan capital. The fact that capital and trained labour are not significant causes for temporary closure, speaks not of their comfortable position of abundance but their insignificant role in the overall organization of industrial production, which is still at a rudimentary stage.

When the scenario is viewed in the territorial dimension (Table 3.44), larger percentages of industrial units are seen to be temporarily closed in Inner Terai and Terai than in Mountain and Hill. In view of the low absolute level and comparatively recent origins of manufacturing activities in Hill and Mountain, this phenomenon should be regarded more as a negative reflection of the deteriorating condition in the predominantly industrialised areas of Terai and Inner Terai than a favourable reflection of the condition in Hill and Mountain. The frequent reasons cited are lack of raw materials specially in the agriculturally more laggard zones of Mountain, Hill and Kathmandu Valley and amongst the Terai, in its mid-eastern, central and western sections. This once again highlights the

Table 3.43 Causes of Temporary Closure of Manufacturing Establishments by Use-based Classifications (1976/77).

	No. of Establishments		Causes of Temporary Closure				
	Total	*Temporarily closed*	*Lack of working capital*	*Lack of trained labour*	*Lack of market*	*Lack of raw materials*	*Others*
	1	2	3	4	5	6	7
I. Consumer Goods	3258 (100.00)	1719 (52.76)	85 (4.94)	74 (4.30)	111 (6.46)	636 (37.00)	813 (47.29)
(i) Durables	164 (100.00)	64 (39.02)	5 (7.81)	9 (14.06)	12 (18.75)	27 (42.19)	11 (17.19)
(ii) Non-durables	3094 (100.00)	1655 (53.49)	80 (4.83)	65 (3.93)	99 (5.98)	609 (36.80)	802 (48.48)
II. Intermediate Goods	186 (100.00)	92 (44.09)	3 (3.26)	8 (8.70)	7 (7.61)	47 (51.09)	27 (29.35)
III. Basic and Capital Goods				NOT AVAILABLE			
IV. Miscellaneous	84 (100.00)	41 (48.81)	–	5 (12.20)	11 (26.83)	13 (31.71)	12 (14.29)
TOTAL	3528 (100.00)	1852 (52.49)	88 (4.75)	87 (4.70)	129 (6.97)	696 (37.58)	852 (46.00)

Note: Figures in parenthesis in column 2 are percentage share of respective values in column 1 and in columns 3 to 7 that of respective values in column 2.

Source: Central Bureau of Statistics, *Census of Manufacturing Establishments, 1976/77*, Kathmandu.

Table 3.44 Causes of Temporary Closing of Manufacturing Establishments by Territorial Zones (1976/77).

Territorial Zones	No. of Establishments		Causes of Temporary Closing					
	Total	Temporarily closed	Lack of working capital	Lack of skilled labour	Lack of market	Lack of raw materials	Lack of long term capital goods	Others
	1	2	3	4	5	6	7	8
MOUNTAIN	33 (100.00)	6 (18.18)	–	1 (16.67)	–	4 (66.67)	–	1 (16.67)
Eastern	11 (100.00)	6 (54.55)	–	1	–	4	–	1
Central	–	–	–	–	–	–	–	–
Western	22 (100.00)	0 –	– –	– –	–	–	–	–
HILL	360 (100.00)	161 (44.72)	11 (6.83)	15 (9.32)	9 (5.59)	67 (41.61)	16 (9.94)	43 (26.71)
Eastern	97 (100.00)	40 (41.24)	2 (5.00)	3 (7.50)	–	22 (55.00)	4 (10.00)	9 (22.50)
Central	253 (100.00)	116 (45.85)	9 (7.76)	11 (9.48)	9 (7.76)	42 (36.21)	12 (10.34)	33 (28.45)
Western	10 (100.00)	5 (50.00)	–	1 (20.00)	–	3 (60.00)	–	1 (20.00)
KATHMANDU VALLEY	608 (100.00)	228 (37.50)	13 (5.70)	15 (6.58)	23 (10.09)	121 (53.07)	13 (5.70)	43 (18.86)
INNER TERAI	278 (100.00)	198 (71.22)	16 (8.08)	16 (8.08)	12 (6.06)	53 (26.77)	27 (13.64)	74 (37.37)
Eastern	19 (100.00)	19 (100.00)	–	5 (26.32)	–	7 (36.84)	–	7 (36.84)
Central	188 (100.00)	115 (61.17)	11 (9.57)	8 (6.96)	9 (7.83)	39 (33.91)	21 (18.26)	27 (23.48)

(Contd.)

(*Table 3.44 contd.*)

Territorial Zones	*No. of Establishments*		*Causes of Temporary Closing*					
	Total	*Temporarily closed*	*Lack of working capital*	*Lack of skilled labour*	*Lack of market*	*Lack of raw materials*	*Lack of long term capital goods*	*Others*
	1	*2*	*3*	*4*	*5*	*6*	*7*	*8*
Western	71	64	5	3	3	7	6	40
	(100.00)	(90.14)	(7.81)	(4.69)	(4.69)	(10.94)	(9.38)	(62:50)
TERAI	2249	1259	48	40	85	451	49	586
	(100.00)	(55.98)	(3.81)	(3.18)	(6.75)	(35.82)	(3.89)	(46.54)
Eastern:	1577	834	26	20	40	240	29	479
	(44.70)	(52.89)	(3.12)	(2.40)	(4.80)	(28.78)	(3.48)	(57.43)
	(100.00)							
Far-Eastern	447	214	8	9	15	60	8	114
	(100.00)	(47.87)	(3.74)	(4.01)	(7.01)	(28.04)	(3.74)	(53.27)
Mid-Eastern	715	426	9	5	12	142	17	241
	(100.00)	(59.58)	(2.11)	(1.17)	(2.82)	(33.33)	(3.99)	(56.57)
Eastern	415	194	9	6	13	38	4	124
	(100.00)	(46.75)	(4.64)	(3.09)	(6.70)	(19.59)	(2.06)	(63.92)
Central	444	307	20	14	28	164	8	73
	(100.00)	(69.14)	(6.51)	(4.56)	(9.12)	(53.42)	(2.61)	(23.78)
Western	228	118	2	6	17	47	12	34
	(100.00)	(51.75)	(1.69)	(5.08)	(14.41)	(39.83)	(10.17)	(28.81)
NEPAL	3528	1852	88	87	129	696	105	747
	(100.00)	(52.49)	(4.75)	(4.70)	(6.97)	(37.58)	(5.67)	(40.33)

Note: Figures in parenthesis in column 2 are percentage shares of respective values in column 1 and those in columns 3 to 8 are that of respective values in column 2.

Source: Central Bureau of Statistics, *Census of Manufacturing Establishments, 1976/77*, Kathmandu.

intimate ties between industrial and agricultural processes in determining their respective fates.

3.5.2 Analysis of Interdependencies

As noted in the previous chapter, statistical correlations between different indicators of a social process when backed by an appropriate theoretical frame can 'indicate' causal dependencies. It would have, therefore, been pertinent to observe correlations between different indicators belonging to both 'production' and 'distribution' components of the industrial process to discern the nature of interdependencies and thus provide important insights into the causes of industrial retardation in the country. However, total lack of statistical information in the desired micro-spatial units, i.e. the districts, for any of the important elements of the industrial process, except for the total population engaged in the industrial sector, has made our attempt infructuous. The information available in the case of the 'manufacturing' sector are limited to only 47 of the 75 districts in 1976/77. We were, therefore, constrained to limit ourselves to deal with only two indicators, namely, percentage of economically active persons in the aggregate industrial (including domestic proto-industry) sector (9i) and gross output per person engaged in manufacturing[137] (10i); the former to capture the quantitative and the latter 'qualitative' aspects of industrial production.

It would be interesting to analyse the correlations of these two indicators of industrial development with other indicators of development (Appendix-9) to deduce causal dependencies, if any.

- No significant correlation is observed between the 'quantity' (9i) and 'quality' (10i) aspects of the industrial process. Allowing for some inadequacies of the data base, this may be seen as a clear manifestation of disarticulation of the different components of the process, both spatial and aspatial. This should particularly indicate that the Nepalese industrial sector is still in a rudimentary stage of 'formal subsumption of labour under capital' and the stage of 'real subsumption' is yet to be attained, when not only size and productivity would go together but a process of 'cumulative causation' would set in to give self-expansionary drive to the industrial activities.
- Percentage of workers in the industrial sector (9i)is seen to have high positive correlation with agricultural output per hectare (NSA) (5a) and value of modern inputs per hectare of agricultural land (7a). This should conclusively establish the strong link between agricultural and industrial prosperity in a predominantly agricultural economy where industrial activities are mere outgrowths of the agricultural sector. However, the high positive correlation with modern inputs in agriculture may not have much to do with the manufacture of agricultural inputs since most of these are imported, but could be merely signs of multicolinearity with high agricultural productivity.
- No significant correlation of % of industrial workers (9i) with % of area under cash crops (6a) and size of land holdings (8a), reflects the inverted and

anemic structure of industrial production dominated by simple processing of cereals and low level of social organization of production.

- Significant positive correlation of % of industrial workers (9i) with literacy rate (3e), school per population distance (12s) and hospital per population distance (13s) signify positive roles of social infrastructure and quality of labour in bringing about a vertical transfer of work force to non-agricultural activities.
- Significant positive correlation of % of industrial workers (9i) with per capital band credit (11s) and average settlement size index (4e) indicates the concentration of industrial activities in urban or large settlement-size areas which are also abound in vital economic infrastructures conducive to industrial development.
- Industrial labour productivity (10i), however, does not seem to respond to any of the above factors affecting the extent/size of industrial production. Besides being a manifestation of weak, anaemic structure of primitive industrialisation, this could also mean structural disarticulation of the stunted manufacturing sector largely disaffected by other sectors of the economy. The only exception perhaps is the positive correlation with agricultural productivity (5a), which once again confirms the close link between agricultural and industrial production. On the contrary positive correlation of industrial productivity with cash crop production (6a) and size of land-holding (8a) reflect a positive contribution of these factors in promoting industrialisation by way of facilitating greater primitive accumulation of capital and supply of vital industrial raw materials. The positive correlation with population growth (1e) may be just spurious in view of the already high labour intensity and low productivity of labour.

3.5.3 Spatial Differentiation of Levels of Industrial Development

In order to delimitate the spatial spread of the industrial process, we would first need to generalise it by constructing a composite index of different indicators of the process in the desired micro-spatial dimension. However, in the light of the observed inadequacies in the data base at the district level we would here first document the 'aggregate' (including domestic proto-industries) and 'manufacturing' components of the industrial process separately and subsequently deduce a generalised picture from them.

3.5.31 Aggregate Industrial Process

As mentioned earlier, districtwise information on the industrial process is limited only to the percentage share of economically active persons in the total secondary production activities for 1971 and no separate information by household and modern manufacturing activities or other variates of the industrial process is available. Therefore, while fully conscious of the limitations of measuring a complex social process by only a small set of variables, we had no other option but to attempt to construct a composite index of the state of the total industrial process based on only the following two indicators:

(1) % of economically active persons in the industrial sector (9i);
(2) gross industrial output per person engaged (10i).

The two indicators are seen to have a quite disparate spatial spread (i.e. C.V. 9i =127.83% and C.V.10i =113.62%) and should articulate to a reasonable extent the distortions in the overall industrial spatial structure.

Following the general method adopted throughout the study, the said indicators are coalesced into a composite index of level of industrial development by principal component analysis[138]. In view of the low correlations between the two indicators and low explanatory powers of the first principal factors (i.e factor loading of first principal component for (9i)=72.98% and for (10i)=26.81%), the composite index may not reflect desired level of objectivity, though the results obtained may be still better than from other methods.

The factor scores of first principal components, which provide the values of the composite index, for each district were arranged in descending order and grouped into 6 categories based on the judiciously selected break-points in the composite index. The figures are presented in Table 3.45 and the spatial pattern thus obtained is depicted in Map 3.3. From close observations at the Table and the Map in the light of the previous discussions on different variates of the industrial process, following inferences can be made:

- A generalised pattern of higher level of industrialisation in Kathmandu Valley and Terai followed by Inner Terai, Hill and Mountain in that order, but punctuated by enclaves of disparate levels, is quite apparent and to that extent confirms the earlier observations.
- In the east-west territorial dimension of the same north-south ecological zone, significant spatial variations in the level of development are noticeable. Whereas the Terai region is seen interspersed with pockets of low levels mostly in its central section, the reverse seems to be the case with Hill and Mountain. Specially conspicuous is the most retarded position of a majority of the districts in the eastern Hill, even behind the generally apprehended most laggard region of the western Hill. Though too much may not be read in statistical derivates based on a data base which is not trustworthy this pattern when read with the previously noted spatial pattern of decline of domestic proto-industries, helps us to draw important inferences about the retrograde impact the extra-verted industrialisation has had in the respective hill regions. However, the slightly better position of most of the districts in central Hill may also be attributed to the same pattern of extra-verted industrialisation taking place in them after their integration with the outside economies by means of modern road networks.
- Coming to more disaggregated micro-level, the disarticulated structure of pseudo-industrialisation with weak multiplier effect is abundantly reflected

Table 3.45 Spatial Differentiation of Levels of Industrial Development: All Industries (1976–77).

Class	Rank	Value**	Districts (Territoial Zone)	Class	Rank	Value**		District (Territorial Zone)	
I	1	3.7.192	Morang	(FET)	IV	37	–0.3256	Darchula	(WM)
	2	3.1090	Rautahat	(MET)		38	–0.3368	Mahottari	(MET)
	3	3.0644	Bhaktapur	(KV)		39	–0.3890	Sindhupal-	
	4	2.2217	Kathmandu	(KV)				Chok	(EH)
	5	2.0665	Lalitpur	(KV)		40	–0.3905	Gulmi	(CH)
						41	–0.4102	Baitadi	(WH)
II	6	1.7272	Udaipur	(EIT)					
	7	1.6311	Manang	(CH)		42	–0.5145	Arghakhan-	(CH)
	8	1.4050	Kaski	(CH)	VI			chi	
	9	1.3454	Bardiya	(WT)		43	–0.5403	Zamjung	(CH)
	10	1.2702	Saptari	(MET)		44	–0.5839	Parbat	(CH)
	11	1.0368	Banke	(WT)		45	–0.5921	Gorkha	(CH)
	12	0.9929	Sunsari	(FET)		46	–0.6076	Dhading	(CH)
	13	0.9635	Dang	(WIT)		47	–0.6093	Rasuwa	(CM)
						48	–0.6180	Tanahu	(CH)
	14	0.5359	Kaviepalan-	(EH)		49	–0.6197	Bajhang	(WM)
			chok			50	–0.6335	Myagdi	(CH)
	15	0.4536	Dhanura	(MET)		51	–0.6374	Rolpa	(WH)
	16	0.4364	Siraha	(MET)		52	–0.6436	Palpa	(CH)
III	17	0.4348	Kanchanpur	(WT)		53	–0.6442	Doti	(WH)
	18	0.3989	Jhapa	(FET)		54	–0.6637	Jajarkot	(WH)
	19	0.3362	Parsa	(ET)		55	–0.6663	Sankhuwasa	
								wa	(EM)

(Contd.)

(*Table 3.45 contd.*)

	20	0.3191	Rupendehi	(WT)
	21	0.3082	Sarlahi	(MET)
	22	0.2926	Chitwan	(CIT)
	23	0.2775	Kailali	(WT)
	24.5	0.1693	Sallyan	(WH)
	24.5	0.1693	Dadeldhura	(WH)
	26	0.1428	Nawalparasi	(CT)
	27	0.1020	Makwanpur	(CIT)
	28	0.0601	Sindhuli	(EIT)
IV	29	–0.0152	Kapilvastu	(OT)
	30	–0.0439	Nuwakot	(CH)
	31	–0.0894	Rukum	(WH)
	32	–0.1474	Bara	(ET)
	33	–0.1648	Baglung	(CH)
	34	–0.2109	Mustang	(CM)
	35	–0.2498	Pyuthan	(WH)
	36	–0.2602	Syangja	(CH)

	56	–0.6778	Bhojpur	(EH)
	57	–0.6973	Dolpa	(WM)
	58	–0/7051	Dailekh	(WH)
	59	–0.7329	Surkhet	(WIT)
	60	–0.7517	Achham	(WH)
	61.5	–0.8060	Kalikot	(WH)
	61.5	–0.8060	Jumla	(WM)
	63	–0.8075	Solukhumbu	(EM)
	64	–0.8466	Dhankuta	(EH)
VI	65	–0.8672	Ilam	(EH)
	66.5	–0.9146	Mugu	(WM)
	66.5	–0.9146	Talejung	(EM)
	68	–0.9457	Bajura	(WM)
	69	–0.9503	Tehrathum	(EH)
	70	–0.9551	Dolakha	(EM)
	71	–0.9710	Khotang	(EH)
	72	–0.9847	Okhaldhnga	(ER)
	73	–0.9866	Ramechhap	(EH)
	74	–0.0026	Humla	(WH)
	75	–0.0590	Penchthar	(EH)

Note: * Including domestic proto-industries and manufacturing industries.
** Factor score of first principal component.

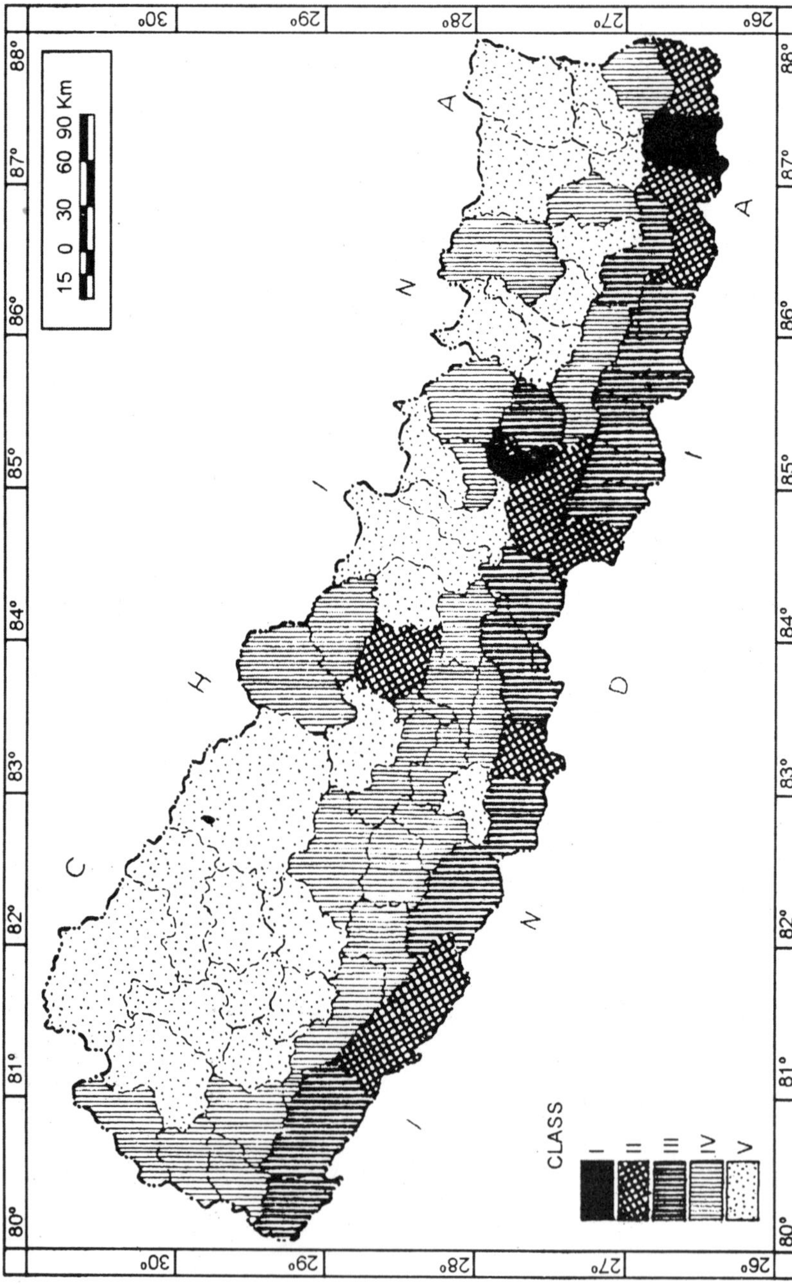

Fig. 3.3 Levels of Aggregate Industrial Development.

in its spatial dimensions. Except for a few enclaves of higher industrial development in far-eastern Terai and Kathmandu Valley, no territorial production complexes with well-articulated spatial division of labour are in sight.

- The gradients of spatial differentiation are not, however, very steep as in many other underdeveloped countries, thereby indicating more of a generalised backwardness of the industrial sector than of a 'dependent development'.
- Certain methodological and statistical inadequacies such as the use of only a small (i.e. 2) number of indicators, inflated productivity figures for districts like Rautahat, Udaipur and Bardiya, higher *average* productivity in figures for western Hill, etc., also seem to have contributed to blurr the real picture of spatial spread of industrial retardation.

3.5.32 Modern Manufacturing Process

In view of the special social significance of the modern manufacturing sector and the general inadequacies observed in the study of aggregate industrial process, we have thought it prudent to construct separate composite indices of manufacturing process in the available spatio-temporal frame and analyse its spatial differentiation. However, in an attempt to study the districtwise processes at two points of time, i.e. 1965 and 1976/77, the selection of indicators of manufacturing development were confined to the following:

(1) % of workers in manufacturing to the total working population;
(2) Gross output per worker;
(3) % of establishments with more than 50 workers to total establishments;
(4) Electricity and fuel consumption per establishment.

Whereas indicator (1) would represent the 'size' of the manufacturing sector in the district, indicators (2), (3) and (4) the 'quality'.

As per the method of construction of composite indices, we found that Kendall's method of additive ranking would generally satisfy the limited purpose of delimitating spatial structure of only the manufacturing sector, despite a number of well-founded methodological objections[139] attributed to it.

The absolute values and rankings of individual indicators by districts for 1965 and 1976/77 are available in Appendix 4 and 5, and the final rank-values and ranking of districts are presented in Table 3.46. The final rank-values after getting them arranged in descending order are grouped into different catagories based on suitably chosen break-points in the rank-values and the emergent spatial structure plotted in Map 3.4.

A close examination of the Tables and Maps enable us to make the following set of observations:

- The overwhelming localisation of manufacturing industries, in terms of major ecological zones, in favour of Terai, Kathmandu Valley and Inner

Table 3.46 Spatial Differentiation of Levels of Industrial Development: Manufacturing Industries (1976–77).

C Class	1965 Rank	Value**	Districts (Territorial Zone)	Class	Rank	1976/77 Value**	District (Territorial Zone)	
I.	1	73	Morang	(FET)	I.	1	169	Morang (FET)
II.	2	69	Banke	(WT)	II.	2	147	Banke (WT)
	3	67.5	Dhanusa	(MET)		3.5	144	Jhapa (FET)
	4	66	Chitwam	(CIT)		3.5	144	Parsa (ET)
	5	63	Parsa	(ET)		5	136	Saptari (MET)
	6	62.5	Jhapa	(FET)		6	134	Sunsari (FET)
						7.5	133	Lalitpur (KV)
	7	55	Lalitpur	(KV)		7.5	133	Rupendelhi (CT)
	8	53.5	Saptari	(MET)		9.5	132	Kapilvastu (CT)
III.	9.5	47.5	Sunsari	(FET)		9.5	132	Surkhet (WIT)
	95	47.5	Bara	(ET)		11	130	Makwanpur (CIT)
	11	47	Kathmandu	(KV)		12	129	Kathmandu (KV)
	12	46.5	Sarlahi	(MET)				
	13	46	Bardiya	(1WT)		13	121.5	Dhanusa (MET)
	14	45.5	Makwanpur	(CIT)		14	119.5	Bardiya (WT)
					III.	15	119	Chitwan (CIT)
	15	44	Rupendehi	(CT)		16	116	Kaski (CH)
						17	114	Siraha (MET)
	16	42.5	Bhaktapur	(KV)		18.5	112	Nawalparasi (CT)
						18.5	112	Kanchanpur (WT)
IV.	17.5	38	Rautahat	(ET)		20	104.5	Bara (ET)
	17.5	38	Nawalparasi			21	103	Sarlati (MET)
				(CT)		22.5	101	Bhaktapur (KV)
	19	36	Siraha	(MET)		22.5	101	Kailali (WT)

(*Contd.*)

(*Table 3.46 contd.*)

20	32.5	Kapilvastu	(CT)		24	92	Dang	(WIT)
21	30.5	Kanchanpur			25.5	90.5	Udaipur	(EIT)
			(WT)		25.5	90.5	Tahahu	(CH)
22	27.5	Mahottari	(MET)		27.5	88	Rautahat	(ET)
					27.5	88	Mahottari	(MET)
23	25.5	Kailali	(WT)		29	84.5	Kavrepalam-chok	(EH)
					30	77	Ilam	(EH)
					31	69.5	Solukhumbu	(EM)
					32	68.5	Palpa	(CH)
					33	57.5	Sindhuli	(EIT)
					34	51	Nuwakot	(CH)
					35	47	Darchula	(WM)
				VI.	36	46.5	Baglung	(CH)
					37	40	Syangja	(CH)
					38.5	38.5	Dhankuta	(EH)
					38.5	38.5	Doti	(WH)
					40	38	Bhojpur	(EH)
					41	37	Dolakha	(EM)
					42	35	Parbat	(CH)
					43	33	S. Palchok	(EH)
					44	23.5	Rolpa	(WH)
					45	21.5	Okaldhunga	(EH)
					–	N.A.	Tehrathin	(EH)
					–	N.A.	Baitadi	(WH)

Note: Total Rank Values.
(see Appendix 18 and 19).

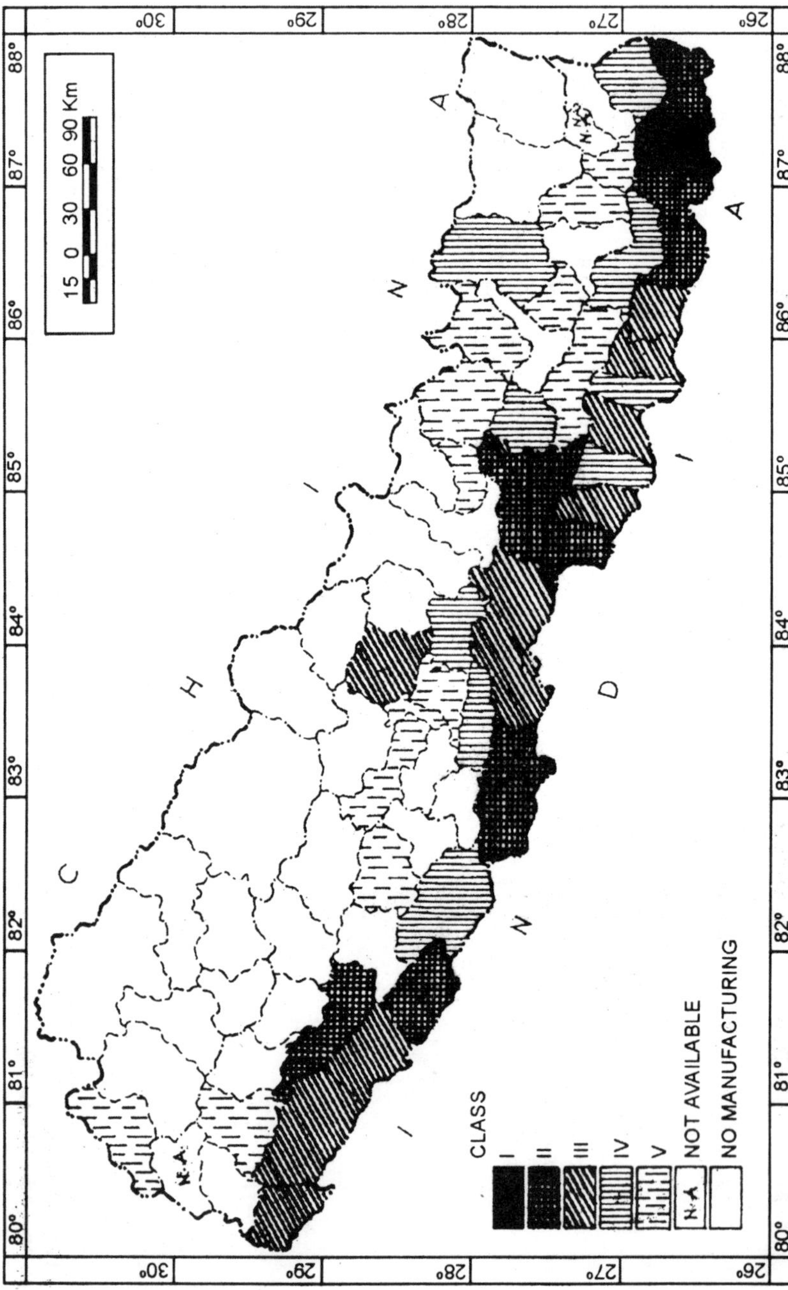

Fig. 3.4 Levels of Development of Manufacturing (1276/77).

Terai is confirmed by the fact that whereas in 1965 all the 23 manufacturing districts belonged to these zones, in 1976/77 out of 47 manufacturing districts 18 were in Terai (total districts = 18), 6 in Inner Terai (total districts = 6), 3 in Kathmandu Valley (total districts = 3), 17 in Hill (total districts = 33) and 3 in Mountain (total districts = 15).

- At the micro-level, the existence of dysfunctional enclaves of high development along major trading outposts of Morang-Jhapa in far-eastern Terai, Parsa-Makwanpur-Kathmandu Valley in the central north-south axis, Rupendehi-Kapilvastu in central Terai and Banke-Surkhet in western Terai surrounded by vast hinterlands of little manufacturing activities, amply demonstrate an extraverted and disarticulated industrial spatial structure.
- In the temporal dimension, despite the spatial spread of manufacturing activities from 23 districts in 1965 to 47 districts in 1976/77, no basic change in the general spatial pattern is observed, which is statistically substantiated by a positive and significant (at 1% level of confidence) rank correlation (i.e. r = 0.6029) between the two composite indices.
- In terms of movements of individual districts in the composite ranking also no major change is noticeable. For example, out of the first ten ranking districts in 1965 and 1976/77, only Dhanusa, Chitawan and Bara were displaced by Rupendehi, Kapilvastu and Surkhet in 1976/77.
- Morang, the first-ranking district in far-eastern Terai is seen to have substantially increased its lead over the second-ranking Banke in west Terai, thus indicating a marked trend in increasing centralisation of industrial production, even though the general gradients of the industrial nodes, are not found to be very high[140].
- Even though of late manufacturing avtivities seem to be spreading along the newly eatablished road network, no discernible production complexes are in sight and the new spatial spread merely seems to strengthen the already established extraverted spatial structure.
- Even if no information on location of manufacturing activities by rural and urban settlements are available, it is generally understood (also supported by positive significant correlation between size of industrial labour force (9i) and average settlement size index (4e) as seen earlier) that most of the production units are concentrated in the major urban areas of Terai along the border with India. With the spread of transportation networks to the inner heartlands, there is noticeable shift in the location of manufactories along the foothills or break-of-bulk points. This should be a logical horizontal (spatial) response to the vertical (sectoral) shift (though marginal) to 'import-substitution' industrialisation from the earlier 'export-oriented' one.

3.5.33 In view of the discernible variation in the industrial spatial structure obtained by delimitation of levels of 'aggregate' and 'manufacturing' industrial development (partly due to differences in the structure of domestic proto-industry and modern manufacturing, and partly because of certain methodological inadequacies), it would be worthwhile to cross-classify the grouping of districts by the two composite indices of development. This should mitigate the methodological inadequacies encountered earlier and provide a composite picture of the state of industrial process with due weightage given to the modern manufacturing sector.

Table 3.47 Cross-Classification of Spatial Variations in Levels of Development of Total Industries and Manufacturing Industries (1976/77).

Lavels of Development of Manufacturing Industries	*Levels of Development of Total Industries*					
	I	*II (Code*	*III number*	*IV of*	*V districts)*	*VI*
I	59					
II	51,49	72, 61, 60, 67	58, 68, 70, 54	71	57	
III	50	73, 31	63, 55, 62, 69, 75, 65, 74	67		
IV	66	56, 52	23	64	30, 34	16, 3
V			53	26, 15, 37, 32, 24	46, 19, 38, 40	25, 4, 21
VI		6	42,48	41, 7, 39, 36, 47*	35, 29, 28, 27, 5, 14, 38, 43, 2, 8, 44, 45	11, 9, 10, 1, 13, 18,* 20, 22, 12, 17

Note: For code number of districts, see Appendix-1.
* Level of development of manufacturing industries 'not available'.

Table 3.47 has been generated from the said cross-classification and the results summerised as follows and depicted in Map. 3.5.

Category	*No. of Districts*	*Code No. of Districts*	*Delineation of Regions*
1. Very High	3	59, 51, 49	Level (I) in one and not less than (II) in another
2. High	10	72, 61, 60, 50, 58, 68, 70, 54, 73, 31	Levels (I) and (II) in one and not less than (III) in another
3. Medium	14	66, 56, 52, 71, 63, 55, 62, 69, 75, 65, 74, 67, 23, 64.	Not less than (III) in both, excluding the first two categories
4. Low	23	6, 53, 57, 26, 15, 37, 32, 24, 30, 34, 42, 48, 16, 3, 46, 19, 33, 40, 41, 7, 39, 36, 47	At least (V) in one and any level in the other, excluding the first three categories
5. Very low	25	25, 4, 21, 35, 29, 28, 27, 5, 14, 38, 43, 2, 8, 44, 45, 11, 9, 10, 1, 13, 18, 20, 22, 12, 17	Other than the first four categories

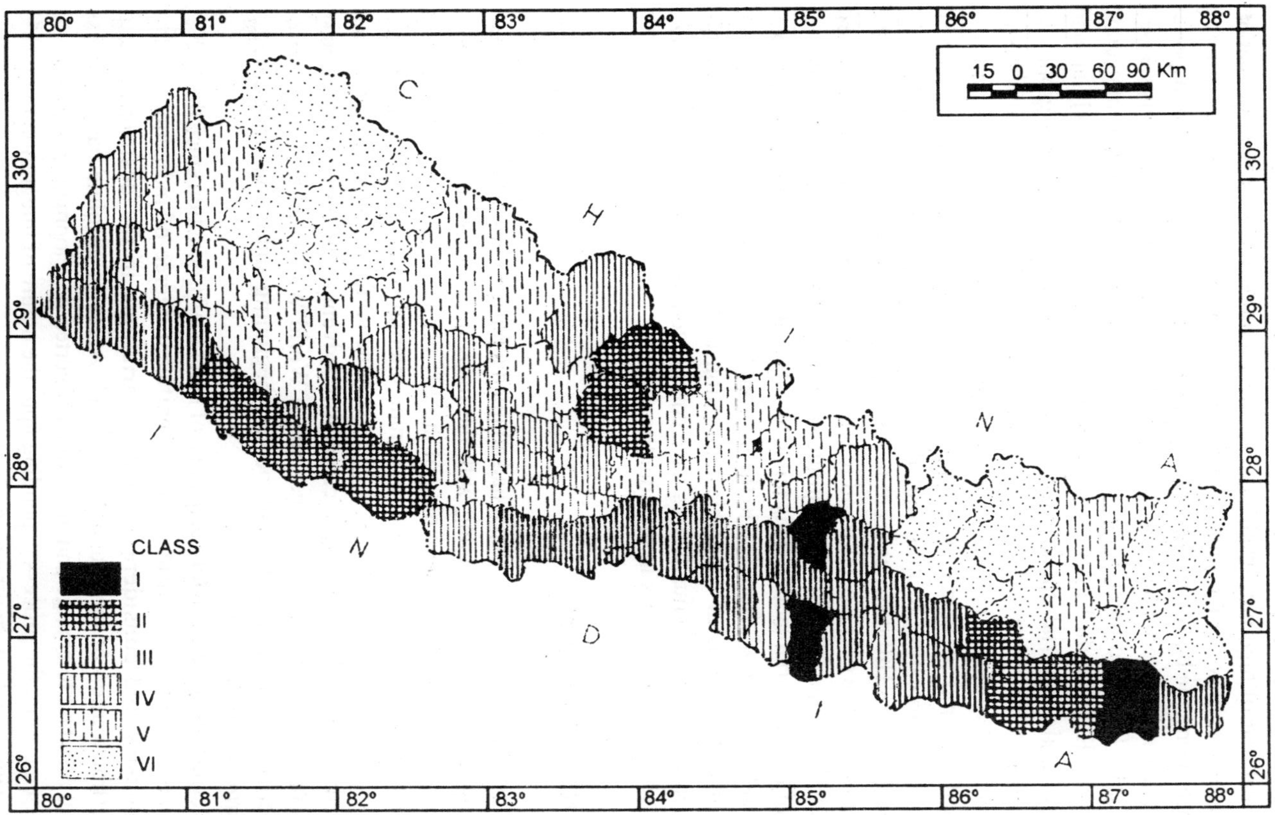

Fig. 3.5 Levels of Aggregate Industrial Development Cross-Classified by Levels of Development of Manufacturing.

It is interesting to note that the results seem to provide a fairly accurate picture of the state of aggregative industrial process in the country. Whereas the three top industrial districts-Morang, Kathmandu and Lalitpur, have been the historical seat of high industrialistion, the next ten districts represent the earlier mentioned enclaves of higher industrial growth around the major trading outposts along the border with India or at the break-of-bulk points of transportation nodes in the interior heartlands. The next group of 14 medium-industrialised districts of Terai and Inner Terai (except Kavre in eastern Hill in the immediate vicinity of Kathmandu Valley), seem to form an outer ring immediately around the principal industrial enclaves of the higher order. The last two groups of industrially most depressed 48 districts (all except two Inner Terai districts of Sindhuli and Surkhet) belong to the outermost 'periphery' of the chronically doomed Hill and Mountain. Even among these more depressed micro-spatial units, it is interesting to note that the traditionally better-placed and well-endowed eastern Hill districts seem to fare worse than their counter-parts in the western Hill. However, socially and in terms of natural zones the most secluded districts of western Mountain constitute the biggest spatial entities at the lowest rung of the industrial ladder. This tends to substantiate the fact that both 'isolation' and 'integration', from and to the metropolitan economy, have been the two complimentary forms of economic retardation in Nepal. In other words, both endogenous and exogenous factors have contributed towards the aggravation of underdevelopment process in the country.

3.6 CONCLUSIONS

- During the 19th century Nepal had attained a fairly high state of craft production, which started declining with the mass influx of British-India factory made goods since the beginning of the 20th century. Apart from the adverse impact of exogenous factors, retrograde internal social structure dominated by a heavily centralised state was not conducive for primitive accumulation and development of industrial capitalism. Advent of modern manufacturing, heralded by the economic exigencies of World War II, ushered in an extroverted industrial process from the very beginning and it could not develop firm endogenous roots.
- Despite the general historical decline of industrial production since the 1920s, there is found a persistence of a significant degree of indigenous proto-industry and considerable spatial variations in the destruction and restructuration of the 'natural economy'. Areas of absolute backwardness but resistant to change and areas of extroverted development can be seen to be emerging, the process depending upto the nature of integration to outside economy and internal tenacity.
- A generalised pattern of chronically anemic and inverted industrial structure is reflected in excessively higher share of elementary processing consisting

of agro-based and forest-based industries and a negligible share of production goods industries. Overall low level of industrial production in the country is characterised by a high degree of its localisation in Terai (specially far-eastern Terai), and Kathmandu Valley.

- There has been a deceleration of growth rates in all the attributes of industrial production except fixed capital, since the beginning of seventies. Moreover, 'intermediate' goods industries have lower growth rates than consumer goods industries, thereby confirming continued intra-sectoral disarticulation. One also observes a greater deceleration of durable consumer goods industries which illustrates the limitation of industrialisation strategy geared to the demands of a narrow upper strata of the population. In the spatial dimension, the areas of higher level of production exhibit slower growth rates. These signs of premature monopolisation seem to have compelled some disperasion (but not significant) of industries towards the more backward Hill and Mountain zones.
- Industrial productivity in the country is not only low at the absolute aggregate level, but there are wide intra-sectoral and intra-territorial variations in them indicating high social and spatial disarticulation.
- General level of capital intensity is very low and is not increasing at satisfactory rate. The low level of technology in use is reflected in low per capita consumption of electricity and low share of technical labour to total labour.
- Industrial production is primarily organised for 'private' appropriation of social surplus. The few state-owned units of 'production goods' industries seem to be merely preparing grounds for the spread of the private sector. Significant degree of premature monopolisation is observed in the form of ownership of most of the industries by few dominant social groups and families, particularly people of Indian origion or Indian nationals.
- The prevalence of a substantial proportion of 'unpaid family labour' engaged in manufacturing adequately demonstrates the primitive nature of organisation of production. Undissolved ties of the industrial labour with agricultural production can be said to acount for the backward relations of production in the industrial sector. The backward nature of relations of production is also characterised by maximisation of 'absolute' surplus values as against the 'relative' surplus value, or in Marx's worlds 'formal subsumption of labour under capital' as against 'real subsumption of labour under capital'.
- External dependence for both technological and raw material inputs in industries is seen to have increased over time. The existing strategy of pseudo-industrialisation can be seen to have oscillated between the two poles of 'import-substitution' (i.e. geared to the 'home market') or 'export-promotion' (i.e. geared to the external market) industrialisation. But the primarily 'home market'-based industrialisation seems to be confronted with two problems: firstly, constriction of the internal market due to gross social inequality and low purchasing power of the masses; and secondly,

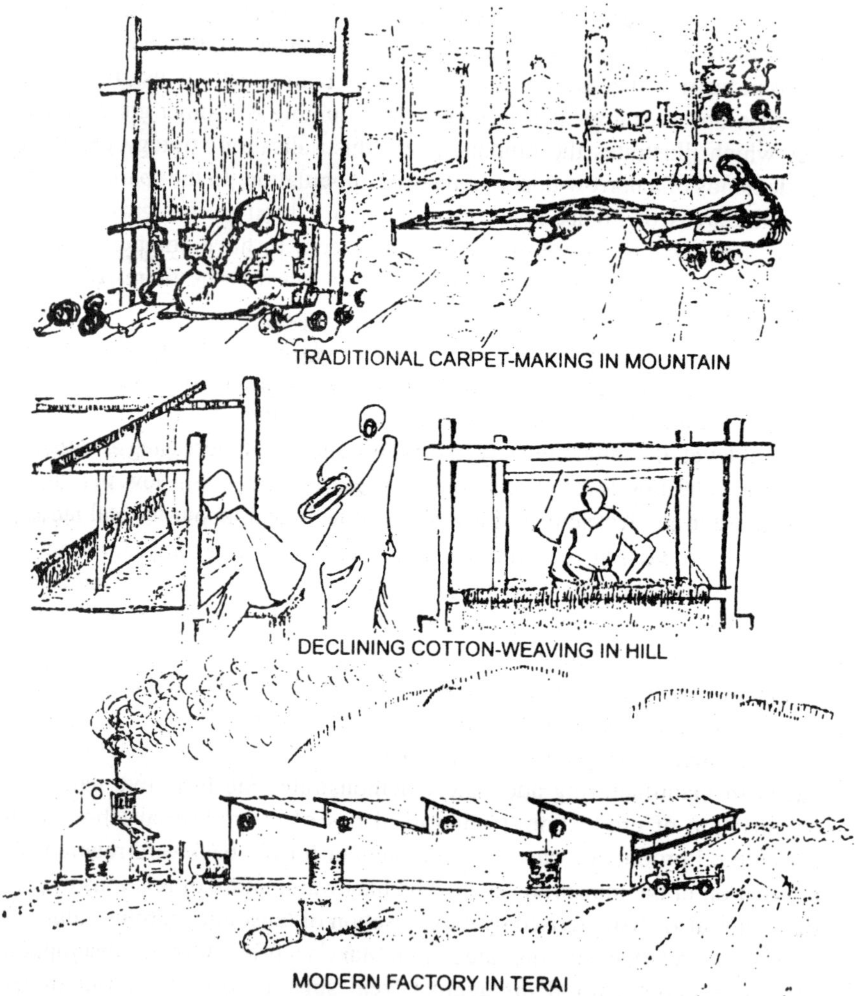

Fig. 3.6 Spatial Differentiation of Industries.

preemption of the existing internal market (mostly composed of the minority upper classes) by exogenous capital.

- The apparently contradictory *lack of credibility* for external finance and *over-dependence* on the same is evident in different branches of industry and territorial zones of industial location. Private Indian capital has played a significant role in the 'industrialisation' of the country, but the absolute size of capital investment for productive purposes is not big. There is virtually no private 'foreign' investment (i.e. other than from India) in the industrial sector.
- The aggregate condition of industrial retardation can be further understood from the extremely low level of capacity utilization and high rate of temporary closure of industrial units.
- High positive correlation of agricultural development with industrial development in the country reflects a strong link between the agrarian and the industrial processes. But this may merely be an expression of predomination of elementary agro-processing activities in the manufacturing sector and not that of articulation of sectoral interdependence found in higher stages of economic development.
- In the territorial dimension, the prevailing condition of the industrial sector is manifested in the appearance of isolated points of industrial localisation along points of superior articulation with the outside economies or at the traditional seat of state authority in the midst of a vast indigent hinterland, thus giving rise to an 'extraverted' and 'disarticulated' industrial spatial structure.

REFERENCE

1. The earliest form of industry has been the 'domestic industry', which is mere processing of raw materials in peasant family that produces them, and is a necessary adjunct of natural economy. When the domestic industry is separated from patriarchal 'agriculture and takes the form of an independent vocation but when goods are produced only to the order of a fixed consumer, it is known as 'artisan' production. Once the artisan starts producing for an unknown, impersonal market he transforms himself into a 'handicraftsman' or a petty commodity producer, though in real life the two forms are hardly to be distinguished. When the workshop of a master 'craftsman expands to assemble many workers under one roof and there develops division of labour within each craft, as against mere *social* division of labour between different crafts earlier, the industry takes the form of 'manufacture'. It constitutes a *bridge* to higher form of social organisation of industrial production as here the workers work with means of production and raw materials provided to them, and instead of their being paid for the total value of the finished product as in domestic industry earlier they are paid with a mere wage. The highest form of industry is the 'modern factory' when machine reduces the role of manual labour, the division of labour within each craft is developed to an infinite extent and form of organisation of production is carried to a qualitatively higher level. (See Lenin, V.I. (1899) *The*

Development of Capitalism in Russia, Progress Publishers, Moscow (1977 edn.); Mandel, E. (1970), *Marxist Economic Theory*, Vol. I, Monthly Review Press, New York).
2. Mandel, *op. cit.*, p. 119.
3. For Marx's definition of 'formal subsumption' and 'real subsumption', see Footnote 114 below.
4. Sutcliffe, R.B. (1971), *Industry and Underdevelopment*, Addison Wesley Publishing Company, London, See also Chapter 2 above.
5. Lenin, *op. cit*, p. 40.
6. Despite occasional divergence of opinions in the matter of interpretation and relative emphasis to be placed on individual conditions, these three preconditions of development of industrial capitalism can be seen to run through major Marxist works. For example, see Marx, K. (1976), *Capital*, Vol. I, Penguin New Left Review edition, London (particularly Part-8); Dobb, M. (1946), *Studies in Development of Capitalism*, Routledge and Kegan Paul, London (1972 edn.); Mandel, *op. cit.*, Brenner, R. (1977), "The Origins of Capitalist Development: a Critique of Neo-Smithian Marxism", *New Left Review*, No. 104, July–August.
7. See, among others, Baran, P. (1957), *The Political Economy of Growth*, People's Publishing House, New Delhi (1962 edn.); Sutcliffe, B. (1972), "Imperialism and industrialisation in third world" in Sutcliffe, B. and Owen, R. (eds.), *Studies in the Theory of Imperialism*, Longman, London; Warren, B. (1973) "Imperialism and Capitalist Industrialisation", *New Left Review*, 81: 3–4; Bernstein, H. (1982), "Industrialization, Development and Dependence" in Alavi, H. and Shanin, T. (eds.), *Introduction to the Sociology of "Developing Societies"*, Macmillan, London; Bagchi, A.K. and Bannerjee, N. (eds.) (1981), *Change and Choice in Indian Industry*, K.P. Bagchi and Co., Calcutta; Varshney, A. (1984), "Political Economy of Slow Industrial Growth in India", *Economic and Political Weekly*, September 1.
8. Bagchi, A.K. (1976), "De-industrialization in India in the Nineteenth Century: Some Theoretical Implications", *The Journal of Development Studies*, Vol. 12, No. 2, p. 137.
9. See Amin, S. (1979), *Unequal Development*, Oxford University Press Delhi, pp. 200–202; Kundu, A. and Raza, M. (1982), *Indian Economy: The Regional Dimension*, Spektrum Publishers and Distributors, New Delhi.
10. See Section 4.11 below.
11. Baran, *op. cit.*, pp. 210–11.
12. See Section 4.1.1. below.
13. Dobb, *op. cit.*, pp. 16–62.
14. Mandel, *op. cit.*, p. 123.
15. As Dobb remarks, "... full flowering of industrial capitalism demands not only a transfer of title to wealth into the hands of the bourgeois class, but a concentration of the ownership of wealth into much fewer hands." (Dobb. *op. cit.*, p. 178).
16. See, among others, Standing, G. (1981), "Migration and Mode of Exploitation: Social Origin of Immobility and Mobility", *The Journal of Peasant Studies*, Vol. 8, No. 2.
17. The concominant 'concentration' of capital in fewer hands and 'dispossession' of previous owner has been central in the analysis of development of industrial capitalism in Marxist literature. (Dobb, *op. cit.*, p. 185). This should be the essence of Marx's well-known exposition, "So-called primitive accumulation... is nothing else than the historical process of divorcing the producer from the means of production". (Marx, *op. cit.*, pp. 874–75).

18. As Lenin observes: "... the transformation of the peasantry into rural proletariat creates a market mainly for articles of consumption, whereas its transformation into a rural bourgeoisie creates market mainly for means of production" (Lenin, *op. cit.*, p. 168).
19. See Nayyar, D. (1981), "Industrial Development in India: Growth or Stagnation?" and Bagchi, A.K. (1981), "Reinforcing and Offsetting Constraints in Indian Industry" in Bagchi and Banerjee, *op. cit.*
20. See Section 1.3.2. above.
21. Massey, D. "Towards a Critique of Industrial Location Theory" in Peet, R. (ed.) (1977), *Radical Geography: Alternative Viewpoints on Contemporary Social Issues*, Maarfa Press, Chicago, p. 196.
22. Industries are known to be 'rooted' to the source of raw material or 'tied' to the market or be 'footloose' depending upon the overriding influences of location of raw materials or market or none (Sutcliffe, R.B. (1971), *op. cit.*, p. 124). However, this formulation in the neo-classical tradition of 'industrial location theory' takes transport costs as the determining variate of industrial production and can be held true only at lower stages of development.
23. See Kundu and Raza, *op. cit.*
24. Regmi, D.R. (1960), *Ancient Nepal*, Firma K.L.M., Calcutta, and Bajracharya, D.B. (1974), *Lichhavi Kalko Abhilekh* (Nepali), Kathmandu.
25. *Ibid.*
26. Of the superior qualities of iron and copper manufactures of Nepal, Kirkpatrick writes, "... the iron of Nepal is not, perhaps, surpassed by that of any other country" and goes on to say European copper did not appear to be of superior quality compared with Nepali copper (Kirkpatrick, W.J. (1811), *An Account of the Kingdom of Nepal*, Manjushri Publishing House, New Delhi (1971 edn.), p. 176). Similarly Hamilton remarks, "The iron of different mines is of very different qualities. Some being so excellent that, even without being converted into steel, it makes knives and swords". (Hamilton, F.B. (1819), *An Account of the Kingdom of Nepal*, Manjushri Publishing House, New Delhi (1971 edn.), p. 78.) Whereas Kirkpatrick and Hamilton have adequately dealt with the flourishing metal-crafts industry and "a very coarse kind" of cotton textiles of Kathmandu Valley, Hodgson (1971) talks of "excellence" of metal-workers of Dhankuta in eastern Hill and the copper manufacturers of Pokhara in western/central Hill. Brown sugar processed from sugarcane is applauded by Kirkpatrick as "much more refined... than that which is usually met with in Bengal". (Kirkpatrick, *op. cit.*, p. 129). Of the extensive scale and high quality production of paper in the Hills and Valley of Nepal Kirkpatrick finds them "strong" and "useful", Hamilton calls them "a very strong paper, remarkably well-fitted for packages", and Hodgson after remarking that "it would probably surprise the paper-makers of England" terms them "better than any Indian paper", (see, Regmi, M.C. (1984), *The State and Economic Surplus Production, Trade and Resource Mobilisation in Early 19th Century Nepal*, Kathmandu).
27. The foundation of systematic munitions production was laid with the establishment of a factory, later known as Jangi Megjin, in Kathmandu under the supervision of French technicians in 1793 after the Nepal–China war. This was expanded to employ as many as 306 technicians and other workers on the eve of 1814–16 Nepal–British war. In Pyuthan, in western Hill, rifles of Enfield model were manufactured to the tune of 501 rifles a year in 1811, which was subsequently raised to 2101 rifles. Another munitions factory commissioned in Those, an iron mining area in the

eastern Hill, later in 1875 was equipped to produce nine rifles daily (Regmi, M.C. (1978), *Thatched Huts and Stucco Palaces: Peasants and Landlords in 19th Century Napal,* Vikas Publishing House Pvt. Ltd. New Delhi, pp. 37–40.

In the words of Orfeur Cavanagh (1851): "There is a foundry at Kathmandu and a large manufactory of fire arms at Peutana, about 15 marches distant. The guns are of brass (copper and zinc) and bored by machinery worked by water power... The rifles and muskets in use with the Gorkha Army are of fair construction, but with rude flint locks... It is supposed that in case of emergency, the government could supply muskets and accoutrements sufficient to equip upward of 100,000 men" (Quoted in *ibid.*).

28. *Ibid.*
29. Seddon et. al. (1981), *Peasant and Workers in Nepal*, Vikas Publishing House Pvt. Ltd., New Delhi, p. 184.
30. "Radha Kissen Chamaria, a Marwari important in Calcutta's jute processing and exporting business, was chiefly responsible for the establishment of Nepal's largest jute mill (i.e. Biratnagar Jute Mills) in 1936. Chamaria had already built a jute mill at Katihar, a town in Bihar about 75 miles south of Biratnagar. The tarai area around Biratnagar had become a major jute-growing area by the 1930s. and the price of jute was high. Chamaria persuaded his friend, Judha Shamsher, Rana Prime Minister of Nepal at the time, to set up a holding company financed jointly by the two of them. Aish Narayan Singhania, Chamaria'a brother-in-law and manager of Chamaria's mill at Katihar, moved to Biratnagar to manage the mill there and was instrumental in establishing Biratnagar's first large rice mill in 1937, a cotton mill in 1942, and a sugar mill in 1946." (Gaige, F. (1975), *Regionalism and National Unity in Nepal*, University of California Press, Berkley and Los Angeles, p. 37).
31. According to one well-informed source, of the total investment in 63 companies upto 1950/51, 70 million rupees were in Indian currency and a pitiable 2.1 million rupees in Nepalese currency. (H.P. Giri (1977) cited in Poudyal, S.R. (1983), *Planned Development in Nepal*, Sterling Publishers, New Delhi, p. 68). Though the respective currency figures may not necessarily represent the ratio of shares by the two sides, it may give general idea about the extent of hegemony exercised by the Indian capitalists.
32. Industrial Services Centre (1982), *Industrial Sectoral Plan Study* (1980/81–1990/91), Vol. I, (Revised Edition), Kathmandu, p. 17.
33. See Bhattarai, B.R. (1983), "Nepalese Nationalism and Nationality Question", *Frontier*, Calcutta, April 16.
34. Mandel has rightly observed that unlike Western Europe where accumulation of money capital, usurer's capital, merchant capital and commercial capital took place in the hands of a bourgeois class, in other pre-capitalist civilizations capital remained unchangingly under the arbitrary power of the despotic and all-powerful state (Mandel, *op. cit.*, p. 123).
35. See Lohani, G.P. (1977), "Nepalko arthik chintanma bhoomi ra janko sthitile prastut gareka kehi bisangatiharu (Nepali) *Roop Rekha* 200th Special Issue, Vol. XVIII, No. 8, Kathmandu.
36. Rawat, P.C. (1974), *Indo–Nepal Economic Relations*, Sterling Publishers, New Delhi, p. 223.
37. See Seddon et. al., *op. cit.*
38. See, among others, Kansakar, V.B.S. (1974), *Population Change in Nepal: A Study of Mobility During 1911–61* (Unpublished Ph.D. Dissertation), Department of

Geography, Patna University; Caplan, L. (1970) *Land and Social Change in East Nepal: A Study of Hindu Tribal Relations*, London.

39. Dobb, *op. cit.*, p. 26.
40. Baran, *op. cit.*, p. 207.
41. See Bhasin, A.S. (1970), *Documents on Nepal's Relations with India and China (1946–66)*, Mumbai.
42. See Shrestha, B.P. (1962), *An Introduction to Nepalese Economy*, Ratna Pustak Bhandar, Kathmandu (1981 edn.) and Seddon et. al., *op. cit.*
43. Shrestha, *op. cit.*, p. 137.
44. The term 'proto-industry' is coined here to differentiate pre-manufacturing stage of secondary production activities from 'artisan' 'handicraft' etc. which have a definite connotation of their own (see Section 3.1.1 above), but to incorporate all of them in a generalized form. However, it should not be confused with 'proto-industrialization' or 'proto-industrial system', propounded by the neo-Chayanovians as a separate or transitional mode of industrial production in between feudalism and industrial capitalism. (For the latter view, see Kriedte et. al. (1981), *Industrialization Before Industrialization*, Cambridge University Press, Cambridge).
45. National Planning Commission Secretariat, National Accounts Project (1979)... *Manufacturing, Financing... etc. (1976/77)*, Kathmandu, p. 32.
46. Industrial Services Centre (1982), *Industrial Sectoral Plan Study* (1980/81–1990/91), Vol. I, (Revised Edition), Kathmandu.
47. Frequent change of nomenclature and definition for the same set of economic activities makes the empirical study in a dynamic frame particularly difficult. Moreover, the erroneous official definition of 'cottage industry' with respect to a predetermined limit of capital investment rather than a determinate mode of articulation of forces and relations of production, renders the available statistical information virtually useless for a scientific study. For example, whereas the Industrial Policy of 1973 had defined 'cottage and village industry' as an industry with fixed assets not exceeding Rs. 200 thousand, the Industrial Policy of 1981 defines 'Cottage industry' as "an industrial enterprise in which investment in machinery, equipment and tools does not exceed Rs. 200.000 in value and fixed assets do not exceed Rs. 500.000 in case of rural and Rs. 800.000 in case of urban areas. " (Nepal Industrial Development Corporation (1982), *Industrial Policy and Acts of His Majesty's Government of Nepal*, Kathmandu, p. 12.
48. *Sample Survey of the Cottage and Small Scale Industries 1972–73* (CBS, Kathmandu), lists 63, 'industry class' of products for the country as a whole and 53, 33, 56 and 49 respectively for eastern, central, western and far-western zones.
49. The 'input-based' classification is made on the basis of dominant raw material/input used and the 'use-based' classification by the dominant use of the principal industrial product is put to. Because of widely varying commodity composition the typologies of industrial classification here do not conform to the usual typologies adopted in the case of manufacturing industries (see Section 3.3.1 below).
50. Also see Seddon et al., *op. cit.*, p. 195.
51. See Poudyal, *op. cit.*, p. 105.
52. However, certain fragmentary studies of some remote areas of this zone have revealed a familiar pattern of decline of domestic proto-industries, particularly woolen and cotton textiles, leather products, etc. in the aftermath of increasing penetration of factory-made goods from India. (See among others, New Era (1976), *Bajhang Small Area Development Programme Survey Report*, Kathmandu).

53. See Sen, A. (1982), *The State, Industrialization and Class Formations in India*, Routledge and Kegan Paul, London, p. 123.
54. Lenin, V.I. (1897), "The Handicraft Census of 1894–95 in Perm Gubernia and General Problems of "Handicraft Industry" in *Collected Works*, Vol. 2, Progress Publishers Moscow, 1972, p. 359.
55. See Seddon et. al., *op. cit.*
56. Overseas trade statistics for 1979/80 shows that "handicrafts", specially woolen goods like carpets, were the fifth leading export items and their contribution was 14.8% of the total exports in that year. (Upadhyaya, G.R. (1983), "Cottage and Village Industries for Economic Development in Nepal" in *Nepal Industrial Digest*, Silver Jubilee Issue, NIDC, Kathmandu, p. 61).
57. Asian Regional Team for Employment Promotion (1974), *A Challenge to Nepal: Growth and Employment*, Bangkok.
58. Commander, Simon (1985), "Proto-Industrial Production as a Barrier to Industrialization? Case of North Indian Sugar Industry 1850–1980", *Economic and Political Weekly*, March 23, p. 514.
59. For example, a similar pattern of spatial differentiation in the destruction of 'natural economy' is reported in the case of Peru. See Bradby, B. (1980), "The destruction of natural economy" in Wolpe, H. (ed.), *The Articulation of Modes of Production*, Routledge and Kegan Paul, London.
60. Manufacturing industries have been defined in successive industrial censuses as those industrial establishments "employing ten or more persons, or using auto-machines".
61. The 'input-based' and 'use-based' typologies of industrial classification used here are based on: Raj, K.N. (1976), "Growth and Stagnation in Indian Industrial Development" "*Economic and Political Weekly*, Annual Number, February; Shetty, S.L. (1978), "Structural Retrogression in the Indian Economy since Mid-Sixties" *Economic and Political Weekly*, Annual Number, February; Varshney, *op. cit.*, and others.
62. Since successive census of manufacturing establishments do not provide separate information on the few industries that can be classified as 'basic goods' and 'capital goods' industries, some idea on their size is sought to be driven home through a separate 'use-based' classification of industries in the 'public' sector as in Table 3.12 as virtually all the industries belonging to these two sub-groups happens to be in the 'public' sector.
63. See Hoffmann, W.G. (1958), *The Growth of Industrial Economics*, Oxford University Press, Mumbai. Though Hoffmann's schema of continually declining ratio of the net output (value-added) in the consumer-goods industries to that in the capital-goods industries in predetermined orders with the corresponding rise in the level of industrialization of the society cannot be applied mechanically for all situations, its general validity with certain methodological reservations cannot be denied. (See Sutcliffe, R.B. (1971) *op. cit.*).
64. More developed industrial economies are characterized by stronger interconnection and complimentariness of different branches of manufacturing industries, manifested in higher ratio of intermediate (or 'semi-manufactories') to the final products, whereas reverse is the case underdeveloped economies (Tyagunenko, V.L. et. al. (ed.) (1973), *Industrialization of Developing Countries*, Progress Publishers, Moscow, p. 164).
65. For the definition of the typology and the method of classification with concrete examples of industries, see Habeeb, A. (1979), *Characteristics and Processes of*

urbanization in Colonial India—A Case Study of Calcutta and its Hinterland (1850–1921), (Unpublished Ph. D. Dissertation), CSRD/SSS/JNU, New Delhi.

66. See, Industrial Services Centre (1982), *Industrial Sector Plan Study* (1980/81–1990/91), Vol. I, (Revised edition), Kathmandu, p. 37.
67. See, HMG/N, Ministry of Finance (1980), *Highlights of Public Enterprises in Nepal for the F.Y. 1977/78*, Corporation Coordination Division, Kathmandu.
68. Since there exists no systematic weighted index of industrial production in the country, we have followed the "preliminary attempt" recently made by Industrial Services Centre. (See Industrial Services Centre (1982) *op. cit.*).
69. See, HMG/N, Ministry of Industry (1983), *Industrial Profile*, Kathmandu.
70. This includes 230 hotels and lodges, out of which 169 (i.e. 73.48%) are located in Bagmati (158) and Narayani (11) zones. For the rest of the study, however, hotels and lodges are not included in 'industry' but in 'trade'.
71. For example, a serious error is suspected in the estimate of rice and oil milling employment in 1972/73 census, resulting in an over-estimation of employment by possibly as much as 40% (See Industrial Services Centre (1982) *op. cit.*, p. 24). However, we have no means to ascertain and rectify such errors.
72. The figures of annual growth rates provided by Industrial Services Centre for 1965/66–1972/73, 1972/73–1977/78 and 1965/66–1977/78 are slightly lower than obtained by us. (*Ibid.*). Still they are quite high compared to other countries. For example, the annual growth rates of production on manufacturing industries for 1960–70 and 1970–76 were 6.7% and 4.5% respectively for "low income countries" and 5.7 % and 3.2 % respectively for "industrialized countries" (The World Bank (1983), *World Development Report 1983*, Oxford University Press, New Delhi).
73. As Sutcliffe has rightly observed, "it is impossible to define a qualitative change such as industrialization in purely qualitative terms" because "many activities which are counted as industrial or manufacturing in fact involve very little industrial activity beyond simple processing of a primary product". (Sutcliffe, R.B. (1971) *op. cit.* p. 16.)
74. Sutcliffe, B. (1972) *op. cit.*, p. 180.
75. In the absence of separate information on the few 'basic' and 'capital' goods industries it is not possible to have a comparative view of their growth rates. Nonetheless, because of their extremely low absolute level and near-zero initial base, small absolute increase would give a disproportionately high growth rate and hence would be misleading for comparative purposes.
76. It is interesting to note that the growth pattern of industry groups in Nepal tend to vary almost in the reverse order to that in India for the relevant period. (See, Ahluwalia cited in Varshney *op. cit.* and Bhagavan, M.R. (1985), "Capital Goods Sector in India: Past and Present Trends and Future Prospects", *Economic and Political Weekly*, March 9). This may be a reflection on the significant differences in the historical experiences of the two countries, and would thus require of us to look for different explanations to the industrial stagnation and structural retrogression than usually advanced in the case of India.
77. Of the more notable contributors to the continuing Indian debate may be cited: Raj, *op. cit.*; Mitra, A. (1977), *Terms of Trade and Class Relations: An Essay in Political Economy*, Frank Cass, London; Shetty, *op. cit.*; Patnaik, P. (1981), "An Explanatory Hypothesis on the Indian Industrial Stagnation" in Bagchi and Bannerji, *op. cit.*;

Bagchi, A.K. (1981), *op. cit.*; Nayyar, *op. cit.*; Mundle, S. (1981), "Growth, Disparity and Capital Reorganisation in Indian Economy: Some Speculations", *Economic and Political Weekly*, Annual Number, March. A critical review and concise account of the debate is available in Bagchi and Banerjee, *op. cit.*, and Varshney *op. cit.* A number of mutually reinforcing and mutually conflicting explanations advanced for Indian Industrial stagnation include the following set of factors: poor performance of the agricultural sector, shift in terms of trade against industry, unequal income distribution and resulting lack of demand, declining levels of public investment, increasing inefficiencies in the industrial structure resulting from government controls and policies, etc.

78. Because of gross overestimation of industrial labour in 1972/73, as already noted, the measure of return per labour for the year may not be reliable and growth rates based on it would naturally be spurious. Hence we have found it prudent to take into account only the overall growth rate for the period 1965 to 1976/77.

79. Even after allowing for some suspected discrepancy in the census data itself, manufacturing value added per labour engaged in Nepal is seen to be among the lowest in the world as reflected in the following figures for relevant countries (all the figures are in US dollar at 1976 standard conversion rates):

<u>Value added/Labour for selected Countries (1976).</u>

1.	Nepal	-$	386.40
2.	Bangladesh	-$	870.40
3.	India	-$	1398.30
4.	Sri Lanka	-$	2653.40
5.	Ethiopia	-$	3694.50
6.	Bolivia	-$	4793.40
7.	Fiji	-$	4851.48
8.	U.S.A.	-$	31610.70

(Source: United Nations (1982), *Yearbook of Industrial Statistics*, 1980 Edition, Vol. 1, General Industrial Statistics, New York.)

80. See, Mundle, *op. cit.*, p. 397.

81. Mandel, *op. cit.*, p. 162.

82. Lenin, *op. cit.*, p. 40.

83. Comparative figures of capital/labour ratios for other economies are as follows (the figures are in US dollar at the standard conversion rates for the corresponding years):

1.	Ethiopia (1976)	-$	277.80
2.	India (1977)	-$	415.90
3.	Nepal (1976/77)	-$	695.58
4.	Fiji (1976)	-$	1095.27
5.	Sri Lanka (1979)	-$	1716.30
6.	Bolivia (1976)	-$	1985.30
7.	U.S.A.	-$	2183.10

(Source: United Nations (1982), *op. cit.*).

84. Poudyal and others, however, seem to hold a different view of the level and growth of the capital intensity condition. Even if their contention of capital intensity as being 'high' and 'increasing' with time does not stand to empirical scrutiny, the theoretical validity of the reasoning for having encouraged capital intensive techniques under the pressure of foreign 'aid' donors and sponsors of industries in the country would have to be acknowledged. (See Poudyal, *op. cit.*, pp. 96–98.)

85. See, Nepal Rastra Bank (1977), *Industrial Survey Report (Nepali)*, Kathmandu, Table No. 7.
86. Even if scale of production or plant size is usually taken as "an indicator of the technique of production" (see Nagaraj, R. (1985), "Trends in factory Size in Indian Industry, 1950 to 1980: Some Tentative Inferences" *Economic and Political Weekly*, February 3, among others). We have thought it more prudent to analyze it in this section of 'distribution' conditions in keeping with our consistent position that size of production unit or scale of operation constitutes an important pre-condition for the overall organization of production and channelisation of the social surplus.
87. A comparative view of size distribution of industrial units by labour engaged, for other economies at different levels of development may be had from the following table:

Enterprises	*% of Industrial Enterprises by Countries*				
	USA 1958	*Britain 1961*	*FRG 1963*	*Japan 1963*	*India 1961*
1–10 workers	54.3	71.8	43.4	73.9	93.0
11–50 workers	30.4	12.0	32.6	21.1	2.0
51–100 workers	6.9	8.5	10.1	2.8	0.2
100 workers and above	8.4	7.7	13.9	2.2	0.2
Non-classified	–	–	–	–	4.6

Source: Shirokov, G.K. (1973), *Industrialization of India*, Progress Publishers, Moscow, p. 268.

88. 'Ancillarisation' refers to a process of capital re-organization where, "corporate capital finds a number of advantages in farming out the earlier stages of production to small ancillary units while itself undertaking only some strategic stages of production, such as the final assembly" (Mundle, *op. cit.*, p. 401).
89. It may be noted that in 1976/77 88.37% of all manufacturing units with less than 10 labour each were engaged in cereal and oil processing activities.
90. Banaji, J. (1980), "Summary of Selected Parts of Kautsky's The Agrarian Question" in Wolpe, *op. cit.*, p. 87.
91. *Ibid.*
92. As Lenin remarks, "The growth of small production among the peasant signifies the appearance of new industries the conversion of new branches of raw material processing into independent spheres of industry, progress in the social division of labour, the *initial process of capitalist development*, while the swallowing-up of small by large establishments implies a further step forward by *capitalist development*, while the swallowing-up of small by large establishments implies a further step forward by capitalism, leading to the triumph of its higher forms" (Lenin (1897) *op. cit.*, p. 382, emphasis added).
93. Some interesting studies on the changing pattern of factory sizes and correlation of plant size with capital intensity, labour productivity etc. have been made in the case of other economies and mutually contradictory conclusions and explanations advanced. For a brief resume of the different positions held on the issue, specially with respect to India, and the latest situation in Indian industry, i.e. general shift towards smaller size units, etc., see Nagaraj, *op. cit.*
94. Ishikawa (1961) and Watanabe (1974) cited in-*ibid.*, p. M–31.
95. Industrial enterprises with "investment in machinery, equipment and tools" exceeding Rs. 0.2 million in value are officially classified into 'small' 'medium' and 'large'

corresponding respectively to the fixed capital investment of less than NRs. 2 million, 2 million to 10 million and above 10 million (Nepal Industrial Development Corporation (1982), *Industrial Policy and Acts of His Majesty's Government of Nepal 2037 (1981)*, Kathmandu, p. 12).

96. Fahrenkrog has provided a concise definition of 'ownership' and 'possession' of means of production thus: "ownership is the power to appropriate and dispose of the product obtained whereas possession is the ability to put the means of production to work" (Fahrenkrog, G. (1984), "Questions of Method in Regional Analysis" in O'Keefe, P. (ed.), *Regional Restructuring Under Advanced Capitalism*, Croom Helm, London, p. 23).

97. An industry in Nepal may be organized and registered as 'sole proprietorship', 'partnership', 'private limited company' or 'public limited company' as defined by the various industrial Acts enacted by the government. These forms of juridical ownership are essentially defined by the number and the nature of collaboration of individual investors. According to the Nepal Company Act of 1964, a 'private limited company' is limited to 50 shareholders and its incorporation demands a subscription of capital by at least two investors, and for a 'public limited company' with unlimited number of shareholders, by at least seven. (Industrial Services Centre (1982), *Investors Guide to Nepal*, Kathmandu, p. 35). Hence, as is understood in the common parlance, all 'public limited' enterprises should not be taken necessarily as the state-owned ones, because the state may own a majority share in some and none in others.

98. Of the 21 public limited companies engaged in manufacturing activities in 1976, the state had 100% shares in seven units more than 50% shares in four, less than 50% shares in another four and none in others; thus an aggregate of 84% shares of paid-up capital in all manufacturing industries organized as public limited companies. (Mahat, R.S. (1981), *Capital Market, Financial Flows and Industrial Finance in Nepal*, Sajha Prakashan, Lalitpur (Nepal), p. 303.

99. For a complete list of manufacturing units organized as 'public enterprises', see HMG/N, Ministry of Finance (1980), *op. cit.*

100. However, many of the present-day 'public enterprises' had been originally established in the private sector and to that extent their share for the earlier period as projected from the current legal status could be slightly misleading. Also there are enough evidences of rise in the absolute number of public limited industrial enterprises in the later years (See, Mahat, *op.cit.*, p. 60), even though their share to the total enterprises may have declined.

101. See, various plan documents of National Planning Commission, Kathmandu.

102. This is so because the Indians tend to register the enterprises in the name of natives for extraneous consideration. As Gaige, in speaking about the industrial investment in Terai remarks: "This cannot be documented by reference to Industry Department records because Indian investors have found it advantageous to associate themselves with hill people, particularly those who have government connections, in order to obtain government licenses for their industries. Therefore, Industry Department records often list hill people as owner and managers of industries in which they have little or no capital investment" (Gaige, *op. cit.*, pp. 37–38).

103. Security Sale-Purchase Centre Ltd. (1981), *Study on Share Ownership of Principle Public Limited Companies in Nepal* (Nepali), Kathmandu.

104. For the retarding effects of early monopolies and comprador–landlord classes on the development of industrial capitalism, see Baran, *op. cit.*

105. Central Bureau of Statistics, *Census of Manufacturing Establishments, 1976–77*, Kathmandu.
106. Security Sale-Purchase Centre Ltd., *op. cit.*, Table 4.
107. Lenin, V.I. (1894), "What the 'Friends of the People' are" in *Collected Works*, Vol. 1, Progress Publishers, Moscow, 1972, p. 223.
108. Brenner, *op. cit.*, p. 32.
109. Nepal Rastra Bank (1977), *Industrial Survey Report* (Nepali), Kathmandu, Table No. 7.
110. See Lenin (1897), *op. cit.*, p. 362.
111. Among others see Seddon *et. al.*, *op. cit.*, p. 168.
112. Janchboojh Kendra (1974), *Mechi dekhi Mahakali* (Nepali), Part–I, Kathmandu, p. 462. Though lacking in correct analytical perspective, a recent report of the Task Force on Migration provides enough empirical evidences of this phenomenon of cross-migration (See Task Force on Migration (1983), *Internal and International Migration in Nepal: Summary and Recommendations*, National Commission on Population, Kathmandu).
113. For lucid expositions on different contradictory roles of migratory labour in advancing or retarding social relations of production in different conditions, see Lenin (1899) *op. cit.*, Banaji, *op. cit.*, Standing *op. cit.*, and Meillassoux, C. (1980), "From reproduction to production: A Marxist-approach to economic anthropology" in Wolpe, *op. cit.*, among others.
114. Marx provides brilliant exposition on two distinct stages of labour process on its take-over by capital. In the first stage, surplus value is extracted by merely extending the length of working day under the existing level of labour productivity, i.e. production of 'absolute' surplus value, which he terms as *formal subsumption of labour under capital.* This can be said to be a characteristic of the period of manufacture. In the second stage, technical process of labour itself is revolutionized so that greater mass of use value can be created with the same amount of labour, i.e. production of 'relative' surplus value. This qualitatively higher stage of capitalist mode of production is called by him as *real subsumption of labour under capital*, and is a characteristic of the modern factory. (See Marx (1976), *op. cit.*, Appendix I.)
115. Banerjee, N. "Is small beautiful?" in Bagchi and Banerjee, *op. cit.*, pp. 288–89.
116. See footnote 114 above.
117. After Marx, the 'circuit' of capital or industrial production may be constructed as follows:

$$M—C^{L}_{MP}—P—C'—M'$$

Where, M = Money capital; C = Commodity;
L = Labour power; MP = Means of production (i.e. instruments and materials of labour);
P = Process of production; C′ = Commodity with added value (i.e. finished product); M′ = Money capital after realization of value.

(See Kay, G. (1975), *Development and Underdevelopment: A Marxist Analysis*, Macmillan, London, pp. 30–31.)

118. The share of imports of 'machinery and transport equipment' to total imports in Nepal is seen progressively rising from 3.17%, 8.41% to 20.12% in the 1950s, 1960s and 1970s respectively. And India accounted for 90.82%, 87.47 % and 47.68% of total imports of these commodities in the successive periods. (See Table 4.24 below.)

119. As a direct result of the closing of Indian market for the Nepalese manufacture under this Protocal "nine out of ten synthetic textiles and six out of seven stainless steel units, a match factory, a woolen mill and a cotton textile unit lay idle in the early seventies". (Nath, Tribhuvan (1975), *The Nepalese Dilemma (1960–74)*, Sterling Publishers Pvt. Ltd., New Delhi, p. 70.
120. Under this scheme exporters to third countries other than India were entitled to keep a certain percentage of hard currency earned to import goods of their choice. (See Chapter 4 below.)
121. ARTEP, *op. cit.*
122. See Bagchi, A.K. (1981), *op. cit.*, Nayyar, *op. cit.*, among others.
123. In the words of Baran, "... just as investment tends to become self-propelling, so lack of investment tends to become self-perpetuating." (Baran, *op. cit.*, p. 208).
124. Central Bureau of Statistics, *Census of Manufacturing Establishments*, 1972/73 and 1976/77, Kathmandu.
125. See Mahat, *op. cit.*, pp. 8–9, for proportions of 'internal' to 'external' sources of industrial finance in different economies and arguments, mostly of Anglo-Saxon scholarship, for or against a higher share of one or the other source.
126. Here finance from 'foreign agencies' include only such as forwarded *directly* for industrial investment by recognized agencies and not channeled through NIDC (whose major sources are 'foreign') or invested by private foreign entrepreneurs.
127. External finance as percentage of total finance was found as 98.7, 93, 92.7, 89.6, 87.7, 72.4, 70.9, 56.6, 54.4, 30.9 and 9.6 respectively for cement, diary, tea, jute, electricity, construction, brick and tile, food processing, match, sugar and cigarette industries. (*Ibid.*, p. 221.)
128. See, Central Bureau of Statistics, *Census of Manufacturing Establishments, 1976/77.*
129. See, NIDC (1980), *Audhyogik Jagat* (Nepali), Vol. 5, No. 1, Kathmandu.
130. Rawat, *op. cit.*, pp. 228–29.
131. These figures of total industrial investment are negligible compared to the investment on trade which was reported to be worth Rs. 155 million in 1956. (*Ibid.*)
132. Scholz, J.T. (1977), *Policy Processes and Rural Development: A Study of Land Reform in Nepal* (Unpublished Ph.D. Dissertation), University of California, Berkley, p. 260.
133. For example, Union Carbide have recently established a dry cell manufacturing unit through their subsidiaries in Calcutta.
134. See, Sengupta, R.P. (1981), "Measurement of Steel Capacity: Bhilai Steel Plant—A Case Study" in Bagchi and Banerjee, *op. cit.*
135. Nepal Rastra Bank (1977), *op. cit.*, Table 12.
136. *Ibid.*, Table 15.
137. In the absence of total industrial output figures (i.e. for both domestic proto-industry and manufacturing sectors) by districts, the output figures only for manufacturing in the respective districts were used, and for districts with no manufacturing activities average output figures for respective ecological–hydrographic zones were used.
138. See Section 1.6 above.
139. See Kundu, A. (1980), *Measurement of Urban Processes: A Study in Regionalisation*, Popular Prakashan, Mumbai, p. 34.
140. Because of its very nature of assigning equal weights and doing away with the magnitude of class intervals of different variables, ranking method minimizes the differences in the absolute values of the variables; hence the gradients would expectedly by not very sharp.

4 Proliferation of Circulation Capital

4.1 INTRODUCTION

After assessing the conditions of the principal production sectors of the economy in the preceding chapters, we shall now investigate into the conditions of economic integration or activities related to circulation. In this chapter the merchant and financial capital operating within and without the social economy are singled out for detailed analysis in the given spatio-temporal frame. The analysis of the current situation of the sub-sectors would be preceded by brief accounts of the related theoretical issues and historical antecedents.

4.1.1 Theoretical Underpinnings

We need to be clear about certain conceptual issues related to the role of circulation capital in structuration of under-development in a transitional society of the kind of Nepal not only because circulation capital, whose major components are merchant/commercial and interest-bearing/money-dealing capital[1], "plays the crucial role in the articulation between capitalist and pre-capitalist economies, and because it provides the appropriate medium for the cooperation of foreign and native capital"[2], but also because it is a "necessary factor in the development of capitalism, a necessary wheel in the mechanism of a *poorly developed* capitalist society"[3]. We would, however, confine ourselves only to the issues which are directly relevant to the present study and in which there is some divergence of opinion amongst radical academics.

4.1.11 Merchant Capital and Underdevelopment

By definition, the "pure form of merchant's capital is the purchase of a commodity in order to sell this same commodity at profit".[4] Algebrically, its circuit is quite simply M-C-M' i.e. purchase and sale of the same commodity for different amounts of money. This simple but integral economic act has varying significance in different historical stages of society, and has given rise to several debates amongst development economists.

Perhaps the most widespread confusion is about equating the presence of any form of capital in society with the development of capitalist mode of production. This is rooted in the failure to realise the simple fact that "(T)rade was born of the uneven development of production in different communities"[5] and hence trading or merchant capital could be (not necessarily though) a contemporary occurrence with this unevenness long before the advent of capitalism[6]. Moreover, there is a fundamental difference in the nature and economic significance of production and circulation of commodities in different social formations. Whereas in pre-capitalist formations "it is surpluses above necessity—which are traded" and "not means of production and means of subsistence required for reproduction", capitalism "necessarily produces its product as a commodity"[7].

Another area of debate concerns the role of merchant capital in structuring the production process of society or reacting upon the social mode of production in which it operates. Notwithstanding the long held position of Marxists that the development of merchant capital "is incapable by itself of promoting and explaining the transition from one mode of production to another"[8] and that "the dissolving effect depends very much on the nature of the producing communities between which it operates"[9], there is a discernible tendency to exaggerate the progressive role of merchant capital in dissolving pre-capitalist societies and heralding a capitalist society[10]. Particularly the 'massive efflorescence of merchant's capital', characteristic of 'the period of transition from feudalism to capitalism and the early stages of development of capitalism'[11], to be seen in many of the present-day Third World Societies has aggravated the confusion about the progressive or regressive role of merchant capital in these societies.

The correct line of argument in this debate should be set in the celebrated enunciation of Marx in *Capital*, Vol. III, namely, "The independent development of merchant's capital... stands in inverse proportion to the general economic development of society"[12]. The 'independent' or the sole, form of capital assumed by merchant's capital in society, is the crucial parameter of our current concern. In order to understand its fuller implications, we have to first understand the dynamics of the relation between productive and circulation capital. It is well known formulation of the Marxist labour theory of value that surplus value arises in production and not in exchange, and merchant capital as capital functioning in the sphere of circulation pockets surplus-value in the form of average profit at the expense of the profit of productive capital. However, in so far as it performs the function of *realizing value* by mediating between the producer and the consumer, it is entitled to receive a profit equivalent to the general rate of profit (calculated not on the total productive capital alone, but on the total productive plus merchant capital). Yet the bitter truth remains that the surplus-value embodied in the value of commodities produced and to be shared as profits by different capitals remains the same, and the profits of productive and merchant capital are thus inversely related[13].

This dilemma assumes graver proportions in the case of underdeveloped countries where merchant capital exists as the sole, and hence 'independent', form of capital within the indigenous economy but as an agent of foreign industrial capital in the context of global economy. This apparent paradox of simultaneously retaining and losing its 'independence' by the merchant capital has doubly depressing consequences for the underdeveloped countries by way of, firstly, repressing general economic development in proportion to the 'independence' of merchant capital, and secondly, reorganisation of the whole economy to the requirements of external economic interests, which Kay very aptly refers to as the *'specifica differentia* of underdevelopment'[14]. Because here merchant capital derives its profits from two sources: surplus value of productive capital in the developed countries and the surplus product of non-capitalist producers in the underdeveloped countries. This would not only strengthen and prolong the merchant phase of capital but would increasingly turn the indigenous merchant capital into comprador capital. Thus the doubly regressive role of conserving the archaic formation and giving an extravert orientation to the economy would be played by merchant capital in the present-day underdeveloped countries, unlike its progressive role of preparing grounds for transition to capitalism in the case of developed countries in the past. The reorganisation of production required by this pattern of trade would need so little capitalisation that there would be no direct involvement of productive capital on a significant scale[15].

A further area of discord has been the characterisation of trade relations between the developed and underdeveloped economies. It was Emmanuel[16] who attempted a radical theorisation of international trade relations in place of the traditional comparative costs doctrine and the subsequent terms of trade explanations. But his explanation of 'unequal exchange' in trade relations between poor (low wage) and rich (high wage) countries in terms of differing wage levels but equalisation of profit rates through mobility of capital resulting in net drain of value from poor to rich countries, has been criticised by subsequent authors[17] as being methodologically invalid. Alternative explanations have instead been advanced consistent with the law of value. It has been rightly stressed that so long as there is a general rate of profit ruling in the economy and different branches of industry have different organic composition of capital, unequal exchange between commodities produced at different technical level would be the natural rule and would be perfectly consistent with the law of value. Extending the same analogy to the international level, goods produced in economies with higher than average organic composition of capital, or higher labour productivity, would sell above their value and those produced in economies with lower than average composition of capital, or lower labour productivity, would sell below their value. Every transaction between the two would involve a drain of value out of the underdeveloped economy and would thus reduce the pace of accumulation there. Thus despite the differences in characterising the mechanism of value transfer[18] it is generally accepted that trade relations between primary-products exporting underdeveloped economy and finished-products-exporting developed economy would be marked by 'unequal exchange' to the net detriment of the former.

4.1.12 Financial Capital and Underdevelopment

Just as trade was born of uneven development of production in different communities, so was credit born of the uneven development of production among different producers within the same community[19]. Hence not only the history but also many of the characteristics and social implications of interest-bearing capital through its various historical forms are similar to those of merchant capital. It may therefore be necessary at the outset to distinguish between different historical forms of interest-bearing capital.

Usurer's capital, which "lives in the pores of production"[20], is the oldest form of capital predominating in pre-capitalist societies. With the advent of the banking system as a special business of money-dealing in the place of private money-dealers and usurers and with the change in the character of the borrowers to a potential capitalist (industrial or merchant) as against a primarily consumptionist previously interest-bearing capital can be said to have acquired a marked distinction from the usurer's capital while retaining the same basic nature or character[21]. Whereas the mass of this capital 'existing outside the production process' and 'yet affected by and affecting it in several ways' may be termed as *financial capital*[22], the integration of financial and industrial capital in such a manner that 'the relationship ceases to be at arm's length and in which the banks are the dominant partners' would give rise to *finance capital.*[23] Thus the structure of money-dealing capital in a pre-capitalist, transitional society with a marked presence of bank-capital may be better understood in terms of 'financial capital', and it is in this sense that the term is used throughout this study.

By these very definitions, interest-bearing capital in its different historical forms can be visualised to play different roles in reorganising the production process in society. The reactionary role of usurer's capital in preserving the archaic social relations, particularly semi-feudalism, has been well-highlighted[24] and generally accepted. The "revolutionary effect" of usury in pre-capitalist societies in the form of "ruining the feudal lord and small-scale producers, on the one hand, and centralising the conditions of labour into capital on the other", as visualised by Marx[25], may not be sufficiently felt in the present-day. Third World conditions where the fulfillment of "the other prerequisites of capitalist production" are increasingly getting remoter under the interventionist impact of metropolitan capital. As regards the role of financial capital or bank capital, in the backward formations it is so indissolutely linked with usurer's capital that it is hardly, likely to be any different. Moreover, the general tendency of 'loan capital' to move 'in the opposite direction to that of industrial capital', as expressed in the higher interest rates enjoyed by the former over the latter[26], may be more operative in the less industrialised conditions, and proliferation of financial/bank capital in them may further depress the development of industrial capital.

In the international plane, finance capital as the principal vehicle of domination of 'a vast majority of debtor states' by 'a handful of usurer states' has been the core of modern theory of imperialism[27]. In the case of the more depressed Third World Countries, however, where the possibilities of direct foreign capital investments are dimmer, metropolitan capital has devised subtle ways of penetrating through 'aid', both bilateral and multilateral. This 'aid as imperialism' is intended not only to ensure steady transfer of value from underdeveloped countries through debt-servicing, etc. by trapping them in a vicious 'debt trap', but also to create and sustain a class within these countries that would permanently ally with imperialism and prepare grounds for future private investments[28]. Thus the ultimate results of these acts of 'sweetening the pills of exploitation' would be counter-productive for the underdeveloped countries, and hence any scientific analysis of the causative factors of underdevelopment should take into account these apparently non-economic factors.

4.1.13 Spatial Implications

Basically a mediating process between the producer and the consumer, or between the producers themselves, the spatial implications of circulation activities would be totally determined by the locales of production and consumption. Hence they would be overwhelmingly space-forming than space-contingent. As it is the large settlements or urban areas where "the geographies of production and consumption interlock"[29], circulation capital would tend to centralise there and hence aggravate spatial inequality. Moreover, since circulation capital "tends to centralise and concentrate itself into monopolies even faster than productive capital"[30], translated into spatial terms proliferation of circulation capital would mean proportionate increase in spatial disparateness. In a situation of extreme backwardness and extravert orientation of economy circulation capital by its greater articulation with outside economy would give a further outward tilt to the overall spatial organisation of the economy.

4.1.2 Historical Antecedents

In keeping with the distinctive historical significance of different branches of circulation capital as outline in the preceding section, the historical contours of commercial/merchant and money-dealing capital in Nepal may be sketched separately and their combined spatial articulation summed up ultimately.

4.1.21 Merchant Capital

As mentioned in the earlier chapter, annals of history bear adequate testimony to a fairly well developed mercantile interactions of Kathmandu Valley with India and Tibet, thus confirming that "foreign trade antedates domestic trade"[31]. On closer analysis it is also discerned that the observed prevalence of merchant capital was mostly confined to entrepot trade between India and Tibet rather than the Nepalese indigenous trade[32]. The exigencies of nature and history were so placed that of the few prominent trans-Himalayan passes which provided trade routes between Indian sub-continent and Central Asia, particularly Tibet, the ones just north of Kathmandu Valley were the lowest (i.e. below 14000 ft.) and the most favourably located. Moreover, settlements along the Nepalese mid-montane provided favourable entrepot for the traders as winter snows closed the Himalayan passes and malaria and monsoons made the jungle-belt to the south impregnable in summer[33].

Besides the entrepot trade that was the predominant form of trade and an 'independent' economic activity of professional traders mostly confined to Kathmandu Valley, trade in subsistence goods, both in barter terms and mediated through money, was practised between the peoples of diverse physiographic zones as governed by the territorial division of labour forced by nature. For, such essentials as salt were not to be found in Nepal. With the increased interactions with the outside economy and aggravation of both social and spatial unevenness, trade in conspicuous consumption goods, and monopolised by Kashmiri and Gosain traders from India, kept on flourishing with passing time. The political unification of the country led to the bourgeoning of administrative centres throughout the country, which in turn attracted mercantile activities that were mainly performed by specialised traders from Kathmandu Valley.

With the semi-colonial integration of the country to British India after the Sugauli Treaty of 1816 the traditional middleman role of Nepal in the India-Tibet trade was gradually weakened and increasingly replaced by bilateral trade with India. The qualitative transformation in this process was made with the extension of Indian railway networks to the southern Nepalese borders by the end of the 19th century, which created a vast export market for timber and agro-produce of Nepal Terai and facilitated penetration of Nepalese internal market by British Indian manufactures. The gradual dwindling of entrepot trade with the direct plying of steam ship between Indian and Chinese ports after the 19th century and its final collapse with the opening-up of direct India-Tibet trade route via Chumbi Valley (Sikkim) in 1904, marked the end of significant role played by entrepot trade in the Nepalese economy. Thus the near continuous stream of India-Nepal-Tibet trade was finally broken up into two separate segments of Nepal-Tibet and Nepal India trade, with the increasing domination of the latter both in volume and social implication. The domination of mercantile interactions with India in the total external trade was further aggravated with the trade treaty of 1923 allowing for free flow of British Indian goods to Nepal. With the near cessation of Nepal-Tibet trade after the Tibetan revolution and intensification of economic integration of the country to India after the 1950s, the total domination of India in the matter of external trade of Nepal was completed. This historical transformation of the nature of external trade of Nepal may be schematically depicted as in Fig. 4.1.

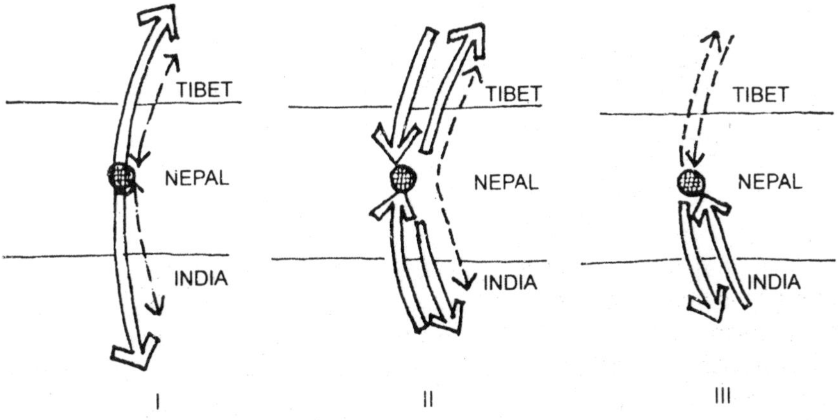

Fig. 4.1 Evolution of External Trade Pattern.

Though no registered account of the volume of Nepal–India trade is available prior to 1875, a collection of import-export figures from sundry sources, as presented in Table 4.1 provides important insights into the historical pattern of growth of trade between the two countries. The hitherto existing balance of trade in favour of Nepal prior to the Sugauli Treaty (1816) is seen to have reversed immediately after the Treaty, which was the logical economic manifestations of the semi-colonial integration of the country to the then vast British empire. The phenomenal expansion of trade in the late 19th century could be viewed as the sign of vastly increased economic integration to British India in the aftermath of extension of railways to the Tẹrai borders. The redeeming feature of the relation was the restoration of trade balance in favour of Nepal, which was the result of massive exports of timber and agro-products from the freshly cultivated Terai. However, the gradual deindustrialisation of Nepal after the first quarter of 20th century (see Chapter 3.1.2) and the lack of structural transformation of society to match the changes in India in between the two World Wars, set in a motion of adverse exchange relations between the two economies, which culminated in a severe adverse balance of payment against Nepal by the 1950s.

Table 4.1 Volume of Nepal-India Trade During the 19th and Early 20th Century.

(In Rs. Million)

Years	*Export Value*	*Import Value*	*Export/Import Ratio*
1809–10[1]	0.364	0.710	5.120
1830–31[2]	1.000	1.600	0.625
1890–91[3]	1.720	1.290	1.333
1895–96[4]	1.834	1.362	1.346
1900–01[3]	2.360	1.630	1.448
1911–12[5]	4.368	2.213	1.973
1915–16[5]	3.949	2.070	1.908
1920–21[5]	5.969	2.820	2.117
1924–25[5]	5.820	2.794	2.083

Source: 1. Buchanan cited in Regmi, M.C. (1971), *A Study in Nepali Economic History 1768–1846*, Manjushri Publishing House, New Delhi, pp. 150–51.
2. Brian H. Hodgson quoted in *ibid*, p. 170.
3. Sen, J. (1977), *Indo-Nepal Trade in the Nineteenth Century*, Firma KLM Private Ltd., Calcutta, p. 28.
4. Stiller, L.F. (1972), "A Note on Himalayan Trade", *Journal of the Tribhuvan University*, Vol. III, No. 1, Kathmandu, November, p. 28.
5. Banskota, N.P. (1981), *Indo-Nepal Trade and Economic Relations*, B.R. Publishing House, Delhi, p. 23.

As a corollary to the predominance of primary production and marginal interactions of entrepot trade with indigenous production system, the structure of export-import trade of Nepal throughout history can be expectedly seen to have been characterised by that of a typical underdeveloped country, i.e. export of primary produce and import of manufactures. Only in the case of trade with Tibet, besides the re-export of manufactured products from India, certain locally processed or manufactured items like metal-ware, ivory goods, wooden vessels and coarse varieties of cloth were exported and subsistence goods like salt and animals and animal products from Tibet were bartered with foodgrains and spices from Nepal. The structure of bilateral trade with India was from the beginning a typical case of 'unequal exchange' between the primary produce with low labour content from Nepal and manufactures with relatively high labour content from India. This pattern, however, is seen to have undergone changes with increasing adversity against Nepal with the passage of time. For example, whereas the import of manufactured goods in the 19th century was limited to the luxury consumptions of the upper classes and the net drain of value away was camouflaged under the favourable balance of trade, with the rapid deindustrialisation of the countryside after the first quarter of the 20th century the volume of import of manufactures increased disproportionately in relation to the export of primary produce, mostly grains and timber, and the net drain of value away from the economy was aggravated by declining balance of trade. The scenario in the first and second decades of the 20th century is empirically captured in Tables 4.2 and 4.3.

Table 4.2 Structure of Exports to India in Early 20th Century.

(Rs. '000)

Commodities	*1913–1914*		*1920–1921*	
	Value	*%*	*Value*	*%*
1. Cattle	3399	7.85	2980	4.99
2. Dye stuffs	867	2.00	1561	2.62
3. Fruits, Vegetables and Nuts	726	1.68	6878	11.52
4. Rice Husked	6897	15.94	8261	13.84
5. Rice Unhusked	9039	20.89	10953	18.35
6. Hides of cattle	2067	4.78	704	1.18
7. Jute (Raw)	3623	8.37	2888	4.84
8. Ghee	3186	7.36	5461	9.15
9. Linseed	953	2.20	1636	2.74
10. Mustards Rope	3098	7.16	4905	8.22
11. Spices	1260	2.91	1119	1.87
12. Tobacco	1237	2.86	1697	2.84
13. Others	6923	16.00	10650	17.84
TOTAL	43275	100.00	59693	100.00

Source: Adapted From Banskota, N.P. (1981), *Indo-Nepal Trade and Economic Relations*, B.R. Publishing House, Delhi, p. 25.

Table 4.3 Structure of Imports from India During Early 20th Century.

Commodities	*1913–1914*		*1920–1921*	
	Value (Rs. '000)	*%*	*Value (Rs. '000)*	*%*
1. Twist and Yarn	2142	10.46	2272	8.06
2. Piece goods	7583	37.03	10313	36.57
3. Metals and Metalware	1983	9.68	2231	7.91
4. Oils	1039	5.07	1163	4.12
5. Salt	1202	5.87	1490	5.28
6. Spices	1199	5.85	1856	6.58
7. Sugar	1024	5.00	1767	6.27
8. Tobacco	745	3.64	908	3.22
9. Others	3563	17.40	6293	22.31
TOTAL	20480	100.00	28203	100.00

Source: Adapted From Banskota, N.P. (1981), *Indo-Nepal Trade and Economic Relations*, B.R. Publishing House, Delhi, p. 25.

Evolution of social class base of traders constitutes an important ensemble in historically defining the role of merchant capital in social development. In the Nepalese history, by the very nature of predominance of external trade, that too entrepot trade, and a very low articulation of social division of labour in the indigenous economy, the social base of the mercantilists are known to be either totally independent of the production system or too inarticulated necessitating direct state intervention. Though an indigenous community of Newar traders fully engaged in 'buying to sale and selling to buy 'is known to have emerged in the Kathmandu Valley since quite early times, by the 17th and 18th century they were reduced to acting as mere retailers and most of the wholesale trade was monopolised by Indian merchants, particularly Gosains and Kashmiris, who had their agents or establishments at different commercial centres in India, Nepal and Tibet[34]. After a temporary expulsion of these 'outsiders' in the wake of a fierce pseudo-nationalistic passion whipped up during the state unification campaign, they are known to have staged a comeback with greater vengeance after the Sugauli Treaty[35]. Also there were ample instances of Tibetan traders travelling down south to the Indian border and Indian traders travelling to Nepalese Terai towns and hills for enacting direct commodity exchanges. In the absence of a local merchant class that could effectively counter the influences of the foreign traders and to directly appropriate commercial profit and tax revenue, the Nepalese state at least from 19th century onwards is known to have directly intervened in external trade through the establishment of trade depots at strategic points and exercising total monopoly of trade in certain commodities or in certain routes. Apart from the subtle form of state trading, the ruling families and nobility are known to have directly controlled much of the external trade from early times[36]. Perhaps it was only the Newar traders amongst the indigenous social groups, who exercised a dominant control in Nepal-Tibet trade till the 1950s and controlled much of the trade in inner countryside, that could be called genuine merchant-capitalists. The new merchant class that emerged in the Terai after the late 19th century was either directly connected with feudal land-owning classes or consisted of immigrants from India who had little stake in the reproduction of the indigenous socio-economic system. The petty traders of the high Mountains, who combined agriculture with barter trade for their subsistence, could hardly be termed mercantalists, except perhaps some professional trading groups like Bhotias of Oolangchung and Sherpas of Namchebazar (both in eastern Mountain) and Thakalies of Tukche (central Mountain), who did manage to diversify their occupation after the cessation of Tibetan trade[37].

On the basis of the foregoing historical overview, it would be pertinent to summerise the essential characteristics of merchant capital in Nepal and the historical impediments in its progressive transformation into production capital, thus remaining a factor in the aggravation of underdevelopment. We may summarily state that:

- Despite the fairly long life of merchant capital in the economy and society of Nepal and despite its proliferation with time, it was not really big in absolute size. The trade with British India though had increased over time, had a narrow base for unlimited expansion because of limited commodities of exchange and greater interests of British colonialists to procure soldiers than goods. The Tibetan market was not very wide because of its scanty population and treacherous terrain, and the scope of entrepot trade got snapped after the opening up of Chumbi Valley route.
- It was mainly confined to entrepot trade, which was little integrated to the indigenous production system and hence had little stake in its expanded reproduction. In other words, this nature of 'independence' of merchant capital was antagonistic to the development of production capital, as originally theorised by Marx.
- Internal trade was more in luxury consumption goods than in subsistence and production goods, and thus had little impact in the production system.
- Trade was mostly controlled by alien merchant capitalists, specially the British Indians, whose fate was more closely tied with the British colonial economy. The indigenous feudal-mercantilists, who also controlled a sizeable trade, expended their commercial profits in luxury consumption rather than in productive investment. The early monopoly in trade, both private and state, was also not conducive for expanded reproduction of capital, as it killed the drive of 'free' competition.
- With the widening of already existing gap in the level of social development vis-à-vis the British Indian economy, the major trading partner, and development of 'unequal exchange' relations with it, which was to aggravate further with the passing time, merchant capital became a fetter than liberator of productive forces in the society.
- Because of physical seclusion of much of the countryside for the lack of transportation linkages across rugged terrains, merchant capital was further constrained from performing the 'historic' role of dissolving the primitive society; it thus continued to survive in the pores of old society.

4.1.22 Money-Dealing Capital

Commensurate with the fairly high stage of development of foreign trade with India and Tibet (China) money as medium of exchange had made an early appearance in the Nepalese history, for even elsewhere in history money is known to have been necessitated by foreign trade long before its use in internal trade[38] Thus just prior to the political unification of the country in the 18th century, wide circulation of currency at least in and around Kathmandu Valley principalities is manifest in minting of silver coins in Kathmandu and their being sent as the principal legal tender in circulation in Tibet[39]. Prevalence of money-dealing capital in the form of usurer's capital even in the countryside is evident from the well-known legal formulation of 17th century king Ram Shah of Gorkha in fixing the interest rate at 10%.

After the semi-colonial integration of the country to British colonial India in the first quarter of the 19th century, a number of factors such as remittances by Nepalese soldiers in British Indian army, increased penetration of merchant capital from outside and enhanced revenue extraction in cash by the state, could be expected, to have increased the scope of money-dealing capital in the country's economy. However, massive injection of money into the economy, perhaps unprecedented in the society's history, was to be witnessed in the wake of sudden boost of Nepalese timber and agro-products exports triggered by the extension of Indian railways to Nepal Terai. But the windfall gains from trade were pocketed by the Rana rulers and the nobility, and got expended in the construction of palatial buildings and conspicuous consumption that ultimately applied a break to larger circulation of money in the society. Still the enhanced role of money in the general economy then is reflected in the establishment in 1880 of 'Tejarathi' system of providing loans to the people of Kathmandu Valley at 5% interest against bullion as colateral security as well as to government servants against recovery from their salary at the source. Though the activities of this fore-runner of the modern banking system were extended to other areas of the country with the turn of the century, since it did not accept deposits and advanced loans against collateral securities only, it spawned money just as 'money' but not as 'capital'[40] Standardization of land revenue on money terms and extension of the system of its realisation in cash to all parts of the country (previously it was confined only to the Terai and western Mountain-Hill) by the first decade of the 20th century (see Chapter 2.1.2 above), also indicates the newly acquired significance of money in the economy. Regular remittances by emigrant workers to Indian cities and high amount of cash brought back by over 200 thousand Nepalese soldiers in British Indian army during the First World War, played a very important role in monetising the hill economy.

The exigencies of Second World War and a set of internal and external factors, as pointed out in the earlier chapter, resulted in the birth of modern industrial capital in the country in the 1930s, and as a corollary to the same historical process the first commercial bank, the Nepal Bank Ltd., was established in 1937 with the state owning 51% of the paid-up capital and the rest by private financiers. Still, the establishment of the first central bank of the country, i.e. Nepal Rastra Bank, was to await till 1956 and dealing in the country's foreign currency till 1960 was entrusted to the Indian Reserve Bank, thus indicating total financial dependence on India. Only the somewhat favourable historical coincidences of the early 1960s, as explained in the earlier chapter, gave rise to a number of specialised and commercial banks and financial institutions under the state aegis[41], which sought to channelise accumulated money-capital to the advantage of new alignments of the ruling classes. However, as a natural outcome of the low development of productive forces in society much of the countryside remained outside the effective interplay of money in the economy, and whatever money-dealing capital existed assumed the form of usury monopolised by private money-lenders, land-lords and merchants.

Significant insights into the history of money in Nepalese society, in general, and fluctuations in relative strength of the economy vis-à-vis that of India, in particular, may be obtained from a study of changing relations of Nepali currency (NC) with Indian currency (IC). Table 4.4:

Table 4.4 Annual Average NC/IC Exchange Rate (1876–1960).

Years	*Exchange Rate*
1876	120
1932	128
1937	144
1941	128
1945	83
1950	104
1955	177
1960	161

Note: Exchange Rate is in Rs. N.C. per Rs. 100 I.C.

Source: 1. Shrestha, B.P. (1962), *An Introduction to Nepalese Economy*, Ratna Pustak Bhandar, Kathmandu (1981 edn.), p. 173.

2. Pant, Y.P. (1970), *Problem in Fiscal and Monetary Policy: A Case Study of Nepal*, C. Hurst, London, p. 161.

The exchange rate is seen to have remarkably stabilized from the last quarter of 19th to the first quarter of the 20th century; thereby indicating relative soundness in relations between the two economics. With the rise in imports of Indian manufactures in the face of rapid deindustrialisation of Nepal after the first quarter of the 20th century, the exchange rate is seen to have turned increasingly unfavourable towards Nepal. However, the favourable turn in trade relations during the Second World War and heavy remittances in Indian currency by Nepalese soldiers after the war, not only checked the downward slide of NC but gave it a temporary upper hand; only to restart a down-hill journey soon after. The catastrophic slide of NC during the 1950s in the face of renewed and recharged economic aggrandisement of Indian monopoly capital after the stage-managed political change of 1951, is too recent to recapitulate. The net result was a massive flight of accumulated money-capital to India, as the money hoards were found to be safter in Indian currency and in Indian coffers.

The logical inferences to be drawn from a study of the history of money in Nepal, which are relevant for the articulation of underdevelopment process, are thus:

- Money has been increasingly mediating acts of economic exchanges in the society, but it has been mostly confined to exchanges with outside economy and thus has not been able to increase the velocity of internal exchanges;
- Because of low differentiation of the economy and hegemony exercised by feudals and comprador mercantile classes who controlled the state, the

overwhelming proportion of money was acquired as 'revenue' and accumulated as 'hoard', rather than circulated as 'capital';

- Money that went into circulation was confined to mercantile activities and seldom found its way into production purposes. In the countryside, money largely took the form of usurer's capital, which merely reproduced existing and retrograde social relations of production;
- With the increasing domination of Indian economy and accumulation of money hoard in Indian currency because of its greater stability and credibility, the 'potential capital' was systematically drained towards the more stronger Indian economy.

4.1.23 Spatial Differentiation

Because of low absolute level of circulation activities concomittant with the low level of social development aggravated by physiographic constraints, their spatial differentiation may not be marked in Nepalese history. Nevertheless, by the very nature of extreme physical diversities and discernible historical changes in the pattern of economic circulation particularly with regard to external integration, the spatial characteristics of the process should assume definite relevance.

Since external trade, specially entrepot trade between India and Tibet, constituted the major economic circulation activity and it required traversing across diverse physiographic zones, natural factors like attitudinal position of Himalayan passes and alignments of courses of mountain rivers, etc. seem to have exercised decisive influence in the original spatial configuration of circulation activities (see Fig. 4.2) As mentioned earlier, both natural and social factors made Kathmandu Valley the most ideal location as an entrepot and it graduated into a focal point of trading activities for the entire hilly region. Backed by the politico-administrative apparatus of the state capital, it retained its supremacy as the principal trading centre throughout history. After the establishment of a unified state incorporating petty hill principalities, it played a centripetal role[42] in mediating the whatever meagre economic interactions that took place along the east-west hilly spine.

Because of its natural advantages for varied agricultural production and proximity to India for exchange of commodities, the Terai region is known to have "the most developed market economy[43] at least since the 18th century. However, the economic interactions were invariably oriented towards India and there was "almost total lack of commercial intercourse between hill region and Terai" as the "two regions had almost nothing to offer in exchange to each other."[44] The commercial importance of Terai was unduly enhanced and extraversion in spatial interactions greatly increased after the extension of Indian rail-heads to selected towns just across the Terai. Of the two major trading zones that developed subsequently, namely eastern Terai with Bengal on the one hand and western Terai with North-West Provinces and Oudh on the other, the former transacted almost three times more trade in value than the latter[45], thus indicating

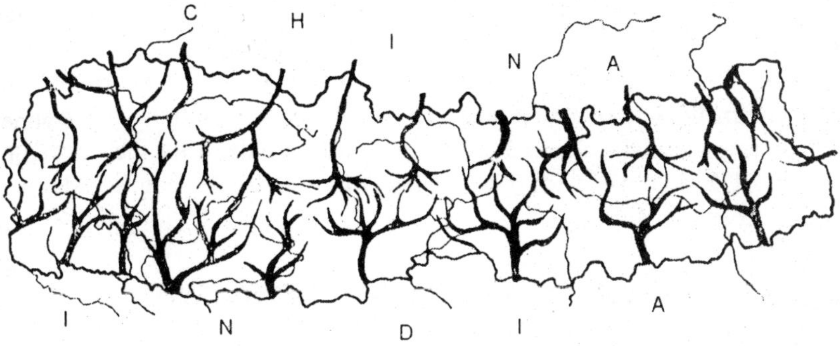

BEFORE 1950s

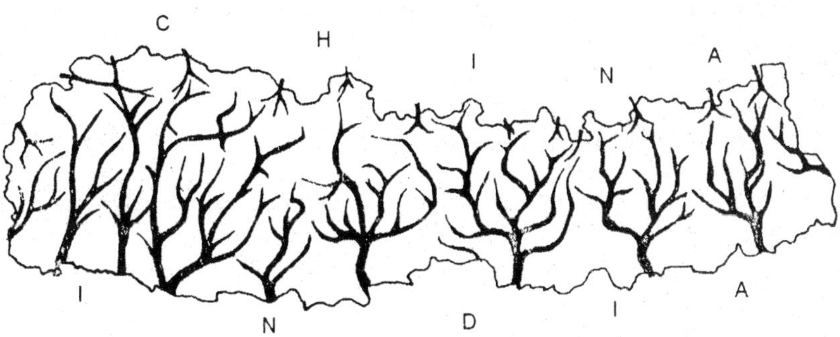

AFTER 1950s

Fig. 4.2 Principal Trade Routes Before and After 1950s.

the domination of eastern Terai in economic circulation activities. The pattern can be assumed to have continued even afterwards.

In the central east-west hilly spine, as a natural consequence to the predominance of subsistence peasant and artisan production, trade was "generally related to the needs of subsistence and was seldom and independent means of livlihood"[6]. The inhabitants of hill regions travelled to nearest Terai markets to exchange their primary produce for salt, kerosene, cloth, etc., or at times to the nearest Indian towns with money. But due to the lack of economic complimentarities and due to transportation constraints across rugged hills and torrential rivers, there was "almost total lack of trade and other intercourse between eastern and western parts"[47].

In the northern-most Mountain region, trade was always a part of economic life. But the form of trade varied from barter of Tibetan salt and animal produce with food-grains from hill regions as a suplimentary means of subsistence in the majority of cases, and wholesale entrepot trade as an exclusive profession in other cases. Also the volume of trade and level of overall economic prosperity varied according to the importance of entrepot trade across the relevant trade routes[48].

In the spatio-temporal dimensions, the traditionally disarticulated and extraverted commercial spatial structure and its further aggravation with near-total orientation towards the South and from it towards India after the cessation of commercial intercourse with Tibet (China) by the 1950s, can be adequately captured from Fig. 4.2.

4.2 ARTICULATION OF MERCHANT CAPITAL WITHIN

Articulation within here essentially concerns with the first and last acts in the circuit of circulation capital in a pre-capitalist economy integrated to the metropolitan economy[49] (i.e. purchase of commodities from the direct producer and sale of the imported and locally acquired commodities, both primary and secondary, to the direct consumers or retailers) plus the acts of primitive exchanges within the indigenous social economy.

4.2.1 Level of Marketisation

In the absence of a systematic inventory of the total economic activities mediated through the market mechanism, not to speak of their disaggregration into spatio-temporal dimensions, it is virtually impossible to make a quantitative estimation of extent of marketisation of the Nepalese economy. Within the prevailing data constraints we have sought to piece together information from sundry sources and earlier fragmentary studies to arrive at a reasonable account of the level of marketisation.

4.2.11 Measures of the extent of household cash expenditure incurred on different commodities and services, as presented in Appendix-6 helps us to form an opinion about the role of market in reproducing the household economy in a society presumed to be overwhelmingly dominated by use-value production and characterised by economic disarticulation. A recapitulation of micro-level studies of earlier students[50] and our own delineation of historical contours of the process of merchant capital should, however, preclude any such absolutist formulations. Even though it is still impossible to gauge the exact proportion of income realised and expenditure incurred in cash, it is clear that the absolute level of marketisation of the economy in larger parts of the country is quite dismal. Spatial differentiation of the attribute, on the other hand, appears quite significant. Not only do Kathmandu Valley and Terai in general and important urban settlements in particular, have high proportion of income accrued as 'business profit', cash expenditure on various consumption goods tends to increase progressively from Mountain-Hill to Terai and from west to east, thus indicating a spatial pattern of increasing marketisation along the same territorial dimensions.

4.2.12 Some idea of the absolute level of marketisation of the economy by different territorial zones can be obtained from the proportion of principal agricultural produce (i.e. rice, wheat, maize and potato) entering into the market (i.e. inter-district flow) and the share of total cereal grains acquired through the market (Table 4.5). In not taking into account the marketed value of such subsistence goods as salt, kerosene, etc. and other manufactured products like cloth, which have been the traditional items of exchange, the said measures of only the agricultural produce may be a gross underestimation of overall level of marketisation; nevertheless, in view of the predominantly agrarian nature of the economy, it should present a fair approximation of the real picture, at least in a relative sense over territorial zones. At the macro-level it is seen that about 30% of the major agricultural produce enters into the market[51]. Viewed in the territorial frame, a progressive decline from north to south, except for the Kathmandu Valley, is observable, which fully conforms to the spatial differentiation of level of agricultural development and availability of marketable surplus, as brought out in the earlier chapter. Along the east-west territorial dimension, whereas the progressive decline in the level of marketisation from east to west in Mountain and Hill is quite understandable, a higher proportion of marketed value in western Terai and Inner Terai may have to be explained in terms of greater economic inequality and thus greater appropriation of marketable surplus in those areas than in their eastern counterparts. The measure of level of marketisation with respect to total commodity flow (i.e. inclusive of total exports and imports) and total foodgrain consumption, also provides the same pattern of spatial differentiation, but of higher degree.

4.2.13 For a total picture of level of marketisation a composite measure of all the commodities (i.e. both indigenously produced and imported and both primary and manufactured products) exchanged through various forms of markets, including periodic and mobile markets, in a dynamic frame, is required. In the absence of the desired statistical data we have sought to calculate density distribution of trading establishments with respect to total households and per caput sale by territorial zones (Table 4.6).

A very low level of commodity exchange through markets is evident from the low figures of the number of trading establishment per 1000 households and per caput sale per month[52]. Wide disparity in territorial dimensions marked by highest concentration in Kathmandu Valley followed by Terai, Inner Terai and Hill respectively, however, fully conforms to the historical pattern of development of merchant capital in the country. In the micro-spatial terms, higher levels of marketisation seen in the central eastern Terai-central Inner Terai-Kathmandu Valley (or, Birgunj–Hetauda–Kathmandu) axis and around the traditional trading outposts of Terai, like Biratnagar in far-eastern, Birgunj in central-eastern, Bhairahawa in central and Nepalgunj, in western Terai, further confirms the continuation of the same historical pattern. In the most depressed areas of Hill, the central section is seen to be at a higher level of development of marketisation,

Table 4.5 Marketing Condition of Agricultural Commodities* by Territorial Zones (1971/72).

(Rs. Million)

Territorial Zones	*Total inflow to*	*Total Cutflow from*	*Intra-regional Flow*	*Total Produce marketed*	*Total Commodity flow*	*Total Production*	*Total Consumption (7) =*	*% of (4) to (6)*	*% of (5) to (7)*
	(1)	*(2)*	*(3)*	*(4)=(2)+(3)*	*(5)=(1)+(4)*	*(6)*	*(6)+(1)–(2)*	*(8)*	*(9)*
MOUNTAIN	17.197	9.718	0.909	10.627	28.124	184.216	132.295	5.77	–
Eastern	5.957	6.393	0.290	6.683	12.640	79.408	78.972	8.42	16.01
Central	3.165	1.681	–	1.681	4.846	20.957	22.441	8.02	21.59
Western	8.375	1.644	0.619	2.263	10.638	84.151	30.882	2.69	11.71
HILL		108.364	65.985	22.418	88.403	196.767	869.397	911.776	10.17
21.58		Eastern	18.291	55.178	7.247	62.425	80.716	335.507	298.62
18.61	27.03		Central	39.424	9.534	6.844	16.378	55.802	320.638
350.528	5.11	15.92		Western	50.649	1.273	8.327	9.600	60.249
213.252	262.628	4.50	22.94						
KATHMANDU VALLEY	55.416	3.208	17.813	21.021	76.437	168.975	221.983	12.44	34.56
INNER TERAI	35.004	114.394	5.043	119.437	154.441	341.801	262.411	34.94	58.85
Eastern	21.239	10.138	0.329	10.467	31.706	75.868	86.979	13.79	36.45
Central	11.963	68.139	4.714	72.853	84.816	163.214	107.038	44.64	79.24
Western	1.802	36.117	–	36.117	37.919	102.709	68.394	35.16	55.44
TERAI	41.738	671.195	54.266	726.16	767.888	1691.096	1061.639	42.94	72.33
Eastern:	39.549	437.609	30.552	468.161	507.700	1114.245	716.185	42.02	70.89
Far-Eastern	16.863	159.919	0.050	159.969	176.822	324.551	181.495	49.29	97.43
Mid- Eastern	11.539	184.312	2.638	186.95	198.489	452.835	280.062	41.28	70.87
Eastern	11.147	93.378	27.864	121.242	132.389	336.859	254.628	35.99	55.99
Central	0.491	116.655	14.529	131.184	131.675	314.482	198.318	41.71	66.40
Western	1.698	116.931	9.884	126.815	128.513	262.369	147.136	48.33	87.34
NEPAL	258.019	864.500	101.148	965.648	1223.667	3255.467	2648.986	29.66	46.19

Note: * Agricultural commodities include rice, wheat, maize and potato.

Source: HMG/N, Ministry of Food, Agriculture and Irrigation (1976), *Report on Trade Flow Survey of Agricultural Commodities Particularly Cereal Grains in Nepal 1971/72*, Department of Food and Agricultural Marketing Services, Bag Bazar, Kathmandu.

which is not surprising in view of its historically closer proximity to Kathmandu Valley and subsequent greater integration with the outside economy. As per the remote Mountain zone, though no statistical data are available, common knowledge of the economy of the area indicates a significant level of marketisation[53]. A recent survey of marketing in a central Mountain district[54] establishments this point and brings out that there are about 10.61 trading establishments per 1000 households. This appears quite reasonable compared to the figures for other zones cites here.

Table 4.6 Level of Development of Marketing by Territorial Zones (1979/80).

Territorial Zones	*No. of trading establishments per 1000 households**	*Per caput sale per month* (Rs.)*
MOUNTAIN	N.A.	N.A.
HILL	3.82 (0.50)	4.31 (0.30)
Eastern	3.31 (0.43)	2.13 (0.15)
Central	4.14 (0.54)	5.64 (0.40)
Western	3.16 (0.41)	2.53 (0.18)
KATHMANDU VALLEY	27.85 (3.65)	55.00 (3.89)
INNER TERAI	6.47 (0.85)	8.95 (0.63)
Eastern	4.01 (0.53)	2.01 (0.14)
Central	8.48 (1.11)	14.62 (1.03)
Western	6.20 (0.81)	8.12 (0.57)
TERAI	8.48 (1.11)	17.58 (1.24)
Eastern	7.40 (0.97)	16.78 (1.19)
Far-Eastern	14.42 (1.89)	26.39 (1.87)
Mid-Eastern	4.03 (0.53)	4.32 (0.31)
Eastern	7.14 (0.94)	30.65 (2.17)
Central	10.01 (1.31)	20.92 (1.48)
Western	14.60 (1.91)	18.35 (1.30)
NEPAL	7.63 (1.00)	14.15 (1.00)

Note: *The absolute figures may be slightly inflated because of their being weighted by household and population based on 1976 mid-term census.
– Figures in parenthesis are location factors.

Source: Central Bureau of Statistics (1981) Report of Internal Trade Survey (Study) 1979/80 (Nepali), Kathmandu.

4.2.2 Structure of Commerce

The nature of commodities traded in terms of their intensity of value content (i.e. whether primary or secondary produce) and their immediate utility (i.e. whether for direct consumption of for production purposes) would indicate the state of exchange relations and thus the level of societal development. We have, therefore, attempted to analyse the structure of commerce by types of commodities traded classified into relevant categories. However, in the absence of the more relevant measure of the total *value of the said commodities traded*, our use here of the total *number of trading establishments* dealing *primarily* in the particular commodities would not only not account for the differences in the sizes of the trading establishments but the value of commodities traded by them as *secondary* items would be left out. Within these obvious limitations, Table 4.7 provides territorial distribution pattern of trading establishments dealing primarily in different commodities categorised into relevant groups.

The fact that two-thirds of the total trading units in the country primarily deal in basic subsistence goods of food-grains and cloth should amply reflect the primitive nature of commodity exchanges. There is no distinct pattern of territorial variations in this basic structure of commerce, though a generally high proportion in Hill and Inner Terai than in Kathmandu Valley and Terai is observable.

If the commodity groups are to be categorised into 'primary' and 'secondary' products[55], it is interesting to note that the percentage of shops dealing in secondary products (irrespective of the intensity of their processing) outnumber the ones dealing in primary products by 50 to 40, the remaining being unable to be classified. This otherwise perfectly logical pattern, however, reveals an important social logic behind it in the context of an economy overwhelmingly dominated by primary production. There is no other way of satisfactorily explaining this phenomenon other than by the historical fact of prevalence of 'external' trade over 'internal' trade in the country, i.e. there is less marketisation of indigenous production, and whatever commodities are internally circulated are mostly imported. In the micro-spatial dimensions the variations in the said pattern are not marked, except for a higher proportion of establishments dealing in primary produces in western Hill and central Inner Terai and significantly lower than national average of the same in western Inner Terai and eastern Terai. These, however, could be manifestations of different social realities; like a small number of trading units dealing in secondary products and a large number of those dealing in primary produces in the more depressed western Hill, and comparatively greater flow of secondary goods in the agriculturally more advanced Terai sub-zones.

The categorisation of marketed commodity groups by 'use-based 'classification (Table 4.8) shows an expectedly high proportion of shops dealing in consumer goods (i.e. 85.07%) and virtually insignificant ones for intermediate (i.e. 6.58%) and capital-cum-basic (i.e. 0.22%) goods. This once again confirms the retarded and inverted structure of economy as brought out in the preceding chapter. The apparently low share of durable consumer goods (i.e. 5.11%) as against an excessively high share of non-durable consumer goods (i.e. 79.96%), however, could be and underestimation of the real value of the former whose relatively high intensity of value could not be adequately reflected in the number of trading units dealing in them. In the territorial dimension, the pattern is almost identical reflecting the basically direct-consumption oriented marketisation in the country However, a discernible variation observable in the form of higher proportion of consumer-durable goods in far-eastern Terai (i.e. 8.57%) and Kathmandu Valley (i.e. 7.83%) is quite compatible with the greater prosperity of these areas and their tighter integration with the metropolitan economy.

Table 4.7 Territorial Distribution of Trading Establishments by Types of Commodities Sold (1979/80).

(%)

Territorial Zones / *Commodity Groups*	*(1)*	*(2)*	*(3)*	*(4)*	*(5)*	*(6)*	*(7)*	*(8)*	*(9)*	*(10)*	*(11)*	*(12)*	*(13)*	*(14)*	*(15)*	*(16)*	*Total*
MOUNTAIN	–	–	–	N–	O–	T–	–	A	V	A	I	L	A	B	I	E	
HILLS	0.56	2.99	2.92	40.70	29.88	–	0.03	1.06	3.25	0.40	0.10	0.07	–	14.23	0.90	2.92	100.00
Eastern	1.49	3.43	9.99	34.13	38.60	–	0.15	0.60	2.53	0.45	–	–	–	4.02	1.34	3.13	100.00
Central	0.19	3.19	0.97	40.83	28.57	–	–	1.06	3.67	0.39	0.14	0.10	–	17.13	0.87	2.90	100.00
Western	1.10	0.37	0.37	55.68	18.32	–	–	2.20	1.83	0.37	–	–	–	17.22	–	2.56	100.00
KATHMANDU VALLEY	0.52	2.89	1.73	42.15	20.32	0.66	2.98	1.76	3.44	4.25	0.23	0.72	0.49	1.99	2.86	12.98	100.00
INNER TERAI	1.02	2.46	1.78	42.41	28.67	0.25	0.34	2.21	3.48	1.44	0.51	0.51	0.34	6.45	0.93	7.21	100.00
Eastern	2.73	2.27	1.82	47.73	33.18	0.91	–	1.36	6.36	0.45	–	–	1.82	0.45	–	0.90	100.00
Central	0.16	1.12	2.25	55.06	23.76	0.16	0.16	2.57	3.05	2.25	0.96	0.80	–	0.80	1.77	5.14	100.00
Western	1.49	5.06	0.89	15.47	34.82	–	0.89	2.08	2.38	0.60	–	0.30	–	20.83	–	15.18	100.00
TERAI	2.08	2.67	1.34	36.43	28.73	0.67	0.81	1.63	4.56	1.51	0.21	1.38	0.13	6.84	2.85	8.16	100.00
Eastern:	2.49	2.23	1.58	33.31	27.42	0.67	0.91	1.47	5.68	1.82	2.22	1.39	0.17	7.91	3.62	9.10	100.00
Far-Eastern	2.13	1.95	1.91	32.58	26.77	0.50	0.91	1.18	4.54	1.72	0.09	1.63	0.32	1.86	5.22	16.70	100.00
Mid-Eastern	0.49	2.99	1.70	38.27	29.94	1.46	0.57	2.75	7.93	2.43	–	1.05	–	6.55	2.51	1.38	100.00
Eastern	5.28	1.96	0.85	29.47	25.98	0.17	1.28	0.68	5.45	1.36	0.68	1.28	0.09	20.70	1.79	2.98	100.00
Central	0.08	2.87	0.80	45.57	32.64	0.48	0.80	1.92	2.95	1.04	0.32	1.76	0.08	1.36	0.56	6.78	100.00
Western	2.62	4.18	0.96	38.97	29.73	0.87	0.44	1.92	1.83	0.78	0.09	0.96	–	8.54	2.27	5.84	100.00
NEPAL	1.32	2.77	1.79	39.14	26.98	0.50	1.12	1.59	3.94	1.92	0.22	0.89	0.20	7.19	2.30	8.14	100.00

Note: Commodity Groups.

(1) Agricultural inputs and other apio-products.
(2) Mineral products, ores and Industrial chemicals other then petroleum.
(3) Petroleum and petroleum products.
(4) Foodgrains, beverages and tobacco.
(5) Textiles, shoes etc.
(6) Building materials.
(7) Furniture and other furnishing goods.
(8) Books and stationaries
(9) Chemicals and drugs.
(10) Hardware and electrical accessories.
(11) Industrial, commercial and agricultural machineries and implements.
(12) Motors, Motor-cycles, cycles and their parts.
(13) Waste products.
(14) Departmental stores and provisional goods.
(15) Watches, musical instruments and jewelleries.
(16) Miscellaneous.

Source: Central Bureau of Statistics (1981), *Report on Internal Trade Survey (Study) 1979/80*, (Nepali), Kathmandu.

Table 4.8 Territorial Distribution of Trading Establishments by 'Use-Based' Classification of Commodities Sold (1979/80).

Commodity Groups	*Consumer Goods*			*Intermediate Goods*	*Basic and Capital Goods*	*Miscellaneous Goods*	*Total*
Territorial Zones	*Total*	*Non-durable*	*Durable*				
MOUNTAIN	NOT AVAILABLE						
HILL	90.52	89.15	1.37	6.47	0.10	2.92	100.00
Eastern	81.82	80.03	1.79	14.91	–	3.13	100.00
Central	92.62	91.26	1.36	4.35	0.14	2.90	100.00
Western	95.62	95.25	0.37	1.84	–	2.56	100.00
KATHMANDU VALLEY	80.47	72.64	7.83	6.29	0.23	12.98	100.00
INNER TERAI	86.44	83.56	2.88	5.85	0.51	7.21	100.00
Eastern	89.53	89.08	0.45	9.55	–	0.90	100.00
Central	90.22	85.40	4.82	3.69	0.96	5.14	100.00
Western	77.37	76.47	0.90	7.44	–	15.18	100.00
TERAI	84.74	79.00	5.74	6.89	0.21	8.16	100.00
Eastern:	83.53	76.60	6.83	7.14	0.22	9.10	100.00
Far-Eastern	76.41	67.84	8.57	6.81	0.09	16.70	100.00
Mid-Eastern	92.00	86.01	5.99	6.64	–	1.38	100.00
Eastern	87.99	83.56	4.43	8.35	0.68	2.98	100.00
Central	88.60	85.24	3.36	4.31	0.32	6.78	100.00
Western	85.44	81.43	4.01	8.63	0.09	5.84	100.00
NEPAL	85.07	79.96	5.11	6.58	0.22	8.14	100.00

Note: Commodity groups in Table 4.7 are classified as follows (Code numbers of commodity groups):
1. Consumer goods (i) Non-durable 4, 57, 8, 9, 14; (ii) Durable 10, 12, 18.2. Intermediate goods 1, 2, 3, 6, 13; 3. Basic and capital.

Thus it is evident that, the structure of commerce in the country is largely undifferentiated, highly inverted and divorced form the indigenous production process.

4.2.3 Social Relations of Exchange

Exchange "is a surface phenomenon of economic life, reflecting the underlying economic and social organisation of production", and thus, "exchange relations are not general, but specific to each mode of economic organisation that shapes them"[56]. The apparently significant scale of commodity exchanges in Nepalese economy, therefore, needs to be qualified by the concrete level of social relations of exchange to gauge its full implications in articulation the underdevelopment process. We would here attempt to sketch out the same with respect to different forms of commodity market, scale of operation of commercial activities and the mode of organization of exchange. However, non-market exchanges operationalised through a coercive mechanism of social dependence and debt bondage that are a hallmark of every pre-capitalist society, with Nepal as no exception, would be beyond our current per view for obvious reasons.

4.2.31 The route a commodity traverses from the direct producer or the organizer of production process, before reaching the ultimate consumer entails the essence of social relations of exchange. The simplest and the lowest level of exchange relations is without doubt the change of hand from the direct producer to the direct consumer with no intermediary. The usual form of market for such simple economic transaction is the *periodic market* organised of a pre-determined date and place, when the direct producers can interrupt their production work and exchange their produce either of barter basis or cash terms. The fact that in Nepal there is a wide prevalence of this primitive form of Market (Table 4.9) is a testimony to the existing low level of social relations of exchange. In the absence of information on the terms of exchange (i.e. whether barter or cash) and the structure of merchandise exchanged, it would not be possible for us to award social grading to this generalised primitive form of marketing. The common knowledge, nevertheless, permits us to state that basic subsistence goods of both indigenous production (brought by direct producers) and imported from outside (put up by the small-time petty retailers) are exchanged in these markets both on barter and monetary terms. Greater prevalence of this form of market, though only in absolute terms, in the more marketised economy of Terai than in Hill and Mountain and more in eastern than in central and western sub-zones of the same ecological zone, should, however, be regarded as a positive indicator of marketing development because of the known increasing order of physical and social disarticulation from south to north and from east to west.

Table 4.9 Distribution of Periodic Markets by Territorial Zones (1981).

'Development Region'	*Ecological Zone*	*No. of Periodic Markets*			
		Mountain	*Hill*	*Terai*	*Total*
1. Eastern		52	77	234	363
	(i)	(80.00)	(74.04)	(49.68)	(56.72)
	(ii)	(14.33)	(21.21)	(64.46)	(100.00)
2. Central		11	21	149	181
	(i)	(16.92)	(20.19)	(31.63)	(28.28)
	(ii)	(6.08)	(11.60)	(82.32)	(100.00)
3. Western		–	4	77	81
	(i)	–	(3.85)	(16.35)	(12.66)
	(ii)	–	(4.94)	(95.06)	(100.00)
4. Far-Western		2	2	11	15
	(i)	(3.08)	(1.92)	(2.34)	(2.34)
	(ii)	(13.33)	(13.33)	(73.33)	(100.00)
TOTAL		65	104	471	640
	(i)	(100.00)	(100.00)	(100.00)	(100.00)
	(ii)	(1016)	(16.25)	(73.59)	(100.00)

Note: Figures in parenthesis are percentages.
1. Column percentage.
2. Row percentage.

Source: Misra, I.R. and Satyal, M.R. (1981), *Development of Agricultural Marketing and the Improvements of Rural Marketing in Hill Areas*, (mimeo.), Kathmandu.

The primitive form of full-time petty traders, cut-off from the production activities, is that of mobile traders or hawkers. This form of marketing is known to be more prevalent in the Terai, than in the rest of the country, though it is spreading to interior hills with the extension of road networks[57]. These petty howkers are, however, hardly to be differentiated from the up-rooted peasants or semi-proletariat and their role as mediator between the producer and consumer scarcely conducive for enhancing social division of labour in view of their own unstable class position.

Socially more important exchange activity is that of permanent or professional trading, which can be differentiated in 'wholesaling' and retailing' according to the nature of their specialisation in the process of meditation between the producer and consumer. By definition, retailing entails selling to direct consumers, goods purchased from wholesaler or direct producer and implies smaller scale operation and thus lesser possibilities of accumulation. On the contrary, wholesaling essential implies greater articulation of marketing process both in vertical (economic) and horizontal (spatial) dimensions, dealing invariably in exchange-value and thus destined to enhance commodity circulation and capital accumulation. Disaggregation of total trading establishments into 'retail', 'wholesale' and 'mixed' units in the territorial frame has been presented in Table 4.10. The fact that about 95% of total units are engaged in retailing while less than 2%

Table 4.10 Nature of Trading Activities by Territorial Zones (1979/80).

Territorial Zones	*Number of Trading Establishments*			
	Retail	*Wholesale*	*Mixed*	*Total*
1. MOUNTAIN	N.A.	N.A.	N.A.	N.A.
2. HILL	2887	27	102	3016
	(95.72)	(0.90)	(3.38)	(100.00)
Eastern	661	3	7	671
	(98.51)	(0.45)	(1.04)	(100.00)
Central	1961	22	89	2072
	(94.64)	(1.06)	(4.30)	(100.00)
Western	265	2	6	273
	(97.07)	(0.73)	(2.20)	(100.00)
3. KATHMANDU	3340	37	82	3459
VALLEY	(96.56)	(1.07)	(2.37)	(100.00)
4. INNER TERAI	1094	34	51	1179
	(92.79)	(2.88)	(4.33)	(100.00)
Eastern	215	–	5	220
	(97.73)		(2.27)	(100.00)
Central	598	6	19	623
	(95.99)	(0.96)	(3.05)	(100.00)
Western	281	28	27	336
	(83.63)	(8.33)	(8.04)	(100.00)
5. TERAI	6595	165	254	7014
	(94.03)	(2.35)	(3.62)	(100.00)
Eastern	4420	55	139	4614
	(95.80)	(1.19)	(3.01)	(100.00)
Far-Eastern	2126	22	56	2204
	(96.46)	(1.00)	(2.54)	(100.00)
Mid-Eastern	1169	18	49	1236
	(94.58)	(1.46)	(2.96)	(100.00)
Eastern	1125	15	34	1174
	(95.83)	(1.28)	(2.90)	(100.00)
Central	1124	84	75	1253
	(89.70)	(6.70)	(5.90)	(100.00)
Western	1081	26	40	1147
	(94.25)	(2.27)	(3.49)	(100.00)
NEPAL	13916	263	489	14668
	(94.87)	(1.79)	(3.33)	(100.00)

Note: Figures in parenthesis are now percentages.
Source: Central Bureau of statistics (1981) *Report on Internal Trade Survey (Study) 1979/80* (Nepali), Kathmandu.

in wholesaling with the rest in both, amply speaks of the backward nature of commerce in the country. The very low wholesale/retail ratio either implies extreme monopolisation of commerce or extreme non-specialisation, both of which do not expedite circulation process or enhance production efficiency. In the Nepalese case, however, because of the observed domination of internal market, commercial process is retarded. To cite the observations of Seddon et. al. this context:

".. there has been a remarkable expansion of small-scale commerce involving small retailers and petty traders dealing in imported goods; these now constitute the most numerous stratum– and the most vulnerable – in a hierarchy which extends from foreign manufacturers through Indian and Nepalese merchants to the small retailers and their customers in the towns and villages"[58].

In the micro-spatial dimensions no discernible variation in the proportions of wholesale and retail establishments is visible except for central Terai and western Inner Terai which have a lower average proportion of retailing establishments. However, the centralisation of wholesale establishments in Terai (i.e. 62.74% of total wholesale units) and Kathmandu Valley (i.e. 14.07%) is commensurate with their greater integration with the metropolitan economy and also with their greater access to wholesale dealership of indigenous production.

4.2.32 Further information on social relations of exchange or state of development of commerce may be obtained from the scale of trading activities, both in terms of total value exchanged and number of persons engaged[59]. The size of trading establishments is important for the accumulation of surplus not in the sense of increasing labour productivity as in industrial production but solely as a means of enhancing capability to exercise monopoly and manipulate prices which forms the real basis of accumulation in the commercial process.

Tables 4.11 and 4.12 provide the relevant zone-wise and urban node-wise scale of commerce in terms of monthly sale and number of persons engaged per trading establishment we find that in the absolute sense the value of monthly sale and number of persons engaged appear to be reasonably high, quite contrary to expectations for a backward economy. This may be due to sampling bias in favour of larger marketing centres. The discernible variations in the size of establishments specially with respect to total monthly sale per establishment, enable us to delimitate areas of greater potential for commercial accumulation along Terai and Kathmandu Valley, particularly along the historical entrepot trade route through Birgunj-Hetauda-Kathmandu axis. The size of establishments in Hill are seen to be the smallest, thereby establishments their relatively more backward position in the whole of country.

Table 4.11 Scale of Commerce and Social Relations of Exchange by Territorial Zones (1979/80).

Territorial Zones	*Monthly sale per trading establishment (Rs. '000)*	*No. of persons per trading establishment*	*% of hired employees to total employees*	*Monthly sale person engaged (Rs. '000)*
I. MOUNTAIN	N.A.	N.A.	N.A.	N.A.
II. HILL	5.616	1.93	6.24	2.915
Eastern	3.486	2.11	4.30	1.652
Central	6.513	1.92	5.88	3.387
Western	4.041	1.50	16.63	2.697
III. KATHMANDU VALLEY	11.008	2.08	20.36	5.292

(Contd.)

(*Table 4.11 contd.*)

IV. INNER TERAI	7.602	2.18	16.39	3.493
Eastern	2.642	2.96	9.92	0.893
Central	9.319	2.05	14.41	4.547
Western	7.637	1.90	26.88	4.009
V. INNER TERAI	11.293	2.27	24.72	4.976
Eastern	12.101	2.18	24.17	5.561
–Far-Eastern	10.342	2.38	20.43	4.352
–Mid-Eastern	5.645	1.95	30.03	2.892
–Eastern	22.199	2.03	26.45	10.909
Central	11.287	2.63	24.62	4.293
Western	8.060	2.25	26.97	3.575
TOTAL	9.764	2.15	19.64	4.548

Source: Central Bureau of Statistics (1991), *Report of Internal Trade Survey (Study) 1979/80* (Nepali), Kathmandu.

Table 4.12 Scale of Commerce and Social Relations of Exchange by Town Panchayats (1979/80).

Territorial Zones/ Town Panchayats		*% of hired to total persons engaged*	*Monthly sale per establish-ment (Rs. '000)*	*Monthly sale per person engaged (Rs. '000)*
	HILL			
Eastern	1. Ilam	5.88	5.703	4.294
"	2. Dnankuta	1.43	2.943	1.114
Central	3. Pokhara	5.19	13.103	4.490
"	4. Tansen	16.60	9.491	4.277
	KATHMANDU VALLEY			
	5. Kathmandu	23.55	13.078	6.018
	6. Lalitpur	12.28	6.308	3.646
	7. Bhaktapur	5.81	3.080	1.781
	INNER TERAI			
Central	8. Hetauda	15.78	11.183	4.554
"	9. Bharatpur	14.50	8.869	4.765
Western	10. Tribhuvan Nagar (Dang)	18.86	6.780	2.862
"	11. Birendra Nagar (Surkhet)	35.77	6.630	4.959
	TERAI			
Eastern	12. Bhadrapur	23.36	19.103	5.178
"	13. Biratnagar	22.36	16.667	5.778
"	14. Dharan	18.60	6.100	3.475
"	15. Rajbiraj	43.14	6.535	3.104
"	16. Lahan	30.22	3.00	1.467
"	17. Janakpur	42.76	5.912	2.966
"	18. Birgunj	33.67	19.553	8.442
Central	19. Butwal	29.06	16.051	5.945
"	20. Siddhartha Nagar (Bhairahawa)	29.39	9.447	2.441
Western	21. Nepalgunj	25.20	7.355	3.130
"	22. Dhangadi	37.36	9.463	3.103
"	23. Mahendra Nagar	13.42	9.983	8.107
	TOTAL	22.74	10.872	4.871

Source: Central Bureau of Statistics (1981), *Report on Internal Trade Survey (Study) 1979/80* (Nepali), Kathmandu.

In the absence of a detailed break-up of total commercial assets and the real income accruing to the trading firms, it is difficult to assess economic viabilities of commercial activities in the country. Considering a moderate 19.64% of total employes as hired for the whole of the country and a low 6.24% of the same in Hill, commercial pursuit appears to be primarily guided by subsistence needs than by accumulation drive. In this context, Blaikie et. al's estimation (based on their study of central Nepal) that "only 30% of enterprises offered real prospects of capital accumulation"[60] appears quite reasonable.

Correlating low absolute level of marketisation and preponderance of subsistence consumer goods traded (as brought out in the earlier section), with high proportions of small size retail shops managed by the self, it can be safely deduced that the nature of social relations of exchange is quite backward and marked by exchange of use-value as against the essential circulation of exchange-value in higher social formations. Furthermore, the widely presumed prevalence of involuntary involvement of peasants in the market for distress selling and buying characteristically of a pre-capitalist agrarian economy, which Bhaduri terms as "forced commerce" [61], makes the overall nature of social relations of exchange in Nepal quite retrograde.

4.2.33 An analysis of mode of social organisation of commerce and ownership distribution of trading establishments by important social groups should further clarify the nature of social relations of exchange.

In the absence of desired statistical information, it can be safely deduced from the earlier observations of prevailing dominance of small-scale and retail trading that private appropriation of commercial profit should be the principal mode of organisation of commerce. However, as brought out in the historical overview of the process earlier, low development of social division of labour and highly centralised nature of the state has resulted in significant degree of state intervention in mercantile activities since earlier times. In the wake of populist waves sweeping the countries of under-developed world after World War II, it is but natural for the ruling classes of Nepal as well to go in for more direct state intervention in the commercial process. Consequently, apart from near monopoly in some sectors of export-import trade, the state has significant hold or monopoly in the internal circulation of commodities like food, agricultural inputs, construction materials, fuel, etc., which are channelled through a number of 'public' enterprises and their branches in important centres of the country[62]. But the basic idea of direct state intervention, as determined by the class-character of the state, appears to be only to prepare ground for ultimate private take-over, which is evident from the dismantling of public sector rice export companies in the early 1980s and leaving the field wide open for private mercantilists. Also the essentially urban and more prosperous area bias of state organisation of trade is evident from the heavy or near total concentration of commercial public enterprises in Kathmandu Valley and Terai[63].

Even among the private mercantilists certain social groups, particularly Newars, Marwaris of Indian descent, Thakalis, etc., are seen to occupy a position of monopoly by virtue of their initial baptism in entrepot trade, closer contacts with foreign agents, identification of trade with a particular caste, etc. The traditional hold of Indian merchants even in internal trade is seen further strengthened because of the pattern of development of internal trade just as a mechanical extension of external trade. In the territorial dimension, whereas the Newars and other ethnic groups like Thakalis are found in dominant position in Hill and interior parts of the country, the Indian merchants have a sway in Terai and bigger urban areas[64].

In sum, such monopolistic (whether state or private) structure of organisation of commerce in a backward economy cannot be regarded as conducive for a healthy development.

4.2.34 Merchant capital in Nepal has been historically an appendage of metropolitan capital. Subsequent pattern of social development are apprehended to have not alleviated but further aggravated this position. Hence, pending a detailed analysis of external trade in the next section, it would be relevant to assess the extent of this nexus to define the nature of social relation of exchange.

In the lack of a detailed account of commodities traded by their sources (i.e indigenous or imported), we can form and idea from the pattern as observed in some selected localities (Table 4.13). The fact that as much as 66.08% of total commodities traded in Nepalgunj (western Terai) and 55.96% in Dharan (far-eastern Terai) were reported to be directly imported should establish beyond doubt the essentially 'comprador' nature of merchant capital in the country. Even in other surveyed urban places, the share of commodities 'purchased from indigenous manufacturers' ranged from low 26.98% in Bhairahawa (central Terai) to an insignificant 7.79% in Nepalgunj; the large part of the remaining being accounted as 'purchased from wholesalers', which is just a vieled form of 'indirect import.'

Table 4.13 Source of Purchase of Commodities by Traders in Principal Trading Centres of Terai (1975/76).

(Rs. Million)

S. No.	*Trading Centres/ Territorial Zones*	*Total*	*Imported*	*Purchased from indigenous manufacturers*	*Purchased from wholesellers*	*Others*
1.	Dharan/Far-Eastern Terai	31.04	17.37	2.84	10.06	0.78
		(100.00)	(55.96)	(9.14)	(32.44)	(2.51)
2.	Birgunj/Eastern Terai	63.61	15.91	11.52	30.42	5.75
		(100.00)	(25.01)	(18.11)	(47.82)	(9.04)
3.	Bhairahawa/Central Terai	68.41	17.07	18.46	19.38	7.16
		(100.00)	(24.95)	(26.98)	(28.33)	(10.47)
4.	Nepalgunj/Western Terai	72.00	47.58	5.61	13.78	5.03
		(100.00)	(66.08)	(7.79)	(19.14)	(6.99)

Note: Figures in parenthesis are percentages.

Source: Central Bureau of Statistics (1976), *Results of Internal Trade Pilot Survey, 1975/76* (Nepali) Kathmandu, Table 2.

When the dominant position of Indian merchants in the ownership of trading establishments is added to the overwhelming proportion of imported commodities traded, the 'comprador' nature of merchant capital in the country gets substantiated beyond any doubt.

4.2.4 Spatial Relations of Exchange

One the basis of the foregoing historical overview and current social processes it can be argued that spatial structure of exchanges in Nepal are essentially a function of two contradictory processes; firstly, marked territorial diversity and strategic geo-political positioning which necessitates or encourages primitive inter-regional and inter-national exchanges; and secondly, extreme inter- and inter-regional physical inaccessibility and lack of economic complimentarity which thwarts intra- and inter-regional exchanges. The combined spatial manifestations of these processes may be analysed in terms of the extent and structure of inter-regional exchanges and spatial organisation of marketing.

4.2.41 Extent of Inter-Regional Exchanges

In the absence of a detailed inventory of inter-regional movement of all commodities, we have here sought to proximate the picture of inter-regional economic interactions through the analysis of inter-regional movement of only foodgrains, which, however, constitute the overwhelming proportion of indigenous commodity production and the single largest group of commodities exchanged.

Table 4.14 provides the volume of inter-regional inflow-outflow of principal agricultural commodities, namely rice, wheat, maize and potato, based on a survey of inter-district flow of these commodities in 1971/72. Though the absolute values of commodity flows may not be reliable and may be biased towards more accessible areas of Terai, Inner Terai and Kathmandu Valley, the Table and Fig. 3.3 provide a useful picture of inter-regional exchange relations during the 1970s. A cursory glance should suffice to outline the principal directions of commodity flows and identify major nodes of economic interactions as manifested in the number of out-flows and inflows originating from and terminating at the particular territorial zone. Both in terms of gross volume of commodities and number of flows, the general pattern of economic exchanges to be observed is predominantly in the north-south territorial dimension, with a net flow of goods from the south to the north. There is a virtually non-existent or negligible flow in the east-west territorial dimension, specially amongst the same ecological sub-zones. The observed pattern, however, is fully consistent with the natural and historical factors which have always determined the course of interactions in the north-south directions, but with fluctuating magnitude.

Along the east-west territorial dimension, discernible variation in the magnitute of the said pattern is noticeable; i.e. a progressive decline from east to west. This may be explained in terms of higher level of commodity production and greater physical accessibility in eastern and central sub-zones than in the

Table 4.14 Inter-Regional Inflow-Outflow Matrix for Principal Agricultural Commodities (1971/72).

Inflow to / *Outflow From*		*Eastern Mountain*	*Central Mountain*	*Western Mountain*	*Eastern Hill*	*Central Hill*	*Western Hill*	*Kathmandu Valley*	*Eastern Inner Terai*	*Central Inner Terai*
(1)		(2)	(3)	(4)	(5)	(6)	(7)	(8)	(9)	(10)
1. Eastern Mountain		[290]	–	–	5311	–	–	–	–	–
	(i)	–	–	–	(89.16)	–	–	–	–	–
	(ii)	–	–	–	(9.63)	–	–	–	–	–
2. Central Mountain		–	–	–	–	3165	–	–	–	–
	(i)	–	–	–	–	(100.00)	–	–	–	–
	(ii)	–	–	–	–	(33.20)	–	–	–	–
3. Western Mountain		–	–	[619]	–	–	–	–	–	–
	(i)	–	–	–	–	–	–	–	–	–
	(ii)	–	–	–	–	–	–	–	–	–
4. Eastern Hill		1368	–	–	[7247]	–	–	1350	1774	–
	(i)	(7.48)	–	–	–	–	–	(7.38)	(9.70)	–
	(ii)	(21.40)	–	–	–	–	–	(42.08)	(17.50)	–
5. Central Hill		–	1070	–	–	[6844]	396	373	–	7072
	(i)	–	(2.71)	–	–	–	(1.00)	(0.95)	–	(17.94)
	(ii)	–	(63.65)	–	–	–	(31.06)	(11.63)	–	(10.38)
6. Western Hill		–	–	–	–	–	[8327]	–	–	–
	(i)	–	–	–	–	–	–	–	–	–
	(ii)	–	–	–	–	–	–	–	–	–
7. Kathmandu Valley		–	–	–	13769	6260	–	[17813]	–	25459
	(i)	–	–	–	(24.85)	(11.30)	–	–	(45.94)	
	(ii)	–	–	–	(24.95)	(65.66)	–	–	(37.36)	
8. Eastern Inner Terai		2181	–	–	4862	–	–	–	[329]	–
	(i)	(10.27)	–	–	(22.89)	–	–	–	–	–
	(ii)	(34.12)	–	–	(8.81)	–	–	–	–	–

(*Contd.*)

(*Table 4.14 contd.*)

Inflow to Outflow From		*Eastern Mountain*	*Central Mountain*	*Western Mountain*	*Eastern Hill*	*Central Hill*	*Western Hill*	*Kathmandu valley*	*Eastern Inner Terai*	*Central Inner Terai*
(1)		(2)	(3)	(4)	(5)	(6)	(7)	(8)	(9)	(10)
9. Central Inner Terai		–	611	–	–	18	–	544	–	[4714]
	(i)	–	(5.11)	–	–	(0.15)	–	(4.55)	–	–
	(ii)	–	(36.35)	–	–	(0.19)	–	(16.96)	–	–
10. Western Inner Terai		–	–	–	–	–	732	–	–	–
	(i)	–	–	–	–	–	(40.62)	–	–	–
	(ii)	–	–	–	–	–	(57.50)	–	–	–
11. Far Eastern Terai		1844	–	–	13529	–	–	–	–	–
	(i)	(10.94)	–	–	(80.23)	–	–	–	–	–
	(ii)	(28.84)	–	–	(24.52)	–	–	–	–	–
12. Mid-Eastern		279	–	–	5928	–	–	–	5282	–
	(i)	(2.42)	–	–	(51.37)	–	–	–	(45.78)	–
	(ii)	(4.36)	–	–	(10.74)	–	–	–	(52.10)	–

(*Table 4.14 contd.*)

Inflow to Outflow From		*Western Inner Terai*	*Far Eastern Terai*	*Mid-Eastern Terai*	*Eastern Terai*	*Central Terai*	*Western Terai*	*India*	*Tibe*	*Total Inflow*
(1)		(11)	(12)	(13)	(14)	(15)	(16)	(17)	(18)	(19)
1. Eastern Mountain		–	151	495	–	–	–	–	–	5957
	(i)	–	(2.53)	(8.31)	–	–	–	–	–	(100.00)
	(ii)	–	(0.09)	(0.27)	–	–	–	–	–	(0.69)
2. Central Mountain		–	–	–	–	–	–	–	–	31.65
	(i)	–	–	–	–	–	–	–	–	(100.00)
	(ii)	–	–	–	–	–	–	–	–	(0.37)

(*Contd.*)

(*Table 4.14 contd.*)

3. Western mountain		1910	–	–	–	–	6469	–	–	8379
	(i)	(22.80)	–	–	–	–	(72.20)	–	–	(100.00)
	(ii)	(5.29)	–	–	–	–	(5.53)	–	–	(0.97)
4. Eastern Hill		–	13739	60	–	–	–	–	–	18291
		–	(75.11)	(0.33)	–	–	–	–	–	(100.00)
		–	(9.59)	(0.03)	–	–	–	–	–	(2.12)
5. Central Hill		–	–	–	–	30513	–	–	–	39424
	(i)	–	–	–	–	(77.40)	–	–	–	(100.00)
	(ii)	–	–	–	–	(26.16)	–	–	–	(4.56)
6. Western Hill		27731	–	–	–	–	22918	–	–	50649
	(i)	(54.75)	–	–	–	–	(45.25)	–	–	(100.00)
	(ii)	(76.78)	–	–	–	–	(19.60)	–	–	(5.86)
7. Kathmandu valley		–	–	938	8990	–	–	–	–	55416
	(i)	–	–	(1.69)	(16.22)	–	–	–	–	(100.00)
	(ii)	–	–	(0.51)	(9.63)	–	–	–	–	(2.41)
8. Eastern Inner Terai		–	–	14196	–	–	–	–	–	21239
	(i)	–	–	(66.83)	–	–	–	–	–	(100.00)
	(ii)	–	–	(7.70)	–	–	–	–	–	(2.46)
9. Central Inner Terai		–	–	893	2954	6943	–	–	–	11963
	(i)	–	–	(7.46)	(24.69)	(58.04)	–	–	–	(100.00)
	(ii)	–	–	(0.48)	(3.16)	(5.95)	–	–	–	(1.38)
10. Western Inner Terai		–	–	–	–	1070	–	–	–	1802
	(i)	–	–	–	–	(59.38)	–	–	–	(100.00)
	(ii)	–	–	–	–	(0.92)	–	–	–	(0.21)
11. Far Eastern Terai		–	50	1490	–	–	–	–	–	16863
	(i)	–	–	(8.84)	–	–	–	–	–	(100.00)
	(ii)	–	–	(0.81)	–	–	–	–	–	(1.95)
12. Mid-Eastern Terai		–	50	2638	–	–	–	–	–	11539
	(i)	–	(0.43)	–	–	–	–	–	–	(100.00)
	(ii)	–	(0.03)	–	–	–	–	–	–	(1.33)

(*Contd.*)

(*Table 4.14 contd.*)

1		2	3	4	5	6	7	8	9	10
13. Eastern Terai		–	–	–	–	–	–	848	–	7428
	(i)	–	–	–	–	–	–	(7.61)	–	(66.64)
	(ii)	–	–	–	–	–	–	(26.43)	–	(10.90)
14. Central Terai		–	–	–	–	91	145	–	–	255
	(i)	–	–	–	–	(18.53)	(29.53)	–	–	(51.93)
	(ii)	–	–	–	–	(0.95)	(11.39)	–	–	(0.37)
15. Western Terai		–	–	–	–	–	–	–	–	–
	(i)	–	–	–	–	–	–	–	–	–
	(ii)	–	–	–	–	–	–	–	–	–
16. India		663	–	126	11681	–	–	93	3082	27925
	(i)	(0.11)	–	(0.02)	(1.93)	–	–	(0.02)	(0.51)	(4.62)
	(ii)	(10.37)	–	(7.66)	(21.17)	–	–	(2.90)	(30.40)	(40.98)
17. Tibet		58	–	1518	98	–	–	–	–	–
	(i)	(3.46)	–	(90.68)	(5.85)	–	–	–	–	–
	(ii)	(0.91)	–	(92.34)	(0.18)	–	–	–	–	–
TOTAL OUTFLOW		6393	1681	1644	55178	9534	1273	3208	10138	68139
	(i)	(0.74)	(0.19)	(0.19)	(6.38)	(1.10)	(0.15)	(0.37)	(1.17)	(7.88)
	(ii)	(100.00)	(100.00)	(100.00)	(100.00)	(100.00)	(100.00)	(100.00)	(100.00)	(100.00)

Note: *Principal agricultural commodities include vice, wheat, maize and potato.

– Figures in principal diagonal indicate inter district flows with the region.

– Figures in parenthesis are percentages; (i) Row percentage (ii) Column percentage.

Source: HMG, Ministry of food, Agriculture and irrigation (1976), *Report on Trade Flows Survey of Agricultural Commodities Particularly Cereal Grains in Nepal, 1971/72*, Department of Food and Agricultural Marketing Services, Bag Bazar, Kathmandu.

(*Table 4.14 contd.*)

(1)		(11)	(12)	(13)	(14)	(15)	(16)	(17)	(18)	(19)
13. Eastern Terai		–	–	2871	[27864]	–	–	–	–	11147
	(i)	–	–	(25.76)	–	–	–	–	–	(100.00)
		–	–	(1.56)	–	–	–	–	–	(1.29)
14. Central Terai		–	–	–	–	[14529]	–	–	–	491
	(i)	–	–	–	–	–	–	–	–	(100.00)
	(ii)	–	–	–	–	–	–	–	–	(0.06)
15. Western Terai		1698	–	–	–	–	[9884]	–	–	1698
	(i)	(100.00)	–	–	–	–	–	–	–	(100.00)
	(ii)	(4.70)	–	–	–	–	–	–	–	(0.20)
16. India		4778	145979	163369	81434	78129	87544	–	–	604803
	(i)	(0.79)	(24.14)	(27.04)	(13.46)	(12.92)	(14.47)	–	–	(100.00)
	(ii)	(13.23)	(91.28)	(88.64)	(87.21)	(66.97)	(74.87)	–	–	(69.96)
17. Tibet		–	–	–	–	–	–	–	–	1674
	(i)	–	–	–	–	–	–	–	–	(100.00)
	(ii)	–	–	–	–	–	–	–	–	(0.19)
TOTAL OUTFLOW		36117	159919	184312	93378	116655	116931	–	–	864500
	(i)	(4.18)	(18.50)	(21.32)	(10.80)	(13.49)	(13.53)	–	–	(100.00)
		(100.00)	(100.00)	(100.00)	(100.00)	(100.00)	(100.00)	–	–	(100.00)

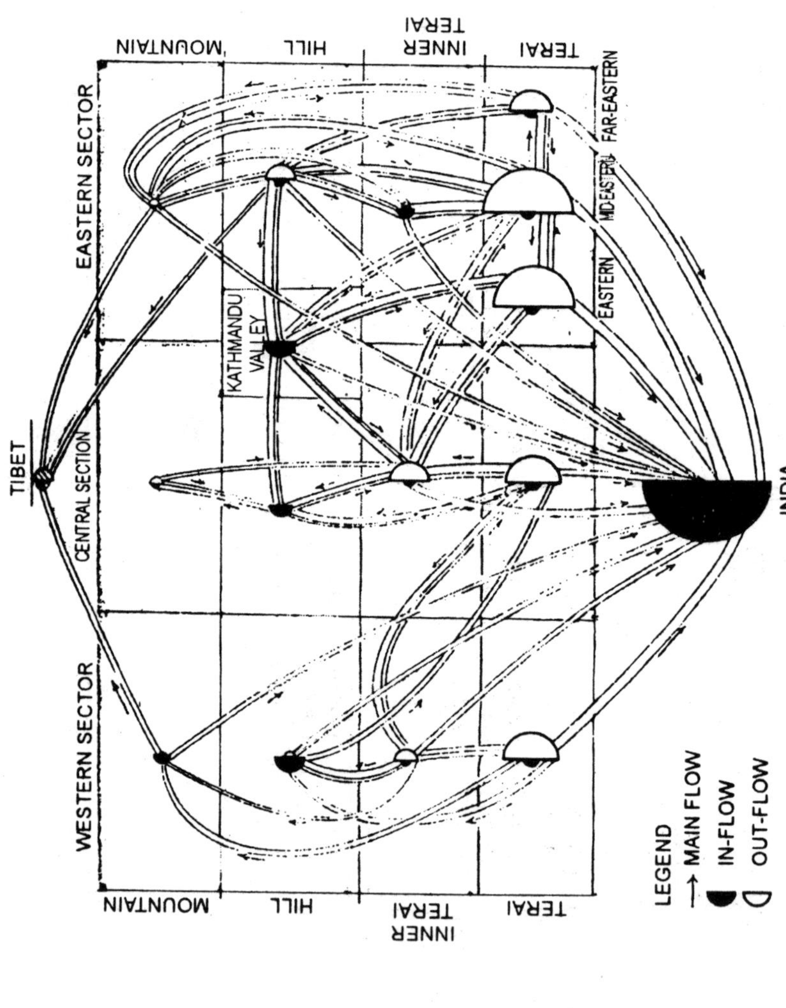

Table 4.3 Inter-Regional Inflow-Outflow of Agricultural Commodities (1971/72).

western. Similarly, progressive aggravation in the outflow/inflow ratio from east to west is fully concomittant with the more depressed state of the economy in western Mountain and Hill than in their counterparts eastwards.

In terms of micro-spatial units, the greatest number of two-way economic linkages are observed in central Inner Terai and Kathmandu valley, on the one hand, and eastern and central Hill, on the other. These sub-zones are hence areas of highest inter-regional economic articulations. However, when the overall spatial articulation of exchange relations is considered it is found that the Terai has greater linkages-both in terms of volume of commodities and number of trade flows-with India; when matched with negligible economic interactions in the larger east-west-territorial frame. This clearly substantiates our arguments that the spatial structure of the economy is externally-integrated (extraverted) and internally fragmented (disarticulated). The scenario would be more apparent if an inter-regional inflow-outflow matrix of total commodity flows inclusive of manufactured goods, both indigenous and imported, could be constructed; which is beyond our capacity at present.

In the context of gradual aggravation of uneven economic development in the country and greater integration of the economy with improved means of transport since the early 1970s, the changing spatial structure of commerce would also demand a fresh investigation. For want of comparative data of commodity flows for recent years, we have constructed an inter-regional inflow-outflow matrix of foodgrains marketed by the premier public sector marketing agency, National Food Corporation, in 1981/82, as presented in Table 4.15 and Fig. 3.4. We note in the Tables and Maps for the two periods that there is a marked polarisation of flows in the conventional north-south directions, with virtual absence of east-west interactions and cessation of previous meagre outflows from north to south. Thus both in terms of volume of commodities exchanged and intensity of trade flows, the near one-way flow from Terai to Hill is unmistakable. In micro-spatial dimensions, the primacy of Kathmandu Valley in commodity procurement and distribution is seen to have enhanced and number of outflows to other sub-zones from far-eastern and mid-eastern Terai increased. Another significant development in commodity exchanges to be observed over the decade is the importation of grains from foreign countries as against exportation in early 1970s.

In sum, the 'extra-version' and 'disarticulation' of spatial structure has definitely been aggravated over the period.

4.2.42 Structure of Inter-Regional Exchanges

The real socio-spatial significances of inter-regional exchanges lie more in the commodity structure than in mere magnitude of the exchanges; because, as already noted in the earlier section, the 'unequal exchange' relation essential for accruing commercial profit is facilitated more in the exchanges of commodities which have different organic composition of capital. In the absence of a detailed inventory of commodities traded in inter-regional dimensions and their relative prices at different places, we have sought to draw a generalised picture of the

Table 4.15 Inter-Regional Inflow-Outflow Matrix for Food-Grains* (1981/82).

(M. Ton)

Inflow to / Outflow From		Eastern Mountain	Central Mountain	Western Mountain	Eastern Hill	Central Hill	Western Hill	Kathmandu Valley	Eastern Inner Terai	Central Inner Terai	Western Inner Terai	Far-Eastern Terai	Mid-Eastern Terai	Eastern Terai	Central Terai	Western Terai	Foreign Countries	Total Inflow
		1	2	3	4	5	6	7	8	9	10	11	12	13	14	15	16	
1. Eastern Mountain	(i) (ii)	[..]	–	–	–	–	–	715 (62.39) (18.39)	–	–	–	238 (20.77) (1.27)	193 (16.84) (1.86)	–	–	–	–	1146 (100.00) (1.32)
2. Central Mountain	(i) (ii)	–	[..]	–	–	755 (100.00) (98.95)	–	–	–	–	–	–	–	–	–	–	–	755 (100.00) (0.87)
3. Western Mountain	(i) (ii)	–	–	50	–	–	174 (13.13) (100.00)	8 (0.60) (0.21)	–	–	81 (6.11) (5.96)	–	–	–	18 (1.36) (0.28)	1044 (78.79) (14.44)	–	1325 (100.00) (1.52)
4. Eastern Hill	(i) (ii)	–	–	–	540	–	–	1019 (17.18) (26.22)	658 (11.09) (100.00)	–	–	2593 (43.71) (13.85)	1662 (28.02) (15.98)	–	–	–	–	5932 (100.00) (6.81)
5. Central Hill	(i) (ii)	–	–	–	–	3492	–	2145 (23.71) (55.18)	–	–	–	–	–	253 (2.80) (4.58)	5941 (65.68) (21.41)	–	707 (7.82) (5.52)	9046 (100.00) (10.38)
6. Western Hill	(i) (ii)	–	–	–	–	–	[..]	–	–	–	1278 (58.95) (94.04)	–	–	–	–	890 (41.05) (12.31)	–	2168 (100.00) (2.49)
7. Kathmandu Valley	(i) (ii)	–	–	– –	6 (0.02) (0.79)	–	–	[..]	–	19110 (66.31) (100.00)	–	2211 (7.67) (11.81)	1246 (4.32) (11.98)	5086 (17.65) (91.99)	540 (1.87) (8.31)	–	627 (2.18) (4.90)	28820 (100.00) (33.07)
8. Eastern Inner Terai	(i) (ii)	–	–	–	–	–	–	–	[..]	–	–	–	1145 (100.00) (11.01)	–	–	–	–	1145 (100.00) (1.31)

(Contd.)

(*Table 4.15 contd.*)

9. Central Inner Terai	(i) (ii)	–	–	–	–	–	–	–	–	[..]	–	12359 (66.07) (66.00)	6156 (32.91) (59.18)	190 (1.02) (3.44)	–	–	–	18705 (100.00) (21.47)
10. Western Inner Terai	(i) (ii)	–	–	–	–	–	–	–	–	–	[1175]	–	–	–	–	2763 (100.00) (38.21)	–	2763 (100.00) (3.17)
11. Far-Eastern Terai	(i) (ii)	–	–	–	–	–	–	–	–	–	–	[2191]	–	–	–	–	2432 (100.00) (19.00)	2432 (100.00) (2.79)
12. Mid-Eastern Terai	(i) (ii)	–	–	–	–	–	–	–	–	–	–	546 (100.00) (2.92)	[12]	–	–	–	–	546 (100.00) (0.63)
13. Eastern Terai	(i) (ii)	–	–	–	–	–	–	1 (0.01) (0.03)	–	–	–	–	–	[–]	–	–	7779 (99.99) (60.79)	7780 (100.00) (8.93)
14. Central Terai	(i) (ii)	–	–	–	–	2 (0.05) (0.26)	–	–	–	–	–	780 (18.10) (4.17)	–	–	[–]	2534 (58.81) (35.04)	993 (23.04) (7.76)	4309 (100.00) (4.95)
15. Western	(i) (ii)	–	–	–	–	–	–	–	–	–	–	–	–	–	–	[509]	259 (100.00) (2.02)	259 (100.00) (0.30)
16. Foreign Countries	(i) (ii)	–	–	–	–	–	–	–	–	–	–	–	–	–	–	–	[-]	–
TOTAL OUTFLOW	(i) (ii)	–	–	–	–	763 (0.88) (100.00)	174 (0.20) (100.00)	3887 (4.46) (100.00)	658 (0.76) (100.00)	19110 (21.93) (100.00)	1359 (1.56) (100.00)	18727 (21.49) (100.00)	10402 (11.94) (100.00)	5529 (6.35) (100.00)	6499 (7.46) (100.00)	7231 (8.30) (100.00)	12797 (14.69) (100.00)	87136 (100.00) (100.00)

Note: * Food-grains include rice, wheat and maize, and only marketed by Nepal Food Corporation.
* Figures in principal diagonal indicate intra-regional flows.
* Figures in parenthesis are percentages: (i) Row%, (ii) Column percentage.

Source: Nepal Food Corporation, *Annual Progress Report, F.Y. 1981–82* (Nepali), Head Office, Kathmandu.

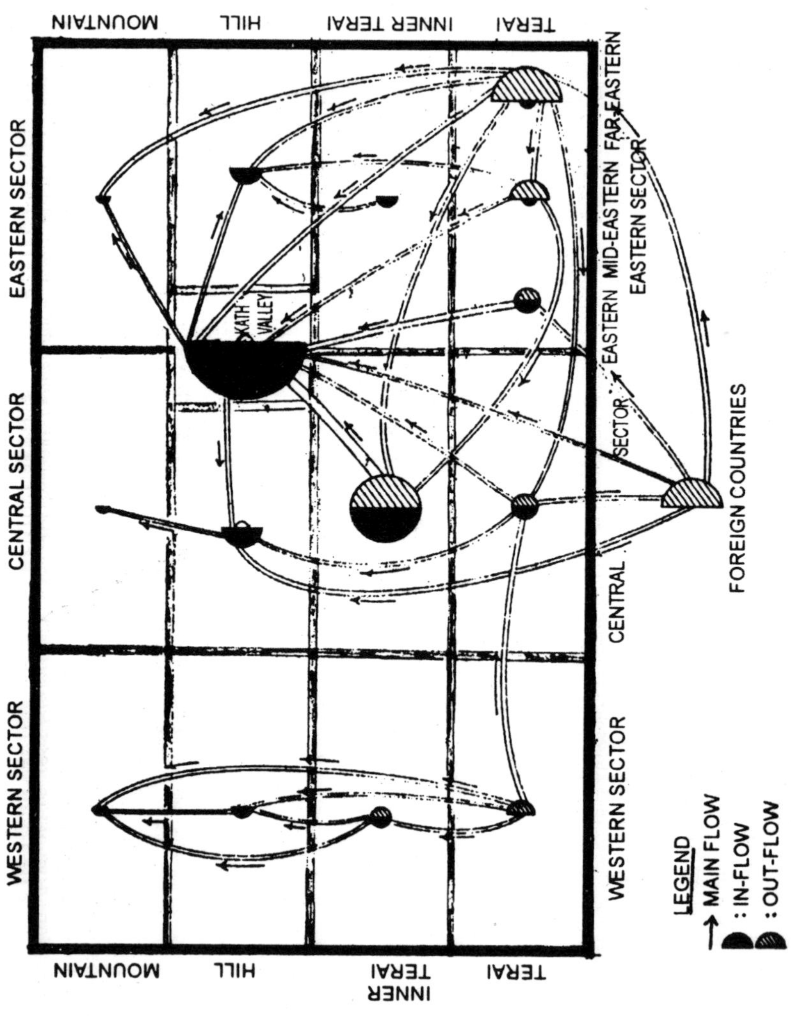

Table 4.4 Inter-Regional Food-Grain Flows (1980/81).

situation by means of study of commodity structures for certain representative areas.

It is well-known that an overwhelming proportion (i.e. 73.20%) of export from Hill to Terai is made up of primary products and the rest of elementary processed or unclassifiable goods[65]. On the other hand the imports invariably comprise of manufactured products. Even though the pattern is fairly understandable in view of the already observed 'unequal specialisation' in territorial division of labour, such exchanges are the classic case of 'unequal exchange' and would result in net flow of surplus from Hill to Terai. Moreover in and exchange relation characterised by a simultaneous presençe of pre-capitalist monopoly on the part of professional trader (i.e. seller of manufactured products) and distress selling and buying on the part of peasants, the over-all loss to hill economy would be further aggravated. Much of the goods purchased by hill-dwellers are however, merely passed-on by the Terai counterparts as much of it is imported from outside. Thus the Terai trader would just act as a mediator between the metropolitan capital and hill economy and the net drain of surplus would eventually be towards the metropolitan economy.

The structure of inter-regional trade in a central Hill area[66] is no different. In it the primary products also constitute a formidable share (i.e. about 35%) of imports along with the manufactured goods; whereas the exports are constituted totally of primary produces.

The structure of trade in Mountain[67] follows the pattern of Hill, but with greater proportion of primary products in imports. Thus the net social implication of exchange relations remain the same, i.e. net flow of surplus away from the Mountain.

For want of time-series data it is difficult to ascertain the changing pattern of structure of inter-regional exchanges; but micro-level studies conducted in areas of greater physical accessibility and greater integration with outside economy[68] and our own impressionistic observation of the situation, suggest that with further deindustrialisation of Hill and Mountain and manipulation of consumption habits of people, dependence on imports of goods for simple subsistence and conspicuous consumption is increasing throughout the country-side. It thus perpetuates the retrograde exchange relations deterimental to the more backward areas of Hill and Mountain.

4.2.43 Spatial Organisation of Marketing

As brought out in the historical review of the commercial process, the primary reliance on entrepot trade has historically tended to distribute market places in Nepal along major north-south trade routes; i.e. starting from the nearest entry point from India along the southern border to break-of-bulk point between Terai and Hill, to rest-places in mid-hills along major river basins or valley, ultimately to the Mountain pass leading to Tibet. This spatial pattern has been described in one of the semi-official reports as;

"judging from the spatial design of existing markets in the Far Western Development Region which is valid for much of the country, one see a tree like pattern or a dendritic system. The base generally is the town or market centre opposite the Indian railhead and emanating from this base in tree-like manner the link extends to other market centres in the hills"[69].

Within this basic pattern, significant alterations in distribution of market places as determined by politico-administrative and economic factors are to be noticed. By the very nature of low socio-economic differentiation and greater role of state in the economic process, market places, particularly in the interior countryside, have always tended to coincide with administrative centres. With the organisation of state administration along an ascending hierarchy of village, district, zone, region and state, the market place hierarchy also have tended to develop along the same line and their location coincides with the location of administrative head-quarters. However, it would be too simplistic to construct a spatial organisation of marketing mechanistically on these lines alone.

With an increased integration of the economy with the outside world and extension of road-networks to the interior hinterlands, the spatial organisation of marketing have been increasingly governed by proximity to collection and distribution points. Whereas the 'distribution' points would be near the areas of population concentration, 'collection' points would very according to the source of acquisition, i.e. import or local production. Since imported commodities consitute a dominant proportion of internally marketed goods, collection points in Terai along the Indian border would be a foregone necessity. The internal collection needs would give rise to collection points mostly in Terai and in selected areas of Hill. The distribution points, on the other hand, would occur at the road terminus and break-of-bulk point along the transition zone between Terai and Hill. Moreover, distribution points for imported luxury consumption goods would have to coincide with the seats of state bureaucracy and feudal lords, i.e. the 'urban' places.

In the absence of information on individual market places the foregoing logic of size and spatial distribution of market places can be captured from the marketing attributes of urban places is seen in Table 4.16 and Fig. 4.5. It is quite evident that the traditional administrative-cum-trading centre of Kathmandu and subsequently emerged trading outposts along the Terai border are the places of overwhelming centralisation of trading activities. The emergence and flourishing of new trading centres like Bharatpur in central Inner Terai and Pokhara in central Hill represent the changes in spatial organisation of marketing brought about by deeper penetration of merchant capital into the interior heartland. Still, the retainment of original position of primacy by Kathmandu (i.e. about one-third of total internal trade transactions), rise of market places along points of direct integration with metropolitan economy or its interior outpost and the absence of higher order market places in greater parts of countryside, all combine together to provide a spatial structure of commerce marked simultaneously by extreme dysfunctionality, extroversion and disarticulation.

Table 4.16 Distribution of Trading Activities by Town Panchayats (1979/80).

	Territorial Zones/ Town Panchayats	Share of total trading establishments (%)	Share of total monthly sale (%)	Share of total persons engaged (%)
HILL		9.1	8.52	10.44
Cenl. East.	1. Ilam	0.72	0.38	0.43
	2. Dhankuta	1.18	0.32	1.40
	3. Pokhara	4.65	5.60	6.08
	4. Tansen	2.55	2.22	2.53
KATHMANDU VALLEY		37.30	38.73	34.73
	5. Kathmandu	29.31	35.25	28.54
	6. Lalitpur	4.10	2.38	3.18
	7. Bhaktapur	3.89	1.10	3.01
INNER TERAI		9.10	7.36	7.89
West. Cent.	8. Hetauda	2.14	2.20	2.35
	9. Bharatpur	4.35	3.55	3.63
	10. Tribhuwannagar	1.58	0.98	1.67
	11. Birendranagar	1.03	0.63	0.24
TERAI		41.15	45.38	46.93
Western Central Eastern	12. Bhadrapur	1.62	2.85	2.68
	13. Biratnagar	8.03	12.30	10.37
	14. Dharan	4.93	2.77	3.88
	15. Rajbiraj	1.59	0.95	1.50
	16. Lahan	0.99	0.27	0.91
	17. Janakpur	3.17	1.73	2.83
	18. Birgunj	4.77	8.58	4.95
	19. Butwal	4.62	6.82	5.58
	20. Bhairahawa	3.17	2.76	5.50
	21. Nepalgunj	4.66	3.15	4.91
	22. Dhangadi	2.25	1.96	3.07
	23. Mahendranagar	1.35	1.24	0.75
	ALL	100.00	100.00	100.00

Source: Central Bureau of Statistics (1981), *Report on Internal Trade Survey (Study) 1979/80 (Nepali)*, Kathmandu.

This should also preclude the existence of a functional hierarchy of market places and a defined pattern of spatial distribution. Though we have no means empirically verify the scenario, sundry studies have confirmed that there exists no regularity in the hierarchy of distribution of market places, except along the transportation nodes and administrative centres[70]. Similarly, the average distance to different catagories of market places from the settlement nodes are found to be quite prohibitive for greater economic interaction in much of the countryside[71].

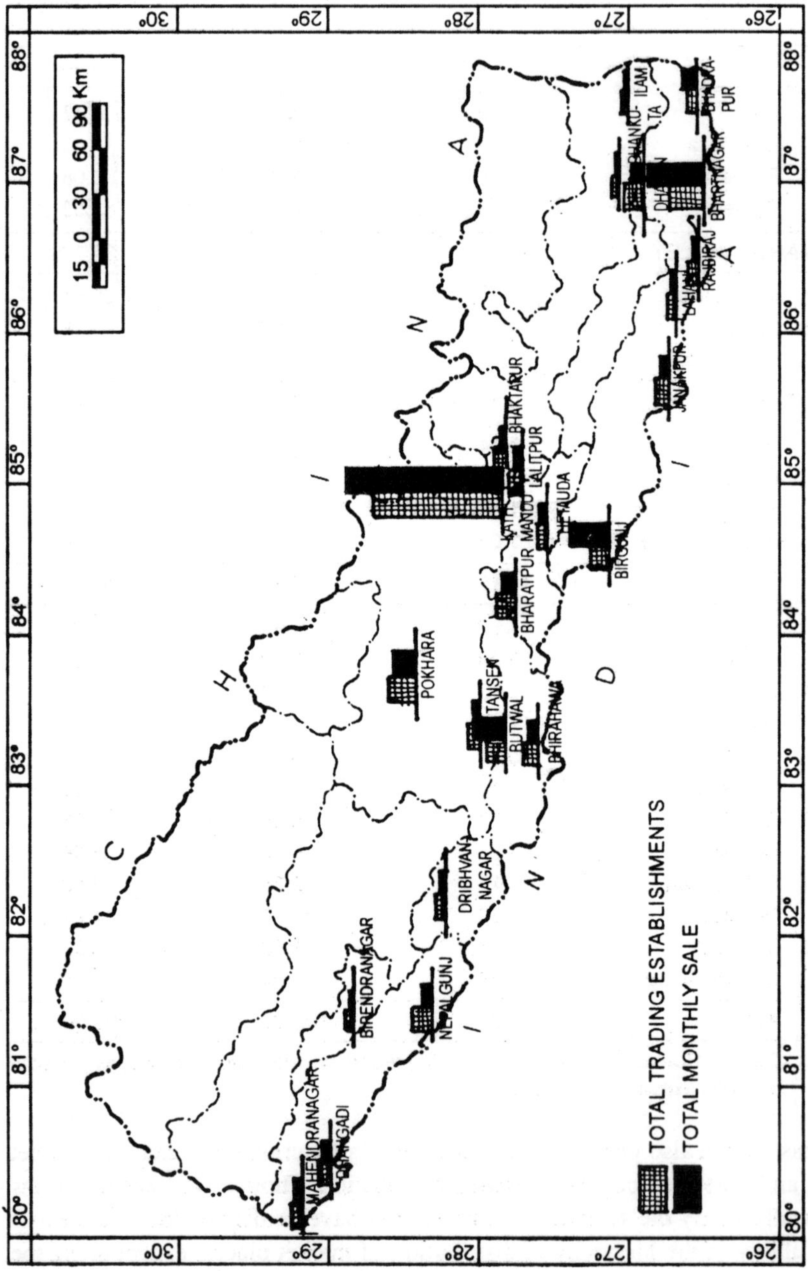

Fig. 4.5 Distribution of Trading Activities by Town Panchayats (1979/80) (% Share).

Thus in conclusion it can be stated that articulation of merchant capital within is marked by a low level of marketisation of the economy, divorce of commercial process from the indigenous production process, backward and retrograde social relations of exchange and disarticulated and extraverted commercial spatial structure.

4.3 ARTICULATION OF MERCHANT CAPITAL WITHOUT

The process of articulation of merchant capital without essentially involves the second and third points of exchanges in the four point circuit of merchant capital i.e. selling the primary products of home country to metropolitan capital and buying manufactured goods from the latter to ultimately sell in the former. In the following section we would be attempting to analyse different characteristics and processes of merchant capital engaged in the said acts, with a view to outline its role in modifying the social and spatial structure of Nepal.

4.3.1 Role of Foreign Trade in the Economy

Though foreign trade has historically been the principal form of mercantile activity in Nepal, as compared to other members of the fraternity in the South-Asian region Nepal's regarded as the most "inward-looking" economy[72]. Despite the apparently small size[73] of import-export trade, what is of more interest to the students of underdevelopment process in Nepal is the rate of increase of its magnitude and its growing role in the overall social process.

As evident from Table 4.17, there has been a fourfold (or more than twelve-fold at current prices) rise in absolute size of export-import trade in a little more than two decades since the mid-1950s when the real integration of the economy with the metropolitan economy started. Also, the fact that the rise in import size was about double that of export provides significant pointers towards the retrograde nature of the whole affair, which demands a serious probe for any meaningful appraisal of underdevelopment process operating in the society.

Table 4.17 Value and Index of Total Exports and Imports at Constant Price.

(Rs. in Million)

Fiscal Year	*Export*		*Import*		*Total*	
	Value	*Index (1956–57 = 100)*	*Value*	*Index (1956–57 = 100)*	*Value*	*Index (1956–57 = 100)*
1956/57	93.784	100	166.887	100	260.671	100
1960/61	193.950	207	368.025	221	561.975	216
1965/66	224.332	239	467.669	280	692.001	265
1975/76	392.537	419	656.024	393	1048.561	402
1979/80	251.831	269	926.808	555	1178.639	452

Note: Export and Import Values have been deflated by the price index complied by Reejal, P.R. (1982), *Nepal's Foreign Trade and Economic Development: 1956/57 to 1979/80* (mimeo.), CEDA, Kathmandu, Appendix 1:3, p. 9.

Source: Nepal Rastra Bank, *Quarterly Economic Bulletin*, (Various issues), Kathmandu.

The real social significance of the extent of economic integration without, as measured by the value of export-import trade, can be understood when it is related with the size of total economic production of society, as measured by the GDP. From Table 4.18 it is seen that the size of foreign trade has tended to hover below 20% of the GDP (except in 1964/65), which would indicate not as yet a dominant position of merchant capital in the economy. But a closer look at the temporal trend and disaggregation of the ratio by import and export components would convey some serious portents for the economy. If the rather exceptional situation of foreign trade in the later half of the 1960s is left aside for the time being an increasing hold of foreign trade in the economy is discernible which is particularly reflected in the gradual rise of total foreign trade/GDP raito from 12.31% in 1970/71 to 19.57% in 1978/79, to a slight drop to 18.02% in 1979/80. The retrograde nature of this rise in the ratio can be better appreciated when it is realised that, except for the exceptional years towards the end of 1960s, about two-thirds of the value of trade was in the form of imports. After 1975/76 not only this proportion had increased but the export/GDP ratio had actually declined. With such a distorted and retrograde structure of foreign trade expansion in its absolute size only amounts to strengthening the process of underdevelopment.

Table 4.18 Size of Foreign Trade as Related to Gross Domestic Product (1964/65–1979/80).

Fiscal Year	*Exports as % of GDP*	*Imports as % of GDP*	*Exports and Imports as % of GDP*
1964/65	7.87	14.62	22.49
1965/66	5.43	11.32	16.75
1966/67	6.64	7.50	14.15
1967/68	5.48	6.66	12.14
1968/69	7.16[1]	9.37[1]	16.53[1]
1969/70	5.58	9.87	15.44
1970/71	4.49[1]	7.82[1]	12.31[1]
1971/72	5.01	8.56	13.58
1972/73	6.33	9.87	16.20
1973/74	5.36	9.08	14.44
1974/75	5.37	10.95	16.32
1975/76	6.82	11.39	18.21
1976/77	6.74	11.62	18.36
1977/78	5.34	12.60	17.94
1978/79	6.07	13.50	19.57
1979/80	3.85	14.17	18.02

Note: [1] Provisional.
Source: Adapted from Reejal, P.R. (1982), *Nepal's Foreign Trade and Economic Development: 1956/57 to 1979/80* (mimeo.), CEDA, Kathmandu, Appendix 1.4.

The growing role of foreign trade in the economy, and its social implications, can be further understood from the rising share of tax revenue from foreign trade (i.e. custom duty) in the total state budget revenue (Table 4.19)

Table 4.19 Share of Customs Duty in State Budget Revenue.

Fiscal Year	*Customs duty as Imports duty*	*% of Total Exports duty*	*Budget Revenue Total duty on Foreign trade*
1950/51	–	–	13.98
1955/56	–	–	17.91
1960/61[(1)]	–	–	35.32
1965/66	36.58	6.07	43.19*
1970/71	30.11	3.76	34.05*
1975/76	28.37	3.38	32.13*
1980/81[(1)]	28.95	3.33	32.34*

Note: [(1)] Revised estimate.
* The total may be slightly higher than the sum of share of 'exports' and 'imports' duties because of some values which could not be classified into any of the two.

Source: HMG/N, Ministry of Finance (1982), *Budget in Nepal (1951/62–1981/82)*, Revenue Administration Training Center, Kathmandu.

Not only has this share risen from 13.98% in 1950/51 to a record 43.19% in 1965/66 to stabilize thereafter at around one-third of the total state revenue, but a staggering 85 to 90% of the custom duty was realised through import trade alone. This should establish beyond doubt to what extent the ruling classes have developed a vested interest in forging an unequal alliance with metropolitan capital.

What is amply evident from this cursory survey is the growing role of merchant capital allied with metropolitan capital in articulating the underdevelopment process in Nepalese society.

4.3.2 Volume and Direction of Trade: Dependence on India

Historical transformation of merchant capital in Nepal from a mediator of the economies of India and Tibet (China) in the form of entrepot trade via Nepal, to an exclusive appendage of Indian economy by the beginning of 1950s, has been sketched out earlier. The continuation of semi-colonial relations with India formalised by periodic treaties[74], virtual cessation of trade with Tibet after the early 1960s, compulsions of land-locked (or India-locked) geographical positioning, widening gap in the level of socio-economic development of India and Nepal, etc., on the one hand, and periodic divergence in the interests of metropolitan capitalist powers in the Himalayan region, on the other, are seen to have given rise to two opposing tendencies of integration of the Nepalese economy to the world imperialist order; i.e. at times exclusively under the hegemony of Indian monopoly capital and at other times with greater direct participation of other more prominent guardians of metropolitan capital. The decisive strength of the former tendency which comes from historical and geographical factors coupled with the qualitative divergence in the interests of rival centres of metropolitan capital, the dominant position of India in the matter of foreign trade 'partners', of Nepal may not be contested. Still, in the wake of increased inter-imperialist rivalry for maintaining hegemony over smaller countries like Nepal, the indigenous mercantile powers have got greater opportunity to 'diversify ' their external trade activities, which should have social and spatial implications. It would thus be pertinent to investigate this phenomenon with the help of some statistical support.

Tables 4.20 and 4.21 indicates the relative share of India[75], the Tibetan region of China and other 'overseas' countries in the total import-export trade and also shows their decadal growth ratios from end of 1950s to end of 1970s. A gradual loosening of monopoly hold of India from a staggering 96.35% of total external trade in the 1950s to a some-what moderate 53.30% in the 1970s and reciprocal rise in the case of 'overseas' countries from 2.74% to 46.70% during the same period is the apparent hallmark of change in external trade pattern. The negligible share of the other geographically contiguous area, i.e. Tibetan region of China[76], substantiates the end of entrepot trade and testifies total orientation of economic interactions without from the southern border. In terms of the import-export compotents there is a sharper fall in the share of export than in that of import vis-à-vis India. The trend is contrary vis-à-vis other countries. This contradicts the falsity of the apparent loosening of trade dependence on India. This more expressedly manifest in the reduction of export/import ratio from 49.70% in the 1950s to 34.0% in the 1970s. In terms of the actual increase in volume of trade by destinations the astounding 200 fold rise in the case of 'overseas' countries is more of a statistical illusion in view of the abysmally low starting base. Therefore, the comparatively moderate 7-fold increase in total trade with India with a massive initial base could be regarded as of greater significance for the articulation of social process in the country.

Significant variations observed in decadal growth ratios of trade volumes by partner countries could unfold important social dynamics governing the operation of merchant capital in the country. As observed in the preceding sections, a set of internal and external historical specificities had combined to make the decade of 1960s one of the most propitious periods for expansion of economic interactions without. This is amply reflected in the higher growth ration of foreign trade during 1950s–60s, specially that of export to 'overseas' countries, which was a phenomenal 400-fold. This apparently progressive development, much celebrated by the ruling class apologists as the historic loosening of traditional stranglehold of Indian monopoly capital in the country's economy and 'diversification' of trade to third countries, is just a camaflouging of essential dependence on India. Pending the analysis of commodity structure of trade in the next section, it can be said, on the basis of historical facts that this apparent 'diversification 'of trade away from India was merely a means or result of playing with the minor contradictions between the different factions of the custodians of metropolitan capital by restoring to oneself the original middleman status

Table 4.20 Volume of Trade and Export/Import Ratio by Major Destinations (1950s to 1970s).

	Export			Import			Total			Export/Import Ratio (%)		
	1950s	*1960s*	*1970s*	*1950s*	*1960s*	*1970s*	*1950s*	*1960s*	*1970s*	*1950s*	*1960s*	*1970s*
1. India	105.86 (98.33)	363.35 (74.94)	556.36 (47.78)	212.83 (95.40)	643.24 (92.32)	1634.08 (55.49)	318.69 (96.35)	1006.59 (85.19)	2190.44 (53.30)	49.7	56.5	34.0
2. Tibet	1.50 (1.39)	2.99 (0.62)	N.A.	1.49 (0.67)	5.01 (0.72)	N.A.	2.99 (0.90)	8.00 (0.68)	N.A.	100.5	59.7	N.A.
3. Overseas	0.296* (0.27)	118.53* (24.45)	608.12 (52.22)	8.77 (3.93)	48.52 (6.96)	1310.77 (44.51)	9.07 (2.74)	167.05 (14.14)	1918.89 (46.70)	3.4	244.3	46.4
TOTAL	107 (100.00)	484.87 (100.00)	1164.49 (100.00)	223.09 (100.00)	696.77 (100.00)	2944.85 (100.00)	330.75 (100.00)	1181.64 (100.00)	4109.34 (100.00)	48.3 (100.00)	69.6 (100.00)	39.5 (100.00)

Note: 1950s, 1960s and 1970s refer to triennum averages of 1957/58–1959/60, 1967/68–1969/70 and 1977/78–1979/80 respectively. Figures in parenthesis are percentages.

Source: Nepal Rastra Bank, *Quarterly Economic Bulletin* (Various Issues), Kathmandu.

Table 4.21 Growth Ratio of Import-Export Trade by Major Destinations.

	Import			Export			Total		
Destination	*1950s–1960s*	*1960s–1970s*	*1950s–1970s*	*1950s–1960s*	*1960s–1970s*	*1950s–1970s*	*1950s–1960s*	*1960s–1970s*	*1950s–1970s*
1. India	3.02	2.54	7.68	3.43	1.53	5.26	3.16	2.18	6.87
2. Tibet	3.35	–	–	1.99	–	–	2.68	–	–
3. Overseas	5.53	27.01	149.44	400.43	5.13	2054.46	18.42	11.49	211.56
TOTAL	3.12	4.23	13.20	4.50	2.40	10.82	3.57	3.48	12.42

Source: Derived from Table 4.21.

of passing on goods to and fro amongst the common trade partners, albeit illegally this time. This can be seen to have been operationalised through the officially devised trade schemes to 'subsidise' trade with third countries; like the by now thoroughly discredited Exporters' Exchange Entitlement (EEE) scheme, or more infamously referred to as 'bonus voucher scheme[77], in force from 1962/63 to 1978. Such schemes of entitling/exempting exporters to hard currency economies (or those other than India) to retain a specified proportion (i.e. up to 60%) of total value of exports for importing any commodity at will, could not but lead to proliferation of illegal and fictitious trade practices in the form of overinvoicing indigenous exports or re-exporting smuggled Indian goods to claim higher bonus for importing luxury goods that could be ultimately smuggled out to Indian markets[78]. Such indirect resort to entrepot trade and large-scale illegal practices were the principal factors that were to provide an illusion of diversification of trade.

Despite the continued dependence on India, the expansion of trade relations with other economies is also significant[79] and deserves probing into in terms of its role to distort the economic structure of the country. Since mercantile articulation with third countries has stabilized only in the 1970s and data are available for this short period only, it would be useful to observe growth pattern of trade by economic and regional classification of countries as provided in Table 4.22. Leaving aside the domination of the South Asian region, wherein lies the single dominant partner India, the most significant trend to be observed is the expansion of trade, particularly import trade with 'developed' countries. The expansion of exchange relations with economies at higher level of social productivity of labour at the expense of ones with more or less the same level aggravates 'unequal exchange' relations as defined earlier. The significant growth in trade (also the import component,) with 'centrally planned' economies (i.e. USSR and China in our context) could, however, be largely accounted to 'commodity aid' to finance construction projects, which seem to have been erroneously recorded as general imports.

In terms of individual trade partners[80] it is interesting to note that after India it is Japan which occupies the second dominant position by way of higher imports from it. Similarly, increasing integration of the economy with the more prominent citadels of metropolitan capital is evident from the important position in partnership hierarchy enjoyed by the U.S.A, West Germany, U.K. and important outposts of metropolitan capital nearer the region, like South Korea, Singapore and Hongkong. In general, a pattern of greater export to other underdeveloped countries (e.g. Bangladesh, Mauritius, Pakistan and Malaysia) and greater import from the developed countries, is clearly discernible, whose economic rationale and social implications are obvious.

All in all, the continued domination of India, on the one hand, and increasing integration with advanced capitalist countries or their props in the nearer region, on the other, amply speak of the retrograde role of merchant capital in aggravating the underdevelopment process.

Table 4.22 Direction of Trade by Economic and Regional Classification of Countries (1972/73 and 1978/79).

S. No.	Classification of Countries*	Export		Import		Total		Export/Import Ratio (%)	
		1972/73	1978/79	1972/73	1978/79	1972/73	1978/79	1972/73	1978/79
1.	Developed	19.98	23.38	11.29	23.70	13.62	23.59	64.79	48.81
2.	Developing	26.62	14.89	3.09	12.35	9.40	13.19	314.95	59.68
3.	Developing–Capital Surplus	–	0.01	–	–	–	0.003	–	∝
4.	Centrally Planned	5.73	6.64	1.63	11.53	2.73	12.54	128.32	28.50
5.	South Asian	47.67	55.08	83.99	52.42	74.26	53.30	20.77	51.99
	TOTAL	100.00	100.00	100.00	100.00	100.00	100.00	36.59	49.48

Note: * The grouping of countries has been done in accordance with the World Bank classification.

Source: Derived from Bista, N.K. (1981), *Import-Export Structure and Trade Expansion in South Asia (Nepal)*, (mimeo.), CEDA, Kathmandu, p. 24.

4.3.3 Structure and Terms of Trade

The more important question, than whom the exchange relations are carried with (which is important only in a general politico-economic sense) is the intensity of value content of the commodities exchanged. It is this which really determines the nature of exchange relations and their social implications. It is with this in mind that we seek to analyse the commodity structure and terms of trade of Nepal in a dynamic frame.

4.3.31 Structure of Commodities Exchanged

In the absence of time-series data in a more useful commodity classification, e.g. input-based or use-based, and in view of the clumsiness of analysis of a large number of unclassified commodities, we have sought to use SITC commodity groups to study commodity composition of trade from the 1950s to the 1970s for the total foreign trade and with the dominant partner India. A different typology has however been devised for trade with overseas countries during the 1970s only.

Tables 4.23 and 4.24 indicate the volume and percentage of different commodity groups imported and exported in total trade and that with India. Looking at the structure of exports first, it is seen that group '0', i.e. 'food including live animals' wherein rice constitutes the major share, and group '2', i.e. 'crude materials, inedibles except fuels' wherein jute and animal products like hides and skin occupy a prominent place, constitute an overwhelming proportion of total exports though in a slightly declining order. If group '0' to '4' are assumed as primary produces and the rest as manufactures, primary goods are seen to constitute 96.09%, 79.20% and 76.58% of total value of exports in the Fifties, Sixties and Seventies respectively. This is a clear manifestation of the prevailing backward nature of exchange relations. In the temporal frame, noticeable rise in the share of manufactured goods in the 1960s should be easily explicable in terms of spurious growth of export-oriented industries like stainless steel and synthetic textiles as already noted in the previous chapter. The failure to sustain the same pattern of growth in the subsequent decade adequately speaks of the inherent fragility of the productive base of the economy.

The structure of imports on the contrary is characterized by the predominance of manufactured products, which increase from 47.25% of the total imports in 1950s to 73.4% in the 1970s. This glaring pattern of export of primary produce and import of manufactures makes the exchange relations of Nepal a typical case of an underdeveloped economy. The retrograde nature of this pattern of exchange relations is further confirmed by the fact that an overwhelming proportion of manufactured imports are consumption-oriented than production – oriented, even if the share of 'machinery and transport equipment' in total import is seen to be rising of late. However, the increasing dependence on technological imports without any sign of improvement of indigenous productive base would

Table 4.23 Structure of Exports: Classified by Major Commodity Groups.

Code No. (1)	S.I.T.C Commodity Groups (2)	Total Exports (I)			Exports to India (II)			Exports to India as % of Total Exports (III)		
		1950s (3)	1960s (4)	1970s (5)	1950s (6)	1960s (7)	1970s (8)	1950s (9)	1960s (10)	1970s (11)
0.	Food (including live animals)	78197 (72.63)	250361 (51.64)	400213 (34.37)	76847 (72.39)	249344 (51.74)	215585 (38.75)	98.30 (1.00)	99.59 (1.00)	53.87 (1.127)
1.	Tobacco and Beverages	1210 (1.12)	2175 (0.45)	9153 (0.79)	1207 (1.14)	2122 (0.44)	927 (0.17)	99.75 (1.01)	97.56 (0.98)	10.13 (0.212)
2.	Crude Materials, Inedibles except Fuels	23793 (22.10)	130450 (26.90)	467498 (40.15)	23778 (22.40)	130357 (27.05)	290964 (52.30)	99.94 (1.01)	99.93 (1.01)	62.24 (1.303)
3.	Mineral Fuels and Lubricants	35 (0.03)	21 (0.004)	427 (0.04)	4 (0.004)	20 (0.004)	427 (0.08)	11.43 (0.12)	95.24 (0.96)	100.00 (2.093)
4.	Animal and Vegetable Oils and Fats	546 (0.51)	1003 (0.21)	14312 (1.23)	538 (0.51)	966 (0.20)	14070 (2.53)	98.53 (1.00)	96.31 (0.97)	98.31 (2.058)
5.	Chemicals and Drugs	231 (0.21)	1277 (0.26)	1928 (0.17)	227 (0.21)	1165 (0.24)	1411 (0.25)	98.27 (1.00)	91.23 (0.92)	73.18 (1.532)
6.	Manufactured Goods Classified Chiefly by Materials	1687 (1.57)	87285 (18.00)	214738 (18.44)	1648 (1.55)	85929 (17.83)	14261 (2.56)	97.69 (0.99)	98.45 (0.99)	6.64 (0.139)
7.	Machinery and Transport Equipments	22 (0.02)	273 (0.06)	2914 (0.25)	22 (0.02)	272 (0.06)	2182 (0.39)	100.00 (1.01)	99.63 (1.00)	74.88 (1.567)
8.	Miscellaneous Manufactured Articles	827 (0.77)	11696 (2.41)	52523 (4.51)	823 (0.77)	11385 (2.36)	3891 (0.70)	99.52 (1.09)	97.34 (0.98)	7.41 (0.155)
9.	Miscellaneous (n.e.s.)	1105 (1.03)	326 (0.07)	753 (0.06)	1065 (1.00)	326 (0.07)	644 (0.12)	96.38 (0.98)	100.00 (1.01)	85.52 (1.790)
	TOTAL	107660 (100.00)	484866 (100.00)	1164485 (100.00)	106159 (100.00)	481877 (100.00)	556363 (100.00)	98.61 (1.00)	99.38 (1.00)	47.78 (1.00)

Note:
- Triennum averages of 1957/58–1959/60, 1967/68–1969/70 and 1977/78–1979/80 are taken for 1950s, 1960s and 1970s respectively, to minimize yearly fluctuations.
- For 1950s and 1960s, exports to India also include exports to 'overseas countries'.
- Figures in parenthesis in columns (I) and (II) are percentages, and those in column (III) Location Factors to respective totals.

Source: Nepal Rastra Bank, *Quarterly Economic Bulletin* (Various issues), Kathmandu.

Table 4.24 Structure of Imports: Classified by Major Commodity Groups.

(in Rs. '000)

Code	S.I.T.C. Commodity Groups	Total Imports (I)			Imports from India (II)			Imports from India (III)		Total Imports
		1950s	1960s	1970s	1950s	1960s	1970s	1950s	1960s	1970s
0.	Food (including live animals	49219 (22.06)	116129 (16.67)	342656 (11.64)	47868 (22.49)	114653 (17.82)	297204 (18.19)	97.26 (1.019)	98.73 (1.069)	86.74 (1.563)
1.	Tobacco and Beverages	18468 (8.28)	8873 (1.27)	35258 (1.20)	18462 (8.67)	8165 (1.27)	27674 (1.69)	99.97 (1.048)	92.02 (0.997)	78.49 (1.414)
2.	Crude Materials, Inedibles except Fuels	10119 (4.54)	49296 (7.07)	71811 (2.44)	10063 (4.73)	45394 (7.06)	52449 (3.21)	99.45 (1.042)	92.08 (0.997)	73.04 (1.316)
3.	Mineral Fuels and Lubricants	15800 (7.08)	67931 (9.75)	314125 (10.67)	14512 (6.82)	66722 (10.37)	49060 (3.00)	91.85 (0.963)	98.22 (1.064)	15.62 (0.281)
4.	Animal and Vegetable Oils and Fats	8491 (3.81)	8369 (1.20)	26432 (0.90)	8491 (3.99)	8361 (1.30)	19295 (1.18)	100.00 (1.048)	99.90 (1.082)	73.00 (1.316)
5.	Chemicals and Drugs	9288 (4.16)	50028 (7.18)	316384 (10.74)	9278 (4.36)	46613 (7.25)	198169 (12.13)	99.89 (1.047)	93.17 (1.009)	62.64 (1.129)
6.	Manufactured Goods Classified Chiefly by Materials	81774 (36.65)	285846 (41.02)	997920 (33.89)	81610 (38.35)	261384 (40.64)	589807 (36.09)	99.80 (1.046)	91.44 (0.990)	59.10 (1.065)
7.	Machinery and Transport Equipments	7079 (3.17)	585991 (8.41)	592522 (20.12)	6429 (3.02)	51250 (7.97)	252913 (15.48)	90.82 (0.952)	87.47 (0.947)	42.68 (0.769)
8.	Miscellaneous Manufactured Articles	13990 (6.27)	50873 (7.30)	254779 (8.65)	13488 (6.34)	40000 (6.22)	142202 (8.70)	96.41 (1.011)	78.63 (0.852)	55.81 (1.006)
9.	Miscellaneous (n.e.s.)	8863 (3.97)	830 (0.12)	9664 (0.33)	2644 (1.24)	695 (0.11)	5307 (0.32)	29.83 (0.313)	83.73 (0.907)	54.92 (0.990)
	TOTAL	223092 (100.00)	696766 (100.00)	2944849 (100.00)	212828 (100.00)	643237 (100.00)	1634076 (100.00)	95.40 (1.00)	92.32 (1.00)	55.49 (1.00)

Note: Triennum averages of 1957/58–1959/60, 1967/68–1969/70 and 1977/78–1979/80 are taken for 1950s, 1960s and 1970s respectively, to minimize yearly fluctuations.

Figues in parenthesis in columns (I) and (II) are percentages, and in column (III) Location Factors.

Source: Nepal Rastra Bank, *Quarterly Economic Bulletin* (Various issues), Kathmandu.

perpetuate rather than mitigate the structurally inverted and distorted nature of the economy.

As per the commodity composition of foreign trade by major trading partners, no meaningful variation in the pattern from the general picture is noticeable. For example, in the case of exports to India the share of primary products is seen to have, dropped from 95.93% in the 1950s to 79.43% in 1960s, only to rise to the same level of 93.83% in the '70s. The only tangible difference in the commodity composition of primary exports in the '50s and '70s has been that the place of commodity group '0', i.e. rice and other cereals, in the 50s has been taken by group '2', i.e jute and other industrial raw materials, in the '70s. Also considering the dominant share of India in both import and export of every major group of commodities, except for the import of mineral fuels etc. and export of petty manufacturer, it can be concluded with fair degree of certainty that it is ultimately the commodity structure of trade with India that decides the overall foreign trade structure.

Some significant observations can be made from the commodity group-wise export/import ratios particularly with respect to trade with India (Table 4.25). It is seen that Nepal had an adverse balance of trade with India in all commodity groups, except group '2', i.e. jute, animal products, etc. In the case of group '0', i.e. food etc., and group '4', i.e. live animals etc., the import and export seem to be quite balanced. This could mean that due to poor physical and economic integration of different territorial units of the country the same commodities, specially foodgrains, animals, etc., are exported to India from one part of the country and imported back at other parts. This should further substantiate our apprehensions about the existence of a 'disarticulated' and 'extraverted' spatial structure in the country.

Table 4.25 Export/Import Ratio by Major Commodity Groups.

S.I.T.C. Commodity Groups	*Export/Import Ratio*			
	Total			*India*
	1950s	*1960s*	*1950s*	*1960s*
0. Food (including live animals)	1.589	2.156	1.168	0.725
1. Tobacco and Beverages	0.066	0.245	0.260	0.033
2. Crude Materials Inedibles except fuels	2.351	2.646	6.510	5.548
3. Mineral Fuels and Lubricants	0.002	0.0003	0.001	0.009
4. Animal and Vegetable Oils and Fats	0.064	0.120	0.541	0.729
5. Chemicals and Drugs	0.025	0.026	0.006	0.007
6. Manufactured Goods Classified Chiefly by Materials	0.021	0.305	0.215	0.024

(*Contd.*)

(*Table 4.25 contd.*)

S.I.T.C. Commodity Group	Export/Import Ratio			
	Total			India
	1950s	1960s	1950s	1960s
7. Machinery and Transport Equipments	0.003	0.005	0.005	0.009
8. Miscellaneous Manufactured articles	0.059	0.230	0.206	0.027
9. Miscellaneous (n.e.s.)	0.125	0.393	0.134	0.121
TOTAL	0.483	0.696	0.395	0.340

Note: Figures of triennum averages of 1957/58–1959/60, 1967/68–1969/70 and 1977/78–1979/80 are taken for 1950s, 1960s and 1970s respectively.
Source: Tables 4.23 and 4.24

Coming to the commodity structure of trade with countries other than India, i.e. 'overseas' countries, because of there being a relatively smaller number of commodities, the exports are presented by individual commodities (Table 4.26) and the imports by use-based classifications (Table 4.27). It is not surprising to note that jute and rice constitute the dominant export commodities. Whereas jute export is seen to maintain a consistently dominant position (despite its declining share)[81], that of rice is marked by extreme fluctuations; which reflects the fragile and unstable base of even the primary product in the country. As per the import structure which almost completely consists of manufacturer, non-durable consumer goods with a dominant share of textiles etc. constitute the major components of imports. This should bear an additional testimony to the pathetic extent of deindustrialisation of the country. Though the growth ratio of 'capital goods' imports may appear comparatively impressive, the limited number of commodities and heavy domination of 'aircraft and spare parts' in total value do not make it a particularly welcome phenomenon.

Table 4.26 Share of Major Commodities in Total Overseas* Exports (1971/72–197879).

(%)

Year/ Commodities	Jute and Jute Products	Rice	Hides and Skins	Carpets	Handi-crafts	Others	Total
1971/72	87.57	–	3.33	0.92	1.02	7.16	100.00
1972/73	61.24	–	8.59	1.84	3.95	24.74	100.00
1973/74	53.56	17.24	6.88	2.18	4.04	16.10	100.00
1974/75	48.09	2.30	3.62	9.07	10.50	26.42	100.00
1975/76	45.32	–	9.36	3.48	4.79	37.05	100.00
1976/77	43.72	–	15.17	7.68	5.66	27.77	100.00
1977/78	38.77	23.04	12.68	3.98	5.70	15.83	100.00
1978/79	33.36	28.71	15.17	5.39	4.89	12.48	100.00

Note: *Countries other than India.
Source: Trade Promotion Centre (1979), *Nepal Overseas Trade Statistics, 1978–79*, Kathmandu.

Table 4.27 Structure of Overseas Imports by Use-based Classification of Commodities.

Year *Commodity Groups*	*1971/72*	*1974/75*	*1978/79*	*Ratio Growth in 1978/79 over 1971/72*
1. Consumer Goods	72.08	35.82	38.08	9.62
(i) Consumer Non-durables	55.44 (47.47)[1]	29.52 (21.02)[1]	28.83 (22.81)[1]	9.46
(ii) Consumer Durables	16.64	6.30	9.25	10.12
2. Intermediate Goods	–	21.83 (18.80)[2]	15.22 (12.99)[2]	1.81[3]
3. Capital Goods	14.16	14.90	16.22	20.84
4. Basic Goods	–	9.65	9.05	2.43[3]
5. Miscellaneous	13.76	17.79	21.43	28.35
TOTAL	100.00	100.00	100.00	18.20

Notes: [1] % share of textiles and readymade garments, which were the single largest item of import throughout.

[2] % share of petroleum products, which were the 2nd largest item of import from 1974/75 onwords.

[3] Growth ratio in 1978/79 over 1974/75.

* Commodities were classified as follows: *Consumer Non-durables:* 1. Textile, 2. Readymade garments, 3. Office equipments and Stationery, 4. Medicines, 5. Spices, 6. Milk (Skimmed, condensed and powder); *Consumer Durables:* 1. Motor, Motorcycle and Spare Parts, 2. Radio, Transistor and Tape-recorder, 3. Electrical Goods; *Intermediate Goods:* 1. Iron Rod, Sheets and Corrugated Sheet, 2. Petroleum Products; *Capital Goods:* 1. Machineries and Parts, 2. Tractor and Spare Parts, 3. Aircraft and Spare Parts, 4. Telecommunication Equipments, 5. Scientific Research Equipments; *Basic Goods*; 1. Fertilizers, 2. Cement; Miscellaneous:1. Miscellaneous.

Source: Trade Promotion Center (1979), *Overseas Trade Statistics*, Kathmandu.

Apart from the universal primary-export and manufacture-import syndrome of underdeveloped trade structure, which is found valid in Nepal, another general characteristic supposedly is the pronounced primacy of few commodities in total value of exports. In the case of Nepal, again, the generally believed high concentration of few products in total value of exports, as evident from the high share of jute, rice and animal products observed earlier, has been officially acknowledged by no less an authority as the UNCTAD[82]. Nor only is the concentration index seen high, but it is also seen as one of the highest as compared to other similarly placed countries, thereby further confirming the acuteness of dependency and underdevelopment.

4.3.32 Terms of Trade

Adverse terms of trade in exchange relations with developed economies is another widely encountered hallmark of underdeveloped economies. Because of their monopoly hold over the means of production and distribution the advanced capitalist economies are found in a position to manipulate the prices of their export commodities and dictate import prices of commodities from backward economies to their advantages. Consequently there is wide variation in the rate of change of import and export prices, the export prices of commodities in underdeveloped economies generally registering a low growth as against a high growth of import prices from developed economies, thus giving rise to adverse terms of trade against the underdeveloped economy. Thus in addition to the generalised form of 'unequal exchange' resulting from the transformation problem of value into prices this concrete form of relative decline in barter terms of trade acts as a mechanism of transfer of value from a backward to an advanced economy.

In the absence of a reliable price index of commodities exported and imported by destinations for a reasonable length of time we have sought to generate our own import and export price indices for India and the overseas' countries for 1974/75–1981/82 making certain assumptions[83] for calculating net barter terms of trade (Table 4.28). Despite a number of lacunae in the construction of the indices, it is interesting to note that terms of trade with India over the year has deteriorated with some fluctuations. It has fluctuated more markedly vis-a-vis 'overseas' countries, the trade has been declining after the favourable position during the initial few years. However, in view of the overall domination of India in the total trade, the net effect could reasonably be assumed to have been detrimental to Nepal

Table 4.28 Net Barter Terms of Trade of Nepal with India and 'Overseas' Countries (1974/75–1981/82).

Year	*Export Price Index (Px)*		*Import Price Index (Pm)*		*Net Barter Terms of Trade Px x 100*	
	India	*Overseas*	*India*	*Overseas*	*India*	*Overseas*
1974–75	100.0	100.00	100.00	100.00	100.00	100.00
1975–76	79.2	122.9	98.0	101.7	80.8	120.8
1976–77	84.2	159.7	105.5	110.8	80.3	144.1
1977–78	120.4	205.2	105.2	125.1	114.4	164.0
1978–79	122.6	199.5	117.2	144.7	104.6	137.9
1979–80	150.4	254.9	141.0	170.3	106.6	149.7
1980–81	144.3	216.7	158.2	168.4	91.2	128.7
1981–82	126.3	172.2	162.2	167.3	77.9	102.9

Note: 1. The Export Price Index is constructed as follows:

$$EPI_t = \sum_{i=i}^{10} P_{it} W_{it}$$

Where, EPI_t = Export Price Index for year *t*.

P_{it} = Index of export unit value for commodity *i* in year *t*.

$$W_{it} = \text{Weight } \frac{x_{it}}{1^{10} x_{it}}.$$

2. The Import Price Index for 'overseas' is constructed as follows:

$$MPI_t = \sum_{i=1}^{12} P_{it} W_{it}.$$

Where, MPI_t = Import Price Index for year *t*.

P_{it} = Index of export unit value of country *i* in year *t*.

$$W_{it} = \text{Weight } \frac{M_{it}}{\sum_{t=1}^{11} m_t}.$$

The adverse impact made by trade relations with overseas countries on the Nepalese economy can be had when we consider the domination of jute export in total export of the country and see it against the definite decline in world terms of trade in jute and jute products:

Year	*1970*	*1971*	*1972*	*1973*	*1974*	*1975*	*1976*	*1977*	*1978*	*1979*
World Terms of trade of jute	133	124	119	100	104	100	78	77	84	71

Source: UNCTAD (1982), op. cit., p. 217.

The official sources of Nepal have also acknowledged that Nepalese jute products have been sold at 50% of the production cost, in the hope of getting compensated by super-profits to be accrued through re-export of luxury goods to India imported with the earnings from jute exports to overseas countries under the bonus voucher scheme[84]

4.3.4 Spatial Organisation of Foreign Trade

In view of the historically important role played by foreign trade in decisively tilting the spatial organisation of the country towards the south, examination of its current position assumes relevance.

Differentiation of areas of production and consumption and location of 'gateway junctions' that physically link indigenous economy with the outside world, constitute the most important elements in spatial organisation of foreign trade. Viewed in terms of the four broad territorial units along the east-west dimensions (Table 4.29), it is observed that the eastern sector with a heavy centralisation of jute and other agricultural products occupies the foremost position in the total size of exports. The central sector on the other hand (including Kathmandu Valley) that houses the citadels of state bureaucracy and principal nodes of population concentration accounts for an overwhelming share of total imports. The share of economically more laggard western and far-western sectors is logically found negligible. In terms of net balance of trade as measured by export/import ratio, only the eastern sector is seen to have positive balance of trade and the rest of the areas are net drainers of value. In the temporal frame, the spatial variations, i.e. high share of total export of the eastern sector and an overwhelming share of total imports into the central sector, get accentuated further. This spatial pattern of export-import trade broadly differentiates the areas of production and consumption and fully conforms to the historical loci of merchant capital in the country. Though no break-up by micro-spatial units are available, by relating the commodity structure of trade as observed earlier with this broad pattern of spatial differentiation it can be fairly well surmised that whereas Terai is the major contributor in exports, Kathmandu Valley and other nodes of state bureaucracy account for much of the imports. The same spatial pattern holds good in the case of import-export trade with India as well, in view of the near identical commodity structure of trade.

Looking at the micro level, the decisive role in defining the spatial configuration of foreign trade seems to have been exercised by the historico-geographical compulsions of land-lockedness and the resultant radial spread of trade and transit routes from important transit points along the southern border to the nearest sea-port of Calcutta for 'overseas' trade and to major urban areas in the contiguous regions of India. As is the tendency of merchant capital to centralise around principal gateway junctions along the major transportation arteries, principal centres of foreign trade are seen to have grown just across the Indian border facing the rail-heads. Leaving aside the by no means insignficant components of illegal trade across the open Nepal-India border, the spatial distribution of foreign trade can be studied with respect to the specified connecting nodes along the border, which number 16 along the Indian border for 'overseas' trade, and 8 along the Tibetan (Chinese) border. In the case of general trade with India there are 18 main and 123 sub-customs offices located approximately at 4 miles interval on an average in the 500 miles long Indo-Nepalese border[85]. It is interesting to note that of the 16 identified connecting points (i.e. as recognised by the Nepal-India Trade agreement) for transacting foreign trade across Indian border 12 are just across the Indian rail-heads and 14 are connected with Indian road networks[86] In the east-west territorial dimensions a greater concentration of connecting points is seen in the eastern Terai, which is quite logical in view of its stronger production base within and its proximity to Calcutta port. Apart from the historical concentration of gateway junctions in the Terai has risen to prominence with increased diversification of trade away from India is the Kathmandu airport which has direct connections with major cities of South and South-East Asia. Most of the low bulk 'overseas' trade is increasingly transited through it.

The relative significance of individual connecting points can be better gauged from the size and share of export-import trade channelled through them. Table 4.30 provides for overall import-export volume through principal getway junctions of Biratnagar, Birgunj, Bhairahava and Nepalgunj for 1966 and Table 4.31 gives a disaggregation of trade volume with India, Tibet and 'overseas' countries for 1980–81. On the basis of the tables conclude that foreign trade in Nepal demonstrated a tendency of centralising around the major trading nodes of Biratnagar, Birgunj, Bhairahawa, Nepalgunj and Kathmandu.

Table 4.29 Import-Export Trade with overseas Countries by Terrotorial Zones (1974/75-1978/79)

(%)

Territorial Zones	Import			Export			Export/Import	
	1974/75	*1976/77*	*1978/79*	*1974/75*	*1976/77*	*1978/79*	*1976/77*	*1978/79*
1. Eastern Sector	19.7	11.6	10.7	55.9	53.2	60.2	278.89	330.15
2. Central Sector (including Kathmandu Valley)	71.7	78.2	79.4	36.7	43.1	34.5	33.55	25.46
3. Western Sector	5.0	6.7	6.6	3.5	0.5	0.8	4.77	7.55
4. Far-Western Sector	3.6	3.5	3.3	3.9	3.2	4.5	55.77	80.43
NEPAL	100.00	100.00	100.00	100.00	100.00	100.00	60.87	58.63

Source: 1. Trade Promotion Center (1979), *Nepal Overseas Trade Statistics 1978-79*, Kathmandu, for 1976/77 and 1978/79 figures.
2. Central Bureau of Statistics (1982), *Statistical Pocket Book Nepal 1982*, Kathmandu, for 1974/75 figures.

Table 4.30 Volume of Export–Import Through Major Custom Points (1966).

(Rs. Million)

Custom Point	*Export*	*Import*	*Total*	*Export/ Import (%)*
1. Biratnagar	133.345 (31.28)	86.305 (17.93)	219.650 (24.20)	154.50
2. Birgunj	25.124 (5.89)	164.288 (34.14)	189.412 (20.87)	15.29
3. Bhairahawa	11.720 (1.75)	44.758 (9.30)	56.478 (6.22)	26.19
4. Nepalganj	20.150 (4.73)	22.760 (4.73)	42.91 (4.73)	88.53

Note: Figures in parenthesis are percentages to the country total.
Source: Central Bureau of Statistics, cited in Okhda (1970).

In terms of individual nodes, Biratnagar is seen to account for the largest share (i.e. 31.28%) of export and Birgunj the largest share of import (i.e. 34.14%) in 1966 and the same pattern is seen to have continued till 1980–81, but with somewhat reduced share because of emergence of newer nodes. The pattern of nodal concentration is easily explicable in terms of the fact that Birgunj has historically been the 'gateway to Kathmandu'. Biratnagar, with its location in the agriculturally and industrially the most advanced region and its good connectivity with Indian railway system, has been the most important trading outpost linked with the metropolitan economic system. Similarly, Bhairahawa and Nepalgunj continue to be the satellitic centres in their respective territorial zones to serve as outposts of metropolitan economy. The exchange points along the Mountain and Hill are too diminutive reflecting upon the depressed economy of their hinterlands.

In sum, the overall spatial organisation of foreign trade is characterised by a decisive orientation towards India, creation and centralisation of trading outposts along the Southern border and polarisation around selected nodes.

4.4 OPERATION OF MERCHANT CAPITAL IN TOURIST TRADE

4.4.0 The theoretical dilemma of classifying tourism activity whether in 'production' or 'circulation' sphere may be largely resolved by deciding which components is pre-dominant in the total economic process. Though production of significant measure of 'services' cannot be denied, on close examination it is not hard to see that this is essentially in the process of realization of value of a commodity already produced, and in that sense it assumes a secondary economic importance. For example, much of the 'income' in tourism is seen to realize through lodging and fooding in the hotel and restaurant, transportation and sales of souvenirs.[87] It needs no explanation that the production and sale of 'service' component in hotels and restaurants are far out weighed by the act of realizing and already existing value in the building and furnishing of the hotels and

Table 4.31 Volume of External Trade by Major Custom Points (1980/81).

(Rs. Million)

Territorial Zones/ Custom Points*	Import				Export				Export/Import Ratio
	India	Tibet	Overseas	Total	India	Tibet	Overseas	Total	
MOUNTAIN									
Eastern									
1. Olangchung	–	0.05	–	0.05	–	0.26	–	0.26	5.45
2. Lamabagar	–	0.32	–	0.32	–	0.72	–	0.72	2.23
3. Tatopani	–	20.63	–	20.63	–	23.10	–	23.10	1.12
Central									
4. Rasuwa	–	8.31	–	8.31	–	1.64	–	1.64	1.97
5. Larke	–	0.39	–	0.39	–	0.39	–	0.39	1.00
6. Mustang	–	0.31	–	0.31	–	0.45	–	0.45	1.44
Western		NOT			AVAILABLE				
HILL									
Eastern									
7. Pasupatinagar	9.21	–	–	9.21	4.23	–	2.27	6.50	0.71
Western									
8. Jhulaghat	11.89	–	–	11.89	6.62	–	–	6.62	0.56
KATHMANDU VALLEY									
9. Tribhuvan Airport	N.A.	–	272.57	N.A.	N.A.	–	102.90	N.A.	N.A. (0.38)**
INNER TERAI									
Western									
10. Koilabas	116.91[1]		4.47	121.38	13.53	–	–	13.53	0.11

(Contd.)

(*Table 4.31 contd.*)

*Territorial Zones/ Custom Points**	*Import*				*Export*				*Export/Import Ratio*
	India	*Tibet*	*Overseas*	*Total*	*India*	*Tibet*	*Overseas*	*Total*	
TERAI									
Eastern									
Far-Eastern									
11. Mechi	155.84[2]	–	9.17	165.01	43.86	–	169.56	213.42	1.29
12. Biratnagar	281.48	–	121.87	403.35	58.53	–	314.23	372.76	0.92
Mid-Eastern									
13. Rajbiraj	6.47	–	–	6.47	3.14	–	–	3.14	0.48
14. Siraha	7.55	–	53.37	60.92	4.67	–	–	4.67	0.08
15. Jaleswar	77.82	–	6.64	84.45	9.73	–	3.49	13.21	0.16
16. Sarlahi	3.71	–	–	3.71	0.11	–	–	0.11	0.03
Eastern									
17. Gaur	21.16	–	–	21.16	9.88	–	–	9.88	0.47
18. Birgunj	1052.80[3]	–	345.32	1398.12	98.91	–	180.78	279.69	0.20
Central									
19. Bhaira hawa	201.64	–	41.89	243.53	26.51	–	3.29	29.80	0.12
20. Krishnanagar	36.37	–	4.41	40.78	8.21	–	–	8.21	0.20
Western									
21. Napalgunj	93.53	–	14.76	108.29	29.39	–	30.57	59.96	0.55
22. Kailali	19.35	–	12.67	32.02	33.17	–	15.04	48.21	1.51
23. Kanchanpur	53.64	–	–	53.64	143.09	–	–	143.09	2.67

Note: * Include hereby Custom posts: **export/import ratio for 'overseas' trade only.

[1] Including Rs. 85.32 million for import of trucks for temporary usage.

[2] Including Rs. 85.01 million for import of trucks for temporary usage.

[3] Including Rs. 100.62 million for import of trucks for temporary usage.

Source: Records of Department of Customs, Ministry of Finance, HMG/N, Kathmandu.

production of food-items. Similarly, the acts of transportation of tourists (note *not goods*) to various destinations or guiding them do not produce any value but are merely prelude to selling them goods and services produced elsewhere. Thus, at best tourism can be categorized as belonging to the sphere of export trade, but with reduced acts of exchanges. Moreover, in an underdeveloped and backward economy, which has to import a large chunk of commodities to be 'sold' to the tourist, the business of tourism may be only a form of entrepot trade, when imported goods are re-exported, but here the 'foreign' consumer himself would be at his door.

Since our immediate concern here is to probe into the role of tourism in modifying the social and spatial structure of Nepal, we would pass on to that.

4.4.1 Status of Tourism in the Economy

Inspired by great natural possessions of Himalayan Mountains and fair amount of cultural endowments, tourism has been considered a medium of ready realization of income by the ruling classes of Nepal. Hence the pronouncement—that amongst the 'four' main foreign exchange earners, namely ex-servicemen, foreign aid, trade and tourism, the state "has to be more dependent upon trade and tourism and should consider both to be permanent and essential sources of increasing national income and earning foreign exchange"[88]. Perhaps in keeping with the same dictum, there has been a phenomenal expansion of the tourism sub-sector in the economy of the country from a low base in the beginning of the 1960s. (Table 4.32). Not only has the volume of tourist flow increased more than 26 times and the earnings by an incredible six hundred times with an accompanying rise in per capita earning, the share of earning from tourism in the total receipts of convertible foreign exchange is seen to have progressively increased from a mere 1.23% in 1962 to 23.42% in 1978 to get stabilized at 23.26% in 1981[89]. Whether the ratio has been inflated due to the failure of other branches of the economy to contribute to the foreign exchange or not, the size of this branch of economic activity has definitely expanded and its role in articulating the total economic structure of society enhanced. Looking at the rate of growth of tourist arrivals and total earnings from tourism during the successive periods from 1962 onwards, however, a slackening of the rate is discernible after 1974, thus implying the inherent structural weaknesses of the economy or the limits of tourism activity itself to sustain a constant growth over time.

In terms of total capital investment in tourism-oriented activities like hotels, travel and tours, etc. (Table 4.33), a distinct acceleration is visible during 1970/71–1980/81. As against the 4-fold growth in investment in hotels during the decade, the investment in travel and tours was 18 fold. Also the absolute value of investment of NRs 218.512 million in 1980–81 constituted 43.0% of total investment in manufacturing activities for the same year. This is a further confirmation of growing economic significance of tourism in the country.

Table 4.32 Growth Trends of Tourist Arrivals and Gross Foreign Exchange From Tourism (1962–1981).

Year	Tourist Arrivals			Total Earning[1]			Earning per Capital (US$)	Earning from Tourism as % of total Receipts of Convertible Foreign Exchange
	Number	Index	Annual Growth Rate[2] (%)	In '000 US$	Index	Annual Growth Rate (%)		
1962	6179	100		78	100		12.62	1.23
1966	12567	203	17.04	399	512	33.65	31.75	3.70
1970	45970	744	28.53	1309	1678	26.64	28.48	4.82
1974	89838	1454	16.15	9079	11640	37.40	101.06	17.58
1978	156123	2527	13.47	27801	35642	25.38	178.07	23.42
1981	161669	2616	1.16	51831	66450	20.12	320.60	23.26

Note:
1. 'Total Earning' is for the Fiscal Year ending with the first half of the corresponding years cited in the Table, as the Fiscal Year starts from July 16 and ends July 15.
2. The growth rates have been calculated by the formula, $G(t\text{–}1),\ t = At = A_{t-1} / \frac{(A_t + A_{t-2})}{2}$, growth rate between the times $t - 1$ and t; A = Attribute.

Source: HMG/N, Ministry of Tourism (1982), *Annual Statistical Report 1981*, Department of Tourism, Kathmandu and Nepal Rastra Bank (1982), *Quarterly Economic Bulletin*, Kathmandu.

Table 4.33 Capital Investment in Tourism-Oriented Activities (1970/71 and 1980/81).

(Rs. Million)

	1970/71	*1980/81*	*Decadal Growth Ratio*
1. Hotels	52.307	208.412	3.984
2. Travels and Tours, etc.	0.550	10.100	18.364
TOTAL	52.857	218.512	4.134

Source: HMG/N, Department of Industries, Kathmandu.

From the point of view of generating employment, however, this sub-sector of economy cannot be said to have attained any degree of social significance. Though no authentic records of size of employment for the total sub-sector is available, one report puts the number of employed in hotels to be around 2000 and another 500 for other related activities in 1971[90]. A later study estimated about 700–8000 persons in 1974–75 to be employed in "producing goods and services consumed by tourists", which figure represented only 0.2% of the labour force in the country[91].

The dichotomous role of tourism in the economy is hence apparent, which should get further clarified in later sections.

4.4.2 Social Implications of Tourism

In the social formation hegemonised by the landlord-mercantile classes and in an economic sub-sector essentially seen as one of the main "foreign exchange earner", the ultimate social implication of the act may not be hard to forecast as that of strengthening this class hegemony internally and reproducing the linkages with metropolitan capital externally. It would therefore be relevant to investigate this aspect of the phenomenon with available empirical support.

4.4.21 Commensurate with the low level of social development and accompanying low mobility of indigenous people, the business of tourism in the context of Nepal essentially implies foreign tourists-internal cross-movement of local people being marginal and unrecorded and out-flow being heavily outnumbed by in-flow[92]. The apparently upper class-biased nature of tourism, therefore, may be discerned from such proxy measures as the country of origin, purpose, mode of travel, category of hotel stayed in, per capita expenditure of tourist, etc.

The fact that of the total tourist arrival in the country in 1981, 42.8% were from Asia including 30.29% from India and the rest from Western Europe (i.e. 40.2%), North America (i.e. 10.6%) and other parts of the world (i.e. 6.4%) indicates the relative domination of tourists from high-income societies[93] Similarly, the predominance of tourists traveling by air (i.e. 89% of total tourists in 1966 and 88% in 1981) over those travelling by land routes, and, according to purpose of visit, dominance of those for 'pleasure' (i.e. 79% of the total tourists in 1981) over those for other purposes, indicates the high-class bias in the whole affair.

The pattern of exchange limited to upper strata of society is all the more evident from the disaggregation of tourists by class-status of their hotels and the share of total expenditure incurred by each category, as presented in Table 4.34. Nearly 32% of total tourists with about 47% of total expenditure between them are seen to be the occupants of 4 and 5 star hotels. Their economic significance would be seen much more if their per capita per day expenditure and resultant income accruing to the hoteliers from them is taken into account. For the relatively larger share of gross expenditure of lower-class tourists is merely due to their average longer stay. The pattern of domination of higher-class tourists would be further manifest if only the tourists from countries other than India, which consists about 70% of the total, is considered.

Table 4.34 Percentage of Tourists and their Share in Total Expenditure by Class of Hotels (1974/75).

	From Countries other than India		*From India*		*Total*	
Hotel Class	*% of Visitors*	*% of total Expenditure*	*% of Visitors*	*% of total Expenditure*	*% of Visitors*	*% of total Expenditure*
1. 1–Star Hotel and lodging	30.67	20.50	53.67	28.52	36.61	21.39
2. 2– and 3 Star Hotel	26.73	26.54	24.05	32.82	26.04	27.24
3. 4– and 5 Star Hotel	39.46	48.83	10.24	32.08	31.92	46.97
4. Private Home	3.14	4.14	12.04	6.58	5.44	4.41

Source: Derived from Burger, V. (1978), *The Economic Impact of Tourism in Nepal: An Input-Output* Analysis (Ph. D. Dissertation, microfilmed), Cornell University, Ithaca, Table 15, p. 119.

The inevitable social implications of this nature of economic activities confined to the consumption needs of the upper strata of society is a cancerous growth of economy little related to the average life of society, and logically dependent on the metropolitan economy. The mushrooming of luxury hotels, running of the only cashino in South Asia, flooding of markets with conspicuous consumption goods, which would obviously have an adverse 'demonstration effects' on the budding middle classes, are all outward manifestations of this spurious growth primarily triggered by tourism in Nepal. Naturally, the current development pattern of tourism in Nepal is found to be 3 times as more capital-intensive as the manufacturing sector, and with this lopsided capital-labour ratio in a labour surplus economy an impossible rate of capital investment of some NRs 4 billion per annum is estimated to be necessary to employ the annual increase in the country's labour force[94]

4.4.22 External Dependence through Tourism

The logical outcome of luxury-oriented and capital-intensive economic activities in a backward formation would be heavy dependence on the metropolitan economy for its reproduction. Before coming to this investigation it has to be recapitulated in advance that as a corollary to the larger political-economy of 'dominance-dependence' between India and Nepal, the tourism sub-sector of Nepal has from the beginning been a mere extension of tourism market of India, or a 'secondary destination' of regional tourism market in Asia. It may just be enough to quote from the official *Nepal Tourism Master Plan* of 1972 in this context:

> "... the dependence on the Indian tourism – like in other sectors of the economy of Nepal – has been most influenced in shaping the present status of tourism in the country.
>
> "Basically this dependence would not give cause for concern since most of the tourism in Asian countries is interconnected same way or the other, were it not for the fact that the present situation is much less beneficial to Nepal than it is to India. Given the present situation where more than two-thirds of the visitors to Nepal are organized travellers handled by Indian travel agents which functions as intermediate agents, much of the tourists' travel budget remains with the Indian agents which often pay the hotels in Nepal in non-convertible currency."[95]

The phenomenon of this external dependence can be empirically observed with the help of Tables 4.35 and 4.36. Despite some inherent limitations, both at the conceptual and empirical level, in determining the "final payment" to different factors "expressed as proportion of expenditure" Table 4.35 provides a useful indication of total "leakage" taking place to outside economies, both Indian and 'Overseas', through this principal "foreign exchange earner", i.e. tourism. Final payments to foreign factors from the expenditure of different category of tourists classified by 'purpose' and 'income level' (reflected in star-categorization of hotels), are seen to range from 24.7% for the 'trekker with porters' to 40.9% for general pleasure tourists staying in 4- and 5-star hotels and to 44.8% for Indian tourists staying in 'private homes', which is quite considerable and seems to tally with estimates of earlier observers.[96] Of the total transfer of payments to outside economy, India quite understandably is seen to account for the predominant share ranging from 16.5% for Indian tourists staying in 'private homes to 31.0% for general tourists travelling for 'business and official'

Table 4.35 Share of Payments to Different Factors in the Expenditure of Tourists by Category (1974/75).

Factors	Expenditure by Category of Tourists											
	Pleasure Tourists				Trekkers			Business	Indians			
	1 Star and lodge	2 and 3 Star Hotel	4 and 5 Star Hotel	Private Home	Organised	With Parlers	Without Porters	Official and others	1–Star Hotel lodge	2 and 3 Star Hotel	4 and 5 Star Hotel	Private Home
I. Foreign Factors	31.5	36.7	40.9	38.9	36.2	24.7	27.3	38.2	32.3	29.4	33.7	44.8
1. India	23.7	27.9	30.4	29.9	28.4	20.1	21.4	31.0	17.7	18.5	24.2	16.5
2. Overseas	7.8	8.8	10.5	9.0	7.7	4.6	5.9	7.1	14.6	10.9	9.5	28.3
II. Nepalese Factors	68.5	63.3	59.1	61.1	63.8	75.3	72.7	61.8	67.7	70.6	66.3	55.2
1. Payroll	13.8	14.5	13.0	12.2	9.7	8.7	12.2	13.1	15.2	14.6	11.6	11.1
2. Payment to Sherpas and Porters	–	–	–	–	16.8	18.6	–	–	–	–	–	–
3. Gross Profit	21.3	21.0	24.5	19.0	14.7	13.5	18.9	22.7	22.0	22.1	28.9	13.8
4. Government	12.2	11.8	11.2	11.3	6.3	6.7	10.7	11.0	12.4	13.8	11.6	15.2
*5. Non-Surveyed Industries	20.4	14.7	9.5	17.7	15.3	27.2	30.2	14.1	16.8	18.2	13.1	13.9
6. Others	0.8	1.3	0.9	0.8	1.0	0.6	0.7	0.9	1.3	1.9	1.1	1.2
TOTAL	100.0	100.0	100.0	100.0	100.0	100.0	100.0	100.0	100.0	100.0	100.0	100.0

Note: *'Non surveyed industries' include Agriculture, Miscellaneous Industries and Services and Distribution.

Source: Derived from Burger, V. (1978), *The Economic Impact of Tourism in Nepal: An Input-Output Analysis* (Unpublished Ph.D. Dissertation), Cornell University, Table 26, pp.188–193.

purposes. In general trekkers and low-income tourists staying in low-class hotels are seen to be the best for ensuring larger retention of income from tourism within the social economy.

Table 4.36 Direct and Indirect Imports Required in Some Tourism-Oriented 'Industries' (1974/75).

(%)

Category	*Imports*		
	From India	*From Overseas*	*Total*
1. 4- and 5-Star Hotel	25.3	6.2	31.5
2. 2- and 3-Star Hotel	14.3	2.1	16.4
3. 1-Star Hotel and Lodge	6.1	0.4	6.5
4. Local Restaurant	8.5	0.0	8.5
5. Travel Agency	23.9	6.3	30.2
6. Trekking Agency	22.8	7.4	30.2
7. Transportation-air	32.7	17.3	50.0
8. Transportation-tourists	36.9	5.6	42.5
9. Transportation-goods	27.8	0.0	27.9
10. Transportation-taxi	44.9	0.0	44.9
11. Electricity	9.0	3.6	12.5
12. Printing	47.0	0.0	47.0
13. Repair and Maintenance	27.8	0.1	27.9
14. Jewellery and Curios	24.9	0.0	24.9
15. Carpets	47.0	0.0	47.0

Source: Adapted from Burger, V. (1978), *The Economic Impact of Tourism in Nepal, An Input-Output Analysis* (Unpublished Ph.D. Dissertation), Cornell University, Ithaca.

A simplerer idea of external economic nexus of tourism can be obtained from the share of direct and indirect imports to total expenditure of different 'industries' connected with tourism (Table 4.36). It is interesting, but quite logical, to note that the share of import value varies from the lowest of 6.5% in 1-Star hotel and lodge and 8.5% for local restaurant to as high as 50% for air-transportation and 74% each for printing and carpets. Again, quite expectedly the share of India in total imports is seen to be dominant in all the observed 'industries'.

The logical conclusion emanating from the foregoing analysis is that tourism in Nepal is basically performing a mere mediatory role between the producers and consumers of an alien economy and thus has no firm roots in the indigenous economy.

4.4.23 Impact of Internal Social Structure

Despite the observed exogenously implanted nature of tourism in Nepal the very fact that it is operating in and is sustained by the local system, and also the basic historic-materialist theoretical formulations of assigning primary role to the *internal* factors in any social process, demand that the internal social base of such a dysfunctional development be probed.

Observation in earlier sections have established that the feudal-mercantile classes exercise a total hegemony over the Nepalese social-polity and tourism by the nature of its development should come under this broad ambit. At the more concrete level, the pattern of 'industrial loans' disbursed by State-operated NIDC, which are heavily biased in favour of tourism-oriented activities, particularly luxury hotels, should provide enough hints as to the essential class base of tourism and establish its nexus with the said class-state. Also, from general observations it can be reasonably assumed that tourism with its known linkages with metropolitan capital forms the most profitable avenue for investment of 'primary capital' accumulated by the traditional feudal mercantile classes.

In the absence of more reliable information, we have sought through Table 4.37 to differentiate ownership of total capital investment in tourism-oriented activities by dominant social groups. A cursory glance through it would suffice to conclude that the two traditional ruling families, Ranas and Shah, and

Table 4.37 Capital Investment in Tourism-Oriented Activities by Dominant Social Groups (Upto 1980–81).

(Rs. Million)

Social Goups Tourism Oriented	*Hotels*	*Travels and Tours and other Tourism business*	*Total*
1. Newars	227.748 (16.47)	13.800 (18.40)	241.548 (16.57)
2. Ranas and Shahs	589.922 (42.65)	24.529 (32.70)	614.451 (42.14)
3. Hill Brahmin and Chhetris	140.898 (10.19)	18.080 (24.11)	158.978 (10.90)
4. Terai–Brahmin and Chhetris	0.738 (0.05)	–	0.738 (0.05)
5. Marwaris and Indians	319.814 (23.12)	6.600 (8.80)	326.414 (22.39)
6. Others	44.304 (3.20)	6.196 (8.26)	50.50 (3.46)
7. Public Ltd. Cos.	59.602 (4.31)	5.800 (7.73)	65.402 (4.49)
TOTAL	1383.026 (100.00)	75.005 (100.00)	1458.031 (100.00)

Note: Figures in parenthesis are percentages.
Source: Records of HMG/N, Department of Industries, Kathmandu.

Marwaris and Indian monopoly capitalists exercise clear hegemony in the tourism sub-sector. Close on their heels are seen the indigenous mercantile groups, the Newars. The overwhelming dominance of these traditional mercantile and landed interests (particularly Ranas and Shahs) in the burgeoning tourism sub-sector amply proves that tourism is a mere overgrowth of the traditional economic structure of society. Also, any casual observation of the ownership pattern of big luxury hotels in Kathmandu, i.e. mostly by the ruling Shah and Rana families in collaboration with Indian monopoly capitalists, should suffice to realize the retrograde comprador-mercantile class essence of tourism in the country.

By the very nature of extraverted, top-heavy and capital intensive development of tourism in the country, the 'multiplier effect' expected to result from the promotion of circulation activities, could be largely rules out. However, as implied in certain observation in Table 4.35 above, some tourist activities particularly the once related to the low-income pleasure tourists and trekkers, can be seen to provide some impetus to the growth of other related economic activities by way of providing markets to their goods and services. Consequently some growth in petty commodity production along the major tourist routes, specially those of trekking, can be envisaged, but which would by no means be enough to make an impact on a social scale. The hitherto marginal impact of tourism in indigenous production structure of society can very well be generalized from the observations of other scholars in one of the more famous tourism-oriented locality, i.e. Pokhara:

> "A survey in Pokhara Valley at a time when over 10,000 tourists had visited Pokhara in the previous twelve months revealed that of 100 households interviewed only five were selling eggs, 5 were selling vegetables, 2 were selling fruits, and 4 were selling peanuts... It would appear that the cropping pattern around Pokhara has hardly changed in spite of the fact that the town has the largest potential effective demand from tourists and officials[97]

4.4.3 Spatial Implication of Tourism

The hallmark of the so-called "Nepal-style tourism" is said to be a "sporting, recreative and cultural holiday".[98] This innocuous phraseology, however, provides a significant tool to make a spatial differentiation of tourism activities in the country. The spatial logic of the said attributes can be discerned thus:

'Sporting' – in terms of mountaineering, trekking, hunting etc., a nature specific activities, mostly favoured by Mountain and Hill.

'Cultural' – a social-history determined phenomenon, located long historical sites and urban nodes i.e. mostly in Kathmandu Valley.

'Recreational' – a mixture of both natural and social attributes, not particularly location-specific.

It would be interesting to see to what extent the present spatial configurations of tourism activities in the country conform to this professed logic.

The fact that an overwhelming proportion of tourists (i.e. 87.89% of arrivals and 91.12% of departures in 1981) travel by air and the only international airport is located in Kathmandu, should set the stage for spatial differentiation of tourism activities in the country. Table 4.38 provides spatial distribution of tourist arrival/departure by principal entry/exit points. Of the remaining 12% (approx). arrival and 9% (approx.) departure by land routes, Bhairahawa (Central Terai) and Birgaunj (central-eastern Terai) are seen to account for the major share. Since these two nodes are the nearest entry points to Kathmandu from Indian border, the Kathmandu-centred movement of tourists can be easily discerned. Reverting

Table 4.38 Distribution of Tourists by Important Entry and Exit Point.

Entry and Exit Points	*Tourist Arrivals*		*Tourist Departures*	
	Numbers	*Percentages*	*Numbers*	*Percentages*
LAND ROUTES	19585	12.11	14360	8.88
1. Jhapa (F.E.T.)	3055	1.89	1836	1.14
2. Birgunj (E.T.)	7495	4.64	4850	3.00
3. Bhairahawa (C.T.)	9035	5.59	7674	4.75
*AIR ROUTES	142084	87.89	147306	91.12
4. Kathmandu (K.V.)	142084	87.89	147306	91.12
i) Via Indian Cities	117547	72.71	116610	72.13
ii) Via Dacca	5546	3.43	3621	2.24
iii) Via Sri Lanka	1369	0.85	3967	2.45
iv) Via Rangoon	665	0.41	1053	0.65
v) Via Bangkok	16957	10.49	22055	13.64
TOTAL	161669	100.00	161666	100.00

Note: Figures include Indian tourists.
* Kathmandu has been subsequently air-linked with Hongkong, Karachi and Dubai. Tourist flows in these routes have yet to be studied.

Source: HMG, Ministry of Tourism (1982), *Annual Statistical Report 1981*, Department of Tourism, Kathmandu.

to the exclusively Kathmandu-based air-route by the next-port of-call of tourists before arrival at and after departure from Kathmandu, Indian cities are seen to claim an overwhelming share of total arrivals or departures, thus providing a spatial seal to the previously observed economic relations of heavy dependence on India.

The spatial distribution of internal movement of tourists cannot be made on the same lines for lack of relevant data. As hotels are seen to be the nearest physical symbols of tourism activities in the country, the pattern of capital investment in hotels by territorial zones over the years (Table 4.39) should provide fairly accurate spatial distribution of tourism inside the country. The apprehended primacy of Kathmandu in tourism is once again confirmed by its staggering share of 89.07% of total investment in hotels. The differentiations of rest of the country remain only of academic interest; though western and central Hill, eastern Mountain and central Inner Terai are seen to account for a heavy share of investment in hotels within their respective zones. However, in view of the 'point- oriented' rather than 'area-oriented' nature of hotel investment, in particular, and tourism development, in general, it would be misleading to talk in terms of territorial zones. For example, all investments in central Inner Terai is known to be centralized in Chitwan, almost all investment in eastern Mountain around the Everest region and 76.25% of the total western Hill in Pokhara. Thus, the only trend to be observed is the high degree of localization along certain nodes of specific natural or cultural (mostly former) significance. Kathmandu, however, could be taken as a special case of spatial manifestation of high degree of commercial monopolization as well.

Table 4.39 Capital Investment in Hotels by Territorial Zones (uptill 1980/81).

(Rs. Million)

Ecological Zones	*'Development' Zones*	*Eastern*	*Central*	*Western*	*Far-Western*	*Total*
1. MOUNTAIN		8.196	3.669	2.564	–	14.429
	(i)	(48.42)	(0.35)	(5.74)		(1.28)
	(ii)	(56.80)	(25.43)	(17.77)		(100.00)
2. HILL		2.360	29.086	32.994[1]	–	64.44
	(i)	(13.94)	(2.74)	(73.85)		(5.73)
	(ii)	(3.66)	(45.14)	(51.20)		(100.00)
3. KATHMANDU		–	1002.098	–		1002.098
VALLEY	(i)		(94.46)			(89.07)
	(ii)		–			–
4. INNER TERAI		–	19.673[2]	–	0.994[3]	20.667
	(i)		(1.85)		(38.14)	(1.84)
	(ii)		(95.19)		(4.81)	(100.00)
5. TERAI		6.372	6.320	9.138	1.612	23.442
	(i)	(37.64)	(0.60)	(20.45)	(61.86)	(2.08)
	(ii)	(27.18)	(26.96)	(38.98)	(6.88)	(100.00)
TOTAL		16.928	1060.846	44.676	2.606	1125.058
	(i)	(100.00)	(100.00)	(100.00)	(100.00)	(100.00)
	(ii)	(1.50)	(94.29)	(3.97)	(0.23)	(100.00)

Note: Figures in parenthesis are percentages, (i) Column percentages; (ii) Row percentage.

[1] Out of which Rs. 25.157 million is in Pokhara only.

[2] All in Chitwan.

[3] All in Surkhet.

Source: Records of HMG/N, Department of Industry, Kathmandu.

The distribution pattern of tourist expenditures across major centers (Table 4.40) also largely confirms the extreme localization of tourism activities in the country. The fact that Kathmandu has a runaway lead over others not only in terms of expenditure of star-hotel occupying pleasure tourists but that of the trekkers (though in a slightly reduced intensity) should set at rest the argument that natural factors condition the spatial distribution of tourism; for it is anybody's knowledge that, there are far better areas of natural beauty than the Kathmandu Valley. But it is the profit-maximisation logic and monopoly rule of merchant capital that has a final say in where to locate its area of operation.

Table 4.40 Territorial Distribution of Expenditure of Tourists by Types (1974/75).

Territorial Units	*Share of Expenditure as % of Total Expenditure*							*Estimated Total Expenditure*	
	Pleasure Tourists				*Trekkers*				
	1-Star Hotel and lodge	*2 and 3 Star Hotel*	*4 and 5 Star Hotel*	*Private Home*	*Organised*	*With Porters*	*Without Porters*	*Rs. '000*	*%*
Kathmandu	91.1	91.5	94.0	91.4	60.5	60.3	79.8	87,104	81.3
Pokhara	7.9	2.4	1.1	8.6	0.7	5.4	8.1	2,891	2.7
Tiger Tops (Chitwan)	0.0	4.1	3.6	0.0	1.1	0.0	0.0	2,233	2.1
Others*	1.0	2.0	1.3	0.0	38.2	34.3	12.1	14,951	13.9
Total	100.00	100.00	100.00	100.00	100.00	100.00	100.00	–	–
Estimated total Expenditure excluding Air-fare (Rs. '000)	12,971	17,158	34,030	2,243	27,689	8,465	4,621	107,179	100,0

Note: * 'Others', include Pokhara-Jomsom Annapurna region; Namche Bazar and Everest Approach; Longtang, Helambu, Gosaikund; etc.

Source: Adapted from Burger, V. (1978), *The Economic Impact of Tourism in Nepal: An Input-Output Analysis* (Unpublished Ph.D. Dissertation), Cornell University, Ithaca.

The only touristic activity to be of some significance for the other areas outside Kathmandu Valley, is trekking. Even in this, leaving aside Kathmandu Valley, heavy localization along Pokhara-Jomson and Everest region is clearly manifest (Table 4.41). This again seems to be a function of both natural and social factors, though some advantages may be conceded to 'natural' monopoly of these areas of exceptional natural beauty.

Table 4.41 Trekking Permits Issued by Major Trekking Areas (1976 and 1981).

Area/Territorial Zone	*1976*		*1981*		*Growth Ratio*
	Number	*%*	*Number*	*%*	
1. Sagarmatha (Everest) Region (Eastern Mountain)	4214	28.30	5804	19.67	1.38
2. Langtang–Helambu (Eastern Hill-Central Mountain)	2014	13.52	3051	10.34	1.51
3. Annapurna Region (Pokhara) (Central Hill-Mountain)	4137	27.78	2180	7.39	0.53
4. Manang (Central Mountain)	961*	6.45	438	1.48	0.46
5. Jomsom-Muktinath (Central Mountain)	3053	20.50	14435	48.93	4.73
6. Jumla-Rara (Western Mountain)	73	0.49	10	0.03	0.14
7. Others	367	2.46	2145	7.27	5.84
TOTAL	14892	100.00	29500	100.00	1.98

Note: *For nine months in 1977.
•Figures do not include trekkers going around Kathmandu and Pokhara Valleys.
Source: For trekking permits figures for 1976, Gurung, H. (1978), "Tourism Trends in Nepal" in *Nepal Industrial Digest*, Vol. 8, No.1, Kathmandu and for 1981, Department of Tourism (1982), *Annual Statistical Report 1981*, Kathmandu.

Thus aided by both monopoly of nature and monopoly of merchant capital, with a decisive role of the latter, the social and spatial structure of tourism is found to be highly centralized, dysfunctional and extraverted.

4.5 ARTICULATION OF FINANCIAL CAPITAL WITHIN

We have in the preceding section analysed the marked growth of merchant capital operating within and without the economy of Nepal and have also observed its increasing role in articulating the social and spatial structure of the country. It would now be relevant to study the status of its close ally, financial capital as defined earlier.

4.5.1 Size and Growth of Financial Capital

Quantitative estimation of the size of financial capital in the economy demands at least the information on the proportion of social product monetized[99] and an account of total social wealth accruing from both internal and external sources, not to speak of the social distribution of wealth. In the absence of a systematic statistical account of the economy in the desired frame, we have to take recourse to sundry micro-level studies to draw a broad picture of the situation.

In a predominantly agrarian economy, the status of money-dealing capital in the agricultural sector should indicate the overall status in the economy. As may be recapitulated from Chapter II, the role of money-dealing capital or pre-capitalist credit is quite significant in the agricultural domain. However, since a mere 12% of gross product or a total of 20% of total income in the countryside seems to have been monetized (i.e. if the more externally integrated eastern Mountain area of IRDP Khandbari is to be taken as a standard case applicable for the whole of the country)[100], the role of money in the absolute scale does not appear very significant. On the contrary, the extent of monetization of the economy of 'urban' areas and important settlement nodes in the countryside seem quite high, ranging from 90.5% in Kathmandu to 48% in Mahendranagar (Western Terai)[101]. Also the significant scale of cash expenditure of households, primarily for importation of subsistence goods from outside, cautions us against underestimating the role of money and credit in the rural economy. With the enhanced integration of the economy with outside world primarily through trade as observed earlier and the resultant commoditisation of the economy and polarisation of society, the area of operation of financial capital can be assumed to have been definitely widened.

In the absence of information on total size of 'money engaged in breeding money',[102] we have to rely entirely on the size of money-capital channelised through the official financial institutions, which though constituting the total size of organized financing in the country may fall far short of capturing the total size of money-capital operating through unorganised channels[103]. Ratio of total assets of financial institutions to the GDP as presented in Table 4.42 should

Table 4.42 Ratio of Total Assets of Financial Institutions to Gross Domestic Product (1965–1979).

Year	*Total Assets of Financial Institutions*		*Gross Domestic Product (GDP)*		*Assets/GDP Ratio (%)*
	Amount	*Growth Index*	*Amount*	*Growth Index*	
1965	777	100	5602	100	13.9
1970	1832	236	8768	157	20.9
1975	4798	618	15074	269	31.8
1979	9315.4	1198	23351	417	39.89

Note: Assests and GDP amount are at current prices.

Source: 1, Security Marketing Centre Ltd. (1980), *Resource Structure of Some Financial Institutions and the Development of Security Market in Nepal*, Kathmandu.

2. Mahat, R.S. (1981), *Capital Market, Financial Flows and Industrial Finance In Nepal*, Sajha Prakashan, Kathmandu, Table 2.6, p. 48.

provide an idea of the size of financial capital as related to the total size of the economy. It is clear that though the absolute size of the ratio is quite low[104] compared to other economies moving along the capitalist path, both the rise in the ratio (i.e. from 13.9% in 1965 to 39.89% in 1979) and the growth index of absolute size (i.e. from 100 in 1965 to 1198 in 1979), is definitely significant.

Disaggregrating the growth trend by types of financial institutions, a more illuminating picture of increasing role of financial capital by its size and nature can be obtained. Table 4.43 provides gross volume, percentage to the total and growth index of different financial institutions. The very limited types of financial institutions confined to the traditional central bank, commercial banks, development banks and others including Life Insurance and provident funds, is certainly a manifestation of low level of development of financial capital under the capitalist social formation.[105]

The gradual decline in the original predominance of the central bank and the corresponding rise of commercial banks during the period 1965–1969 is sure sign of burgeoning of financial capital along the path of capitalist mode of production[106].

4.5.2 Social Relations of Financing

Historically 'money-breeding money' has assumed different forms and performed different social roles in different social formations. Hence to asses the exact role of financial capital in articulating the underdevelopment process in the concrete social formation of Nepal, it would be pertinent to analyse social relations of financing in its various ensembles.

4.5.21 As mentioned earlier no statistical data are available for financial flows channelised through private money-lenders, merchants, land-lords, etc. though it is widely believed and supported by findings of Agricultural Credit Surveys that private sources account for a substantial proportion of financial flows in the countryside. Nevertheless, the pre-capitalist nature of these financial flows can be fairly well ascertained and to that extent can be left out from our immediate perview of 'financial capital' in the strict literal sense. In the absence of information on total volume of financial capital in operation, it is not possible to measure the 'degree of institutionalization', i.e. share of assets of financial institutions to total financial assets, which should naturally grow with higher levels of economic development.

As per the nature of organisation of financial institutions in Nepal all of them are organised as 'public enterprises' either with total state control or a majority share of state in them[107]. The heavy involvement of the state in financial organisation is in keeping with the modified strategy of metropolitan capital after World War II to promote collective control by indigenous ruling classes through state machinery in view of weak position of local bourgeoisie in most of the Third World Countries. Only with the advent of 1980s has the local

Table 4.43 Volume and Growth of Assets of Financial Institutions (1965–1979).

(Rs. Million)

Year	*Central Bank*			*Commercial Bank*			*Development Bank*			*Other Financial Institutions*			*Total*		
(as of mid-July)	*Amount*	*% of total*	*Growth Index*	*Amount*	*% of total*	*Growth Index*	*Amount*	*% of total*	*Growth Index*	*Amount*	*% of total*	*Growth Index*	*Amount*	*%*	*Growth Index*
1965	553.0	71.1	100	162.4	20.9	100	42.1	5.4	100	19.8	2.6	100	777.3	100.0	100.0
1970	1130.7	61.7	205	519.2	28.3	320	109.7	6.0	261	73.0	4.0	369	1832.6	100.0	236
1975	2231.7	46.5	404	1831.2	38.2	1128	491.3	10.2	1167	244.1	5.1	1233	4798.3	100.0	617
1979	3806..9	40.9	688	3918.6	42.1	2413	973.3	10.45	2312	622.4	6.7	3143	9321.2	100.0	1199

Note: The amount of assets are at current prices.

1. Central Bank: Nepal Rastra Bank.
2. Commercial Banks: 1. Nepal Bank Ltd., 2. Rastriya Banijya Bank.
3. Development Banks: 1. Nepal Industrial Development Corporation, 2. Agricultural Development Bank.
4. Others: 1. Rastriya Beema Sansthan, 2. Provident Fund Corporation, 3. Credit Guarantee Corporation (P) Ltd., 4. Security Marketing Center.

Source:

1. For figures for 1965, 1970 and 1975, Mahat, R.S. (1981), *Capital Market, Financial Flow and Industrial Finance in Nepal*, Sajha Prakashan, Kathmandu, Table 2.4, p. 44.
2. For figures for 1979, Security Marketing Centre Ltd. (1980), *Resource Structure of Some Financial Institutions and the Development of Security Market in Nepal*, Kathmandu, Nepal Rastra Bank, *Quarterly Economic Bulletin*, Kathmandu, and HMG/N, Ministry of Finance (1980), *Highlights of Public Enterprises in Nepal for the F.Y. 1977/78*, Corporation Coordination Division, Kathmandu.

bourgeoisie gained some confidence to collaborate with metropolitan finance capital to establish the first bank as a joint venture[108].

The nature of social relations of financing may be further clarified by the distribution of ownership of deposits of commercial banks as in Table 4.44. It is clear that an overwhelming proportion of deposits is owned by private bank with foreign collaboration, the share of 'foreigners' and 'private individuals' should rise further. Though in the absence of relevant data it is not possible to ascertain the actual source of money hoarded by the production sector, however, on the basis of the study of the structure of economy so far it may not be wrong to assume that bulk of this capital hoard originates in the agricultural sector.

Table 4.44 Ownership Classification of Deposit of Commercial Banks*.

(Rs. Million)

Ownership	*Deposits of Commercial Banks*			*Growth Ratio*
	1977 (mid-July)	*1980 (mid-Jan)*	*1982 (mid-Jan)*	*1982 over 1977*
Foreigners	243.0 (11.82)	138.7 (4.67)	127.4 (2.99)	0.52
Government and Non-Government enterprises and organizations	496.7 (24.17)	831.2 (28.01)	1476.4 (34.61)	2.97
Private individuals	1315.4 (64.01)	1997.6 (67.32)	2659.2 (62.34)	2.02
TOTAL	2055.1 (100.00)	2967.5 (100.00)	4265.4 (100.00)	2.08

Note: * Excluding inter bank deposits.
Figures in parenthesis are percentages.

Source: Nepal Rastra Bank, *Commercial Banking Statistics*, Various issues, Kathmandu.

4.5.22 Financial capital essentially reproduces itself by claiming revenue/interest from different economic activities rather than by directly participating in the production process and appropriating surplus labour. But its immediate association with 'circulation' or 'production' phases in the circuit of capital, has different significance in articulating the social process. Therefore, it would be worthwhile to examine the sectoral distribution and condition of disbursion of credit[109]

Table 4.45 gives the classification of credit of commercial banks by principal economic activities. It is apparent that with nearly 60% of total credit advanced going to 'business' purposes, financial capital merely acts as an ally of merchant capital. The next highiest share ranging from 20–26% is observed to go to 'consumption' purposes, which means that it is only performing the retrograde role of usurer's capital. On the whole a mere 8.96% to 15.04% of total bank credit is found to be going to productive purposes, even if all the loans to agriculture and industrial sector are assumed to be utilised for productive purposes, which is quite unlikely. Thus it is not hard to conclude that the burgeoning financial capital in the country is not a medium of economic progress but just an ally of merchant capital which we have already established as an appendage of metropolitan capital.

Table 4.45 Purposewise Classification of Credit of Commercial Banks[1].

(Rs. Million)

Purposes	*1977 Mid-July*	*1980 Mid-January*	*1982 Mid-January*
1. Agricultural	20.5 (1.69)	23.3 (0.95)	61.6 (1.64)
2. Industrial	88.0 (7.27)	305.4 (12.46)	503.4 (13.40)
3. Business[2]	728.2 (60.17)	1571.7 (61.92)	2105.4 (56.04)
4. Transport, Services and Storage	68.4 (5.65)	65.7 (2.68)	69.4 (1.85)
5. Consumption	283.6 (23.43)	493.7 (20.14)	975.5 (25.96)
6. Financial (purposes unclassified)	21.5 (1.78)	45.2 (1.84)	41.7 (1.11)
TOTAL	1210.2 (100.00)	2451.0 (100.00)	3757.0 (100.00)

Note: 1. Excluding investment on Government Bonds and Shares of Government enterprises.
2. Advances against bills for collection of Bills purchased and discounted are included in business purposes.
– Figures in parenthesis are percentages.

Source: Nepal Rastra Bank, *Commercial Banking Statistics*, (Various issues), Kathmandu.

The retrograde nature of financial capital as an ally of merchant capital and a veiled form of usurer's capital, is further confirmed from the 'security' distribution of outstanding credits of commercial banks. It is found that the approximate break-up of loan securities all through the 1960s and 1970s were: foreign trade (bills and goods): 30%; gold, silver etc. house-land: 20% ; grains and other agricultural production: 35%[110].

Of the already minimal credit extended to 'productive' activities, the practical inefficacy of it is reflected in the higher share of 'short-term' loans than that of 'medium term' loans (Table 4.46). This is a clear manifestation of use of credit more for consumption objectives rather than for the expansion of the productive base of the economy.

The irony of the retrograde nature of financial capital is amply borne out by the loan disbursement pattern of even the so-called development banks like Agricultural Development Bank. It is observed that the 'development' loans tend to promote more of the 'circulation' component than the 'production' component of the production activities. As already noted in the previous chapter, primary share of NIDC loans over the years has gone to investment in hotels.

Table 4.46 Commercial Bank's Lending in Priority Sectors.

	Mid-July 1977	*Mid-January 1980*	*Mid-January 1982*
1. Agricultural Sector	18.8 (45.97)	65.3 (43.68)	64.8 (35.53)
Short Term	7.6	49.3	47.3
Medium Term	11.2	16.0	17.5
2. Cottage and Small Scale Industries	19.9 (48.66)	45.4 (30.37)	67.9 (37.23)
Short Term	7.7	17.0	37.5
Medium Term	12.2	28.4	30.4
3. Service Sector	2.2* (5.38)	38.8 (25.95)	49.7 (27.25)
TOTAL	40.9 (100.00)	149.5 (100.00)	182.4 (100.00)

Note: * Excluding hire purchase credit to trucks, buses, cars, etc.
Figures in parenthesis are percentages.

Source: Nepal Rastra Bank, *Commercial Banking Statistics*, (Various issues), Kathmandu.

The collusion of the state with the forces of external integration than with those of strengthening indigenous production base is also reflected in the retrograde interest rates charged on loans for different purposes[111].

Thus it is amply evident that not only the social relations of financing are backward but are retrograde to the extent of distorting the economic structure by disproportionately strengthening the 'circulation' component of the economy internally and promoting unequal integration externally.

4.5.3 Spatial Differentiation of Financial Capital

By the very nature of higher mobility and greater tendency to centralise and concentrate, the spatial distribution of financial capital would be expected to be more disparate. Within the given data constraints we would here be investigating the financial spatial structure primarily with respect to the mass of capital channelised through commercial banks, which commanded about 40% of instituionalized finance in 1979.

4.5.31 Table 4.47 gives the historical pattern of distribution of bank branches by territorial zones. The data shows that there is a high centralisation of banks in Terai and Kathmandu Valley and gradual dispersion to Hill and Mountain to encompass all the territorial units by the 1980s. A similar pattern of gradual expansion from east to west in the respective ecological zones, with some exceptions in Inner Terai and Mountain, is also observable. This spatio-temporal pattern of distribution of financial capital is quite in conformity with the distribution of agricultural and industrial production and perhaps even more closely with that of spatial loci of merchant capital, as observed in the preceding sections.

Table 4.47 Growth Trends in The Distribution of Commercial Bank Branches by Territorial Zones (1950–1980).

Territorial Zones	*Commercial Bank Branches*							
	1950		*1960*		*1970*		*1980*	
	No.	*%*	*No.*	*%*	*No.*	*%*	*No.*	*%*
MOUNTAIN	–	–	–	–	2	2.50	18	7.47
Eastern	–	–	–	–	1	1.25	7	2.90
Central	–	–	–	–	–	–	3	1.24
Western	–	–	–	–	1	1.25	8	3.32
HILL	–	–	3	18.75	15	18.75	60	24.90
Eastern	–	–	1	6.25	6	7.50	20	8.30
Central	–	–	2	12.50	7	8.75	30	12.45
Western	–	–	–	–	2	2.50	10.	4.15
KATHMANDU VALLEY	1	14.29	1	6.25	15	18.75	40	16.60
INNER TERAI	–	–	–	–	8	10.00	18	7.47
Eastern	–	–	–	–	1	1.25	3	1.24
Central	–	–	–	–	4	5.00	11	4.56
Western	–	–	–	–	3	3.75	4	1.66
TERAI	6	85.71	12	75.00	40	50.00	105	43.57
Eastern:	5	71.43	8	50.00	29	36.25	76	31.54
–Far-Eastern	2	28.57	4	25.00	9	11.25	31	12.86
–Mid-Eastern	1	14.29	2	12.50	12	15.00	27	11.20
–Eastern	2	28.57	2	12.50	8	10.00	18	7.47
Central	–	–	3	18.75	6	7.50	15	6.22
Western	1	14.29	1	6.25	5	6.25	14	5.81
NEPAL	7	100.00	16	100.00	80	100.00	241	100.00

Note: Figures are for mid-July of the year.
Source: Nepal Rastra Bank, *Quarterly Economic Bulletin* (Various issues), Kathmandu.

On the other hand, in view of the fewer number of public financial enterprises and their total subsumption to state control, their total centralisation in Kathmandu Valley may not be very surprising.

A more illuminating picture of spatial distribution of financial capital may be obtained by the distribution pattern of the total deposits and credits of commercial banks by territorial zones (Table 4.48). Though no time-series data are available for earlier periods, the situation at the end of 1970s and the beginning of 1980s indicates extreme localisation in Kathmandu Valley, which accounted for a staggering 56.92% of deposits and 47.73% of credit in 1982. Apart from this over-centralisation in the capital region, a generalised pattern of increasing centralisation from Mountain to Terai in north-south territorial dimension and in central sub-zone in east-west territorial dimension is observable. This pattern of spatial distribution of bank capital is fully in keeping with the general spatial differentiation of the economy, except for greater degree of centralization in

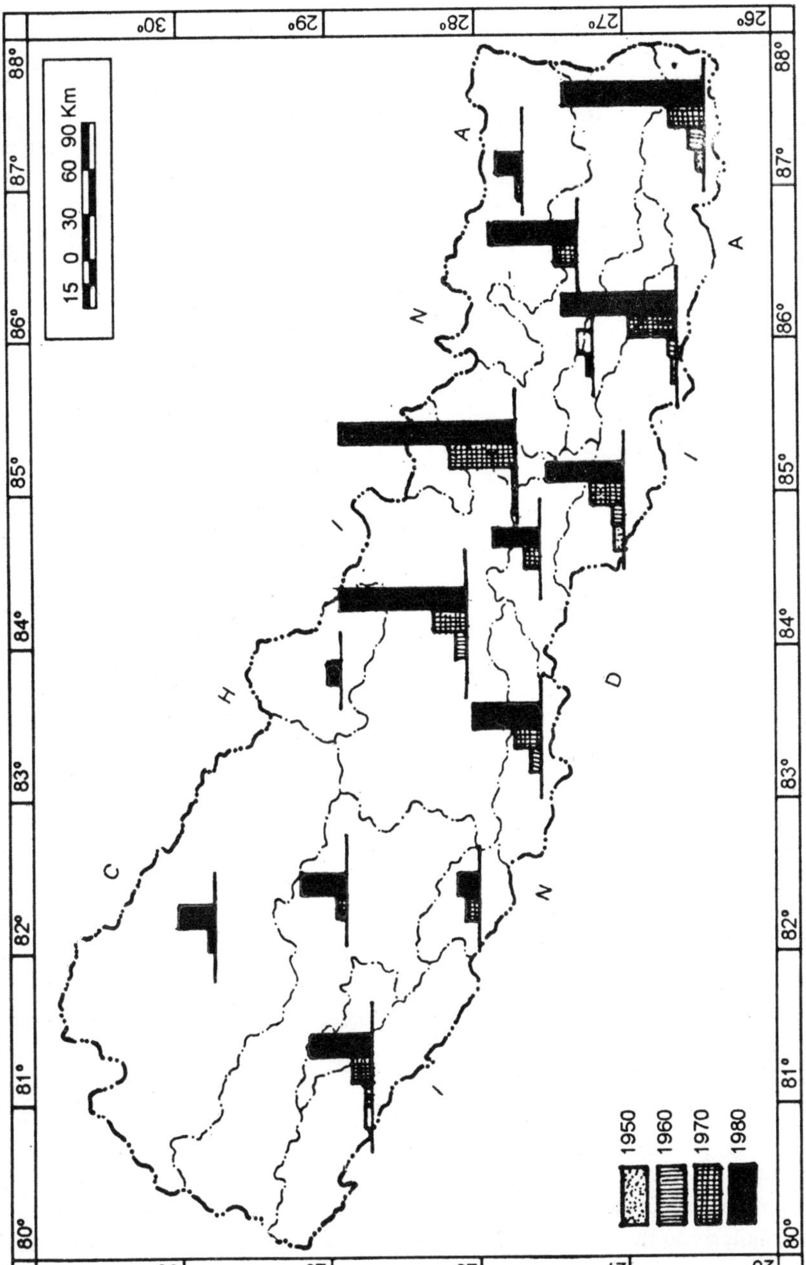

Fig. 4.6 Growth of Commercial Bank Branches.

Kathmandu Valley in the present context. This may be largely explicable in terms of observed in closer alliance of merchant and financial capital, both of which favour the centralisation at Kathmandu Valley, the mercantile and bureaucratic nodes of the country.

Table 4.48 Distribution of Deposits and Credits of Commercial Banks Territorial Zones (1978 and 1982).

(In Rs. Million)

Territorial Zones	*Total Deposits*				*Total Credits*			
	1978		*1982*		*1978*		*1982*	
	Amount	*%*	*Amount*	*%*	*Amount*	*%*	*Amount*	*%*
MOUNTAIN	36.4	1.54	83.2	1.95	13.3	0.68	29.8	0.72
Eastern	15.8	0.67	39.2	0.92	7.7	0.39	19.0	0.46
Central	3.1	0.13	9.0	0.21	1.8	0.09	3.8	0.09
Western	17.0	0.72	35.0	0.82	3.8	0.19	7.0	0.17
HILL	183.4	7.75	423.6	9.91	124.4	6.35	292.7	7.08
Eastern	44.6	1.89	104.1	2.43	28.7	1.47	70.3	1.70
Central	144.0	4.82	265.2	6.20	84.2	4.30	195.4	4.72
Western	24.8	1.05	54.3	1.27	11.5	0.58	27.0	0.65
KATHMANDU VALLEY	1482.3	62.66	2433.7	56.92	953.0	48.67	1974.6	47.73
INNER TERAI	96.0	4.06	194.5	4.55	47.8	2.44	126.0	3.05
Eastern	6.1	0.26	14.6	0.34	2.8	0.14	6.7	0.16
Central	64.1	2.71	131.2	3.07	36.2	1.85	105.0	2.54
Western	25.8	1.09	48.7	1.14	8.8	0.45	14.3	0.35
TERAI	567.7	24.00	1140.6	26.60	819.6	41.86	1713.9	41.43
Easterns:	402.6	17.02	825.1	19.30	685.2	34.99	1359.7	32.87
–Far-Eastern	220.3	9.31	353.4	8.27	393.8	20.11	713.2	17.24
–Mid-Eastern	31.9	3.46	207.6	4.86	171.9	8.78	304.1	7.35
Eastern	100.4	4.24	264.1	6.18	119.5	6.10	342.4	8.28
Central	81.9	3.46	165.3	3.87	41.8	2.13	102.8	2.48
Western	83.2	3.52	150.2	3.51	92.6	4.73	251.4	6.08
NEPAL	2365.8	100.00	4275.6	100.00	1958.1	100.00	4137.0	100.00

Source: Nepal Rastra Bank (1982), *Commercial Banking Statistics*, No. 7, Kathmandu, May.

The spatial distribution of the financial process by quality and financial flow across territorial zones may be observed in terms of bank density, per capita bank deposit and credit and credit/deposit ratio, as presented in Table 4.49. The worst features of spatial disparateness in the distribution of financial capital are manifest, particularly in the case of per capita distribution of bank deposit and credit. Per capita deposit and credit in Kathmandu Valley are more than 11 times and more than 9 times the respective national averages in 1982. Over time there is no discernible variation in the ratios.

Table 4.49 Level of Development of Banking Territorial Zones (1978 and 1982).

Territorial Zones	*Per Capita Bank Deposit (Rs.)*		*Per Capita Bank Credit (Rs.)*		*Credit/Deposit Ratio*	
	1978	*1982*	*1978*	*1982*	*1978*	*1982*
I. MOUNTAIN	35.72	78.12	13.05	27.98	0.37	0.36
Eastern	36.16	80.00	17.62	38.78	0.49	0.48
Central	63.16	187.50	31.58	79.17	0.50	0.42
Western	34.76	66.41	7.77	13.28	0.22	0.20
II. HILL	31.24	72.05	21.19	49.79	0.68	0.69
Eastern	24.61	57.87	15.84	39.08	0.64	0.63
Central	44.65	101.88	32.98	75.07	0.74	0.74
Western	16.47	36.76	7.64	18.28	0.46	0.50
III. KATHMANDU VALLEY	2038.93	3168.88	1310.87	2571.09	0.64	0.81
IV. INNER TERAI	92.13	152.19	45.87	98.59	0.50	0.65
Eastern	20.47	42.07	9.40	19.31	0.46	0.46
Central	156.72	262.93	88.51	210.42	0.56	0.80
Western	77.01	112.73	26.27	33.10	0.34	0.29
V. TERAI	119.19	188.97	172.08	283.95	1.44	1.50
Eastern:	114.57	194.32	194.99	320.23	1.70	1.65
Far-Eastern	242.89	260.43	434.18	525.57	1.79	2.02
Mid-Eastern	47.92	106.35	100.59	155.79	2.10	1.46
Eastern	111.80	281.86	133.07	365.42	1.19	1.30
Central	115.84	172.19	59.12	107.08	0.51	0.62
Western	153.51	180.96	170.85	302.89	1.11	1.67
NEPAL	176.26	284.66	145.89	275.43	0.83	0.97

Source: Nepal Rastra Bank (1982), *Commercial Banking Statistics*, No. 7, Kathmandu, May.

The interpretations of varying credit/deposit ratio, however, would demand some prior theorising. Whereas in the capitalist social formation credit would be primarily directed towards the spheres of production and higher credit/deposit ratio would be a positive indicator of development, in the pre-capitalist formations much of the credit would be merely in the form of usurer's capital leading to ultimate ruination of the borrower and hence could not be regarded as a positive indicator. Thus the same quantitative value of the ratio could mean different things in different situations. Coming to the cases of Nepal, it is interesting to note that whereas the ratio is above unity (i.e. more credit than deposit)in Terai and its sub-zones except central Terai, it is below unity in rest of the territorial zones of the country. Also it is seen decreasing from south to north and from east to west in the familiar pattern of spatial differentiation of other economic attributes. Except for the case of Kathmandu Valley (i.e. more deposit than credit), rest of the pattern is easily explicable in terms of the basic economic structure of the respective spatial units. Whereas the areas with higher deposit than credit are predominantly agricultural areas with some surplus but no avenue for its investment, the other way round is the case with other areas, who need more capital for investment but fall short of it[112]. The exceptional case of Kathmandu Valley may have to be explained partly in terms of greater 'hoarding' resorted to by absentee landlords based in Kathmandu who siphon off agricultural surplus from outside areas into the banks centralised there, and partly in terms of the flow of foreign capital which makes its initial entry into Kathmandu but may be ultimately invested somewhere else. Thus the inter-regional financial flows trickle towards the more developed Terai from the backward Hill and Mountain.

A further characteristic of the quality of financial capital by territorial zones may be obtained by a cross-classification of credit/deposit ratios of bank deposits per capita. The higher deposit per capita and lower credit/deposit ratio would indicate a backward/retrograde social relations of financing usually characterised as usurer's capital or just 'financial' capital. A higher deposit per capita accompanied by higher credit/deposit ratio would on the other hand indicate a more progressive social relations of financing. Thus only the Terai regions show a progressive and more advantageous social relations of financing, while the rest a regressive one.

4.5.32 Analysis of Interdependencies

The social and spatial characteristics of financial (bank) capital in Nepal can be further generalised from the analysis of interdependencies between different indicators of development. When the statical correlations of bank deposit per capita (S11) with other indicators (Appendix 9) are analysed, keeping within broader conceptual frame, the following observations can be made:

- Bank credit per capita is not seen to have any significant correlation with any of the indicators of agricultural and industrial development, thereby overruling any positive link of financial capital in productive economic activities.
- It is seen to have significant positive correlation with non-agricultural labour force (E_2), which is quite understandable in view if the known concentration of non-agricultural labour force in the 'tertiary' sector and the observed alliance of bank capital with merchant and bureaucratic capital.
- The positive significant correlation with the index of urbanisation (E_4) amply substantiates the over-centralisation of financial capital in urban places.

It can be concluded that the financial capital in Nepal is socially regressive and is characterised by backward and retrograde social relations of financing, and spatial disparateness marked by over-centralisation in the mercantile and bureaucratic centres, particularly Kathmandu Valley. This thus can be seen as one of the key agents for aggravation of underdevelopment process.

4.6 ARTICULATION OF FINANCIAL CAPITAL WITHOUT

Growing articulation of the Nepalese economy with metropolitan economy through various relation of commodity and labour exchanges has been already acknowledged. In view of close alliance between different forms of circulation capital and in view of capital export being one of the important mechanism of reproduction of neo-colonial relations in the present global order, the investigation of the status of the financial capital in articulating this relation becomes imperative. It may be necessary to clarify at the outset that for the lack of reliable documentation of financial flows across the political frontiers of siamese-twin-like formations of India and Nepal at the private/unofficial level, our attempt here would be confined to the financial interactions At the official/state level and this should be taken as only a pointer to the real situation.

4.6.1 Magnitude of Finanacial Linkage Without

To assess the financial linkages without, it may be necessary to summerise the magnitude of general economic linkages first. A quick survey of the single column presentation of b.o.p. (balance of payment) available only for the mid-1970s onwards[113], would enable one to realise that the violently fluctuating b.o.p (although slightly favorable for most of the years in question) has been sustained by an increasing dose of foreign loans. This has been so because the constant deficit in merchandise and service exchanges has not been balanced even by a continuously rising 'unreqitted transfers' mostly comprised of remittances from emigrant workers at the private level and foreign 'grants' at the state level resulting in an ever fluctuating deficit or surplus (mostly former) 'current account balance'. In the absence of b.o.p. accounts for the verification of a longer temporal trend, some idea may be gained from the composition of receipts and expenditure of convertible foreign exchnage since the mid-1950s[114]. It is evident that during the earlier period a favourable balance has been maintained, apart from the merchandise exports, by 'Gorkha' remittances and later with increasing earning from tourism and heavy doses of foreign 'aid' (both grants and loans). What is abundantly clear from these observations is the increasing penetration of financial capital in the guise of 'aid', which demands closer scrutiny.

The ever increasing magnitude of foreign capital and economies growing reliance upon it has been a topic of major concern of late[115]. From Table 4.50, not only is the gross volume of foreign 'aid' in the last 30 years seen to have increased by almost 60 times, its tremendous straglehold in the destiny of the economy is apparent from the fact that it constituted almost two-thirds of total public sector 'development' expenditure during the successive plans. The most disquietening aspect is the growing dependence on foreign capital to the extent of 74.6% of total planned outlay in the proposed Seventh Plan, after it had fallen to 45% in the Fourth Plan from 100% in the First Plan.

Table 4.50 Share of Foreign 'Aid' in Public Sector Development Expenditure During Different Plans.

(Rs. Million)

Plan/Period	*Development Expenditure*	*Foreign 'Aid' (Gross)*	*Foreign 'Aid' as % of Development Expenditure*
First Plan (1956–61)	382.9	382.9	100.0
No Plan Year (1961–65)	86.2	70.6	81.9
Second Plan (1962–65)	614.7	478.3	77.8
Third Plan (1965–70)	1639.1	919.8	56.1
Fourth Plan (1970–75)	3356.9	1509.1	45.0
Fifth Plan (1975–80)	8870.6	4264.1	48.1
Sixth Plan (1980–85)	21750.0	13260.0	61.0
Seventh Plan (1985–90)	30150.0	22500.0	74.6
TOTAL	66850.4	43384.8	64.90

Source: 1. Various Plans, National Planning Commission, HMG/N_1 Kathmandu.
2. HMG/N_1 Ministry of Finance (1981), *Accelerated Development of Nepal, Development Prospects and Foreign Assistance Required for the 1980s*, Vol. I, Kathmandu.

Further idea of role of foreign capital in the economy may be obtained by relating it with such measures of the economy as the GDP, 'development' budget and merchandise imports (Table 4.51). Whereas its relation with development budget for respective years is a logical replica of relation with plan outlays, it is seen to constitute about one-third of total merchandise imports on an average. The real social significance of foreign capital is, however, felt in comparison with the GDP, which is seen to have risen from 2.58% of GDP in 1965/66 to 5.69% in 1980/81. Compared to other similarly placed economies, particularly those in South Asia, Nepal's foreign 'aid' dependence is known to be on the higher side[116].

Table 4.51 Dimensions of Foreign 'Aid' as Related to GDP, Development Budget and Imports (1965–66 to 80–81).

Year	*'Aid' as Percentage of*		
	GDP	*'Development' Budget*	*Merchandise Imports*
1965–66	2.58	63.61	22.84
1970–71	3.39	65.19	43.37
1975–76	2.91	40.81	25.52
1980–81	5.69	57.20	34.11

Source: 1. The World Bank (1981), *Nepal Policies and Prospects for Accelerated Growth*, October, 15.
2. HMGN, Ministry of Finance (1982), *Budget in Nepal (1951/52–1981/82)*, Revenue Administration Training Centre, Kathmandu.
3. Nepal Rastra Bank, *Quarterly Economic Bulletin* (Various issues).

A more relevant measure to gauge the magnitude of foreign financial capital would be the size of debt in both absolute terms and as related to the total population, as shown in Table 4.52. It is interesting to note that the total debt has increased nearly 50times over the 15 year period (i.e. from 1964/65 to 1980/81) and the per capita debt 22 times over 1971–81. As compared to other 'low income countries', however, the measure of public debt as percentage of GNP appears not very significant[117].

Table 4.52 Direct and indirect Outstanding External Debt (1964/65–1980/81).

(Rs. Million)

	Outstanding debt			*Growth Index of total debt*	*Per Capita debt (Rs.)*
	Direct	*Indirect*	*Total*		
1964–65	28.9	15.8	44.7	100	N.A.
1970–71	38.7	37.2	75.9	170	14.97
Mid-July 1975	190.2	42.5	23.7	521	N.A.
	(89.06)	(–)	(72.80)		
1980–81	2204.0	29.0	2233.0	4996	332.61
	(77.32)	(–)	(76.34)		

Note: Figures in parenthesis are percentage share of Asian Development Bank (ADB) and International Development Association (IDA).

Source: HMGN, Ministry of Finance, *Economic Survey* (Various years) and Nepal Rastra Bank, *Quarterly Economic Bulletin* (Various issues), Kathmandu.

4.6.2 Structure of Finance and Social Implications

In the light of virtually non-existent private capital investment form of financial linkages without, the study of structure and social implications of external financial flows in the context of Nepal would again boil down to the study of that of foreign 'aid'.

4.6.21 An analysis of growth trends of 'aid' inflows into the country by sources and conditions of disbursement should provide valuable insights into its ultimate social implications, for it is more the conditions of import rather than the import per se of capital that has a bearing in shaping the course of the economy, Table 4.53 provides break-up of capital inflow by bilateral and multi-lateral sources and terms of grant and loan in a temporal frame. It is seen that up to the 1960s all the aid was in the form of 'grants' and came from entirely bilateral sources. Since then the proportion of loans from multilateral agencies have progressively risen to assume a significant proportion of 43% by the 1980s. This pattern is fully consistent with the known path chartered by metropolitan capital in its self-assigned 'civilizing mission' to the underdeveloped societies particularly after the World War II[118]. It is quite understandable in terms of the accumulation imperatives of capital. Till the end of the Sixties capital inflow was usually in the form of 'grants' through bilateral channels to sufficiently commodities and stabilise the economy and prepare the ground for ultimate commercial exploitation through

Table 4.53 'AID' Inflow to Nepal by Types and Sources (1960/61–1980/81).

Year	*Bilateral*			*Multilateral*			*All*		
	Grant	*Loan*	*Total*	*Grant*	*Loan*	*Total*	*Grant*	*Loan*	*Total*
1960/61	224.474 (98.67)	–	224.474 (98.67)	3.027 (1.33)	–	3.027 (1.33)	227.051 (100.00)	–	227.501 (100.00)
1965/66	175.300 (98.15)	3.300 (1.85)	178.600 (100.00)	–	–	–	175.300 (98.15)	3.300 (1.85)	178.600 (100.00)
1970/71	270.685 (89.29)	32.458 (10.71)	303.143 (100.00)	–	–	–	270.685 (89.29)	32.458 (10.71)	303.143 (100.00)
1971/72	227.261 (80.90)	26.914 (9.58)	254.175 (90.48)	14.776 (5.26)	11.973 (4.26)	26.749 (9.52)	242.037 (86.16)	38.887 (13.84)	280.924 (100.00)
1975/76	307.685 (60.85)	23.069 (4.56)	330.754 (65.41)	52.032 (10.29)	122.868 (24.30)	174.900 (34.59)	359.717 (71.14)	145.937 (28.86)	505.654 (100.00)
1980/81	692.472 (45.85)	166.016 (10.99)	858.488 (56.84)	163.058 (10.80)	488.706 (32.36)	651.764 (43.16)	855.530 (56.65)	654.722 (43.35)	1510.252 (100.00)

Note: Figures in parenthesis are low percentages.
Source: HMG/N, Ministry of Finance (1982), *Budget in Nepal (1951/52–1981/82)*, Revenue Administration Training Center, Kathmandu.

the 'debt trap' of loans channelised increasingly through the multilateral agencies. It may be recapitulated in this context from Table 4.52 above that Asian Development Bank and International Development Association accounted for 76.34% of total outstanding debt in 1980–81 after making their debut only in the beginning of Seventies. Consequent upon the increasingly pumping–in of loans, the economy's debt-service liability is reported to have reached 2.5% of total export earning and 5% of convertible export earning in 1980/81[119]. Thus Nepal's absorption into the familiar machination of neo-colonial exploitation through financial capital and subjection into the never-ending cycle of external financial dependency as seen in the more prominent 'underdevelopment' economies of Latin America and other parts of the Third World, gets largely confirmed.

However, the story would not end there. The much talked about and largely true, politico-strategic aspect of foreign capital inflow to this country[120] sought to be wooed by rival imperialist powers needs to be examined to realise the true implications of foreign capital in the economy. A review of capital inflow in the form of bilateral 'grant' by major 'donors' over the years[121] would unfold the dynamics of 'politics' having prevailed over 'economics' in the initial years and gradual reversal of the position in later years.

4.6.22 Sectoral Distribution of Foreign Capital

The real social implications of external financial linkages may be assessed from the mode of sectoral investment of the imported capital. In the absence of a sectoral break-up of capital investment since the early Fifties, when the capital inflow first made its debut, it may not be possible to empirically verify the trend. However, taking into consideration the high share of foreign capital in development expenditure in different plans and cross-classifying it with sectoral decomposition of total outlays in different Plans (see Appendix-10) a revealing set of observations can be made. The fact that transportation and communication received largest share of investment till the 4th plan (or till mid-seventies) provides an important insight into the familiar role of foreign capital in preparing the base for market penetration and laying the infrastructure for private investment, so frequent a modus operandi of metropolitan capital in backward and underdeveloped societies.[122]

Purpose-wise allocation of foreign 'aid' from 1974/75 to 1982/83 (Table 4.54) also confirms the same pattern, though it must be just a minor replica of the earlier picture when the magnitude of domination of transportation and communication sub-sector must have been much more pronounced. The fact that after the transportation and communication infrastructure was laid the emphasis gradually shifted to power (i.e. mostly hydroelectric power, which also has a strong export potential) indicates the sequences of preparation made by metropolitan capital to export more capital. The rise in investment share of agriculture with an emphasis on 'integrated development' programmes to strengthen the base of small peasantry is entirely in keeping the new World Bank programmes enunciated after the early 1970s.[123]

Table 4.54 Purposewise Allocation of Total Foreign 'Aid' Disbursement (1974/75–1982/83).

Purposes	1974–75	1977–78	1980–81	1982–83*
1. Agriculture, Irrigation and Forestry	14.02	17.44	20.51	27.74
2. Industry and Commerce	10.99	8.12	4.46	11.90
3. Power	1.99	24.49	35.87	21.35
4. Transport and Communication	62.99	34.38	28.15	16.42
5. Social Services and others	10.01	15.56	11.02	22.59
	100.00	100.00	100.00	100.00

Note: *Estimates
Source: HMG/N, Ministry of Finance, *Economic Survey* (Various Years), Kathmandu.

A better idea of the investment trend for a longer period may be available from the sectoral distribution pattern of total 'aid' inflow from major bilateral and multilateral sources, namely India, USA and IDA-ADB (Table 4.55). The fact that the largest bilateral 'donor' India should have directed 62.8% of its total 'aid' to transportation and communication and another 27.2% to irrigation, power, etc., reveals a very significant role of external financial capital in articulating the Nepalese economy. Leaving aside the politico-strategic content[124] of this pattern of Indian 'aid', the layouts and sequences of construction of transportation and

Table 4.55 Purposewise Allocation of Foreign 'Aid' by Major Sources.

(%)

Purposes/Sources	India (from 1951 to 1980)	U.S.A. (upto 1979/80)	I.D.A and A.D.B. (upto 1981)
1. Transport and Communication	62.8	20.7	17.25
2. Irrigation, Power and Water Supply	27.2	–	38.13
3. Agriculture Forestry and Allied	0.8	19.3	13.40
4. Industries	1.1	8.7	10.42
5. Social Services and Local development	3.6	36.1	9.84
6. Administrative and Technical assistance	4.5	10.7	8.44
7. Miscellaneous	–	3.5	1.71
	100.0	100.0	100.0

Source: Derived from Poudyal, S.R. (1982), *Foreign Aid in Nepal*, CEDA, Kathmandu.

communication networks (see Chapter 5.4 below) reveal a strong economic motive for strengthening markets for Indian goods and capital investment. In the case of U.S. 'aid', the larger proportion in 'social services and local development' followed by transportation and communication and agriculture, indicates a strong combination of both political and economic intents. The late entrants IDA and ADB, on the other hand, are seen to have directed their finances (mostly in 'loans') to power, transportation and communication and agriculture, which seem to have been motivated by preparing grounds for private capital investments as envisaged by the parent body, the World Bank.

Besides the sectoral distribution of foreign finance, the forms of their remittances, e.g. in 1981, 40.7% of total 'aid' committed were as 'technical assistance' and 59.3% as 'capital assistance',[125] also tend to create structural imbalances and lead to permanent dependence on the exogenous economy. Moreover, by the very motivation of metropolitan capital and by the inherent structural weaknesses of the 'recepient' economy, a large proportion of invested capital is known to revert back directly to the metropolitan destinations[126].

4.6.23 Financial capital as a social relation should logically promote certain class configurations in society which are conducive to its continued reproduction. Within the present world imperialist order, promotion and/or preservation of capitalist classes would be the natural concern of metropolitan financial capital even during its operation in backward and underdeveloped formations. In the context of Nepal, however, since foreign financial flow takes place exclusively in the form of 'aid' the preservation and strengthening of the present class and state structure becomes more direct and glaring. This may be better expressed in the words of a seasoned observer thus:

> "... aid has assisted the monarchy both directly and indirectly to create a better-equipped and better trained army and to put a large number of potentially restive, educated young men on the bureaucratic payrolls... Thus, in the short run at any rate, foreign assistance has enhanced the monachy's chances of survival and has inhibited the growth of pressures for fundamental change"[127].

Besides the direct 'bribing' of ruling classes to serve the interests of imperialism, the sectoral distribution of finances as observed in the preceding pages also reveals a subtle form of promotion and sustainance of class configurations which would both act as an ally of imperialism and be resistant to revolutionary change. Whereas the opening of markets through expansion of circulation networks and enhancement of consumption needs of upper strata of the populace have greatly strengthened the might of comprador mercantile classes, various 'integrated development programmes have sought to check rapid class differentiation in the countryside and insulate against revolutionary upheavls. Moreover, the proliferation of management and technical jobs and general expansion of the bureaucracy can be said to have led to the growth and stabilization of the "middle classes"[128]

4.6.3 Spatial Implications

In the absence of a separate inventory of spatial distribution of various components of foreign capital in the country, it may not be possible to construct a systematic configuration of the same. Nevertheless, in view of the dominant share of foreign capital in all the plan outlays to date a broad generalisation of spatial implications of foreign finances can be made from the spatial disaggregation of Plan outlays. Also, the spatial configuration of certain sectoral projects like roads may be taken as proxy for that of foreign finances as well.

Spatial allocation of 'development' projects during successive Plans are known to be heavily biased in favour of Terai, particularly its eastern wing, and Kathmandu Valley.[129] Hence it is quite logical to assume the same spatial pattern for the disbursement of external financing. Territorial and sectoral distribution of foreign financed projects as in 1981 (Table 4.56) also reveals the same pattern of high centralisation in Terai, but the picture is not very clear due to high percentage (i.e. 45.65%) of projects not spatially identified. However, on the basis of past experiences and general observations it can be assumed with reasonable certainty that large proportion of the unidentified ones would go to Terai and Kathmandu Valley.

Further clarity on the spatial distribution of foreign financing would be obtained if the sectoral and territorial distribution of foreign financing as given in the same Table are cross-classified. It is quite understandable to observe that whereas Terai and Inner Terai account for bulk of financing in the sub-sectors of agriculture, industry and commerce and power and physical infrastructure, the Hill and Mountain account for almost total allocation in 'community and local development' and Kathmandu Valley claims the largest share in 'social services and infrastructures'. This pattern of spatial distribution provides significant insights into the location imperatives of financial capital in the country. Terai and Inner Terai are seen as the exclusive locales for more 'productive' investment of capital. On the other hand Kathmandu Valley is the greater beneficiary of direct-consumption oriented investment and Hill and Mountain seem to be forced to live on sheer 'altruism'[130], because of their greatly eroded productive base. Thus metropolitan capital is seen to be following differing tactics in according to the differing economic structure of the regions, i.e. pamper the bureaucracy in Kathmandu, silence the restive peasantry in Hill and Mountain and economically exploit the resources in Terai and Inner Terai. This is fully in keeping with the neo-colonial rationale propagated through World Bank etc.

However, the stage of full economic exploitation does not seem to have been attained yet. This is evident from low overall financial investment in 'productive' sectors of economy, i.e. only about one-third of total external financing. As the major thrust is as yet in building physical and social infrastructures, the spatial 'beneficiaries' of foreign capital would be the selective nodes of economic prosperity and bureaucratic authority, i.e. areas of Terai and Kathmandu Valley. And to that extent foreign capital can be said to have aggravated the disparateness in spatial structure.

Table 4.56 Territorial and Sectoral Distribution of External Financing (1981).

(In thousand US dollars)

Technical Zones	Sectors	Agriculture, Irrigation and Forestry	Industry Mining and Commerce	Power and Physical Infra-structure	Social Services Infra-structure	Community and Local Development	Miscellaneous	Total
1. Mountain		32.8	–	5236.6	6.5	2530.00	–	7805.9
	(i)	(0.04)		(4.71)	(0.01)	(14.18)	–	(2.61)
	(ii)	(0.42)		(67.09)	(0.08)	(32.41)	–	(100.0)
2. Hill		10296.3	243.3	23995.4	1548.9	13430.5	108.3	49622.7
	(i)	(11.80)	(2.04)	(21.60)	(2.65)	(75.28)	(0.87)	(16.59)
	(ii)	(20.75)	(0.49)	(48.36)	(3.12)	(27.07)	(0.22)	(100.0)
3. Kathmandu Valley		140.5	130.0	3327.5	10078.9	–	1285.1	14962
	(i)	(0.16)	(1.09)	(2.99)	(17.25)		(10.29)	(5.00)
	(ii)	(0.94)	(0.87)	(22.24)	(67.36)		(8.59)	(100.0)
4. Inner Terai		–	1231.9	4502	8.2	–	–	5742
	(i)		(10.32)	(4.05)	(0.01)			(1.92)
	(ii)		(21.45)	(78.40)	(0.14)			(100.0)
5. Terai		49420.2	1117.9	27309.4	1924.3	45	4596.8	84413.60
	(i)	(56.63)	(9.36)	(24.58)	(3.29)	(0.25)	(36.81)	(28.22)
	(ii)	(58.55)	(1.32)	(32.35)	(2.28)	(0.05)	(5.45)	(100.0)
6. Non-specified		27383.4	9216.9	46739.3	44864.6	1835.9	6496.9	136537.0
	(i)	(31.39)	(77.19)	(42.07)	(76.78)	(10.29)	(52.03)	(45.65)
	(ii)	(20.06)	(6.75)	(34.23)	(32.86)	(1.34)	(4.76)	(100.0)
NEPAL		87273.2	11940.0	111110.2	58431.4	17841.4	12487.1	299083.3
	(i)	(100.00)	(100.00)	(100.00)	(100.00)	(100.00)	(100.00)	(100.00)
	(ii)	(29.18)	(3.99)	(37.15)	(19.54)	(5.97)	(4.18)	(100.00)

Note: Figures in parenthesis are percentages, (i) Column percentages; (ii) Row percentages.
Source: Compiled from UNDP (1982), *The Resident Representative's Annual Report on Development Cooperation to Nepal 1981*, Kathmandu.

4.7 CONCLUSTIONS

General level of marketiasation of the indigenous economy (measured both in terms of the total indigenous produce circulated through markets and the number of trading, establishments per unit households and per capita sale) is quite low. The economy is also not marked by self-sufficiency or autarchy, as is evident from the significant amount of cash expenditure on subsistence goods not locally produced. There is significant spatial variation in the levels of marketisation, declining from south to north and from east to west. The primacy of Kathmandu Valley is however quite marked.

- The commodity structure of commerce is largely direct-consumption oriented and divorced from the indigenous production process.
- The social relations of exchange is marked by primitiveness as reflected in predominance of retailing and small-scale operations, circulation of use-values than exchange-values, etc. On the other hand there is strong tendency of commercial monopolisation in terms of ownership by dominant mercantile groups. The 'comprador' character of merchant capital is also well manifested.
- The general pattern of marketed commodity flows is predominantly in the north-south territorial dimension, with a net flow of goods from south to north. There is a vertually non-existent or negligible flow in the east-west territorial dimension, specially among the same ecological sub-zones. Whereas the primacy of Kathmandu in terms of inter-regional commercial linkages is well-articulated, the Terai areas have greater linkages and commercial exchanges with India than with other territorial zones within the country. In terms of commodity structure of inter-regional exchanges as well there is evidence of 'unequal exchange' resulting in a net flow of value from north to south, i.e. from Mountain-Hill to Terai, which is ultimately drained away from the economy.
- The spatial organisation of marketing is marked by a heavy centralisation of higher order market place in Kathmandu Valley and in Terai just across the Indian border and a total absence of them in the larger parts of the country. Thus the spatial structure of commerce is simultaneously marked by extreme dysfunctionality, internal fragmentation (disarticulation) and outward-orientation.
- The dependence of the economy on foreign trade is increasing with time. The retrograde nature of the process is not only marked by low export/import ratio but also by the increasing volume of imports and declining exports.
- The apparent slackening of dependence on India is illusory. This is so not only because almost half of total external trade is still transacted with India but the apparent reduction is brought out by reduction of exports rather than of imports. Diversification of trade to countries other than India has led to

direct integration of the economy with more powerful centres of metropolitan capital and has aggravated the relations of external dependence.

- The characteristic features of unequal exchange between exports of primary products and imports of finished products as seen in the case of underdeveloped economies in general are not only present in acute scale, but the exchange relations are further marred by increasing imports of consumption oriented than production-oriented manufactures. Also, the primacy of few commodities, like jute and rice, in total value of exports further confirms the typically underdeveloped structure of foreign trade in Nepal.
- Terms of trade with major partners are seen fluctuating violently and turning adverse in general. Terms of trade with the dominant partner India have turned against Nepal and further aggravated over the years.
- The spatial distribution of export-import values clearly differentiate areas of production (i.e. from where more export takes place) and areas of 'consumption' (i.e. to which more import takes place) in the country. Whereas eastern parts of the country in general and Terai in particular are seen to be the principal areas of production or export, 'central' parts of the country in general and Kathmandu Valley in particular, are the principal areas of consumption or imports.
- The landlocked position of the country and excessive dependence of India for external economic interactions has given rise to a distorted spatial structure marked by centralisation of major trading nodes in Terai. The essentially extractive nature of trade relations is spatially manifest in the growth of satellitic centres at major 'gateway junctions' along the southern border, e.g. Biratnagar in east, Birgunj in Central-East, Bhairahawa in central and Nepalgunj in West.
- Tourism, within the prevailing framework of underdeveloped socio-economic structure of Nepal, is merely a form of 'entrepot trade' where imported goods are re-exported albeit to foreign consumers who are present at the door.
- Role of tourism in the economy as the largest 'foreign exchange earner' and the major avenue for capital investment has been rising phenomenally.
- Its social role is, however, suspect in view of marginal employment generated within the sub-sector.
- By all the related attributes like mode of travel, star-category distribution of hotels, etc., the upper-class bias in the growth of tourism is apparent. Also, the heavily capital-intensive nature of development has resulted in a cancerous growth of economy little related to the average life of society and logically dependent on exogenous support.
- Tourism in Nepal has been merely an extension of the Indian economy. Since much of the 'earnings' from tourism are leaked to alien economies by various mechanisms of surplus transfer, tourism is basically performing a mere mediatory role between the producers and consumers of alien economy and thus has developed no roots in the indigenous economy.

- Tourism by the nature of its development in Nepal has been a mere outgrowth of traditional feudal-mercantile capital dominated socio-economic structure allied with metropolitan capital and has proved a profitable avenue for the investment of indigenous primitive capital in alliance with metropolitan merchant capital.
- Because of the capital-intensive nature of development and its retrograde class-bias tourism has tended to be highly space-specific and has given rise to dysfunctional spatial enclaves in addition to further enhancement of socio-spatial primacy of Kathmandu.
- Aided by both monopoly of nature and monopoly of merchant capital, with a decisive role of the latter, the social and spatial structure of tourism in Nepal is found to be highly centralised, dysfunctional and extraverted. Hence, despite its fragile social roots, both in terms of scale and nature of development, tourism has acted as an additional mechanism of aggravation of underdevelopment of society.
- Financial capital in general is still in a primitive stage of development, but the size of institutionalised finance more particularly bank capital, is showing a rapid growth.
- Social relations of financing is found to be backward and retrograde, as manifested in the large proportion of organised financing going in for mercantile activities and consumption purposes. The short-term loans given are more than medium or long term loans. Also financial capital is seen abetting the general distortion of the structure of the economy by disproportionately strengthening the 'circulation' component of the economy internally and promoting unequal integration externally.
- There is extreme spatial disparity in the distribution of bank capital, particularly in favour of the mercantile and administrative centre of Kathmandu Valley. In the dynamic frame as seen in the inter-regional differentials in credit/deposit ratios, a pattern of transfer of economic surplus in the form of bank capital is seen to be taking place from the more retarded areas of Hill and Mountain to the better-off areas of Kathmandu Valley and Terai.
- As characterised by backward and retrograde social relations of financing and tendency to over-centralise spatially, burgeoning financial capital is observed to be one of the principal agents of underdevelopment of the space economy.
- Dependence of the economy on external finance is increasing. The evolution of financial integration of the economy to metropolitan economy is following, with some exceptions of politico-strategic overtones, the same pattern of neo-colonial integration as seen in the case of other underdeveloped countries. But the integration is still at the initial stage and the degree of financial depreciation as observed elsewhere is yet to be seen.
- External financial capital, mostly in the form of 'aid' (both 'soft' loans and grants), has gone to prepare ground for later mercantile exploitation, i.e. it is mostly confined to infrastructure-building.

- Spatial concentration of external finance in economically more 'viable' and politically more important areas, has led to further spatial disparateness.
- The general proliferation of circulation capital divorced from the indigenous production process is likely to further aggravate economic retardation of the country and lead to a path of neo-colonial underdevelopment as seen elsewhere.

REFERENCES

1. These different terminologies are seen to have widely varying connotations in the strict economic sense. For example, Sau has taken 'merchant's capital' as general form of capital and divided its circulation component into 'commercial capital' and 'money-dealing capital' (See Sau, R. (1982), *Trade, Capital and Underdevelopment: Towards a Marxist Theory*, Oxford University Press, Calcutta, pp. 57–59). However, we have used the terms in their common parlance and classified them accordingly.
2. Keyder, C. (1982), *The Definition of a Peripheral Economy: Turkey 1923–1929*, Cambridge University Press, Cambridge, p. 7.
3. Lenin, V.I. (1897), "The Handicraft Census of 1894–95 in Perm Gubernia and General Problems of 'Handicraft Industry'" in *Collected Works*, Vol. 2, Progress Publishers, Moscow (1972 edn.), p. 442.
4. Lenin, V.I. (1899), *Development of Capitalism in Russia*, Progress Publishers, Moscow (1977 edn.), p. 373.
5. Mandel, E. (1971), *Marxist Economic Theory*, Vol. I. Monthly Review Press, New York, p. 210.
6. In Marx's own words:

   "There is.... not the least difficulty in understanding why merchant's capital appears as the historical form of capital long before capital established its own domination over production. Its existence and development to a certain level are in themselves historical premises for the development of capitalist production (1) as premises for the concentration of money wealth, and (2) because the capitalist mode of production presupposes production for trade selling on a large scale, and not to the individual customer... " (Marx, K., "Historical Facts about Merchant's Capital", in Marx, K. (1978), *Capital*, Vol. III, Progress Publishers, Moscow, p. 327).
7. Brenner, R. (1977), "The Origins of Capitalist Development : A Critique of Neo-Smithian Marxian", *New Left Review*, No. 104, p. 50, and Marx, K., "Results of the Immediate Process of Production', in Marx, K. (1979), *Capital*, Vol. I, Penguin Books/New Left Review, Harmondsworth, Appendix-I, pp. 949–50.
8. Marx (1978), *op. cit.*, p. 327.
9. Marx, K. (1977a), *Grundrisse*, Penguin Books Harmondsworth, p. 858.
10. See the famous 'transition debate' in Hilton, R. et al. (eds.) (1954), *The Transition from Feudalism to Capitalism*, People's Book House, Patna.
11. Brewer, A. (1980), *Marxist Theories of Imperialism*, Routledge and Kegan Paul, London, p. 47.
12. Marx (1978), *op. cit.*, p. 328.
13. For detailed expositions on these lines, see, among others, Marx, K. (1978), *op. cit.*, Part IV, and Kay, G. (1975), *Development and Underdevelopment: A Marxist Analysis*, Macmillan, London.

14. Kay, *op. cit.*, pp. 99–103.
15. *Ibid.*, p. 102.
16. Emmanuel, A. (1972), *Unequal Exchange: A Study in the Imperialism of Trade*, New Left Books, London.
17. See, among others, Battelheim, C., "Theoretical Comments", in *Ibid*, Appendix-I; Kay, *op. cit.*; Sau, R. (1978), *Unequal Exchange, Imperialism and Underdevelopment: An essay on the Political Economy of World Capitalism*, Oxford University Press, Calcutta; Bharadwaj, K. (1984), "A Note on Emmanuel's 'Unequal Exchange'," *Economic and Political Weekly*, Review of Political Economy, July.
18. For example, Amin has advanced the thesis of 'unequal specialization' to explain the inequality in relations between the economies of 'centre' and 'periphery'. This put very simply, says international specialisation is determined by absolute cost levels and cost levels depend on productivity and wages; the countries of the 'centre' having got huge lead in productivity can ensure lowers costs even at the time of wage increase and retain ascendency in 'unequal specialisation', which reflects in international exchange relations in the form of net advantage to the 'centre' and disadvantage to the 'periphery' (See Amin, S. (1979), *Unequal Development*, Oxford University Press, Delhi).
19. Mandel, *op. cit.*, p. 210.
20. Marx (1978), *op.cit.*, p. 598.
21. *Ibid.*, pp. 600–07.
22. Bottomore, T. et. al. (eds.) (1983), *A Dictionary of Marxist Thought*, Basil Blackwell, London, p. 177.
23. *Ibid.*, p. 173.
24. See, Bhaduri, A. (1973), "A study in Agricultural Backwardness under Semi-Feudalism, *The Economic Journal*, Vol. 83, No. 329, March; and Prasad, P.H. (1974), "Reactionary Role of Usurer's Capital in Rural India", *Economic and Political Weekly*, Special Number, August.
25. Marx (1978), *op. cit.*, p. 597.
26. *Ibid.*, p. 489.
27. See, Lenin, V.I. (1916), "Imperialism, the Highest Stage of Capitalism", in *Collected Works*, Vol. 22, Progress Publishers, Moscow.
28. See, among others, Hayter, T. (1971), *Aid as Imperialism*, Penguin Books, Harmondsworth; Buyers, T.J. (ed.), (1972), *Foreign Resources and Economic Development: A Symposium on the Report of the Pearson Commission*, Frankcass, London; Payer, C. (1974), *The Debt Trap: The IMF and the Third World*, Penguin Books, Harmondsworth; Feder, E. (1976), "The New World Bank Programme for the Self-Liquidation of the Third World Peasantry", *The Journal of Peasant Studies*, Vol. 3, No. 3, April, pp. 343–52.
29. Berry, B.J.L. (1967), *Geography of Market Centres and Retail Distribution*, Prentice-Hall, London. p. 2.
30. Kay, *op. cit.*, p. 96.
31. Sau, *op. cit.*, p. 24.
32. Stiller, L.F. (1972) "A Note on Himalayan Trade", *Journal of the Tribhuvan University*, Vol. VII, No. 1, November, Kathmandu, p. 2.
33. Gurung, H.B. (1970), *Geographical Setting – Nepal: A Profile*, Nepal Council of Applied Economic Research, Kathmandu, pp. 10–11.
34. Regmi, M.C. (1971), *A Study in Nepali Economic History*, Manjushri Publishing House, New Delhi, p. 24; Stiller *op. cit.*, p. 4; Adhikary, K.K. (1975), "A Brief

Survey of Nepal's Trade with British India during the latter half of the 19th Century", *Contributions to Nepalese Studies*, Vol. 2. No. 1, CNAS, Kathmandu, February, p. 189.

35. This is evident from the following report of Brian H. Hodgson, the first British Resident in Kathmandu after the Sugauli Treaty: "It appears ... that at this present time (December 1831), there are, in the great towns of the valley of Nepal, fifty-two native and thirty-four Indian merchants engaged in foreign commerce, both with the South and the North... A third of such of these merchants as are natives of the plains have come up subsequently to the establishment of the Residency in 1816, since which period as is thought by the oldest merchants of Kathmandu, the trade has been trebled." (Quoted in Regmi (1971), *op. cit.*, p. 169).
36. Regmi, D.R. (1965), *Medieval Nepal*, Vol. II, Firma KLM Private Ltd., Calcutta, p. 511.
37. See Furer–Haimendorf, C.V. (1975), *Himalayan Traders*, John Murrey, London.
38. Mandel, *op. cit.*, p. 217.
39. According to D.R. Regmi, "The Nepalese rulers earned a profit of half a million rupees out of the mint on this account" (Regmi (1965) *op. cit.*, p. 534), not an insignificant amount for the given era.
40. See Marx (1978), *op. cit.*, p. 428, for social implications of different forms of money.
41. The following financial institutions, which are still the premier institutions in the country, were established, in order of their incorporation, as follows; Nepal Industrial Development Corporation (NIDC), to promote private sector industrial financing–1959; the Cooperative Bank, 1963; Provident Fund Corporation, in 1963; the Rastriya Banijya Bank—a state-owned commercial bank–1965; the Land Reform Savings Corporation in 1966, which was merged with the Cooperative Bank to form Agricultural Development Bank in 1967; National Insurance Corporation in 1968; Credit Guarantee Corporation (P) Ltd., 1974; Security Marketing Centre, 1976.
42. Regmi, M.C. (1984), *The State and Economic Suplus: Production, Trade and Resource Mobilisation in Early 19th Century Nepal*, Kathmandu, p. 131.
43. Regmi (1971), *op. cit.*, p. 20.
44. Regmi (1984), *op. cit.*, p. 131.
45. Sen, J. (1977) *Indo–Nepal Trade in the Nineteenth Century*, Firma KLM Private Ltd., Calcutta, pp. 143–44.
46. Regmi (1971), *op. cit.*, p. 20.
47. Regmi (1984), *op, cit.*, p. 131.
48. For the differences in the pattern of trade and level of prosperity amongst traders of Olangchung, Arun Valley, Namchebazar, Kali Gandaki, Dolpo, Karnali and Mahakali, See Furer–Haimendorf, *op. cit.*
49. See, Kay, *op. cit.*, p. 120.
50. For example, Mc. Dougal (Mc Dougal, C. (1969), *Village and Household Economy in Far-Western Nepal*, Tribhuvan University, Kathmandu) and Caplan (Caplan, A.P. (1972), *Priests and Cobblers: A Study of Social change in a Hindu Village in western Nepal*, Chandler Publishing Company, San Fransisco), in separate studies of western Nepal and Caplan (Caplan, L. (1970), *Land and Social Change in East Nepal: A Study of Hindu-Tribal Relations*, Routledge and Kegan Paul, London.) in a study of eastern Nepal have exploded the myth of pre-capitalist autarchy that was supposed to have characterised a backward hill economy. Blaikie et. al. (Blaikie, P., et. al. (1980),

Nepal in Crisis: Growth and Stagnation at the Periphery, Oxford University Press, Delhi), in a survey of Central Nepal have confirmed the earlier conclusions.

51. This favourably compares with the earlier estimation of also 30% of total food grains traded through marketing channels. (Shrestha, G.R. (1978), *Foodgrains Distribution System in Nepal*, Nepal Food Corporation, Kathmandu, p. 8).
52. The first countrywide "Internal Trade Survey (study)" undertaken by the Central Bureau of Statistics in 1979/80 on which this study is based records only the trade transactions in settlement nodes with more than 30 trading establishments in Terai and with more than 20 in Hill but none in Mountain, and completely ignores the periodic markets and mobile trading activities. Thus the level of marketisation based on these data would be an underestimation.
53. See, Furer–Haimendorf, *op. cit.*
54. I.R.D.P. (1979), *Marketing Survey of Farm Produce, Livestock, Cloth and Storage Needs in Rasuwa–Nuwaket Districts*, Project Coordinator's Office, Kathmandu. p. 7.
55. For want of a more detailed break-up of commodities the commodity groups in Table 4.7 may be re-classified as follows:

Classification	*Commodity Group Code No.*
1. Primary	1, 4
2. Secondary	2, 3, 5, 6, 7, 8, 9, 10, 11, 12, 14, 15
3. Miscellaneous	13, 16

56. Bhaduri, A. (1983), *Economic Structure of Backward Agriculture*, Macmillan, Delhi, p. 1.
57. In some parts of the remote Mountains the seasonally wandering traders, like Taralis of Dolpa, are known to combine mobile trading with animals husbandry and cultivation. (See Furer–Haimendorf, *op. cit.*)
58. Seddon, D. et. al. (1981), *Peasants and Workers in Nepal*, Vikas Publishing House Pvt. Ltd., New Delhi, p. 187.
59. Since there is no production of value and hence extraction of surplus-value in the process of circulation, the number of persons engaged is significant only as the measure of total value transacted by them in which proportion they can share surplus value already expropriated in the production process. (See, also *Ibid.*, p. 189.)
60. Blaikie, et. al., *op. cit.*, pp. 155–56.
61. See Bhaduri, *op. cit.*, Chaps I and II.
62. The important 'public enterprises' in the wholesale and retail trade sector with their number of branches till 1977/78 (in parenthesis) are follows:
    1. Nepal Food Corporation (62);
    2. National Trading Limited (22);
    3. Tobacco Development Company (15);
    4. Fuel Corporation (11);
    5. Nepal Oil Corporation (13);
    6. Jute Development and Trading Corporation (1);
    7. Agriculture Inputs Corporation (-) ;
    8. Cottage Industry and Handicraft Emporium (P) Ltd.
63. See HMG/N, Ministry of Finance (1980), *Highlights of Public Enterprises in Nepal for the F.Y. 1977/78*, Corporation Coordination Division, Kathmandu.
64. Disaggregation of membership of Chamber of Commerce in selected urban places by caste/ethnic group reveals that 54.73% of total members in Pokhara (Central Hill) are

Newars and traders of Indian Origin constitute 42.69% of total members in Bhairahawa central Terai) (Sheddon et. al., *op. cit.*, p. 205).

65. For example, a survey conducted by GDI/CEDA showed that 73.20% of export from Hill to Terai consisted of primary products. (Ojha, D.P. and Weiss, D. (1972), *Regional Analysis of Kosi Zone/Eastern Nepal*, GDI/CEDA, Berlin/Kathmandu, pp. 89–90.
66. See Zehender, W. et. al. (1975), *The Influence of Kathmandu on the Axis Bidoor/ Trishuli Bazaar-Dhunche*, Draft Report Submitted to German Development Institute, Kathmandu.
67. See *Ibid.*
68. See Blaikie et. al., *op. cit.*
69. CEDA (1973–75), *Regional Development Study (Nepal)*, Part IIa, Kathmandu, p. 266.
70. See Shrestha, C.B. (1973–74), "The System of Central Places in the Arniko Rajmarge Area of Nepal", *The Himalayan Review*, Vol, VI. No. 5–6, Nepal Geographical Society, Kathmandu.
71. The mean distances to various categories of market places from the rural nodes in Rasuwa and Nuwakot districts were found as follows:

(in miles)

District/Territorial Zone	*Mean distance to the nearest*		
	Local Bazar	*Central Bazar*	*Market Town*
1. Rasuwa (Central Mountain)	6.5	16.34	30.56
2. Nuwakot (Central Hill)	4.1	8.83	12.49

Source: IRDP (1979), *Marketing Survey of Farm Produce, Livestock, Cloth and Storage Needs in Rasuwa–Nuwakot Districts,* Project Coordinators Office, Kathmandu.

72. Naqvi, S.N.H. "Trade Policy for the Sub-Region-Pakistan, India, Bangladesh, Sri Lanka and Nepal—During the 1980s" Paper presented to ESCAP (23 April–4 May 1979), Bangkok, as cited in Bista, N.K. (1981), *Import-Export Structure and Trade Expansion in South Asia (Nepal)*, (mimeo.), CEDA, Kathmandu, p. 59.
73. Nepal's share in total world export was a mere 0.11% and that of import 0.21% in 1978/79 (*Ibid.*, p. 65).
74. For a review of different treaties signed by the governments of Nepal and India from time to time, see Banskota, *op. cit.*
75. Because of long (about 500 miles) and open border with India, specially along the economically more important Terai, and strong socio-economic proximities and interactions across the political border, it has never been possible to accurately document the actual volume of trade transactions with India. According to one estimate about one-third of total trade flows between the two countries go unrecorded. (ARTEP (1974), *A Challenge to Nepal: Growth and Employment*, Bangkok, p. V2.) Hence these figures on India should be regarded as an underestimate.
76. Trade with mainland China is transacted through sea-routes via Calcutta port, and is included in the 'overseas' section.
77. For a review of EEE and other periodic schemes like Dual Exchange scheme adopted by the government from time to time to encourage trade with countries other than India, see among others, Rana, P.S.J.B., "Indo-Nepalese Trade Today and its Policy

Implications for Nepal", in CEDA (1969), *Trade and Transit: Nepal's Problem with her Southern Neighbour*, Occasional Paper No. 1, Kathmandu; Rawat, P.C. (1974), *Indo-Nepal Economic Relations*, National Publishing House, Delhi, Banskota, *op. cit.*

78. According to one observer as much as Rs. 150 million, or about 30% of total export was realized through re-export of goods to India in 1969 (Rana, PSJB, *op. cit.*, p. 4).
79. Nepal has formal bilateral agreement on trade with 66 countries (in 1981) (Banskota, *op. cit.*, p. 103), though agreements by themselves do not amount to actual trade relations.
80. See Trade Promotion Centre, *Nepal Overseas Trade Statistics* (Various issues), Kathmandu.
81. Jute export was gradually replaced by carpets and garment exports to overseas countries after the Eighties.
82. UNCTAD has constructed indices of concentration "diversification" of export structure of different countries. Though both the indices measure the intensity of commodity shares in the total export, the concentration index "discriminates more finely between countries which are relatively more concentrated in their export structure" and the "diversification" index "discriminates more finely between countries which are relatively more diversified", and both indices range between zero and 1.0, with latter representing the most extreme concentration. The indices for selected countries at different levels of development are given as below:

Country	*"Diversification" Index*		*Concentration Index*	
	1970	*1978*	*1970*	*1978*
1. Nepal	0.972	0.934	0.597	0.361
2. Afghanistan	0.937	0.938	0.307	0.302
3. Bangladesh	–	0.898	–	0.383
4. India	0.654	0.647	0.139	0.130
5. Sri Lanka	0.935	0.861	0.584	0.482
6. Ethiopia	0.889	0.916	0.603	0.766
7. Uruguay	0.915	0.778	0.433	0.238
8. Japan	0.430	0.464	0.131	0.192
9. U.S.A.	0.325	0.359	0.099	0.107

Source: UNCTAD (1982), *Handbook of International Trade and Development Statistics*, Supplement 1981, United Nations, New York, Table 4.5, pp. 212–15.

83. For the convenience of availability of data by disaggregation of countries and unit value indices of commodities, only a seven year period from 1974/75 to 1981/82 is considered. The export price indices for India and 'overseas' countries are constructed by aggregating a set of 10 commodities each selected on the basis of relative importance among commodities for which annual quantity and unit value data are available. For India these were: rice, maize, herbs, dry ginger, timber, purified butter, raw jute, jute cutting, jute goods and oil seeds, which together accounted for 45 to 70% of total export; and for 'overseas' these were: rice, pulses, catechu, large cardamom, dry ginger, herbs, bristle, carpets, hide and skins and raw jute, which together accounted for 60 to 80% of total export. As regards to the import price index, the wholesale price index of India was taken as proxy, for India,

and for 'overseas' an aggregation of export unit value indices of 12 countries selected on the basis of their relative importance in total imports by Nepal and the availability of export unit value indices.

84. Rana, PSJB *op. cit.*, pp. 4–5.
85. Rawat, *op. cit.*, p. 104.
86. Bajracharya, B.B. and Shrestha, C.B. (1981), *Transport Communication Linkage in Nepal* (mimeo.), CEDA, Kathmandu.
87. In the case of Nepal it was found that about 95% of 'direct' tourist expenditure was incurred in hotels and restaurants, travel and trekking agencies, air and road transportation and purchase of carpets and curios. (Burger, V. (1978), *The Economic Impact of Tourism in Nepal: An Input-Output Analysis* (Ph.D. Dissertation-Microfilmed), Cornell University, Ithaca, p. 86).
88. National Planning Commission, *Fourth Plan*, quoted in Department of Tourism (1972), *Nepal Tourism Master Plan*, HMGIN, Ministry of Commerce and Industry, Kathmandu, p. 143.
89. However according to one study the gross foreign exchange earned from tourism in 1974/75 itself was NRs. 150 million, or about 30% of total foreign exchange earnings. (Burger, *op. cit.*, p. 312).
90. Department of Tourism, *op. cit.*, pp. 145–16.
91. Burger, *op. cit.*, p. 301.
92. For example, in 1981 as against the total inflow of tourists from outside of 161,669 the outflow of Nepalese tourists (of course only registered or travelling by air) was 23,839. This, however, would be an underestimation in view of large number of Nepalese travelling to India by road for pilgrimage, etc., which is never recorded.
93. Wherever not mentioned all the statistical data are from, $HMGN_1$, Ministry of Tourism, *Annual Statistical Report*, (Various issues), Department of Tourism, Kathmandu.
94. Burger, *op. cit.*, p. 301.
95. Department of Tourism, *op. cit.*, p. 77.
96. Whereas *Nepal Tourism Master Plan* in 1972 estimated the 'leakage' from hotel business to vary from "30% for construction and not less than 50% for the operation, including food and beverages" (p. 78), the ARTEP report in 1974 estimated the leakage from the entire tourism and tourism-oriented economic sub-sectors to vary from a minimum of 26% to a maximum of 38% (ARTEP, *op. cit.*, p. VII–13).
97. Seddon, D. et al. (1981), *Peasants and Workers in Nepal*, Vikas Publishing House Pvt. Ltd., New Delhi, p.
98. Department of Tourism, *op. cit.*, p. 164.
99. Though financial capital can accrue and get circulated in both monetary and non-monetary forms (See Goldsmith, R.W. (1969), *Financial Structure and Development*, Yale University Press, New Haven and London, pp. 15–16), money is the generally accepted medium of exchange and can thus be taken as an essential but not an exclusive basis for operation of financial capital in the particular economy.
100. See CEDA (1975), *Regional Development Study (Nepal)* Part IIIb, Kathmandu.
101. See Nepal Rastra Bank (1978), *Report on Household Budget Survey*, (different series), Kathmandu.
102. Marx uses the term "money-breeding money" to describe forms of latent money-capital in pre-capitalist societies. (Marx (1977b), *op. cit.*, p. 86.)
103. According to the Agricultural Credit Review Survey, 1976/77, rural agricultural households obtain 76% of their total loan from private or non-institutional sources.

But it would be inadvertent to conclude that this 76: 24 ratio should reflect the generalized ratio of size of private and institutional financial agencies in the country. Because, for one, institutional agencies as they are centralized in urban areas would be lending more to non-agricultural sectors and, for another, not all loans advanced by private agencies in backward rural areas can be categorised as money-capital, in the strict sense of the term but would only be a form of usurer's capita.). (See, Marx (1978), *op. cit.*, p. 600, for the distinction between usurer's capital and interest-bearing capital in the capitalist sense.)

104. The financial asset/GDP ratio is quite understandably seen to be high and rising with higher stages of capitalist development, whereas the law of financial development would be modified in the socialist mode. The relevant ratios for selected countries for 1963 were as follows (in %): Pakistan – 37; India – 53; Thailand – 47; Venezuela – 66; U.S.S.R.– 44; U.S.A. – 167; Switzerland – 272 (Goldsmith, *op. cit.*, p. 209).
105. Societies at higher levels of capitalist development are known to have more varied forms of financial intermediaries like savings bank, building societies, mortgage banks, investment trusts, trustee organizations, unit trusts, etc., in addition to the traditional ones.
106. For the periodisation of society based on the type of dominant financial institutions for each epoch, see Goldsmith, *op. cit.*, p. 34.
107. Whereas all other financial institutions are under state control, the state owns 51% share in Nepal Bank Ltd., and in the case of Credit Guarantee Corporation (P) Ltd., The Central Bank owns 66% share and other two banks the remaining share.
108. The Nepal Arab Bank Limited was established in 1984 with the collaboration of Dubai Bank Ltd. which already had its activities and branches in Pakistan, Bangladesh, Sri Lanka, Hong Kong, Kuwait, UAE, UK and USA.
109. Though Marx uses the term 'credit' to mean only advance of loans under capitalist mode of production, saying "... credit as an essential, developed relations of production appears *historically* only in circulation based on capital or on wage labour" (Marx (1977a), *op. cit.*, p. 535), we use it in the common parlance of all loans under all conditions.
110. Nepal Rastra Bank, *Quarterly Economic Bulletin*, various issues.
111. For instance, the loan rates of NIDC effective from July 16, 1976 for all industries irrespective of their social significance e.g. basic industries, import-substituting industries, export-promoting industries, agro-industries, tourism 'industry' (including hotels) were the same i.e. 11% (*Ibid.*, 1982, p. 32).
112. This pattern in Nepal fully conforms with the general pattern envisaged by Mandel. (See Mandel, *op. cit.*, p. 219.)
113. See Nepal Rastra Bank, *Quarterly Economic Bulletin* (various issues), Kathmandu.
114. See *Ibid.*
115. See for example, Poudyal, S.R. (1982), *Foreign Aid in Nepal*, CEDA, Kathmandu; Integrated Development Systems (1983), *Foreign Aid and Development in Nepal*, Kathmandu; Dharmdasani, M.D. (1984), *Political Economy of Foreign Aid in the Third World: A Case Study of Nepal*, Shalimar Publishing House, Varanasi.
116. Foreign 'Aid' as percentage of GDP and total government expenditure for countries of South Asia in 1981 was as follows:

Country	*As Percentage of GDP*	*As Percentage of Total Govt. Expenditure*
Nepal	5.4	38.2
Bangladesh	8.5	45.6*
India	0.9	7.0
Pakistan	3.2	17.4**
Sri Lanka	8.9	25.7

* for 1981/82.
** for 1980.

117. For 1970 and 1976 respectively, the external public debt as % of GNP was 0.3 and 3.2 for Nepal and 14.2 and 20.9 for other 'low income countries'. (The World Bank, *World Development Report 1983*, Oxford University Press, New Delhi.)
118. For a review of the historical evolution and characteristics of the 'new style aid-giving' through multilateral agencies like IDA and regional banks under the aegis of World Bank and IMF, the foremost international mediators of metropolitan capital, and the experiences of major foreign capital dependent economies, see Payer, *op. cit.*
119. UNDP (1982), *The Resident Representative's Annual Report on Development Cooperation to Nepal 1981*, Kathmandu, p. ii.
120. See Mihaly, *op. cit.*, for a commendable review of international 'aid' politics in Nepal in the Fifties and Sixties.
121. See HMG/N, Ministry of Finance, *Economic Survey* (Various issues), Kathmandu.
122. See among others, Griffin, K. "Pearson and the Political Economy of Aid" in Byres (1972), *op. cit.* and Feder, E. (1976), "The New World Bank Programme for the Self-liquidation of the Third World Peasantry", *The Journal of Peasant Studies*, Vol. 3, No. 3, April, pp. 343–52.
123. The infamous Mc Namara thesis to 'help the poor' as presented in address to the board of Governors of World Bank in Nairobi in September 1973, was to bring about a number of 'small green revolutions' in the small-holder sector in lieu of the disastrous big Green Revolution of the 1960s. For an excellent critique of this strategy, see Feder, *op. cit.*
124. See Mihaly, *op. cit.*, pp. 46–47.
125. UNDP, *op. cit.*, p. iv.
126. An analysis of local and foreign factors in foreign 'aided' projects in Nepal revealed that of the total project cost 56% was foreign cost and 44% local cost, and of the total foreign 'aid' only 35.24% was retained in the indigenous economy (Pant, T.N. "Foreign Aid and Agricultural Development in Nepal" in Integrated Development Systems, *op. cit.*, pp. 188–89).
127. Gaige, F. (1975), *Regionalism and National Unity in Nepal*, University of California Press, Berkley and Los Angeles, p. 200.
128. See also Misra, C. and Sharma, P. "Foreign Aid and Social Structure: Notes on Intra-state Relationship" in Integrated Development Systems, *op. cit.*
129. Approximate regional allocation of 'development' projects till the 1980s were as follows: Terai – 29%; Kathmandu Valley – 34%; Mountain and Hill – 14%; Not specified – 23% (Upadhyay, J. and Shrestha, B.R. (1981), *External Assistance and Nepal's Hill Agriculture*, Paper Prepared for Seminar on Nepal's Experience in Hill Agricultural Development, Kathmandu, April 3, pp. 6–7).

130. This is also evident from the implementation of eight 'Integrated Rural Development Projects' through foreign 'aid' in the Mountain and Hill areas, which can be listed as follows: Rasuwa/Nuwakot (central Mountain and Hill) and Mahakali (western Mountain and Hill) IRDP financed by World Bank; Sagarmatha (eastern Mountain) IRDP by ADB, IFAD, EEC; Kosi Hill Area (eastern Mountain and Hill) RDP by UK; Rapti (western Hill) IRDP by USAID, Lamosangu-Jiri (eastern Mountain) IHDP by Switzerland and Karnali-Bheri (western Mountain and Hill) by Canada.

5 The Nature of Organisation of Space

- ***Introduction***
  - — Theoretical Premises
  - — Historical Antecedents
- ***Territorial Distribution and Mobility of Population***
  - — Territorial Distribution of Population
  - — Mobility of Population
- ***Settlement System and Urbanisation***
  - — Characteristics of Settlement System
  - — Pattern of Spatial Distribution of Settlements
  - — Population-Size Distribution of Settlements
  - — Hierarchic Arrangement of Settlements
  - — Characteristics and Processes of "Urbanisation"
  - — Level and Speed of Urban Process
  - — Hierarchical Structuring of Urban Places
  - — Economic Base of Urban Places
  - — Interdependence of 'Spatial Form' and 'Social Process'
- ***Nature of Spatial Integration***
  - — Evolution of Spatial Linkages
  - — Existing Patterns of Spatial Linkages
  - — Articulation of Spatial Linkages
- ***Spatial Differentiation of Composite Levels of Development***
- ***Conclusions.***

5.1 INTRODUCTION

In the preceding chapters we have analysed the nature of underdevelopment of Nepal in the vertical [sectoral] dimensions. The spatial issues were dealt with only in the context of the concerned economic sectors. In keeping with our analytical frame sketched in the beginning of the study, it would now be imperative to analyse the cumulative spatial manifestations of the sectoral processes. This is sought to be done in terms of the observations of the territorial spread and mobility of population, the formation of settlement system and the process of urbanisation, the patterning and articulation of spatial linkages, and finally, spatial differenciation of composite levels of development/underdevelooment. To begin with, additional theoretical premises of the issues are sketched out and historical antecedents reconstructed so as to understand the 'concrete' in terms of the 'general' and view the 'present' in the light of the 'past'.

5.1.1 Theoretical Premises

The basic postulates on the interrelations of social and spatial processes have been brought out in Chapter 1, which should be directly relevant for the discussions in this chapter and need not be retold. Particularly the analytical position of viewing spatial formation as the *manifestation* of and to a lesser degree a *causative factor* in the particular configuration of social formation needs to be firmly grasped, as this provides for analysing the nature of organisation of space in terms of the historical stage of social mode of production.

In addition to the previously sketched general analytical framework on the dynamics of organisation of space, it may be relevant here to briefly dwell on the specific "component[s] of the spatial structure"[1] such as settlements, transport and communication linkages etc. and the territorial spread of population, "the most important condition for the material life of society and the basis and the subject of all social production"[2], so that their inclusion in the study of organisation of space may not appear out of place.

Population is the natural precondition of the social development and the primary productive force of all mankind. Hence the laws of its motion, particularly its territorial organisation and migratory redistribution, would be indissolutely interlinked with the law of motion of society[3]. In other words, territorial spread and mobility of population would reflect the inherent spatial structure of the given social process. It would, therefore, be logical to precede an analysis of the nature of organisation of space in a particular social formation with a study of the territorial organisation and migratory redistribution of population.

Population settles in space, giving rise to "settlements". A simple definition of a settlement would thus be, "territorial grouping of population"[4], or, 'the spatial form in which the settling of people takes place'[5]. But just as the spatial spread of population is governed by the social production process, more so is their 'grouping in settlements' or the crystallization of their "outward expression" in a certain system of settlement is dependent ultimately on the mode of social production, or more exactly 'reproduction'[6]. Thus "the laws of the correspondence of the form of settlement to the mode of social production" can be seen as inherent in all social formation[7]. Viewed in the historical perspective of evolution of social forms of organisation of production in society and the emergence of forms of settlements, this relation can be adequately established. The rise of higher forms of organisation of society can be seen marked by, among other characteristics, the "successive replacement of individual fields of settlements by settlement network and finallly by settlement systems"[8]. In other words, concomitant with the rise in the social division of labour there would be rise in spatial division of labour and hence a more ordered pattern of spatial distribution of settlements, a higher differentiation by economic activities and population size-classes and a better articulation of settlement hierarchy[9]. Allowing for the operational impact of other extraneous factors like 'natural and cultural milieus', the distortions in the different aspects of territorial organisation of settlements[10] should indicate the nature of underdevelopment as manifested in the spatial dimensions.

The separation between town and country has been the "foundation of every division of labour that is well developed" and the whole economic history of the society is said to be "summed up in the movement of this antithesis"[11]. The characteristics and processes of 'urbanisation' have, therefore, constituted a major domain of the study of spatial manifestation of underdevelopment in the Third World Countries[12]. Though there is considerable difference of opinion amongst academics in defining the concept of urbanisation and the role of cities in social development[13], the more scientific approach would be to define urbanisation as "a process of the reorganisation of space through spatial redistribution of population among a hierarchical system of settlement in response to vertical shifts within the workforce"[14] and visualize the character and social role of city as varying under different historical stages of, development[15]. Thus, under condition of 'development' when urbanisation is a horizontal [territorial] response to genuine vertical (sectoral) changes in the economy, cities would act as locales of both production and consumption, would play a *generative* role in the economy and their spatial organisation would possess healthy attributes like a well-articulated hierarchical system, etc. In a condition of absolute backwardness 'marked by domination of feudalism' cities would be primarily locales of military-administrative authority parasiting on the agricultural hinter-land and their spatial organisation geared to the efficient extraction of absolute surplus value and policing needs. In a situation of 'modern underdevelopment' under the reign of merchant capital, on the other hand, 'dependent urbanism' would arise where "the urban form exists as a channel for the extraction of quantities of surplus from a rural and resource hinterland for purposes of shipment to the major metropolitan centres"[16]. Whereas in both the latter cases of 'pseudo-urbanisation' the horizontal movement of people from the rural to urban areas is not accompanied by proportionate vertical shift in the economy, in the matter of spatial organisation the 'dependent urbanism' of merchant capitalism achieves "a spatial integration above and beyond that typical of the parochialism of the feudal era"[17]. In a transitional semi-feudal, semi-capitalist situation the urbanism would also possess a hybrid character in both it's a spatial and spatial dimensions. Thus the analysis of the various attributes of urbanism would constitute an important aspect of the study of organisation of space in the given social formation.

Spatial integration is one of the most important processes of spatial organisation. The 'structural elements' in a spatial integrative process include not only nodes or the human settlement systems but also "various channels or linkages through which exchanges or interactions within the system take place"[18]. The spatial linkages like different means of transport and communication[19] occupy increasingly dominant position in the overall spatial organisation with the rise in the production and circulation of exchange value in the economy. This is so because 'the longer the turnover time of given capital, the smaller is its annual yield of surplus value' and the 'turnover time of a given capital is equal to the production time plus the circulation time'[20]. Thus as goaded by its accumulation imperative to reduce the cost and the time involved in the movement; capital would constantly strive to 'drive beyond every spatial barrier' and 'annihilate space with time':

"While capital must on one side strive to tear down every spatial barrier to intercourse, i.e. to exchange, and conquer the whole earth for its market, it strives on the other side to annihilate this space with time .... The more developed the capital ... the more does it strive simultaneously for an even greater extension of the market and for greater annihilation of space by time"[21].

Conversely, the less the rule of capital in the economy the less would be the development of 'physical conditions of exchange', as in semi-autarchic, use value based feudal, semi-feudal formations. In pre-capitalist formations marked by 'Asiatic' features, i.e. entrenchment of a strong centralised state authority, just as the settlement system is governed by the politico-administrative imperatives so would be the pattern of spatial integration. In a colonial, semi-colonial setting, however, the 'accumulation imperatives' of foreign capital, primarily in the mercantile form, would in phases[22] give rise to an essentially extroverted spatial integrative pattern geared to deeper penetration of market in the 'periphery' and swifter transhipment of commercial booty to the metropolitan 'Centre'. The analysis of the patterning and articulation of spatial linkages should, therefore, help to discern both the aspatial and spatial structure of the prevailing development/underdevelopment process.

Ultimately the spatial differentiation of composite levels of development determined by the aggregation of different indicators of development and based on a consistent theoretical frame, should sum up the aggregate spatial structure of the total social process.

5.1.2 Historical Antecedents

Identification of the historical contours of the process of spatial organisation in Nepal in the light of the above conceptual frame would provide the datum for measuring the process in the current context. Accordingly, the historical perspective can be drawn in terms of: (i) territorial spread of population; and (ii) evolution of settlement system and spatial linkages.

5.1.21 Territorial Spread of Population

The historical sequences of colonisation of the present state of Nepal has been important in determining the current form of spatial organisation. Though delving into too distant a past may not be relevant it is important to note that with the mysterious fossilization of the original Austric people in the hot-humid valleys, the central east-west hilly spine with Kathmandu Valley as the nerve centre appears to have been the established habitation zone of the primitive people. With the turn of the Christian era and rapid rise and fall of civilizations in the neighbouring Indian plains, periodic waves of 'refugees' continued to throng the tranquil secluded valleys of Nepal Hills and subsequently introduced social and spatial changes in the area. The most significant socio-spatial changes, however, were to be followed with the massive immigration of plain Hindus with superior technologies and social organisation from 12th to 14th century A.D. Not only did their labour-intensive wet-rice cultivation technology and attendant social organisation give a tremendous impetus to the hitherto sluggish population growth, but they were more prone to occupy fertile river valleys and less rugged terrains against the higher altitude occupancy of the earlier communal-tribal people, who got pushed further north or higher-up in the Hill and Mountain region. Thus arose distinct demarcation of the areas of habitation by peoples of different socio-cultural formations. Meanwhile occasional influx from Tibet continued by way of northern Mountain, who occupied only the more rugged parts along the Himalayas, and pockets of southern fringe of thickly forested and hot-humid Terai, particularly the central-western and central-eastern sections, got gradually encroached upon and settled by inhabitants of neighbouring Gangetic plains. Thus at the time of formation of a centralised state in mid-18th century broad areas of habitation had been demarcated and the principal zones of population concentration which emerged were the Kathmandu Valley, east-west spine of mid-hills and selected pockets of Terai.

The establishment of the unified state and subsequent territorial expansion along the foot-hills of the Himalayas, from Teesta in east to Sutlej in the west, acted as a big stimulant to population growth and spatial spread with greater mobility. However, with the semi-colonial integration with British India in the first quarter of the 19th century and reversion to a primarily inward-looking process of development, population spread was confined to the mid-hills and deliberate conversion of some of the previously inhabited lands to thick forests were resorted to provide natural defensive barriers to incursions from the southern plains[23]. Still, the economic imperatives of enhanced revenue needs of the state kept encouraging the colonisation of Terai through induced immigration of more heat-resistant cultivators from the Gangetic plain. Nonetheless the inherent low level of man-nature interactions and general economic slack in the midst of recurrent political upheavals is suspected to have repressed population growth between 1750 and 1850 maintained a situation of general labour scarcity[24]. Subsequent internal socio-political stabilization and massive clearance of Terai forests in the wake of extension of Indian railway networks to the Nepalese borders to the end of the 19th century provided entirely new dimensions to the increased rate of population growth and a southward tilt in spatial concentration of population. Together with this, a queer pattern of territorial spread and mobility of population was observable in the form of emigration of semi-pauperised peasants from Nepal hills to the contiguous hill areas of Sikkim, Darjeeling, Assam, etc. for permanent settlement or to the cities of India for temporary employment, and immigration of feudal lords and cultivators to Nepal Terai from adjoining plains of India[25]. Thus by the first quarter of the 20th century the broad pattern of territorial spread and mobility of population was laid, which was to continue with minor variations.

Table 5.1 provides territorial distribution and growth of population from 1911 the year when the first rudimentary census was taken. It is interesting to note that the total population declined until 1930 and then gradually rose with an increasing rate during the successive decades. Though the authenticity of the enumerations prior to 1952/54 cannot be vouched, the general trend may be indicative, if not reflective, of the real situation. Whereas the initial decline in population may be attributed both to high death rates and large-scale enrolment of mercenaries and their heavy casualties in British armies during the 1st World War[26], the rise in population from 1930s onwards could be seen as a response to the significant socio-economic changes that took place since then as narrated in previous chapters. In terms of ecological zones the relative shares were: 58.40% in Mountain and Hill, 36.44% in Inner Terai and Terai and 5.16% in Kathmandu Valley by 1911. This distribution pattern continued with minor fluctuations till the 1950s. Also there is no discernible pattern or significant spatial variation in the inter-censal rate of growth of population. This is a clear substantiation of the apprehension that accentuation of south-ward tilt in population concentration is a phenomenon of recent origin.

5.1.22 Settlement System and Spatial Linkages

Settlement as territorial groupings of population and formation of settlement system as the reorganisation of space through redistribution of population among a hierarchical system of settlement, can be historically appraised in the spatio-temporal frame in line with the historical sequences of evolution of the production process and population spread as delineated earlier.

In view of near absence of the vertical differentiation of the social process based on subsistence primary production, the earliest spatial organisation of population grouped in primitive rural habitats is to be differentiated along technical considerations of pattern of grouping of shelters dictated by natural i.e., physiographic climatic factors. The universally communal nature of primitive societies, however, gave birth to small clustered groupings of shelters as against a dispersed pattern to be seen later with the advent of parcellized, private ownership of means of production, particularly land. The initial differentiation in the rural habitat types in Nepalese history were perhaps in the form of greater spatial dispersions of *Khasa* people of western hill against a more compact grouping of *Kiratas* in the east as determined by faster class differentiation or evolution of private property in the former society than in the latter. The first rural-urban divide was, however, to be witnessed in Kathmandu Valley, where, greater degree of social division of labour facilitated by higher natural productivity of

Table 5.1 Territorial Distribution and Growth of Population (1911–1952/54).

Territorial Zones	*1911*			*1920*			*1930*			*1942*			*1952/54*		
	Population	*%*	*Average annual growth rate (%)*	*Population*	*%*	*Average annual growth rate (%)*	*Population*	*%*	*Average annual growth rate (%)*	*Population*	*%*	*Average annual growth rate (%)*	*Population*	*%*	*Average annual growth rate (%)*
Mountain + Hill	3292911	58.40	–	3144843	56.42	–0.51	3139845	56.75	–0.02	3819931	60.79	1.65	4979713	60.31	2.4
Kathmandu Valley	290879	5.16	–	306909	5.51	0.60	262233	4.74	–1.56	325139	5.17	1.81	410995	4.98	2.1
Inner Terai + Terai	2054959	36.44	–	2122036	38.07	0.36	2130487	38.51	0.04	2138579	34.03	0.03	2865917	34.71	2.7
NEPAL	5638749	100.00	–	5573788	100.00	–0.13	5532574	100.00	–0.07	6283649	100.00	1.08	8256625	100.00	2.5

Source: United Nations (1980), *Population of Nepal*, ESCAP, Bangkok.

soil plus favourable location as an entrepot trade centre, gave rise to Greek-like city states quite early in the history[27]. In the greater parts of the populated hill-sides, on the other hand, noticeable variations in the *form* of spatial organisation were introduced with the advent of Hindu immigrants from Indian plains during 12th and 14th century A.D., whose 'dispersed' pattern of settlements along less rugged terrains and river valleys conducive for wet-rice cultivation were in sharp contrast to the more 'concentrated' settlements of indigenous dwellers on higher Hills and Mountains. Nonetheless the essentially disarticulated rural spatial organisation with no hierarchical differentiation, prevailed throughout. At the time of state unification in mid-18th century the only settlement nodes with a semblance of 'urban' character were the three towns of Kathmandu Valley, viz. Lalitpur, Kathmandu and Bhaktapur[28]. These towns had acquired the character of European 'feudal agglomerations' combining politico-administrative functions and craft production and trade with substantial agricultural production. Naturally a 'system' of settlements did not develop and there was little economic interactions between these prosperous urban nodes with the indigent hinterlands except for the tribute extraction activities of the state centred on these nodes. Amidst the highly fragmented space economy, north-south trade routes passing through more prosperous principalities like Palpa, in Makwanpur and Vijayangar and aligned along river valleys upto the Himalayan passes, had developed resembling an axial pattern of spatial organisation.

After the formation the centralised state with Kathmandu as its capital, not only was there a gradual rise in the primacy of the Valley but a loosely articulated system of administrative centres, later attracting trading functions, was established throughout the country. However, the overall backward economic structure with little inter-regional complimentarity compounded by physical extremity and inaccessibility, could not have permitted interactive social and spatial linkages to develop. Also with the closing of approach routes from the south to the hills and evacuation of quasi-military and other settlements[29] in those areas to convert them into forest barriers after the military defeat at the hand of the Britishers, a temporary phase of inward-looking and autarchic spatial organisation was introduced in the first half of the 19th century.

The whole pattern of organisation of space underwent a fundamental change after the extension of Indian railway networks to the Nepalese border. A number of trading centres emerged just across the rail-heads and road-terminii all along the Terai border from Jhapa/Morang, to Nepalgunj[30], to organize shipments of forest and agricultural products to India and forward imported manufactured goods to Nepal. Rudimentary roads connecting those centres were also extended across the Terai to the foot-hills. Subsequently centres of population concentration and trading functions flourished along the piedment areas and zones of contact between different ecological zones particularly in the foothills in Inner Terai[31].

Further spatial reorganisation was carried out in the aftermath of increased semi-colonial integration of the country with British India after the Treaty of 1923. This was initiated by the construction of the modern roads, railways and rope-ways, all designed to connect the internal economic hub of Kathmandu with India[32].

With the advent of the 2nd world war and addition of rudimentary industrial functions to the already existing trading outposts along the southern border, further distortions in spatial stucture with increased outward-orientation were effectuated.

On the other hand, the natural outcome of increased economic integration of the country with British Indian colonial economy was the deindustrialisation of the country and decline of indigenous craft-production centres in the hills and Kathmandu Valley[33]. At the macro-level the integration of the economy as a primary product exporting and manufacture importing appendage to the metropolitan capital resulted in a failure to bring about vertical transfer of workforce to the non-primary sector, continued emigration of pauperised peasants and artisans to Indian cities and a general failure at 'urbanisation'. Consequently, notwithstanding the mushroom growth of trading centres along the southern border, in the absence of productive activities they continued to get stunted and remained mere overgrown villages. By the 1950 the three traditionsl towns of Kathmandu Valley were the principal urban nodes in the country. Moreover five out of the ten urban places and 82.58% of total urban population were concentrated in the Valley (see Table 5.2). The sluggishness in urban growth can be understood from the fact that the decadal growth ratio of the three largest urban nodes during 1942–1952/54 was only 1.38 as against the overall population growth ratio of 1.31 for the same period.

Table 5.2 Population Growth of 'Urban' Areas,* 1942–1952/54.

'Urban' areas	*1942*	*1952/54*	*Percentile increase*
1. Kathmandu	68,594	106.570 (44.77)	55.36
2. Lalitpur	34,685	42.183 (17.72)	21.62
3. Bhaktapur	27,864	32.118 (13.49)	15.27
4. Nepalgunj	N.A.	10.813 (4.54)	–
5. Birgunj	N.A.	10.037 (4.22)	–
6. Thimi	N.A.	8.657 (3.64)	–
7. Biratnagar	N.A.	8.060 z(3.39)	–
8. Kirtipur	N.A.	7.038 (2.96)	–
9. Janakpur	N.A.	7.037 (2.96)	–
10. Malangawa	N.A.	5.551 2.33	–
TOTAL	N.A.	238.064 (100.00)	–

Note: * Settlement with more than 5000 population.
Figures in parenthesis are column percentages.

As per the overall condition of spatial organisation in the country, in the beginning of the 1950s, it could be summarised as one of 'pre industrial isolation' slowly getting encroached upon by colonial integrative mechanisms. This is amply borne out by a very low development of modern transportation and communication networks and their inevitable outward-orientation as in the colonial set-up. Moreover, whereas the spatial structure of the large part of the country was marked by extreme fragmentation and disarticulation, parts of the Terai were getting separately integrated into the larger system of India and a dendritic pattern of social and spatial integration from the Indian rail-heads to the far-flung hamlets in the countryside were taking shape along the traditional north-south trade and transportation arteries.

The historical evolution of the spatial structure of the county can be schematically presented as in Fig. 5.1. which bears a striking resemblance to that of Peru[34] through different historical stages.

5.2 TERRITORIAL DISTRIBUTION AND MOBILITY OF POPULATION

As outlined earlier territorial organisation and migratory redistribution of population would reflect the inherent spatial structure of the given social process. Hence it would be useful to analyse the territorial distribution of population in Nepal before we attempt to investigate the tangible physical form of spatial organisation. However, it may be clarified at the outset that the limited contextual purpose makes this study only an exercise in a definite aspect of 'population geography' but not that in 'demography' as such, so that only those aspects of population dynamics as are directly relevant in articulating the ultimate spatial structure may be dealt with.

5.2.1 Territorial Distribution of Population

5.2.11 The historical overview of the extent and trends of territorial spread of population have broadly identified the zones of habitation in Nepal. The scenario since the 1950s when integration with the metropolitant economy increase should permit us to view the territorial population dynamics as a concrete manifestation of socio-spatial process of underdevelopment.

Percentage share in total population and crude density of population by geographical area for each territorial zone during the successive censuses since 1952/54 are presented in Table 5.3. The skewed pattern of population distribution is not only self-evident from the disproportionately higher share of population compared to the geographical area Kathmandu Valley and Terai than in the rest of the areas, but the pattern is seen getting further skewed with the passage of time, except for the improvement in land-man ratio in Inner Terai. The same pattern is more clearly reflected in the spatio-temporal variations in crude population density. The extent of spatial unevenness in population

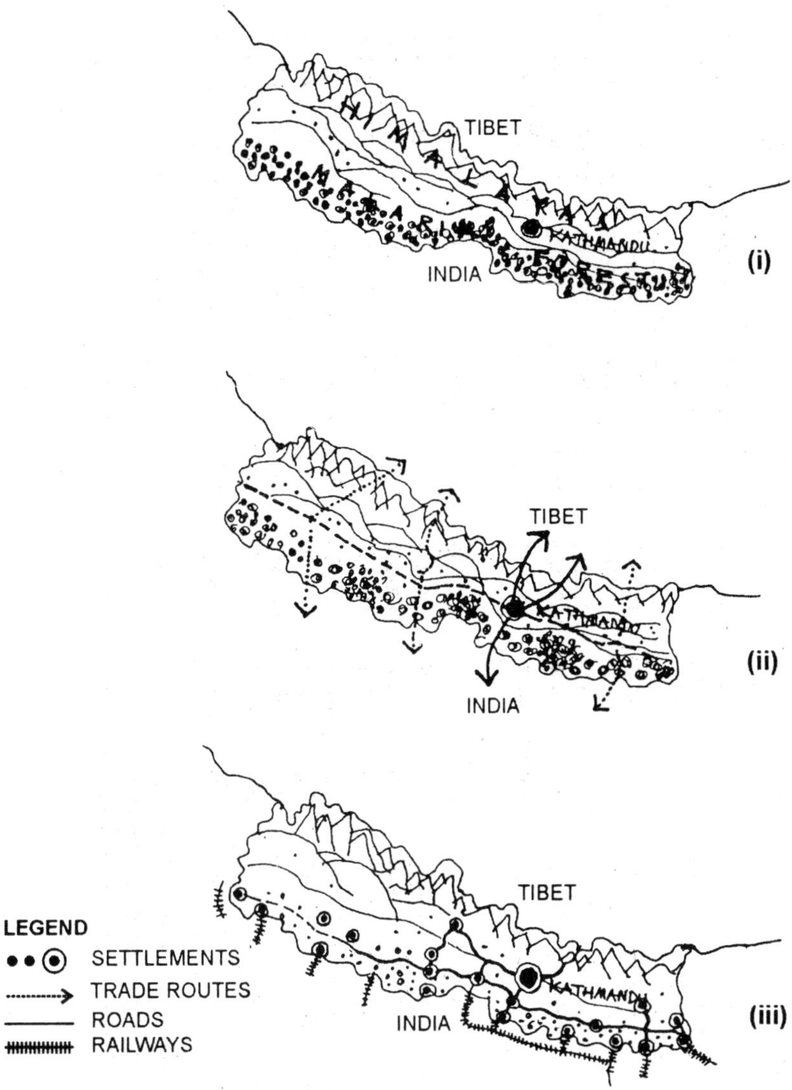

Fig. 5.1 Evolution of Spatial Organization.

distribution in Nepal can, therefore, be characterised as one of the most notable in the world[34a]. This extreme skewness in the spatial distribution of population would not only have its natural implications for overall spatial organisation, but, when looked at in a dynamic frame, provide important insights into the dynamics of the social process in operation. For, as against the nature deterministic explanations of the "logical-empiricists", the density differentials over different territorial zones can be seen as a combined result of both historical and natural factors. For example, the lowest density in western Terai, even behind Hill and

Table 5.3 Population Distribution and Density by Territorial Zones, 1952/54 to 1981.

Territorial Zones	*1952/54*			*1961*			*1971*			*1981***		
	Population	*%*	*Density (per sq. mile)*	*Population*	*%*	*Density (per sq. mile)*	*Population*	*%*	*Density (per sq. mile)*	*Population*	*%*	*Density (per sq. mile)*
MOUNTAIN HILL	4979713	60.3	127.2	5531307	58.7	141.3	6167309	53.4	157.5	7104577	47.30	181.5
Eastern	1708816	20.7	171.7	1886722	20.0	189.6	2036240	17.6	204.6	2283687	15.20	229.5
Central	1754123	21.2	134.9	1946502	20.7	149.7	2296941	19.9	176.7	2652298	17.66	204.0
Western	1516774	18.4	93.6	1698083	18.0	104.8	1834128	15.9	113.2	2168592	14.44	133.9
KATHMANDU VALLEY	410995	5.0	1393.2	459990	4.9	1559.3	618911	5.4	2098.0	766820	5.11	2599.4
INNER TERAI	476500	5.8	88.6	536509	5.7	99.7	848535	7.3	157.7	1113108	7.41	206.9
Eastern	189228	2.3	96.9	193666	2.1	99.2	260031	2.2	133.2	347545	2.31	178.0
Central	197957	2.4	77.1	244236	2.6	95.1	420684	3.6	163.8	499316	3.32	194.4
*Western	89315	1.1	103.7	98607	1.0	114.5	167820	1.5	194.9	266247	1.77	309.2
TERAI	2389417	28.9	237.9	2885190	30.7	287.3	3921228	33.9	390.5	6035946	40.18	601.1
Eastern	1806049	21.9	318.9	2213282	23.5	390.8	2974150	25.7	525.1	4246446	28.27	749.7
Central	348179	4.2	267.8	400357	4.3	308.0	521836	4.5	401.4	959197	6.39	737.8
Western	235189	2.8	76.4	271551	2.9	88.2	425242	3.7	138.2	830303	5.53	269.8
NEPAL	8256625	100.0	150.5	9412996	100.0	171.6	11555983	100.0	210.6	15020451	100.0	273.8

Note: *Excluding Surkhet district; **Based on provisional census figures.

Source: 1. United Nations (1980), *Population of Nepal,* ESCAP, Bangkok.
2. Central Bureau of Statistics, *Statistical Pocket Book Nepal 1982*, Kathmandu.

Mountain sub-zones of the same hydrographic zone, uptill 1961, is reflection on its late colonisation due to historical exigencies rather than on its inferior natural attributes. Similarly, only a politico-economic approach can explain the case of population distribution in Inner Terai, which was one of the most ancient seats of human occupation[35] but was 'historically' allowed to stagnate into inhospitable malaria-infested zone till it was 'historically' reopened for cultivation with active collaboration of metropolitan capital in the 1950s.[36]

In view of the extreme physiographic diversities, which is a major determinant in a society based on subsistence cultivation a better insight into the essential characteristics of spatial distribution of population may be obtained from the study of spatio-temporal variation in 'physiological' densities rather than mere 'crude' densities[37]. In the absence of regional break-up of land areas by their useability under different levels of technology, densities per 'cultivated' area by different territorial zones for 1971 are calculated and presented in Table 5.4. Also presented are crude density figures for 1971 and 1981 at a more disaggregated level. It is interesting to note that the territorial distribution pattern of 'crude'

Table 5.4 Population Density Per Geographical and Cultivated Area by Territorial Zones (1971–1981).

(Population/Sq. Km)

Territorial Zones	*Density per geographical area*			*Density per cultivated area*
	1971	*1981*	*% Change*	*1971*
MOUNTAIN	19.47	22.11	13.56	1103.24
Eastern	36.25	40.42	11.51	1433.58
Central	7.32	6.82	–6.84	850.77
Western	15.49	18.25	17.82	927.17
HILL	92.69	106.25	14.63	1243.07
Eastern	112.00	125.81	12.33	1152.42
Central	97.67	114.26	16.99	1300.95
Western	71.35	80.93	13.43	1269.35
KATHMANDU VALLEY	564.19	699.02	23.90	1294.8
INNER TERAI	57.07	82.92	45.30	476.30
Eastern	55.43	74.09	33.66	604.72
Central	73.17	105.16	43.72	482.51
Western	45.59	72.19	58.35	390.76
TERAI	153.91	232.56	51.10	344.86
Eastern:	208.48	297.66	42.78	357.60
Far-Eastern	164.02	288.17	75.69	310.32
Mid-Eastern	248.00	334.91	35.04	360.56
Eastern	126.29	251.37	70.54	415.86
Central	163.00	262.72	61.18	302.09
Western	52.91	103.31	95.26	328.12
NEPAL	79.32	103.10	29.98	612.04

Note: Cultivated area for 1981 not available.

Source: 1. Central Bureau of Statistics, *Statistical Pocket Book 1982*, Kathmandu.
2. APROSC Data Bank, Kathmandu.

and 'physiological' densities for major physical ecological zones are almost in reverse order. It shows that whereas there is greater localisation and higher population pressure[38] per unit of actually habitated land in Mountain and Hill, there is a relatively even spread and less pressure in Inner Terai and Terai. The social and spatial implications of these differences are significant. However, the inferences drawn for and abstract society, i.e. assuming a uniform social organisation of production, would be misleading, because a higher man/cultivated-land ratio with a 'peasant proprietorship' (as in Hill and Mountain) would give a 'dispersed' form of spatial organisation whereas a lower ratio with greater concentration of landholdings (as in Terai) would give a 'concentrated' form. It is also interesting to note that the inter-regional variability of 'physiological' density is significantly lower (C.V.1971=54.62%) than the 'crude' density (C.V.1971=109.28%), thus indicating a lower variation in the actual spatial form of population distribution.

5.2.12 Further insights into spatial distribution of population in a temporal frame may be obtained from inter-censal growth ratios and average annual growth rates (Table 5.5). Against the consistently rising average annual growth rate of population in the successive census periods at the macro-national level,[39] the growth rates at the micro-regional level, except for the Terai, appear quite erratic. Such erratic fluctuations in population growth are definite manifestations of inherent structural contradictions in the social process which should have corresponding spatial repercussions. However, a consistent trend to be observed is a rising growth rate from north to south, i.e. from Mountain to Terai, quite in keeping with the pattern of socio-economic development as observed in the previous chapters. This may have some significance for theoretical generalisations and counters the fatalistic arguments of the neo-Malthusians and concurs with the position of radical academics, that there generally exists "a positive correlation between population growth and production growth"[40]. But the generalisations based on narrow empirical observations may not be stretched too far and may be understood only within the framework of prevailing social mode of production as emphasized by Marx that "... every special historic mode of production has its own special laws of population, historically valid within its limits alone"[41] Viewed at the micro-regional levels, whereas there is remarkable stability and near uniformity in the growth rates in Mountain-Hill, spurts of extreme rates both in temporal and spatial dimensions are discernible in the case of Terai and Inner Terai, reflecting the historical specificities that were possibly behind such fluctuations in growth rates. For example, the extremely high average annual growth rates of 11.90% in eastern Terai during 1952/54–61, 6.91% in western Terai during 1971–81 and 5.58% and 5.45% respectively in central and western Inner Terai during 1961–71, coincide with the immediate aftermath of malaria-eradication programme and large-scale opening up of virgin lands, for cultivation in those regions. At the absolute level of population increase during 1952/54–1981, more than a three-fold increase in western Terai and Inner Terai followed by more than 2½ times increase in the rest of the Terai and central Inner Terai, help differentiate areas of high

Table 5.5 Inter-censal Growth of Population by Territorial Zones (1952/54 to 1981).

Territorial Zones	*1952/54–1961**		*1960–1971*		*1971–1981*		*1952/54–1981**	
	Growth ratio	*Average annual growth rate (%)*	*Growth ratio*	*Average annual growth rate (%)*	*Growth ratio*	*Average annual growth rate (%)*	*Growth ratio*	*Average annual growth rate (%)*
MOUNTAIN + HILL	1.11	1.32	1.11	1.06	1.15	1.40	1.43	1.28
Eastern	1.10	1.11	1.08	0.76	1.12	1.15	1.34	1.00
Central	1.11	1.50	1.18	1.67	1.15	1.45	1.51	1.54
Western	1.12	1.63	1.08	0.77	1.18	1.69	1.43	1.33
KATHMANDU VALLEY	1.12	1.45	1.35	3.05	1.24	2.18	1.87	2.25
INNER TERAI	1.13	1.55	1.58	4.70	1.31	2.75	2.34	3.08
Eastern	1.02	0.26	1.34	2.99	1.34	2.94	1.84	2.12
Central	1.23	3.05	1.72	5.58	1.19	1.73	2.52	3.49
*Western	1.10	1.42	1.70	5.45	1.59	4.72	2.98	4.13
TERAI	1.21	2.42	1.36	3.13	1.54	4.41	2.53	3.36
Eastern	1.23	2.28	1.34	3.00	1.43	3.63	2.53	2.99
Central	1.15	2.01	1.30	2.69	1.84	6.28	2.75	3.82
Western	1.15	2.07	1.57	4.59	1.95	6.91	3.53	4.78
NEPAL	1.14	1.65	1.23	2.10	1.30	2.70	1.82	2.16

Note: *Growth rates are calculated for 9 years (1952–1961) and 29 years (1952–81) for the Eastern Sectors, 7 years (1954–1961) and 27 years (1954–1981) for the Central and Western Sectors and 8 years (1953–61) and 28 years (1953–81) for Zonal average and Nepal.

The growth rate is calculated by using the formula $\left[\sqrt[t]{\frac{P_i}{P_o}} - 1\right] \times 100$ where P_o = Population at the beginning of the period; P_i = Population at the end of the period; t = No. of years.

Source: Derived from Table 5.3.

population concentration and rapid spatial reorganisation from the lagging ones in Mountain and Hill.

Looking at the picture of growth of population during 1971–81 at further disaggregated level of districts (see Appendix 8, E-1) it is evident that areas of highest growth are concentrated along far-eastern and Western Terai, with rest of the Terai and Inner Terai with high to moderate growth, Kathmandu Valley, Hill and most of Mountain with low growth and parts of Mountain with absolute decline in population. The spatial configuration at a glance reveals that the dynamics of population growth is more conditioned by the possibility of horizontal spread of population to "colonisation frontiers"[42] than by vertical shifts within the work force.

The essentially retrograde nature of population growth and spatial redistribution is also borne out from Appendix-9 which gives the correlation matrix of selected development indicators. The fact that distribution of population growth (E_1) has highest positive and significant correlation with distribution of percentage of households owning more than 5 acres of cultivated land (A-8), (or, an indicator of greater availability of land, or of greater concentration in landholdings, or of both) suggests the essentially pre-capitalist nature of population growth[43]. On the other hand, positive correlations also with industrial labour productivity (I-10) and cash crop production (A-6), provide indication of emerging capitalistic stimulants for population growth. However, the lack of significant positive correlations with many of the indicators of development rules out this possibility to any significant scale.

Pending further investigation into the growth and spatial redistribution pattern of population as articulated through the scale and direction of its mobility, it can be tentatively generalised that the nature of population growth and distribution in the country is essentially 'conservative'. The spatial implications of such a process would also he obviously not as spectacular as that of the vertical shifts in work force would have been.

5.2.2 Mobility of Population

5.2.20 As our immediate concern here is to document spatial rearrangement of population through inter-regional mobility, we would be dealing only with the permanent shift or 'migration' of population[44]. Also population mobility would be seen essentially as a response to the social and spatial uneven development specific to the given stage of social mode of production and as a mechanism of spatial integration and interaction.

Historically, population mobility within and without the state boundary in Nepal has been traced to the dual imperatives of internal socio-economic crisis and external stimulation particularly after the semi-colonial integration of the country with British India. Continuation of the same internal and external situation rather in an aggravated form and further articulation of social and spatial uneven development particularly after the 1950s, should provide the initial setting for probing into the phenomenon at the present.

5.2.21 In the absence of empirical information on population mobility by different typologies of migrants, we have found it prudent to consider all population absent for more than six months at the time of enumeration as a proxy measure for 'permanent migration', howsoever elusive the mere six months gap may prove in ascertaining the real picture. Moreover, the absence of even this minimum information in the 1971 census, has constrained us to analyse the migratory movements by different territorial zones only for 1952/54 and 1961 (Table 5.6). It is evident that people in motion for long duration constitute as much as 2.56% of total population in 1952/54 and the proportion is seen to have increased to 3.95% in 1961.[45] The more significant aspect of the phenomenon with greater social and spatial implications is that an overwhelming proportion of migrants originate from economically more laggard Mountain and Hill (94.39% of total migrants in 1952/54 and 89.15% in 1961) and head mostly for regions outside the country (91.36% in 1952/54 and 84.9% in 1961), that too mostly to India (72.55% in 1952/54 and 78.11% in 1961). The only redeeming feature in this otherwise avowedly 'primitive' type of population mobility triggered by the 'push' mechanism of law man-nature interactions and retrograde social relation of production rather than by the social momentum of higher modes of production 46 is the increasing destination of migrants to areas within the country (i.e. from 8.64% of total migrants in 1952/54 to 15.09% in 1961)[47]. However, the already confirmed nature of internal population shift to "colonisation frontiers" of forested areas of Terai and Inner Terai, makes this pattern of mobility no less retrograde and 'conservative'.

The predominantly extra-state orientation of population mobility may to some extent be checked by considering the crossflow of population across the international border. Territorial distribution of volume of 'emigration' and 'immigration' and their ratios are presented in Table 5.7. It is quite understandable, keeping in view the historical pattern of population movement across the international border, that emigration from the country should be almost three times the immigration into it, and in the sub-territorial dimensions only Terai should be the net 'importer' and all the net 'exporter', the central Hill exporting a staggering 131 times more population than importing from outside the country. The apparent analogy of 'unequal exchange' in the net 'export' of population from the economically more retarded Hill and Mountain and 'import' by the more vibrant Terai to and from the more developed outside economy, and its inevitable retrograde implications for aggravating spatial uneven development, should need no elaboration.

5.2.22 A more serious concern from the view point of internal articulation of social and spatial structure should be of the inter-regional mobility of population *within* the country. Also, a better inventory of internal population shift in the horizontal plane may be obtained from place-of-birth data by relevant territorial zones. Table 5.8 provides net inter-regional mobility of population by the same method for 1952/54,1961 and 1971. At the aggregate level, the absolute volume

Talble 5.6 Migration of Population* within and Outside the Country by Territorial Zones (1952/54 and 1961).

Territorial Zones	*1952/54*				*1961*			
	Total migrants	*Migrants as % of total population*	*% of Total migrants*		*Total migrant*	*Migrants as % of total population*	*% of Total migrants*	
			Within country	*Outside country*			*Within country*	*Outside country*
MOUNTAIN + HILL	204696 (94.39)	3.98	7.42	92.58	344852 (89.15)	5.87	11.52	88.48
Eastern	58941 (27.18)	3.33	15.93	84.07	99552 (25.74)	5.03	19.11	80.89
Central	100752 (46.46)	2.48	4.72	95.28	166868 (43.14)	7.90	9.81	90.19
Western	45003 (20.75)	6.46	2.30	97.70	78432 (20.28)	4.41	5.44	94.56
KATHMANDU VALLEY	4766 (2.20)	1.15	38.92	61.08	14520 (3.75)	3.06	51.18	48.82
INNER TERAI	4651 (2.14)	0.97	16.88	83.12	10174 (2.63)	1.86	34.29	65.71
Eastern	2342 (1.08)	1.22	17.68	82.32	5172 (1.34)	2.60	35.40	64.60
Central	1796 (0.83)	0.74	4.12	95.88	4234 (1.09)	1.66	33.28	66.72
Western	513 (0.24)	0.57	57.89	42.11	768 (0.20)	0.77	32.42	67.58
TERAI	2740 (1.26)	0.11	33.21	66.79	17249 (4.46)	0.59	44.76	55.24

(Contd.)

(*Table 5.6 contd.*)

Eastern	2384 (1.10)	0.13	35.23	64.77	13533 (3.50)	0.61	47.13	52.87
Central	202 (0.09)	0.06	19.31	80.69	2766 (0.72)	0.69	31.34	68.66
Western	154 (0.07)	0.07	20.13	79.87	950 (0.25)	0.34	50.00	50.00
NEPAL	216853 (100.00)	2.56	8.64	91.36	386834 (100.00)	3.95	15.09	84.91

Note: * Those who are absent for more than six months. Figures in parenthesis are column percentage.
Source: Central Bureau of Statistics, *Population Census of Nepal,* 1952/54 and 1961, Kathmandu.

Table 5.7 Pattern of Emigration and Immigration by Territorial Zones (1961).

Territorial Zones	*Emigration*		*Immigration*			
	No. of Persons (1)	*% (2)*	*No. of Persons (3)*	*% (4)*	*Net Balance (5)*	*Ratio of 1 to 3*
MOUNTAIN + HILL	305.267	92.94	9.190	8.35	–296.077	33.22
Eastern	80.591	24.54	7.781	7.07	–72.810	10.36
Central	100.502	30.60	769	0.70	–99.733	130.59
Western	74.164	22.58	640	0.58	–73.524	115.88
KATHMANDU VALLEY	7.089	2.16	1.890	1.72	–5.199	3.75
INNER TERAI	6.626	2.02	349	0.32	–6.277	18.99
Eastern	3.341	1.02	36	0.03	–3.305	92.81
Central	2.766	0.84	200	0.18	–2.566	13.83
Western	519	0.16	113	0.10	–406	4.59
TERAI	9.498	2.89	98.632	89.62	89.134	0.10
Eastern	7.155	2.18	57.275	52.04	+50.120	0.12
Central	1.899	0.58	37.134	33.74	+35.235	0.05
Western	444	0.14	4.223	3.84	+3.779	0.11
NEPAL	328.470	100.00	110.061	100.00	–218.409	2.98

Source: Derived from Kansakar V.B.S. (1974), *Population Chance in Nepal: A study of Mobility During 1911–61* (Unpublished Ph.D. Dissertation), Department of Geography, Patna University, Table 6.17.

Table 5.8 Net Inter-Regional Migration* in Nepal (1952/54 to 1971).

Territorial Zones	*1952/54*			*1961*			*1971*		
	In-Migration	*Out-Migration*	*Net Migration*	*In-Migration*	*Out-Migration*	*Net Migration*	*In-Migration*	*Out-Migration*	*Net Migration*
MOUNTAIN + HILL	602	11371	–10769	15841	121828	– 105997	52513	393235	– 340922
Eastern	244	7233	– 6989	5364	74846	– 69492	17498	186843	– 169345
Central	358	4138	– 3780	5694	38326	– 32632	29952	140642	– 110890
Western				4783	8656	– 3873	5063	65750	– 60687
KATHMANDU VALLEY	7678	1460	+6218	24748	20131	+ 4617	26440	45484	– 19044
INNER TERAI	688	579	+ 109	36351	29424	+ 6857	9733	49692	– 39959
Eastern	201	407	– 206	5345	10552	– 5207	6385	37916	– 31531
Central	487	172	+ 315	27560	2118	+ 25372	1223	2095	– 872
Western				3446	16754	–13308	2125	9681	– 7556
TERAI	4762	320	+ 4442	101507	6984	+ 94523	418435	18510	+ 399925
Eastern	3497	294	+3203	72030	3848	+ 68182	185799	10267	+ 175532
Central	1265	26	+ 1239	8307	2591	+ 5716	161751	6504	+ 155247
Western				21170	545	+ 20625	70885	1739	+ 69146
NEPAL	13730	13730	± 0	178437	178437	± 0	506921	506921	± 0

Note: *Based on place of birth date by districts.
Source: Central Bureau of Statistics, *Population Census, Nepal,* 1952/54, Part-I, Vol. 3, p. 259; 1961, Vol. II, pp. 30–31 and 1971, Tables 8 and 10.

of total internally mobile population appears quite low, reflecting the low level of socio-spatial differentiation in the country. However, significant growth in the percentage of such population from a negligible 0.17% of the total in 1952/54 to 1.90% in 1961 and 4.39% in 1971 is a testimony to the increasing socio-spatial differentiation as brought out in the earlier chapters. In the territorial frame, it is established beyond doubt that whereas Mountain and Hill have been the constant net 'losers' and Terai constant net 'gainer' of population, Kathmandu Valley and Inner Terai have changed from a position of net gainer till 1961 to that of net loser by 1971. Also, in the spatio-temporal frame, the in-migration/out-migration ratio in Terai is seen to have increased from 14.88 in 1952/54 to 22.61 as against very low but slightly rising ratios in Mountain and Hill. Whereas the erratic fluctuations in in-migration/out-migration ratios in Inner Terai is quite understandable in view of the unstable social nature of this literally transitional zone of late colonisation, the drastic decline in the ratio in the predominantly 'urban' Kathmandu Valley should provide serious food for thought in the nature of distorted development in this 'centre' of the 'periphery'. The whole scenario when backed by the politico-economic processes in operation in different territorial zones, conclusively establishes an increasingly uneven structuration of space tilted towards the south.

Articulation of spatial structure of the country may be better understood through the observation of inter-regional population transfer in a dynamic frame. With the same object in mind, Tables 5.9 and 5.10 have been constructed to provide matrices of inter-regional mobility of population in 1961 and 71 and the same depicted in Fig. 5.2. A cursory glance at the Tables and Fig. suffices to differentiate not only areas of different degrees of mobility but also principal loci of population movement that would ultimately reflect the changing pattern of spatial oraganisation in the country. Though the two matrices are not strictly comparable at the disaggregated levels of territorial zones, because of different enumeration units adopted in the successive censuses, combining together contiguous sub-zones of Hill and Mountain on one side and Terai and Inner Terai on the other, broad inter-regional crossflows of population can be constructed and compared. It is expected that the dominant currents of population flows are invariably oriented from Mountain Hill to Inner Terai-Terai, that too within the same hydrographic zone, and there is negligible horizontal movement within the same physical-ecological zone. The only exception of a more balanced in-migration/out-migration flows and interactions with diverse regions, is to be seen in the case of Kathmandu Valley, the traditional politico-administrative and financial-mercantile capital. Not only is there a 'vertical' transfer of population from the rural hinterland to this traditional seat of 'urban' functions (which we shall probe in the next section), but in- and out-migration occurs here by way of frequent transfer of politico-administrative personnel and out-migration of traditional Newar mercantalists of the Valley to all corners of the country. Nevertheless, this somewhat positively integrative population mobility seen with respect to the Kathmandu Valley is too small in absolute scale to affect the overall

Table 5.9 Matrix of Inter-regional Migration of Population* (1961).

IN-MIGRATION TO / OUT-MIGRATION FROM		Eastern Hill	Central Hill	Western Hill	Kathmandu Valley	Eastern Inner Terai	Central Inner Terai	Western Inner Terai	Eastern Terai	Central Terai	Western Terai	Total Out-Migration
(1)		(2)	(3)	(4)	(5)	(6)	(7)	(8)	(9)	(10)	(11)	(12)
1. Eastern Hill			909	293	14339	4314	2914	32	51347	303	368	74846
	(i)	[21296]	(1.21)	(0.39)	(19.16)	(5.77)	(3.89)	(0.04)	(68.63)	(0.40)	(0.49)	(100.00)
	(ii)		(15.96)	(6.13)	(57.94)	(80.71)	(10.58)	(0.93)	(71.29)	(3.65)	(1.74)	(41.94)
2. Central Hill		443		2878	7802	67	18139	246	2096	5955	700	38326
	(i)	(1.16)	[39963]	(7.51)	(20.36)	(0.17)	(47.33)	(0.64)	(5.47)	(15.54)	(1.83)	(100.00)
	(ii)	(8.27)		(60.17)	(31.53)	(1.26)	(65.88)	(7.14)	(2.91)	(71.69)	(3.31)	(21.48)
3. Western Hill		40	1843		438	9	130	2918	166	245	2867	8656
	(i)	(0.46)	(21.29)	[13658]	(5.06)	(0.10)	(1.50)	(33.71)	(1.92)	(2.83)	(33.12)	(100.00)
	(ii)	(0.75)	(32.37)		(1.77)	(0.17)	(0.47)	(84.68)	(0.23)	(2.95)	(13.54)	(4.85)
4. Kathmandu Valley		3717	2060	519		116	4529	105	6873	1124	1088	20131
	(i)	(18.46)	(10.23)	(2.58)	[19980]	(0.58)	(22.50)	(0.52)	(34.14)	(5.58)	(5.40)	(100.00)
	(ii)	(69.42)	(36.18)	(10.85)		(2.17)	(16.45)	(3.05)	(9.54)	(13.53)	(5.14)	(11.28)
5. Eastern Inner Terai		381	20	16	36		11	12	10072	3	1	10552
	(i)	(3.61)	(0.19)	(0.15)	(0.34)	[176]	(0.10)	(0.11)	(95.45)	(0.03)	(0.01)	(100.00)
	(ii)	(7.12)	(0.35)	(0.33)	(0.15)		(0.04)	(0.35)	(13.98)	(0.04)	(—)	(5.91)
6. Central Inner Terai		126	333	8	729	8		3	944	16	21	2188
	(i)	(5.76)	(15.22)	(0.37)	(33.52)	(0.37)	[482]	(0.14)	(43.14)	(0.73)	(0.96)	(100.00)
	(ii)	(2.25)	(5.85)	(0.17)	(2.95)	(0.15)	–	(0.09)	(1.51)	(0.19)	(0.10)	(1.23)
7. Western Inner Terai		25	117	879	59	–	18		1.26	1.66	15364	16754
	(i)	(0.15)	(0.70)	(5.25)	(0.35)		(0.11)	[7.88]	(0.75)	(0.99)	(91.70)	(100.00)
	(ii)	(0.47)	(2.05)	(18.38)	(0.34)		(0.07)		(0.17)	(2.00)	(72.57)	(9.39)

(Contd.)

(*Table 5.9 contd.*)

IN-MIGRATION TO / OUT-MIGRATION FROM		Eastern Hill	Central Hill	Western Hill	Kathmandu Valley	Eastern Inner Terai	Central Inner Terai	Western Inner Terai	Eastern Terai	Central Terai	Western Terai	Total Out-Migration
(1)		(2)	(3)	(4)	(5)	(6)	(7)	(8)	(9)	(10)	(11)	(12)
8. Eastern Terai		595	108	35	1145	829	442	23		389	282	3848
	(i)	(15.46)	(2.81)	(0.91)	(29.76)	(21.54)	(11.49)	(0.61)	[60002]	(10.11)	(7.33)	(100.00)
	(ii)	(11.11)	(1.90)	(0.73)	(4.63)	(15.51)	(1.61)	(0.67)		(4.68)	(1.33)	(2.16)
9. Central Terai		19	265	10	117	2	1340	82	277		479	2591
	(i)	(0.73)	(10.23)	(0.39)	(4.52)	(0.08)	(51.72)	(3.16)	(10.69)	[991]	(18.49)	(100.00)
	(ii)	(0.35)	(4.65)	(0.21)	(0.47)	(0.04)	(4.87)	(2.38)	(0.38)			(1.45)
10. Western Terai		8	39	145	83		10	25	129	106	226	545
	(i)	(1.47)	(7.16)	(26.61)	(15.23)		(1.83)	(4.59)	(23.67)	(19.45)	[4380]	(100.00)
	(ii)	(0.15)	(0.68)	(3.03)	(0.34)		(0.04)	(0.73)	(0.18)	(1.28)		(0.31)
TOTAL IN-MIGRATION		5354	5694	4783	24748	5345	27533	3446	72030	8307	21170	178437
	(I)	(3.00)	(3.19)	(2.68)	(13.87)	(3.00)	(15.43)	(1.93)	(40.37)	(4.66)	(11.86)	(100.00)
	(ii)	(100.00)	(100.00)	(100.00)	(100.00)	(100.00)	(100.00)	(100.00)	(100.00)	(100.00)	(100.00)	(100.00)

Note * Based on 'place of birth' data.
- Figures in parenthesis are percentages; (i) Row percentage; (ii) Column Percentage.
- Figures in principal diagonal are intra-regional inter-district migrations.
- 'Hill' includes 'Mountain'.

Source: Central Bureau of Statistics, *Population Census-1961*, Vol. II, Kathmandu, pp. 30–33.

Table 5.10 Matrix of Inter Regional Migration of Population* (1971).

In-migration to / *Out-migration from*		*Eastern mountain*	*Central mountain*	*Western mountain*	*Eastern Hill*	*Central Hill*	*Western Hill*	*Kathmandu Valley*	*Eastern Terai*	*Central Terai*	*Western Terai*	*Total out-migration*
-		(1)	(2)	(3)	(4)	(5)	(6)	(7)	(8)	(9)	(10)	
1. Eastern Mountain		–	9	7	8390	1350	7	3485	21215	3353	100	379.16
	(i)	–	(0.02)	(0.02)	(22.13)	(3.56)	(0.02)	(9.19)	(55.95)	(8.84)	(0.26)	(100.00)
	(ii)	–	(0.74)	(0.33)	(47.95)	(4.54)	(0.14)	(13.18)	(11.42)	(2.07)	(0.14)	(7.48)
2. Central Mountain		–	–	1	11	602	1	141	61	1262	16	2095
	(i)	–	–	(0.05)	(0.53)	(28.74)	(0.05)	(6.75)	(2.91)	(60.24)	(0.76)	(100.00)
	(ii)	–	–	(0.05)	(0.06)	(2.02)	(0.02)	(0.53)	(0.03)	(0.78	(0.02)	(0:41)
3. Western Mountain		5	13	–	4	112	1428	136	33	64	7886	968
	(i)	(0.05)	(0.13)	–	(0.04)	(1.16)	(14.75)	(1.40)	(0.34)	(0.66)	(81.46)	(100.00)
	(ii)	(0.08)	(1.06)	–	(0.02)	(0.38)	(28.20)	(0.51)	(0.02)	(0.04)	(11.13)	(1.91)
4. Eastern Hill		5054	64	9	–	7936	52	10216	149401	13309	802	186843
	(i)	(2.70)	(0.23)	–	–	(4.25)	(0.03)	(5.47)	(79.96)	(7.12)	(0.43)	(100.00)
	(ii)	(79.15)	(5.23)	(0.42)	–	(26.67)	(1.03)	(38.64)	(80.41)	(8.23)	(1.13)	(36.36)
5. Central Hill		225	1000	91	346	–	1421	8681	2572	123378	2928	140642
	(i)	(0.16)	(0.71)	(0.06)	(0.25)	–	(1.01)	(6.17)	(1.83)	(87.72)	(2.08)	(100.00)
	(ii)	(3.52)	(81.77)	(4.28)	(1.98)	–	(28.07)	(32.83)	(1.38)	(76.28)	(4.13)	(27.74)
6. Western Hill		30	–	1928	19	2710	–	616	242	3816	56389	65750
	(i)	(0.05)	–	(2.93)	(0.03)	(4.12)	–	(0.94)	(0.37)	(5.80)	(85.76)	(100.00)
	(ii)	(0.47)	–	(90.73)	(0.11)	(9.11)	–	(2.35)	(0.13)	(2.36)	(79.55)	(12.97)
7. Kathmandu Valley		682	122	53	4863	15172	1350	–	8276	12373	8138	45484
	(i)	(1.50)	(0.27)	(0.12)	(10.69)	(33.36)	(2.97)	–	(18.20)	(27.20)	(4.70)	(100.00)
	(ii)	(10.68)	(9.98)	(2.49)	(27.79)	(50.99)	(26.66)	–	(4.43)	(7.65)	(3.02)	(8.97)
8. Eastern Terai		359	5	17	3741	368	41	1708	–	3729	299	10267
	(i)	(3.50)	(0.50)	(0.17)	(36.44)	(3.58)	(0.40)	(16.64)	–	(36.32)	(2.91)	(100.00)
	(ii)	(5.62)	(0.41)	(0.80)	(21.38)	(1.24)	(0.81)	(6.46)	–	(2.31)	(042)	(2.03)

(Contd.)

(*Table 5.10 contd.*)

In-migration to *Out-migration from*		Eastern mountain	Central mountain	Western mountain	Eastern Hill	Central Hill	Western Hill	Kathmandu Valley	Eastern Terai	Central Terai	Western Terai	Total out-migration
		(1)	(2)	(3)	(4)	(5)	(6)	(7)	(8)	(9)	(10)	
9. Central Terai		29	10	11	111	1426	50	1141	3399	–	327	6505
	(i)	(0.45)	(0.15)	(0.17)	(1.71)	(21.92)	(0.77)	(17.54)	(52.25)	–	(5.03)	(100.00)
	(ii)	(0.45)	(0.82)	(0.52)	(0.63)	(4.80)	(0.99)	(4.32)	(1.83)	–	(0.46)	(1.28)
10. Western Terai		1	–	8	8	76	713	316	150	407	–	1739
	(i)	(0.06)	–	(0.46)	(0.46)	(4.37)	(41.00)	(18.17)	(8.63)	(23.40)	–	(100.00)
	(ii)	(0.02)	–	(0.38)	(0.05)	(0.26)	(14.08)	(1.20)	(0.08)	(0.25)	–	(0.34)
TOTAL IN-MIGRATION		6385	1223	2125	17498	29752	5063	26440	185799	161751	70885	506921
	(i)	(1.26)	(0.24)	(0.42)	(3.45)	(5.87)	(1.00)	(5.22)	(36.65)	(31.91)	(13.98)	(100.00)
	(ii)	(100.00)	(100.00)	(100.00)	(100.00)	(100.00)	(100.00)	(100.00)	(100.00)	(100.00)	(100.00)	(100.00)

Note: * Based on 'place of Birth' data.
Figures in parenthesis are percentages: (i) Row percentage; (ii) Column percentage.
'Terai' includes 'Inner Terai'.

Source: Central Bureau of Statistics, *Population Census 1971*, Vol. II, Part I, Kathmandu, Tables 8 and 10.

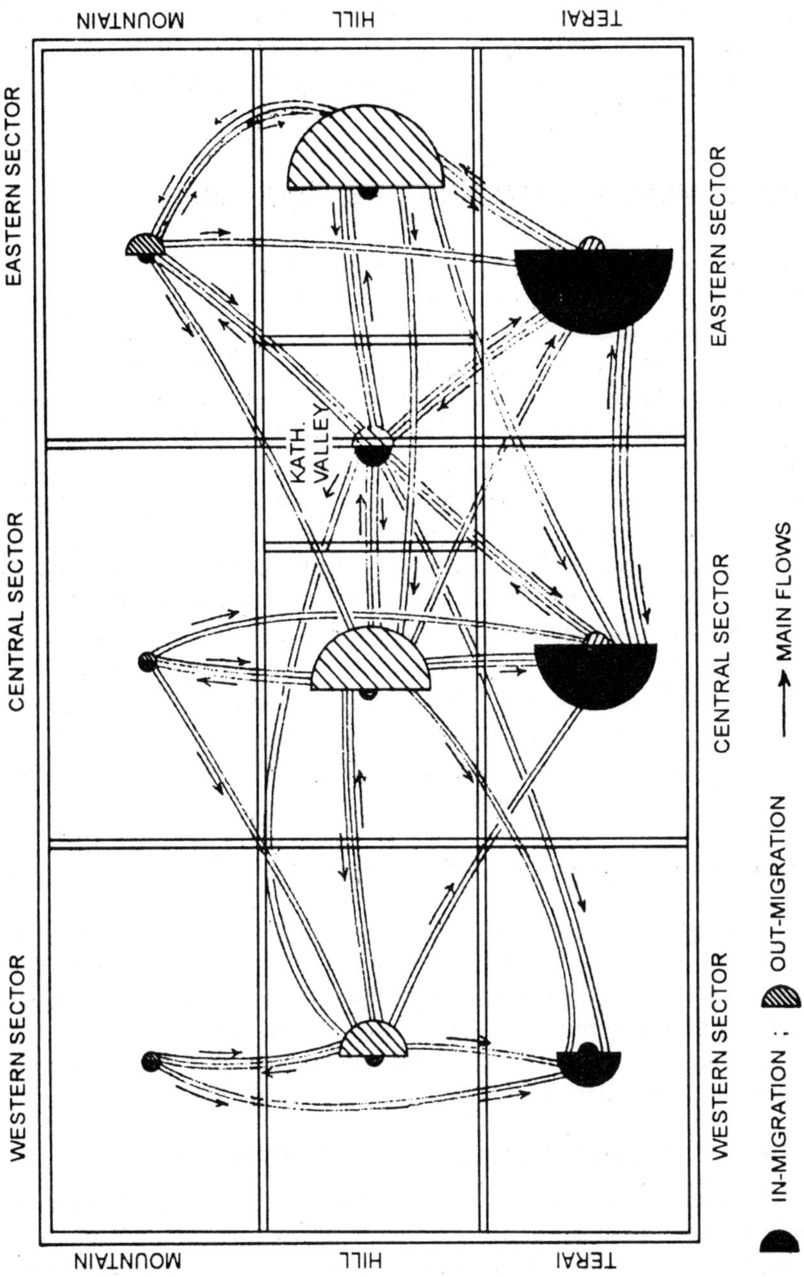

Fig. 5.2 Inter-Regional Migration of Population (1971).

structure of mobility, which as ever remains internally stunted and disarticulated and oriented towards southern parts of the country and towards India.

However, this generalised appraisal of spatial distribution and mobility of population at the abstract and undifferentiated level needs to be differentiated along various structural characteristics, e.g. rural-urban divide, to get an actual configuration of spatial organization, which we shall consider in the next sections.

5.3 SETTLEMENT SYSTEM AND URBANISATION

The generalised study of territorial distribution and mobility of population ought to be followed by the study of the concrete manifestation of spatial redistribution of population as a response to the socio-economic process, to construct a fair picture of organisation of space. As brought out in the discussion of theoretical framework earlier the formation of settlements is the concretisation of that process at the spatial level. Settlements evolve from the individual points of localisation of population through a 'settlement network' to a 'settlement system' charecterised by an interacting hierarchy of settlements of different 'rural' and 'urban' mixes with the successive levels of socio-economic development. Thus the study of system of settlements as a 'holistic spatio-temporal process' should get the primary emphasis in an exercise to delimit the spatial structure of underdevelopment. A separate evaluation of the characteristics and processes of 'urban' segment of the total system of settlements should also be considered in a transitional society integrated to the global neo-colonial process such as Nepal. Within the obvious data constraints, we would first investigate the total system of settlements with predominant rural component and then proceed on to a more intensive dissection of the process operating in the 'urban' component only.

5.3.1 Characteristics of Settlement System

With an initial supposition of a low level of articulation in the hierarchy of settlements as a 'system' and in the absence of desired statistical information in a spatio-temporal frame, our investigation of the condition of system of settlements here would be confined to a general appraisal and territorial differentiation of settlement networks of mostly rural types in terms of their pattern of spatial distribution, population size-class and hierarchical articulation, if any.

5.3.11 Pattern of Spatial Distribution of Settlements

The obvious form of spatial organisation of an economy which is predominantly primary-production based and which has been integrated within world imperial system in a later stage is a rural one with occasional 'urban' nodes. Table 5.11 provides a statistical testimony to the overwhelmingly large concentration of population in rural settlements with little temporal variation. Though because of the changes in the micro-units of enumeration in the 1971 census it is not possible to empirically verify the temporal trend in the change of number of rural settlements yet from the marginal shift in the share of population away from rural to urban places throughout the period (i.e. from 2.9% in 1952/54 to 6.4% in 1981) and from marginal decrease in the number of rural places during 1952/54–1961 (i.e. a decrease of 1.13%), it can be safely assumed that there has been marginal change in the structure of settlements over the years.

Table 5.11 Distribution of the Population by Rural-Urban Residence in 1952/54, 1961, 1971 and 1981.

Census year	*Sector*	*Number of localities*[(a)]	*Population*	*Percent*
1952/54	Rural	28760	8018630	97.1
	Urban	10	237995	2.9
	Total	28770	8256625	100.00
1961	Rural	28446	9076774	96.4
	Urban	16	336222	3.6
	Total	28462	9412996	100.00
1971	Rural	3915	11094045	96.0
	Urban	16	461938	4.0
	Total	3931	11555983	100.00
1981	Rural	N.A.	14066118	93.6
	Urban	23	956721	6.4
TOTAL		N.A.	15022839	100.00

Note: [(a)] In the 1952/54 and 1961 censuses, the village was the enumeration area. In 1971, the panchayat which is a grouping of adjacent villages and hamlets, was the unit of enumeration. Hence the fall in the number of rural localities between 1961 and 1971.

Source: Central Bureau of Statistics, Kathmandu.

The spatial form assumed by individual rural places, e.g. dispersed or nucleated, and the pattern of their territorial distribution, e.g. uniform, random or clustered, should be a reflection of and have significant bearing upon the spatio-social process. However, the study of these basic aspects of settlement process have been often divorced from the broader politico-economic process. In most studies the discernible variations in individual settlement forms in Nepal, e.g. predominantly linear–nucleated in Mountain, dispersed in Hill and clustered-nucleated in Terai, Inner Terai and Kathmandu Valley (see Fig.5.3), have been without a sense of originality defined as a function of mere topographical differentials[48]. No doubt latitudinal variations and accompanying physical altributes have their impact on settlement forms and their spatial distribution[49], more dominantly at the initial sages of habitation and at lower level of socio-economic development and conversely in decreasing magnitude with higher stages of development, but for the student of political economy of underdevelopment the social factors assume primary importance and in the case of Nepal the given variations in settlement forms can be adequately explained in socio-economic terms. For instance, apart from the physiographic determinants which must have been crucial at the initial stages, the dispersed-clustered form of settlement along

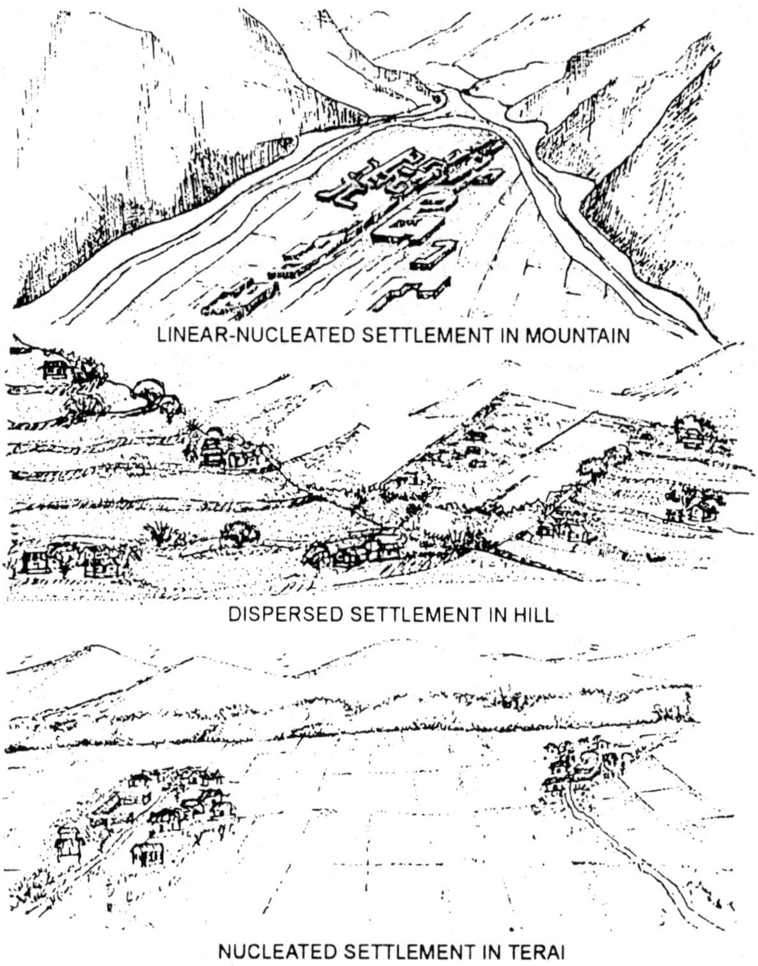

Fig. 5.3 Spatial Variations in Settlement Forms.

river valleys and hospitable plateaus in the Mountain fully conform to the subsistence trade and pastoralism-oriented economy and primitive communilism-tinged society. The predominantly 'dispersed' form of settlements, to the point of extreme scattering of individual houses all over the terraced slopes of the Hill are a natural reflection of the individuated peasant proprietorship form of semi-feudal economy. Also the nucleated settlements of the Mountain zone inhabited by aboriginal tribal groups and the settlements of Kathmandu Valley along the junctions of trade routes and administrative centres and of late along the modern roads in the Hill, adequately testify the 'social' origin of settlement types. Similarly, the nucleated settlements in Terai and Inner Terai, reflect a higher differentiation of society and greater socialisation of production abetted by the possibility of greater centralisation of means of production, i.e. land, and greater division of labour. The nucleated forms in Kathmandu Valley have also been a function of greater division of labour and socialisation of production facilitated by greater availability of productive land and early development of market economy. Apart from this generalised picture of territorial differentiation of settlement forms, at the macro level the usual picture is one of extreme dispersion and uneven spatial distribution of settlements resulting in inefficient organisation of space which once historically created by a particular spatio-social process proves difficult to change in order to achieve a spatio-social rationalisation.

From the viewpoint of spatial reorganisation as a response to the social process, a more critical aspect is the pattern of spatial distribution of settlements; for, whereas a 'clustered' and 'uniform' pattern of distribution would facilitate operation of economies of scale and grater inter-settlement interactions leading to socio-economic advancement and would be a reflection on higher stages of development, the 'random' distribution would represent the opposite scenerio. The commonly used statistical measure of nearest neighbour index[50] would have provided a better idea of this pattern, but the absence of desired statistical information at the settlement level has constrained us to generalise the picture from non-empirical observations and from settlement densities and expected nearest neighbour distance as presented in Table 5.12. Commensurate with the low level of socio-economic development based on primary production and the correspondingly higher influence of natural factors in the spatio-social process, randomness is seen to be the dominant tendency in spatial distribution of settlements, the degree of randomness varying in proportion to the degree of physiographic differentiation and mode and level of socio-economic development, i.e. greater uniformity and clustering in Terai and Kathmandu Valley, greater randomness in Hill and a mixed pattern but with differing intensity in Inner Terai and Mountain. The only regularity to be seen in the spatial distribution of settlements across different ecological-altitudinal zones is their 'dendritic' alignments along river valleys and transportation routes, particularly in Mountain and Hill. Eradication of Malaria in lower hot-humid valleys and alignment of modern roads along valley bottoms, are seen to have accelerated the process of concentration of settlements in valley bottoms in Hill areas[51].

In the absence of a medium of empirical verification of the pattern of spatial distribution of settlements, some general idea of degree of concentration or dispersion of settlement and inter-settlement distances can be had from territorial variations in settlement density and expected mean nearest neighbour distances as presented in Table 5.12. Though the analytical poverty of the arithmetic measure of density of settlements devoid of the information on their population-size and areal extent is obvious, in the ordinal scale the measure is seen to explain significant variation in pattern of distribution of settlements over different territorial zones. Whereas, in the absolute geopraphical plane, the wide dispersion of settlements in the rugged Mountain and significant concentration/agglomeration in the plain areas of Terai and Kathmandu Valley is quite understandable and

Table 5.12 Density and Excepted Mean Nearest Neighbour Distance of Rural Settlements* by Territorial Zones (1971).

Territorial Zones	*No. of Settlements*	*Density of Settlements*		*Mean nearest Neighbour Distance (Km.)*	
		Per 100 sq. km. for Geographical area	*Per 100 for sq. km. of Cultivated area*	*Between Localities*	*Between Hamlets**
	1	*2*	*3*	*4*	*5*
I. MOUNTAIN	424	0.89	50.18	5.30	1.77
A. Eastern	168	1.40	55.45	4.22	1.41
B. Central	46	0.65	75.41	6.21	2.07
C. Western	210	0.73	43.66	5.85	1.95
II. HILL	1796	3.25	43.52	2.78	0.93
A. Eastern	565	3.95	40.65	2.16	0.84
B. Central	775	3.40	45.30	2.71	0.90
C. Western	446	2.44	43.47	3.20	1.07
III. KATHMANDU VALLEY	143	13.04	29.92	1.38	0.46
IV. NNER TERAI	236	1.53	12.77	4.04	1.35
A. Eastern	86	1.83	20.00	3.69	1.23
B. Central	77	1.62	10.69	3.93	1.31
C. Western	73	1.22	10.46	4.53	1.51
V. TERAI	1316	5.07	11.36	2.22	0.74
A. Eastern	969	6.79	11.65	1.92	0.64
i. Far-Eastern	150	3.18	6.02	2.80	0.93
ii. Mid Eastern	499	8.56	12.44	1.71	0.57
iii. Eastern	320	8.59	17.61	1.71	0.57
B. Central	208	5.70	10.56	2.09	0.70
C. Western	134	1.67	10.34	3.87	1.29
NEPAL	3915	2.69	20.74	3.05	1.02

Note: * 'Settlement' here refers to the census enumeration unit of 'panchayat which is grouping of several hamlets.

** Obtained by multiplying 'panchayat' unit by number of 'wards', i.e. 9 'wards' in each 'panchayat'.

may be largely explicable in terms of initial natural differentials later on aggravated by uneven socio-economic development, the relatively higher settlement density in the physically more rugged Hill than in the more level Inner Terai (notwithstanding the inclusion of much of inhospitable Hill tracts in them) should be largely accounted to the differences in historical sequences of colonisation as explained earlier[52]. The distribution of settlement density with respect to the actual habitable area (here proximated by cultivated area), on the other hand, reflects a comparatively greater degree of concentration in Mountain and Hill than in Terai and Inner Terai, which is quite expected in view of the general paucity and extreme localisation of cultivable land in the former zones. A better idea of spatial distribution of settlements can be provided by the average inter- settlement distance as measured by 'expected mean nearest neighbour distance'[53], which is here seen to vary with topographical disparateness and socio-economic backwardness observed firstly along with north-south ecological divide and secondly along east-west socio-economic zonings. In summary and at the broad level of generalisation, the organisation of space in Nepal as manifested in the form and spatial distribution of settlements is seen to be highly inefficient, the degree of inefficiency varying from Mountain to Terai along natural and social differentials.

5.3.12 Population-Size Distribution of Settlements

A better picture of functional efficiency of a system of settlements may be obtained from the analysis of population-size distribution of settlements in a spatio-temporal frame. Though the measure of absolute size of a settlement by its abstract population content devoid of its structural decomposition may be deceptive, particularly in a labour surplus and primary production based economy, the population base can be taken as a safe proxy measure for various economies of scale or agglomeration. However, the absence of settlements level time-series data has compelled us here to attempt to draw a generalised picture on the basis of the 'panchayat' level data for a single point of time. Also, it may be relevant to clarify at the outset that keeping within the espoused analytical framework of considering the system of settlements as a holistic rather than a segmented 'urban' or 'rural' phenomenon, both the urban and rural places are considered together for the analysis.

Tables 5.13 and 5.14 provide a size-wise distribution of number of settlements and their population share by relevant territorial zones. In terms of the country as a whole, it is seen that a staggering 93.57% of total settlements containing 82.96% of total population belong to size-classes of less than 5000 population. Some idea of actual abysmal size of these settlements with their inherent functional inefficiency for articulating the development process can be had when it is recapitulated that each of these enumeration units of a 'panchayat' consists of several separate settlement units. The largely undifferentiated and disarticulated system of settlements is evident from a near non-existent hierarchical structure with a mere 24 (or 0.61%) settlements accounting for 5.04% of the total population lying above the 10,000 population-size mark. In the meso and micro territorial dimensions, except for the Kathmandu Valley with its long history of urban development and to some extent the up-coming far-eastern Terai, there is no discernible variation in the universally low differentiation of settlement structures. However, amongst the territorial units of generally stunted

Table 5.13 Territorial Distribution of Settlements by Size Classes (1971).

No. of Settlements by Size Classes Territorial Zones		*100,000* 1	*50,100,000* 2	*20–50,000* 3	*10–20,000* 4	*5–10,000* 5	*3–5,000* 6	*2–3,000* 7	*1–2,000* 8	*1,000* 9	*Total* *10 = 1 to 9*
I. MOUNTAIN		–	–	–	–	12	84	125	130	73	424
	(i)					(5.24)	(7.52)	(7.89)	(14.87)	(70.87)	(10.79)
	(ii)					(2.83)	(19.81)	(29.48)	(30.66)	(17.22)	(100.00)
A. Eastern		–	–	–	–	8	41	61	51	7	168
	(i)					(3.49)	(3.67)	(3.85)	(5.84)	(6.80)	(4.27)
	(ii)					(4.76)	(24.40)	(36.31)	(30.36)	(4.17)	(100.00)
B. Central		–	–	–	–	1	–	3	16	26	4
	(i)					(0.44)		(0.19)	(1.83)	(25.24)	(1.17)
	(ii)					(2.17)		(6.52)	(34.78)	(56.52)	(100.0)
C. Western		–	–	–	—	3	43	61	63	40	210
	(i)					(1.31)	(3.85)	(3.85)	(7.21)	(38.83)	(5.34)
	(ii)					(1.43)	(20.48)	(29.05)	(30.00)	(19.05)	(100.00)
II. HILL		–	–	1	—	91	567	724	395	21	1799
	(i)			(20.00)		(39.74)	(50.76)	(45.71)	(45.19)	(20.39)	(45.19)
	(ii)			(0.06)		(5.06)	(31.52)	(40.24)	(21.96)	(1.17)	(100.00)
A. Eastern		–	–	–	–	16	183	256	108	3	566
	(i)					(6.99)	(16.38)	(16.16)	(12.36)	(2.91)	(14.4)
	(ii)					(2.83)	(32.33)	(45.23)	(19.08)	(0.53)	(100.00)
B. Central		–	–	1	–	40	218	314	192	12	777
	(i)	–		(20.00)		(17.47)	(19.52)	(19.82)	(21.97)	(11.65)	(19.77)
	(ii)			(0.13)		(5.15)	(28.06)	(40.41)	(24.71)	(1.54)	(100.00)
C. Western		–	–	–	–	25	166	154	95	6	446
	(i)					(10.92)	(14.86)	(9.72)	(10.87)	(5.83)	(11.35)
	(ii)					(5.61)	(37.22)	(34.53)	(21.30)	(1.35)	(100.00)

(*Contd.*)

(*Table 5.13 contd.*)

III. KATHMANDU VALLEY		1	1	1	–	3	39	53	48	–	146
	(i)	(100.00)	(100.00)	(20.00)		(1.31)	(3.49)	(3.35)	(5.49)		(3.71)
	(ii)	(0.68)	(0.68)	(0.68)		(2.05)	(26.71)	(36.30)	(32.88		(100.00)
IV. INNER TERAI		–	–	–	3	42	100	59	32	1	237
	(I)				(17.65)	(18.34)	(8.95)	(3.72)	(3.66)	(0.97)	(6.03)
	(II)				(1.27)	(17.72)	(42.19)	(24.89)	(13.50)	(0.42)	(100.00)
A. Eastern		–	–	–	–	5	32	34	14	1	86
	(i)					(2.18)	(2.86)	(2.15)	(1.60)	(0.97)	(2.19)
	(II)					(5.81)	(37.21)	(39.53)	(16.28)	(1.16)	(100.00)
B. Central		–	–	–	3	22	36	10	7	–	78
	(I)				(17.65)	(9.61)	(3.22)	(0.63)	(0.80)		(1.98)
	(II)				(3.85)	(28.21)	(46.15)	(12.82)	(8.97)		(100.00)
C. Western		–	–	–	–	15	32	15	11	–	73
	(I)					(6.55)	(2.86)	(0.95)	(1.26)		(1.86)
	(II)					(20.55)	43.84)	(20.55)	(15.07)		(190.00
V. TERAI		–	–	9	14	81	327	623	269	8	1325
	(I)			(60.00)	(82.35)	(35.37)	(29.27)	(39.33)	(30.78)	(7.77)	(33.71)
	(II)			(0.23)	(1.06)	(6.11)	(24.68)	(47.02)	(20.30)	(0.60)	(100.00)
A. Eastern		–	–	2	12	66	241	431	221	2	975
	(I)			(40.00)	(70.59)	(28.82)	(21.58)	(27.21)	(25.29)	(1.96)	(24.80)
	(II)			(0.21)	(1.23)	(6.77)	(24.72)	(44.21)	(22.67)	(0.21)	(100.00)
B. a. Far-Eastern		–	–	2	10	36	57	38	9	1	153
	(I)			(40.00)	(58.82)	(15.72)	(5.10)	(2.40)	(1.03)	(0.97)	(3.89)
	(II)			(1.31)	(6.54)	(23.53)	(37.25)	(24.84)	(5.88)	(0.65)	(100.00)
b. Mid-Eastern		–	–	–	1	27	138	253	81	1	501
	(I)				(3.88)	(11.79)	(12.35)	(15.97)	(8.27)	(0.97)	(12.74)
	(II)				(0.20)	(5.39)	(27.54)	(50.50)	(15.17)	(0.20)	(100.00)

(*Contd.*)

(*Table 5.13 contd.*)

No. of Settlements by Size Classes Territorial Zones		*100,000* 1	*50,100,000* 2	*20–50,000* 3	*10–20,000* 4	*5–10,000* 5	*3–5,000* 6	*2–3,000* 7	*1–2,000* 8	*1,000* 9	*Total* *10 = 1 to 9*
c. Eastern		–	–	–	1	3	46	140	131	–	321
	(I)				(5.88)	(1.31)	(4.12)	(8.84)	(14.99)		(8.17)
	(II)				(0.31)	(0.93)	(14.33)	(43.61)	(0.81)		(100.00)
B. Central		–	–	–	2	53	47	131	25	–	210
	(I)				(11.76)	(2.18)	(4.21)	(8.27)	(2.86)		(5.34)
	(II)				(0.95)	(2.38)	(22.38)	(62.38)	(11.90)		(100.00)
C. Western		–	–	1	–	10	39	61	23	1	135
	(I)			(20.00)		(4.37)	(3.49)	(3.85)	(2.63)	(0.97)	(3.43)
	(II)			(0.74)		(7.41)	(28.89)	(45.19)	(17.04)	(0.74)	(100.00)
NEPAL		1	1	5	17	229	1117	1584	874	103	3931
	(I)	(100.00)	(100.00)	(100.00)	(100.00)	(100.00)	(100.00)	(100.00)	(100.00)	(100.00)	(100.00)
	(ii)	(0.03)	(0.03)	(0.13)	(0.43)	(5.83)	(28.42)	(40.30)	(22.23)	(2.62)	(100.00)

Note: Figures in parenthesis are percentages (i) Column percentage; (ii) Row percentage.

Source: Central Bureau of Statistics, *Population Census-1971*, Vol. I, Table 4, Kathmandu.

Table 5.14 Territorial Distribution of Population by Size Classes of Settlemants (1971).

Population by Size Classes of Settlements / Territorial Zones		>100,000	50–100,00	20–50,000	10–20,000	5–10,000	3–5,000	2–3,000	1–2,000	<1,000	Total
I. MOUNTAIN		–	–	–	–	69036	308034	311434	192067	50855	931426
	(i)					(4.97)	(7.43)	(7.93)	(13.26)	(65.88)	(8.05)
	(ii)					(7.41)	(33.07)	(33.44)	(20.62)	(5.46)	(100.00)
A. Eastern		–	–	–	–	46660	153192	152013	77533	4956	434374
	(i)					(3.36)	(3.70)	(3.87)	(5.40)	(6.42)	(3.76)
	(ii)	–	–	–	–	(10.74)	(35.27)	(35.00)	(17.85)	(1.14)	(100.00)
B. Central		–	–	–	–	5810	–	7629	21375	17083	51897
	(i)					(0.42)		(0.19)	(1.49)	(22.13)	(0.45)
	(ii)					(11.20)		(14.70)	(41.19)	(32.92)	(100.00)
C. Western		–	–	–	–	16566	154822	151792	93159	28816	445955
	(i)					(1.19)	(3.74)	(3.87)	(6.48)	(37.33)	(3.86)
	(ii)					(3.71)	(34.72)	(34.04)	(20.89)	(6.46)	(100.00)
II. HILL		–	–	20611	–	557179	2108997	1795234	647545	17305	5146871
	(i)			(13.75)		(40.15)	(50.88)	(45.72)	(45.06)	(22.42)	(44.54)
	(ii)			(0.40)		(10.83)	(40.98)	(34.88)	(12.58)	(0.34)	(100.00)
A. Eastern		–	–	–	–	91793	689120	638659	179749	2553	1595793
	(i)					(6.51)	(16.63)	(16.26)	(12.51)	(3.31)	(13.81)
						(5.75)	(43.18)	(40.02)	(11.26)	(0.16)	(100.00)
B. Central		–	–	20611	–	323646	808913	766886	312795	10636	2225934
	(i)			(13.75)		(23.32)	(19.52)	(19.53)	(21.77)	(13.78)	(19.26)
	(ii)			(0.93)		(14.54)	(36.34)	(34.45)	(14.05)	(0.48)	(100.00)

(*Contd.*)

(*Table 5.14 contd.*)

Population by Size Classes of Settlements / *Territorial Zones*		*>100,000*	*50–100,00*	*20–50,000*	*10–20,000*	*5–10,000*	*3–5,000*	*2–3,000*	*1–2,000*	*<1,000*	*Total*
C. Western		–	–	–	–	141680	610964	389689	155001	4116	1237022
	(i)					(10.21)	(14.74)	(9.92)	(10.79)	(5.33)	(10.70)
	(ii)					(11.45)	(49.39)	(31.50)	(12.53)	(0.33)	(100.00)
III. KATHMANDU VALLEY		150402	59049	40112	–	17769	139273	134726	77580	–	618911
	(i)	(100.00)	(100.00)	(26.77)		(1.28)	(3.36)	(3.43)	(5.40)		(5.36)
	(ii)	(24.30)	(9.54)	(6.48)		(2.87)	(22.50)	(21.77)	(12.53)		(100.00)
IV. INNER TERAI		–	–	–	41037	257838	379041	147148	54216	913	880193
	(i)				(18.39)	(18.58)	(9.15)	(3.75)	(3.77)	(1.18)	(7.62)
	(ii)				(4.66)	(29.29)	(43.06)	(16.72)	(6.16)	(0.10)	(100.00)
A. Eastern		–	–	–	–	30773	122442	81912	23991	913	260031
	(i)					(2.22)	(2.95)	(2.09)	(1.57)	(1.18)	(2.25)
	(ii)					(11.83)	(47.09)	(31.50)	(9.23)	(0.35)	(100.00)
B. Central		–	–	–	41037	132952	136681	25403	11237	–	347410
	(i)				(18.39)	(9.58)	(3.30)	(0.65)	(0.78)		(3.01)
	(ii)				(11.81)	(38.27)	(39.34)	(7.31)	(3.23)		(100.00)
C. Western		–	–	–	–	94014	119918	39833	18988	–	272753
						(6.77)	(2.89)	(1.01)	(1.32)		(2.35)
	(i)					(34.47)	(43.97)	(14.60)	(6.96)		(100.00)
V. TERAI		–	–	89126	182099	503630	1209303	1538224	464895	7225	3994502
	(i)			(59.48)	(81.61)	(36.29)	(29.18)	(39.17)	(32.25)	(9.36)	(34.57)
	(ii)			(2.23)	(4.56)	(12.61)	(30.27)	(38.51)	(11.64)	(0.18)	(100.00)

(*Contd.*)

(*Table 5.14 contd.*)

A. Eastern	(i)	–	–	65603	152006	419292	893844	1059079	378014	6246	2974150
	(i)			(43.78)	(68.12)	(30.21)	(21.57)	(26.97)	(26.30)	(8.09)	(25.74)
	(ii)			(2.21)	(5.11)	(14.10)	(30.05)	(35.61)	(12.71)	(0.21)	(100.00)
a. Far-Eastern		–	–	65603	124719	241301	227235	96636	15150	985	772589
	(i)			(43.78)	(55.89)	(17.39)	(5.48)	(2.46)	(1.12)	(1.28)	(6.69)
	(ii)			(8.49)	(16.14)	(31.23)	(29.41)	(12.51)	(2.09)	(0.13)	(100.00)
b. Mid-Eastern		–	–	–	14294	159588	504852	523319	143123	668	1445844
	(i)				(6.41)	(11.50)	(12.18)	(15.87)	(9.96)	(0.87)	(12.51)
	(ii)	–	–	–	(0.99)	(11.04)	(34.92)	(43.11)	(9.90)	(0.05)	(100.00)
c. Eastern		–	–	–	12999	18403	161757	339124	218741	4593	755617
	(i)				(5.93)	(1.33)	(3.90)	(8.64)	(15.22)	(5.95)	(6.54)
	(ii)				(1.72)	(2.44)	(21.41)	(44.88)	(28.95)	(0.61)	(100.00)
B. Central					30087	26773	168633	324630	44987	–	595110
	(i)				(13.48)	(1.93)	(4.07)	(8.27)	(3.13)		(5.15)
	(ii)				(5.06)	(4.50)	(28.34)	(54.55)	(7.56)		(100.00)
C. Western		–	–	23523	–	57505	146826	154515	41894	979	425242
	(i)			(15.70)		(4.14)	(3.54)	(3.93)	(2.92)	(1.27)	(3.68)
	(ii)			(5.53)		(13.52)	(34.53)	(36.34)	(9.85)	(0.23)	(100.00)
NEPAL		150402	59049	149849	223136	1387840	4144648	3926758	1437103	77198	11555983
	(I)	(100.00)	(100.00)	(100.00)	(100.00)	(100.00)	(100.00)	(100.00)	(100.00)	(100.00)	(100.00)
	(II)	(1.30)	(0.51)	(1.30)	(1.93)	(12.01)	(35.87)	(33.98)	(12.44)	(0.67)	(100.00)

Note: Firgures in parenthesis are percentages: (i) Column parcentage; (ii) Row percentage.
Source: Central Bureau of Statistics, *Population Census-1971*, Vol. 1, Kathmandu, Table 4.

settlement structure, the Mountains areas are seen to be at the lowest rung of the ladder with as much as 47.88% of settlements with less than 2,000 population and none with more than 10,000 population.

The increase in average size and disparity in the sizes of settlements are generally regarded as the characteristic features of higher level of urbanisation and organisation of system of settlements in underdeveloped societies. We have therefore constructed an 'average settlement size index'[54] reflecting the composite effect the average settlement size and disparity in their distribution for each territorial zone as in Table 5.15. Even if the absolute value of the index may be highly inflated because of acceptance of 'panchayat' as the basic unit of settlement, in the ordinal scale it is seen to provide fairly good indication of the level of urbanisation or polarised development of hierarchical structure of settlements. Whereas the mean sizes of the settlements are quite small and there is little inter-regional variations in them the coefficients of variation of settlement sizes are significantly large and inter-regional variations in them equally marked,

Table 5.15 Average Settlement Size Index by Territorial Zones (1971).

Territorial Zones	*Mean Size of Settlements ('000 Population)*	*Standard Deviation of Settlement Size ('000 Population)*	*Coefficient Variation of Settlement Size (%)*	*Average Settlement Size Index ('000 Population)*
I. MOUNTAIN	2.288	1.450	63.4	3.207
a. Eastern	2.717	1.471	54.1	3.513
b. Central	1.130	1.130	100.0	2.260
c. Western	2.198	1.337	60.8	3.011
II. HILL	3.001	1.605	53.5	3.859
a. Eastern	2.925	1.210	41.4	3.426
b. Central	2.942	1.842	62.6	4.095
c. Western	3.099	1.539	49.7	3.864
III. KATHMANDU VALLEY	4.404	13.787	313.0	47.563
IV. INNER TERAI	4.034	2.27	56.3	5.311
a. Eastern	3.163	1.435	45.4	3.814
b. Central	4.994	2.823	56.5	6.590
c. Western	4.034	1.980	49.1	5.006
V. TERAI	3.166	2.407	76.0	4.996
a. Eastern	3.199	2.467	77.1	5.101
i. Far-Eastern	5.405	4.732	87.5	9.548
ii. Mid-Eastern	3.042	1.468	48.3	3.750
iii. Eastern	2.393	1.199	50.1	2.994
b. Central	2.955	1.580	53.5	3.800
c. Western	3.359	3.129	93.2	6.270
NEPAL	3.094	3.311	107.0	6.639

Source: Central Bureau of Statistics, *Population Census-1971*, Vol. I, Table 4, Kathmandu.

which must be largely due to the inclusion of small number of urban areas with wide gaps in population sizes. It is interesting note that the composite effect of the mean settlement size and coefficient of variation of settlement size is aptly reflected in the average settlement size index and Kathmandu Valley is seen to have nearly five times greater the value of the index than that of the next highest of far-eastern Terai. Even in terms of the absolute size (though of the 'panchayat' unit) only Kathmandu Valley is seen to have the index value more than 10,000 population, far-eastern and western Terai and central western Inner Terai with value between 5,000 to 10,000 population and all the remaining areas with value of less than 5,000 population. This empirically substantiates the low level of urbanisation and development of settlement systems in the country. Also it is conclusively established that only Kathmandu Valley—the traditional centre of state authority and commercial activity—and some parts of Terai and Inner Terai-areas of extraverted mercantile and industrial activities-show some semblence of urbanisation and better organisation of settlement systems.

However, for the correct assessment of the phenomenon of spatial organisation as manifested in the system of settlements, which is essentially dynamic process, the temporal trend of the process assumes greater significance. Due to lack of comparable data for such an analysis it was not possible to carry out any meaningful study. It is nevertheless noticeable that settlements along major highways, break-of-bulk points and trading outposts along the Indian border have highest growth ratios, e.g. Syangja, Putalibazar, Pokhara, Ilam in Hill, Hetaura, Bharatpur in Inner Terai and Bhairahawa, Biratnagar, Bhadrapur, Butwal, Nepalgunj in Terai[55]. On the other hand, after the decline of trans-Himalayan trade with Tibet after the 1950s, prominent trading centres of the Mountain are seen to have actually been depopulated, e.g. Oolangchunggola and Tukuche. In the previously densely populated areas of higher average sized settlements like of Kathmandu Valley and mid-eastern Terai there is discernible general stagnation in the growth of settlements and some signs of polarisation marked by higher growth ratios of greater sized settlements, particularly in Kathmandu Valley.

5.3.13 Hierarchic Arrangement of Settlements

The foregoing analysis has established a very low differentiation in the hierarchy of settlements as measured by the population-size of settlements, except in a few areas like Kathmandu Valley. However, a more important aspect from the viewpoint of political economy of development process is the extent of articulation of hierarchical system of settlements through functional linkages between centres of different orders. For, a healthy spatial structure is marked by a well-developed and functionally integrated hierarchy of settlements wherein the number of settlement increases and inter-settlement distances tend to decline regularly from the higher to the lower levels of hierarchy. A whole gamut of Central Place theories from Christaller-Losch downwards have attempted to define this system of functional hierarchy of settlements and the pattern of their spatial distribution, which remain largely true despite their extra-historical methodological short-comings.[56] In the case of Nepal, however, a low level of hierarchical differentiation of inhabited points even by their population-sizes and equally low differentiation and spatial articulation of socio-economic processes as brought out in previous chapters precludes any significant degree of functional articulation of hierarchical structure of settlements. Moreover, absence of settlement level data thwarts our attempt to analyse the state and nature of hierarchic arrangement of settlements in a comprehensive frame.

The development of functional hierarchy of settlements is governed by the level of socio-economic development and can be distinguished only with respect to the type and level of central functions performed by the given inhabited points to the points in the system of settlements. In a backward and underdeveloped economy like Nepal, where the number of central functions available for the larger areas are limited and are highly centralised around few points, the only central functions available for the general society and which can be taken as variables to determine spatial variations in the functional articulation of hierarchical structure of settlements, can be the administrative and commercial functions. But the essentially parasitic nature of these 'functions' should not be ignored and the hierarchical structure of space based on them can at best provide loci of only the *circulation* component and not the total social *production* process that should really be articulated in the genuine hierarchical structure of settlements.

With in the existing constraints of availability of data, we have found it prudent to take the marketing centres with more than 30 trading establishments in Terai, Inner Terai and Kathmandu Valley and more than 20 establishments in Hill as provided by the internal Trade Survey undertaken by Central Bureau of Statistics in 1979/80 as the proxy for the central places and analyse their spatial distribution pattern (Table 5.16). Even though the lower order central places and places with central functions other than the commercial services are left out, the said measure should represent a fairly large percentage of higher order central places as it includes such vital attributes of centrality as the urban functions (since all town panchayats are included), banking services and export-import activities. However, as all the central places are assumed to be of the same order the level of centrality or its place in the hierarchical order, has been conspicuously unaccounted for, and we have no way to gauge the 'hierarchic distance'[57] between the places which determines the functional efficiency of the system of places. Nevertheless, even while assuming the unlikely possibility of even distribution of settlements over the physical spaces of widely varying ruggedness, we have weighted the number of total settlements in a given territorial zone by the 'settlement distance', which mathematically is the square root of the reciprocal of the settlement density, while measuring the spatial distribution of central places in terms of total number of settlements so that the widely varying densities of settlements in different zones are taken care of. From the table, it is seen that in the macro-dimension of the country as a whole the number of central places (though only of relatively higher order as defined earlier) per 100 settlements is just near

Table 5.16 Distribution of Central Places* per 100 Settlements 100 by Territorial Zones.

Territorial Zones	*No. of Central Places per 100 Settlements by "Settlement Distance**"*	*No. of Trading Establishments per Central Place*
I. MOUNTAIN	N.A.	N.A.
II. HILL	1.904	24.37
a. Eastern	1.653	21.71
b. Central	2.089	26.67
c. Western	1.706	17.93
III. KATHMANDU VALLEY	3.892	266.23
IV. INNER TERAI	1.621	39.53
a. Eastern	1.213	27.25
b. Central	2.644	39.50
c. Western	1.024	56.00
V. TERAI	2.119	54.41
a. Eastern	2.426	50.16
i. Far-Eastern	3.657	71.16
ii. Mid-Eastern	2.380	29.40
iii. Eastern	1.716	61.79
b. Central	1.701	69.61
c. Western	1.831	60.58
NEPAL	1.960	49.62

Note: * A Central Place is defined here as a market place with more than 30 trading establishments in Terai and more than 20 in Hills.

** Settlement distance is calculated by using the following formula:

$d = \frac{A}{S}$, where d = settlement distance

A = area of the region

S = No. of settlements in the region.

Source: 1. Central Bureau of Statistics, *Report on Internal Trade Survey (Study), 1979/80*, (Nepali), Kathmandu, 1981.

2. Central Bureau of Statistics, *Population Census-1971*, Vol. I, Kathmandu, 1975.

about 2, which is a pathetic low for any meaningful articulation of hierarchical system of settlements. In the micro-spatial dimension Kathmandu Valley, far-eastern Terai, central Inner Terai and central Hill are seen to have a better distributional pattern of central places than the rest of the areas. Moreover, if the number of trading establishments per central place is to be taken as proxy for the number of central functions and ranks assigned to the places accordingly, Kathmandu Valley and Terai, except the mid-eastern Terai, are seen to have higher order of central places than the rest. And if the numerical distribution of central places is to be weighted by their rank order, then the superiority of Kathmandu Valley and Terai in the distribution of central places per unit of settlements would be multiplied further. Still the apprehended uneven distribution of hierarchic distances of central places even in those better placed areas, make the settlement networks highly dysfunctional and unresponsive to the socio-economic development needs.

Even though we have no means to empirically verify the pattern of hierarchic arrangement and spatial distribution of settlements in general and central or urban places in particular some micro-level studies have observed a pattern of centralisation of higher order places in close proximity against the theoretical rule of increasing distance between the higher order centres. It is also observed that the spheres of influence of the centres are neither circular nor hexagonal as prescribed by Christaller but very asymmetrical as governed by a number of natural and social factors like the topographical barriers and purchasing power of the populace[58]. Also, following from the account given in the previous chapter of the principal directions of inter- regional trade in the north-south axis, a 'dendritic' pattern of organisation of marketing centres starting from the trading outposts of Terai bordering with India through the inland assembly and whole-sale market to the small retailing centres in remote Hill and Mountain can be observed as in Fig. 5.4 after Johnson.[59]

As in all backward societies with a historical legacy of a strong centralised state power another pattern that can be observed consists of a system of politico-administrative centres ranging from village/town panchayat centre to district, zonal, regional and national capital centre as presented in Fig. 5.5. But the marketing and administrative centres are not different in most cases, and thus a harmonius blending of two separate settlement systems of a 'dendritic' market system and a polarised politico-administrative system gives rise to a dichotomous system marked simultaneously by internal polarisation and external dependence.

5.3.2 Characteristics and Processes of "Urbanisation"

Keeping within the methodological premise of viewing 'urbanisation' as a total "process of reorganisation of space and system of settlements in response to changes in the regional structure of the economy"[60], practical considerations of realities of general disarticulation between social processes and spatial forms in the backward and transitional societies like Nepal demands a separate and intensive probing into the characteristics and processes of 'urban' sub-system in the total spatial network; for, it is this component of the settlement system that weilds significant influence in articulating the spatial structure. However, the small *scale* of the urban phenomenon and its relatively short history, at least in the macro spatio-social dimension, in Nepal does not permit an empirical investigation of the desired rigour; hence our attempt here shall be confined to a general study of the level and speed of the urban process, the hierarchical structuring of the urban places and their socio-economic attributes and implication. This will be attempted in a spatio-temporal frame, wherever possible.

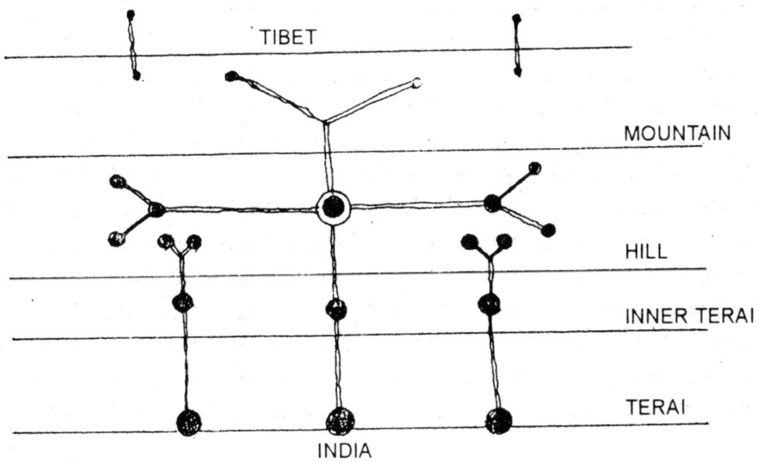

Fig. 5.4 Dendritic Market System.

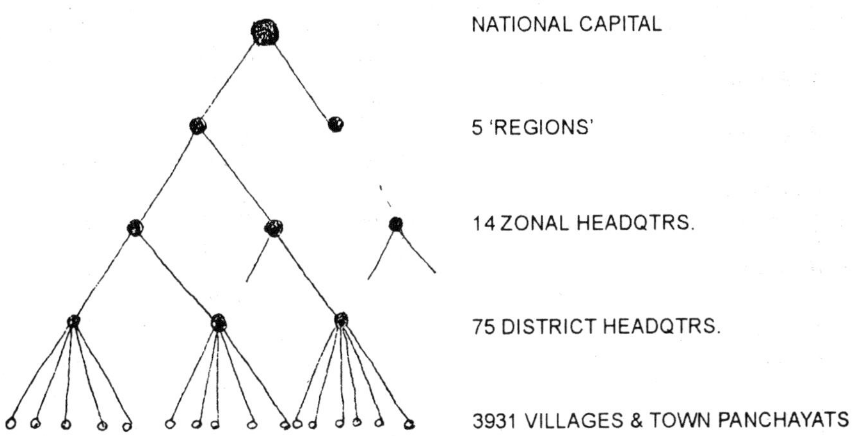

Fig. 5.5 Politico-Administrative System.

5.3.21 Level and Pace of the Urban Process

As measured by the percentage of total population residing in designated 'urban' areas (see Table 5.11) Nepal is undoubtedly one of the least urbanised societies in the world. Moreover, unlike in other large-sized underdeveloped countries like India, the *scale*, or the absolute size, of the urban population is also not significant. Hence, the study of the urban process, particularly with reference to its role in defining the spatial structure of society, assumes significance in the context of Nepal only as much as there is discernible territorial differentiation and temporal variation in the *level* of urbanisation.

Of the number of statistical measures in use, we have found more appropriate and convenient to use urban/rural ratio (U/R) of the population[61] for ascertaining spatio-temporal variations in the level of urbanisation in Nepal. Table 5.17 at once brings forth the staggering disparity in the level of urbanisation by territorial zones, for a low absolute level of the phenomenon in the macro frame. But, a closer look reveals that urbanism is almost totally confined to the Kathmandu Valley. In the spatio-temporal frame, despite a marginal rise in the macro dimension largely aided by the emergence of fresh enclaves of urban population concentration, there is a discernible trend of decline or erratic fluctuation in the urban/rural ratio in the major areas of higher levels of urbanisation like Kathmandu Valley and eastern Terai. This may be likened to the process of 'urban atrophy' and de-urbanisation in the aftermath of the direct colonial integration of the society to the metro-politan economy as seen elsewhere[62]. The parallel scenario is

Table 5.17 Levels of Urbanization by Territorial Zones (1952/54–1981).

Territorial Zones	*Urban Population as % or Rural Population*			
	1952/54	*1961*	*1971*	*1981*
1. MOUNTAIN* + HILL	–	0.29 (0.08)	0.56 (0.13)	1.22 (0.18)
A. Eastern	–	0.30 (0.08)	0.36 (0.09)	1.04 (0.15)
B. Central	–	0.54 (0.15)	0.19 (0.27)	2.31 (0.34)
C. Western	–	–	–	–
2. KATHMANDU VALLEY	91.86 (30.93)	90.16 (24.37)	67.57 (16.24)	90.13 (13.25)
3. INNER TERAI	–	–	1.95 (0.47)	8.20 (1.21)
A. Eastern	–	–	–	–
B. Central	–	–	4.00 (0.96)	14.28 (2.1)
C. Western	–	–	–	8.67 (1.28)
4. TERAI	1.77 (0.60)	3.66 (0.99)	4.30 (1.03)	7.34 (1.08)
A. Eastern	3.96 (1.33)	4.05 (1.09)	3.78 (0.91)	8.49 (1.25)
B. Central	–	–	6.12 (1.47)	5.93 (0.87)
C. Western	4.82 (1.62)	6.18 (1.67)	5.86 (1.41)	14.50 (2.13)
NEPAL	2.97 (1.00)	3.70 (1.00)	4.16 (1.00)	6.80 (1.00)

Note: • Figures in parenthesis are location quotients.
* There is no urban population in Mountain. It has been clubbed with Hill, just because boundaries of census districts till 1961 intermingle with the two zones.

Source: Central Bureau of Statistics, *Population Census*, 1952/54, 1961, 1971, 1981 Kathmandu.

not unexpected in view of the semi-colonial pattern of integration of Nepalese society to the metropolitan economy, albeit late. However, significant dissimilarities in the two situations, i.e. the classical colonial situation and the semi-colonial mode of external integration with still dominant tendency of introversion and seclusion, and their varying implications for spatial organisation and urbanisation should not be overlooked.

Further clarity on the spatio-temporal variations in the distribution of urban population and the temporal trends of urbanisation can be obtained by analysing the changing shares and rates of growth of urban population by individual places and designated territorial zones as presented in Table 5.18. It is clear that the capital centre of Kathmandu Valley still accounts for an overwhelming share of total urban population in the country, though the share is seen to be falling sharply. This conforms to the known pattern of heavy concentration of urban population around the politico-administrative capital of the small, centralised states with unbroken links with feudal past[63]. More pertinent aspect for assessing the current dynamics of the spatio-social process is the emergence of newer enclaves of urban population concentration and their widely varying rates of growth. Both in terms of the number of urban places and the share of urban population, there is seen a distinct and consistent shift in favour of Terai and Inner Terai. Another interesting and highly significant aspect of the 'urbanisation' process is the absence of consistent growth[64] of any of the major urban places even in the favourably positioned Terai and Inner Terai; but persistent emergence of newer places in newer areas particularly favoured with road networks and high agricultural growth aided by opening up of previously forested lands for cultivation[65]. When this pattern is crowned with the sluggish growth rates of almost all the old urban centres, not to speak of the outright death of the smaller urban places in and around Kathmandu Valley (e.g. Banepa) and in mid-eastern Terai, the hypothesis of urban atrophy and de-urbanisation developed in the colonial context appears to be more or less applicable in the present-day context of Nepal. Even at the macro-level, the moderate growth rates of urban population of 4.40% during 1952/54–61, 3.23% during 1961–71 and 7.55% during 1971–81[66] when weighted by the natural population growth rates of 1.65%, 2.05% and 2.70% for the respective periods do not appear very significant. Thus the peculiarity of the urban process in Nepal is distinguished more by absolute stagnation at low levels as in the medieval feudal context and resembling the model of colonial de-urbanisation, than by 'hyper-urbanisation' or 'pseudo-urbanisation'[67] as in other more prominent underdeveloped countries. On the other hand, the emergence and higher growth rates of urban places in Nepal in locations economically and physically more integrated with the metropolitan economy, particularly after the 1970s, give a strong temptation to equate the scenario with that of other underdeveloped countries and characterise the process as 'dependent urbanism'[68]. But this is dampened by the low absolute scale and unintegrated pattern manifested in changing locales and erratic growth pattern. The urban phenomenon in Nepal, thus, appears at a historic cross-road of a pre-capitalist era increasingly moving

Table 5.18 Distribution and Growth of Urban Population by Towns and Territorial Zones (1952/54–1981).

Torritorial Zones/ Town Panchayats	*1952/54*		*1961*			*1971*			*1981*		
	Total population	*% of Total urban population*	*Total population*	*% of Total urban population*	*Average annual growth rate (%)*	*Total population*	*% of Total urban population*	*Averge annual growth rate*	*Total population (%)*	*% of Total urban population*	*Average annual growth rate (%)*
(1)	*(2)*	*(3)*	*(4)*	*(5)*	*(6)*	*(7)*	*(8)*	*(9)*	*(10)*	*(11)*	*(12)*
I. HILL	–	–	16237	4.83	–	34344	7.43	7.80	83376	8.71	9.28
Eastern	–	–	5688	1.69	–	7299	1.59	2.53	23609	2.47	12.45
1. Illam	–	–	–	–	–	7299	1.59	–	9773	1.02	2.96
2. Dhankuta	–	–	–	–	–	–	–	–	13836	1.45	–
3. Banepa	–	–	5688	1.69	–	–	–	–	–	–	–
Central	–	–	10549	3.14	–	27045	5.85	9.87	59767	6.25	8.35
4. Pokhara	–	–	5413	1.61	–	20611	4.46	14.30	46642	4.38	8.51
5. Tansen	–	–	5136	1.56	–	6434	1.39	2.28	13125	1.37	7.39
II. KATHMANDU VALLEY	196777	82.53	218092	64.87	1.30	249573	54.03	1.38	363507	38.00	3.83
6. Kathmandu	106579	44.73	121010	35.99	1.60	150402	32.56	2.20	235160	24.58	4.57
7. Lalitpur	42183	17.70	47713	14.19	1.56	59049	12.79	2.15	79875	8.35	3.06
8. Bhaktapur	32320	13.56	33877	10.08	0.59	40122	8.68	1.70	48472	5.07	1.91
9. Thimi	8657	3.63	9719	2.89	1.46	–	–	–	–	–	–
10. Kirtipur	7038	2.95	5764	1.71	–2.52	–	–	–	–	–	–
III. INNER TERAI	–	–	–	–	–	16194	3.50	–	96861	10.12	19.5
Central	–	–	–	–	–	16194	3.50	–	62394	6.52	14.45
11. Hetauda	–	–	–	–	–	16194	3.50	–	34792	3.64	7.95
12. Bharatpur	–	–	–	–	–	–	–	–	27602	2.89	–
Western	–	–	–	–	–	–	–	–	34467	3.60	–
13. Tribhuvan Nagar	–	–	–	–	–	–	–	–	20608	2.15	–

(*Contd.*)

(*Table 5.18 contd.*)

14. Birendra Nagar	–	–	–	–	–	–	–	–	13859	1.45	–
IV. TERAI	41498	17.42	101893	30.31	11.88	161837	35.03	4.63	412977	43.17	9.82
Eastern	30685	12.88	86076	25.60	13.76	108227	23.43	2.32	254152	26.56	8.89
Far-Eastern	8060	3.38	49353	14.68	17.98	73102	15.83	4.00	145451	15.20	7.12
15. Bhadrapur	–	–	–	–	–	7499	1.62	–	9761	1.02	2.67
16. Biratnagar	8060	3.38	35355	10.52	15.72	45100	9.76	2.45	93544	9.78	7.57
17. Dharan	–	–	13998	4.16	–	20503	4.44	3.90	42146	4.41	7.47
Mid-Eastern	12588	5.28	25954	7.72	9.47	221126	4.79	–1.50	65059	6.80	11.39
18. Rajbiraj	–	–	5232	1.56	–	7832	1.70	4.12	16444	1.72	7.70
19. Lahan	–	–	–	–	–	–	–	–	13775	1.44	–
20. Janakpur	7037	2.95	8928	2.66	3.02	14294	3.09	4.81	34840	3.64	9.32
21. Katihani	–	–	5073	1.51	–	–	–	–	–	–	–
22. Malangawa	5551	2.33	6721	2.00	2.42	–	–	–	–	–	–
Eastern	10037	4.21	10769	3.20	0.89	12999	2.61	1.90	43642	4.56	12.86
23. Birgunj	10037	4.21	10769	3.20	0.89	12999	2.81	1.90	43642	4.56	12.86
Central	–	–	–	–	–	30087	6.51	–	53702	5.61	5.97
24. Bhairahawa	–	–	–	–	–	17272	3.74	–	31119	3.25	6.04
25. Butwal	–	–	–	–	–	12815	2.77	–	22583	2.36	5.83
Western	10813	4.54	15817	4.7	4.86	23525	5.09	4.05	105123	10.99	16.15
26. Nepalgunj	10813	4.54	15817	4.7	4.86	23525	5.09	4.05	34015	3.56	3.76
27. Bhungarhi	–	–	–	–	–	–	–	–	27274	2.65	–
28. Mahendra Nagar	–	–	–	–	–	–	–	–	43834	4.58	–
NEPAL	238275	100.00	33622	100.00	4.40	461038	100.00	3.23	956721	100.00	7.55

Note: Ratio of growth for individual towns and for territorial concern are not comparable; on the latter are inflated (or deflated) due to inclusion (or conclusion) or newly born (or dead) urban centre in the zone in between the two points of time.

Source: Central Bureau of Statistics, *Population Census*, 1952/54, 1961 and 71 and Statistical Pocket Book: Nepal 1984, Kathmandu.

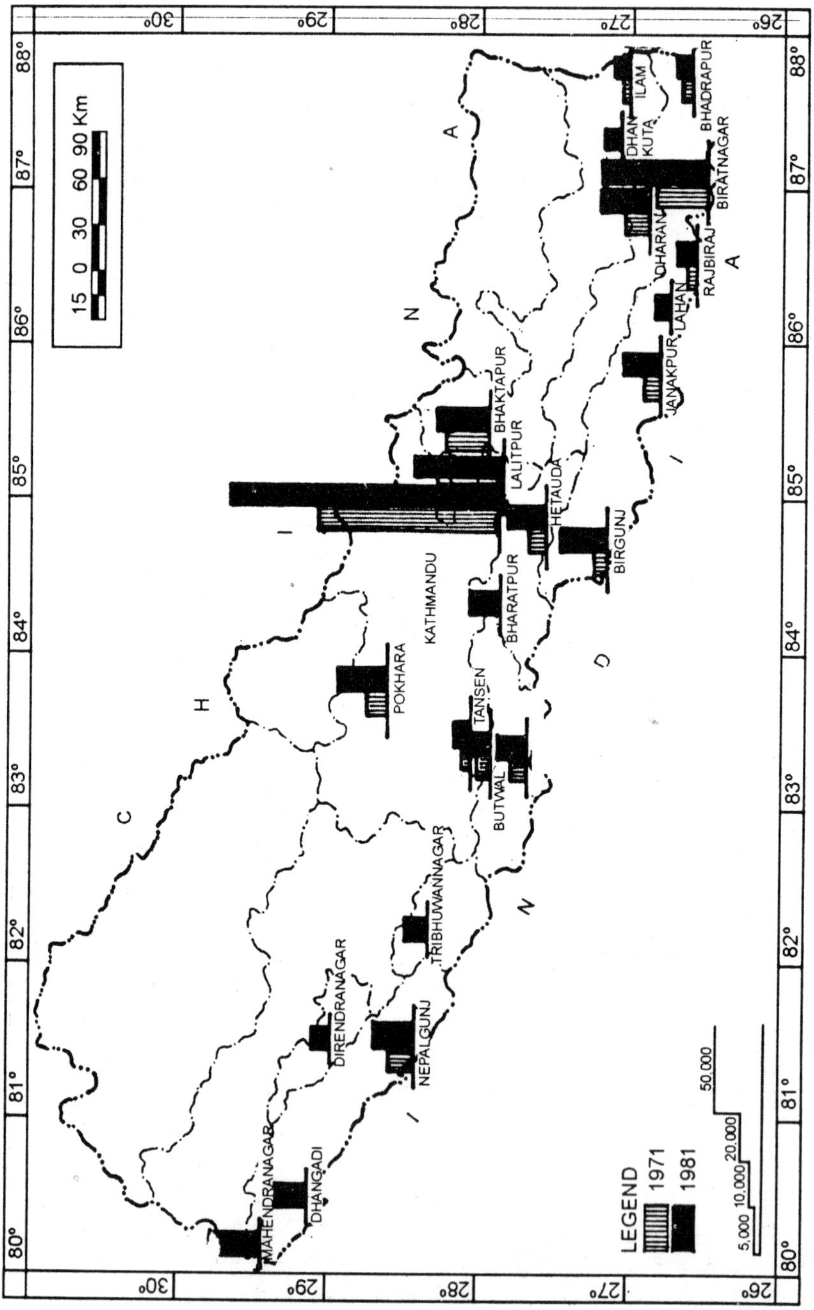

Fig. 5.6 Distribution of Urban Population.

towards 'dependent urbanism'. Such generalisations demand the analysis of many other characteristics of urbanisation which we shall attempt in the following sections.

The true nature of the growth of urban places can be ascertained by decomposing their rate of growth as due to natural increase and migration. In the absence of reliable data for the purpose we have made a crude attempt to estimate the proportion of migrants in each urban place by calculating the expected size of the population and deducting the actual size from it as in Table 5.19. Also percentage of population born outside the respective territorial zones (in the absence of information at lower spatial units, or whether residing inside or outside the municipal boundary even when born within the broad territorial zone) are tabulated to cross–check the proportion of migrants as derived from above calculation. The two sets of figures are by no means comparable, nor do they independently represent the exact proportion of migrants, because a number of other factors like change in municipal boundaries are also responsible for population growth which the first method cannot ascertain. This is so as all persons born outside the territorial zone cannot be assumed to have migrated only during the two census periods in question as is sought to be conveyed by the second set of figures. Consequently some significant generalisations about the growth trends of towns in different territorial zones can be made. Leaving aside the case of Pokhara where the municipal boundary has expanded between the two census periods, the *proportion of migrants* to the towns is rather negligible both by absolute value and as compared to similar situations elsewhere[69]. In terms of individual towns and principal territorial zones, the proportion is even lower in older, major urban places and in Kathmandu Valley. Old and prominent centre like Bhaktapur is also suspected to have experienced net outmigration. This further substantiates the hypothesis of general urban atrophy and stagnation, and, rules out a situation of large-scale convergence of rural "refuges" to give rise to 'urban involution' as in the cities of many other underdeveloped countries[70], but the situation is seen changing after the 1970s. Judged by the regional place-of-birth data of urban population, a broad trend of relatively higher migration into Terai and Inner Terai towns is observable, which is quite consistent with the general pattern of population movement as noted earlier.

Table 5.19 Urban Migration Pattern (1971).

Territorial Zone/ Town Panchayat	*Estimated Migrants as % of total Urban Population**	*Persons born Outside the Territorial Zone as % of total Urban Population*
A. Eastern Hill	N.A.	5.4
1. Illam		
B. Central Hill		
2. Pokhara	67.77	3.3
3. Tansen	1.09	9.6
C. Kathmandu Valley		
4. Kathmandu	1.26	13.0

(*Contd.*)

(*Table 5.19 contd.*)

Territorial Zone/ Town Panchayat	*Estimated Migrants as % of total Urban Population**	*Persons born Outside the Territorial Zone as % of total Urban Population*
5. Lalitpur	0.85	5.3
6. Bhaktapur	–3.63	3.0
D. Central Inner Terrai		
7. Hetauda	N.A.	31.1
E. Eastern Terai		
8. Bhadrapur	N.A.	54.7
9. Biratnagar	3.80	47.5
10. Dharan		54.1
11. Rajbiraj	18.03	27.5
12. Janakpur	23.34	17.6
13. Birgunj	–1.66	32.4
F. Central Terai		
14. Bhairahawa	N.A.	48.1
15. Butwal	N.A.	67.2
G. Western Terai		
16. Nepalgunj	17.49	35.0

Notes: * Migrants were estimated as the excess population over the expected population of the urban place calculated by assuming a constant natural growth rate ® of 2.07% during 1961–1971 and using the formula $P_{71} = P_{61}$ (1 + r) 10.

Source: Central Bureau of Statistics, *Population Census-1971*, Kathmandu.

5.3.22 Hierarchical Structuring of Urban Places

The very rationale of the social process that leads to progressive differentiation of urban and rural spatial forms, i.e. enhancement of social productivity of labour through the operationalisation of economy of scale, spatially manifested as the concentration of a significant quantity of the social surplus product at one point in space, demands a hierarchic structuring of the urban places in different size-classes and functionally related with one another in a definite pattern commensurate with the historical stage of social development. Significant theoretical generalisation and empirical studies have already been made on the pattern of this hierarchic structuring and a separate branch of urban study, on what is commonly known as 'rank-size relationship' of urban places has emerged[71]. In view of the small number of urban places and a relatively short history of urbanisation in the case of Nepal, our attempt at the analysis of the hierarchical pattern of urban places will be confined to the investigation of size-class distribution of towns, their variability in rankings and the nature of their rank-size relationship.

Table 5.20 gives the distribution of urban places by number and population share into a five-tier size-class from 1952/54 to 1981. We observe that though the number of urban places with more than 100,000 population has been limited to one centre/and the concentration of urban population in the largest size town remains overwhelming, there has been a distinct trend of strengthening the previously feeble structure at the middle both in terms of number of places and share in the total urban population. Even though the trend could be construed as a positive development the euphoria cannot be sustained because of the still top-heavy

Table 5.20 Distribution and Growth of Urban Population by Size-Class of Towns (1952/54–1981).

Size-class of Towns	1952/54			1961				1971				1981			
	No. of Towns	Population	% of Total Population	No. of Towns	Population	% of Total Population (%)	Average Annual Growth Rate	No. of Towns	Population	% of Total Population (%)	Average Annual Growth Rate*	No. of Towns	Population	% of Total Population (%)	Average Annual Growth Rate*
I. > 100,00	1	106,579	44.73	1	121,019	35.99	1.60	1	150,402	32.56	2.20	1	235,160	24.58	4.57
II. 50–100,000	–	–	–	–	–	–	–	1	59,049	12.79	–	2	173,419	18.13	3.06
III. 20–50,000	2	74,503	31.27	3	116,945	34.78	1.14	5	149,849	32.44	2.12	13	457,569	47.83	5.86
IV. 10–20,000	2	20,850	8.75	3	40,584	12.07	2.98	5	73,574	15.93	3.46	5	71,039	7.43	8.54
V. 5–10,000	5	36,343	15.25	9	57,675	17.15	7.84	4	29,064	6.29	7.12	2	19,534	2.04	10,40
TOTAL	10	238,275	100.00	16	336,222	100.00	2.73	16	461,938	100.00	2.83	23	956,721	100.00	5.59

Note: * Compound growth rate of towns which have existed through the two points of time.
Source: Derived from Table 5.18.

structure for the low absolute level of urbanism, and the discernible weakening of the lower base. The pattern can be better understood and the implications better appreciated when the magnitude and variation of growth rates by size-classes (Table 5.21) is analysed. It is evident from the Table that, characteristic to the situation of transitional societies, lower order towns have higher mean growth rates and higher dispersions in rates indicating the ephemeral nature of urbanisation. Though the scenario is seen improving with the rise in mean growth rates and decline in dispersions, the comparative slugglishness in average growth rates of middle order towns entails a retrograde trend in the overall process of urbanisation.

Table 5.21 Means and Dispersions of Growth Rates of Towns by Size-Classes (1952/54–1981).

Size Class of Town	*1952/54–1961*				*1961–1971*				*1971–1981*			
	N	*X*	*S*	*V*	*N*	*X*	*S*	*V*	*N*	*X*	*S*	*V*
I. > 100,000	1	1.60	–	–	1	2.20	–	–	1	4.57	–	–
II. 50-100,000	–	–	–	–	–	–	–	–	1	3.06	–	–
III. 20-50,000	2	1.14	0.49	44.91	3	2.12	0.31	14.76	5	5.86	2.55	43.69
IV. 10-20,000	2	2.98	1.99	69.10	3	3.46	0.98	29.88	5	8.54	2.58	30.70
V. 5-10,000	5	7.84	5.46	135.82	4	7.12	4.67	73.14	4	10.40	2.37	45.75

Note: N = Number of towns;
X = Mean growth rate;
S = Standard deviation of growth rates;
V = Coefficient of variation of growth rates (%).

Source: Derived from Table 5.18.

Dynanism of the urban process is generally reflected in the movement of towns across size-classes. To gauge the situation in Nepal 'transition matrices' showing the movement of towns across size-classes during successive decades were constructed as in Table 5.22 and the result summerised in Table 5.23. It is clear that proportion of towns remaining in the same size-class is significant, substantiating a general pattern of stagnation as observed earlier even though the 'mobility' is seen to have increased in recent decades. Whereas the increase in mobility and 'death' of nearly one-third of towns of the lowest class during 1961-71 speaks of ephemerality rather than the dynamism of the process, the scenario is seen to have significantly improved during 1971–81.

Table 5.22 Transition Matrices of Number of Town in Population Size Group at Successive Dates.

	(i) Size Group	*Numbers of Towns in 1961*						
		I	*II*	*III*	*IV*	*V*	*VI**	*Total*
No. of Towns in 1958/54	I	1	0	0	0	0	0	1
	II	0	0	0	0	0	0	0
	III	0	0	2	0	0	0	2
	IV	0	0	0	2	0	0	2
	V	0	0	1	0	4	0	5
	*VI	0	0	0	1	5	0	6
	TOTAL	1	0	3	3	9	0	16/10

(*Contd.*)

(*Table 5.22 contd.*)

	(ii) Size Group	*I*	*II*	*III*	*IV*	*V*	*VI**	*Total*
				Numbers of Towns in 1971				
No. of Towns in 1961	I	1	0	0	0	0	0	1
	II	0	0	0	0	0	0	0
	III	0	1	2	0	0	0	3
	IV	0	0	2	1	0	0	3
	V	0	0	1	1	2	5	9
	*VI	0	0	0	3	2	0	5
	TOTAL	1	1	5	5	4	5	16/16

	(ii) Size Group	*I*	*II*	*III*	*IV*	*V*	*VI**	*Total*
				Numbers of Towns in 1981				
No. of Towns in 1971	I	1	0	0	0	0	0	1
	II	0	1	0	0	0	0	1
	III	0	1	4	0	0	0	5
	IV	0	0	5	0	0	0	5
	V	0	0	0	2	2	0	4
	*VI	0	0	4	3	0	0	7
	TOTAL	1	2	13	5	2	0	23/16

Note: The matrices shows the distribution of urban places by size classes at the beginning and end of the period. Whereas the row entries for each class, show the classes in which the places ended the period, the column entries, for each class at the end of the period, show in which size class the places had started the period. (Method derived from Robson, as cited in Habeeb, *op. cit.*, p. 74).

* Group VI denote non-urban places.

Table 5.23 Birth, Death and Movement by Size Classes of Urban Places During 1952/54–1981.

	No. of Urban Places at the end of the Period		
	1952/54–1961	*1961–1971*	*1971–1981*
1. Urban places remaining in the same class	9	6	8
2. Moving to lower class	–	–	–
3. Moving to higher class	1	5	8
4. Born during the period	6	5	7
5. Dead during the period	–	5	–
TOTAL :	16	16	23

Source: Derived from Table 5.22.

Variability of the ranks of urban places as measured through their average rank, range in change of ranks during the determinate period, etc., is another indication of dynamism or otherwise in the reconstruction of the urban system. Table 5.24 was constructed to gauge this dynamism. As apprehended, generally a high degree of immobility and stability in ranks was observed. Some variability seen at lower levels may be mainly due to the addition of newer centres particularly during 1971-81. Only the consistent rise in the ranks of the centres like Biratnagar and Pokhara may be attributed to their essential dynamism.

Table 5.24 Variability of the Ranks of Urban Places at Each Census.

Urban Places	*Rank in*				*Average Rank*	*Range of Rank*	*Net Gain or Loss (–) During the Period*
	1952/54	*1961*	*1971*	*1981*			
1. Kathmandu	1	1	1	1	1	0	0
2. Biratnagar	7	3	3	2	3.75	5	+5
3. Lalitpur	2	2	2	3	2.25	1	–1
4. Bhaktapur	3	4	4	4	3.75	1	–1
5. Pokhara	–	13	7	5	9.33	8	+8
6. Mahendranagar	–	–	–	6	–	–	–
7. Birgunj	5	7	11	7	7.5	6	–2
8. Dharan	–	6	6	8	6.67	2	–2
9. Janakpur	9	9	10	9	9.25	1	0
10. Hetauda	–	–	9	10	9.5	1	–1
11. Nepalgunj	4	5	5	11	6.25	7	–7
12. Bhairahawa	–	–	8	12	10	4	–4
13. Bharatpur	–	–	–	13	–	–	–
14. Dhangadhi	–	–	–	14	–	–	–
15. Butwal	–	–	12	15	13.5	3	–3
16. Tribhuvan Nagar	–	–	–	16	–	–	–
17. Rajbiraj	–	14	13	17	14.67	4	–3
18. Birendra Nagar	–	–	–	18	–	–	–
19. Dhankuta	–	–	–	19	–	–	–
20. Lahan	–	–	–	20	–	–	–
21. Tansen	–	15	16	21	17.33	6	–6
22. Illam	–	–	15	22	18.5	7	–7
23. Bhadrapur	–	–	14	23	18.5	9	–9
24. Thimi	6	8	–	–	–	–	–
25. Malangawa	10	10	–	–	–	–	–
26. Kirtipur	8	11	–	–	–	–	–
27. Banepa	–	12	–	–	–	–	–
28. Matihani	–	16	–	–	–	–	–

From the politico-economic point of view of spatial organisation, a more relevant issue than the size-neutral ranking is the rank-size distribution and hierarchic distance amongst the urban places. Following from the earlier observations of unusually highly skewed pattern of spatial distribution of urbanisation, high population concentration in the largest single town and total immobility of towns in the upper size-classes, the form of rank-size distribution of urban places in Nepal at the general level appears to be the 'primate' type, than the 'log-normal' or 'polynucleated' one[72]. The degree of primacy as represented by the usual ratio of the population of the largest town to the second largest in the country is seen to be 2.53, 2.54, 2.55, and 2.51 respectively during 1952/54, 1961, 1971 and 1981 which is sizeable by any standard. In fact the ratio would be multiplied if the three urban centres of Kathmandu Valley were considered as one, which they are for all practical purposes. These three cities of Kathmandu Valley, due to their spatio-social proximity, can be taken as joint primate at the apex of the loosely articulated (more politico-administratively than economically and physically) national urban system, if the loose arrangement can be referred to at all by the term 'system'. The theoretical explanation for this high degree of primacy may be found in a cumulative operation of these interrelated factors; bureaucratic-commercial capital of a highly centralised, feudal state,[73] lack of spatial integration of the economy in a national system etc.

A more reliable account of the hierarchical structuring of urban places in Nepal could have been obtained from the assessment of 'hierarchical distance' between them, as mentioned earlier, but the absence of economic or physical interactions between many of the urban places except through the mediation of the primate capital city, precludes the practicality of such an exercise. Moreover, it is common knowledge that many of the urban places, particularly those near the Indian border, have greater interactions with the higher order cities in neighbouring Indian than with those within the country.

5.3.23 Economic Base of Urban Places

The very definition of urban spatial form as 'a horizontal response to the vertical shifts within the work force', implies a non-primary economic activity as the base for urban areas. However, as already mentioned previously, urban process is conditioned by the historical stage of social development and the economic base of urban places can vary widely according to the stage of development and the characteristics of the specific social formation. Since it is this qualitative aspect of urbanisation rather than the quantitative aspect of population size that is crucial in the articulation of spatial form and the social process, we have sought to assess the situation in Nepal by means of sectoral decomposition of urban labour force according to the typology of 'sectors' adopted in Chapter-1. It was found imperative to look into the phenomenon along the size-class and territorial groupings of the urban places to ascertain quality of urbanism both in vertical and horizontal scales.

First let us analyse the general and macro picture. About one-third of the total urban labour force is seen still engaged in primary-production activities, about a meagre one-eighth in non-primary production and more than half in economic integration or 'circulation' activities. With its overwhelming component of 'services', or practically, administrative and policing activities. Pending further analysis at the disaggregate level, this is enough to liken the pattern of urbanisation to a medieval feudal agglomeration where fortresses and trading posts attracted accretion of indigenous peasant communities to give a 'half-urban half-rural' spatial formation[74]. Also, this amply highlights the significant differences in the nature of urbanisation in Nepal from that in many of the other underdeveloped countries with a colonial past or high degree of integration with metropolitan economy, where a blighted urban growth with highly inflated informal service sector occupations of the "floating population" seem to be the general feature of urbanisation. But the difference is not qualitative but only quantitative, commensurate with the variations in historical experiences particularly with reference to the history of integration with metropolitan economy and the pace of internal socio-economic differentiation.

Coming to the scenerio at the disaggregate level, in terms of size-classes of towns there is no significant variation in the sectoral composition of labour force (Table 5.25). There is, however, a high incidence of 'services' activities in the first-order towns. This essentially confirms the nature of a thwarted urbanisation in an agrarian economy, the process being geared around only the 'extractive' and 'consumption' drive of a narrow section of the ruling classes. The pattern is different in the first-order town, i.e. the capital city of Kathmandu, where there is greater centralisation of administrative and policing function of the state.

Table 5.26 provides the territorial disaggregation of the sectoral composition of the urban labour force. The dependence of the urban labour force on primary production activities is found significant everywhere; the proportion of labour force engaged in this sector varying from about one-fourth of the total in the industrually more developed eastern Terai to a staggering two-thirds in the laggard eastern Hill. Even in the capital region of Kathmandu Valley with a long history of urbanisation, labour force dependent on the primary-sector is nearly one-third the total. Except for the markedly higher concentration of service sector in the Kathmandu Valley, of non-primary production sector in eastern Terai and a generally high value of trade and commerce sector in Terai, there is a significant degree of similarity in the sectoral composition of urban labour force in all the territorial zonings, not withstanding a marginally overall superior position of Terai and Kathmandu Valley than Hill and Inner Terai. This spatial pattern of distribution of quality of urbanism fully conforms to the spatial differentiation of level of socio-economic development as brought out in the earlier chapters.

To summarize, the urbanisation process in Nepal is essentially retarded and thwarted, the urban places are primarily locales of parasitic activities of circulation and consumption of surplus values and the general articulation of social process tends to lead to "ruralization of the city" rather than to "urbanization of the countryside"[75].

5.3.3 Interdependence of 'Spatial Form' and 'Social Process'

Basing on the theoretical formulations of a dialectical relationship between 'spatial form' and 'social process', as brought out earlier, it would be interesting to investigate the extent to which they are interdependent in the context of Nepal. In the absence of statistical information on other aspects of spatial formations and more reliable methods of empirical verifications of the processes, we would here propose to draw general inferences on the mode and extent of interaction between 'space' and 'society' by observing and judiciously interpreting the statistical correlations between the 'settlement size index', which as interpreted by Arriaga also indicates the level of urbanisation by spatial units, and other indicators of socio-economic development as presented in Appendix 9. Though, by the very technique of statistical analysis and less reliability of data base, all

Table 5.25 Sectoral Composition of Urban Labour Force by Size-Class of Towns (1971).

(%)

Size-Class of Towns	*Production Sector*			*Economic Integration Sector*			*Total*
	Primary Production	*Non-primary Production*	*Sub-total*	*Trade and Commerce*	*Services*	*Sub-total*	
I. > 100,000	15.06	7.60	22.66	16.80	60.54	77.34	100.00
II. 50–100,000	35.97	17.12	53.09	12.63	34.28	46.91	100.00
III. 20–50,000	43.48	16.26	59.74	15.66	24.60	40.26	100.00
IV. 10–20,000	39.23	9.47	48.70	20.74	30.56	51.30	100.00
V. 5–10,000	33.67	12.30	45.97	19.95	34.08	54.03	100.00
ALL	32.86	12.48	45.34	16.71	37.95	54.66	100.00

Source: Central Bureau of Statistics, *Population Census- 1971*, Vol. 5, Table 45, Kathmandu.

Table 5.26 Sectoral Composition of Urban Labour Force by Territorial Zones (1971).

Size-Class of Towns	*Production Sector*			*Economic Integration Sector*			*Total*
	Primary Production	*Non-primary Production*	*Sub-total*	*Trade and Commerce*	*Services*	*Sub-total*	
I. HILL	60.08	5.56	65.65	16.97	17.38	34.35	100.00
A. Eastern	70.79	2.19	72.98	6.00	21.02	27.02	100.00
B. Central	57.24	6.45	63.71	19.86	16.43	36.29	100.00
II. KATHMANDU VALLEY	29.84	10.15	39.99	14.28	45.73	60.01	100.00
III. INNER TERAI	58.89	7.50	66.39	10.76	22.85	33.61	100.00
A. Central	58.89	7.50	66.39	10.76	22.85	33.61	100.00
IV. TERAI	27.94	18.06	45.98	20.75	33.27	54.02	100.00
A. Eastern	24.22	21.88	46.07	19.86	34.07	53.93	100.00
B. Central	39.92	9.20	49.12	19.36	31.52	50.88	100.00
C. Western	30.38	11.33	41.71	26.55	31.74	58.29	100.00
NEPAL	32.85	12.48	45.34	16.71	37.95	54.66	100.00

Source: Central Bureau of Statistics, *Population Census-1971,* Vol. 5, Table 45, Kathmandu.

the observed relations cannot be accepted at face value, the following inferences can be drawn from the correlation matrix;

- The settlement size index (E_4) is seen to have significant positive correlations with as many as eight other indicators of development. This can be safely interpreted as indicative of high interdependence of spatial organisation and economic development in the country.
- The very high correlation of the index with percentage of non-agricultural labour (E_2) is quite understandable. But one should be cautious in interpreting the causal relations. Whereas non-agricultural activities may be essentially associated with higher settlement size index or greater degree of urbanisation, the vice versa may not be necessarily true as confirmed by a large proportion of urban labour force in primary-production activities as mentioned in the preceding section.
- The index is seen to have varied interrelationship with different indicators of agricultural development. Whereas agricultural output per hectare (A_5) and use of modern inputs per hectare (A_7) are seen to have significant positive correlations with level of urbanisation, production of commercial crops (A_6) and land relations (A_8) seem to be independent of and not affecting urbanisation. The situation may be slightly confusing; because, in view of the known pattern of overwhelming share of chemical fertilizers in the total input which are invariably imported and channelised through the urban centres, high correlation of use of inputs and urbanisation index may be understandable. But high agricultural-productivity, in a backward and underdeveloped economy with less articulation of backward and forward economic linkages, may not necessarily coincide with higher urbanisation index, given the nature of spurious urbanisation as observed earlier. Nevertheless, the observed correlation may have significant implications in that the urban places in Nepal are seen to be mere over-grown villages with strong ties with the agricultural economy. The very fact that production of commercial crops (A_6) and land relation (A_8) are unrelated to urbanisation index, abundantly speaks of the hiatus between agricultural and urbanisation processes; in other words growth or location of urban places may have been conditioned by the possibilities of extraction of surplus product from the agricultural sector but urban places may not have interacted to change the course of agricultural processes. The conclusion is fully in line with the realities of urbanisation in the underdeveloped countries.
- The index is seen to have a significant positive correlation with the *scale* of industrial development (I_9) but not with the industrial labour productivity (I_{10}). Again the same argument as given earlier may be extended to explain the phenomenon, namely that whereas the meagre industrial activities may have been logically concentrated in the urban places the spurious urban process in return may not have interacted to further the industrial process. The appraisal of industrial process in the earlier chapter and that of urban process in the preceding section should confirm this.

- High positive correlations of the index with banking (S_{11}), health (S_{12}) and educational (S_{13}) institutions and literacy (E_{13}) may be quite understandable and logical in that these central functions, or their results, may be highly location specific.

5.4 NATURE OF SPATIAL INTEGRATION

Of the different processes of spatial organization under investigation in this chapter, spatial integration constiutes one of the most significant aspects. Linkages relate largely to transportation and communication networks, as well as to all media through which information, goods and people move between the various nodes. However, in the immediate context of attempting to investigate the spatial structure of underdevelopment and given the backward stage of social formation increasingly under the spell of circulation capital in Nepal, the more relevant component of spatial linkages to be studied would be 'the physical conditions of exchange', or the means of transportation. We would this attempt in the ensuing pages to delineate the evolutionary dynamics and territorial differentiation and articulation of transportation networks, particularly roadways and air-ways, with a view to assess their interactive roles in the process of 'development of underdevelopment'.

5.4.1 Evolution of Spatial Linkages

The essential dynamics of evolution of the fragile transportation network, both in the temporal sequence of their construction and territorial alignments, were seen in the previous section to be primarily guided by the accumulation imperatives of metropolitan capital, both in its direct economic or indirect politico-strategic manifestations, till the 1950s. Rather the 1950s marked the real historical beginning of the end of physical isolation of the country. The development of transportation networks since then has taken place under the same politico-economic dispensation, within and without and has been but the function of the same imperatives, albeit in a changed form whenever necessary.

The sequential evolution of road and aviation networks, for they are also technically to be the principal forms of linkages in a land-locked and rugged mountainous physical environs, during the successive decades till the 1980s are presented in Figs. 5.7, 5.8, 5.9 (Appendix 7). Though the real picture has been slighty blurred because of the non-availability of time-series information on the lay-out of other roads below the hierarchical category of highways, it throws enough light to discern the politico-economic process that has given rise to the determinate forms of transportation networks. It is marked by an apparently contradictory scenario of heavy outward-orientation as in a colonial setting, on the one hand, and equally heavy convergence towards the capital centre as in an 'Asiatic'–feudal setting, on the other. The given 'spatial form', however, is fully consistent with the 'social process' delineated in the earlier chapters, i.e. processes

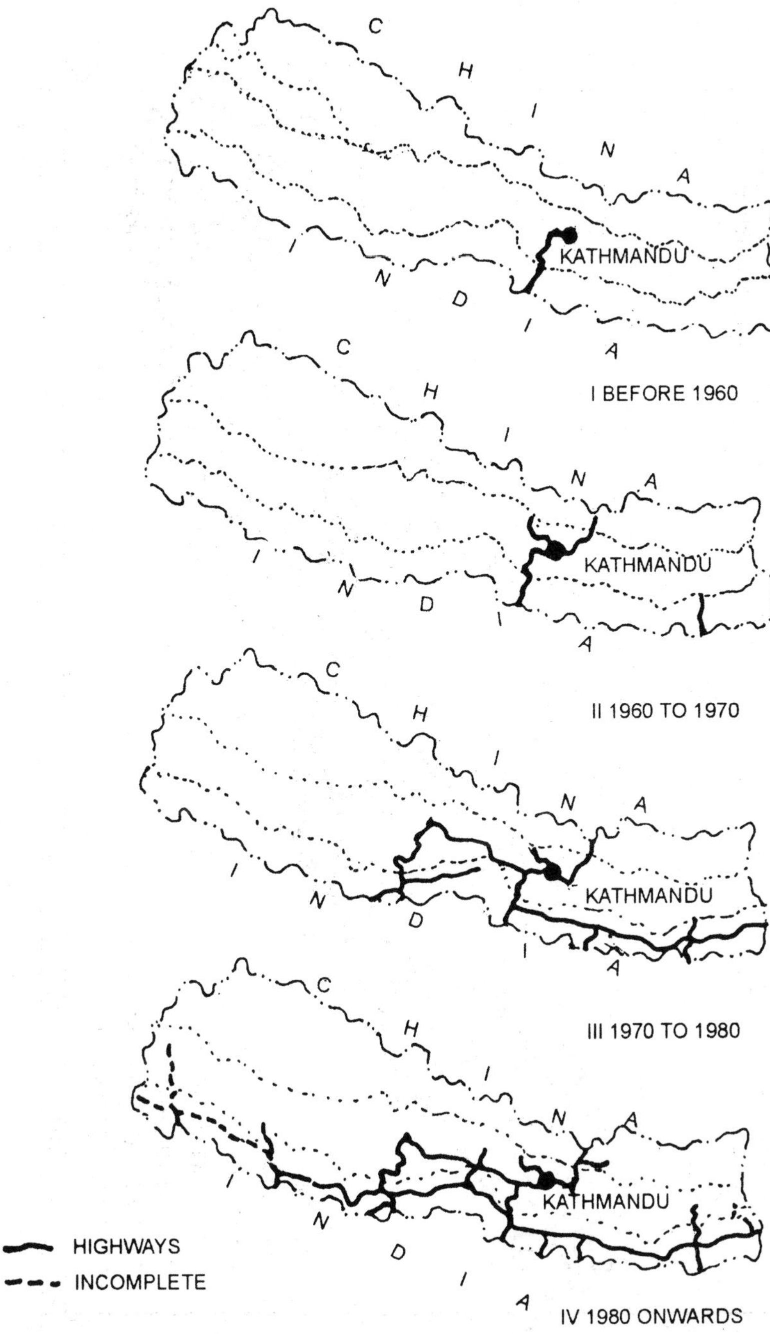

Fig. 5.7 Evolution of Spatial Linkages.

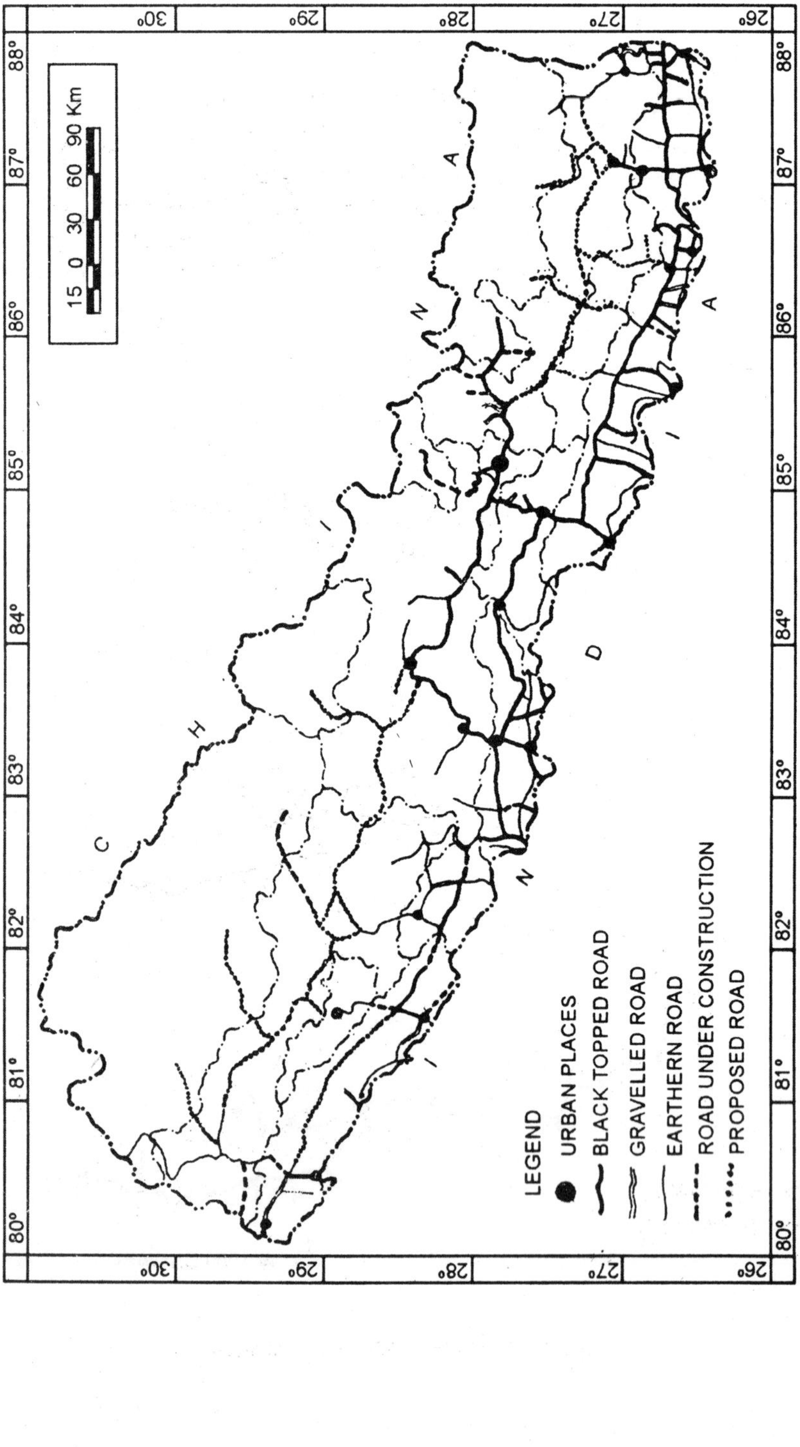

Fig. 5.8 Nepal Road Network.

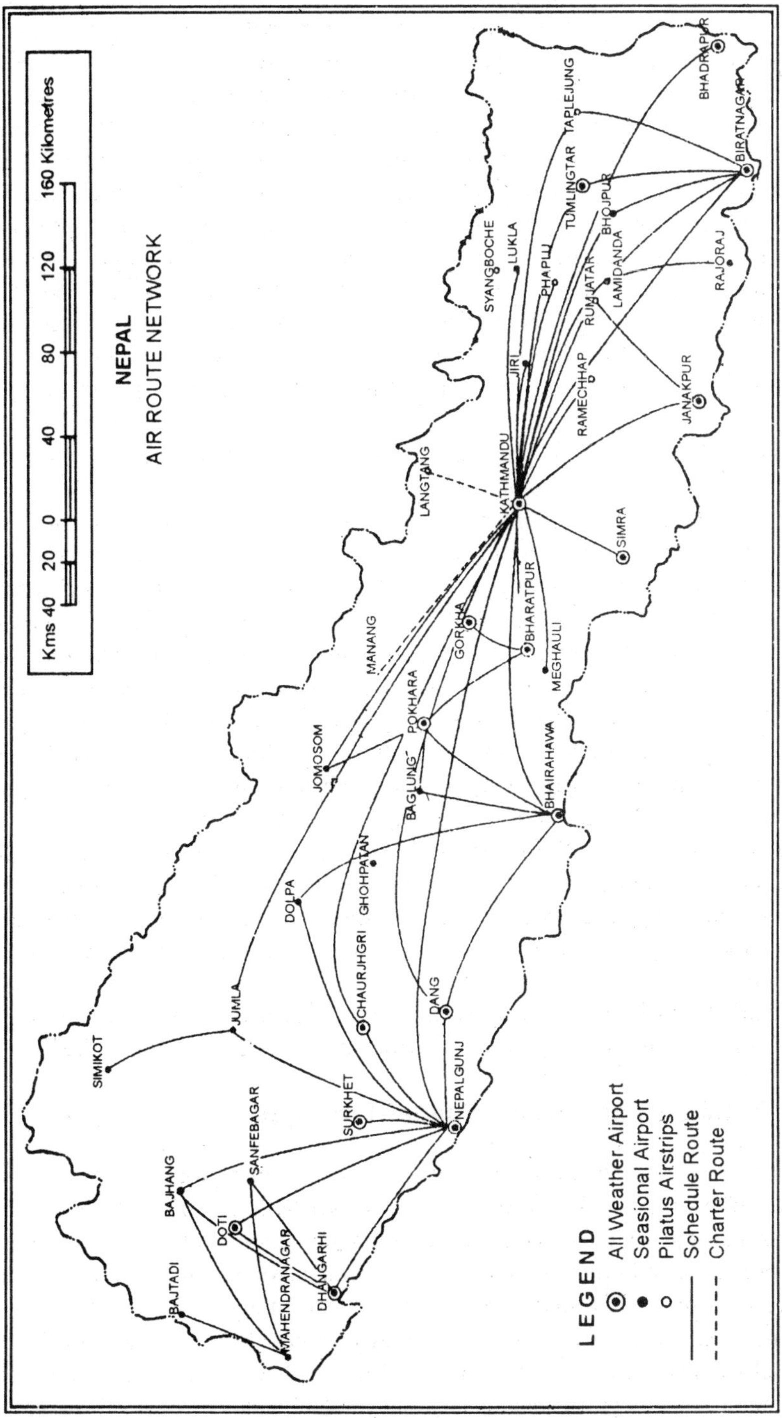

Fig. 5.9 Nepal Air Route Network.

marked by strong conservative feudal forces commandered by a centralised state and the rising centripetal forces of merchant capital tied to the dynamics of metropolitan capital. If only the sequential evolution of road networks inclusive of all catagories of roads is taken into account one can see strong resemblance, though with some situation-specific differences, to the pattern of development transport networks in other underdeveloped countries as hypothesized by Taaffe, Morrill and Gould[76]. Despite the absence of a direct colonial experience and a land-locked physical setting, the semi-colonial pattern of external integration to British India since the 19th century and its continuation with the super-imposition of neo-colonial features under independent India subsequently, makes the case of spatial integration of Nepal not fundamentally different from this general model. Of course, the possibility of ultimate development of a self-centred route network under the colonial (semi-colonial) dispensation has been discounted even conceptually[77], and the debate need not be extended to the case of Nepal as it is seen to be still in the middle phases, at most the beginning of the third phase of the model, of sequential development.

The development of transport network in Nepal has also been sought to be explained away by politico-strategic motivation of different funding agents,[78] which appears to be true after a glance at the nature of road alignments funded by different sources (Appendix-7), but this in no way precludes the basic economic imperatives behind the pattern of development of transport, networks. When the increasing articulation of merchant capital in general and with outside economies in particular, as observed in the previous chapter, is matched with the pattern of extension of transport networks to the interior hinterlands, the mercantile imperatives of the efforts gets easily substantiated, as rightly emphasized by Marx in his celebrated formulation of "annihilation of space by time",

Viewing the pattern of development of transport networks in the light of the internal class relations, besides articulating the interests of the rising mercantile forces of both indigenous and comprador varieties, it can be seen to have been motivated by the enhancement of tribute-extraction and policing power of the centralised state[79] for, by their physical alignments along less-inhabited places, sophisticated and import-based building technology, etc., many of the high-investment roads are found to have contributed little socio-economically[80].

5.4.2 Existing Patterns of Spatial Linkages

Lopsided spatial structures reflected in grossly uneven regional distribution of transport networks are found to be the universal hallmark of underdeveloped societies, particularly those with a direct colonial history. However, both natural and historical specificities of Nepal, i.e. extreme physiographic diversities and absence of a direct colonial experience and late integration to metropolitan economy, seem to have entailed the spatial linkages to be more ill-developed universally than developed unevenly. In the virtual absence of rail lines and relatively minor social significance of air transport, the analysis of level of spatial linkages here would be focussed on the road networks only.

The poor level and growth of road linkages at the macro level is evident from Table 5.27. Though much ado is made by the interested quarters about the so-called impressive growth of road networks over the years, the falsity of the seemingly high growth rate gets uncovered when it is realised that the starting base is too insignificant and the growth ratios during successive points of time are seen to have slackened after the mid-sixties. Moreover, not only are the average population size and geographical area per unit of road length found still too high to benefit from the road networks (assuming an even spatial distribution of population and road networks), the addition of gross road length as compared to the increase in population does not appear significant.

Table 5.27 Level and Growth of Road Linkages.

Year	*Road Length*		*Average Influenced Population per km.*	*Average Influenced area per km. (Sq. km.)*
	Total Length (km.)	*Growth Ratio*		
1951	376	–	21250	378
1956	624	1.66	13600	228
1962	1193	1.91	7970	119
1965	2049	1.72	5130	69
1970	2504	1.22	4600	57
1975/76	3444	1.38	3594	42
1980/81	5021	1.46	2869	29
1982/83	5546	1.10	2894	27

Source: HMG/N, Ministry of Works and Transport, *Nepal Road Statistics 1983*, Department of Roads, Kathmandu.

Table 5.28 Distribution of Road Length by Territorial Zones (As on July 1983).

(Km.)

Territorial Zones	*Unweighted Length*		*Unweighted Length**	
	Total	*%*	*Total*	*%*
MOUNTAIN	81	1.46	187	1.69
Eastern	81	1.46	187	1.69
Central	–	–	–	–
Western	–	–	–	–
HILL	1458	26.29	2836	25.70
Eastern	406	7.32	901	8.16
Central	682	12.30	1565	14.18
Western	370	6.67	370	3.35
KATHMANDU VALLEY	590	10.64	1286	11.65
INNER TERAI	750	13.52	1224	11.09
Eastern	44	0.79	68	0.06
Central	337	6.08	622	5.64
Western	369	6.65	534	4.84

(Contd.)

(*Table 5.28 contd.*)

Territorial Zones	*Unweighted Length*		*Unweighted Length**	
	Total	*%*	*Total*	*%*
TERAI	2666	48.07	5504	49.87
Eastern	1664	30.00	3363	30.47
Central	560	10.10	1306	11.83
Western	442	7.97	835	7.57
NEPAL	5546	100.00	11037	100.00

Note: • Road lengths of all hierarchical structural categories and types given in *Nepal Road Statistics, 1983* are taken into consideration to calculate unweighted total length.

* Weight to different types of roads are arbitrarily awarded as follows: Black Top–3; Gravel–2; Earthern–1.

Source: HMGN, Ministry of Works and Transport, *Nepal Road Statistics, 1983*, Department of Roads, Kathmandu.

However, the real social implications of road networks can be better ascertained through the spatial distribution pattern of the networks and further, through various measures of road density. As is evident from Table 2.28, there is an overwhelming concentration of road networks in Terai, Inner Terai and Kathmandu Valley and large areas of Mountain and Hill have not and inch of motorable road[81]. This is fully in keeping with the natural and social leverage enjoyed by former areas over the rest of the territories.

Further generelisations of politico-economic significance can be made from the territorial differentiation of road densities as measured against geographical area, population and a combined areal-population measure of 'population distance' as presented in Table 5.29. Though the limitations of the average density measures particularly in a situation of extreme physiographic differentiations are obvious, they are found quite useful in an ordinal scale to depict inter-regional variations of the attribute. As observed earlier, the road density at the macro-level is found to be very low[82]. The more appalling is the degree of inter-regional variations, heavily in favour of Kathmandu Valley, followed by Terai and Inner Terai. Leaving aside the consistently dominant position of Kathmandu Valley by any measure of road density, significant variations at the micro-level are observed when the densities are weighted against geographical area and population, concomitant with the variations in population densities of different micro-spatial entities. The average picture, however, can be said to have been represented by the density a weighted against 'population distance'. Accordingly, Kathmandu Valley is understandably found way ahead of the rest and all parts of Terai and Inner Terai (except the eastern Inner Terai) are seen to have density values above the national average. The only incongruent situation appears to be the apparently more favourable road network position in western parts of Terai and Inner Terai. This is quite contrary to reality, and the misleading picture is only a reflection of the low population density of these areas. We may thus conclude that the distribution of road linkages is heavily biased towards Kathmandu Valley, Terai and Inner Terai in the north-south physico-ecological dimensions, and towards the central parts of the country around Kathmandu Valley in the east-west socio-ecological dimensions. This is

Table 5.29 Territorial Variations in Road Density (1983).

Road Density Territorial Zones	Per 100 sq. km. of Geographical Area		Per 10,000 Population		By Population Distance* (x 103)	
	Magnitude (km.)	L.Q.	Magnitude (km.)	L.Q.	Magnitude (km.)	L.Q.
I. MOUNTAIN	0.169	0.04	0.765	0.21	0.360	0.10
Eastern	0.679	0.18	1.672	0.45	1.063	0.28
Central	–	–	–	–	–	–
Western	–	–	–	–	–	–
II. HILL	2.634	0.69	2.479	0.67	2.556	0.68
Eastern	2.839	0.75	2.256	0.61	2.529	0.67
Central	2.993	0.79	2.619	0.71	2.798	0.75
Western	2.026	0.53	2.504	0.68	2.252	0.60
III. KATHMANDU VALLEY	53.783	14.13	7.694	2.08	20.354	5.43
IV. INNER TERAI	4.863	1.28	5.864	1.59	5.341	1.43
Eastern	0.938	0.25	1.266	0.34	1.090	0.29
Central	7.098	1.86	6.749	1.83	6.992	1.85
Western	6.167	1.62	8.543	2.31	7.258	1.94
V. TERAI	10.272	2.70	4.416	1.20	6.732	1.80
Eastern	11.644	3.06	3.918	1.06	6.765	1.80
Central	15.34	4.03	5.838	1.58	9.462	2.52
Western	5.500	1.44	5.323	1.44	5.410	1.44
NEPAL	3.807	1.00	3.692	1.00	3.748	1.00

Note: Unweighted road length as on July 1983 and population for 1981 is used to calculate density.
*Road density to population distance is computed by using the following formulas:

$$\frac{R/P}{\sqrt{\frac{A}{P}}}$$

Where, R = Road length in the given area
P = Population
A = Area.

The actual computed value is multiplied by 1000 to make presentation distinct.

Sources: 1. Road length from Table 5.29.
2. Population and geographical area from, Central Bureau of Statistics, *Statistical Pocket Book, Nepal*, 1984, Kathmandu.

concomitant with the apparently dichotomous mono-centred and extraverted socio-spatial process in operation as observed throughout this study.

But this generalised study of road density misses the point that one major weakness of the essentially neo-colonial transportation system prevalent in the underdeveloped countries like Nepal is their "inadequate interlinkages and intermodal connections and their limited integration into the total spatial economy of these territories"[83]. This can be partly shown by the analysis of hierarchical structure of roads, with the implicit assumption that a better articulated spatial economy would have a better defined hierarchical structure of transport networks. Territorial distribution of road lengths by hierarchic classes and their ratios, analogous to K values of Christaller developed in connection with urban hierarchy[84]. These are presented in Table 5.30. At the macro-level, a distinct hierarchical arrangement of a road system with an increase of length towards upper grade roads is visible, though the ratios were irregular. This is a clear substantiation of the existence of a neo-colonial type of top-heavy hierarchical structure of transportation networks with inadequate interlinkages and intermodal connections represented by lower order roads. At the micro level too, with significant quantitative differences, the identical qualitative pattern of a top-heavy structure is discernible the important exception being that of Kathmandu Valley. The absence of any pattern in the least developed areas of eastern Inner Terai, western Hill and Mountain is inconsequential given their abysimally low values of road lengths of any class.

Table 5.30 Hierarchical Structure of Roads by Territorial Zones (July 1983).

Territorial Zones	*Road Length by Class of Road (km.)*				*Ratio of*	*Ratio of*	*Ratio of*
	High-ways	*Feeder Roads*	*District Roads*	*Urban Roads*	*1 to 2*	*2 to 3*	*3 to 4*
	1	*2*	*3*	*4*	*5*	*6*	*7*
I. MOUNTAIN	–	81	–	–	–	–	–
Eastern	–	81	–	–	–	–	–
Central	–	–	–	–	–	–	–
Western	–	–	–	–	–	–	–
II. HILL	536	587	259	76	0.91	2.27	3.41
Eastern	153	212	32	9	0.72	6.63	3.56
Central	322	212	81	67	1.52	2.62	1.21
Western	61	163	146	–	0.37	1.12	–
III. KATHMANDU VALLEY	11	103	83	404	0.11	1.24	0.21
IV. INNER TERAI	385	285	70	10	1.35	4.07	7.00
Eastern	–	30	14	–	0	2.14	–
Central	224	95	9	9	2.36	10.56	1.00
Western	161	160	47	1	1.01	3.40	47.00
V. TERAI	986	801	643	236	1.23	1.25	2.72
Eastern	508	547	475	134	0.93	1.15	3.54
Central	228	155	112	65	1.47	1.38	1.72
Western	250	99	56	37	2.53	1.77	1.51
NEPAL	1918	1857	1055	726	1.03	1.76	1.45

Sources: HMG/N, Ministry of Works and Transport, *Nepal Road Statistics 1983*, Department of Roads, Kathmandu.

Another way of looking at the level of development of spatial linkages and their social implications can be the measurement of accessibility of inhabitated places from the nearest transportation routes. The fact of a very low average road density, domination of arterial highways in the low articulated system of road networks, greater dispersion of inhabitated places due to topographical extremity and the like, should obviate a very low accessibility both in terms of total population or total area. In the absence of information for a better assessment of the situation, we have found it convenient to concur with the highly generalised observations of earlier scholars. To quote Ender:

> "The basic data are; the area of Nepal, 140000 km, the length of the paved road network, 1600 km, and a distance from the road (on either side) to define accessibility. From these data one finds that only 11% of the total land area is within 5 km. of the paved road. Similarly about 34% of the total area is now within 15 km. of a paved road. On the basis of the distribution of population by district, the auther estimates that 40% of the population has potential access to a paved road..., of those with potential access, 80% are in Terai. Those with potential access are defined to be with 15 km. of a paved road, which allows those in the Terai to make a trip from their village to the road and back in a day by bullock-cart and those in the hills to travel from their villages to the road and back on foot in a day, carrying a load in one direction"[85]

Considering the additional road length since then and including unpaved roads as well, the situation can be assumed to have slightly improved, but not with a qualitative difference.

5.4.3 Articulation of Spatial Linkages

In keeping with our basic postulate of viewing spatial organisation as a dynamic socio-spatial process rather than a static reflection of the social phenomenon, it would now be pertinent to examine how the different spatial units interact with one another by means of transportation linkages. Also, the social implications of different types of spatial linkages, particularly their role in aggravating the underdevelopment process, would be understood in greater depth if they are looked as the connecting medium between two/areas of socio-economic activities rather than as mere medium of circulation *within* a node/area. We would, thus, analyse the process first as operating between various nodes within the given a real units and then between the a real units them selves.

5.4.31 The efficiency of transportation networks within a given spatial unit would depend on the degree of their being able to connect different settlement nodes. To put the same thin the other way round, the efficiency of settlement nodes would depend to a large extent, on the degree of their being connected with other nodes; i.e. the higher the number of transporation linkages terminating in a settlement node, the larger would be the size of the hinterland it interacts with and the greater its efficiency[86]. The statistical technique devised for measuring this phenomenon is the *connectivity index*, which is computed by measuring connectivity among places with reference to their relative position without regard to distance and direction. To study the situation in Nepal, we have sought to take into consideration all settlements with a population of 5,000 and above and more than 9 central functions[87] in different territorial zones and the indices devised to measure the connectivity of network are beta, gama, and alpha[88]. The observation are presented in Table 5.31.

First looking at the country-wide plane, the absolute low level of connectivity as reflected in any of the indices is self-evident. Whereas in the temporal frame some improvement is noticed in connectivity as reflected in beta and gama indices, the alpha index is yet to assume significance. In other words, whereas the average number of direct road connections per 'urban' node (beta index) and proportion of observed direct links to possible direct links (gama index) are improving with time, continuous circuits in the network system (alpha index) have not yet emerged. Even the values of the former two indices are found to be low as lately as 1980. This means that on an average every town has a direct road link with just one other town and this represents only 38% of the possible direct links. Hence their positive socio-economic implications can be hardly considered satisfactory.

In the spatio-temporat dimensions only Central Hill (in effect Kathmandu Valley) has to show consistently some values of beta and gama index. However the absolute values of this region is still too low and it has been surpassed by eastern and central Terai in 'beta' measure and by western Hill in 'gama' measure. By 1980 all the areas of Terai are seen to have developed some degree of connectivity, but amongst Hill and Mountain all except Central and Western Hill have drawn a complete blank. Even though the absence of direct connectivity between urban nodes could also be attributed to the very absence of urban nodes in those areas, earlier observations have established that these areas are too deficient in transportation networks. In a situation of such abject lack of road network it is not at all surprising not to find any circuit formation in the network system.

All in all, the poor articulation of linkages between settlements is a living testimony of the disarticulated spatial structure of the economy as a whole as hypothised earlier.

5.4.32 From the point of view of the articulation of spatial economy at macro level, the nature of inter-regional connectivity and interactions assume greater significance. Hence it would be pertinent to examine the situation, based on the same conceptual premise and methodology as used in the case of inter-nodal direct connectivity but with a different statistical technique.

A matrix of weighted values of different catagories of road, air and railway connections between the regional areal units has been constructed as in Table 5.32. Though awarding of weights to different catagories of transportation networks even when the immediate concern is with number of point connections

Table 5.31 Spatio-Temporal Variations in Road Connectivity (1952/54–1980).

Indices of Connectivity	*1952/54*			*1961*			*1971*			*1980*		
Territorial Zones	*Beta 1*	*Gama 2*	*Alpha 3*	*Beta 4*	*Gama 5*	*Alpha 6*	*Beta 7*	*Gama 8*	*Alpha 9*	*Beta 10*	*Gama 11*	*Alpha 12*
1. Eastern Mountain	–	–	–	–	–	–	–	–	–	–	–	–
2. Central Mountain	–	–	–	–	–	–	–	–	–	–	–	–
3. Western Mountain	–	–	–	–	–	–	–	–	–	–	–	–
4. Far-Western Mountain	–	–	–	–	–	–	–	–	–	–	–	
5. Eastern Hill	–	–	–	–	–	–	–	–	–	–	–	–
6. Central Hill	0.60	0.33	0	0.70	0.33	0	0.70	0.23	0	0.85	0.40	0
7. Western Hill	–	–	–	–	–	–	0.50	0.33	0	0.75	0.50	0
8. Far-Western Hill	–	–	–	–	–	–	–	–	–	–	–	–
9. Eastern Terai	–	–	–	0.70	0.17	0	0.80	0.33	0	0.92	0.32	0
10. Central Terai	–	–	–	0.30	0.17	0	0.70	0.29	0	0.90	0.32	0
11. Western Terai	–	–	–		–	–	–	–	–	0.50	0.25	0

(*Contd.*)

(*Table 5.31 Contd.*)

Indices of Connectivity	*1952/54*			*1961*			*1971*			*1980*		
Territorial Zones	*Beta* 1	*Gama* 2	*Alpha* 3	*Beta* 4	*Gama* 5	*Alpha* 6	*Beta* 7	*Gama* 8	*Alpha* 9	*Beta* 10	*Gama* 11	*Alpha* 12
12. Far-Western Terai	–	–	–	–	–	–	–	–	–	0.60	0.33	0
NEPAL	0.30	0.13	0	0.44	0.17	0	0.61	0.33	0	1.1	0.38	0.03

Note : 1. Different indices of connectivity are calculated as follows :

$$\text{Beta} = \frac{e}{v}$$

where,

$$\text{Gama} = \frac{e}{3(V-2)}$$

e = edges, or no. of road links

$$\text{Alpha} = \frac{e-v+1}{2v-5}$$

v = vertices, or no. of towns.

2. Classification of territorial zones correspond to the official 'development regions', whereby Kathmandu Valley is included in Central Hill and Inner Terai in Terai.

Source: Adapted from Bajracharya, B.B. and Shrestha, C.B. (1981), *Transport and Communication Linkages in Nepal*, CEDA, Kathmandu.

rather than with their magnitude and direction, may be disputed and may have affected the relative strength of different catagories in the final matrix, it was found necessary to account for the differences in time-cost, the speed and relative socio-economic significance of the attributes. Also inclusion of railway networks just across the political border was thought prudent in order to capture the real degree of physical and socio-economic integration of bordering areas with the outside space economy. The result is a matrix of direct inter-regional connectivity of a revealing nature for ascertaining the pattern of spatial integration.

The broad observations to be derived from the matrix are:

- Kathmandu valley has direct connectivity with largest number of areal units, confirming a mono-centric development within;
- Terai areas have greater orientation towards India than the indigenous hinterland;
- There is little or no mutual linkage between different parts of Hill and Mountain or other spatial units in the east-west directions; thus confirming a fragmented and disarticulated spatial structure.
- The principal directions of linkages are oriented in the north-south direction, to coincide with the trade flow dominated by the operation of merchant capital tied to the metropolitan economy.
- Greatest direct connectivity with outside space economies is understandably with India and it is predominently mediated through the Tirai. Direct integration with countries other than India is marginal and is almost exclusively channelised through Kathmandu valley. Thisbroadly differentiates the spatial nodes that act as outposts in articulating unequal relationships with the metropolitan economy.
- Internally areas of greatest direct connectivity are seen to be: Kathmandu Valley-Central Hill, Kathmandu Valley-Eastern Terai, Central Hill-Central Inner Terai, Eastern Hill-Eastern Terai, Western Hill-Western Terai, which broadly represent the dominant arteries of socio-spatial interactions and bear a testimony to the capital city-centred and north-south axial pattern of articulation of spatial econoy.

5.4.33 These connectivity measures, however, fail to provide the actual extent of inter-regional interactions, which is reflected in the volume of flows of passenger and goods traffic between the said spatial units. In the absence of systematic volumetric survey reports or records of such traffic in a spatio-temporal frame, we have sought to generalise the pattern from induced traffic flows between the given spatial units and findings of other micro-leviel studies.

A matrix of inter-regional traffic flows generated from cumulative passenger seats of vehicles registered with the Roads Department is presented in Table 5.33. Though the measure ignores the rate of occupancy of vehicle seats in different routes, cumulative value discriminates against the newer routes, movement of

Table 5.32 Matrix of Inter-Regional Direct Connectivity (As on July 1983).

	Eastern Mountain	Central Mountain	Wastern Mountain	Eastern Hill	Central Hill	Wastern Hill	Kathmandu Valley	Eastern Inner Terai	Central Inner Terai	Western Inner Terai	Eastern Terai	Central Terai	Western Terai	India	Other Countries	Total
	1	2	3	4	5	6	7	8	9	10	11	12	13	14	15	
1. Eastern Mountain	–			2 (7.14)			7 (8.97)				4 (1.76)					13 (2.36)
2. Central Mountain		–			1 (2.94)		3 (3.85)									4 (0.72)
3. Western Mountain			–				1 (1.20)					1 (2.33)	5 (9.43)			7 (1.27)
4. Eastern Hill	2 (15.39)			–			7 (9.97)				10 (11.90)			6 (4.88)	3 (70.00)	28 (5.07)
5. Central Hill		1 (25.00)			–		13 (16.67)		12 (52.17)			8 (18.60)				34 (6.16)
6. Western Hill			2			–	3 (3.85)			3 (12.50)			10 (18.87)	3 (2.44)		19 (3.44)
7. Kathmandu Valley	7 (53.85)	3 (75.00)	1 (14.29)	7 (25.00)	13 (28.74)	3 (15.79)	–		4 (17.39)	1 (4.17)	1^2 (1.29)	3 (6.98)	3 (5.66)	9 (7.12)	12 (80.00)	78 (14.13)
8. Eastern InnerTerai								–	–		(4.76)					4 (0.72)
9. Central Inner Terai					12 (35.39)		4 (5.13)				4 (4.76)	3 (6.98)				23 (4.17)

(*Contd.*)

(*Table 5.32 contd.*)

	Eastern Mountain	*Centtal Mountain*	*Wastern Mountain*	*Eastern Hill*	*Central Hill*	*Wastern Hill*	*Kathmantu Valley*	*Eastern Inner Terai*	*Central Inner Terai*	*Western Inner Terai*	*Eastern Terai*	*Central Terai*	*Western Terai*	*India*	*Other Countries*	*Total*
	1	*2*	*3*	*4*	*5*	*6*	*7*	*8*	*9*	*10*	*11*	*12*	*13*	*14*	*15*	
10. Estern Inner Terai						3 (15.79)	1 (1.28)			–		6 (13.95)	8 (15.00)	6 (4.88)		74 (4.35)
11. Eastern Terai	4 (30.77)			10 (35.71)			12 (15.38)	4 (100.00)			–			50 (40.65)		84 (15.22)
12. Central Terai		1 (14.29)			8 (23.53)		3 (3.85)		3 (13.04)		5 (25.00)	–		29 (17.89)		43 (7.79)
13. Western Terai		5 (71.43)				10 (52.63)	3 (3.58)			6 (25.00)				27 (21.95)		53 (9.60)
14. India			6 (21.43)	6 (21.43)	3 (15.79)		9 (11.54)			8 (33.33)	5 (59.52)	22 (51.16)	27 (50.94)			123 (22.28)
15. Other Countries			3 (10.71)				12 (15.38)								–	15 (2.72)
TOTAL	13 (100.00)	4 (100.00)	7 (100.00)	23 (100.00)	34 (100.00)	19 (100.00)	73 (100.00)	4 (100.00)	23 (100.00)	24 (100.00)	84 (100.00)	43 (100.00)	53 (100.00)	123 (100.00)	15 (100.00)	552 (100.00)

Note: * All types of direct road and air connections and railway stations within 5 km. of the international border as on July 1985 have been taken into account to calculate connectivity index, heights to various categories of physical connections have been awarded arbitrarily as follows: Kotalled road, all weather air-route and railways – 3; Gravelled road – 2; Seasonal air-route and Jeepable road – 1.

* Figures in parenthesis are column percentage.

Source: 1. HMG—Ministry of Works and Transport, *Nepal Road Statistics 1983*, Department of Roads, Kathmandu.

2. Royal Nepal Airlines Corporation, Planning Division, Kathmandu.

Table 5.33 Matrix of Inter-Regional Traffic Flows* (As on May 1984).

	Mountain	*Eastern Hill*	*Central Hill*	*Westeren Hill*	*Kathmandu Valley*	*Eastern Inner Terai*	*Central Inner Terai*	*Western Inner Terai*	*Eastern Terai*	*Central Terai*	*Western Terai*	*Total*
	1	*2*	*3*	*4*	*5*	*6*	*7*	*8*	*9*	*10*	*11*	*12*
1. Mountain	–	–	–	–	–	–	–	–	–	–	–	–
2. Eastern Hill	–	–	–	–	3489 (21.92)	–	–	–	972 (9.02)	–	–	4461 (7.62)
3. Central Hill	–	–	(378)	–	5308 (33.35)	–	569 (10.54)	–	822 (7.63)	4104 (50.31)	–	10803 (18.45)
4. Western Hill	–	–	–	–	–	–	–	–	–	–	1234 (81.51)	1234 (2.11)
5. Kathmandu Valley	–	3489 (78.21)	5308 (49.13)	–	(1559)	–	80 (1.48)	–	5588 (51.86)	1449 (17.76)	–	15914 (27.19)
6. Eastern Inner Terai	–	–	–	–	–	–	–	–	–	–	–	–
7. Central Inner Terai	–	–	569 (5.27)	–	80 (0.50)	–	(25)	–	2769 (25.70)	1981 (24.28)	–	5399
8. Western Inner Terai	–	–	–	–	–	–	–	–	–		280 (18.49)	280 (0.48)
9. Eastern Terai	–	972 (21.79)	822 (7.61)	–	5588 (35.11)	–	2769 (51.29)	–	(15873)	624 (7.65)	–	10775 (18.41)
10. Central Terai	–	–	4104 (37.99)	–	1449 (9.11)	–	1981 (36.69)	–	624 (5.79)	(5121)	–	8158 (13.94)
11. Western Terai	–	–	–	1234 (100.00)	–	–	–	280 (100.00)	–	–	(200)	1514 (2.59)
TOTAL	–	4461 (100.0)	10803 (100.0)	1234 (100.0)	15914 (100.0)	–	5599 (100.0)	280 (100.0)	10775 (100.0)	8158 (100.0)	1514 (100.0)	58538 (100.0)

Note: *Traffic flows have been measured in terms of cumulative passenger seats of vehicles registered with the Roads Department uptil May, 1984.
§ Figure in principal diagonal are intra-regional flows.
§ Figures in parenthesis are column percentage.

Source: Based on records of HMG/N, Ministry of Works and Transport. Department of Transport Management. Babar Mahal, Kathmandu.

more important goods traffic is not taken into account and movement across the international border (which is very significant in the case of Terai) is left out of the picture, yet the matrix is seen to provide important insights into the extent of inter-regional interactions in the country. As a natural corollary to the very absence of land transport networks (air transport has been left out of the analysis for the lack of comparable data) all of Mountain areas are seen to have no vehicular interactions and eastern and western sections of Hill and Inner Terai have only marginal inter-regional interactions. Once again, largest share of total inflow or outflow of traffic is claimed by Kathmandu Valley,[89] followed by areas adjoining it and eastern Terai, confirm the by now well-established characteristics of the spatial economy centralised around selected nodes. Centralisation around Kathmandu Valley becomes all the more glaring when a cumulative assessment of traffic flows to and from sub-ecological units around the Valley is made. Except for the highest inter-regional flows between the two most dominant nodes of Kathmandu Valley and eastern Terai, which is fully consistent with the logic of socio-spatial articulation, the higher inter-regional traffic flows are noticed to be confined to adjoining territorial zones, particularly between the corresponding plain and hill areas. This pattern of heavy convergence of movements around the primate-capital city areas and relatively shorter average trip lengths of passenger traffic,[90] in addition to the total absence of vehicular movements in large parts of the country, is a clear manifestation of weak inter-regional linkages and disarticulated spatial structure. Also, the pattern of higher traffic movements in the south direction within the same hydrographic socio-ecological zone, can be safely reaffirmed as the manifestation of extraverted spatial structure.

Combined inter-regional movement of passenger and goods traffic should have provided the holistic picture of the nature of spatial articulation. In the absence of such data in the desired frame we have no option but to cite the findings of earlier micro-level studies in a generilsed form in support of our characterisation of the spatial structure in Nepal. Among others, Ender's study of frieght flows along important routes and to/from prominent nodes clearly brings out the directional distribution of freight flows as being heavily oriented from south (Terai) to north (Kathmandu Valley, Hill) and concentrated around Kathmandu Valley, particularly along Birgunj-Hetauda-Kathmandu corridor[91]. Our own findings of inter-regional trade flows in the previous chapter also confirms this pattern.

Passenger and freight movement by air is also reported to conform to this broad pattern of convergence around Kathmandu, on the one hand, and greater movement in the north-south direction within the same hydrographic zone, on the other[92].

The nature of spatial integration as brought out by the foregoing analysis is seen to be clearly marked by the apparently contradictory scenario of polarisation around the capital city zone of Kathmandu Valley, on the one hand, and outward-orientation towards India along a north-south dendrite stretching from Mountain to Terai.

5.5 SPATIAL DIFFERENTIATION OF COMPOSITE LEVELS OF DEVELOPMENT

After having analysed the separate aspects of spatial manifestations of the social process it would now be pertinent to sum up the total scenario. This we propose to do through spatial differentiation of the composite levels of social development as measured by an index constructed by aggregating a number of indicators of sectoral development. The underlying assumption behind this, as also brought out in the analytical frame earlier, is that the nature and pattern of spatial distribution of unevenness in development/underdevelopment would not only vary with the historical stage of development of society but would also be a key variable in the overall organisation of space.

5.5.1 Before attempting to analyse the spatial differentiation of the composite social process, it may be necessary to dwell briefly on the selection of indicators and the construction of the composite index.

In this analysis we have retained the indicators pertaining to the agricultural and industrial sectors as already discussed. Two more sub-groups of indicators of 'general economic base' and 'social services and infrastructure' development [See Appendix-8] have been added to capture the total picture of the multi-dimensional phenomenon of development/underdevelopment within the given data constraints. Whereas the inclusion of rest of the indicators such as availability of schools (S-13), hospital beds (S-12), bank credit (S-11), level of 'urbanisation' (E-4), proportion of non-agricultural labour force (E-2) as positive indicators of development may be quite understandable, that of inter-censal growth of population (E-1) in a labour surplus economy can be disputed. This indicator has been included here merely to account for the large-scale territorial redistribution of population as a result of inter-spatial socio-economic differentials. Literacy rate (E-3) has been separately included not only to gauze the 'qualitative' aspect of the population but also to account for the role of non-formal education particularly in the Mountain zone and the known pattern of Terai to avail of educational facilities in the neighbouring areas of India. However, several important variables in the development/underdevelopment process of a transitional society such as transportation and communication facilities, energy use, etc., had to be left out for want of data at the desired micro level.

The logic of formation of sub-groups of indicators has been rooted in the subjective judgement of the researcher, but the grouping has been consciously resorted to as the composite index constructed by treating the first principal factor obtained from the sub-group as the new variables "alleavates the necessity of taking more than one principal factor since the correlations among the variables in a sub-group are generally high"[93].

The indicators have been aggragated by using the method of first principal component on the correlation matrix [See Appendix-9] first to obtain indices of development for different sub-groups of indicators and finally the composite index of overall development. Spearman rank correlations for different indices of development have been calculated (Table 5.34) to observe the variations in spatial distribution of levels of development of different aspects of the social process as represented by different sub-groups of indicators. It is seen that different indices have high and positive correlation with one another, except for the " Social services and infrastructure" development with agricultural and industrial development. This may, however, merely indicate coincidental pattern of disparate or retarded development rather than high sectoral interdependence in view of the previously observed disarticulated structure of the economy.

Table 5.34 Rank Correlations Between Different Indices of Development.

Index of Dev. / *Index of Dev.*	*I*	*II*	*III*	*IV*	*V*
I	1.0000				
II	0.6051	1.0000			
III	0.5885	0.7132	1.0000		
IV	0.6320	0.3096	0.3202	1.0000	
V	0.8372	0.7336	0.7203	0.6258	1.0000

Note: I – Index of general economic base.
II – Index of agricultural development.
III – Index of industrial development.
IV – Index of social services and infrastructure development.
V – Index of composite development.

5.5.2 The factor scores of first principal component for individual districts are arranged in descending order and grouped into homogeneous classes by chosing suitable cut-off points through subjective judgements keeping in view the purpose of the exercise, i.e. spatial differentiation of levels of development/underdevelopment, rather than 'regionalisation', They are presented in Table 5.35. and plotted in Fig. 5.10.

Table 5.35 Spatial Differentiation of Composite Level of Development.

Class	*Rank* (1)	*Factor Scores of First Principal* (2)	*Districts (Territorial Zones)* (3)	
I	1.	15.1751	Kathmadhu	(KV)
II	2.	8.5485	Bhaktapur	(KV)
	3.	7.6914	Lalitpur	(KV)
III	4.	4.0459	Morang	(FET)
IV	5.	2.4186	Sansari	(FET)
	6.	2.1428	Jhapa	(FET)

(*Contd.*)

(*Table 5.35 contd.*)

Class	*Rank* (1)	*Factor Scores of First Principal* (2)	*Districts (Territorial Zones)* (3)	
V	7.	1.78194	Parsa	(ET)
	8.	1.67376	Kaski	(CH)
	9.	1.5635	Banke	(WT)
	10.	1.1635	Chitwan	(CIT)
VI	11.	0.76058	Rupendehi	(CT)
	12.	0.6572	Bara	(ET)
	13.	0.5566	Makwanpur	(CIT)
	14.	0.4144	Saptari	(MET)
	15.	0.3943	Dhanusha	(MET)
	16.	0.3206	Manang	(CM)
	17.	0.3148	Nawalparasi	(CT)
	18.	0.2487	Dhankuta	(EH)
	19.	0.2253	Dang	(WIT)
	20.	0.1871	Parbat	(CH)
	21.	0.0351	Tanahu	(CH)
	22.	–0.0428	Rautahat	(ET)
	23.	–0.0468	Siraha	(MET)
	24.	–0.0911	Kailali	(WT)
	25.	–0.1118	Palpa	(CH)
	26.	–0.1256	Sarlahi	(MET)
	27.	–0.1369	Udaipur	(EIT)
	28.	–0.1459	Kanchanpur	(WT)
	29.	–0.2436	Lamjung	(CH)
	30.	–0.3129	Mustang	(CM)
	31.	–0.3431	Tehrathum	(EH)
	32.	–0.3485	Mahottari	(MET)
	33.	–0.3665	Sindhuli	(ETT)
	34.	–0.3723	Bardiya	(WT)
	35.	–0.3814	Kapilvastu	(CT)
	36.	–0.3852	Dandeldhura	(WH)
	37.	–0.3992	Gulmi	(CH)
	38.	–0.4215	Syangja	(CH)
	39.	–0.5176	Kavre	(EH)
	40.	–0.6032	Illam	(EH)
	41.	–0.6462	Baglung	(CH)
	42.	–0.7469	Pyuthan	(WH)
	43.	–0.7522	Baitadi	(WH)
	44.	–0.7532	Surkhet	(WIT)
	45.	–0.7619	Arghakhanchi	(CH)
	46.	–0.7697	Sankhuwasabha	(EM)
	47.	–0.8333	Nuwakot	(CH)
	48.	–0.8697	Myagdi	(CH)
	49.	–0.8843	Darchula	(WM)
	50.	–0.9233	Okhaldhunga	(EH)
	51.	–0.9240	Panchathar	(EH)
	52.	–0.9534	Bhojpur	(EH)
	53.	–0.9598	Gorkha	(CH)
	54.	–0.9966	Rasuwa	(CM)

(*Contd.*)

(*Table 5.35 contd.*)

55.	−1.0073	Sallyan	(WM)
56.	−1.0822	Solukhumbu	(EM)
57.	−1.1472	Dolakha	(EM)
58.	−1.2129	Taplejung	(EM)
59.	−1.2436	Sindhupalchok	(EH)
60.	−1.2587	Dhanding	(CH)
61.	−1.8777	Rukum	(WH)
62.	−1.4640	Rolpa	(WH)
63.	−1.4909	Khotang	(EH)
64.	−1.5630	Rameshhap	(EH)
65.	−1.6019	Achham	(WH)
66.	−1.7262	Dolpa	(WM)
67.	−1.7518	Doti	(WH)
68.	−1.7795	Bajhang	(WM)
69.	−1.8427	Dailekh	(WH)
70.	−1.8532	Jajarkot	(WH)
71.	−1.8761	Mugu	(WM)
72.	−1.9010	Kalikot	(WM)
73.	−1.9310	Bajura	(WM)
74.	−1.9360	Jumla	(WM)
75.	−2.1015	Humla	(WM)

It can be generally observed that:

- Whereas the spatial disparateness in development is very pronounced at the higher levels, at the middle and lower levels there is virtually no trace of spatial differentiation. This is a clear indication of the extremely polarised spatial structure, but with no attendant development of an ordered spatial system.
- In the broader territorial dimension, the areas at higher levels of development are seen centralised around selected pockets of Kathmandu Valley, Far-eastern Terai and points of superior physical and economic articulation with the outside world and centres of mercantile and administrative functions within. These 'blisters' of spurious growth are seen surrounded by the vast indigent hinterland of not only the nature-baited Mountain and Hill but also the favourably endowed Terai, particularly the western and mid-eastern sections. This should indicate the rising supremacy of 'social' factors in designing the spatial structure of the country.
- Looking at the further disaggregated level of administrative districts, the state capital centre of Kathmandu, followed by the two other districts of the Valley i.e. Bhaktapur and Lalitpur, are seen far ahead of the remaining districts. This should clearly establish the continuing domination of monocentric pattern of development geared around the locales of principal surplus-appropriating class as in a feudal setting. However, the emerging pattern of 'extraverted' development is manifest in the higher position in the development matrix occupied by the traditional outposts of metropolitan capital such as Morang (Biratnagar) and adjoing districts of far-eastern Terai, Parsa (Birgunj), Banke (Nepalgunj), Rupendehi (Bhairahawa) and Dhanusha

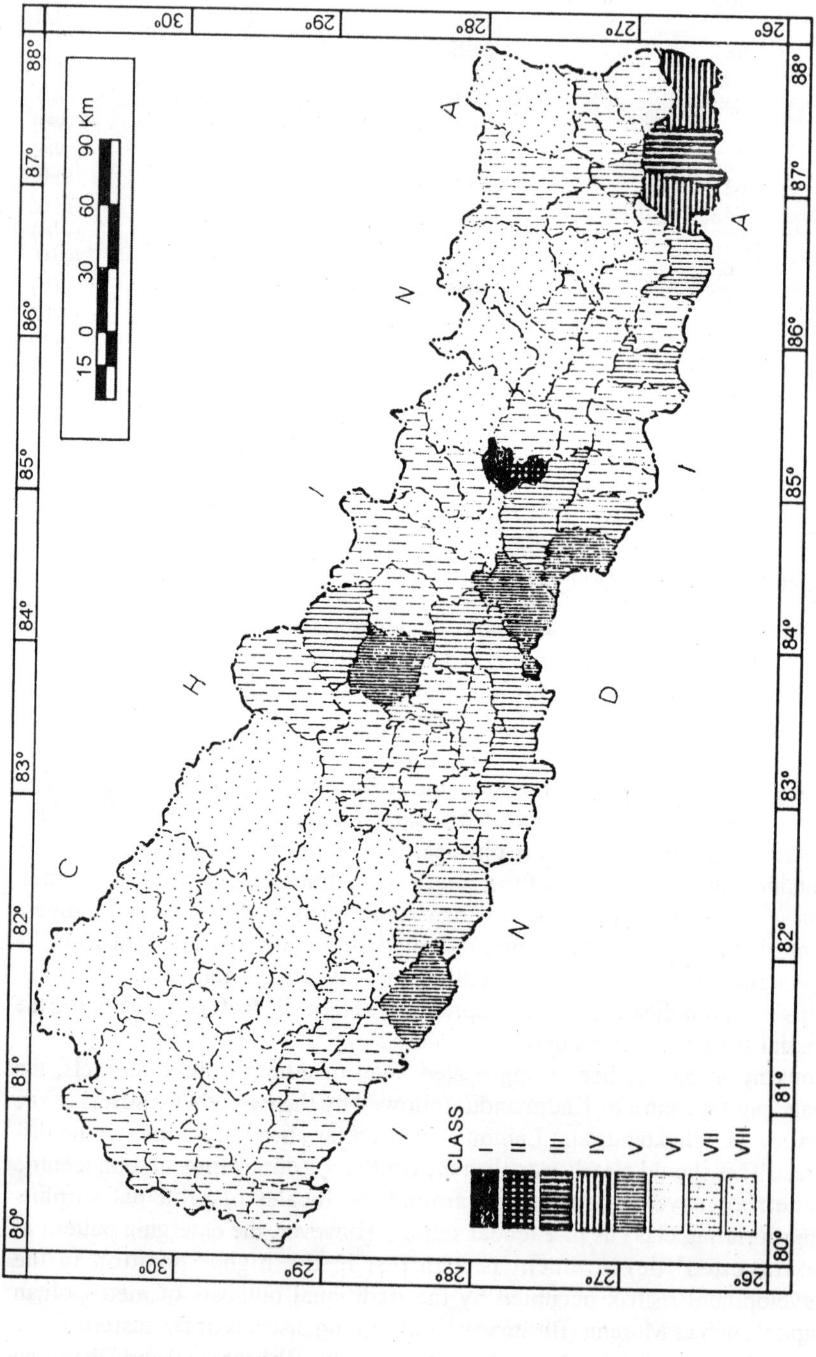

Fig. 5.10 Composites Levels of Development.

(Janakpur). The sudden cataputting of Kaski (Pokhara) in central Hill and Dhankuta (Dhankuta) in eastern Hill can also be explained in terms of their newly acquired status of outposts at the head of roads projecting into the hinterland. Moreover, in view of the significant overlapping of locales of internal bureaucratic authority and external mercantile interests, also abated by superior natural attributes, all these factors cumulatively can be envisaged as having exercised causal impact in the spatial differentiation of a transitional, pre-capitalist economy.

A time-series analysis with the inclusion of more spaceforming variables would have provided further confirmation of the causal relations in the observed dichotomous spatial structure of underdevelopment of Nepal marked by extreme polarisation at one end and equally extreme spatial non-differentiation at the other end. But on the basis of these fragmentary observations subsumed under a consistent theoretical frame, it can be safely generalised that spatial unevenness in development/underdevelopment in Nepal is a function of 'conservation' of pre-capitalist monopolistic structures, on the one hand, and uneven development within and penetration from without of capitalism, on the other. However, the non-differentiating (or disarticulating) tendency of pre-capitalist structures seem to be having an upper hand in the countrywide plane.

5.6 CONCLUSIONS

- The evolution of spatial organisation in Nepal has tended to follow the pattern of colonised countries marked by gradual extrovertedness, though at a slower pace and in a more guarded manner because of lack of direct colonial experience.
- Territorial population dynamics should be seen as a concrete manifestation of inherent socio-spatial process.
- Spatial configuration of inter-censal population growth rate reveals that the dynamics of population growth in more conditioned by the possibility of horizontal spread of population to 'colonisation frontiers' than by vertical shifts within the work force. Thus the nature of spatial spread and growth of population in Nepal is essentially 'conservative' and not as significant in redesigning the spatial form.
- Movement of population is directed more towards outside the country than within. The absolute volume of total internally mobile population is quite low, reflecting upon the low level of socio-spatial differentiation.
- The pattern of net inter-regional migration of population over time conclusively establishes an increasingly uneven structuration of space heavily tilted towards the south, i.e. Terai. The dominant currents of population flows are invariably oriented from Mountain-Hill to Inner Terai-Terai, that too within the same hydrographic (vertical) zone, and there is negligible horizontal movement within the same physico-ecological zone.

- Rurality is the hallmark of organisation of space in Nepal. Significant inter-regional variability in the forms of rural settlements, e.g. dispersed in Hill and nucleated in Terai, and the pattern of their spatial distribution, e.g. random in Hill and more uniform in Terai, is not only a function of natural differentials of territorial zones but both a subject and object of social organisation of production. In general, the form and spatial distribution of settlements is seen to be highly inefficient.
- An overwhelming proportion of settlements have a very small average population-size. There is a very low differentiation of size-class structure of settlements, except in Kathmandu Valley, thus reflecting upon the low economic differentiation of society. Consequently the 'average settlement size index,' or the mean expected size of the settlement in a region, is found very low for all the territorial zones, except the Kathmandu Valley, whose primacy is quite pronounced.
- Spatial distribution of growth rates of settlements are found very erratic, thus reflecting upon the transitional nature of the society. Whereas settlements along newly constructed highways, at break-of-bulk points and encompassing trading outposts along the Terai border with India have shown highest growth ratios, prominent settlements of Mountain are seen actually depopulated in the wake of the decline in economic interactions with Tibet.
- There is very low differentiation and articulation of functional hierarchy of settlements. Not only are the number of central places per unit settlements a pathetic low, but their hierarchic distances are apprehended to be uneven, thus giving rise to dysfunctional settlement networks.
- In the absence of a well articulated national settlement system, separate aspatial or spatial sub-systems seem to be in operation simultaneously, e.g. a 'dendritic' market system and a polarised politico-administrative system.
- Not only is the general level of urbanisation very low but the *scale* of urbanisation, i.e. absolute size of urban population, is also not significant. There is extreme localisation of urbanism in Kathmandu Valley, the traditional seat of 'feudal urban agglomeration,' though there is a distinct and consistent shift in favour of Terai and Inner Terai.
- General growth rate of urban population is quite sluggish. Whereas the growth rates of larger and older urban places are marginal some of the smaller and older urban places have actually declined. This bears a strong resemblence to the pattern of urban atrophy and de-urbanisation seen in the aftermath of colonial conquest of a society. Moreover, the growth of urban population is seen mostly due to natural growth rather than from migration.
- Even if the hierarchical structuring of urban places does not appear marked at the absolute level because of small number of places, the top-heavy structure is quite pronounced when viewed at the relative level.
- The rate of movement of towns across size-classes and variability in rankings is seen not significant, thereby further confirming general urban stagnation.

- Rank size distribution of urban places is found to be of 'primate' type than a 'log-normal' one. The nature of urbanisation thus resembles that of under developed societies.
- The economic base of urban places is found to be very weak with about 33% of the total population still engaged in primary-production and more than 50% in 'circulation' activities. Thus the pattern of urbanisation resembles more to a medieval-feudal agglomeration of' 'half-urban half-rural' character, than one of 'hyper-urbanisation' or 'pseudo-urbanisation' encountered today in other underdeveloped countries. The urbanisation process is seen essentially retarded and thwarted, the urban places are seen to be primarily locales of parasitic activities of circulation and consumption of surplus values and the general articulation of social process is found leading to "ruralization of the city" rather than to "urbanization of the countryside".
- The sequence of evolution and the current pattern of spatial linkages in Nepal show heavy outward orientation (extra-verted) as in a colonial setting, on the one hand, and equally heavy convergence towards the capital centre (mono-centred) as in an 'Asiatic-feudal' setting, on the other.
- Both natural and historical specificities of Nepal, i.e. extreme physiographic diversities and absence of a direct colonial experience and late integration to metropolitan economy, seem to have made the spatial linkages more ill-developed universally than developed unevenly. Still the disparity in distribution is quite glaring for a low overall development of the transportation linkages.
- In terms of inter-regional direct connectivity and highest share of traffic to Kathmandu Valley, orientation of linkages and flows predominantly in north-south direction, greater linkages and interactions of Terai with India. The composite nature of spatial integration is thus seen to be clearly marked by the apparently contradictory scenario of excessive polarisation around the capital city, on the one hand, and outward-orientation towards India along a north-south dendrite stretching from Mountain to Terai on the other. This may be cited as typical mode of spatial integration' in a semi-feudal, semi-/ neo-colonial society.
- The spatial structure of development/underdevelopment to be generalised from spatial differentiation of composite levels of development shows on the one hand a dichotomous structure marked by extereme polarisation around the traditional state capital of Kathmandu and increasing polarisation around points of higher physical and economic integration with outside world (particularly India) and equally extreme spatial non-differentiation of the vast hinterland. Thus it can be generalised that spatial unevenness in development/underdevelopment in Nepal is a function of 'conservation' of pre-capitalist monopolistic structure and uneven development within and penetration from without of capitalism (of the mercantile form).

REFERENCES

1. Lappo, G.M. and Povovarov, Yu.L., "Settlement in the USSR", in Bourne, L.S. et. al. (ed.) (1984), *Urbanization* and *Settlement Systems: International Perspectives*, Oxford University Press, p. 335.
2. Valentey, D.I., "Introduction", in Valentey, D.I. (ed.) (1978), *The Theory of Population: Essays in Marxist Research*, Progress Publishers, Moscow, p. 10.
3. This should be the logical implication of Marx's well-known observation: "... in fact every special historical mode of production has its own special laws of population, historically valid within its limits alone "[Marx, K., *Capital*, Vol. I, Progress Publishers, Moscow (1978 edn.), p. 591].
4. Kovalev, S.A., "Population Geography", in Valentey (ed.), *op. cit.*, p. 100.
5. Pokshishevsky, V.V., "Population Distribution", in *Ibid*, p. 70.
6. As Pokshishevsky correctly points out, since the "geography of the consumer pole" of the process of social reproduction is also important in the distribution of population and its employment it would be more correct to speak in terms of 'social reproduction' [*Ibid.*, p. 71, Foot Note].
7. V.G. Davidovich cited in *Ibid.*, p. 72.
8. Lappo, *op. cit.*, p. 336.
9. This is defined by Alam as: "In a well-developed and functionally integrated hierarchy of settlements the number of settlements increases and inter-settlement distances tend to decline regularly from the higher to the lower levels of hierarchy" ["The National Settlement System of India", in Bourne, L.S., et. al. (ed.), *op. cit.*, p. 468].
10. For example, the settlement system in deemed to be distorted if : "(1) the distribution is marked by a significant clustering of large-sized settlements in pockets or corridors of development, (2) Such settlements are disproportionately more numerous, and (3) the inter-settlements distance range of such settlements is much less when compared to the settlements in lower size range" [*Ibid.*, p. 470].
11 Marx, K. and Engels, F., "The City, the Division of Labour, and the Emergence of Capitalism", in Abu-Lughed, J. and Hay, R. (ed.) (1979), *Third World Urbanization*, Methuen, New York (Reprinted), p. 22.
12. See, among others, McGee, T.G. (1971), *The Urbanisation Process in the Third World*, G. Bell and Sons, London: Habeeb, A. (1979), *Characteristics and Processes of Urbanisation in Colonial India: A Case Study of Calcutta and its Hinterland (1850–192)* (unpublished Ph.D. Dissertation), CSRD/SSS/JNU, New Delhi.
13. For a concise review of the debate spanning different schools of thought, see Habeeb, *op. cit.*, pp. 4–11.
14. Raza, M., "Foreword", in Premi, M.K. (1980), *Urban Out Migration: A Study of its Nature, Causes and Consequences*, Sterling Publishers Pvt. Ltd., New Delhi, p. vii.
15. As Marx observes:

    "The history of classical antiquity is the history of cities, but the cities founded on landed property and on agriculture; Asiatic history is a kind of indifferent unity of town and countryside (the really large cities must be regarded here merely as royal camps as works of artifice... erected over the economic construction proper); the Middle Ages (Germanic period) begins with land as the seat of history, whose further development then moves forward in the contradiction between town and countryside; the modern [age] is the urbanization of the countryside, not ruralization of the city as in antiquity" [Marx, K. (1977a), *Grundrisse*, Penguin Books, Harmendsworth, p. 479].

16. Harvey, D. (1973), *Social Justice and the City*, Edward Arnold, London (1976 edn.), p. 232.
17. *Ibid*, p. 258.
18. Mabogunge, A.L. (1980), *The Development Proces: A Spatial Perspective*, Hutchinson, London, p. 61.
19. Marx calls the means of transport and communication as "physical conditions of exchange" [Marx. (1977a), *op. cit.*, p. 524].
20. See, Marx, K. (1977b), *Capital*, Vol. II, Progress Publishers, Moscow, and Harvey, D. (1975), "The Geography of Capitalist Accumulation: A Reconstruction of the Marxian Theory", in Peet, R. (ed.) (1977), *Radical Geography: Alternatives Viewpoint on Contemporary Social Issues*, Marroufa Press, Chicago.
21. Marx (1977a), *op. cit.*, p. 539.
22. On the basis of the study of a number of underdeveloped countries of Africa, Asia and Latin America having sea ports and with a direct colonial experience, Taaffe, Morrill and Gould have proposed a four phase sequence of development of transport networks. In the *first*, pre-colonial phase, each small port has a small trading hinterland with which it is linked by short and inconsequential routeways. The *second* phase coincides with the period of colonial rule and begins with the emergence of the first major penetration lines from the sea coast to the interior. It is marked by the differential growth of coastal ports and the enhancement of the economic importance of the inland transportation terminals. The penetration lines are motivated by the needs to connect the colonial headquarters with interior areas for political and military control and to tap areas of exploitable minerals and export-oriented agricultural production. The *third* phase is marked by the greater emphasis on lateral interconnections based on feeder routes to expand tributary areas. Theoretically the process should continue until all the ports, interior centers and major intermediate nodes are linked. The *fourth* phase is marked by an emphasis on high priority linkages until a fairly complete and coherent network of routes has emerged. A new process of concentration, similar to that noticed in the second phase, begins to take place. [Taaffe, E.J., Morrill, R.L., and Gould, P.R., (1963), "Transport expansion in underdeveloped countries: a comparative analysis" *Geographical Review*, Vol. 53, No. 4, pp. 503–29].
23. For example, previously extensively cultivated Inner Terai areas of present day Chitwan and Makavanpur were allowed to revert to a natural state of thick, malerial forests after 1816 to block the routes of possible invasion of Kathmandu Valley. [Oldfield, H.A. (1880), *Sketches from Nepal*, Vol. I, Allen, London, p. 56].
24. Poffenberger, M. (1980), *Patterns of Change in the Nepal Himalaya*, Macmillan, Delhi, p. 39.
25. See, Regmi, M.C. (1971), *A Study in Nepali Economic History 1768 –1846*, Manjushri Publishing House, New Delhi: Caplan, L. (1970), *Land and Social Change in East Nepal: A Study of Hindu Tribal Relations*, Routledge and Kegan Paul, London: Kansakar, V.B.S. (1973–74). "History of Population Migration in Nepal", in *The Himalayan Review*, Vol. VI, No. 5–6, Nepal Geographical Society, Kathmandu; Kansakar, V.B.S. (1974), *Population Change in Nepal: A Study of Mobility During 1911–61.* (Unpublished Ph.D. Dissertation), Department of Geography, Patna University; Poffenberger, *op. cit.*; Dahal, D.R. (1983), "Economic Development through Indigenous Means: A case of Indian Migration in the Nepal terai", in *Contribution to Napalese Studies*,Vol. II, No. 1, CNAS, Kathmandu, December; among others, for the documentation of this migratory process. However, their analysis of

the process along the 'ecological niche' hypothesis will have to be replaced by a more scientific historico-materialist approach of seeing it as the composite result of both the natural and social factors.

26. A total of 200,000 Napalese soldiers, i.e. 20% of total economically active population, were enlisted for the 1st World War, out of which at least 20,000 were killed. [Peet, R.C. (1978), *Migration, Culture and Community: A Case Study from Rural Nepal* (Ph.D. Dissertation, Microfilmed), Columbia University, U.S.A., p. 442].
27. Fairly reliable accounts of Chinese traveler Wuan Chuwan, who visited, the Valley in 7th century A.D., substantiate a developed 'urban' culture based on craft production and trade at the time in the Valley. Other not very authentic accounts based on chronicles of later years give the date of foundation of the three major urban places as follows: Lalitpur–10th century B.C.; Kathmandu–6th century A.D.; and Bhaktapur–14th century A.D. [Kansakar (1974), *op. cit.*, p. 296].
28. Population sizes of the three urban places at the time of state unification in 1769 were given as: Lalitpur–24 thousand houses; Kathmandu–22 thousand houses; and Bhaktapur–12 thousand houses [Giuseppe, F. (1807), *An Account of the Kingdom of Nepal*, Asiatic Researches, Vol. II, Ch. XVII, pp. 310–11]. The estimates appear to be highly exaggerated when compared with the more reliable population figures of 30,000 each for Lalitpur and Bhaktapur in the second half of the 19th century as provided by Daniel Wright [Kansakar (1974), *op. cit.*, p. 297].
29. Regmi, M.C. (1984), *The State and Economic Surplus: Production, Trade Resource Mobilisation in 19th Century Nepal* (to be published), Kathmandu, p. 16.
30. Important settlements with predominantly export-import trading functions that sprung up or flourished in Nepal terai at the end of 19th and beginning of 20th century were, from east and west: Bhadrapur, Biratnagar, Janakpur, Birgunj, Bhairahawa, Nepalgunj and Dhangadi, their counterpart centers in the Indian side of the border with the rail heads being: Galgalia, Farbisganj–Jogbani, Jayanagar, Raxaul, Nautanwa, Rupadiya and Gaurifanta, respectively. [Dahal, *op. cit.*, p. 7–8]. For an extensive list of trade route and system of transport and trade registration stations along Nepal–India border from Darjeeling in east to Kumaon in west during the 19th century, see Sen, J. (1977), Indo–Nepal Trade in the Nineteenth century, Firma K.L.M. Private Ltd., Calcutta, Chapters 4 and 5.
31. The prominent centers along the foot-hills or Inner Terai, from east to west, are: Dharan, Lahan, Sindhulimarhi, Simara, Hetauda, Narayanghat, Butwal, Tulsipur and Surkhet [Kansakar (1974), *op. cit.*, p. 107].
32. This is amply evident from the alignments and sequences of construction of the modern transportation and communication networks in the country, which were as follows: installation of 22 km. ropeway from Matatirtha (Kathmadu Valley) to Dhursingh (near Bhimphedi) in 1927; completion of the construction of 42 km. all weather gravel road from Bhimphedi to Amlekhgunj and 47 km. railway from Amlekhgunj to Raxaul (India) by 1927; construction of second rail link between Jayanagar (India) and Janakpur in 1937 and its extension to Bijalpur (both in mid-eastern Terai) in 1938; extension of ropeway from Matatirtha to Teku (Kathmandu Valley) by 7.5 km. in 1947. (Shrestha, R.L. "Transport Sector—A Review", in Banskota, M. and Bista, N.K. (ed.) (1980), *Nepal's Economy—An Overview*, CEDA, Kathmandu.)
33. See Section 3.1.2 above.
34. See Salinas, P.W. "Mode of Production and Spatial Organisation in Pero, in Moulaert, F. and Salinas, P.W. (eds.) (1983), *Regional Analysis and the New International Division of Labour*, Kluwer Nijhoff, The Hague pp. 79–94.

34a. Karan and Jenkin noted way back in the late 1950s that: "Few parts of the world are more empty than the snow–covered ranges of northern Nepal; few parts are more crowded than the Kathmandu Valley..." [Karan P.P. and Jenkin, W.M. (1960), *Nepal: A Cultural and Physical Geography*, University of Kentucky Press, Lexington, P. 51]. The only difference since then and now is that the density in Kathmandu Valley has doubled and in Terai trebled.

35. See, Section 1.4 above.

36. For an account of the active involvement of Ford Foundation and other custodians of metropolitan capital in the malaria-eradication programme and clearance of Rapti valley for human occupation, see Mihaly, E.B. (1965). *Foreign Aid and Politics in Nepal: A Case Study*, Oxford University Press. London.

37. Population density with respect to the total geographical area is referred to as 'crude' density and that with respect to cultivable area as 'physiological' density [Clarke, J.I. (1965), *Population Geography*, Pergamon Press, Oxford, (1972 edn.), pp. 29–30]. We have slightly misappropriated the term 'physiological' for 'cultivated' area in the absence of desired information on 'cultivable' area.

38. The term 'population pressure' is used here in a relative and concrete sense of existing backward stage of social formation and not in the absolute and abstract sense of neo-Malthusians.

39. The annual population growth rates for Nepal during 1950–60, 1960–70 and 1970–80 respectively were 1.65, 2.10 and 2.20 as against the world average of 1.84, 1.99 and 1.88.

40. Bondestam, L. "The Political Ideology of Population control" in Alavi, H. and Shanin, T. (1982), *Introduction to the Sociology of 'Developing Societies'*, Macmillan, London, p. 254.

41. Footnote 3 above.

42. Zelinsky (1971), cited in Forbes, D.K. (1984), *The Geography of Underdevelopment*, Croom Helm, London. P. 143.

43. See *Ibid.*

44. For a terminological distinction and different politico-economic implications of 'circulation' (or 'circular migration') and 'migration' (or 'permanent migration') of population, see *Ibid*, pp. 162–63.

45. The same growth trend is expected to have continued in subsequent years and by 1971 the proportion of total long-term migrants was estimated be way over 5% of total population. [Rana, R.S.J.B. and Thapa, Y.S. "Population Migration: Nature and Scope", in Upadhyaya and Abuevu (1974), *op. cit.*, p. 45].

46. For a typology of population mobility at different stages of social development and with different socio-economic implications as provided by Peterson, see Mabogunje, *op. cit.*, p. 239.

47. A survey on migration of agriculture labour conducted in the mid-1970s revealed that the percentage of labour migrating within the country was 31.70, which is just double the proportion in 1961. [National Planning Commission Secretariat (1978), *A Survey of Employment, Income Distribution and Consumption Patterns in Nepal* (Summary Report, Vol. IV), HMG/N, Kathmandu p. 83.

48. Almost all the sketchy mentions of settlement pattern in a geographical study of Nepal from Karan and Jenkin (*op. cit.*) downwards are guilty of this analytical sterility.

49. Bose provides an account, with somewhat nature-deterministic flavour, of distribution of settlements over different altitudinal zones in Indian Himalayas, which should

hold more or less true for the corresponding altitudinal zones of Nepal as well. [Bose, S.C. (1972), *The Geography of the Himalaya*, National Book Trust, Delhi, p. 96–97].

50. The nearest neighbour index measures the deviation of any spatial pattern of distribution of points from randomness. The index R is calculated as the ratio of the actual mean distance between nearest neighbour point in a given area ($\overline{D}_O$) to the mean expected distance of random distribution of the same number of points in the same area ($\overline{D}_r$). O_r :

$$R = \frac{\overline{D}_O}{D_r} = \frac{\overline{D}_O}{\frac{1}{2}\sqrt{\frac{N}{A}}} = 2\,\overline{D}_O\sqrt{\frac{N}{A}}$$

where, N = Number of settlements;
A = Area of the place.

The ratio R ranges from O, when there is maximum aggregation of all the points at one location, through 1 which represents a random distribution up to 2.15 which represent even distribution. [Mahmood, A (1977), *Statistical Methods in Geographical Studies*, Rajesh Publications, New Delhi, p. 72–73.]

51. See Blaikie, P., et. al. (1980), *Nepal in Crisis: Growth and Stagnation at the Periphery*, Oxford University Press, Delhi.

52. A more accurate appraisal of the absolute degree of crude settlement density may be obtained by multiplying the given values by the number of hamlets proximated by the number of 'wards' in each enumeration unit of a 'panchayat', i.e. nine wards in each panchayat.

53. See, footnote 50 above.

54. The index has been defined as

$S_j = U_j\,(C_j^2+1)$, where S_j = average size index for *j*th region.
U_j = mean size of the settlement in the *j*th region,
C_j = Coefficient of variation of settlement size.

[See Kundu, A. (1980), *Measurement of Urban Processes: A Study in Regionalisation*, Popular Prakashan, Mumbai, p. 36.] In fact the index can be written as

$$S_j = \frac{\sum_{i=1}^{n} U_j^2}{\sum_{i=1}^{n} U_j^1}$$ where U_{ij} = Population of the *i*th settlement in the *j*th region, and interpreted as the expected value of the size of the settlement for the given population. Whereas Kundu has considered only urban population both in the numerator and denominator to construct average town size index and interpret as the expected value of the size of the town for the urban population. [*Ibid*], Habeeb, after Arriaga, has used the index to measure degree (level) of urbanization and interpret as the expected value of the size of the cities for the given region by taking urban population in the numerator and total population in the denominator. [Habeeb, *op. cit.*, p. 54].

55. Other studies have also established the identical pattern of stagnation of off-road settlements and high growth of on-road ones. To quote Blaikie et. al. in this context: "Centres such as Walling, Armadi, Aryabhanjyang, Majuwa, Khaireni, Dumre, and Bimalnagar all show recent and rapid growth, having had little sign of significant

commercial activity before the building of the roads which pass through them... There is sufficient evidence to show that the rate of growth of the small, new urban centers on the road is significantly greater than that of centers off the road, of whatever size; there is also a strong indication that larger centers on the road have grown at a greater rate than the larger centers off the road". [Blaikie et al. *op. cit.*, p. 133].

56. For a critique of Chirstaller–Losch Theory of Central places from a historic-materialist position, See Saushkin, Yu.G. (1980), *Economic Geography: Theory and Methods*, Progress Publishers, Moscow.
57. For the definition and operational significance of 'hierarchic distance', see Kundu, *op. cit.*, p. 38. Though he defines the measure in the context of system of urban settlements, it should be relevant for the system of settlement as a whole.
58. See Shrestha, C.B. (1973–74), "The System of Central Places in the Arniko Rajmarga Area of Nepal", in *The Himalayan Review*, Vol. VI, No. 5–6, Nepal Geographical Society, Kathmandu.
59. Johnson, E.A.J. (1971), *The Organisation of Space in Developing Countries*, Harvard University Press, Cambridge, p. 86.
60. Habeeb, *op. cit.*, p. 18.
61. Since Arriaga's method of measuring the degree (level) of urbanisation by obtaining the average of the size of cities where the urban population resides is implicit in our "average settlement size index" constructed earlier, which shall again be utilized to analyse interdependencies between different spatio-social processes in the later section, we have sought to use here the simple index of the ratio of total urban to only rural (not as conventionally both urban and rural) population in the region, for the purpose, as this would show greater disparity in space besides having other conceptual advantages. [See Kundu, *op. cit.*, p. 34].
62. For a historical appraisal of the process in the classic case of colonial India, see Habeeb, *op. cit.*
63. See Alam, *op. cit.*, among others.
64. High growth followed by a fast decline seems to be a general rule for new urban centers in underdeveloped countries. For example, see Davidovich, F., "Brazilian Urban Settlement," in Bourne et. al. *op. cit.*, p. 429.
65. The pattern becomes all the more glaring when the newly designated town panchayats after 1971 are taken into consideration; namely, Dhankuta, at the head of newly built Dharan–Dhankuta road; Lahan, along East-West highway; Bharatpur, at the T–junction of east-west and north-south highways, Tribhuvannagar and Birendranagar, at break-of-bulk points between plains and Hills; Dhangadi and Mahendranagar, in the literal 'Naya Muluk' (i.e. new country) of Western Terai and along the Indian border.
66. The growth rates would be much lower if only the growth rates of the real 'urban' component of the population are considered by discounting the growth due to mere change in the designation of settlements from 'rural' to 'urban' in the successive censuses.
67. See, McGee, *op. cit.*, among others.
68. See Section 5.1.1 above.
69. Arriaga's study of urban population growth in Chile, Mexico and Venezuela showed that natural increase accounted for 58–70% of urban population growth. See Mabogunje, *op. cit.*
70. See McGee, *op. cit.*
71. For a concise review of theoretical generalizations on patterns of rank-size relationships of urban places, see Berry, B.J.L., "City Size and Economic Development", in

Jakobson, L. and Prakash, V. (eds.) (1971), *Urbanization and National Development*, Sage Publications, Beverly Hill, and, for empirical studies of the same in different countries, Bourne et. al. *op. cit.*, An excellent review of the general theory of urban primacy and an original exposition of the theory of 'colonial primacy' is available in Habeeb, *op. cit.*

72. The rank-size distribution of a system of urban places is said to be "log-normal" if, when logarithm of rank after the urban places are arrayed in decreasing order of size, a linearity is obtained, and is regarded as normal pattern when there are distinct but not overwhelmingly dominant first-order cities. This is also referred to as simple "rank-size distribution". Where the largest city has overwhelming domination over the whole system or where the actual population of the largest city exceeds the expected from the straight-line relationship, a condition of "primary" is said to exist. And when the settlement system is decentralized or focused around two or more major cities, a "decentralized or polynucleated" distribution is said to prevail. [See Berry, *op. cit.*, and Alam, *op.*, *cit.*]
73. Alam on the basis of three city index of primary for all the states of India concludes that primacy is pronounced (i) in states with expatriate settlement, (ii) in states with a strong feudal background and (iii) in peripheral states where all development activities are concentrated in a single city [Alam, *op. cit.*, p. 462].
74. See historical accounts of pattern and quality of urbanization in different countries like USSR, Poland, India, in Bourne et al., *op. cit.*
75. See footnote 15 above.
76. See footnote 22 above.
77. See, for example, Mabogunje, *op. cit.*, p. 289–90.
78. Mihaly has provided interesting exposures of politico-strategic motivations and behind-the-scene intrigues indulged in by different capitalist-imperialist powers, particularly India and the U.S.A., while undertaking the construction of transport networks in Nepal. To quote him:
"The road from Kathmandu to Raxaul... not only opened the Kathmandu market to trade with India, but it facilitated the defence of Kathmandu by the Indian Military. Gaucher airport, then only airfield in Nepal, made possible quick and reasonably reliable travel from Delhi, Calcutta, and Patna to Kathmandu. The runway was only long enough for Dakota aircraft and was not designed for expansion which would permit larger aircraft coming from other countries (oı over the mountains) to land. Such an expansion required the construction of an entirely new runway—a project which was not taken up for a decade and then only by the United States" [Mihaly, *op. cit.*, p. 46–47].
Further: "Both India and the United States had turned down Napalese requests to undertake it [i.e. a survey for an east-west road], both arguing that a road across Nepal, was not yet an economic proposition. India, moreover was not eager to assist in a project which would lead to the reduction of Nepal's dependence on India. The road would offer a means of traversing Nepal without entering India and utilizing the Indian road or rail system" (*Ibid.*, pp. 99–100].
79. To quote Blaikie et. al. in this context:
"The less on provided by the events of 1950–1, when the Ranas-largely through their inability to move troops swiftly within the country–were unable to put down armed insurrection within Nepal, and their dependence on the operation of the Indian railways for east-west communications, were not lost on the king. Indeed, we would

argue that considerations of internal security provide a major underlying motive for the governments concern with the development of a modern transport system, although the objectives of economic development and political unity are frequently invoked". [Blaikie *et. al. op. cit.*, 4].

80. A plethora of studies to gauze the 'impact' of different roads have been conducted to date. Despite the analytical sterility of many of these studies they provide important empirical information. For a review of these works see Shrestha, R.L. (1980), *Impact of Kathmandu Raxaul Highway (Tribhuban Rajmarg) on Nepalese Economy (1956–1975)*, G.S. Agarwal, Kathmandu.
81. Even as late as 1982/83, 25 of the total 75 districts (13 out of 15 in Mountain and 12 out of 33 in Hill) with did not have any kind of motorable road. Another 14 (1 in Mountain, 10 in Hill, 2 in Inner Terai and 1 in Terai) had only unpaved/seasonal road connections. [Derived from *Nepal Road Statistics, 1983.*]
82. Compared against the world average of 10 km. of road length per 100 sq. km. of geographical area (for 1980), the corresponding value for Nepal, i.e. 3.807 km. per 100 sq. km. (for 1983), is found to be nearly three times less. [Bajracharya, B.B. and Shrestha, C.B. (1981), *Transport and Communication Linkages in Nepal*, CEDA, Kathmandu, p. 28.]
83. Mabogunje, *op. cit.*, p. 293.
84. Bajracharya and Shrestha, *op. cit.*, p. 44.
85. Ender, G.P. (1980), *The Development of Road Transportation in Nepal and its Relationship to Agriculture Development* (Unpublished Ph.D. Dissertation), Cornell University, Ithaca, p. 105.
86. Kundu, *op. cit.*, p. 37.
87. Adapted from Bajracharya and Shrestha, *op. cit.*
88. The *beta* index measures the ratio of the number of road links popularly written as edges(e) to the number of urban settlements called vertices (v). The *gama* index measures the proportion of observed direct links to the number of maximum possible direct links among a set of urban settlements. The *alpha* index measures circuits in a network system. A circuit refers to a series of road links among towns all of which can be approached without retracing. As a set of urban settlements is connected by more direct routes the values of these three indices increase. [Hagget, P. (1969), *Location Analysis in Human Geography*, Edward Arnold, London, pp. 236–240.] Kundu also has used an index resembling *beta* index to measure connectivity of urban nodes, which he terms as Average Connectivity Index (*op. cit.*, p. 37).
89. One study has estimated the total traffic flow to or from Kathmandu to be still higher, or about 40% of total travel (Ender, *op. cit.*, p. 83).
90. Ender, after a survey of traffic movements along prominent road routes and between selected settlement nodes in Nepal, has found an inverse relationship between trip lengths and number of trips, and has rightly concluded it to be the evidence of weak inter-regional linkage (*ibid*, pp. 78–79).
91. *Ibid*, pp. 94–97.
92. See Bajracharya and Shrestha, *op. cit.*

6 Summary of Findings and Conclusions

The important findings of this study and conclusions arisen therefrom may be summarised as follows:

1. Social development should be seen as a process triggered by the contradictions between forces and relations of production in a given social formation. Development and underdevelopment may be considered antithetical to each other in that, whereas 'development' within a given social formation would be full realisation of productive potentials of the society or transformation to higher social formation, 'underdevelopment' would be the opposite condition of non-realisation of full potential of development and/or blockage to transformation to higher formations under the cumulative impacts of prevailing endogenous and exogenous conditions.
2. Space should not be seen as 'external' to but as immanent in the development process such that one may define development as a combined' socio-spatial process'. Within the implied dialectic of the relation between spatial and social processes, spatial formation may be viewed as the *manifestation of* and to a lesser degree a *causal factor in* the particular social formation. Consequently the spatial structure of a particular social formation may be located in the production and reproduction logic of the given formation.
3. The current social and spatial structure of development/underdevelopment of Nepal should be viewed in the light of its peculiar historical and natural spacificities including; late and induced, and hence uneven 'feudalisation' under the aegis of a strong centralised state power; no direct colonial but only semi-colonial integration with the metropolitan power which is still continuing in a new guise; extreme physiographic diversities and natural barriers to socialisation of means of production in large parts of the country constituting of Hill and Mountain; etc.
4. The prevailing structure of the Nepalese economy is seen characterised by very low development of the productive forces as manifested in negligible

sectoral differentiation with the predominance of the primary production sector. Also, there are increasing signs of proliferation of circulation capital and growing articulation of the economy with the metropolitan capitalist economy. The social and spatial structure of development/underdevelopment should, therefore, be analysed in terms of the characteristics and processes of the dominant sectors of the economy both separately and cumulatively.

5. Very low development of productive forces in the agriculture sector is reflected in overwhelming domination of traditional factors of production like land and human and animal labour in total factor inputs. Marked unevenness in the spatial distribution of natural factors of production is compounded by extreme spatial disparateness in the use of modern inputs.
6. The backward and retarded state of agriculture is also manifest in low cropping intensity, predominance of subsistence (cereal) crops in total area and value of production, sluggish growth rate of crop output, declining food surplus (or aggravating food deficit), etc. The minimal 'cash crop' production is highly centralised in the more extravertedly integrated Terai; but not only is its growth rate extremely sluggish but some important export-oriented crash crops like jute is seen declining in the absolute sense. The decline of the few industrial crops like tobacco points towards the lack of required impulses from other sectors of the economy (i.e. industry) for agricultural development.
7. The yield rates of crops, or land productivity, are found not only low but are seen consistently declining over time. Whereas gross land productivity declines from the more depressed Mountain-Hill to Terai, net land productivity and labour productivity vary the other way round; thus giving currency to the Marxist explanation of apparent 'superiority' of small-scale peasant agriculture as due to 'overwork' and 'underconsumption' by the hapless peasants. The spatial differentiation of the holistic picture of the 'health' of the agriculture sector as obtained by cross-classification of spatial distribution of land and labour productivities reveal that only the eastern Terai and Kathmandu Valley, the traditional areas of centralisation of merchant-bureaucratic and industrial capital, are 'healthy' in the midst of chronic morbidity of the vast hinterland.
8. Spatial variations in gross output per-cultivated hectare are more due to the differences in the multiplication of cropping or horizontal expansion of gross cropped area than due to change in yield rates of crops. More than three-fourths of the marginal increase in gross agricultural output is found accounted for by area increase and an insignificant share of less than 2% by yield increase. Modern inputs are seen to have exercised negligible influence in the overall structuration of the agriculture sector, except for their catalytic role in aggravating social disparateness.
9. The backward and retrograde relations of production in agriculture is found reflected in the extremely low and declining average size of land-holding per farm house-hold and pre-ponderence of 'owner-cultivator' subsistence peasantry amidst considerable disparity in the social distribution of vital means

of production-land. The stagnant structure is also manifest in the negligible change in the distribution pattern of land-holding even in a decade marked by the much published official 'land reform' programme, except for the rise in fragmentation of land-holdings. The low degrees of social differentiation accompanied by pre-ponderence of 'owner-cultivator' households as well as the lowest average size of holding to be found in the traditional habitation zone of central east-west hilly spine of the country, may be cited as the typical example of social retardation operationalized through the perpetuation of a marginalized peasantry.

10. Pre-capitalist ground-rent realised primarily through the system of share-cropping constitutes the principal form of appropriation of social surplus in the agriculture sector. However, a number of historical and natural specificities of different parts of the country do make the characterisation of different rented tenure according to premedited concepts not as simple. In the territorial dimensions, areas of better agro-climatic conditions (i.e. Terai, Kathmandu Valley and Inner Terai) and those away from the central state authority (i.e. eastern and western zones) exhibit higher degree of 'feudalisation' than the rest; thus complying with the Marxist theoretical position on the conditions of development of feudalism and with the historical sequence of evolution of agrarian process in Nepal.
11. Of the auxiliary forms of appropriation of social surplus from the agriculture sector such as state taxation, mercantile exploitation and usury practices, the last form is found widespread in both space and time frame and quite retrograde in character.
12. Various types of servile attached-labour system are known to prevail as the mode of extraction of surplus labour from the direct producer other than the small tenant-cultivator. Moreover, rampant underemployment and seasonal out-migration has slackened the process of peasant differentiation and perpetuated the archaic social relations of production. In view of greater polarisation of classes and greater articulation of social contradictions, Terai and Inner Terai logically appear to be more ripened for restructuring of social organisation of production in agriculture.
13. The aggregate agrarian process in Nepal is found characterised by low technical level of production, pre-capitalist (or semi-feudal) relations of production, disarticulation with other sectors of the economy, particularly industry, and a general state of stagnation and retardation. In the territorial dimension it is manifested in the marginally differentiated vast hinterland of Hill and Mountain surrounded by areas of 'extraverted development' along Terai, Inner Terai and Kathmandu Valley.
14. During the 19th century Nepal had attained a fairly high state of craft production, which started declining with the mass influx of British-India factory made goods since the beginning of the 20th century. Apart from the adverse impact of exogenous factors, retrograde internal social structure dominated by a heavily centralised state was not conducive for primitive

accumulation and development of industrial capitalism. Advent of modern manufacturing, heralded by the economic exigencies of World War II, ushered in an extroverted industrial process from the very beginning and it could not develop firm endogenous roots.

15. Despite the general historical decline of industrial production since the 1920s, there is found a persistence of a significant degree of indigenous proto-industry and considerable spatial variations in the destruction and restructuration of the 'natural economy'. Areas of absolute backwardness but resistant to change and areas of extroverted development can be seen to be emerging, the process depending upon the nature of integration to outside economy and internal tenacity.
16. A generalised pattern of chronically anemic and inverted industrial structure is reflected in excessively higher share of elementary processing consisting of agro-based and forest-based industries and a negligible share of production goods industries. Overall low level of industrial production in the country is characterised by a high degree of its localisation in Terai (specially far-eastern Terai) and Kathmandu Valley.
17. There has been a deceleration of growth rates in all the attributes of industrial production except fixed capital, since the beginning of seventies. Moreover, 'intermediate' goods industries have lower growth rates than consumer goods industries, thereby confirming continued intra-sectoral disarticulation. One also observes a greater deceleration of durable consumer goods industries which illustrates the limitation of industrialisation strategy geared to the demands of a narrow upper strata of the population. In the spatial dimension, the areas of higher level of production exhibit slower growth rates. These signs of premature monopolisation seem to have compelled some dispersion (but not significant) of industries towards the more backward Hill and Mountain zones.
18. Industrial productivity in the country is not only low at the absolute aggregate level, but there are wide intra-sectoral and intra-territorial variations in them indicating high social and spatial disarticulation.
19. General level of capital intensity is very low and is not increasing at satisfactory rate. The low level of technology in use is reflected in low per-capita consumption of electricity and low share of technical labour to total labour.
20. Industrial production is primarily organised for 'private' appropriation of social surplus. The few state-owned units of 'production goods' industries seem to be merely preparing grounds for the spread of the private sector. Significant degree of premature monopolisation is observed in the form of ownership of most of the industries by few dominant social groups and families, particularly people of Indian origin or Indian nationals.
21. The prevalence of a substantial proportion of 'unpaid family labour' engaged in manufacturing adequately demonstrates the primitive nature of organisation of production. Undissolved ties of the industrial labour with agricultural production can be said to account for the backward relations of production

in the industrial sector. The backward nature of relations of production is also characterised by maximisation of 'absolute' surplus value as against the 'relative' surplus value, or in Marx's words 'formal subsumption of labour under capital' as against 'real subsumption of labour under capital'.

22. External dependence for both technological and raw material inputs in industries is seen to have increased over time. The existing strategy of pseudo-industrialisation can be seen to have oscillated between the two poles of 'import substitution' (i.e. geared to the 'home market') or 'export promotion' (i.e. geared to the external market industrialisation. But the primarily 'home market'-based industrialisation seems to be confronted with two problems; firstly, constriction of the internal market due to gross social inequality and low purchasing power of the masses; and secondly, preemption of the existing internal market (mostly composed of the minority upper classes) by exogenous capital.
23. The apparently contradictory *lack of credibility* for external finance and *over-dependence* on the same is evident in different branches of industry and territorial zones of industrial location. Private Indian capital has played a significant role in the 'industrialisation' of the country, but the absolute size of capital investment for productive purposes is not big. There is virtually no private 'foreign' investment (i.e. other than from India) in the industrial sector.
24. The aggregate condition of industrial retardation can be further understood from the extremely low level of capacity utilization and high rate of temporary closure of industrial units.
25. High positive correlation of agricultural development with industrial development in the country reflects a strong link between the agrarian and the industrial processes. But this may merely be an expression of predomination of elementary agro-processing activities in the manufacturing sector and not that of articulation of sectoral interdependence found in higher stages of economic development.
26. In the territorial dimension, the prevailing condition of the industrial sector is manifested in the appearance of isolated points of industrial localisation along points of superior articulation with the outside economies or at the traditional seat of state authority in the midst of a vast indigent hinterland, thus giving rise to and 'extraverted' and 'disarticulated' industrial spatial structure.
27. General level of marketisation of the indigenous economy is quite low. The economy is also not marked by self-sufficiency or autarchy, as is evident from the significant amount of cash expenditure on subsistence goods not locally produced.
28. The commodity structure of commerce is largely direct consumption oriented and divorced from the indigenous production process.
29. The social relations of exchange is marked by primitiveness as reflected in predominance of retailing and small-scale operations, circulation of use values rather than exchange-values, etc. On the other hand there is strong tendency

of commercial monopolisation in terms of ownership by dominant mercantile groups. The 'comprador' character of merchant capital is also well manifested.

30. The general pattern of marketed commodity flows is predominantly in the north-south territorial dimension, with a net flow of goods from south to north. There is a virtually non-existent or negligible flow in the east-west territorial dimension. Whereas the primacy of Kathmandu in terms of inter-regional commercial linkages is well-articulated, the Terai areas have greater linkages and commercial exchanges with India than with other territorial zones within the country. The commodity structure of inter-regional trade reveals a pattern of net flow of value from north to south in a relation of 'unequal exchange'.
31. The spatial organisation of marketing is marked by a heavy centralisation of higher order market places in Kathmandu Valley and in Terai just across the Indian border and a total absence of them in the larger parts of the country. The spatial structure of commerce is, thus, simultaneously marked by extreme dysfunctionality, internal fragmentation (disarticulation) and outward-orientation.
32. The dependence of economy on foreign trade is increasing with time. The retrograde nature of the process is not only marked by low export/import ratio but also by the increasing volume of imports and declining exports.
33. The apparent slackening of trade dependence on India is illusory. This is so not only because almost half of total external trade is still transacted with India but the apparent reduction is brought out by reduction of exports rather than of imports. Diversification of trade to countries other than India has led to direct integration of the economy with more powerful centres of metropolitan capital and has aggravated the relations of external dependence.
34. The characteristic features of 'unequal exchange' between exports of primary products and imports of finished products as seen in the case of underdeveloped economies in general are not only present in acute scale, but the exchange relations are further marred by increasing imports of consumption oriented than production oriented manufactures. The primacy of few commodities like jute and rice in total value of exports further confirms the typically underdeveloped structure of foreign trade in Nepal. Terms of trade with major partners are seen fluctuating violently and turning adverse in general.
35. The spatial distribution of export-import values clearly differentiate principal areas of 'production' (i.e. from where more export takes place) around eastern parts of country in general and Terai in particular and principal areas of 'consumption' (i.e. to which more import takes place) around central part of the country in general and Kathmandu Valley in particular. The essentially extractive nature of trade relations and excessive dependence on India for external economic interactions has given rise to a distorted spatial structure marked by centralisation of major trading nodes at principal 'gateway junctions' along the border of Terai with India.

36. Tourism in Nepal can be taken as a form of 'entrepot trade' where imported goods are re-exported albeit to foreign consumers within the country. The upper-class bias and heavily capital-intensive nature of development of tourism has resulted in a cancerous growth of economy little related to the average life of society and logically dependent on exogenous support.
37. Aided by both monopoly of nature and monopoly of merchant capital, with a decisive role of the latter, the social and spatial structure of tourism in Nepal is found to be highly centralised, dysfunctional and extraverted. Hence despite its fragile social roots, both in terms of scale and nature of development, tourism has acted as an additional mechanism of aggravation of underdevelopment of society.
38. Financial capital in general is still in a primitive stage of development but the size of institutionalised finance, or more particularly bank capital, is showing a rapid growth. It is seen abetting the general distortions of the structure of the economy by disproportionately strengthening the 'circulation' component of the economy internally and promoting unequal integration externally.
39. There is extreme spatial disparity in the distribution of bank capital particularly in favour of the mercantile and administrative centre of Kathmandu Valley. The analysis of credit/deposit ratios in the spatio-temporal frame reveals a general pattern of value transfer in the form of bank capital from the more retarded areas of Hill and Mountain to the relatively better off areas of Kathmandu Valley and Terai.
40. The evolution of financial integration of the economy to the metropolitan economy is following, with some exception of politico-strategic overtones, the same pattern of neo-colonial integration as seen in the case of other underdeveloped countries. But the integration is seen to be still at the initial stage and the degree of financial depredation as observed elsewhere is yet to be seen. External financial capital, mostly in the form of 'aid', is currently seen to have gone to prepare ground for later mercantile exploitation, and has generally accentuated the outward-orientation of the space economy.
41. The evolution of spatial organisation in Nepal has tended to follow the pattern of colonised countries towards gradual extrovertedness, but at a slower pace and in more guarded manner because of the absence of direct colonial experience and the attendant imperative of greater exploitation of resources.
42. Spatial configuration of inter-censal population growth rate reveals that the dynamics of population growth is more conditioned by the possibility of horizontal spread of population to 'colonisation frontiers' than by vertical shifts within the workforce. Thus the nature of spatial spread and growth of population in Nepal is essentially 'conservative' and not as significant in redesigning the spatial form. The pattern of net inter-regional migration of population over time demonstrates and increasingly uneven structuration of space heavily tilted towards the south, i.e. Terai.

43. Rurality is the hallmark of organisation of space in Nepal. The form and spatial distribution of settlements is seen to be highly inefficient. There is a very low differentiation of size-class structure of settlements, except in Kathmandu Valley, thus reflecting upon the low economic differentiation of society. Spatial distribution of growth rates of settlements are found very erratic indicating the transitional nature of society. Whereas settlements along newly constructed highways, at break-of-bulk points and encompassing trading outposts in Terai are growing very fast, prominent settlements of Mountain are seen actually depopulated. In the absence of a well-articulated national settlement system, separate aspatial or spatial sub-systems comprising of a 'dendritic' market system and a polarised politico-administrative system, seem to be in operation simultaneously.
44. Both the level and scale of urbanisation are very low. There is extreme localisation of urbanism in Kathmandu Valley, the traditional seat of 'feudal urban agglomeration', though there is a distinct and consistent trend of shift in favour of Terai and Inner Terai. The sluggish general growth rate of urban population and decline of smaller older urban centres bears a strong resemblance to the pattern of urban atrophy and de-urbanisation seen in the aftermath of colonial conquest of a society. The hierarchical structuring of urban places is not very marked and the rank-size distribution pattern is found to be of a feudal 'primate' type. The economic base of towns is found very fragile resembling a medieval feudal agglomeration of 'half-urban half-rural' character. The urban places are seen to be primarily locales of parasitic activities of circulation and consumption of surplus values and the general articulation of social process is found leading to "ruralization of the city" rather than to "urbanisation of the countryside".
45. The sequence of evolution and current pattern of spatial linkages show a heavy outward orientation (extroverted) as in a colonial setting, on the one hand, and equally heavy convergence towards the capital centre (monocentred) as in an 'Asiatic-feudal' setting. The natural and historical specificities of the country seem to have made the spatial linkages ill-developed universally than developed unevenly. The disparities in their development are also glaring. The composite nature of spatial integration is found to be marked by the apparently contradictory scenario of excessive polarisation around the capital city, on the one hand, and outward-orientation towards India along a north-south dendrite stretching from Mountain to Terai, on the other. This may be cited as an example of the typical mode of spatial integration in a semi-feudal, semi-/neo-colonial society (see Fig. 6.1).
46. The spatial structure of development/underdevelopment generalised from the spatial differentiation of composite levels of development also confirms a dichotomous structure marked, on the one hand, by extreme polarisation around the traditional state capital of Kathmandu and increasing polarisation around points of higher physical and economic integration with the outside world and, on the other, by the equally extreme spatial non-differentiation

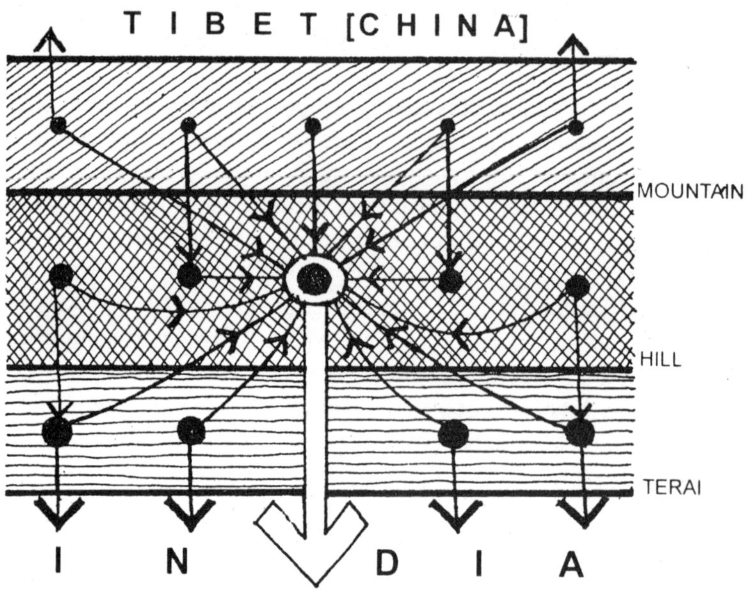

Fig. 6.1 Mono-Central and Extraverted Regional Structure.

(and hence disarticulation) in the vast hinterland. Thus the spatial unevenness in development in Nepal can be seen as the function of both the conservation of pre-capitalist monopolistic structure and also the uneven development or penetration of capitalism (primarily in the mercantile form), though the non-differentiating (or disarticulating) tendency of pre-capitalist structures seem to be having an upper hand on the country-wide plane.

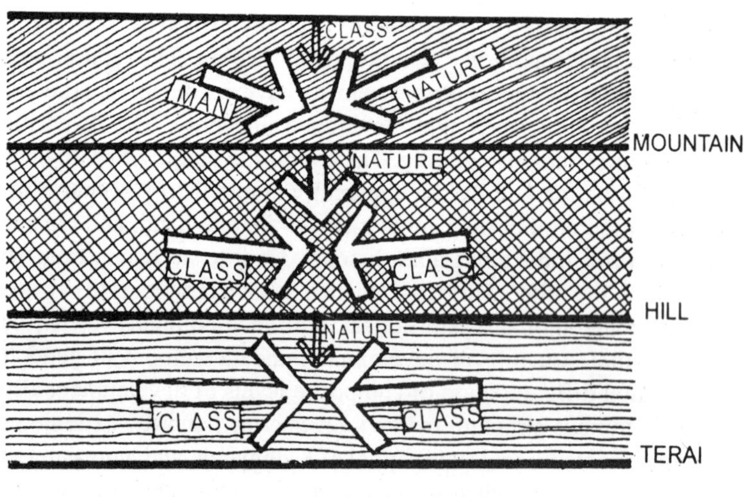

Fig. 6.2 Nature of Contradictions.

On the basis of the findings of this study it can be concluded that the problems of development/underdevelopment of Nepal both in the social and spatial dimensions are essentially the problems of transition of a pre-capitalist society hybridized primarily under the retrograde internal social structure but increasingly mediated by the exogenous capitalist/imperialist interests. Even though the space economy is seen characterised more by the absolute low level of development of the productive forces than by a distortedly developed structure, the recent trends are found to be increasing superimposition of the latter tendency onto the former, as the two are not necessarily exclusive and contradictory. Also the dominant spatial differentiation may be seen in terms of the changing nature of basic contradictions in different territorial zones (Fig. 6.2), which should also provide a 'planning' perspective to 'change' the status quo. Hence without the basic restructuration of the society which would check the above tendencies as well as the forces abating them, the social and spatial problems of development/underdevelopment are not likely to be solved.

Appendices

Appendix 1 Definition of Spatial Units for the Study

Designated Territorial Zones	*Administrative Districts*	*Geographical Area (Sq. Km.)*	*Population (1981)**
MOUNTAIN		47872 s(32.86)	1058269 (7.05)
1. Eastern	1. Taplejung 2. Sankhuwasabha 3. Solukhumbu 4. Dolakha	11982 (8.22)	484335 (3.22)
2. Central	5. Rasuwa 6. Manang 7. Mustang	7094 (4.87)	48374 (0.32)
3. Western	8. Dolpa 9. Jumla 10. Kalikot 11. Mugu 12. Humla 13. Bajura 14. Bajhang 15. Darchula	28796 (19.77)	525560 (3.50)
I. HILL		55346 (37.99)	5880642 (39.1)
4. Eastern	16. Panchthar 17. Ilam 18. Dhankuta 19. Tehrathum 20. Bhojpur 21. Ckhaldhunga 22. Khotang 23. Ramechhap 24. Sindhupalchok 25. Kavrepalanchok	14302 (9.32)	1799352 (11.98)
5. Central	26. Nuwakot 27. Dhading 28. Gorkha 29. Lamjung 30. Tanahu 31. Syangja 32. Kaski 33. Parbat 34. Myagdi 35. Banglung 36. Gulmi 37. Argha-Khanchi 38. Palpa	22790 (15.64)	2603924 (17.34)
6. Western	39. Pyuthan 40. Rolpa 41. Rukum 42. Salyan 43. Dailekh 44. Jajarkot 45. Achham 46. Doti 47. Baitadi 48. Dadeldhura	18254 (12.53)	1477366 (9.84)

(*Contd.*)

(*Appendix 1 contd.*)

7. Kathmandu Valley	49. Kathamandu 50. Lalitpur 51. Bhaktapur	1097 (0.75)	766820 (5.11)
INNER TARAI		15422 (10.59)	1278774 (8.51)
8. Eastern	52. Udaypur 53. Sindhuli	4691 (3.22)	347545 (2.31)
9. Central	54. Makwanpur 55. Chitwan	4748 (3.26)	499316 (3.32)
10. Western	56. Dang-Deukhuri 57. Surkhet	5983 (4.11)	431913 (2.88)
TERAI		25954 (17.81)	6035946 (40.18)
11. Eastern	58. Jhapa 59. Morang 60. Sunsari 61. Saptari 62. Siraha 63. Dhanusha 64. Mahottari 65. Sarlahi 66. Rautahat 67. Bara 68. Parsa	14266 (9.79)	4246446 (28.27)
12. Central	69. Nawalparasi 70. Rupendehi 71. Kapilvastu	3651 (2.51)	959197 (6.39)
13. Western	72. Banke 73. Vardiya 74. Kailali 75. Kanchanpur	8037 (5.52)	830303 (5.33)
NEPAL		145691** (100.00)	15020451 (100.00)

Note: Figures in parenthesis are percentages.

* Provisional.

** After readjustment of boundary with China total area has been changed to 147181 Sq. Km.

Appendix 2 Distributional Characteristics of Nepalese Agriculture

Territorial Zones	*Gint Coeff. of Operational Land Holding*		*Extend of Rented Tenure*				*Average Size of Holding per Household hold (hectare)*	
			Households (%)		*Area (%)*			
	1961	*1971*	*1961*	*1971*	*1961*	*1971*	*1961*	*1971*
MOUNTAIN	–	0.465	–	17.93	–	9.58	–	0.47
Eastern	–	0.407	–	22.50	–	13.03	–	0.54
Central	–	0.572	–	8.99	–	5.14	–	0.63
Western	–	0.454	–	14.08	–	5.05	–	0.37
HILLS	0.420	0.363	34.38	10.66	15.88	6.34	0.45	0.36
Eastern	–	0.352	41.61	18.36	23.38	10.94	0.51	0.41
Central	–	0.369	25.59	6.18	9.21	3.30	0.42	0.34
Western	–	0.355	37.27	8.44	13.34	4.60	0.41	0.34
KATHMANDU VALLEY	0.360	0.390	61.37	45.72	37.36	25.98	0.47	0.48
INNER TERAI	0.629	0.577	28.66	11.30	24.32	13.62	1.51	1.32
Eastern	–	0.565	25.21	10.25	21.72	10.74	0.98	0.81
Central	–	0.483	21.66	3.38	11.21	1.94	1.47	1.11
Western	–	0.559	58.51	34.28	43.05	27.28	2.81	2.71
TERAI	0.577	0.542	52.60	31.41	28.99	18.86	2.44	2.09
Eastern	–	0.532	48.96	34.70	28.38	22.22	2.23	1.86
Central	–	0.528	62.64	15.28	28.44	6.89	2.65	2.15
Western	–	0.500	70.00	30.20	33.24	15.95	4.36	4.21
NEPAL	0.644	0.624	40.36	19.00	25.51	15.80	1.09	0.96

Note: * Including tenant cultivators.
Source: Central Bureau of Statistics, *Sample Census of Agricultural, Nepal* 1961 and 1971, Kathmandu.

Appendix 3 Classification of Industries

I. *Use-based Classification*

1. Consumer Goods
   (a) *Consumer Non-durables:* Oil and grain mill products; bakery; fruit canning and bottling; Sugar refineries; distilleries; animal feeds; tea packing; biri making; cigarettes; yarn and textiles; caps making; printing press; drugs and medicines and soaps; matches; ice and ice cream; foot wear (shoes), Carpets and rugs;
   (b) Consumer Durables: Wooden furniture and construction materials*, metallic vessels; jewelleries and curious;
2. Intermediate Goods
   Jute processing; textile spinning; saw mills; paper; metallic furniture and construction materials*; brick and tiles;
3. Capital Goods**
   Agriculture and machine tools.
4. Basic Goods**
   Cement; electricity.
5. Miscellaneous
   Repairing works; miscellaneous.

II. *Input-based Classification*

1. Agro-based
   (a) Crop-based
   Oil and grain mill products; bakery; fruit canning and bottling; sugar refineries; distilleries; animal feeds; tea packing; biri making; cigarettes; yarn and textiles; textile spinning; jute processing; caps making;
   (b) Animal-based
   foot wear (shoes); carpets and rugs.
2. Forest-based
   Matches; wooden furniture and construction materials; saw mills; paper manufacturing.
3. Mineral-based
   (a) Metallic Mineral
   Metallic furniture and construction materials, metallic vessels; jewelleries and curious;

Note: * Since no separate break-up is available for 'furniture' (Consumer Durable) and 'construction materials' (Intermediate Goods) components, it is arbitrarily grouped 'Wooden' in Consumer Durables and 'Metallic' in Intermediate Goods.

** No separate information available for agriculture and machine tools and cement factories in the successive censuses (see Table 3.12 for use-based classification of public enterprises') and generation of electricity perhaps not included in 'manufacturing'.

(b) Non-metallic mineral
Bricks and tiles; cement*;

4. Chemical-based
Drugs and medicines; soaps;
5. Electricity, gas-based
None.
6. Service-based
Printing press; repairing works.
7. Miscellaneous
Ice and ice cream; Miscellaneous.

Note: No separate information available for 'cement' in the successive industrial censuses.

Appendix 4 Level of Development of Registered Manufacturing (1965).

Territorial Zones/ Districts			Indicators of Development of Registered Manufacturing								Total Rank Value	Item Compose Ranking
			1		2		3		4			
			Value	Rank Value	Value	Rank Value	Value	Rank Value	Value	Rank Value		
I.		MOUNTAIN										
II.		HILL										
III.		KATHMANDU VALLEY										
		1. Kathmandu	1.64	22	13.96	1	4.06	18	3.61	6	47	11
		2. Lalitpur	0.75	19	18.05	3	3.24	16	8.10	17	55	7
		3. Bhaktapur	0.18	5	77.71	22	0.00	5.5	5.03	10	42.5	16
IV.		INNER TERAI										
	Cont-rol	4. Makwanpur	0.04	1	75.56	21	0.00	5.5	8.5	18	45.5	14
	Cont-rol	5. Chitwan	0.25	8	46.15	15	5.00	21	11.1	21	66	4
V.		TERAI										
	Far Eastern	6. Jhapa	0.72	18	85.63	23	0.00	5.5	7.30	16	62.5	6
	Far Eastern	7. Morang	5.36	23	20.43	4	15.66	23	47.88	23	73	1
	Far Eastern	8. Sunsari	0.36	11	59.22	18	0.00	5.5	6.34	13	47.5	9.5
	Md-Eastern Eastern	9. Suptari	0.54	13.5	32.57	10	1.54	11	9.25	19	53.5	8
	Md-Eastern Eastern	10. Siraha	0.13	3	42.71	14	2.94	15	3.21	4	36	19
	Md-Eastern Eastern	11. Dhanusa	0.62	16.5	28.35	9	7.87	22	10.42	20	67.5	3
	Md-Eastern Eastern	12. Mahottari	0.17	4	58.84	17	0.00	5.5	2.59	1	27.5	22
	Md-Eastern Eastern	13. Sarlahi	0.62	16.5	26.64	6	4.00	17	3.62	7	46.5	12

(Contd.)

(*Appendix 4 contd.*)

Territorial Zones/ Districts			*Indicators of Development of Registered Manufacturing*								*Total Rank Value*	*Item Compose Ranking*
			1		*2*		*3*		*4*			
			Value	*Rank Value*	*Value*	*Rank Value*	*Value*	*Rank Value*	*Value*	*Rank Value*		
	Eastern	14. Rautahat	0.12	2	73.04	20	2.70	14	2.73	2	38	17.5
		15. Bara	0.54	13.5	41.53	13	1.67	12	4.75	9	47.5	9.5
		16. Parsa	1.09	20	33.93	11	4.82	20	5.99	12	63	5
Central		17. Nawalparasi	0.21	6.5	44.08	15	0.00	5.5	5.38	11	38	17.5
		18. Rupandehi	0.60	15	28.01	8	2.63	13	4.37	8	44	15
		19. Kapilvastu	0.44	12	38.79	12	0.00	5.5	2.87	3	32.5	20
Western		20. Banke	1.10	21	27.68	7	4.76	19	11.52	22	69	2
		21. Bardiya	0.21	6.5	65.92	19	0.00	5.5	6.64	15	46	13
		22. Kailali	0.34	10	23.95	5	0.00	5.5	3.44	5	25.5	23
		23. Kanchanpur	0.29	9	14.91	2	0.00	5.5	6.5	14	30.5	21

Note: Indicators of development:
1. Workers in manufacturing to total working population* (%).
2. Output per worker (Rs. 000).
3. Establishments with more than 50 workers to total establishments (%).
4. Electricity and Fuel Consumption per establishment (Rs. 000).

For want of districtwise data for 1965, the 'total working population' from 1971 census has been used for weighting workers in manufacturing in 1965; hence the absolute figures are deflated.

Source: Central Bureau of Statistics, *Census of Manufacturing Establishments 1965*, Kathmandu.

Appendix 5 Level of Development of Registered Manufacturing (1976/77)

Territorial Zones/ Districts		Indicators of Development								Total Rank Value	Item Compose Ranking
		1		2		3		4			
		Value	Rank Value	Value	Rank Value	Value	Rank Value	Value	Rank Value		
I.	MOUNTAIN										
Eastern	1. Solukhumbu	0.43	17.5	5.33	6	25.0	44	0.50	2	69.5	31
	2. Dolakha	0.21	12	7.80	8	0.0	9	1.86	8	37	41
	3. Darchula	1.26	28	8.35	9	0.0	9	0.41	1	47	35
II.	HILL										
Eastern	4. Ilam	0.82	21	3.83	3	0.0	9	52.67	44	77	30
	5. Tecrathum	N.A.	–	N.A.	–	N.A.	–	N.A.		–	–
	6. Dhankuta	0.16	10.5	4.15	4	0.0	9	4.5	15	38.5	38.5
	7. Bhojpur	0.23	13	6.01	7	0.0	9	2.0	9	38	40
	8. Okhalchunga	0.11	7.5	2.93	2	0.0	9	0.67	3	21.5	45
	9. Sindhupal Chok	0.10	6	23.47	14	0.0	9	1.39	4	33	43
	10. Kavrepalanchok	0.16	10.5	92.14	38	2.0	20	5.00	16	84.5	29
Control	11. Nuwakot	0.25	14	50.80	23	0.0	9	1.59	5	51	34
	12. Tanahu	0.43	17.5	21.40	13	4.0	32	9.48	28	90.5	25.5
	13. Kaski	2.85	37	126.50	42	3.28	27	2.23	10	116	16
	14. Syangja	0.02	1	32.69	18	0.0	9	2.73	12	40	37
	15. Palpa	0.42	16	12.16	10	2.78	22.5	6.11	20	68.5	32
	16. Parbat	0.13	9	18.95	11	0.0	9	1.60	6	35	42
	17. Baglung	0.07	4.5	29.20	16	0.0	9	5.25	17	46.5	36

(Contd.)

(Appendix 5 contd.)

Territorial zones/ Districts			Indicators of development								Total rank value	Item compose ranking
			1		2		3		4			
			Value	Rank value	Value	Rank value	Value	Rank value	Value	Rank value		
	Eastern	18. Rolpa	0.05	2.5	2.64	1	0.0	9	2.23	11	23.5	44
		19. Doti	0.11	7.5	27.99	15	0.0	9	1.67	7	38.5	38.5
		20. Baitadi	N.A.	–	N.A.	–	N.A.	–	N.A.	–	–	–
III.		KATHMANDU VALLEY										
		21. Kathmandu	3.96	41	81.50	36	3.80	30	7.36	22	129	12
		22. Lalitpur	4.29	42	21.34	12	8.51	39	29.06	40	133	7.5
		23. Bhagatpur	2.54	36	33.53	19	3.03	25	7.17	21	101	22.5
IV.		INNER TERAI										
	Eastern	24. Udaipur	0.07	4.5	173.86	44	0.0	9	12.17	33	90.5	25.5
		25. Sindhuli	0.05	2.5	71.00	32	0.0	9	4.43	14	57.5	33
	Central	26. Makwanpur	1.06	24	53.84	25	8.33	38	40.92	43	130	11
		27. Chitwan	1.73	34	67.01	31	2.86	24	10.34	30	119	15
	Western	28. Dang-doukhuri	0.53	19	54.01	26	1.75	18	9.56	29	92	24
		29. Surkhet	3.55	40	4.47	5	28.57	45	34.5	42	132	9.5
V.		TERAI										
	Far-Eastern	30. Jhapa	6.26	44	42.73	21	13.53	42	17.36	37	144	3.5
		31. Morang	5.58	43	109.40	40	12.34	41	72.42	45	169	1
		32. Sunsari	0.97	23	90.92	37	4.65	33	33.55	41	134	6

(Contd.)

(*Appendix 5 contd.*)

Region	Sub-region	District										
Eastern	Mid-Eastern	33. Saptari	1.67	32	121.86	41	7.25	37	9.40	26	136	5
		34. Siraha	0.84	22	77.52	35	5.43	34	7.59	23	114	17
		35. Chanusa	1.63	30.5	54.16	27	3.13	26	21.63	38	121.5	13
		36. Mahottari	1.28	29	30.44	17	3.65	29	3.66	13	88	27.5
		37. Sarlahi	1.72	33	74.95	33	1.82	19	5.32	18	103	21
	Eastern	38. Rautahat	0.29	15	254.86	45	0.0	9	5.33	19	88	27.5
		39. Bara	1.63	30.5	48.16	22	3.42	28	7.85	24	104.5	20
		40. Parsa	7.00	45	41.37	20	9.60	40	24.97	39	144	3.5
Central		41. Nawalparasi	1.07	25	64.05	29	3.90	31	9.44	27	112	18.5
		42. Rupondehi	3.24	39	62.09	28	6.22	35	10.66	31	133	7.5
		43. Kapilvastu	1.75	37	53.63	24	6.35	36	15.93	35	132	9.5
Western		44. Banke	3.01	38	65.63	30	15.71	43	16.90	36	147	2
		45. Bardiya	0.71	20	155.09	43	2.78	22.5	14.06	34	119.5	14
		46. Kailali	1.14	26	76.62	34	0.0	9	11.41	32	101	22.5
		47. Kanchanpur	1.20	27	100.55	39	2.70	21	8.00	25	112	18.5

Note: Indicators of Development:

1. Workers in registered manufacturing to total working population* (%).
2. Output per worker (Rs. 000).
3. Establishment with more than 50 workers to total establishments (%).
4. Electricity and Fuel consumption per establishment (Rs. 000).

* For want of districtwise break-up for the corresponding year, the total working population for 1971 has been used for weighting the workers in registered manufacturing in 1976/77; Vs hence the absolute figures are inflated.

Source: Central Bureau of Statistics, *Gensus of Manufacturing Establishments 1976/77*, Kathmandu.

Appendix 6 Average Cash Expenditure Pattern of Rural Households by Territorial Zones.

(%)

Territorial Zones	*Eastern Sector*[1]			*Central Sector*[2]			*Western Sector*[1]		
Items	*Mountain*	*Hill*	*Terai*	*Mountain*	*Hill*	*Terai*	*Mountain*	*Hill*	*Terai*
1. Foods Grains and other Foods	17.32	20.25	22.23	26.92	7.49	Not Available	20.65	17.53	19.55
2. Meat	8.65	8.43	7.02	15.14	8.41		18.13	6.60	5.03
3. Furniture etc.	1.57	1.08	1.34	0.29	1.08		1.50	10.5	1.47
4. Clothing	24.03	19.78	19.68	16.50	27.50		33.75	30.23	28.74
5. Agricultural Inputs	0.02	1.08	1.39	0.19	1.75		0.19	0.37	0.40
6. Salt	3.26	2.33	0.90	3.97	2.20		6.84	3.73	1.70
7. Sugar	2.86	2.34	10.14	3.99	3.81		2.12	3.93	3.55
8. Kerosene	2.94	2.26	2.57	2.27	2.34		1.48	1.85	2.20
9. Cigarettes	1.50	2.60	2.99	4.17	6.84		4.12	3.58	2.66
10. Education and Health	9.75	12.07	15.79	12.41	15.30		5.33	9.38	12.48
11. Festivals, Funerals etc.	18.46	20.78	12.84	4.20	15.14		8.48	15.54	10.10
12. Drinks	1.71	2.41	1.00	2.93	2.23		1.38	1.12	2.92
13. Ornaments	1.39	0.27	1.44	N.A.	N.A.		1.05	1.48	1.47
14. Others	4.28	4.31	6.82	6.91	5.90		4.91	4.44	7.67
TOTAL	100.00	100.00	100.00	100.00	100.00	–	100.00	100.00	100.00
Per house hold expenditure per annum (Rs.)	1828.64	2127.68	3375.59	5377.26	3080.79	–	1579.17	1876.82	2418.24

Note: Absolute values of cash expenditure per household in the central sector appear higher and are not comparable with the rest because of the differences in the method and the time of the survey.

Source: 1. CEDA, *Regional Development Study,* (Nepal), Part IIIa and IIa, Kathmandu, May, 1973–July 1975.
2. CEDA, *Impact of Polchara Growth Centre on its Hinterlands: Gandalci Growth Axis, Northern Part*, Kathmandu, June 1977.

Appendix 7 Growth Pattern of Road Network and Airports

(A) GROWTH PATTERN OF ROAD NETWORK*

Period of Completion	Total Length (km.)	'Aided' by
I. Upto 1960		
1. Thankot-Bhainse	114	India
III. 1960 to 1970		
1. Kathmandu-Trishuli	68	India and USA
2. Bhainse-Hetauda	10	USA
3. Hetauda-Raxaul	57	USA
4. Kathmandu-Kodari	114	China
5. Jogbani-Dharan	50	UK
III. 1970–1980		
1. Pokhara-Sunauli	184	India
2. Pathlaiya-Dhalkebar	109	USSR
3. Dhalkebar-Rajbiraj	95	India
4. Rajbiraj-Itahari	69	India
5. Itahari-Kakarbhitta	92	India
6. Naubise-Pokhara	174	China
7. Narayangarh-Butwal	116	UK
8. Bhairahawa-Lumbini	22	(Nepal)
IV. 1980-onwards		
1. Narayangarh-Gorkha	61	China
2. Dharan-Dhankuta	50	UK
3. Hetauda-Narayangarh	78	ADB

(B) GROWTH PATTERN OF AIRPORTS

Period of Completion/Airport	Type	Territorial Zones
I. Period to 1960		
1. Kathmandu	AW	Kathmandu Valley
2. Simara	AW	Eastern Terai
3. Biratnagar	AW	Far-Eastern Terai
4. Bhairahawa	AW	Central Terai
5. Pokhara	AW	Central Hill
II. 1960–1970		
1. Rajbiraj	S	Mid-Eastern Terai
2. Janakpur	AW	Mid-Eastern Terai
3. Gorkha	S	Central Hill
4. Dang	S	Western Inner Terai
5. Bharatpur	AW	Central Inner Terai
6. Dhangadi	AW	Western Terai
7. Meghauli	S	Central Inner Terai
8. Surkhet	AW	Western Inner Terai
9. Nepalgunj	AW	Western Terai
10. Bhadrapur	AW	Far-Eastern Terai
III. 1970–1980		
1. Lukla	S	Eastern Mountain
2. Rumjatar	S	Eastern Hill
3. Tumlingtar	S	Eastern Mountain

(contd.)

(*Appendix 7 contd.*)

(A) GROWTH PATTERN OF ROAD NETWORK*

Period of Completion	*Total Length (km.)*	*'Aided' by*
4. Bhutwal-Kohalpur	251	India
5. Lamosangu-Jiri	110	Switzerland
V. Incomplete		
1. Dhangarhi-Dandeldhura	140	USA
2. Kohalpur-Banbasa	191	(Nepal)
3. Kohalpur-Surkhet	92	(Nepal)
4. Charale-Illam	78	(Nepal)

Note: * Only Highways.
Source: Department of Roads, *Nepal Road Statistics 1983*, HMG/N, Ministry of Works and Transport, Kathmandu, p. 30, And Royal Nepalies Embassy 1985, *Nepal News*, Vol. XIV, No. 23–24, New Delhi, August 1, 0–10.

(B) GROWTH PATTERN OF AIR PORTS

Period of Completion/Airport	*Type*	*Territorial Zones*
4. Lamidanda	S	Eastern Hill
5. Phaplu	S	Eastern Mountain
6. Taplegunj	S	Eastern Mountain
7. Bhojpur	S	Eastern Hill
8. Jiri	S	Eastern Mountain
9. Baglung	S	Central Hill
10. Ramechhap	S	Eastern Hill
11. Jomsom	S	Central Mountain
12. Jumla	S	Western Mountain
13. Chaurjabari	AW	Western Hill
14. Silgadi Doti	AW	Western Hill
15. Mahendranagar	S	Western Terai
16. Safebagar	S	Western Hill
17. Dolpa	S	Western Mountain
18. Bajhang	S	Western Mountain
19. Simikot	S	Western Mountain
20. Baitadi	S	Western Hill

Note: *S = Seasonal ; AW = All Weather.
Source: RNAC, Planning Division, Kathmandu.

Appendix 8 Indicators of Development (Districtwise) (1970s).

Dist. Code No.	District	INDICATORS OF DEVELOPMENT* I				II				III		IV		
		E1	E2	E3	E4	A5	A6	A7	A8	I9	I10	S-11	S-12	S-13
1.	Taplejung	103.42	1.60	14.6	2.864	1450	2.09	5.92	0.64	0.28	7.41	43	0.615	65.85
2.	Sankhuwasbh	108.87	2.25	13.3	3.591	2828	1.40	5.92	2.05	0.76	7.41	21	0.840	44.71
3.	Solukhumbu	106.32	1.69	12.3	2.906	2183	1.32	5.92	7.18	0.55	5.33	22	1.190	24.38
4.	Dolakha	112.39	0.99	10.1	4.348	1614	2.70	53.09	0.62	0.19	7.80	8	0.946	49.37
5.	Rasuwa	111.18	3.93	6.4	1.062	1768	1.16	20.38	0.23	0.87	7.41	25	1.013	73.67
6.	Manang	83.51	8.91	4.7	4.633	2385	0.80	32.18	10.14	5.20	7.41	12	1.295	45.46
7.	Mustang	91.36	6.25	19.5	1.633	1428	0.74	8.34	9.78	1.64	7.41	67	1.377	31.96
8.	Dopla	114.31	3.02	5.3	1.210	2160	0.62	0.34	0.20	1.70	7.41	16	0.661	30.60
9.	Jumla	113.26	1.69	6.2	2.643	1255	1.47	0.34	0.38	0.49	7.41	14	0.649	37.05
10.	Mugu	111.67	4.59	5.2	1.500	812	1.40	0.34	0.14	0.28	7.41	14	0.609	59.31
11.	Kalikot	119.70	1.69	7.7	2.643	823	2.38	0.34	0.42	0.49	7.41	25	0.708	37.33
12.	Humla	113.00	0.77	6.1	1.689	1793	0.95	0.34	0.00	0.11	7.41	3	0.711	19.56
13.	Bajura	120.73	0.45	4.1	3.153	1345	1.89	7.67	0.54	0.22	7.41	3	0.716	47.43
14.	Bajhang	120.43	1.29	9.6	4.094	827	2.62	7.67	0.14	0.85	7.41	6	0.565	37.84
15.	Darchula	120.00	3.41	15.0	3.316	1088	0.78	3.72	13.53	1.39	8.35	12	0.680	60.91
16.	Ilam	120.57	3.38	16.6	3.336	1981	3.50	6.26	3.79	0.48	3.83	34	0.862	61.64
17.	Panchthar	105.02	1.22	13.4	3.212	1611	2.30	1.65	0.75	0.03	6.45	15	1.414	54.56
18.	Tehrathum	102.53	1.31	17.0	3.593	1729	2.95	3.67	0.17	0.24	6.45	26	1.661	67.51
19.	Bhojpur	108.38	2.40	12.1	3.615	1533	2.56	15.91	0.25	0.78	6.01	11	0.856	66.02
20.	Khotang	107.51	1.47	11.7	3.870	1164	2.51	11.66	0.08	0.20	6.45	25	0.562	60.29
21.	Okhaldunga	111.29	2.05	10.9	2.853	1941	2.88	20.18	0.68	0.28	2.93	13	1.209	53.90

(contd.)

(Appendix 8 contd.)

Dist. Code No.	District	INDICATORS OF DEVELOPMENT*												
		I				II				III		IV		
		E1	E2	E3	E4	A5	A6	A7	A8	I9	I10	S-11	S-12	S-13
22.	Ramechhap	103.29	1.33	10.5	4.105	1178	1.47	4.88	1.54	0.17	6.45	20	0.793	48.74
23.	Kavre	120.93	3.10	11.2	2.860	1784	3.48	21.99	0.40	0.52	92.14	28	0.939	77.90
24.	Sindhu–Palchok	112.55	3.48	7.9	3.444	1922	0.44	21.99	0.09	0.81	23.47	9	0.743	42.36
25.	Dhankuta	116.43	3.24	16.1	3.435	2184	3.39	7.81	1.89	0.51	4.15	32	1.737	91.71
26.	Nuratkot	114.96	3.08	7.8	4.886	1594	2.02	4.33	0.37	0.65	50.18	20	1.059	70.82
27.	Dhading	115.61	1.03	5.2	5.835	1400	4.22	20.50	0.25	0.34	25.04	27	1.122	52.98
28.	Gorkha	123.31	2.13	11.6	3.439	1581	1.73	35.36	2.43	0.37	25.04	58	0.899	53.34
29.	Lamjung	122.22	1.50	17.7	2.899	2493	0.60	32.18	1.72	0.47	25.04	16	0.815	83.74
30.	Tanahu	133.04	1.81	17.8	4.872	2084	1.66	16.60	1.21	0.43	21.40	45	1.239	86.29
31.	Kaski	127.00	7.87	24.7	9.247	2554	1.62	26.51	1.35	1.16	126.50	208	1.371	84.63
32.	Syangja	117.86	2.78	18.3	3.011	1288	2.02	31.29	0.17	0.78	32.69	43	0.625	93.27
33.	Parbat	106.26	1.68	17.5	2.855	1174	1.04	57.01	0.58	0.57	18.95	17	1.251	136.55
34.	Palpa	120.68	3.23	21.5	3.303	1230	3.56	11.46	0.26	0.66	12.16	39	0.988	101.60
35.	Arghakhanihi	121.53	1.34	15.0	3.800	1825	2.48	9.52	0.19	0.52	25.04	25	0.749	71.14
36.	Gumli	115.62	1.97	16.6	3.316	1323	4.66	41.71	0.36	0.76	25.04	11	1.040	78.13
37.	Baglung	120.76	2.78	14.0	3.991	1267	1.99	45.17	0.06	1.07	29.20	39	0.789	66.47
38.	Myagdi	114.00	1.11	12.5	2.788	1879	1.75	8.34	0.68	0.29	25.04	58	0.647	91.10
39.	Pyuphan	115.82	3.01	13.0	3.600	2070	4.03	10.70	0.24	1.20	19.47	22	0.744	54.13
40.	Rolpa	108.94	1.61	6.5	3.781	2411	0.81	4.41	0.27	0.96	2.64	6	0.575	42.02
41.	Rukum	129.89	2.53	6.9	4.524	1846	2.00	4.41	0.38	1.51	19.47	5	0.415	42.22
42.	Sallyan	107.48	3.29	9.5	3.849	1770	3.00	9.12	0.36	2.01	19.47	3	0.814	36.10
43.	Jajarkot	112.19	1.07	5.1	4.946	1487	2.48	6.00	0.89	0.40	19.47	6	0.576	38.88

(Contd.)

(*Appendix 8 contd.*)

44.	Dailekh	111.90	0.37	8.4	3.510	1189	2.36	7.88	0.00	0.32	19.47	13	0.531	42.85
45.	Achham	112.62	0.58	6.1	3.046	1353	2.26	7.67	0.10	0.23	19.47	8	0.781	65.55
46.	Doti	118.73	1.48	7.1	2.957	1491	3.65	7.67	0.9	0.18	27.99	8	0.742	32.78
47.	Baitadai	113.53	2.70	14.1	4.447	1371	2.57	12.01	0.41	0.89	19.47	12	0.893	66.72
48.	Dandel–Dhura	144.41	3.63	14.1	4.036	1486	2.63	1.60	0.76	2.01	19.47	11	1.197	45.36
49.	Kathmandu	124.06	46.75	38.3	64.613	5336	0.57	491.31	1.78	4.10	81.50	3176	4.528	169.66
50.	Bhaktapur	131.37	27.11	24.2	13.885	7129	2.20	491.31	0.31	7.18	33.53	56	1.981	216.45
51.	Lalitpur	128.44	26.46	25.0	33.788	4147	3.11	491.31	2.07	5.62	21.34	203	2.437	118.08
52.	Udaipur	138.11	1.94	10.4	3.476	3072	24.92	1.83	14.55	0.35	173.86	16	0.917	43.16
53.	Sindhuli	133.57	1.43	10.1	4.242	3333	20.39	23.95	3.92	0.24	71.00	9	0.959	40.48
54.	Makwanpur	141.79	4.96	11.9	7.522	3706	12.55	86.42	4.36	0.84	53.84	139	0.891	46.48
55.	Chitwan	138.65	6.47	21.2	5.781	3897	24.64	89.15	23.81	0.81	67.01	109	0.601	50.31
56.	Dang	142.71	6.38	10.7	5.703	2980	18.13	11.70	38.98	2.50	54.01	20	0.639	39.13
57.	Surkhet	158.05	2.36	10.7	3.828	2121	7.12	7.21	7.13	0.72	4.474	25	0.931	47.99
58.	Jhapa	192.04	10.58	20.8	8.757	3239	15.57	17.28	61.32	1.75	42.73	325	1.085	76.72
59.	Morang	183.39	19.27	20.0	9.585	3262	22.57	46.92	49.63	6.15	109.40	885	0.948	61.45
60.	Sunsari	143.88	11.79	19.5	10.359	3418	20.31	46.92	50.15	1.44	90.92	320	1.479	67.82
61.	Saptari	130.53	6.30	15.1	3.018	2657	10.12	24.31	29.81	1.04	121.86	198	0.363	56.30
62.	Siraha	124.51	4.89	12.0	2.715	3028	5.12	29.17	23.13	0.77	77.52	61	0.889	58.43
63.	Dhanusha	130.83	9.52	11.9	4.450	2857	5.88	48.95	17.13	1.51	54.16	127	0.758	59.98
64.	Mahottari	128.57	4.97	11.2	4.515	2781	5.11	48.95	21.29	0.70	30.44	31	0.648	53.33
65.	Sarlahi	139.20	5.42	8.2	3.940	2970	5.70	42.46	25.78	0.60	74.95	65	0.899	55.53
66.	Rautahat	133.18	4.11	8.2	2.900	2816	6.26	20.09	20.51	0.57	254.86	37	0.950	48.55
67.	Bara	136.25	5.65	11.5	2.661	3740	7.11	99.41	21.30	0.53	48.16	80	1.193	67.13
68.	Parsa	140.41	12.31	14.7	3.472	3791	6.70	99.41	24.46	1.67	41.37	801	0.876	57.81

(*Contd.*)

(*Appendix 8 contd.*)

Dist. Code No.	*District*	*INDICATORS OF DEVELOPMENT**												
		I				*II*				*III*		*IV*		
		E1	*E2*	*E3*	*E4*	*A5*	*A6*	*A7*	*A8*	*I9*	*I10*	*S-11*	*S-12*	*S-13*
69.	Naval–Parasi	168.65	3.10	15.6	3.672	2985	8.15	78.65	28.36	0.61	64.05	38	0.668	65.95
70.	Rupandehi	155.71	8.10	16.3	4.704	3000	6.00	54.74	32.67	1.01	62.09	100	1.023	52.89
71.	Kapilvastu	131.80	4.98	11.7	2.821	2502	3.85	39.16	32.89	0.62	53.63	24	0.785	50.33
72.	Banke	157.70	15.71	12.3	10.992	3018	5.29	28.13	37.44	2.29	65.63	430	0.917	43.86
73.	Bardiya	194.81	2.32	5.4	4.324	2270	13.63	15.62	80.30	0.18	155.09	63	0.756	39.84
74.	Kailali	189.81	2.71	7.1	3.588	2831	13.43	17.50	74.61	0.49	76.62	436	0.619	37.34
75.	Kanchanpur	241.07	3.24	11.6	5.169	2125	4.71	11.33	46.96	0.07	100.55	56	0.849	42.91

Note: *Indicator of development includes.

I. General Socio-Economic base.
- E-1 Growth of population (1981 as % of 1971).
- E-2 % of non agricultural labour to total labour.
- E-3 Literacy rate.
- E-4 Average settlement size index (i.e. SJ = Uj(C^2J+1) where Uj = mean size of settiemenmt, Cj = C.V. of settlement size).

II. Agricultural Development.
- A-5 Output per hectare of net sown area (NSA).
- A-6 % area under cash crops to gross cropped area (GCA).
- A-7 value of modern inputs per hectare of GCA (Rs.).
- A-8 % of households owning 5 acres of cultivated land.

III. Industrial Development
- I-9 % economically active persons in manufacturing.
- I-10 gross output per person engaged in manufacturing (Rs. 000).

IV Social Services and Infrastructure Development
- S-11 Per capita bank credit (Rs.).
- S-12 Health institutions per 1000 population by population distance.
- S-13 Schools per thousand population (5–15 yrs. of age) by population distance.

Appendix 9 Correlation Matrix of Indicators of Development.

Indicators	E_1	E_2	E_3	E_4	A_5	A_6	A_7	A_8	I_9	I_{10}	S_{11}	S_{12}	S_{13}
E_1	1.0000												
E_2	0.1931	1.0000											
E_3	0.1129	0.6791	1.0000										
E_4	0.0978	0.8828	0.6448	1.0000									
A_5	0.3708	0.7372	0.4969	0.5370	1.0000								
A_6	0.5487	0.1175	0.1080	0.0093	0.4230	1.0000							
A_7	0.0671	0.8579	0.6164	0.8089	0.7276	–0.0202	1.0000						
A_8	0.8001	0.1787	0.0350	0.0142	0.3568	0.6273	–0.0365	1.0000					
I_9	0.1009	0.7841	0.4587	0.5434	0.6141	0.1172	0.6962	0.1196	1.0000				
I_{10}	0.5252	0.2193	0.1127	0.1431	0.4015	0.5555	0.0814	0.5547	0.0714	1.0000			
S_{11}	0.1742	0.8025	0.5742	0.8559	0.4659	0.0953	0.5635	0.1630	0.4021	0.2183	1.0000		
S_{12}	–0.0446	0.7933	0.6854	0.8615	0.5105	–0.0876	0.7521	–0.0835	0.4978	0.0879	0.7360	1.0000	
S_{13}	–0.0415	0.6172	0.6968	0.5520	0.4776	–0.1522	0.7391	0.1674	0.4990	0.0074	0.4000	0.6391	1.0000

Note: For notations of indicators of development, see Appendix 8.

Appendix 10 Sectoral Allocation of Total Outlay under Different Periodic 'Plans'.

(in Million Rs.)

	Periodic Plans	*Agricultural, Irrigation and Forestry*		*Industry, Power and Mining*		*Transport and Communication*		*Social Services*		*Miscellaneous*		*Total*	
		Amount	*%*	*Amount*	*%*	*Amount*	*%*	*Amount*	*%*	*Amount*	*%*	*Amount*	*%*
1.	First Plan (1956–1961)	74.5 (33.6)	22.56 (15.7)	55.00 (23.70)	16.67 (11.06)	124.00 (94.90)	37.58 (44.28)	64 (50.3)	19.39 (23.47)	1250 (11.80)	3.79 (5.51)	330.00 (214.30)	100.00 (100.00)
2.	Second Plan (1962–1965)	81.60 (87.31)	13.60 (14.63)	193 (241.03)	32.17 (40.39)	143.5 (93.54)	23.92 (15.67)	102.70 (95.31)	17.12 (15.97)	– (27.82)	– (4.46)	600.00 (596.82)	100.00 (100.00)
3.	Third Plan (1965–1970)	647.50	2590	697.75	27.9	670.25	26.8	414.50	16.58	70.00	2.8	2500.00	100.00
4.	Fourth Plan (1970–1975)	1171.80	33.10	720.00	20.34	1252.00	35.37	381.50	10.78	14.70	0.42	3540.00	100.00
5.	Fifth Plan (1975–1980)	3167.00	34.44	1799.90	19.57	2527.10	27.48	1703.00	18.52	–	–	9197.00	100.00
6.	Sixth Plan (1980–1985)	10570	31.14	88.10	25.96	5870	17.30	8690	25.60	–	–	33940	100.00

Note: Figures in parenthesis indicate actual expenditure.
Amounts are at current prices.

Source: National Planning Commission, various plans, citedin Central Bureau of Statistics, *Statisciai Pocket Book Nepal 1982*, Kathmandu, and National Planning Commission, *The Sixth Plan 1980–1985 Part I* (A Summary), Kathmandu, 1981.

Bibliography

I: Official Publications, Statistical Reports, etc.

Central Bureau of Statistics, *Population Census—Nepal* 1952/54, 1961 and 1971, (different Volumes), Kathmandu.

Central Bureau of Statistics, *National Sample Census of Agriculture Nepal*, 1961 and 1971, Kathmandu.

Central Bureau of Statistics, *Census of Manufacturing Establishments*, 1965, 1972/73 and 1976/77.

Central Bureau of Statistics, *Sample Survey of the Cottage and Small Scale Industries* 1972–73, Kathmandu.

Central Bureau of Statistics (1976), *Result of Internal Trade Pilot Survey*, 1975/76, (Nepali), Kathmandu.

Central Bureau of Statistics (1977), *The Analysis of the Population Statistics of Nepal.* Kathmandu.

Central Bureau of Statistics, *Statistical Pocket Book—Nepal*, 1982 and 1984, Kathmandu.

Central Bureau of Statistics (1993), *National Sample Census of Agriculture 1991/92*, Kathmandu.

Central Bureau of Statistics (1997), *National Living Standards Survey Report 1996* (Vols. I and II), Kathmandu.

Central Bureau of Statistics (1998), *Census of Manufacturing Establishments 1996/97*, Kathmandu.

Central Bureau of Statistics (2001), *Statistical Year Book of Nepal* 2001, Kathmandu.

Central Bureau of Statistics (2002), *Population Census 2001 National Report*, Kathmandu.

HMG/N, Ministry of Finance, *Economic Survey* (various years), Kathmandu.

HMG/N, Ministry of Finance (1980), *Highlights of Public Enterprises in Nepal for the F.Y. 1977/78.* Corporation Coordination Division, Kathmandu.

HMG/N, Ministry of Finance (1981), *Accelerated Development of Nepal, Development Prospects and Foreign Assistance Required for the 1980s.* Vol. I, Kathmandu.

HMG/N, Ministry of Finance (1982), *Budget in Nepal (1951/52–1981/82)*, Revenue Administration Training Centre, Kathmandu.

HMG/N, Ministry of Food and Agriculture (1971), *Farm Management Study in the Selected Regions of Nepal (1968–69)*, Economic Analysis and Planning Division, Kathmandu.

HMG/N, Ministry of Food and Agriculture (1972), *Agricultural Statistics of Nepal*, Economic Analysis and Planning Division, Kathmandu.

HMG/N, Ministry of Food, Agriculture and Irrigation (1976), *Report on Trade Flow Survey of Agricultural Commodities Particularly Cereal Gains in Nepal, 1971/72*, Department of Food and Agricultural Marketing Services, Kathmandu.

HMG/N, Ministry of Food, Agriculture and Irrigation (1977), *Agricultural Statistics of Nepal*, Agricultural Statistics Division, Kathmandu.

HMG/N, Ministry of Food, Agriculture and Irrigation (1978), *Hand Book of Agricultural Statistics of Nepal*, Agricultural Statistics Division, Kathmandu.

HMG/N, Ministry of Food, Agriculture and Irrigation (1979), *Agricultural Marketing Information, Special Issue*, Food and Agricultural Marketing Services Department, Kathmandu, January 1.

HMG/N, Ministry of Industry (1983), *Industrial Profile*, Kathmandu.

HMG/N, Ministry of Local Development (1979), *Marketing Survey of Farm Produce, Livestock, Cloth and Storage Needs in Rasuwa–Nuwakot Districts*, Project Coordinator's Office, Kathmandu.

HMG/N, Ministry of Tourism, *Annual Statistical Report* (various issues), Department of Tourism, Kathmandu.

HMG/N, Ministry of Works and Transport, *Nepal Road Statistics–1983*, Department of Roads, Kathmandu.

Industrial Services Centre (1982), *Investors Guide to Nepal*, Kathmandu.

International Centre for Integrated Mountain Development (ICIMOD) (1997), *Districts of Nepal-Indicators of Development*, Kathmandu.

Janchboojh Kendra (1974), *Mechi dekhi Mahakali* (Nepal), Part 1–4, Raj Darbar, Kathmandu.

Ministry of Finance (2002), *Economic Survey—F.Y. 2002/2003*, HMG/N, Kathmandu.

National Accounts Project (1979), ... *Manufacturing, Financing... etc (1976/77)*. National Planning Commission Secretariate, Kathmandu.

National Planning Commission (1970), *The Fourth Plan (1970–75)*, HMG/N, Kathmandu.

National Planning Commission (1975), *The Fifth Plan (1975–80)*, HMG/N, Kathmandu.

National Planning Commission (1980), *Draft Sixth Plan (1980–85)* (Nepali), HMG/N, Kathmandu.

National Research Associates (1982), *Nepal District Profile*, Kathmandu.

Nepal Industrial Development Corporation (1982), *Industrial Policy and Acts of His Majesty's Government of Nepal*, Kathmandu.

Nepal Rastra Bank, *Annual Report*, (various years), Kathmandu.

Nepal Rastra Bank, *Commercial Banking Statistics* (various issues), Kathmandu.

Nepal Rastra Bank, *Quarterly Economic Bulletin* (various issues), Kathmandu.

Nepal Rastra Bank (1972), *Agricultural Credit Survey Nepal* 1969/70, Vol, I–IV, Agricultural Credit Division, Kathmandu.

Nepal Rastra Bank (1977), *Industrial Survey Report* (Nepali), Kathmandu.

Nepal Rastra Bank (1978), *Report on Household Budget Survey* (Series 1 to 18), Research Department, Kathmandu.

Nepal Rastra Bank (1980), *Agricultural Credit Review Survey Nepal, 1976/77*, Vol. I–IV, Agricultural Credit Division, Kathmandu.

Nepal South Asia Centre (NESAC) (1998), *Nepal Human Development Report 1998*, Kathmandu.

Security Marketing Centre Ltd. (1980), *Resource Structure of Some Financial Institutions and the Development of Security Market in Nepal*, Kathmandu.

Trade Promotion Centre (1979), *Nepal Overseas Trade Statistics 1978–79*, Kathmandu.

The World Bank, *World Development report* (different years), Oxford University Press, New Delhi.

UNCTAD (1982), *Handbook of International Trade and Development Statistics*–Supplement 1981, United Nations, New York.

UNDP (1982), *The Resident Representative's Annual Report on Development Corporation to Nepal.* 1981, Kathmandu.

United Nations (1980), *Population of Nepal*, ESCAP, Bangkok.

United Nations (1982), *Yearbook of Industrial Statistics* 1980 Edition, Vol. I, General Industrial Statistics, New York.

II. Books and Articles

Abu–Lughod, J. and Hay, R. (ed.) (1979), *Third World Urbanisation*, Methuen, New York (Reprinted).

Adhikary, K.K. (1975), "A Brief Survey of Nepal's Trade with British India During the Latter Half of the 19th Century", *Contribution to Nepalese Studies*, Vol. 2, No. 1 CNAS, Kathmandu, February.

Alavi, H. (1975), "India and the Colonial, Mode of Production", *Economic and Political Weekly*, Special Number, August.

Alavi, H. and Shanin, T. (1982), *Introduction to the Sociology of Developing Societies*, Macmillan, London.

Althusser, L and Balibar, E. (eds.) (1970), *Reading Capital*, New Left Books, London (1979 edn).

Amatya, S.L. (1973/74), "A Study of Agricultural Crop Combination in Nepal", *The Himalayan Review*, Vol. VI, No. 5–6, Nepal Geographical Society, Kathmandu.

Amin, S. (1974), *Accumulation on a World Scale*, Monthly Review Press, New York.

Amin, S. (1979), *Unequal Development*, Oxford University Press, Delhi.

Amin, S. (2003), "Interview", *Frontline*, Vol. 20, No. 2, January 18–31.

APROSC (1978), *Agrarian Reform and Rural Development in Nepal*, (County Review Paper), Kathmandu.

Arrighi, G. and Saul, J.S. (eds.) (1973), *Essays on Political Economy of Africa*, Monthly Review Press, New York.

ARTEP (1974), *A Challenge to Nepal: Growth with Employment*, Bangkok.

Asian Development Bank (1982), *Nepal: Agriculture Strategy Study*, Vol. I and II, Bangkok/Kathmandu.

Bagchi, A.K. (1976), "De-industrialization to India in the Nineteenth Century: Some Theoretical Implications", *The Journal of Development Studies*, Vol. 12, No. 2.

Bagchi, A.K (1981), "Reinforcing and Offsetting Constraints in Industry", in Bagchi, A.K. and Bannerjee, N. (eds.), *Change and Choice in Indian Industry*, K.P. Bagchi and Co., Calcutta.

Bagchi, A.K (1982), *The Political Economy of Underdevelopment*, Cambridge University Press, Cambridge.

Bagchi, A.K. and Bannerjee, N. (eds.) (1981), *Change and Choice in Indian Industry*, K.P. Bagchi and Co., Calcutta.

Bailey, A.M. and Liobera, J.R. (eds.) (1981), *The Asiatic Mode of Production: Science and Politics*, Routledge and Kegan Paul, London.

Bajracharya, B.B. and Shrestha, C.B. (1981), *Transport and Communication Linkages in Nepal* (Mimeo), CEDA, Kathmandu.

Bajracharya, D.B. (1974), *Lichchavi Kalka Abhilekh* (Nepali), Centre for Nepal and Asian Studies, Tribuvan University, Kathmandu.

Banaji, J. (1973), "Mode of Production in India Agriculture: A Comment", *Economic and Political Weekly*, April 17.

Banaji, J (1980), "Summary of Selected Parts of Kautsky's *The Agrarian Question*", in Wolpe, W. (ed.), *The Articulation of Nodes of Production*, Routledge and Kegan Paul, London.

Bannerjee, N. (1981), "Is small beautiful?", in Bagchi, A.K. and Bannerjee, N. (eds.), *Change and Choice in India Industry*, K.P. Bagchi and Co., Calcutta.

Banskota, M and Bista, N.K. (eds.) (1980), *Nepal's Economy—An Overview* (Mimeo), CEDA, Kathmandu.

Banskota, N.P. (1981), *Indo–Nepal Trade and Economic Relations*, B.R. Publishing Corporation, Delhi.

Baran, P. (1957), *The Political Economy of Growth*, People's Publishing House, New Delhi (1962 Edn.).

Bardhan, P. (1984), *Political Economy of Development in India*, Oxford University Press, Delhi.

Bernstein, H. (ed.) (1975), *Underdevelopment and Development: The Third World Today*, Penguin Books, Harmondsworths.

Bernstein, H. (1982), "Industrialization, Development and Dependence", in Alavi, H. and Shanin, T. (eds.), *Introduction to the Sociology of Developing Societies*, Macmillian, London.

Berry, B.J.L. (1967), *Geography of Market Centres and Retail Distribution*, Prentice-Hall, London.

Berry, B.J.L. (1971), "City Size and Economic Development", in Jakobson, L.and Prakash, V. (eds.) (1971), *Urbanization and National Development*, Sage Publication, Berely, Hill.

Bettelheim, C. (1972), "Theoretical Comments", in Emmanuel, A (1972), *Unequal Exchange: A Study in Imperialism of Trade*, New Left Books, London, Appendix–1.

Bhaduri, A. (1973), "A Study in Agricultural Backwardness under Semi-Feudalism", *The Economic Journal*, Vol. 83. No. 329, March.

Bhaduri, A. (1984), *Economic Structure of Backward Agriculture*, Macmillan, Delhi.

Bhagavan, M.R. (1985), "Capital Goods Sector in India: Past and Present Trends and Future Prospects", *Economic and Political Weekly*, March 9.

Bharadwaj, K. (1974), *Production Conditions in Indian Agriculture*, Cambridge University Press, London.

Bharadwaj, K. (1984), "A Note on Emmanuel's Unequal Exchange", *Economic and Political Weekly*, Review of Political Economy, July.

Bhasin, A.S. (1970), *Documents on Nepal's Relations with India and China (1949–66)*, Academic Books Ltd., Mumbai.

Bhattacharya, K.B. and Mishra, C. (eds.) (1997), *Development Practices in Nepal*, Central Department of Sociology and Anthropology, Tribhuvan University, Kathmandu.

Bhattacharya, N. and Saini, G.R. (1972), "Farm Size and Productivity: A Fresh Look", *Economic and Political Weekly*, June 24.

Bhattarai, B.R. (1983), "Napalese Nationalism and Nationality Question", *Frontier*, Vol. 15, No. 35, April 16.

Bhattarai, B.R. (1985), "Prabasi Mazdoorharuko Dohoro Bhoomika: Kehi Saiddhantic Prashnaharu" (Napali), *Nepali Ekta Sandesh* (Organ of All India Nepalese Unity Society) Vol. 5, No. 1.

Bista, D.B. (1968), *Padipur: A Central Terai Village of Nepal*, (Mimeo) USAID/N, Kathmandu.

Bista, D.B. (1982), "The Process of Napalization", in *Anthropological and Linguistic Studies for the Gandake Area in Nepal*, Manumenta Serindica No. 10, Institute for the Study of Languages and Cultures of Asia and Africa, Tokyo.

Bista, D.B. (1990), *Fatalism and Development: Nepal's Struggle for Modernisation*, Orient Longman, Calcutta.

Bista, N.K. (1981), *Import–Export Structures and Trade Expansion in South Asia* (Nepal) (Mimeo), CEDA, Kathmandu.

Blaikie, P. et al. (1980), *Nepal in Crisis: Growth and Stagnation at the Periphery*, Oxford University Press, Delhi.

Blaikie, P. (1981), "Nepal: The Crisis of Regional Planning in a Double Dependent Periphery", in Stohr, W.B. and Taylor, D.R.F. (eds.), *Development from Above or Below*, John Wiley and Sons. Ltd.

Bondestam, L. (1982), "The Political Ideology of Population Control", in Alavi, H. and Shanin, T. (eds.), *Introduction to the Sociology of Developing Societies*, Macmillan, London.

Bose, S.C. (1972), *The Geography of the Himalayas*, National Book Trust, Delhi.

Bottomore, T. et. al. (eds.) (1983), *A Dictionary of Marxist Thought*, Basil Blackwell, Worcester.

Bourne, L.S. et al. (eds.) (1984), *Urbanisation and Settlement Systems: International Perspectives*, Oxford University Press.

Bradby, B. (1980), "The destruction of natural economy" in Wolpe, H (ed.) *The Articulation of Modes of Production*, Routledge and Kegan Paul, London.

Brenner, R. (1977), "The Origins of Capitalist Development: A Critique of Neo-Smithian Marxism", *New Left Review*, No. 104.

Brewer, A. (1980), *Marxist Theories of Imperialism*, Routledge and Kegan Paul, London.

Byres, T.J. (1972), *Foreign Resources and Economic Development: A Symposium on the Report of the Pearson Commission*, Frank Cass, London.

Byres, T.J. (1983), "Historical Perspectives on Sharecropping", *The Journal of Peasant Studies*, Vol. 10, No. 203, January–April.

Caplan, A.P. (1972), *Priests and Cobblers: A Study of Social Change in a Hindu Village in Western Nepal*, Chandler Publishing Company, San Francisco.

Caplan, L. (1970), *Land and Social Change in East Nepal: A Study of Hindu–Tribal Relations*, Routledge and Kegan Paul, London.

Carney, J. et al. (1981), *Regions in Crisis*, Croom Helm, London.

CEDA (1969), *Trade and Transit: Nepal's Problem with her Southern Neighbour* (Mimeo) Occassional Paper No. 1, Kathmandu.

CEDA (1973–75), *Regional Development Study Nepal* (5 Vols), Kathmandu.

Chapagain, D.P. (1976), "Agricultural Productivity Pattern in Nepal and Its Variations", in Dhungana, B. (ed.), *Research Productivity and Mechanization in Napalese Agriculture* (Mimeo), CEDA, Kathmandu.

Chattopadhyay, P. (1972), "On The Question of Mode of Production in India Agriculture: A Priliminary Note", *Economic and Political Weekly*, March 25.

Chattopadhyay, B. and Raza, M. (1975), "Regional Development: Analytical Framework and Indicators", *Indian Journal of Regional Science*, Vol. II, No. 1.

Clarke, J.I. (1965), *Population Geography*, Pergamon Press, Oxford (1972 edn.).

Commander, S. (1985), "Proto-Industrial Production as a Barrier to Industrialisation? Case of North Indian Sugar Industry 1850–1980", *Economic and Political Weekly*, March 23,

Bhusal, G. (2002), *Nepalko Artha-Rajniti: Sankatko Punarutpadan ra Rupantaranko Disha* (in Nepali), Nepal Adhayayan Kendra, Kathmandu.

Bhattarai, B.R. (1999), *Rajnaitik Arthashastrako Ankhijhyal* (from the Keyhole of Political Economy) (in Nepali), Utprerak Prakashan, Kathmandu.

Dahal, D.R. (1983), "Economic Development Throught Indiagenous Means: A Case of Indian Migration in the Nepal Terai", in *Contributions to Nepalese Studies*, Vol. II, No. 1, CNAS, Kathmandu, December.

Dahal, M.K. (ed.) (1998), *Impact of Globalisation in Nepal*, Nepal Foundation for Asian Studies and Friedirich-Ebert Stiftung, Kathmandu.

Dasgupta, B. (1971), "Socio-Economic Classification of Indian Districts—A Statistical Approach", *Economic and Political Weekly*, August 14.

Dasgupta, B. (1984), "Mode of Production and the Extent of Peasant Differentiation in Pre-British Bengal", *Social Scientist*, Vol. 12, No. 8, August.

Dasgupta, B. (1984a), "Sharecropping in West Bengal during the Colonial Period", *Economic and Political Weekly*, Review of Agriculture, March 31.

Dasgupta, B. (1984b), "Sharecropping in West Bengal: From Independence to Operation Barga", *Economic and Political Weekly*, Review of Agriculture, June 30.

Davey, B. (1975), *The Economic Development of India: A Mirxit Analysis*, Spokesman Books, Nottingham.

Davidovich, F. (1984), "Brazilian Urban Settlement", in Bourne, L.S. et. al. (eds.), *Urbanisation and Settlement Systems: International Perspectives*, Oxford University Press.

De Silva, S.B.D. (1982), *The Political Economy of Underdevelopment*, Routledge and Kegan Paul, London.

Dharamdasani, M.D. (1984), *Political Economy of Foreign Aid in the Third World: A Case Study of Nepal*, Shalimar Publishing House, Varanasi.

Dobb, M. (1946), *Studies in the Development of Capitalism*, Routledge and Kegan Paul, London (1978) (edn.).

Emmanuel, A. (1972), *Unequal Exchange: A Study in the Imperialism of Trade*, New Left Book, London.

Endev, G.P. (1980), *The Development of Road Transportation in Nepal and its Relationship to Agriculture Development*, (Unpublished Ph.D. dissertation), Cornell University, Ithaca.

Feder, E. (1976), "The New World Bank Programme for the Self-Liquidation of the Third World Peasantry", *The Journal of Peasant Studies*, Vol. 3, No. 3, April.

Feldman, D. and Fournier, A. (1976), "Social Relations and Agricultural Production in Nepal's Terai", *The Journal of Peasant Studies*, Vol. 3, No. 4, July.

Frank, A.G. (1967), *Capitalism and Underdevelopment in Latin America*, Monthly Review Press, New York.

Frank, A.G. (1969), *Latin America: Underdevelopment or Revolution*, Monthly Review Press, New York.

Frank, A.G. (1978), *Dependent Accumulation and Underdevelopment*, Macmillan, London.

Friedman, J. (1966), *Regional Development Policy: A Case Study of Venezuela*, MIT Press, Massachusettes.

Forbes, D.K. (1984), *The Geography of Underdevelopment*, Croom Helm, London.

Foster–Carter, A. (1978), "The Modes of Production Controversy", *New Left Review*, No. 107.

Foster, J.B. (2002), "The Rediscovery of Imperialism", *Monthly Review*, Vol. 54, No. 6, November.

Furer–Haimendorf, C.V. (1975), *Himalayan Traders*, John Murray, London.

Gaige, F. (1975), *Regionalism and National Unity in Nepal*, Vikas Publishing House Pvt. Ltd., New Delhi.

Goldsmith, R.W. (1969), *Financial Structure and Development*, Yale University Press, New Haven and London.

Gordan, A. (1979), "Stages in the Development of Java's Socio-Economic Formations 700–1979 AC", *Journal of Contemporary Asia*, Vol. 9, No. 2.

Gurung, H, (1981), *Food Systems and Society in Nepal: An Overview* (Mimeo.), New Era, Kathmandu.

Gurung, H. (1983), *Nepal: Some Development Issues (*Mimeo), Kathmandu.

Gurung, H., "Forward" in Pandey, D.R. (1999), *Nepal's Failed Development: Reflections on the Mission and Maladies*, Nepal South Asia Centre, Kathmandu.

Habeeb, A. (1979), *Characteristics and Processes of Urbanization in Colonial India—A Case Study of Calcutta and Its Hinterland (1850–1921)* (Unpublished Ph.D. Dissertation), CSRD/SSS/JNU, New Delhi.

Habib, I. (1963), *The Agrarian System of Mughal India* (1556–1707), Mumbai.

Hagget, P. (1969), *Location Analysis in Human Geography*, Edward Arnold, London.

Hamilton, F.B. (1819), *An Account of the Kingdom of Nepal*, Manjusri Publishing House, New Delhi (1971 edn.).

Harvey, D. (1973), *Social Justice and the City*, Edward Arnold, London (1976 edn.).

Harvey. D. (1975), "The Geography of Capitalist Accumulation: A Reconstruction of the Marxian Theory", in Peet, R. (ed.) (1977), *Radical Geography: Alternative Viewpoints on Contemporary Social Issues*, Marroufa Press Chicago.

Harvey, D. (1981), "The Urban Process under Capitalism: A Framework for Analysis", in Dear, A. and Scott, A.J. (eds.) (1981), *Urbanization and Urban Planning in Capitalist Society*, Methuen, London.

Hayter, T. (1971), *Aid As Imperialism*, Penguin Books, Harmondsworth.

Hindess, B. and Hirst, P.Q. (1975), *Pre-Capitalist Modes of Production*, Routledge and Kegan Paul, London.

Hilton, R. et al. (ed.) (1954), *The Transition from Feudalism to Capitalism*, People's Book House, Patna.

HMG/N, Ministry of Food and Agriculture (1981), *Nepal's Experience in Hill Agriculture Development*, Kathmandu.

Hoffmann, W.G. (1958), *The Growth of Industrial Economics*, Oxford University Press, Mumbai.

Holland, S. (1976), *Capital Versus the Regions*, Macmillan, London.

Industrial Services Centre (1982), *Industrial Sectoral Plan Study (1980/81–1990/91)*, Vol. I. Kathmandu (Revised Edition).

Isard, W. (1956), *Location and Space Economy*, MIT Press, Cambridge, 1972 edn.

Ishi, H. (1982), "Agriculture Labour Recruitment in a Parbate Village in Nepal", in *Anthrological and Linguistic Studies of the Gandaki Area in Nepal*, Institute for the Study of Language and Culture of Asia and Africa, Tokyo.

Integrated Development Systems (1983), *Foreign Aid and Development in Nepal*, Kathmandu.

Jha, K.K. (1978), *Agricultural Finance in Nepal: Analytical Study*, Haritage, New Delhi.

Johnson, E.A.J. (1971), *The Organisation of Space in Developing Countries*, Harvard University Press, Cambridge.

Kansakar, V.B.S. (1973–74), "History of Population Migration in Nepal", *The Himalayan Review*, Vol. VI, No. 5–6, Nepal Geographical Society, Kathmandu.

Kansakar, V.B.S. (1974), *Population Change in Nepal: A Study of Mobility During 1911–61* (Unpublished Ph.D. Dissertation), Department of Geography, Patna University.

Kay, G. (1975), *Development and Underdevelopment: A Marxist Analysis*, Macmillan, London.

Keyder, C. (1981), *The Definition of a Peripheral Economy: Turkey 1923–29*, Cambridge University Press, Cambridge.

Khadka, R.B. (1979), *Emigration in Nepal: A Micro Level Study of Bayalpata Village Panchayat, Achham*, Tribhuvan University, Kathmandu.

Kirkpatrick, W.J. (1811), *An Account of the Kingdom of Nepal*, Manjushri Publishing House, New Delhi (1969, edn.).

Kriedte, P., Medick. H. and Schlumbohm, J. (1981), *Industrialisation before Industrialisation*, Cambridge University Press, Cambridge.

Kundu, A. (1980), *Measurement of Urban Processes: A Case Study in Rationalization*, Popular Prakashan, Mumbai.

Kundu, A. and Raza, M. (1982), *Indian Economy: The Regional Dimension*, Spektrum Publishers and Distributors, New Delhi.

Laclau, E. (1971), "Feudalism and Capitalism in Latin America", *New Left Review*, No. 67, May–June.

Lappo, G.M. and Povovarov, Yu.L. (1984), "Settlement in the USSR", in Bourne, L.S., et. al. (eds.), *Urbanisation and Settlement Systems: International Perspectives*, Oxford University Press.

Lenin, V.I. (1894), "What the 'Friends of the People's Are", in *Collected Works*, Vol. I, Progress Publishers, Moscow, 1972.

Lenin, V.I. (1897a), "A Characterization of Economic Romanticism (Sismond: and our own Native Sismondi's ", *Collected Works*, Vol. 2, Moscow.

Lenin, V.I. (1897b), "The Handicraft Census of 1894–95 in perm Gubernia and General Problems of 'Handicraft Industry'" in *Collected Works*, Vol. 2, Progress Publishers, Moscow, 1972.

Lenin, V.I. (1899), *Development of Capitalism in Russia*, Pogress Publishers, Moscow, 1977.

Lenin, V.I. (1900), "Capitalism in Agriculture" in *Collected Works*, Vol. 4, Progress Publishers, Moscow, 1964.

Lenin, V.I. (1901), "The Agrarian Question and the 'Critics of Marx'", in *Collected Works*, Vol. 5, Progress Publishers, Moscow, 1973.

Lenin, V.I. (1916), Imperialism, The Highest Stage of Capitalism", *Collected Works*, Vol. 22, Progress Publishers, Moscow, 1964.

Lenin, V.I. (1977), "Underdevelopment and Dependency: Critical Notes," *Journal of Contemporary Asia*, Vol. 7, No. 1.

Lipietz, A (1981), "The Structuration of Space, the Problem of Land and Special Policy", in Carney, J. et. al. (1981), *Regions in Crisis*, Croom Helm, London.

Lipton, M. (1977), *Why Poor People Stay Poor: Urban Bias in World Development*, Harvard University Press, Cambridge.

Lohani, G.P. (1967), "Napalma bhoomi–Sambandhama sudhar tarfa bhaeko gatibidhi ra ajasammako upalabdhi" (Nepali), HMG/N, Ministry of Information and Broadcasting, Department of Information, Kathmandu.

Lohani, G.P. (1977), "Nepalko arthic Chintanma bhoomi ra janako sthitile prastut gareka Kehi bisangatiharu" (Nepali), *Roop-Rekha*, Vol. XVIII, No. 8, Kathmandu.

Lotta, R. and Shannon, F. (1984), *America in Decline*, Banner Press, Chicago.

Mobogunge, A.L. (1980), *The Development Process: A Spatial Perspective*, Hutchinson, London.

Magdoff, H. (2002), *Essays on Imperialism and Globalisation*, Cornerstone Publications, Kharagpur.

Mahat, R.S. (1981), *Capital Market, Financial Flows and Industrial Finance in Nepal*, Sajha Prakashan, Kathmandu.

Mahmood, A. (1977), *Statistical Methods in Geographical Studies*, Rajesh Publications, New Delhi.

Mandel, E. (1970), *Marxist Economy Theory*, Vol. I, Monthly Review Press, New York.

Mao Tse-tung (1937), "*On Contradiction*", Foreign Language Press, Peking, 1967.

Marx, K. (1977a), *Grundrisse*, Penguin Books, Harmondsworth.

Marx, K. (1977b), *Capital*, Vol. II, Progress Publishers, Moscow.

Marx, K. (1978), *Capital*, Vol. III, Progress Publishers, Moscow.

Marx, K. (1979), *Capital*, Vol. I, Penguin Books/New Left Review, Harmondsworth.

Marx, K. and Engels, F. (1978), *On Colonialism*, Progress Publisher, Moscow.

Marx, K. and Engels, F. (1979), *Pre-Capitalist Socio-Economic Formation*, Progress Publishers, Moscow.

Massey, D. (1977), "Towards a Critique of Industrial Location Theory", in Peet, R. (ed.) (1977), *Radical Geography: Alternative Viewpoints on Contemporary Social Issues*, Maaroufa Press, Chicago.

Meillassoux, C. (1980), "From reproduction to production: A Marxist approach to Economic anthropology", in Wolpe, W. (ed.), *The Articulation of Modes of Production*, Routledge and Kegan Paul, London.

Mc Dougal, C. (1969), *Village and Household Economy in Far-Western Nepal*, Tribhuvan University, Kathmandu.

Mc Lellan, D. (ed.) (1977), *Karl Marx: Selected Writings*, Oxford University Press, Oxford.

Mihaly, E.B. (1965), *Foreign Aid and Politics in Nepal: A Case Study*, Oxford University Press, London.

Misra, C. and Sharma, P. (1983), "Foreign Aid and Social Structure Notes on Intra-State Relationships", in Integrated Development Systems, *Foreign Aid and Development in Nepal*, Kathmandu.

Mitra, A. (1977), *Terms of Trade and Class Relations*, Frank Cass, London.

Moulaert, F. and Salinas, P.W. (eds.) (1983), *Regional Analysis and the New International Division of Labour*, Kluwer–Nijhoff, the Hague.

Mundle, S. (1981), "Growth, Disparity and Capital Reorganization in Indian Economy: Some Speculations", *Economic and Political Weekly*, Annual Number, March.

Myrdal, G. (1957), *Economic Theory and Under-Developed Regions*, Metheun, London (1969 reprint).

Nagaraj, R. (1985), "Trends in Factory Size in Indian Industry, 1950 to 1980: Some Tentative Inferences", *Economic and Political Weekly*, February 3.

Nath, T. (1975), *The Nepalese Dilemma 1960–74*, Sterling Publishers Pvt. Ltd. New Delhi.

National Commission on Population (1983), *Internal and International Migration in Nepal: Summary and Recommendation*, Task force on Migration, Kathmandu.

National Planning Commission (1974a), *Regional Development Policies*, Report of the Task force, HMG/N, Kathmandu.

National Planning Commission (1974b), *Report of Task Force on Land Use and Erosion Control*, HMG/N, Kathmandu.

National Planning Commission Secretariat (1978), *A Survey of Employment, Income Distribution and Consumption Patterns in Nepal* (Summary Report, Vol. IV), HMG/N, Kathmandu.

Nayyar, D. (1981), "Industrial Development in India: Growth or Stagnation?", in Bagchi, A.K. and Bannerjee, N. (eds.), *Change and Choice in Indian Industry*, K.P. Bagchi and Co., Calcutta.

New Era (1981), Study on Inter-Regional Migration in Nepal, Kathmandu.

Ojha, D.P. and Weiss, D. (1972), *Regional Analysis of Kosi Zone/Eastern Nepal Working Method for Regional Planning in Nepal*, GDI/CEDA, Berlin and Kathmandu.

Okada, F.E. (1970), *Preliminary Report on Regional Development Areas in Nepal*, National Planning Commission, HMG/N, Kathmandu.

O.'Keefe, P. (ed.) (1984), *Regional Restructuring Under Advanced Capitalism*, Croom Helm, London.

Owen, R. and Sutcliffe, R.B. (1972), *Studies in the Theory of Imperialism*, Longman, London.

Pal, M.N. (1975), "Regional Disparities in the Levels of Development in India", *Indian Journal of Regional Sciences*, Vol. II, No. 1.

Palma, G. (1978), "Dependence: A formal theory of underdevelopment or a methodology for the analysis of concrete situations of underdevelopment?", *World Development*, No. 6.

Pandey, D.R. (1999), *Nepal's Failed Development: Reflections on the Mission and Maladies*, Nepal South Asia Centre, Kathmandu.

Pant B.D. (1982), *Statistical Analysis of Economic Activities for Regional Planning in Nepal* (unpublished Ph.D. Dissertation), Indian Statistical Institute, Calcutta.

Pant, Y.P. (1970), *Problems in Fiscal and Monetary Policy: A Case Study of Nepal*, C. Hurst, London.

Patnayaik, P. (1995), *Whatever Happened to Imperialism and Other Essays*, Tulika, New Delhi.

Patnaik, P. (1972), "On the Political Economy of Underdevelopment", *Economic and Political Weekly*, Annual Number, February.

Patnaik, S.C. (1981), *Economics of Regional Development Planning in Third World Countries*, Associated Publishing House, New Delhi.

Patnaik, U. (1971), "Capitalist Development in Agriculture: A Note", *Economics and Political Weekly*, September, 25.

Patnaik, U. (1976), "Class Differentiation within the Peasantry: An Approach to Analysis of Indian Agriculture", Economic and Political Weekly, September.

Patnaik, U. (1979), "Neo-Populism and Marxism: The Chayanovian View of the Agrarian Question and Its Fundamental Fallacy", *The Journal of Peasant Studies*, Vol. 6, No. 4, July.

Payer, C. (1974), *The Debt Trap: The IMF and the Third World*, Penguin Books, Harmondsworth.

Pearce, R. (1983), "Sharecropping: Towards a Marxist View", *The Journal of Peasant Studies*, Vol. 10, No. 203, January–April.

Peet, R. (ed.) (1977), *Radical Geography: Alternative Viewpoints on Contemporary Social Issues*, Marroufa Press, Chicago.

Peet, R. (1979), "Societal Contradiction and Marxist Geography", *Annals of the Association of American Geographers*, Vol. 69.

Peet, R.C. (1978), *Migration, Culture and Community: A Case Study from Rural Nepal* (Ph.D. Dissertation, Microfilmed), Columbia University, U.S.A.

Petras, J. (1978), *Critical Perspectives on Imperialism and Social Class in the Third World*, Monthly Review Press, New York.

Poffenberger, M. (1980), *Patterns of Change in the Nepal Himalaya*, Macmillan, Delhi.

Ponnambalam, S. (1981), *Dependent Capitalism in Crisis: The Sri Lankan Economy, 1948–1980*, Zed Press, London.

Paudyal, S.R. (1982), *Foreign Aid in Nepal* (Mimeo), CEDA, Kathmandu.

Paudyal, S.R. (1983), *Planned Development in Nepal: A Study*, Sterling Publishers, New Delhi.

Pradhan, P. (ed.) (1973), *A New Dimension in Nepal's Development*, CEDA, Kathmandu.

Prasad, P.H. (1974), "Reactionary Role of Usurer's Capital in Rural India", *Economic and Political Weekly*, Special Number, August.

Quami, M. (1982), *Geography of Marxism*, Basil Blackwell, Oxford.

Raj, K.N. (1976), "Growth and Stagnation on Indian Industrial Development", *Economic and Political Weekly*, Annual Number, February.

Rana, P.S.J.B. and Malla, K.P. (eds.) (1973), *Nepal in Perspective*, CEDA, Kathmandu.

Rana, R.S.J.B. (1971), "Regional Variations in the Growth Structure of Crop Production in Nepal", *The Himalayan Review*, Vol. IV, Nepal Geographical Society, Kathmandu.

Rao, C.H.H. (1968), "Farm Size and Yield Per Acre: A Comment", *Economic and Political Weekly*, Vol. 3, No. 37, September, 14.

Rawat, P.C. (1974), *Indo-Nepal Economic Relations*, National Publishing House, Delhi.

Raza, M. "Foreward", in Premi, M.K. (1980), *Urban Out Migration: A Study of Its Nature, Causes and Consequences*, Sterling Publishers Pvt. Ltd., New Delhi.

Reejal, P.R. (1982), *Nepal's Foreign Trade and Economic Development, 1956/57 to 1979/80* (Mimeo), CEDA, Kathmandu.

Regmi. D.R. (1960), *Ancient Nepal*, Firma KLM Private Ltd. Calcutta.

Regmi, D.R. (1965), *Medieval Nepal*, Vol. II, Firma KLM Private Ltd., Calcutta.

Regmi, M.C. (1963–68), *Land Tenure and Taxati n in Nepal*, Ratna Pustak Bhandar, Kathmandu (1978 edn.).

Regmi, M.C. (1971), *A Study in Nepali Economic History 1768–1846*, Manjusri Publishing House, New Delhi.

Regmi, M.C. (1976), *Landownership in Nepal*, University of California, Berkley.

Regmi, (1978), *Thached Huts and Stucco Palaces: Peasants and Landlords in 19th Century Nepal*, Vikas Publishing House Pvt. Ltd. New Delhi.

Regmi, M.C. (1984), *The State and Economic Surplus: Production, Trade and Resource Mobilisation in Early 19th Century Nepal* (to be published), Kathmandu.

Radney, W. (1972), *How Europe Underdeveloped Africa*, Bogle Louverture Publications, London.

Rose, L.E. (1973), *Nepal: Strategy for Survival*, Oxford University Press, Delhi.

Roxborrow, I. (1979), *Theories of Underdevelopment*, Macmillan, London.

Rudra, A. (1968), "Farm Size and Yield Per Acre", *Economic and Political and Weekly*, Special Number, July.

Rudra A. (1970), "In Search of the Capitalist Farmer", *Economic and Political Weekly*, June 27.

Rudra A., et. al. (1969), "Big Farmers of Punjab", *Economic and Political Weekly*, September 20, December 27.

Salinas, P.W., "Mode of Production and Spatial Organisation in Peru", in Moulaerl, F. and Salinas, P.W. (eds.) (1983), *Regional Analysis and the New International Division of Labour*. Kluwer-Nijhoff, The Hauge.

Santos, M. (1977), "Society and Space: Social Formation as a Theory and Method", *Antipode*, Vol. 9, No. 1, February.

Santos, T.D. (1970), "The Structure of Dependence", in Wilber, C.K. (ed.), *The Political Economy of Development and Under Development*, Random House, New York.

Santos, T.D. (1975), "The Crisis of Development Theory and the Problem of Dependence in Latin America", in Bernstein, H. (ed.), *Underdevelopment and Development: The Third World Today*, Penguin Books, Harmondsworth.

S.A.T.A. (1977), *Mountain Environment and Development*, University Press, Kathmandu.

Sau, R. (1973), "On the Essence and Manifestation of Capitalism in Indian Agriculture", *Economic and Political Weekly*, March 31.

San, R. (1978), *Unequal Exchange, Imperialism and Underdevelopment: An Essay on the Political Economy of World Capitalism*, Oxford University Press, Calcutta.

Sau, R. (1982), *Trade Capital and Underdevelopment : Towards a Marxist Theory*, Oxford University Press, Calcutta.

Saushkin, Yu.G. (1980), *Economic Geography: Theory and Methods*, Progress Publishers, Moscow.

Scapini, J.C. (ed.), *Underdevelopment Theories in Latin America* (Mimeo), Institute for Studies on Economic Development, Nepali (Italia).

Scholz, J.T. (1977), *Policy Process and Rural Development: A Study of Land Reform in Nepal* (Unpublished Ph.D. Dissertation), University of California, Berkley.

Security Marketing Centre Ltd. (1981), *Study on Share Ownership of Principle Public Limited Companies in Nepal* (Nepali), Kathmandu.

Seddon, D. et. al. (1981), *Peasants and Workers in Nepal*, Vikas Publishing House Pvt. Ltd., New Delhi.

Sen, A. (1982), *The State, Industrialization and Class Formations in India*, Routledge and Kegan Paul, London.

Sen, A.K. (1962), " An Aspect of Indian Agriculture", *The Economic Weekly*, Annual Number, February.

Sen, J. (1977), *Indo–Nepal Trade in the Nineteenth Century*, Firma K.L.M. Private Ltd., Calcutta.

Sengupta, P. and Sdasyuk G.V. (1968), "Economic Rationalization of India-Problems and Approaches", in *Census of India 1961*, Vol. I, No. 8, New Delhi.

Shah, S. (1981), "Developing an Economy: Nepal's Experience", *Asian Survey*, Vol. XXI, No. 10, October.

Singh, Randhir (2001), "The Return of Karl Marx", Mainstream, May 5.

Sharma, P. (1973–74), "Growth Poie as a Regional Development Strategy in Nepal", *The Himalayan Review*, Vol. VI, No. 5–6, Kathmandu.

Sharma P. and Ojha, D.P. (1975), *Evolution of Nepal's Dependency Relationship with India* (M.S. Term Paper), Cornell University, Ithaca.

Sharma P.S. (1982), *Ineuqality in Land Holdings and Agricultural Development in India: A Regional Analysis* (Unpublished Ph.D. Dissertation), CSRD/SSS/JNU, New Delhi.

Shetty, S.L. (1978), "Structural Retrogression in the Indian Economy Since Mid–Sixties", *Economic and Political Weekly*, Annual Number, February.

Shirokov, G.K. (1973), *Industrialization of India*, Progress Publishers, Moscow.

Shrestha, B.P. (1962), *An Introduction to Nepalese Economy*, Ratna Pustak Bhandar, Kathmandu (1981 edn.).

Shreshtha, C.B. (1973–74), "The System of Central Places in the Arniko Rajmarga Area of Nepal", *The Himalyan Review*, Vol. VI, No. 5 and 6, Nepal Geographical Society, Kathmandu.

Shrestha, G.R. (1978), *Foodgrain Distribution System in Nepal*, Nepal Food Corporation, Kathmandu.

Shrestha, N.R. (1997), *In the Name of Development: A Reflection of Nepal*, University Press of America, Lanham.

Shrestha, R.K. and Sharma, P. (eds.) (1980), *Nepal: Atlas of Economic Development*, Institute of Science and Technology, HMG/N, Kathmandu.

Shrestha, R.L. (1980), *Impact of Kathmandu Raxaul Highway (Tribhuvan Rajmarg) on Nepalese Economy (1956–1975)*, G.S. Agrawal, Kathmandu.

Singh, H. (1978), *Ladhakh-Problem of Regional Development in the Context of Growth Point Strategy* (Unpublished Ph.D. Dissertation), CSRD/SSS/JNU, New Delhi.

Smith, N. (1984), *Uneven Development: Nature, Capital and Production of Space*, Basil Blackwell, Oxford.

Soja, E.W. (1980), "The Socio-Spatial Dialectic", Annals of Association of American Geographers, Vol. 70, No. 2.

Stalin, J. (1938), *Dialectical and Historical Materialism*, New Book Center, Calcutta, 1976.

Stalin, J. (1976), *Problem of Leninism*, Foreign Language Press, Peking.

Standing, G. (1981), "Migration and Modes of Exploitation: Social Origins of Immobility and Mobility", *The Journal of Peasant Studies*, Vol. 8, No. 2, January.

Stiller, L.F. (1972), "A Note on Himalayan Trade", *Journal of the Tribhuvan University*, Vol. III, No. 1, Kathmandu, November.

Stiller L.F. and Yadav, R.P. (1979), *A Study of Nepal's Planning Experience*, CNAS, Kathmandu.

Stilwell, F.J.B. (1978), "Completing Analysis of the Spatial Aspects of Capitalist Development", *Review of Radical Political Economy*, Vol. 10, No. 3, Fall.

Sutcliffe, B. (1972), "Imperialism and Industrialization in the Third World", in Owen R. Sutcliffe, B. (ed.) *Studies in the Theory of Imperialism*, Longman, London.

Sutcliffe, R.B. (1971), *Industry and Underdevelopment*, Addison Wesley Publishing Company, London.

Sweezy, P.M. (1970), *The Theory of Capitalist Development*, Monthly Review Press, New York.

Taylor, J. (1979), *From Modernization to Modes of Production*, Macmillan, London.

The World Bank (1979), *Nepal: Development Performance and Prospects*, South Asia Regional Office, Washington, D.C.

The World Bank (1981), *Nepal: Policies and Prospects for Accelerated Growth*, October, 15.

Tyagunenko, V.L. et. al. (eds.) (1973), *Industrialization of Developing Countries*, Progress Publishers, Moscow.

Upadhyaya, D.C. and Abueva, J.V. (ed.) (1974), *Population and Development in Nepal*, CEDA, Kathmandu.

Upadhyaya, G.R. (1983), "Cottage and Village Industries for Economic Development in Nepal", *Nepal Industrial Digest*, Silver Jubilee Issue, NIDC, Kathmandu.

Upadhyaya, J. and Shrestha, B.R. (1981), *External Assistance and Nepal's Hill Agriculture*, Paper Prepared for Seminar in Nepal's Hill Agriculture Development, (Mimeo), Kathmandu, April 3.

Valentey, D.I. (ed.) (1978), *The Theory Population: Essays in Marxist Research*, Progress Publisher, Moscow.

Varshney, A. (1984), "Political Economy of Slow Industrial Growth in India", *Economic and Political Weekly*, September 1.

Walker, R.A. (1978), "Two Sources of Uneven Development under Advanced Capitalism: Spatial Differentiation and Capital Mobility", *Review of Radical Political Economy*, Vol. 10, No. 3, Fall.

Wallerstine, I. (1974), *Modern World System*, Academic Press, New York.

Warren, B. (1973), "Imperialism and Capitalist Industrialization", *New Left Review*, No. 81.

Warren, B. (1980), *Imperialism, Pioneer of Capitalism*, Verso, London.

Weiner, M. (1971), "The Political Demography of Nepal", in Seminar on Population and Development (July 28–30, 1971), CEDA, Kathmandu.

Wilber, C.K. (ed.) (1970), *The Political Economy of Development and Underdevelopment*, Random House, New York.

Wolpe, H. (ed.) (1980), *The Articulation of Modes of Production*, Routledge and Kegan, Paul, London.

Wolpe, H. "Introduction", in Wolpe, H. (ed.) (1980), *The Articulation of Modes of Production*, Routledge and Kegan Paul, London.

Zaman, M.A. (1973), *Evaluation of Land Reform in Nepal*, HMG/N, Ministry of Land Reforms, Kathmandu.

Zehender, W. et. al. (1975), *The Influence of Kathmandu on the Axis Bidoor/Trisuli Bazar–Dhunche*, Draft Report Submitted to GDI, Berlin, Kathmandu.

Zevering, K.H. (1974), *Agricultural Development and Agrarian Structure in Nepal*, ARTEP, Bangkok.

Index